Microsoft® Visual Basic® .NET Programming:

From Problem Analysis to Program Design

**E. Reed Doke and
Susan Rebstock Williams**

THOMSON

COURSE TECHNOLOGY

Australia • Canada • Mexico • Singapore • Spain • United Kingdom • United States

THOMSON
COURSE TECHNOLOGY
™

Microsoft Visual Basic .NET Programming: From Problem Analysis to Program Design
is published by Course Technology.

Senior Acquisitions Editor:
Amy Yarnevich

Product Manager:
Alyssa Pratt

Development Editor:
Lisa Ruffolo

Production Editors:
Melissa Panagos
Brooke Booth

Senior Marketing Manager:
Karen Seitz

Associate Product Manager:
Mirella Misiaszek

Editorial Assistant:
Jenny Smith

Senior Manufacturing Coordinator:
Trevor Kallop

Cover Designer:
Steve Deschene

Disclaimer:
Course Technology reserves the right to revise this publication and make changes from time to time in its content without notice.

The Web addresses in this book are subject to change from time to time as necessary without notice.

ISBN 0-619-16010-1

Brief
Contents

Table of Contents

14. Advanced Topics: DBMS, SQL, and ASP.NET　521

Preface

Welcome to *Visual Basic .NET Programming: From Problem Analysis to Program Design*. This textbook is designed for a first Computer Science (CS1) course using Microsoft Visual Basic .NET and the Visual Studio .NET integrated development environment (IDE). Traditionally, this course has used C, C++, or Java. However, with the rapidly rising popularity of VB .NET in the computer programming industry, CS1 courses are being revised to include VB .NET. This text was designed and written as a direct result of these advances.

The .NET Framework and VB .NET now implement the key object-oriented (OO) concepts of inheritance and polymorphism, making VB .NET a full-blown object-oriented platform instead of an object-based language. Because of its true object-orientation, its significant departure from VB 6.0 (both in syntax and paradigm), and Microsoft's dominant position in the software industry, CS1 degree programs requiring Java or C++ are now considering VB .NET for their OO programming courses. In addition, VB .NET is ideal for curricula adopting new OO language courses.

This book assumes no prior programming experience.

APPROACH

The text is organized into 15 chapters. Chapter 1 provides the background you need to begin writing VB .NET programs. It introduces basic computer terminology and explores the history of programming languages. It also emphasizes how to solve problems and develop algorithms. Finally, it discusses basic object-oriented programming concepts, and identifies the benefits of the object-oriented approach.

In Chapter 2, you explore the VB .NET development environment by creating a VB .NET project and then compiling and executing a VB .NET program. You also use the visual form designer, examine the debugging tool, and explore the help facility.

Chapter 3 builds upon the concepts and techniques introduced in Chapter 2. You explore the Microsoft .NET Framework, which provides a large, useful library of hundreds of prewritten classes. You then write a VB .NET module definition, and learn how to define variables and data types. You also write basic computational statements and read input from the keyboard.

Chapters 4 and 5 introduce control structures to alter the sequential flow of execution. In Chapter 4, you learn how to write and interpret logical expressions in general, and then focus on one-way, two-way, and multi-way selection statements. Chapter 5 explores the iteration structure, including Do While, Do Until, and For Next statements. You also learn how to create nested structures.

Chapter 6 explains how to use VB .NET supplied classes. You invoke methods in the String class, display message boxes, format numeric output, work with dates, and read and write sequential files.

In Chapter 7, you work with arrays. You define one-dimensional arrays, create String arrays, and declare multi-dimensional arrays. You also learn how to search an array and use the ArrayList class.

Chapter 8 explains how to write graphical user interfaces (GUIs). After exploring the VB .NET GUI classes, you explore GUI design principles. Then you learn how to employ forms, buttons, and labels and handle events.

Chapter 9 discusses writing procedures in detail. It explores the client-server model, reviews the syntax of procedures, and explains how to design and write user-defined procedures and overloaded procedures.

Chapter 10 deals with object-oriented development in more detail. It covers class definitions and explores the three-tier design model. Chapter 11 explains how to implement the object-oriented concepts of inheritance and association.

Chapter 12 is the first of four advanced topics chapters, and explains how to handle exceptions. Chapter 13 explains how to create advanced GUI applications and include graphics. In Chapter 14, you explore ASP .NET and learn how to create integrated systems that interact with a relational database. Chapter 15 introduces the advanced topics of data structures and recursion.

Appendix A explains how to set up an Internet Information Services (IIS) server if you want to run Web applications on your computer.

How to Use the Book

This text was designed to be covered in one semester. Chapters 1 through 9 cover the fundamentals of programming and the VB .NET language; we suggest you cover these chapters in sequence. Because VB .NET is an object-oriented language, OO concepts are discussed as part of the basic topics. However, Chapters 10 and 11 focus specifically on OO program development. You can adjust your depth of coverage in these chapters depending on your level of OO interest. For example, you could skim both chapters, cover Chapter 10 in detail and skip Chapter 11, cover both chapters in depth, or omit both.

The final four chapters cover advanced topics. You can select specific topics and tailor the depth of coverage to meet the requirements of your specific course. These chapters assume that you have already covered Chapters 1 through 9.

- Chapter 12 covers both handling exceptions and writing user-defined exception classes. Exception handling is an important topic and is used in subsequent chapters.

- Chapter 13 illustrates the design and development of advanced GUI applications, and introduces data access classes.

- Chapter 14 introduces both ASP .NET and relational DBMS applications. Note that these topics are introduced, but are not covered in detail. Chapter 14 assumes that the data access classes presented in the latter portion of Chapter 13 have been covered.

- Chapter 15 introduces data structures and recursion. Again, these topics are introduced but not covered in extensive detail.

Features of the book

Every chapter in this book includes the following features. These features are conducive to learning and enable students to learn the material at their own pace.

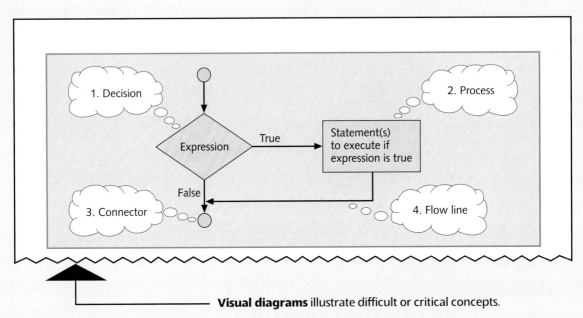

Visual diagrams illustrate difficult or critical concepts.

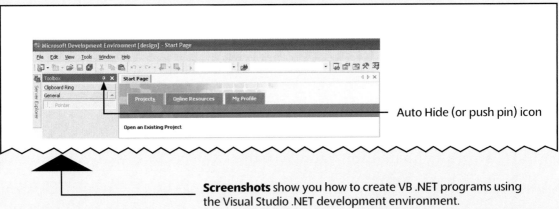

Auto Hide (or push pin) icon

Screenshots show you how to create VB .NET programs using the Visual Studio .NET development environment.

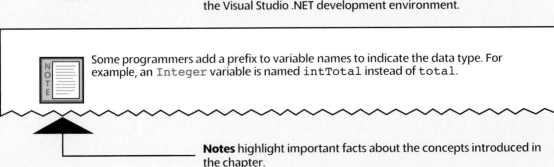

Some programmers add a prefix to variable names to indicate the data type. For example, an `Integer` variable is named `intTotal` instead of `total`.

Notes highlight important facts about the concepts introduced in the chapter.

Features of the book

Example 5-9: Computing an exam average using a For Next loop

```
1.  ' define variables
2.  Dim sum, average As Double
3.  Dim numberOfExams As Integer = 5
4.  Dim counter As Integer
5.  ' begin loop
6.  For counter = 1 To 5 Step 1
7.      Console.WriteLine("Enter an Exam Score: ")
8.      sum = sum + Convert.ToDouble(Console.ReadLine())
9.  Next
10. ' compute & display the average
11. average = sum / numberOfExams
12. Console.WriteLine("The average is: " & Math.Round(average, 1))
```

Start of loop

End of loop

Sample Run:

```
Enter an Exam Score:
85
Enter an Exam Score:
90
Enter an Exam Score:
94
Enter an Exam Score:
89
Enter an Exam Score:
91
The average is: 89.8
```

Discussion:

Lines 2 and 3 define the variables `sum`, `average`, and `numberOfExams` as in the previous examples.

Numbered **examples** illustrate the key concepts with corresponding code. The programming code in these examples is numbered for easy reference, and is often followed by a Sample Run. A discussion also describes what each line in the code does.

Features of the book

PROGRAMMING EXAMPLE: PAYROLL CALCULATION

This programming example demonstrates a program that calculates an employee's pay based on an hourly pay rate, number of hours worked, and eligibility for overtime pay. The program prompts the user to input overtime eligibility, hours worked, and pay rate, and then computes regular pay, overtime pay, and total pay. Finally, it displays the computation results rounded to two decimal positions.

Input   Overtime exempt "Y" or "N", hours worked, and hourly pay rate

Output   The employee's regular pay, overtime pay, and total pay, with the results rounded to two decimal positions

Problem Analysis and Algorithm Design

The purpose of this program is to calculate and print an employee's pay amount. To calculate the pay, you need to know how many hours the employee worked and the normal pay rate. You also need to know whether the employee is eligible for overtime pay; if so, the program calculates the overtime amount and adds it to the regular pay amount. The program should print the pay amount to two decimal places because this is a currency amount.

Variables   Because the program will ask users whether an employee is exempt from overtime pay, and then to enter the pay rate and number of hours worked, you need variables to store this information and the user's input. You also need a variable to store the calculated pay amount. You therefore need the following five data type `Double` variables, one `Boolean`, and one `String`.

```
Dim hoursWorked, rate, regularPay, overtimePay, totalPay As Double
Dim exemptEmployee As Boolean
Dim stringInput As String
```

Formulas   The program uses three formulas to compute the pay amount—one to calculate regular pay, another to calculate overtime pay, and a third to calculate total pay:

```
regularPay = hoursWorked * rate
overtimePay = (hoursWorked - 40) * rate * 1.5
totalPay = regularPay + overtimePay
```

Programming Examples are complete programs that appear in each chapter. These examples include the accurate, concrete stages of Input, Output, Problem Analysis and Algorithm Design, and Complete Program Listing.

Features of the book

1. Correct the following code so that it compiles and executes correctly. Assume the variables have been correctly declared and populated.

   ```
   If hoursWorked Not > 40 Then otPay = 0
   ```

2. Correct the following code so that it compiles and executes correctly. Assume the variables have been correctly declared and populated.

   ```
   If hoursWkd Not > 40 Then
   otPay = 0
   ```

3. What is the output of the following code?

   ```
   If 1 > 2 Or 5 < 6 Then
       Console.WriteLine("True")
   Else
       Console.WriteLine("False")

   End If
   ```

Exercises reinforce study and ensure that students have learned the material.

Features of the book

Programming Exercises challenge students to write VB .NET programs with a specified outcome.

From beginning to end, the concepts are introduced at a pace that is conducive to learning. *The writing style of this book is simple and straightforward, and it parallels the teaching style of a classroom.* Before introducing a key concept, we explain why certain elements are necessary. The concepts introduced are then described using examples and small programs.

Each chapter has two types of programs. The first type are small programs that are part of the numbered Examples (*e.g.*, Example 4-1), and are used to explain key concepts. In most of these examples, each line of the programming code is numbered. The program, illustrated through a Sample Run, is then explained line by line. The rationale behind each line is discussed in detail.

The Programming Examples form the backbone of the book and are designed to be methodical and user-friendly. Each Programming Example starts with a Problem Analysis and is followed by the Algorithm Design. Every step of the algorithm is then coded in VB .NET. In addition to teaching problem-solving techniques, these detailed programs show the user how to implement concepts in an actual VB .NET program. We strongly recommend that students study the Programming Examples very carefully to effectively learn VB .NET.

Quick Review sections at the end of each chapter reinforce learning. After reading the chapter, students can quickly walk through the highlights of the chapter and test themselves using the ensuing Exercises and Programming Exercises. Many readers refer to the Quick Review as an easy way to review the chapter before an exam.

TEACHING TOOLS

The following supplemental materials are available when this book is used in a classroom setting. All instructor teaching tools, outlined below, are available on the Course Technology Web site (*www.course.com*).

Electronic Instructor's Manual. The Instructor's Manual that accompanies this textbook includes:

- Additional instructional material to assist in class preparation, including suggestions for lecture topics.

- Solutions to all the end-of-chapter materials, including the Exercises and Programming Exercises.

ExamView®. This textbook is accompanied by ExamView, a powerful testing software package that allows instructors to create and administer printed, computer (LAN-based), and Internet exams. ExamView includes hundreds of questions that correspond to the topics covered in this text, enabling students to generate detailed study guides that include page references for further review. These computer-based and Internet testing components allow students to take exams at their computers, and save the instructor time because each exam is graded automatically.

PowerPoint Presentations. This book comes with Microsoft PowerPoint slides for each chapter. These are included as a teaching aid for classroom presentations, either to make available to students on the network for chapter review, or to be printed for classroom distribution. Instructors can add their own slides for additional topics that they introduce to the class.

Distance Learning. Course Technology is proud to present online courses in WebCT and Blackboard to provide the most complete and dynamic learning experience possible. When you add online content to one of your courses, you're adding a lot: Topic Reviews, Practice Tests, Review Questions, Assignments, PowerPoint presentations, and, most of all, a gateway to the 21st century's most important information resource. We hope you will make the most of your course, both online and offline. For more information on how to bring distance learning to your course, contact your local Course Technology sales representative.

Solution Files. The solution files for all Programming Exercises and end-of-chapter Programming Examples are available at *www.course.com*.

Before You Start Working with Visual Studio .NET

If you are using your own personal computer to complete the exercises in this book, you first need to install Visual Basic .NET. To do so, follow the instructions that accompany the Microsoft Visual Studio .NET software packaged with this book, accepting the defaults suggested by the Setup wizard. See your instructor or technical support person if you encounter difficulties or have questions about the setup.

To help organize your work, create a work folder on your computer's hard drive for the exercises you will complete.

Acknowledgements

Completing a text like this requires the dedication and hard work of many people. As usual at Course Technology, we were fortunate to find interested, excited, and future-oriented people. The Managing Editor, Jennifer Muroff, provided the initial ideas and assembled a great editorial and production team. When she promoted herself to fulltime mom, we began working with Alyssa Pratt, Senior Product Manager, who continued to provide strong leadership. We are reluctant to say that Alyssa replaced Jennifer, because no one could do that, but Alyssa gently kept all of us on schedule and promptly dealt with issues as they arose. First and foremost on our team was developmental editor Lisa Ruffolo whose contributions have been substantial. In fact, this is the third book that Lisa has edited for us and we specifically requested that she be a part of our team. Many thanks also to Production Editors Melissa Panagos and Brooke Booth. Many others were also involved in the production of this text, including copy editors, quality assurance testers, graphic artists, and proofreaders. Without their contributions, this text would not exist.

We would also like to thank our families for being so understanding about all of the time we had to invest in this project. Although they have become accustomed to our lengthy writing projects, we nonetheless appreciate their continued support and patience.

Finally, we want to acknowledge and thank the team of reviewers who helped to see this project through. Their contributions were always insightful and useful. It would be impossible to produce a book like this without interested and knowledgeable reviewers. We were very fortunate. The reviewers were:

Vanessa Starkey, University of Dayton

Mark Thomas, University of Cincinnati

Socratis Tornaritis, Southern Illinois University, Edwardsville

Dedications

To Sharon Kay (Ellis) Doke (1942 – 1994) and our sons, Dave and Dan—ERD

To Richard and Josh—SRW

1

Introduction to Visual Basic .NET: Background and Perspective

In this chapter, you will:

- O Learn basic computer terminology and component architecture
- O Explore the history of programming languages
- O Recognize the similarities between programming languages and spoken languages
- O Solve problems and develop algorithms
- O Identify basic object-oriented programming concepts
- O Examine the benefits of the object-oriented approach

In some form, information technology shapes many of the things we do each day and how we do them. Your daily routine might resemble the following scenario. Before you leave the house, you check your e-mail and use your cell phone to call a friend. Then you stop to buy gas using a credit card to pay at the pump. At your destination, you use the Internet to research the prices and features of digital cameras, and receive an instant message from a friend who is traveling in Europe. You decide to have lunch at your favorite fast-food restaurant, where you order a hamburger and French fries. The cashier uses a touch screen device to enter information about your order including a special request to hold the pickles. This information instantaneously appears on a monitor in the kitchen while another device prints a receipt. While waiting for your food, you play a game on your personal digital assistant (PDA). Later that afternoon, you use the online services of your bank to pay your electric bill, and then stop by an automated teller machine (ATM) to withdraw $25 in cash. When you get home, you go online to order the digital camera you identified as the best deal in your earlier research, and call in an order for a pizza. The pizza place has a record of your name, address, and details about the pizza you ordered last week, and this information appears on a monitor in front of your order taker so the pizza employee can process your order quickly. In all of these instances—in everything from communications to shopping, from research to entertainment—you use information technology to make things happen.

The pervasiveness of information technology fuels an ongoing need for computer programmers and system developers. All information technology applications—from simple systems that process your order for a hamburger and french fries, to those that generate your cellular phone bill, to intelligent navigation systems that manage missiles and space exploration vehicles—require computer programs to make them work. In learning a computer language, you take the first step toward creating information technology solutions to the problems and opportunities of tomorrow.

In this book, you learn the fundamentals of the Visual Basic .NET programming language, one of the most powerful and popular languages used by software developers. What is more important, you learn good programming practices and problem-solving techniques, and understand how to apply them to solve real-world problems.

In this chapter, you study basic computer terminology and identify the main components of a computer. You learn about the historical evolution of programming languages, and explore similarities and differences between these languages and those that you speak, read, and write. You also gain insight into the problem-solving approach you use to design and develop programs. Finally, you are introduced to key concepts of the object-oriented programming approach and recognize the benefits this approach provides.

UNDERSTANDING BASIC COMPUTER TERMINOLOGY AND COMPONENT ARCHITECTURE

Before learning a programming language, you should understand basic computer terms and the fundamentals of how a computer works. The remainder of this book builds on these fundamentals. Many people think of a computer as a device that can perform complex computations at very high speed. While this characterization is certainly true, computers also perform many other kinds of tasks. The Merriam-Webster Online Dictionary defines a **computer** as "a programmable electronic device that can retrieve, store, and process data." Because data comes in many forms (such as numbers, text, graphics, and video), processing data includes not only making numerical calculations but also manipulating symbols, usually to solve a problem or make a logical decision.

A computer requires both hardware and software to process data. **Hardware** refers to the physical, touchable components of a computer, such as the keyboard and mouse (input devices), monitors, printers, and external storage units (output devices), one or more processors, and memory. The arrangement of these components within a computer is referred to as its **architecture**. In 1945, Hungarian-born mathematician John von Neumann proposed a computer architecture that continues to form the backbone of the computers we use today, nearly 60 years later.

In the von Neumann architecture, a computer has three primary components—input/output devices, memory, and a central processing unit—as shown in Figure 1-1. **Input/output devices** include familiar items such as the keyboard, mouse, monitor, printer, disk drives, and a host of other devices, ranging from scanners and digital cameras to machines that carry out specialized operations on the floor of a manufacturing plant.

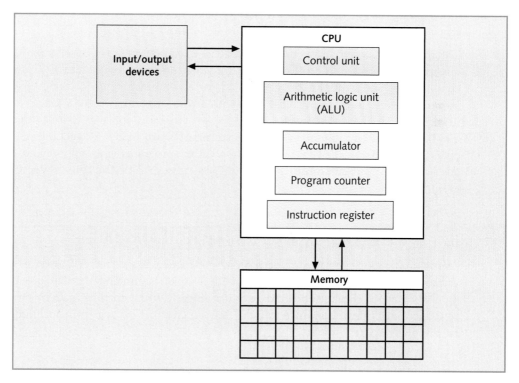

Figure 1-1   Elements of a computer

Memory is a storage device that holds data. There are two basic types of memory: read-only and random access. The contents of **read-only memory (ROM)** are fixed and do not change even when the computer is switched off. For this reason, ROM is also referred to as nonvolatile memory. In most computers you use, ROM contains information necessary to load and initialize (or boot) the operating system. (An **operating system**—such as Microsoft Windows, UNIX, or Linux—provides a default user interface and manages many low-level tasks, such as communicating with input and output devices.) Information stored in **random access memory (RAM)**, on the other hand, is changeable and usually volatile—that is, the contents of RAM are lost when the computer is shut down. When a program runs, values move in and out of RAM at high speeds to carry out program instructions. However, unless the program stores those values on a disk or other output device, they will not be available for further processing later.

The **central processing unit (CPU)** is the brain of the computer. The CPU typically has a set of registers, an arithmetic logic unit, and a control unit. A **register** is a high-speed memory location that holds data in the CPU while it is being processed. Some examples of registers are the **accumulator**, which holds intermediate results of computations carried out by the CPU; the **program counter**, which holds the address of the next instruction to be executed; and the **instruction register**, which holds the instruction currently being executed by the CPU. The **arithmetic logic unit (ALU)** performs addition, subtraction, and other arithmetic operations. The **control unit** directs the flow of operations within the CPU, telling the CPU when and where to fetch the next instruction, how to decode and execute the instruction, and where to store the result.

Software refers to computer programs that are executed or carried out by the hardware. A **computer program** is a set of instructions that directs a computer to perform specific computations and symbol manipulations. There are two major categories of software: application programs and system software. **Application programs** solve a particular problem or perform a specific function for the user. The programs you will write in this book fall into the application program category. **System software** includes operating systems, compilers, editors, device drivers, and a host of other programs that support and enable the development and execution of application programs. Visual Basic .NET (VB .NET) is an example of system software.

EXPLORING THE HISTORY OF PROGRAMMING LANGUAGES

As you are about to discover, modern programming languages are very powerful and enable you to develop sophisticated applications with relative ease, much faster than programmers in the early days of computing could have imagined. On the surface, modern programming languages bear little resemblance to their early counterparts, yet the principal underpinnings remain unchanged.

Machine Language

The earliest programming languages were machine languages. **Machine language** consists of nothing but 0's and 1's, or bits. A **bit** is a binary digit—that is, a bit is either a 0 or a 1. At the machine level, bits are the only things that a computer truly understands. Combinations of bits, or bit patterns, are used to represent (or encode) other pieces of information. For example, a combination of eight bits, or a **byte**, typically represents a single character (such as the letter "a" or the symbol ">").

To illustrate machine language, consider a simple computer that provides only four instructions—clear the accumulator, add the contents of a specified memory location to the accumulator, subtract the contents of a specified memory location from the accumulator, and store the contents of the accumulator in a specified memory location. These four instructions could be represented in binary as combinations of two bits, as shown in Table 1-1.

Table 1-1 Instruction set of a simple machine

Binary Code	Meaning
00	Clear the accumulator
01	Add the contents of a specified memory location to the accumulator
10	Subtract the contents of a specified memory location from the accumulator
11	Store the contents of the accumulator in a specified memory location

Suppose that our simple machine also contains eight memory locations (numbered 0 through 7). Each memory location (or **address**) can be represented as a binary number using a combination of three bits: the first memory location (in binary) would be 000, the second would be 001, and so on.

 Each digit in a binary number represents a power of 2, just as each digit in a decimal number represents a power of 10. For example, the digits in the decimal number 243 represent $[(2 * 10^2) + (4 * 10^1) + (3 * 10^0)] = [(2 * 100) + (4 * 10) + (3 * 1)] = [200 + 40 + 3] = 243$. Similarly, the digits in the binary number 110 represent $[(1 * 2^2) + (1 * 2^1) + (0 * 2^0)] = [(1 * 4) + (1 * 2) + (0 * 1)] = [4 + 2 + 0] = 6$.

Finally, suppose that memory location 000 contains the value 4, memory location 010 contains the value 3, and memory location 110 contains the value 1. The memory contents of our machine would appear as follows:

Address:	000	001	010	011	100	101	110	111
Contents:	4		3				1	

A machine language program to clear the accumulator then performs the computation (4 + 3 − 1) and stores the results in memory location 100 as follows (spaces are added to improve readability):

```
00 01 000 01 010 10 110 11 100
```

After the program executes, memory location 100 will hold the value 6.

Such sets of 0's and 1's are all that computers understand, but are nearly indecipherable to humans. As you can imagine, programming in machine code, particularly as programs grow large, is difficult, time-consuming, and error-prone.

Assembly Language

The cumbersome nature of programming in machine language led to the development of assembly language. **Assembly language** provides a one-to-one correspondence between each machine language instruction and a **mnemonic**—a word or character string that represents the instruction. Assembly language still requires writing a set of single-step instructions, but is much easier for people to read and write. For example, the assembly language instruction set for our simple machine might consist of the mnemonics CLR (for Clear), ADD (for Add), SUB (for Subtract), and STO (for Store). Assembly language also allows you to assign names or **identifiers** to memory locations. Thus, memory locations 000 through 111 might now be referred to as A, B, C, D, E, F, G, and H, respectively. Given this new representation of instructions and memory locations, the program written in assembly language is shown on the left, with explanations on the right:

CLR   Clear the accumulator

ADD A   Add the contents of memory location A to the accumulator

ADD C   Add the contents of memory location C to the accumulator

SUB G   Subtract the contents of memory location G from the accumulator

STO E   Store the contents of the accumulator in memory location E

Assembly language programs require special software, called an **assembler**, to translate the mnemonics and memory location names into the underlying pattern of 0's and 1's of machine code. Different computers have different instruction sets and use different patterns of 0's and 1's to represent those instructions. For this reason, machine languages and assembly languages are unique to the particular machine (or platform) for which they were developed. This means that an assembly language program written for one computer architecture usually will not run on a different computer architecture without significant modification. And, although assembly language is much easier to read and write than machine code, it still requires programmers to write code in a way that is unnatural to many people.

High-level Languages

High-level languages, such as COBOL, Java, and Visual Basic, evolved partially in response to the need for portability and partially in response to the need for more expressive languages that let programmers write instructions in a more natural way. For example, to instruct the computer to execute the simple machine program in VB .NET, you write `E = A + C - G`. Obviously, programs written in high-level languages are much easier to read, write, and maintain, but they are less efficient in terms of the CPU time and memory needed to execute them. This tradeoff is one people are often willing to accept because the labor costs associated with producing and maintaining code that is difficult to read and write usually far outweigh the costs of additional CPU time and memory. However, in cases where CPU resources are scarce (such as onboard navigation systems), a lower-level language is sometimes the language of choice.

Similar to assembly language, programs written in a high-level language require an additional software program called a **compiler** to translate the program to machine code. In general, high-level language processing not only involves compiling, but also linking, loading, and executing. For example, when you write a program in VB .NET, you will use a text editor to enter and save your program. The program you write is referred to as **source code**. For VB .NET programs, source code is saved in a file named *xxx*.vb, where *xxx* is the name you assign to your program (such as *MyFirstProgram*); for Java programs, source code is saved in a file named *xxx*.java. Other high-level languages have similar source file naming conventions.

When you tell the computer to compile a program written in a high-level language, the compiler reads your source code and checks for a variety of errors, such as misspellings. If the compiler does not detect any errors, it translates your source code to machine code (also called **object code**) and stores it in an object file. Another special program called the **linker** then combines your object code with that of other programs in the class libraries. A **class library** is a collection of object files that support the features and functions of a high-level language. For example, all high-level languages include a library of mathematical functions. If your program requires determining the square root of a particular number, you do not have to write the code that actually calculates the square root. Instead you simply call upon the square root function that is built into the math library to do this for you. VB .NET includes an extensive and powerful set of class libraries that enable you to write programs that solve complex problems with relatively few lines of code. You will learn much more about the VB .NET class libraries in later chapters.

When you tell the system to execute (or run) your program, a software program (sometimes called a **loader**) loads the object code into memory and executes the program. Figure 1-2 shows an overview of creating, compiling, and executing a high-level language program.

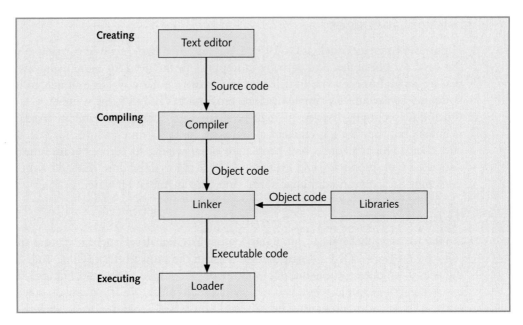

Figure 1-2   Overview of high-level language processing

As you will learn in Chapter 2, the Visual Studio Integrated Development Environment (IDE) provides a text editor for entering source code and software tools for compiling and executing your programs. In Chapter 3, you will learn precisely how the .NET Framework carries out the task of compiling and executing the VB .NET programs you write.

LEARNING A PROGRAMMING LANGUAGE

Learning a programming language is in many ways like learning a foreign language. You must first understand the basic vocabulary of the language. In programming languages, the basic vocabulary is words built into the language, which are referred to as **keywords** or **reserved words**. When you learn a foreign language, you must also learn its structure—that is, how to combine words with other symbols (such as punctuation marks) to form meaningful sentences, paragraphs, and larger groupings of related thoughts (such as chapters in this textbook). In programming languages, **statements** are similar to sentences—a statement consists of keywords, identifiers, and symbols. **Procedures** are similar to paragraphs—a procedure consists of one or more related statements that work together to perform a specific task (such as calculating your grade-point average). **Modules** are similar to chapters in this textbook—a module is a self-sufficient group of related procedures that you can combine with other modules to create applications.

Furthermore, as with a foreign language, you must learn the **syntax**, or rules of the language. This includes spelling, punctuation, and grammar. Although some human languages such as

English, Spanish, and French share many common characteristics, they also have syntactical differences beyond the obvious differences in vocabulary. For example, in Spanish, questions begin with "¿" and end with "?", and adjectives usually follow rather than precede the noun they describe. The Spanish word for school is *escuela*, and the word for large is *grande*. The question "Is Yale a large school?" would be written in Spanish as "¿Es Yale una escuela grande?" Just as each foreign language has its own unique syntax and structure, so does each programming language. For example, in COBOL many statements end with a dot (.), in Java each statement ends with a semi-colon (;), and in VB. NET no end of statement punctuation mark is required.

In human languages, as well as in programming languages, proper structure and syntax is necessary to communicate clearly. However, while most humans would know how to interpret a statement where a needed punctuation mark is omitted or a word is misspelled, compilers are not so forgiving. When the compiler translates your source code to machine language, it checks for syntax errors. A **syntax error** is a mistake in your program that violates one of the language rules. For example, if you omit a needed punctuation mark or misspell one of the keywords, the compiler will inform you that the program has a syntax error; you must correct this error before you can continue.

As with spoken languages, even if a statement is syntactically correct, it may not make sense. In order to communicate effectively, a statement or paragraph must also be logically (or semantically) correct. For example, although the sentence "I have a spot named dog" is syntactically correct, it is nonsensical. While people may be able to guess the proper meaning of such statements, compilers cannot. In a computer program, logical errors of this kind are not detected by the compiler, and as a result, execute whether they should or not. **Logic errors,** also known as bugs, are mistakes in your program that cause it to produce incorrect results. Later in this book, you will learn how to isolate and fix bugs in your programs.

In summary, to learn a programming language, you must learn both the keywords (vocabulary) and the syntax (language rules). To write computer programs that will produce correct results, you must also learn to write statements that are logically (semantically) correct and combine them to solve the problem at hand.

SOLVING PROBLEMS AND DEVELOPING ALGORITHMS

At its heart, computer programming is problem solving. For example, a payroll program takes information such as hours worked and wage rate and uses it to solve the problems of calculating pay and generating a paycheck. A university registration system uses information about courses, students, professors, and classrooms to solve the problems of enrolling students in courses and generating class schedules. Problems for which computer programs are useful almost always require one or more inputs, such as hours worked and wage rate, and produce one or more results or outputs, such as paychecks. A sequence of steps, or an **algorithm**, is used to transform the input(s) into the desired output(s). The input-process-output model for achieving the transformation is shown in Figure 1-3.

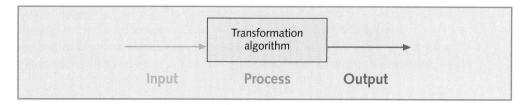

Figure 1-3   Transforming inputs into outputs

Computer programs specify the transformation algorithm—that is, they accept inputs, specify the steps necessary to transform them into the desired outputs, and then generate those outputs. The transformation algorithm is the solution algorithm; the outputs are the solution to the problem. Because programs solve problems, it is critical that programmers embrace a problem-solving approach. A problem-solving approach dictates that you understand the problem at hand, properly identify the available inputs and the desired outputs, and develop a transformation algorithm *before* you begin writing code.

The first step in problem solving is to make sure you understand the problem. Although this step may seem obvious, it is frequently overlooked—especially by novice programmers. Understanding a problem often requires asking questions or doing research to gather more information. This information may concern the number, type, source, or format of the available inputs; the number, type, destination, or format of the desired outputs; or details regarding the sequence of steps needed to make the transformation. For example, consider the problem of calculating a payroll. Suppose a company has two types of employees—hourly and salaried. Hourly employees are paid overtime if they work more than 40 hours in a week. The overtime rate is 1.5 times the hourly wage rate. Salaried employees receive a base salary regardless of the number of hours they work. To calculate payroll and generate a paycheck, you need to have at least four inputs: (1) employee name; (2) hours worked—a number between 0 and 168 (the number of hours in a week); (3) wage rate or base salary—a number greater than 0; and (4) employee type—the letter S or H (representing salaried or hourly). To calculate pay, you must understand the differences between how salaried and hourly employees are paid. Weekly pay for salaried employees is equal to their base salary; weekly pay for hourly employees is equal to their base pay plus overtime compensation (if any). For hourly employees who work 40 hours or less per week, base pay is equal to the wage rate multiplied by hours worked, and overtime compensation is 0. For hourly employees who work more than 40 hours per week, base pay is equal to the wage rate multiplied by 40, and overtime compensation is equal to the hours over 40 multiplied by the overtime rate. To generate a paycheck, you must format weekly pay in currency notation (for example, $425.00), formulate a textual representation of the pay amount ("Four hundred twenty-five and no/100"), and then print these items along with the employee name in the proper positions on the check. When other elements of payroll processing (such as calculating amounts to withhold for payroll taxes and employee benefits) are taken into consideration, the problem becomes much more complex and the need for developing a clear understanding of the problem becomes even greater.

Once you clearly understand the problem to be solved—including the inputs, processes, and outputs—only then can you proceed to the second step in the problem-solving process: developing an algorithm that will lead to a correct solution. Consider a simple and familiar example: the problem of calculating your end-of-semester grade point average (GPA). Assume that course grades are limited to the following values: A, B, C, D, and F. Also assume that an A corresponds to 4 grade points, a B corresponds to 3 grade points, etc. Finally, assume that the desired output (semester GPA) is a decimal number formatted to two decimal digits, such as 3.25. Your semester GPA is the weighted average of your course grades. The weight associated with a course is the number of credit hours earned in that course. With this information in hand and your assumptions validated, you are ready to develop an algorithm.

 In general, you must validate assumptions before you develop an algorithm. Unvalidated assumptions lead to programs that produce wrong results. For example, some schools issue numeric grades (0–100) rather than letter grades, and some schools that issue letter grades use a 5-point scale rather than a 4-point scale.

Example 1-1: Creating a GPA algorithm

To compute your GPA, you must know the letter grade and the number of credit hours associated with each course. These are the inputs. You can determine the average using the following formula:

```
GPA = total grade points / total credit hours
```

An algorithm to compute your semester GPA can be expressed as follows:

Set TotalPoints, TotalHours, and GPA equal to 0

For each course

    Get Grade and CreditHours

    Add CreditHours to TotalHours

    If Grade is an 'A', multiply CreditHours by 4 and add result to TotalPoints

    If Grade is a 'B', multiply CreditHours by 3 and add result to TotalPoints

    If Grade is a 'C', multiply CreditHours by 2 and add result to TotalPoints

    If Grade is a 'D', multiply CreditHours by 1 and add result to TotalPoints

When no more courses

    If TotalHours is not 0, calculate GPA = TotalPoints/TotalHours

A final step in the problem-solving approach is to verify that your algorithm produces correct results. One way to do this is to desk-check your algorithm. **Desk–checking** involves drawing columns by hand that correspond to items in your algorithm. You then create a set of test data and step through your algorithm. As you step through the algorithm, you record the changing values for each item, essentially mimicking the way a computer would execute a program based on your algorithm.

Example 1-2: Desk-checking the algorithm

For the GPA example, desk-checking requires creating a table with columns for grade, CreditHours, TotalPoints, TotalHours, and GPA. To create a set of test data, think of representative input values for the problem you are trying to solve. In this case, assume you completed four courses with the following grades and credit hours:

Grade	CreditHours
A	3
B	2
C	4
A	3

As you step through the algorithm, you record the following information, striking through each value when you replace it with a new value:

Grade	CreditHours	TotalHours	TotalPoints	GPA
~~A~~	~~3~~	~~3~~	~~12~~	
~~B~~	~~2~~	~~5~~	~~18~~	
~~C~~	4	~~9~~	~~26~~	
A	3	12	38	
				38/12 = 3.17

 It is common practice in desk-checking to strike through old values for an item when a new value for that item comes into existence.

After completing these four courses, your semester GPA is 3.17. If desk-checking your algorithm does not produce a correct result—if it produced 10.00 or -0.5, for example—then you must go back and find the logic error in your algorithm.

Until you can demonstrate the validity of your algorithm, it is foolhardy to begin writing code. Although many beginning students object to the time they must invest to understand the problem, design an algorithm, and desk-check it, this approach almost always saves time and frustration in the long run.

IDENTIFYING BASIC OBJECT-ORIENTED PROGRAMMING CONCEPTS

For many years, programmers focused their efforts on the algorithmic approach you have just seen—that is, they defined a set of steps to transform inputs into the desired outputs, and then translated these steps into code. Because this approach to programming is based on sequences of actions, or procedures, it became known as **procedural programming**, and languages that support this approach—COBOL, C, and FORTRAN—are referred to as procedural programming languages.

In recent years, a new approach to programming, the object-oriented (OO) approach, has become popular. Object-oriented programming languages, such as Java and VB .NET, have become the languages of choice for many new systems development projects and particularly for Internet-based applications. Before you begin programming in VB .NET, you should therefore learn some of the basic concepts of object-oriented programming.

Object-oriented programming (OOP) begins by defining a collection of objects that work together to solve the problem at hand. An **object** often corresponds to something in the real world—it is a thing that has characteristics and behaviors. Look around you. You will see many different kinds of objects. If you are at home, you will likely see your book, your computer, your desk, and perhaps your faithful dog. If asked to describe your dog, you might say she is a four-year-old yellow lab named Molly. In describing your dog, you have identified a set of attributes (gender, age, color, breed, and name) for dog objects. If asked what your dog can do, you might say that she barks, eats, sleeps, and knows how to shake hands and roll over. The things your dog can do are called its behaviors, or methods.

Consider another example. A computer program can have many types of objects, such as those that make up the graphical user interface (GUI) and others that are the focus of the problem to be solved. A GUI object, such as a button or a check box, has **attributes**, which are characteristics that have values: the size, the shape, the color, the location, and the caption of a button, for example. GUI objects also have behaviors, or **methods**, which define what the object can do. For example, a button can respond to a click and a check box can show that it is checked or unchecked.

Objects such as dogs and GUI buttons are relatively easy to understand because you can see them and interact with them directly. But computer programs often require other types of objects, called **problem domain objects**, which are specific to the problem being solved. For example, the point-of-sale system at your favorite restaurant deals with order objects and food objects. Like GUI objects, problem domain objects also have attributes and methods, as shown in Figure 1-4. Attributes are characteristics that describe the object. For example, an order object has an order number, date, and amount. A food object, such as a hamburger, has a name and price. Methods give problem domain objects the ability to perform tasks. For example, the methods of an order object might include the ability to set the order date, add a food product to the order, and calculate the order amount. A food object might have methods to set its name and price, give its name and price, and check the availability of the ingredients required to make it.

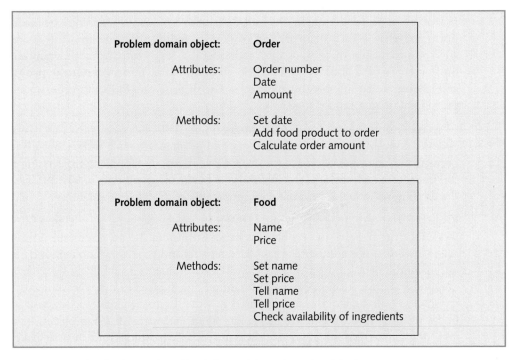

Figure 1-4   Attributes and methods in problem domain objects

Objects interact by sending messages to each other. A **message** asks an object to invoke, or carry out, one of its methods. For example, an order object might send a message to a cheeseburger object asking it to check the availability of its ingredients. Note that to send the message the order object does not need to know the details of how the cheeseburger object carries out this task, but only whether the task is successfully accomplished. If the restaurant is out of cheese, an order for a cheeseburger cannot be filled. The order object needs to know whether the ingredients for a cheeseburger are available, but is not concerned with how the cheeseburger object makes this determination.

Hiding these details illustrates another key concept in OOP known as encapsulation. **Encapsulation** means that the attributes and methods of an object are packaged into a single unit, and what is more important, that you do not need to know the internal structure of the object to send messages to it. You only need to know what an object can do. Encapsulation hides the internal structure of objects as well as the details of how the object carries out its behaviors. This is often referred to as **information hiding**.

A restaurant has many order objects and many food objects, each with a unique identity. The fact that each object has a unique identity is important because it enables you to refer to it or send it a message. For example, when an order object asks a food object to check the availability of its ingredients, it needs to send the message to a particular food object.

When you refer to all food objects as a group, you are talking about the food class. A **class** defines what all objects of the group have in common. When you refer to a specific member of the group, you are talking about an **instance** of the class. Cheeseburger is an instance of the food class, and your pet Molly is an instance of the dog class. When each instance is created, it automatically possesses all of the attributes and methods defined for its class. For example, when a new instance of a food object is created, it automatically has attributes for name and price, and methods to set its name and price, give its name and price, and check the availability of its ingredients.

One of the most powerful concepts in OOP is inheritance. **Inheritance** means a class of objects takes on, or inherits, characteristics of another class and extends them as necessary. For example, some food objects might need additional attributes not common to all members of the food class. Food objects such as coffee and soft drinks need a size attribute (small, medium, or large). Other food objects, such as steaks, need attributes for how they should be cooked (rare, medium, or well-done) while others, such as hamburgers, need attributes for the condiments that are desired (ketchup, mayonnaise, pickles, etc.) If the food class is already defined, a beverage class can be defined by extending the food class to take on the more specific attributes and methods required by a beverage. Similarly, a steak class and a sandwich class can be defined by extending the food class to take on the more specific attributes and methods required by steaks and sandwiches. The beverage class, the steak class, and the sandwich class would then be considered **subclasses** of the food class, and the food class would be the **superclass** of the beverage, steak, and sandwich classes. This relationship is shown in Figure 1-5. Because a superclass specifies general characteristics and subclasses capture more specialized information, diagrams such as the one in Figure 1-5 are called generalization/specialization (or inheritance) hierarchies.

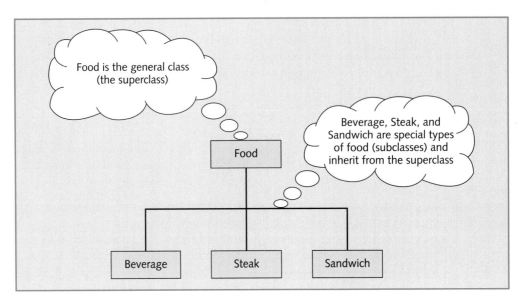

Figure 1-5   A superclass and its subclasses

A final key concept in OOP is **polymorphism**, which literally means "many forms." Polymorphism refers to the way different objects can respond in their own way to the same message, and is related to the inheritance of methods. For example, cellular phone companies offer many service plans. Most service plans include some number of minutes for a fixed monthly fee, and then price excess minutes at a particular rate. Some service plans charge additional fees for roaming outside a given geographic area while others include free nationwide long distance. Some service plans include free calls during certain hours of the day or days of the week and others offer reduced rates for family plans. All the different types of service plans know how to generate a bill, but they follow different rules for doing so. Polymorphism means that the sender of the message "generate bill" does not need to know what type of service plan is involved, but only that the recipient of the message correctly generates a bill when asked.

Understanding concepts such as encapsulation, inheritance, and polymorphism takes time and requires experience in writing OO programs. At this point, you should focus on learning OO terminology and gaining a general idea of the OOP approach. As you read through this book and begin writing programs, you will learn much more about these and other OO concepts.

EXAMINING THE BENEFITS OF THE OBJECT-ORIENTED APPROACH

The OO approach to programming and systems development offers two major advantages over the traditional, procedural approach. The first of these is naturalness. It is natural to think in terms of the objects around you. It is usually not difficult to identify the attributes and behaviors of the objects with which you work and use everyday. Users find it natural to define a problem in terms of the objects that are familiar to them, which can simplify the task of gathering information necessary to understand the problem requirements. People also tend to organize their knowledge in a hierarchy similar to generalization/specialization hierarchies. For example, it is common for people to think of the animal kingdom in terms of categories such as reptiles, mammals, birds, and insects. Each of these categories brings to mind further specialization—when you think about mammals, animals such as dogs, cats, horses, and cows may come to mind. If asked, you could quickly identify another level of subcategories for each of these groups, such as hunting dogs and herding dogs. In addition, you could describe distinguishing attributes and behaviors of each group at each level of the hierarchy.

A second key benefit of the OO approach is reusability. **Reusability** means that classes and objects can be created once and used many times. You can think of each class as a physical component that you can use to build solutions for multiple problems. Once you define a class (create a component), you can use that class (component) to build different kinds of systems. For example, once you create an order class for a restaurant, you can reuse it in other systems that need order objects, often with little or no modification. If the new system has a special type of order that must be handled differently, the existing order class can be extended to a new subclass. You do not have to see the source code for the class to reuse it or extend it. This saves time and makes your job easier.

OOP languages such as VB .NET come with class libraries that contain many predefined classes you can use in your programs. A class library is a perfect example of reusability. For example, VB .NET has a class library that provides common GUI components such as buttons, labels, and check boxes. If a program you are writing requires the user to push a button to initiate some task, you do not need to create a button class from scratch. Instead, you use the button class that is provided in the class library to create a button object for your program.

Do the benefits and popularity of the OO approach mean that the algorithmic approach you studied earlier is no longer useful? No, not at all! As you will see throughout this book, the OO approach still requires you to design algorithms to define the methods (or behaviors) of an object and to describe the ways in which objects interact with one another.

Whether you are writing programs in a procedural or an OOP language, the goal is to write code that is understandable, unambiguous, and most important, produces accurate results every time. Instructions must be clear, precise, properly ordered, and detailed enough to produce desired results. Writing a program requires you to think logically, follow a problem-solving approach, and pay attention to detail. At the same time, programming demands creativity, a willingness to look for new and better ways to solve a problem, and an ability to see how the pieces of a complex problem fit together.

Writing programs is both an art and a science. It requires both creative and analytical talents. Even more so, programming is an applied discipline. You must do programming to learn it. Like developing a good golf swing, writing programs well takes practice. As you proceed through this book, keep in mind that nothing will contribute to your success more than practice.

QUICK REVIEW

1. A computer is a programmable electronic device that can retrieve, store, and process data (such as numbers, text, graphics, and video). Processing data includes not only numerical calculations but also the manipulation of symbols, usually to solve a problem.

2. A computer consists of hardware (physical, touchable components) and software (computer programs). Hardware includes input/output devices, one or more processors, and memory.

3. The arrangement of physical components within a computer is referred to as its architecture.

4. There are two types of memory: read-only memory (ROM) and random access memory (RAM). The contents of ROM are fixed and nonvolatile. Nonvolatile means that the contents remain intact after the computer is shut off. Information stored in RAM is changeable and volatile.

5. A central processing unit (CPU) typically contains several registers, an arithmetic logic unit (ALU), and a control unit.

6. A register is a high-speed memory location that holds data in the CPU while it is being processed. Some examples of registers are the accumulator, which holds intermediate results of computations carried out by the CPU; the program counter, which holds the address of the next instruction to be executed; and the instruction register, which holds the instruction currently being executed by the CPU.

7. The ALU performs addition, subtraction, and other arithmetic operations.

8. The control unit directs the flow of operations within the CPU, telling the CPU when and where to fetch the next instruction, how to decode and execute the instruction, and where to store the result.

9. Software refers to computer programs that are executed or carried out by the hardware. A computer program is a set of instructions that direct a computer to perform specific computations and symbol manipulations.

10. There are two major categories of software: application programs and system software. Application programs solve a particular problem or perform a specific function for the user. The programs you write are application programs. Programs that support and enable the development and execution of application programs are referred to as system software. Operating systems, compilers, editors, and device drivers are examples of system software.

11. The earliest programming languages, known as machine languages, consist only of binary digits (or bits)—that is, only 0's and 1's. Machine code is the only thing computers truly understand, but is almost indecipherable to humans.

12. Assembly language provides a one-to-one correspondence between each machine language instruction and a mnemonic—a word or character string that represents the instruction. Assembly language also allows a programmer to assign names (or identifiers) to memory locations. As a result, assembly language is much easier to read and write than machine language.

13. Assembly language programs require a special software program, called an assembler, to translate the mnemonics and memory location names into the underlying pattern of 0's and 1's of machine code.

14. Similarly, programs written in high-level languages (such as COBOL, Java, and VB .NET) require an additional software program called a compiler to translate the program to machine code. During translation, the compiler also checks for syntax errors.

15. When you write a program, you write source code. If there are no syntax errors, the compiler translates your source code to machine code (or object code). A program called the linker then combines your object code with that of other programs in the class libraries. When you tell the system to execute your program, a program called a loader loads the object code into memory and executes the program.

16. A class library is a collection of object files that support the features and functions of a high-level language.

17. In programming languages, the words that are built into the language are referred to as keywords; sentences are statements; paragraphs are procedures; and chapters are modules.

18. Semantic (or logic) errors are not detected by the compiler. These errors are commonly called bugs.

19. To learn a programming language, you must learn the keywords (vocabulary) and the syntax (language rules). To write computer programs that will produce correct results, you must write statements that are logically correct and combine them in such a way as to solve the problem at hand.

20. The first step in solving a problem is to make sure you understand it. Understanding a problem may require asking questions about the available inputs, the desired outputs, and the sequence of steps needed to transform the inputs into the desired outputs.

21. The sequence of steps used to transform the inputs into the desired outputs is called an algorithm.

22. Desk-checking involves setting up a table with columns that correspond to items in an algorithm, and then tracking the changing values of these items through each step of the algorithm.

23. The traditional approach to programming is based on sequences of actions, or procedures, and is known as procedural programming,

24. Object-oriented programming (OOP) defines a collection of objects that work together to solve a problem.

25. An object often corresponds to something in the real world and has attributes (characteristics) and methods (behaviors).

26. Objects interact by sending messages to each other. A message asks an object to invoke, or carry out, one of its methods.

27. Encapsulation is an object-oriented (OO) concept that refers to the bundling of an object's attributes and methods into a single unit. Encapsulation hides the internal structure of an object as well as the details of how an object carries out its behaviors.

28. A class defines those things that a group of objects have in common. This commonality may include both attributes (characteristics) and methods (behaviors).

29. A specific member of a class is referred to as an instance of the class.

30. Inheritance is an OO concept through which a class of objects takes on (or inherits) characteristics of another class, and then extends these characteristics by specializing them in a particular way.

31. A class that inherits from another class is called a subclass. The class from which a subclass inherits is called its superclass.

32. Polymorphism, which literally means "many forms," is an OO concept referring to the way different objects can respond in their own way to the same message.

33. One major advantage of the object-oriented (OO) approach is naturalness—it is natural for us to think about problems in terms of the objects around us. A second advantage is that it promotes the reuse of classes and objects.

34. Writing programs is an art and a science requiring both creative and analytical talents. It is also an applied discipline. To succeed as a programmer you must practice writing programs.

EXERCISES

1. What is meant by the term "architecture" when referring to computer hardware? Describe the high-level hardware architecture of a typical computer.

2. Name the typical components of a CPU and state the purpose of each.

3. Give examples of at least three input devices and three output devices.

4. Compare and contrast the following terms:
   a. Hardware : : Software
   b. ROM : : RAM
   c. Identifier : : Address
   d. Register : : Memory location

5. Assume a simple machine uses four bits to represent its instruction set. How many different instructions can this machine have? How many instructions could it have if eight bits are used? How many if 16 bits are used?

6. Consider a simple machine with the following instruction set:

Binary Code	Mnemonic	Meaning
000	CLR	Clear the accumulator
001	ADD	Add the contents of a specified memory location to the accumulator
010	SUB	Subtract the contents of a specified memory location from the accumulator
011	STO	Store the contents of the accumulator in a specified memory location
100	MULT	Multiply the value in the accumulator by the contents of a specified memory location
101	LOAD	Load the contents of a specified memory location into the accumulator
110	INC	Add one to the accumulator
111	DEC	Subtract one from the accumulator

Assume that this machine has eight memory locations whose addresses and contents are as shown:

Address:	000	001	010	011	100	101	110	111
Contents:	9		3			5	2	

Write machine language code to perform each of the following calculations. Store each result in the first empty memory location.

a. $(5 * 9) + 3$

b. $(3 + 5) * 9$

c. $(5 * 3) + (2 * 9)$

7. Write the assembly language equivalent for each of the calculations in Exercise 6. Assume that the memory addresses in Exercise 6 can be referred to as A, B, C, D, E, F, G, and H, respectively.

8. What is the advantage of assembly language over machine language? What is the advantage of a higher-level language over assembly language? What is the major disadvantage of higher-level languages?

9. What is the purpose of an assembler? A compiler? A linker? A loader?

10. Compare and contrast the following terms:

a. System software : : Application software

b. Source code : : Object code

c. Syntax : : Semantics

11. Describe the problem-solving approach to computer programming. Why is such an approach needed?

12. Design an algorithm to calculate a customer's bill at a fast-food restaurant. Assume that each item purchased has a price and quantity ordered. For example, a customer might purchase three hamburgers at $1.39 each, two orders of French fries at $.99 each, and one soft drink at $1.09. The algorithm should calculate the total cost of the order, including a 7% sales tax, and then print a sales receipt.

13. Review the algorithm presented earlier in this chapter that calculates a semester GPA, and then complete the following tasks:

   a. Explain why it is unnecessary to check for a grade of 'F' in the GPA algorithm.

   b. Modify the algorithm so that it accommodates the circumstance in which a student withdraws from a course. Assume that when a student withdraws from a course, he or she earns 0 credit hours for that course, the letter grade assigned to the course is a 'W', and that the grade point value for a 'W' is 0.

   c. Modify the original GPA algorithm to alter the assumption of letter grades. Assume instead that a student receives a numeric grade between 0 and 100 for each course.

   d. Assume that in addition to the semester GPA, you also need to calculate the cumulative GPA. What additional inputs are needed? Modify the original GPA algorithm to include this calculation.

14. The electric power company in your community sends you a bill for the electric energy you consume each month. The amount of electric energy you have consumed is determined by reading a meter outside your home. The difference between the meter reading taken this month and the meter reading taken one month ago reflects the amount of electric energy you have used. Assume that your electric meter has five digits, as shown in Figure 1-6.

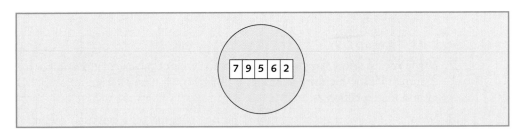

Figure 1-6   An electric meter

The following algorithm calculates the average energy consumption over several months:

Set AvgEnergyUsed, TotalEnergyUsed, NumberOfMonths equal to 0
Get BeginningMeterReading

Set PreviousMeterReading equal to BeginningMeterReading
For each month in the time period
    Add 1 to NumberOfMonths
    Get MeterReading
    Calculate EnergyUsed = MeterReading - PreviousMeterReading
    Add EnergyUsed to TotalEnergyUsed
    Set PreviousMeterReading equal to MeterReading
When no more months
    Calculate AvgEnergyUsed = TotalEnergyUsed / NumberOfMonths

Desk-check the algorithm using 79562 as the beginning meter reading and the follow-ing values for meter readings at the end of months 1, 2, and 3 respectively: 81023, 84777, and 88145. The correct answer for the average energy used over the three-month time period is 2861. Does the algorithm produce the correct result? What potential problems, if any, do you see with the algorithm?

15. Desk-check the algorithm in Exercise 14 again using a different set of test data. This time, assume the value for the beginning meter reading is 87304 and the values at the end of months 1, 2, and 3 are 93102, 98740, and 00753, respectively. The correct answer now for the average energy used is 4483. Does the algorithm produce the correct answer? Why not?

16. Modify the algorithm in Exercise 14 so that it produces the correct result with the test data given in Exercise 14 and with the test data given in Exercise 15, and then desk-check it again. If it does not produce the correct result in both cases, repeat the process of making corrections and desk-checking until the algorithm works. Based on this example, what can you say about the selection of test data?

17. Assume that a university tracks information for two kinds of persons: students and employees. All types of persons have a name, address, and phone number, and know how to tell these things about themselves. All employees have an employee number and a job title, and know how to tell these things about themselves. Similarly, all students have a student number and a GPA, and know how to tell these things about themselves. Assume further that there are two types of employees (faculty and staff), and two types of students (undergraduate and graduate). Faculty members have a monthly salary, and know how to calculate their pay. Staff members have a regular hourly wage and an overtime wage rate, and also know how to calculate their pay. Undergraduate students have a major and an advisor, and know how to tell these things about themselves. Grad-uate students have one or more previous degrees and know how to tell this about themselves.

    a. Create a generalization/specialization hierarchy for this scenario. Identify the attributes and behaviors that are associated with each group at each level in the hierarchy.

    b. List all the characteristics and behaviors of an undergraduate student. What OO concept (encapsulation, inheritance, or polymorphism) makes it possible for an undergraduate student to be able to tell his or her name?

c. Note that faculty and staff both know how to calculate their pay, but use different mechanisms for doing so. What OO concept (encapsulation, inheritance, or polymorphism) makes it possible for faculty and staff to respond to the request to calculate pay in unique ways?

d. What OO concept (encapsulation, inheritance, or polymorphism) enables a calculate pay request to be sent without needing to know the details of how calculations are carried out?

18. Construct a three-level generalization/specialization hierarchy (similar to the one you created for Exercise 17) that represents some area of knowledge (or groups of objects) with which you are familiar. Identify characteristics and behaviors for each group at each level of the hierarchy. Use your diagram to illustrate the concepts of encapsulation, information hiding, inheritance, and polymorphism.

19. Compare and contrast the following terms:

a. class :: instance :: object

b. message :: polymorphism :: method

c. encapsulation :: information hiding

d. inheritance :: attribute :: method

e. superclass :: subclass

f. module :: class library :: reusability

20. Identify and describe the two major advantages of the OO approach.

2

The Visual Studio .NET Development Environment

In this chapter, you will:
- O Explore the Visual Studio .NET development environment
- O Create a project using Visual Basic .NET
- O Compile and execute a Visual Basic .NET program
- O Use the visual form designer
- O Explore the debugging tool
- O Explore the help facility

Chapter 1 introduced you to the fundamental characteristics of computers, programming languages, and objects. You learned about component architecture and the evolution of programming languages. You saw how the syntax and structure of programming languages resembles that of spoken languages, and you learned the importance of taking an algorithmic, problem-solving approach to programming. You also explored object-oriented concepts, such as attributes, methods, inheritance, and encapsulation.

In this chapter, you learn how to use Visual Basic .NET (VB .NET) to write and execute simple programs. You begin by exploring the basic features of the Visual Studio .NET development environment. You learn how to use various tools and windows to create simple applications. You are introduced to the features of the VB .NET debugging tool and help facilities. After completing this chapter, you will have firsthand experience with VB .NET and understand how to use the development environment to create, modify, and execute programs.

EXPLORING THE VISUAL STUDIO .NET DEVELOPMENT ENVIRONMENT

VB .NET is one of several languages supported by Microsoft's Visual Studio .NET integrated development environment. An **Integrated Development Environment (IDE)** is a set of software tools that helps you code, test, and document the programs you write. As you will see, Visual Studio .NET is a powerful tool designed to meet today's demand for the rapid deployment of software systems and Web applications. In this book, you develop applications using the VB .NET programming language. However, the knowledge you gain about the Visual Studio .NET development environment applies to any other .NET language such as C++ .NET, C# .NET, or J# .NET.

Like most IDEs, Visual Studio .NET includes many tools that support software development tasks. These range from simple text editors, to intelligent editors that recognize patterns as you type and can complete code for you, to visual development tools that generate code based on forms you build. Visual Studio .NET makes it easy to organize, compile, and execute your programs, and provides facilities to help you test your programs and isolate errors that keep these programs from running as you intend. Visual Studio .NET also provides extensive help facilities to assist you in the process of writing programs. Together these tools simplify programming tasks, making your job as a programmer easier and reducing the time it takes to develop working programs.

In this chapter, you work through a series of hands-on exercises to become familiar with the basic features of the Visual Studio .NET IDE. After completing these exercises, you will understand the concepts, tools, and windows that are essential for developing VB .NET programs.

Getting Started with VB .NET

To complete the steps in this chapter, you must first install Visual Studio .NET on your computer. (See the Preface of this book if you need to install Visual Studio .NET.) Then you are ready to start working with VB .NET.

To start VB .NET in Windows XP Professional:

1. Click the **Start** button, point to **All Programs**, point to **Microsoft Visual Studio .NET 2003**, and then click **Microsoft Visual Studio .NET 2003**. See Figure 2-1.

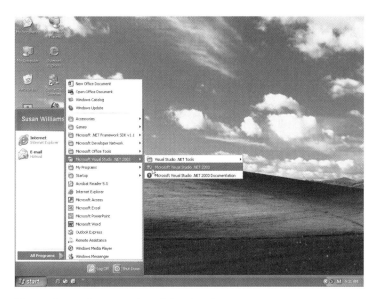

Figure 2-1   Starting Visual Studio .NET

2. A splash screen identifying the Visual Studio .NET languages installed on your computer momentarily appears, and then you see the Microsoft Development Environment (MDE) window. Verify that the MDE window resembles Figure 2-2. (Your screen may vary slightly depending on the settings for your computer.)

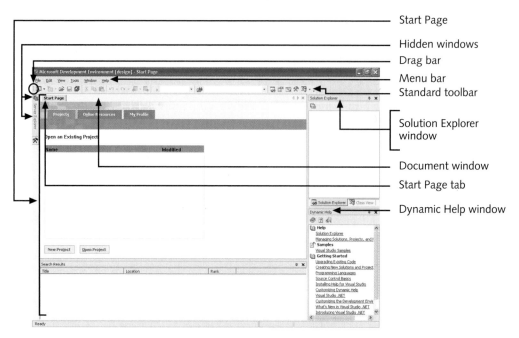

Start Page

Hidden windows

Drag bar

Menu bar

Standard toolbar

Solution Explorer window

Document window

Start Page tab

Dynamic Help window

Figure 2-2   The Microsoft Development Environment

Exploring the Microsoft Development Environment

As shown in Figure 2-2, the MDE includes a menu bar, various toolbars, and several windows. You use the menu bar to select commands that perform tasks such as opening and closing files; opening and closing projects; compiling, executing, and debugging programs; and accessing help facilities.

The toolbars provide buttons for many of the most common commands. To learn the names of these buttons, point to a button until a ScreenTip appears. Visual Studio .NET provides many toolbars, and displays them on a **context-sensitive** basis, which means that it automatically displays toolbars that support the task you are performing. As a result, the current set of toolbars depends on what you are doing. You can reveal or hide specific toolbars by right-clicking any empty space on the toolbar and checking or unchecking a toolbar name. (An alternate way to reveal or hide toolbars is to click Tools on the menu bar, click Customize, and then click the Toolbars tab.) You can change the position of any toolbar by using the drag bar to move it to a new location. (The drag bar is the set of short lines that appears on the left edge of the toolbar.)

The development environment includes a number of different windows. Depending on your configuration, you may not see all the windows shown in Figure 2-2. Notice, however, that the Start Page appears by default as a tabbed page within the document window (also called the main window).

In Figure 2-2, you see two other windows—the Solution Explorer window and the Dynamic Help window. Each of these are explained later in this chapter. Depending on your configuration, additional tabs may be visible at the bottom of the Solution Explorer and Dynamic Help windows, indicating that these windows contain other tabbed panes.

In addition, observe the tabs that appear along the left edge of the main window. These tabs identify hidden windows. **Hidden windows** enable you to keep frequently needed tools and resources readily available without cluttering the IDE. You can reveal a hidden window by moving the mouse pointer over its tab. The hidden window slides out, as in Figure 2-3 (which shows only part of the MDE). When you move the pointer out of the space occupied by the revealed window, it slides back to its hidden position. Figure 2-3 also identifies icons that enable you to display important windows you will learn about later—most notably, the Solution Explorer window, the Properties window, and the Toolbox.

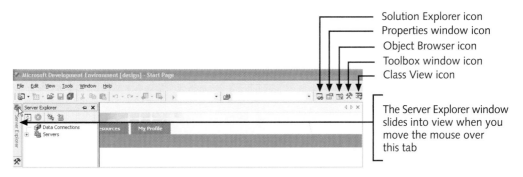

Figure 2-3   Revealing a hidden window

If this is the first time you are using Visual Studio .NET and you accepted the default settings when you installed the software, your screen should closely resemble Figure 2-2. If it does not, the following steps will help you configure your system so that your development environment window matches Figure 2-2 as closely as possible.

To configure your system:

1. Click **Tools** on the menu bar, and then click **Customize**. The Customize dialog box opens. See Figure 2-4.

If you are using VB .NET Standard Edition rather than VB.NET Professional Edition, you may not see all of the items listed in Figure 2-4.

Figure 2-4   The Customize dialog box

2. Click the **Toolbars** tab, if necessary, to select it.

3. Make sure that the only items checked are **MenuBar** and **Standard**. Later, you will customize your settings by adding other toolbars to your configuration.

4. Click **Close** to close the dialog box and apply the changes.

5. If windows other than the Solution Explorer window and Dynamic Help window are visible, close them. You can close any window by clicking the **Close** button (the X in the upper-right corner). Recall that additional tabs may be visible at the bottom of the Solution Explorer and Dynamic Help windows, indicating that these windows contain other tabbed panes. Although additional tabbed panes will not interfere with your work, you can close them if desired. To close a pane, click its tab (to select the pane), and then click its Close button.

6. If the Solution Explorer window is not visible, click the **Solution Explorer** button on the toolbar. The Solution Explorer window appears in the upper-right portion of the development environment.

Another way to make the Solution Explorer window visible is to click View on the menu bar, and then click Solution Explorer.

2

7. If the Dynamic Help window is not visible, click **Help** on the menu bar, and then click **Dynamic Help**. The Dynamic Help window appears in the lower-right portion of the development environment.

8. If the Toolbox does not appear as a hidden window along the left edge of the main window, click the **Toolbox** button on the toolbar. The Toolbox window opens, as shown in Figure 2-5. To hide the Toolbox window, click the **Auto Hide** (or push pin) icon in the Toolbox window title bar, and then move the pointer to the center of the main window.

 Clicking the push pin icon toggles the Auto Hide feature. When the push pin is in the vertical position, the Auto Hide feature is disabled. Clicking the push pin icon when it is in the vertical position enables the Auto Hide feature. This hides the Toolbox window by minimizing it as a tab along the edge of the document window.

Figure 2-5   The Toolbox window

Understanding the Start Page

The Start Page automatically loads in the document window when you start Visual Studio .NET. As shown in Figure 2-6, the Start Page contains three tabs named Projects, Online Resources, and My Profile. The Projects tab contains links to the projects you create. When you are connected to the Internet, the Online Resources tab contains links to a number of useful online resources. The My Profile tab allows you to personalize some of the settings that control the appearance and behavior of the IDE.

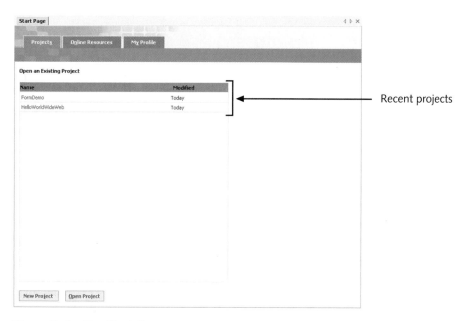

Figure 2-6   The Start Page

In this chapter, you explore the Projects tab. A **project** is a collection of files related to the VB .NET application you are creating. Clicking the Projects tab is one way to begin a new project or continue working on an existing project. When you click the Projects tab, you see a list of projects on which you have recently worked. If this is your first time using VB .NET, none appear on the list. You also see two buttons, as shown in Figure 2-6.

To open a project on the list, click the project name. If you want to work on a project that is not on the list, click the Open Project button to navigate to any project in any folder. Click the New Project button to create a project.

CREATING A PROJECT USING VISUAL BASIC .NET

A programming tradition when learning a new language is to write a program that displays the message "Hello World." For your first VB .NET project, you continue this tradition, but expand the message to "Hello World Wide Web."

When you create a VB .NET project, you must identify the type of project you want to create. Recall that Visual Studio .NET supports several programming languages; therefore, when you create a Visual Basic project, you must identify the project type as Visual Basic. You must also identify the template you want to use and specify the project name and location. A

template is a pattern for creating a specific type of application. VB .NET provides a number of programming templates. In this chapter, you work with two templates: the Console Application template and the Windows Application template. For your first project, you create a console application. A **console application** executes at the command line rather than within the Windows environment.

To create your first VB .NET project:

1. If you have not already done so, start Visual Studio .NET. The Start Page, Solution Explorer window, and Dynamic Help window appear.

2. If it is not already selected, click the **Projects** tab on the Start Page. You see a list of recent projects, together with the Open Project and New Project buttons. If this is the first time you have used VB .NET, the list of projects is empty.

3. Click the **New Project** button to create a project. The New Project dialog box opens, as shown in Figure 2-7.

 If you are using VB .NET Standard Edition rather than VB .NET Professional Edition, you may not see all the Project Types and Templates shown in Figures 2-7 and 2-8.

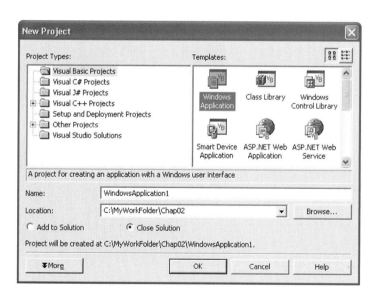

Figure 2-7   The New Project dialog box

4. If it is not already selected, click the **Visual Basic Projects** folder in the Project Types pane. In the Templates pane, you identify the type of application you want to create.

5. To select the console application template, scroll the Templates pane, and then click the **Console Application** icon.

6. In the Name text box of the New Project dialog box, you specify the name of your project. If this is your first console application, the Name text box contains the default project name ConsoleApplication1. Delete the default project name and type **HelloWorldWideWeb** in the Name text box.

7. In the Location text box, you specify the parent folder for your project. Your project will be saved as a subfolder within the folder you specify. If the folder or subfolders you specify do not already exist, VB .NET creates them for you. For this project, specify the Chap02 folder within your work folder as the location. (You can find instructions for creating and naming your work folder in the Preface of this book.) See Figure 2-8.

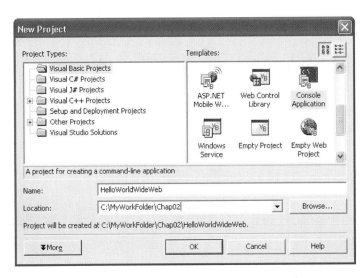

Figure 2-8   Specifying the new project type, template, name, and location

8. Click **OK**. As shown in Figure 2-9, several things happen. The Text Editor toolbar appears below the Standard toolbar; a tabbed page named Module1.vb appears in the document window; and the Properties window appears (along with Dynamic Help) as a tabbed pane in the lower-right window of the development environment. The Solution Explorer window and Properties window contain information about your new project. You see how to use this information shortly.

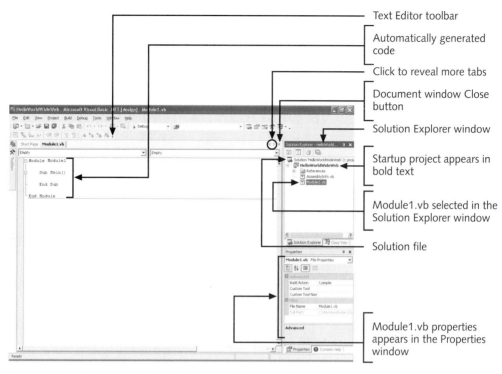

Figure 2-9   Module1.vb, the Solution Explorer window, and the Properties window for the HelloWorldWideWeb project

Take a moment to examine the contents of the Module1.vb document, the Solution Explorer window, and the Properties window. Notice in the Module1.vb document that VB .NET has automatically generated some code for you. This code is based on the Console Application template you selected. You learn the meaning of this code in this and subsequent chapters. Observe also that the Properties window contains information about the file properties of Module1.vb. When you click a different item in the Solution Explorer window, the information in the Properties window changes to reveal the properties of that item.

Also notice that multiple documents (such as the Start Page and Module1.vb) may be open at one time. To select a document, click its tab. The tab for the currently selected, or active, document appears in bold text. In Figure 2-9, Module1.vb is the active document. When working with a large number of documents, you can use the left and right arrows in the title bar of the document window to reveal tabbed pages that otherwise would be out of view. You can close the active document by clicking the Close button in the document window.

If you inadvertently close the Start Page, you can click Help on the menu bar, and then click Show Start Page to bring it back into view. If you inadvertently close the Module1.vb document window, you can reopen it again by double-clicking Module1.vb in the Solution Explorer window.

Understanding How VB .NET Organizes Your Programs

The Solution Explorer window shows the hierarchical arrangement of items that the solution you are building comprises. You should understand the way VB .NET organizes these items and the relationships between them. In VB .NET, the programs you write are named with a .vb file extension. By default, VB .NET names console applications as Module1.vb, Module2.vb, and so forth. You soon learn how to assign more descriptive names to your programs.

Visual Studio .NET uses projects and solutions to organize and manage programs and other files needed in your application. Recall that a project is a mechanism for grouping related files. For instance, a project might contain several program files, image files, and other miscellaneous items. A solution is a container for one or more projects. The solution file appears at the top of the hierarchy in the Solution Explorer window. When a solution contains more than one project, you must designate the **startup project**, which is the project that executes first when you run your application. Most of the solutions you create in this book contain only one project, and by default, VB .NET designates that project as the startup project. In the Solution Explorer window, the project file designated as the startup project appears in bold text, as shown earlier in Figure 2-9.

Notice in Figure 2-9 that in addition to Module1.vb, the HelloWorldWideWeb project contains a References folder and a program module named AssemblyInfo.vb. These items contain information needed by the system to complete your solution and execute your program. The plus and minus icons to the left of items in the hierarchy indicate that you can expand or collapse these items, respectively.

Using the Text Editor

For this example, you use the text editor to alter the contents of Module1.vb so that it displays the message "Hello World Wide Web" when the program executes. The Visual Studio .NET text editor (also called the code editor) provides standard text-editing capabilities, as well as color-coding, code indentation, and code completion features. By default, Visual Basic keywords appear in blue, comments appear in dark green, and other text appears in black. A **comment** is a statement you include in a program for documentation purposes only. You will learn more about comments in Chapter 3. Notice in Figure 2-9 that blocks of code appear at different levels of indentation. Although indentation is not required for your program to work properly, it improves readability and is considered good programming practice. The text editor helps you adhere to this practice by automatically indenting blocks of code as you type.

The text editor includes a code completion feature called **IntelliSense** that helps you complete lines of code by matching words. As you type, the text editor recognizes partial class and method names and suggests possible matches for the name you are typing. To complete the class or method name, you select the appropriate item from a list.

As with most text editors, you can also use the standard Windows shortcut keys to perform standard editing functions such as positioning the insertion point, selecting text, performing cut/copy/paste operations, and searching text.

To modify the contents of the Module1.vb program module:

1. In the Module1.vb document window, position the insertion point at the end of the line that reads "Sub Main ( )" and press **Enter**. A new line opens. Notice that the insertion point automatically indents under the word "Main."

2. Type the following partial line of code: **Console.** (Be sure to type the period.)

   When you type the period at the end of the word Console, a pop-up window opens. See Figure 2-10. This window lists the methods and properties of the Console class. You learn more about this class later. For now, you should recognize that these methods and properties represent choices for completing the partial line of code that you began.

 You can also type Ctrl+J to list the members of a class for statement completion when editing code.

Figure 2-10   The IntelliSense feature

3. In the pop-up window, move the scroll bar down until you see the WriteLine option. Double-click **WriteLine**. Notice that WriteLine is appended to the code you previously typed.

4. Type **("Hello World Wide Web")** immediately after the word WriteLine. Be sure to include the parentheses and double quotation marks. As you type, additional messages and windows appear and offer help and advice on completing the line of code, as shown in Figure 2-11. You learn more about these messages and windows later in this text.

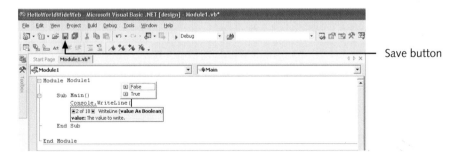

Figure 2-11   Additional IntelliSense messages

5. The tab for Module1.vb now includes an asterisk (*). The asterisk indicates that the contents of Module1.vb have changed and serves as a reminder that your changes need to be saved. Save your work by clicking the **Save** button on the toolbar.

Modifying the Text Editor Settings

When using the text editor, you may find it helpful to customize some of the settings. For example, you may want to change the font type, font size, or color of the text in the code editor window.

To change the font size of the text in the code editor window:

1. Click **Tools** on the menu bar, and then click **Options**. The Options dialog box opens.

2. If it is not already selected, click the **Environment** folder.

3. If necessary, click the **Environment** folder a second time to reveal its contents.

4. Click **Fonts and Colors**.

5. If necessary, select **Text Editor** in the Show settings for list box.

6. In the Size list box, select **12**, and then click **OK**. The text in the code editor window changes to a 12-point font.

It is often helpful to display line numbers in the text editor. This enables you to easily refer to specific lines of code.

To display line numbers within the source code:

1. Click **Tools** on the menu bar, and then click **Options**. The Options dialog box opens.

2. If it is not already selected, click the **Text Editor** folder.

3. If necessary, click the **Text Editor** folder a second time to reveal its contents, and then click the **Basic** subfolder that appears beneath it.

4. Click the **Line numbers** check box to turn on this feature, and then click **OK**. The source code in the text editor window now includes line numbers.

You can use a similar approach to customize many settings within the MDE.

Renaming Module1.vb

It is a common and preferred programming practice to assign descriptive names to the programs you write. Recall that by default, VB .NET names programs as Module1.vb, Module2.vb, and so on.

To rename Module1.vb:

1. In the Solution Explorer window, click **Module1.vb**. The file properties of Module1.vb appear in the Properties window. See Figure 2-12.

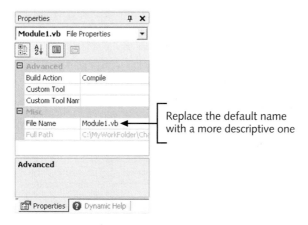

Figure 2-12   The file properties of Module1.vb

2. In the Properties window click the **File Name** property. In the text box to the right of the File Name property, delete the default filename **Module1.vb**, type **HelloWorldWideWeb.vb**, and press **Enter**. This renames the file. See Figure 2-13.

Figure 2-13   Renaming Module1.vb as HelloWorldWideWeb.vb

 An alternate way to change the filename is to right-click the filename in the Solution Explorer window, and then select the Rename option to rename the file.

The filename now reads HelloWorldWideWeb.vb in the File Name property box and in the Solution Explorer window. The tab name in the document window also changes to HelloWorldWideWeb.vb. See Figure 2-14.

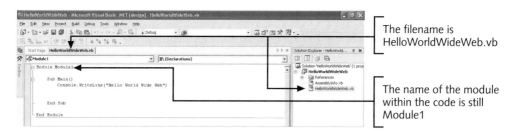

Figure 2-14   The MDE after renaming Module1.vb as HelloWorldWideWeb.vb

Notice that changing the filename had no effect on the code in the HelloWorldWideWeb.vb document. The first line of code still reads `Module Module1`, indicating that within the source code, this program is still identified as Module1. Although it is not required for your program to work properly, it is good programming practice to rename this module in the source code with an appropriate, descriptive name.

    3. To change the module name in the source code, click in the document window. On the first line of code, delete the word **Module1** and type **HelloWorldWideWeb**, as shown in Figure 2-15.

New name of module

Figure 2-15   Renaming Module1 as HelloWorldWideWeb

    4. On the toolbar, click the **Save** button to save your changes to HelloWorldWideWeb.vb.

Setting the Startup Object

You are almost ready to compile and execute your console application. However, because you changed the module name within the source code, you must also change the project properties to identify HelloWorldWideWeb as the startup object. The **startup object** is the module where execution begins when VB .NET runs your application.

To set the startup object:

    1. In the Solution Explorer window, right-click the **HelloWorldWideWeb** project icon.

    2. On the shortcut menu, click **Properties**. The HelloWorldWideWeb Property Pages dialog box opens.

    3. Click the **Startup object** list arrow, click **HelloWorldWideWeb**, as shown in Figure 2-16, and then click **OK**.

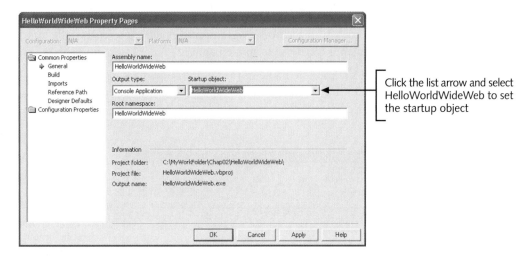

Figure 2-16 The Property Pages dialog box

An alternate way to display the Property Pages dialog box is to select the HelloWorldWideWeb project icon in the Solution Explorer window, and then click either the Properties icon in the Solution Explorer window or the Property Pages icon in the Properties window. See Figure 2-17.

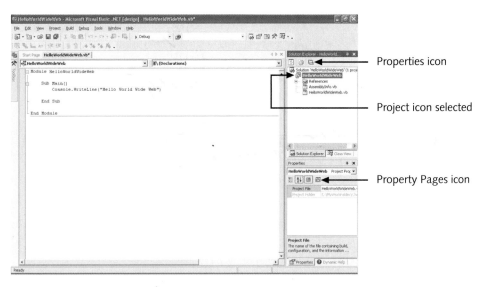

Figure 2-17 Alternate ways to display the Property Pages dialog box

You are now ready to compile and execute your program.

COMPILING AND EXECUTING A VISUAL BASIC .NET PROGRAM

You can compile and execute your program in several ways. You can use options on the Build and Debug menus or toolbars, or use shortcut key combinations. The approach you use is simply a matter of preference. For now, you will use menu options.

To compile and execute your program:

1. Click **Debug** on the menu bar, and then click **Start Without Debugging**.

2. If you have not made an error, an Output window appears informing you that VB .NET successfully built your application. See Figure 2-18. Then a window opens and displays the message "Hello World Wide Web," as shown in Figure 2-19.

Figure 2-18   Output window

Figure 2-19   Window displaying "Hello World Wide Web" message

If you inadvertently clicked Start rather than Start without Debugging, the window displays your message briefly then automatically closes. If you made an error, you will see a message box informing you that there were build errors and asking if you want to continue, as shown in Figure 2-20. Click **No** to view information about the errors. Error messages appear in a Task List pane, as shown in Figure 2-21. You can jump directly from an error message to the line of code that caused the problem by double-clicking the error message.

Figure 2-20   Build error message box

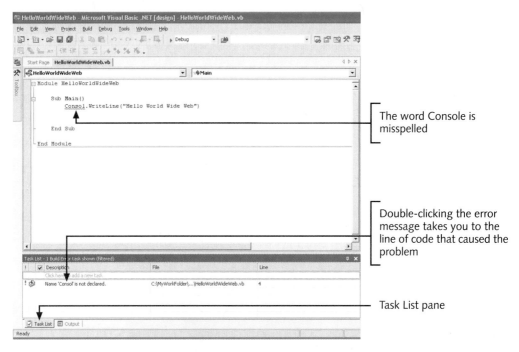

Figure 2-21   An error message in the Task List pane

3. Close the window displaying the "Hello World Wide Web" message by clicking its **Close** button.

4. Close the Output window by clicking its **Close** button.

5. To close the HelloWorldWideWeb solution, click **File** on the menu bar, and then click **Close Solution**.

USING THE VISUAL FORM DESIGNER

Although you will create a number of console applications as you work through this text, you will also create many Windows applications. A **Windows application** is one that runs in the Windows environment. When you create Windows applications, you will use a visual form editor in addition to the text editor.

A visual editor allows you to select icons representing various components (such as buttons, text boxes, and lists), and then place and arrange them on the window. As you manipulate these icons, VB .NET generates the programming statements required to build the form. As you reposition icons or change their properties, the code is dynamically updated to reflect your changes. Using the visual editor, you can quickly create forms for Windows applications, such as the one shown in Figure 2-22.

Figure 2-22   A Windows application form

The visual form editor is known as the Windows Form Designer. When the Windows Form Designer is active, the Toolbox contains visual components such as text boxes, buttons, and labels. You select elements from the Toolbox to design input forms. You use the Properties window to adjust the properties of components on your form, such as changing the color of a button or the font within a text box. As you arrange and manipulate these items, VB .NET generates the source code that makes your form work. In this chapter, you learn how to create a simple Windows application using the Windows Form Designer. You learn much more about the Windows Form Designer in Chapters 8 and 13.

Creating a Windows Application

You will now create a VB .NET project for a Windows application. You use the Windows Form Designer to create an input form for the application. Recall that when you create a project, you must identify the project type and template you want to use, and specify the project name and location.

To create a Windows application:

1. If you have not already done so, start Visual Studio .NET.

2. If it is not already selected, click the **Start Page** tab in the document window, and then click the **Projects** tab.

3. Click the **New Project** button. The New Project dialog box opens.

4. In the New Project dialog box, click the **Visual Basic Projects** folder in the Project Types pane. Click the **Windows Application** icon in the Templates pane.

5. If this is your first Windows application, the Name text box will contain the default project name WindowsApplication1. Delete the default project name and type **FormDemo** in the Name text box.

6. In the Location text box, specify the parent folder for your project. You can accept the default location or use the Browse button to select an alternate location.

7. Click **OK**. As shown in Figure 2-23, the Windows Form Designer appears as a tabbed document labeled Form1.vb [Design]. By default, the Windows Form Designer names files that contain forms as Form1.vb, Form2.vb, and so on.

 If desired, you can change the default filename. To do so, right-click Form1.vb in the Solution Explorer window. On the shortcut menu, select Rename. Delete the default value, and then type a new filename (including the .vb extension). For this example, accept the Form1.vb default filename.

2

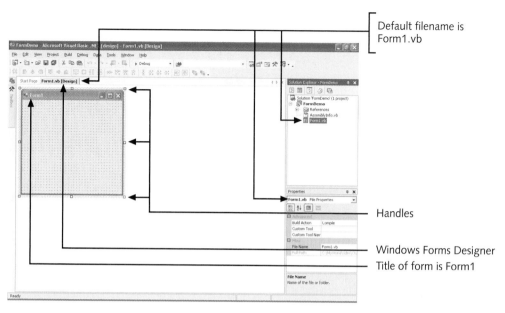

Default filename is
Form1.vb

Handles

Windows Forms Designer

Title of form is Form1

Figure 2-23 The Windows Form Designer

Notice that several additional things happen when you create the Windows Application project. The Layout toolbar appears beneath the Standard toolbar. The Layout toolbar contains buttons that help you control the appearance and position of the components (such as buttons and text boxes) you add to the form. As before, the Solution Explorer window contains information about this project and its associated elements. The Properties window shows the properties of the Form1.vb file. By default, the text that appears in the form's title bar and the name of the form object are Form1. You see how to change these defaults shortly.

Notice also the appearance of the form. The background contains tick marks arranged in a grid. This grid, together with the Layout toolbar, helps you align components you place on the form. The grid is visible only while you are designing the form, and will not appear when your application executes.

Along the outer edges of the form you see small white boxes called handles. A **handle** is a special type of button that allows you to resize a form. When you point to a handle, the pointer changes to a double arrow. When you see the double arrow, you can resize the form by clicking and dragging the handle.

You will now complete steps to customize the form so that it appears as shown in Figure 2-22. First, you change the size, background color, title, and name of the form. Then you add a welcome message and button to the form. Finally, you complete steps to ensure that when your program is running and you click the button, a thank-you message appears in a small window, as shown in Figure 2-24.

Figure 2-24   Thank-you message generated by the FormDemo project

Customizing the Appearance of a Form

You have many options for customizing the appearance of a form. In this chapter, you learn how to change the size, background color, title, name, and position of a form. In Chapters 8 and 13, you will explore additional techniques for creating more complex forms.

To change the size of a form:

1. Click inside the form to select it.

2. Point to the handle in the lower-right corner of the form. When the pointer changes to a double arrow, drag the handle down and to the right to enlarge the form. Release the mouse button when the form is approximately the same size as the form shown in Figure 2-25.

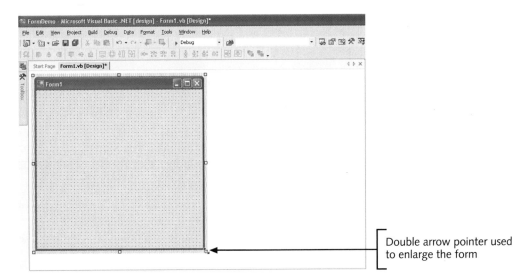

Double arrow pointer used to enlarge the form

Figure 2-25   Enlarging the form

To change the title, name, background color, and position of a form:

1. Make sure that the form is selected.

 An item on a form, including the form itself, is selected when its handles are visible and its properties are listed in the Properties window.

2. Scroll through the Properties window until you see the Text property. You use the Text property to set the text that appears in the title bar of the form. Click the **Text** property to select it. See Figure 2-26. Delete the default value (Form1), type **My First Form**, and press **Enter**. The title of the form changes to My First Form.

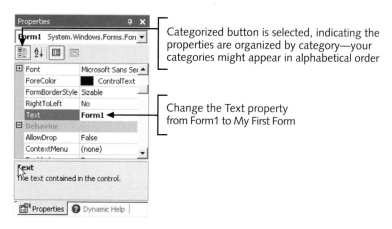

Categorized button is selected, indicating the properties are organized by category—your categories might appear in alphabetical order

Change the Text property from Form1 to My First Form

Figure 2-26   Changing the title of the form

3. Scroll down in the Properties window until you locate the (Name) property. Notice that the default name of the form object is Form1. Although forms will work properly if you accept default names, it is good programming practice to assign meaningful names to form objects and all of the components that you add to them. To change the name of the form object, click the **(Name)** property to select it. See Figure 2-27. Delete the default value (Form1), type **frmFirstForm** and press **Enter**. The name of the form changes to frmFirstForm.

 This book uses naming conventions for form objects and components you add to them. For example, form names begin with the prefix "frm," button names begin with the prefix "btn," and label names begin with the prefix "lbl."

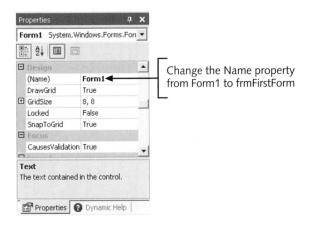

Change the Name property
from Form1 to frmFirstForm

Figure 2-27 Changing the name of the form

4. Scroll up in the Properties window until you locate the BackColor property. Click the **BackColor** property to select it. A list arrow appears next to the current value of this property, as shown in Figure 2-28.

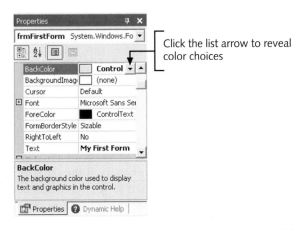

Click the list arrow to reveal
color choices

Figure 2-28 Changing the background color of the form

5. Click the **list arrow** to see the color choices, which are grouped into three different sets: Custom, Web, and System. Click the **Custom** tab, and then click the **white** color square. See Figure 2-29. The background of the form changes from light gray to white.

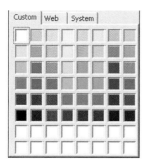

Figure 2-29   Selecting a color from the Custom tab

6. Similarly, scroll down in the Properties window until you locate the StartPosition property. Click the **StartPosition** property to select it. A list arrow appears next to the current value of this property. Click the **list arrow** to see the start position choices, and then click **CenterScreen**. This centers the form on the screen when your program runs.

Adding Components to a Form

To add components to a form, you need the Toolbox. If you have followed the steps in this chapter, the Toolbox appears as a hidden window on the left side of your main window. If you do not see the hidden Toolbox window, click the Toolbox button on the toolbar to open it.

 An alternate way to open the Toolbox is to click View on the menu bar, and then click Toolbox.

You can now position the Toolbox as a hidden window by clicking its Auto Hide icon. Your screen should resemble Figure 2-30.

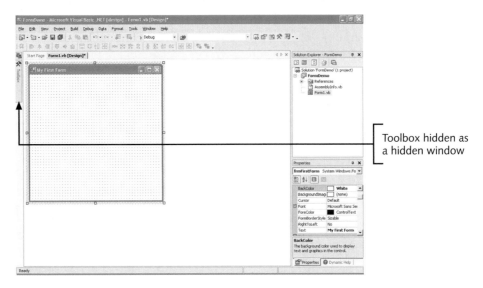

Toolbox hidden as a hidden window

Figure 2-30   The MDE after making changes to the form and hiding the Toolbox

To add a welcome message to your form:

1. Point to the **Toolbox** tab to reveal its contents. You see a number of components, including labels, buttons, and text boxes, as shown in Figure 2-31.

Figure 2-31   Contents of the Toolbox when the Windows Form Designer is active

2. Double-click **Label** to add a label to the form, and then move the pointer toward the center of the main window so that the Toolbox slides back to its hidden position. You see a label on the form. By default, the label name and the label text are "Label1".

3. Drag the lower-right handle to enlarge the label, as shown in Figure 2-32.

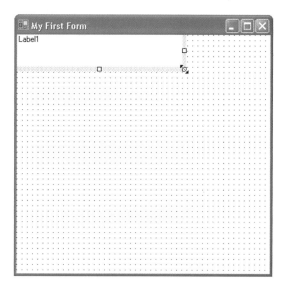

Figure 2-32   Enlarging the label

4. To assign a meaningful name to the label, scroll through the Properties window to locate and select the **(Name)** property. Delete the default value (Label1), type **lblWelcome**, and then press **Enter**.

5. Similarly, locate and select the **Text** property, and then delete the default value (Label1). Type **Welcome to VB .NET**, and then press **Enter**. Notice that the label text changes.

6. To change the color of the label text, select the **ForeColor** property in the Properties window. A list arrow appears next to the current value of this property. Click the **list arrow** to see the color choices. Click the **Custom** tab, and then click the **red** color square. The label text changes to red.

7. To change the label font, select the **Font** property in the Properties window. A button containing an ellipsis (...) appears to the right of the current value of the Font property. See Figure 2-33.

Ellipsis button

Figure 2-33   The Font property and ellipsis button

8. Click the **ellipsis** (**...**) button to open the Font dialog box, shown in Figure 2-34. In the Font pane, scroll down the list and click **Times New Roman**. In the Size pane, scroll down the list and click **18**. Click **OK** to apply the changes and close the dialog box. The label font reflects your changes.

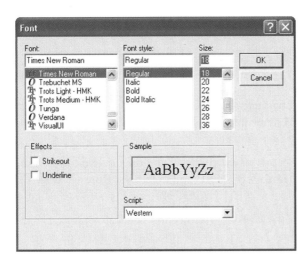

Figure 2-34   The Font dialog box

9. To center the label text within the area occupied by the label, select the **TextAlign** property in the Properties window. Click the **list arrow** in the text box to the right of this property. You see a box with nine rectangles, as shown in Figure 2-35. These rectangles represent the position of the text within the label

component—upper-left, upper-center, upper-right, and so on. Click the rectangle in the center of the box to indicate that you want to center the text in the label.

Figure 2-35   Setting the TextAlign property

10. Point to the label. The pointer changes to a four-headed arrow, called the move pointer, as shown in Figure 2-36. When the move pointer is visible, you can drag a component to a new position on the grid.

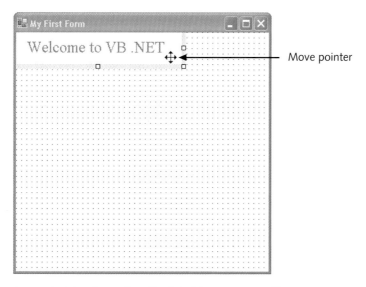

Figure 2-36   Dragging the label to a new position

11. Drag the label to the position shown in Figure 2-37.

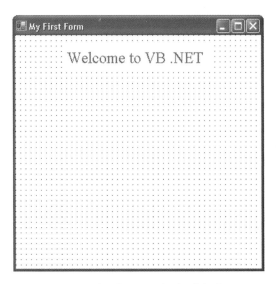

Figure 2-37   The form with the label in its new position

 To center the label horizontally in the form, you can select the label, and then click the Center Horizontally button in the Layout toolbar. Alternately, you can click Format on the menu bar, point to Center in Form, and then click Horizontally.

To add a button to the form:

12. Point to the **Toolbox** tab to reveal the Toolbox. Double-click **Button**, and then move the pointer toward the center of the main window so that the Toolbox returns to its hidden position.

 There are two other ways to add a component to a form. One way is to click a component in the Toolbox. When you move the pointer toward the center of the main window, the pointer changes to correspond to the component type you selected. Drag to draw the component on the form. The other way to add a component is to point to the component in the Toolbox, and then press and hold the left mouse button while you drag the component to the form.

13. Notice that the button is selected (its handles are visible), and thus its properties appear in the Properties window. Drag the button to position it beneath the welcome message label. Enlarge the button and center it horizontally on the form. See Figure 2-38.

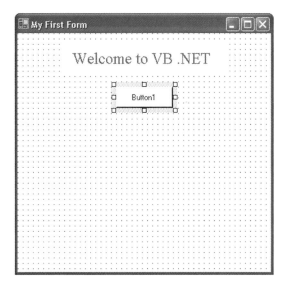

Figure 2-38   Adding the button to the form

14. In the Properties window, select the **(Name)** property and change it to **btnPushMe**.

15. Select the **Text** property and change it to **Push Me**.

16. Select the **Font** property. Change the font to **Arial** and the size to **10**.

17. Select the **BackColor** property and change it to **yellow**. The initial design of your form is now complete, and appears in Figure 2-39.

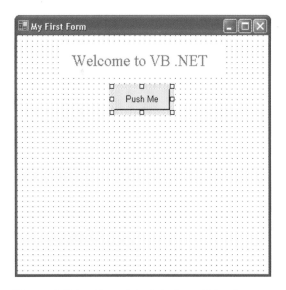

Figure 2-39   Completed design of the form

If you run your project now, you will see a form that contains your welcome message and Push Me button. However, clicking the Push Me button will have no effect. This is because you have not yet identified the action(s) to be taken when the button is clicked. Recall that when the Push Me button is clicked, you want your program to respond by displaying a thank-you message. To build this functionality, use the text editor to add code to your program.

To add code that displays a thank-you message when the Push Me button is clicked:

1. If it is not already selected, select the **Form1.vb [Design]** page in the document window.

2. Double-click the **Push Me** button. You see code similar to that shown in Figure 2-40. VB .NET generated this code based on the actions you completed in the Windows Form Designer. The meaning of this code will be explained in later chapters of this book.

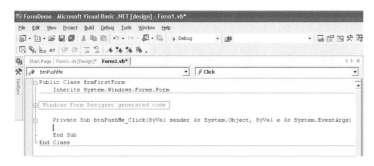

Figure 2-40   Code generated by the Windows Form Designer

3. Notice that the insertion point in the code window is located within a block of code that begins with the words `Private Sub btnPushMe_Click`. This line of code is the beginning of the procedure that is responsible for responding to a click of the Push Me button.

4. At the insertion point, type the following text, as shown in Figure 2-41.

MessageBox.Show("Thank you for using VB .NET")

This code instructs the system to display a thank-you message in a message box. Note the behavior of the IntelliSense feature as you type.

Figure 2-41   Adding the code to make the button work

5. Observe that the tabs for the code editor window and the Windows Form Designer window both include an asterisk, indicating that the contents of these windows have changed since they were last saved. To save the contents of both windows, click the **Save All** button on the toolbar.

By default, VB .NET looks for Form1.vb to begin execution of a Windows application. Because you changed the name of the form, you must identify frmFirstForm as the startup object before you can compile and execute your program.

To set the startup object:

1. In the Solution Explorer window, select the **FormDemo** project icon in the Solution Explorer window, and then click the **Properties** icon.

2. When the FormDemo Property Pages dialog box opens, click the **Startup object** list arrow, click **frmFirstForm**, and then click **OK**.

To compile and execute your program:

1. Click **Debug** on the menu bar, and then click **Start Without Debugging**. An output window opens and tells you whether VB .NET was able to successfully build your project.

   If you have not made any mistakes, your form appears in a window titled My First Form, as shown in Figure 2-42.

Figure 2-42   Output of the FormDemo project

2. In the My First Form window, click the **Push Me** button. A window containing your thank-you message appears, as shown in Figure 2-43.

Figure 2-43   The thank-you message generated by clicking the button

3. Click **OK** to close the thank-you message window, and then click the **Close** button in the My First Form window to close your form. Also close the Output window.

4. If you are not continuing to the next section, close the FormDemo solution by clicking **File** on the menu bar, and then clicking **Close Solution**.

You now have an idea of the power and flexibility of the VB .NET development environment. You have seen how the Toolbox and Properties window work together to help you create applications quickly and easily. Next you learn about two other powerful features of VB .NET: the debugging tool and the help facility.

EXPLORING THE DEBUGGING TOOL

Visual Studio .NET includes a powerful tool commonly known as a debugger. A **debugger** helps you isolate errors that keep your program from running as intended. The debugger has many features, only one of which is introduced in this chapter. You learn more about the debugger later in this text.

In this chapter, you learn how to use the debugger to set breakpoints. A **breakpoint** is a flag that tells the debugger to temporarily suspend execution of your program at a particular point. While program execution is suspended, you can view information about your program that may help you determine the source of a problem. Setting breakpoints is most useful in programs that are more complex than those presented in this chapter—especially in programs that manipulate the values of inputs and other variables or contain code sequences that are repeated multiple times.

Learning how to set a breakpoint is a necessary first step in preparing yourself to use the debugger. Later in this book, you learn techniques for troubleshooting a program after a breakpoint has been reached. At that time, you will begin to understand the real power of the debugger. For now, you learn how to set a breakpoint in a simple program and observe the behavior of the system when it encounters the breakpoint.

Getting Started with the Debugger

Before you begin exploring the VB .NET debugger, you should understand its role. A debugger is intended to help you identify errors in your program that occur while the program is running. The debugger cannot help you find coding errors that prevent your program from being built successfully. Stated another way, VB .NET must be able to successfully build your program before you can use the debugger. Also, remember that while the debugger helps you find logic errors, it does not fix them for you.

Setting Breakpoints

Recall that a breakpoint is a flag in your program that tells the debugger to pause execution of the program. Although you usually set breakpoints in programs so you can test the effects of using variables, accepting input, or repeating code sequences, you can set a breakpoint in the FormDemo solution to test the thank-you message. To illustrate, you will modify the FormDemo program then set a breakpoint after the line of code that displays the thank-you message.

To modify the FormDemo program and set a breakpoint:

1. If necessary, open the **FormDemo** solution. (To open the solution, click **File** on the menu bar, and then click **Open Solution**. Navigate to the FormDemo folder in your Chap02 folder, and then double-click the **FormDemo** solution file.) If it is not already selected, click the **Form1.vb** tab.

 If the Form1.vb tab is not visible, click View on the menu bar, and then click Code.

2. In the code window, position the insertion point at the end of the line of code that displays the thank-you message, press Enter, and then type the following text:

   MessageBox.Show("Have a nice day")

   This causes a second message box to appear after the thank-you message box closes.

3. Right-click the second **MessageBox.Show** statement. A shortcut menu appears, as shown in Figure 2-44.

Figure 2-44   The shortcut menu for inserting a breakpoint

4. Click **Insert Breakpoint** on the shortcut menu. Notice that the second MessageBox.Show statement is highlighted, indicating that the breakpoint has been set. See Figure 2-45.

Figure 2-45   Setting a breakpoint in the code window

When you execute your program in debug mode, program execution is suspended just before this line of code.

To execute your program in debug mode:

1. Click **Debug** on the menu bar, and then click **Start**. Several windows containing information used by the debugger open along the bottom of the main window, and then your form appears.

2. Click the **Push Me** button on your form. As before, the thank-you message appears.

3. Click **OK** to dismiss the thank-you message. The code editor window opens. Notice that the second MessageBox.Show statement is highlighted in yellow, indicating that the breakpoint has been reached. See Figure 2-46. At this point, execution of your program is suspended.

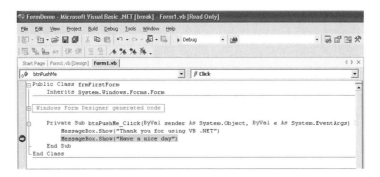

Figure 2-46   Program execution suspended at the breakpoint

By setting a breakpoint at the line of code that displays the second message box, you can troubleshoot the code that is responsible for generating the form and displaying the first message box. For example, what if the thank-you message does not appear, or something goes wrong when it does appear? Although you do not yet know enough about the VB .NET programming language to perform this kind of troubleshooting, later in this book you learn how to perform additional steps to isolate program errors while execution is suspended. At that time, you will see how breakpoints can save time and effort in pinpointing logic errors that lead to unexpected or incorrect results.

4. To resume program execution, click **Debug** on the menu bar, and then click **Continue**. The second MessageBox.Show statement executes, and the window containing your "Have a nice day" message appears.

5. Click **OK** to close the message window, and then close the FormDemo program execution window by clicking its **Close** button.

6. Close the Output window by clicking its **Close** button.

7. Click **File** on the menu bar, and then click **Close Solution** to close the project.

EXPLORING THE HELP FACILITY

The VB .NET development environment includes extensive help facilities that enable you to access help in many different ways. As with most Windows applications, you can search for help on a specific item, browse a table of contents, or scroll through an alphabetized index of topics. In addition, VB .NET includes two other powerful help features—dynamic help and context-sensitive help—that may be new to you. In this section, you explore the help facilities of the VB .NET development environment and learn how to use many of their features.

Accessing Help

You can access most of the help features of VB .NET through options on the Help menu. The Help menu is shown in Figure 2-47.

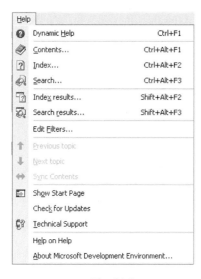

Figure 2-47   The Help menu

When you select an option from the Help menu, a corresponding window opens within the IDE.

To make sure the windows you see resemble the ones in this text as closely as possible:

1. In the document window, close all documents except the Start Page.

2. Close all tool windows, including the Solution Explorer and Dynamic Help windows. Your window should resemble Figure 2-48.

 If FormDemo and HelloWorldWideWeb do not appear in the list of existing projects, click View on the menu bar, and then click Refresh.

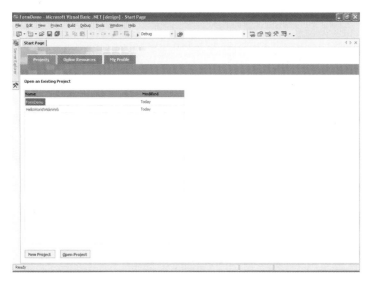

Figure 2-48 The MDE with only the Start Page document open

Exploring the Contents Option on the Help Menu

The Contents option on the Help menu displays a list of help topics in a format that resembles a table of contents.

To open the Contents window:

1. Click **Help** on the menu bar, and then click **Contents**. The Contents window opens.

2. If necessary, select **Visual Basic** in the Filtered by list box.

 Recall that Visual Studio .NET includes several languages other than Visual Basic. Setting the value in this text box to Visual Basic limits the scope of help topics to those associated with Visual Basic. If you change this value, you will see help topics associated with other Visual Studio .NET languages.

3. Notice that the Contents window organizes help topics in a hierarchical fashion. Plus and minus signs to the left of nodes in the hierarchy identify topics that you can expand or collapse, respectively. Expanding a node reveals a list of additional subtopics and documents that pertain to that item. Collapsing a node hides those

details. Click the **plus sign (+)** to the left of the Visual Studio .NET node to expand the node, and then click the **plus sign (+)** to the left of the Visual Basic and Visual C# subnode to see a list of its subtopics. You see the hierarchy shown in Figure 2-49.

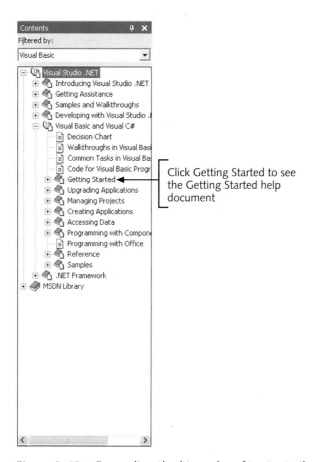

Figure 2-49   Expanding the hierarchy of topics in the Contents window

4. You can click any item in the hierarchy to display a page in the document window. For example, click **Getting Started**. Information about this topic appears in a tabbed page in the document window, as shown in Figure 2-50.

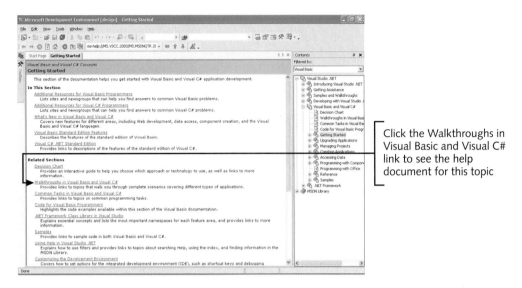

Figure 2-50   The Getting Started help document

5. You can click links within the document window to navigate to pages that contain more detailed information. For example, in the Getting Started document window, click the **Walkthroughs in Visual Basic and Visual C#** link. The help page appears in the document window, as shown in Figure 2-51.

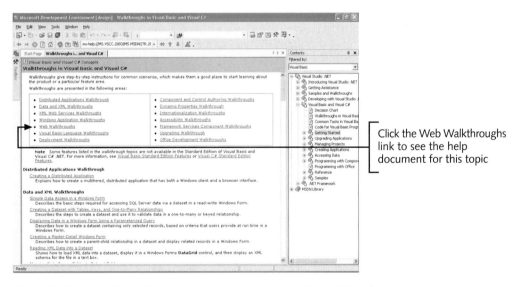

Figure 2-51   The Walkthroughs in Visual Basic and Visual C# help document

6. Click the **Web Walkthroughs** link, and then click the **Creating a Basic Web Forms Page** link to view help information on this topic. See Figure 2-52.

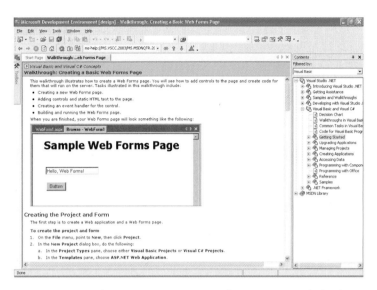

Figure 2-52   The Creating a Basic Web Forms Page help document

7. Close the Creating a Basic Web Forms help document by clicking its **Close** button.

8. Close the Contents window by clicking its **Close** button.

Exploring the Index Option on the Help Menu

The Index option on the Help menu displays a list of help topics in alphabetical order.

To open the Index window:

1. Click **Help** on the menu bar, and then click **Index**. The Index window opens, as shown in Figure 2-53.

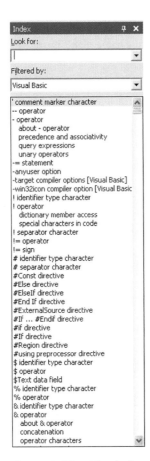

Figure 2-53   The Index window

2. If necessary, select **Visual Basic** in the Filtered by list box.

3. You can locate an item in the index by scrolling through the list. For example, scroll down and click **.NET Framework**. The help page for this item appears in the document window, as shown in Figure 2-54.

Figure 2-54   The .NET Framework help document

4. An alternate way to locate a topic in the index is to specify the topic in the **Look for** text box. As you type, the system locates items in the index that match your specification. When you click an item on the list, a help page opens within the document window. For example, click the **Look for** text box, and press the **Del** key to delete its current contents. Type **forms** to locate this term in the index. As you type, notice how the system selects the item in the index that most closely matches your specification. Press **Enter** to display the currently selected help page. You see the information shown in Figure 2-55.

Figure 2-55   Using the Look for option of the Index window

Some items in the index have multiple help pages (or targets) associated with them. For example, try looking for help on Web Forms. An Index Results window listing two targets appears within the IDE. Double-click an item on this list to open the desired help page.

Some items in the index serve only as a mechanism for identifying a group of related help pages. These items are referred to as parent entries and do not have help pages associated directly with them. When you click one of these items, you will see an Empty Index Entry page, which prompts you to select one of the child entries.

5. Close the Forms help document by clicking its **Close** button.

6. Close the Index window by clicking its **Close** button. If it is open, also close the Index Results window.

Exploring the Search Option on the Help Menu

The Search option on the Help menu allows you to search the database of help pages for those that contain a specific word or phrase. A list of pages that contain the word or phrase appears in a Search Results window. When you select an item from this list, the associated help page appears in the document window.

To open the Search window:

1. Click **Help** on the menu bar, and then click **Search**. The Search window opens, as shown in Figure 2-56. Some of the check boxes that appear beneath the Search button might be checked, depending on your configuration.

Figure 2-56   The Search window

2. Type **breakpoints** in the Look for text box. If any of the check boxes that appear beneath the Search button are checked, uncheck them and then click **Search**. A Search Results window opens, listing 137 topics. Double-click the third item on the list to open the Using the Breakpoints Window help document. See Figure 2-57.

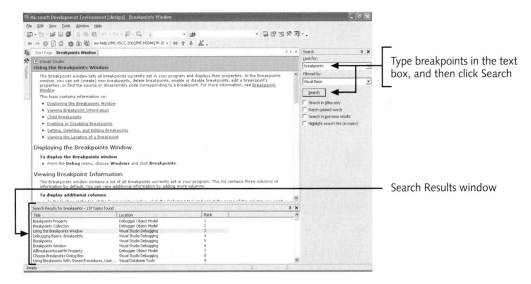

Figure 2-57   Using the Breakpoints Window help document

3. You can search for matches in titles only, match related keywords, search in previous results, and highlight search hits. Revise your search by clicking the **Search in titles only** check box. This limits the search to pages that include the keyword in the title. Also, click the **Highlight search hits (in topics)** check box so that the

keyword for which you are searching will be highlighted in the resulting help pages. Click **Search**.

4. Notice that the Search Results window now includes only 12 entries. Double-click the first item in the list to open the associated help document. Observe that the word "breakpoints" is highlighted, as shown in Figure 2-58.

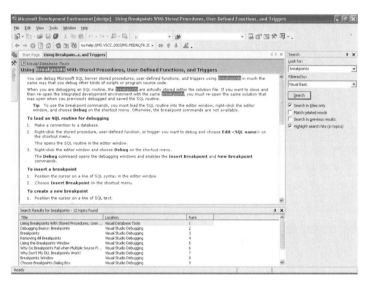

Figure 2-58   Revising the search

5. Close the Search, Search Results, and help document windows.

Exploring the Dynamic Help Option on the Help Menu

The Dynamic Help option on the Help menu is a powerful feature that identifies help topics in response to actions you take.

To see how Dynamic Help works:

1. Open the Start Page, Solution Explorer, and Properties windows.

2. Click **Help** on the menu bar, and then click **Dynamic Help**. The Dynamic Help window appears as a tabbed pane along with the Properties window, as shown in Figure 2-59.

Because the Dynamic Help feature responds to actions you take, the information you see in the Dynamic Help window may differ somewhat from Figure 2-59.

2

Figure 2-59   The Dynamic Help window

3. Click the **Solution Explorer title bar** to select the Solution Explorer window. Notice that the contents of the Dynamic Help window change to provide links to help pages that deal with the Solution Explorer.

4. Open the **FormDemo** project. In the Solution Explorer window, click the **View Designer** icon to view the form in design mode. See Figure 2-60.

The View Designer icon

Figure 2-60 The View Designer icon in the Solution Explorer window

The input form you designed earlier in this chapter appears in the document window, and the contents of the Dynamic Help window change to reflect help topics associated with the Windows Form Designer.

5. In the Form1.vb [Design] document window, click the **Push Me** button to select it. Notice that the contents of the Dynamic Help window change to reflect help topics that deal with buttons, as shown in Figure 2-61.

Figure 2-61 The Dynamic Help window with the Push Me button selected

The Dynamic Help feature responds in a similar fashion to actions you take as you work with various windows, tools, and elements of VB .NET.

Exploring Context-Sensitive Help

Another powerful help feature in VB .NET is context-sensitive help. This option does not appear on the Help menu, but you can invoke it by pressing the F1 key.

To see how context-sensitive help works:

1. Continuing from the steps in the previous section (with the Push Me button selected), press the **F1** key. A page describing the Button class opens in the document window, as shown in Figure 2-62. You learn more about the Button class and the information presented on this help page in later chapters of this book.

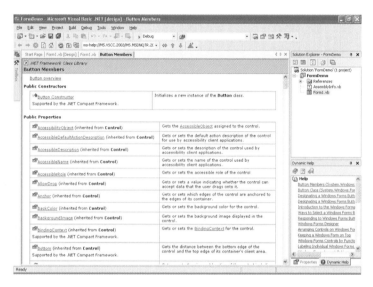

Figure 2-62   Context-sensitive help for the Push Me button

2. Click the **Form1.vb [Design]** tab to return to the Windows Form Designer window. Double-click the **Push Me** button to open the code window. You see the code and the breakpoint you created earlier in the document window.

3. If necessary, position the insertion point at the beginning of the word **MessageBox** on the line of code where the breakpoint is set. Observe that the contents of the Dynamic Help window change to provide links to pages that provide MessageBox information.

4. Press the **F1** key. A page describing the MessageBox class opens in the document window.

5. Click the **Form1.vb** tab to return to the code window. Click the word **Private**, and then press the **F1** key. Information about the Private keyword appears in a document window, as shown in Figure 2-63. Close Visual Studio .NET.

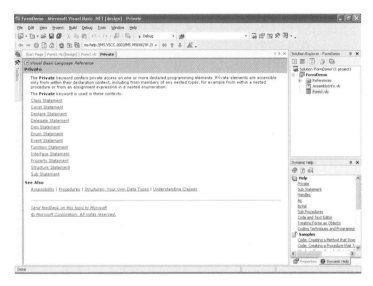

Figure 2-63 Context-sensitive help for the Private keyword

You can press the F1 key at any time to obtain help on virtually any keyword, component, window, or other element of VB .NET.

QUICK REVIEW

1. Visual Studio .NET is an Integrated Development Environment (IDE). An IDE is a set of software tools that helps you code, debug, and test a system as you develop it.

2. Visual Basic .NET (VB .NET) is one of the programming languages supported by the Visual Studio .NET IDE.

3. The Visual Studio .NET IDE includes tools that assist you with text editing, visual form editing, program compilation and execution, debugging, and program organization and management.

4. VB .NET provides many options that allow you to customize the appearance of your screen and the tools that you use. This includes the ability to pin tools to the development environment as hidden windows.

5. The Visual Studio .NET IDE provides templates (or patterns) for creating different kinds of applications, such as console applications and Windows applications.

6. A console application runs at the command line, whereas a Windows application runs in the Windows environment.

7. VB .NET uses a hierarchical arrangement of solutions and projects to organize the programs you write. Solutions and projects can be thought of as containers. A project contains the files that an application comprises. A solution contains one or more projects. Solutions with multiple projects are sometimes needed for large systems. The Solution Explorer window provides an organized view of these containers.

8. The VB .NET text editor supports color-coding, indentation, and code completion features.

9. You can customize the text editor settings to change the size of the code text or display line numbers, for example.

10. The startup object is the module where execution begins when VB .NET runs your program.

11. To compile and execute a VB .NET program, you can use options on the Build and Debug menus.

12. The VB .NET visual form editor, known as the Windows Form Designer, is a visual development tool that generates code from forms you build.

13. The Properties window allows you to set and modify properties of objects in the forms designer window.

14. To customize a form, you can change its appearance, such as its size, background color, and title, and you can add components, such as labels, buttons, and text boxes.

15. A debugger is a tool that helps you identify problems that prevent your program from running as intended.

16. A breakpoint is a flag that instructs the debugger to temporarily suspend execution of your program. While execution is suspended, you can perform steps to locate the source of the error.

17. The help facility of VB .NET provides many options for accessing help, including the Contents window, the Index window, the Search window, dynamic help, and context-sensitive help.

EXERCISES

1. What is an IDE? What are the major benefits of using an IDE? What are the drawbacks?

2. What are the major tools in the Visual Studio .NET IDE and what are the primary features of each?

3. What is the difference between a text editor and a visual form editor?

4. What is the purpose of the Solution Explorer? The Toolbox? The Properties window? Describe how these tools work together when you are creating a Windows application.

5. Compare and contrast the following terms: project, solution, and program.

6. What does it mean to add a breakpoint to a program? How are breakpoints useful?

7. What primary kinds of help are available to you in VB .NET? Which do you think you will prefer? Why?

8. What is meant by the term "startup project?" How do you identify the startup project?

9. What is meant by the term "startup object?" When is it necessary to set the startup object? How do you set the startup object?

10. What is the purpose of the ForeColor property of a label? What is the purpose of the Text property of a button?

11. How do you "hide" a tool window?

12. What is a hidden window? Why is it helpful to hide tool windows?

13. What is the major difference between a console application and a Windows application?

14. What are two good programming practices identified in this chapter?

15. What is the difference between the Contents option and the Index option on the Help menu?

16. What is the purpose of a debugger? When can one be used?

17. What is the difference between Visual Studio .NET and Visual Basic .NET?

18. What is a console application? How does a console application differ from a Windows application?

19. Use the help facilities of Visual Studio .NET to do the following:

   a. Use the Index window to find information on the Button class.

   b. Use the Search feature of the help facility to find information on "responding to button clicks".

   c. Describe the similarities and differences between dynamic help and context-sensitive help.

20. Do you think that IDE code generation tools, like the one you used in this chapter, will one day replace the need for programmers? Why or why not?

PROGRAMMING EXERCISES

1. Create a Windows application. Set the background color of the form to light green. Change the title of the form to "My First Program". Set the start position so that your form appears in the center of the screen when you run it. Add the label "This is my first program" to the form. Set the label text to dark blue. Set the background color of the label to yellow. Change the font of the label to Comic Sans MS, bold, point size 20. Adjust the size of the label and the form so that the entire label is visible. Center the label text within the label. Position the label in the center of the form. Assign a meaningful name to the label using the naming conventions adopted in this text. Save and run your project.

2. Enlarge the form you began in Programming Exercise 1 and add a button to the form. Set the button text to "What is my name?" Assign a meaningful name to the button using the naming conventions adopted in this text. Set the background and foreground colors as well as the font of the button text according to your preferences. Adjust the size of the button if necessary. Position the "This is my first program" label near the top center of the form. Center the "What is my name?" button beneath the label. Save your project and run your form.

3. Continue your work from Programming Exercise 2 and add the code necessary to make the button work. When the button is pressed, display a MessageBox with the message "My name is *your name*" (where *your name* is your actual name). When the message box is closed, display a second message: "VB .NET is fun". Save your project and run your form.

4. Continuing from Programming Exercise 3, make sure the form is selected. In the Properties window, change the name of the form from Form1 to frmMyFirstForm. Change the startup object accordingly. Save your project and run your form.

5. Continuing your work from Programming Exercise 4, add a breakpoint to suspend execution before the second message box is shown. Save your project and run your form in debug mode. When the breakpoint is reached, resume program execution and verify that your program responds as it should.

6. Create a console application that displays your name, address, telephone number, and date of birth, each on a separate line.

7. Create a Windows application that uses four buttons to display your name, address, telephone number, and date of birth, respectively. Accept the default values for the button names. Change the text of each button to reflect its purpose—such as Display Name or Display Address. Resize each button as needed to accommodate the text you assign to it. Enlarge the form and position the buttons horizontally across the top on the form. Make the buttons a uniform size and align the tops of the buttons with equal horizontal spacing between them. (*Hint*: Hold down the Ctrl key while you select the buttons, and then use the buttons on the Layout toolbar (or the options on the Format menu) to resize them, align them, and make the horizontal spacing equal.) Change the title of the form to "Personal Information". Add the code to make each of the buttons work—that is, when a button is clicked, display a message box containing the requested information. Save and run your project.

8. What do you notice about the position of the form and the message boxes? How could you ensure that the form and message boxes will appear in the center of the form?

9. Examine the code generated by the Windows Form Designer. What do you notice about the code? Why is it important to assign meaningful names to form components?

Introducing the Microsoft .NET Framework and Visual Basic .NET

In this chapter, you will:
- Explore the Microsoft .NET Framework
- Write a Visual Basic .NET module definition
- Define Visual Basic .NET variables and data types
- Write basic computational statements
- Read input from the keyboard

Chapter 2 explored the Visual Studio .NET Integrated Development Environment (IDE) and illustrated how to enter and run simple Visual Basic .NET (VB .NET) programs and how to create small console and windows projects. In this chapter, you are introduced to the Microsoft .NET Framework and learn some of the fundamentals of the VB .NET programming language. The power in VB .NET comes, in part, from the large, useful .NET library containing hundreds of prewritten classes. These classes provide methods you invoke to accomplish tasks ranging from computation and number formatting to establishing network connections and accessing relational databases. Many of these supplied classes and their methods are illustrated in this and subsequent chapters. In this chapter, you learn how to write a module definition, declare variables, and write basic computational statements so you gain a fundamental understanding of the .NET Framework and some of the VB .NET language syntax. This chapter focuses on introducing the .NET Framework, and working with VB .NET variables, while Chapter 4 explores using the class library in more detail.

EXPLORING THE MICROSOFT .NET FRAMEWORK

The central component of VB .NET is the .NET Framework. This Framework consists of the three key parts identified in the following list and shown in Figure 3-1.

- Compilers for VB .NET and other supported .NET languages
- The Common Language Runtime (CLR)
- The Framework Class Library (FCL)

Each of these is described in more detail in the following sections.

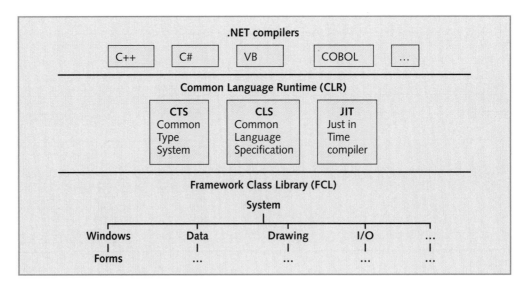

Figure 3-1   The .NET Framework

Note that the Visual Studio IDE you used in Chapter 2 is not a part of the .NET Framework. Instead, it interfaces with the .NET Framework to assist you in creating applications.

The Microsoft .NET Compilers

VB .NET is one of several compilers included in the .NET Framework. In addition to VB .NET, the Framework includes C++, C# (pronounced C sharp), J#, and even COBOL. You can view a current list of the supported languages at *www.microsoft.com*.

You learned in Chapter 1 that a compiler has two primary purposes: to check your source code for valid syntax and then translate it into executable form. All of the Framework compilers check syntax and translate your source code into a language called **Microsoft Intermediate Language (MSIL)** or simply **Intermediate Language (IL)**. However, IL is not executable machine language; instead it is the language used by the CLR, which then translates IL into executable code. All of the .NET compilers produce IL. This means that you can write one program in C++, another in C#, and another in Visual Basic (VB), and all the programs can interact with each other.

The Common Language Runtime

One of the responsibilities of the CLR is to connect the IL files coming from the various .NET compilers, translate these into executable files, and then manage the execution of the code in this file. Figure 3-2 illustrates this process.

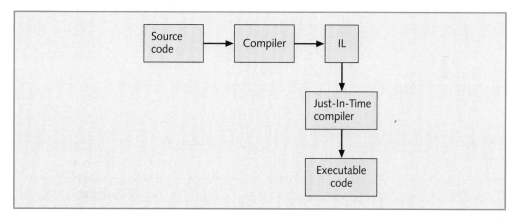

Figure 3-2 Compiling and executing

The CLR consists of three important pieces:

- The **Common Type System (CTS)** defines the standard .NET data types for all of the .NET programming languages. A **data type** determines the kind of data to be stored and the way it is stored in memory. In this chapter, for example, you work with numbers containing decimal positions, numbers without decimals, and character data. A data type can be as simple as `Integer` and as complex as a class, containing data you can access and methods you can invoke. Data types are explored further later in this chapter.

- The **Common Language Specification (CLS)** contains the rules for language interoperability. These rules include specifications such as naming requirements, data type definitions, and argument passing conventions. All .NET languages must follow the CLS rules.

- The **Just-In-Time (JIT) compiler** translates IL into executable, processor-specific machine language. This translation is done just before the application is to be executed, thus the name just-in-time.

In addition, the CLR allocates and reclaims memory while the application is running.

The Framework Class Library

An **assembly** is a file containing IL. The FCL consists of approximately 100 assemblies, each of which contains one or more classes. These assemblies have a suffix of .dll (System.dll, System.Windows.Forms.dll, etc.). Each class has methods that you invoke to accomplish a task, and several have attributes containing data you can retrieve. For example, the `Math` class has methods such as `Pow`, which does exponentiation, and `Sqrt`, which computes the square root of a value. The `Math` class also contains the constant values for PI and the natural log base E. Methods and attributes in the .NET classes are called **members**.

The classes in the FCL are organized logically into **namespaces**. Namespaces are arranged into a hierarchy, as shown in Figure 3-3.

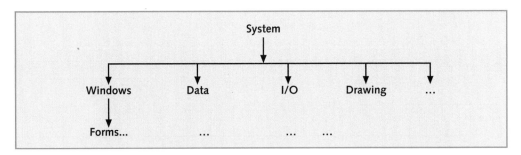

Figure 3-3   The .NET FCL namespaces

A namespace can contain both classes and other namespaces. `System` is the root of all other namespaces, but also contains several classes such as `Math`, `Console`, and `String`. Incidentally, you can create your own namespaces and assign classes you write to a namespace that you define.

The Framework compilers do not automatically search all namespaces for classes used by your code. Instead, you use the keyword `Imports` to tell the compiler the specific namespaces to access. If you omit the `Imports` statement, the compiler cannot locate the class and error messages result. You specify a namespace by writing the hierarchy names separated with periods. To illustrate, the `Forms` namespace would be specified as `System.Windows.Forms`. This means the `Forms` namespace is contained in the `Windows` namespace, which in turn is in the `System` namespace. You give the compiler access to the classes in a namespace by writing the keyword `Imports` at the beginning of your code, followed by the namespace. The `System` namespace (but not its subordinate namespaces) is accessed automatically by the compiler. This means that if you use only classes in the `System` namespace, then you do not need to include the `Imports` statement.

Table 3-1 lists selected namespaces and shows a few of the classes within each namespace. Chapter 2 showed you how to access .NET Help. You can use the Visual Studio .NET Help facility to explore the various methods of the classes in the FCL.

Table 3-1 Selected FCL namespaces

Namespace	Selected Classes
System	Array Console Convert DateTime Exception TimeSpan String Math
System.Collections	ArrayList
System.IO	StreamReader StreamWriter
System.Data	DataRow DataTable DataSet
System.Data.OleDb	OleDbCommand OleDbConnection OleDbDataAdapter OleDbParameter
System.Windows.Forms	Button CheckBox Form Label Menu MenuItem RadioButton TextBox

WRITING A VISUAL BASIC .NET MODULE DEFINITION

In Chapter 2 you explored the VB .NET IDE by writing a module definition named HelloWorldWideWeb. This section describes this module in more detail. Example 3-1 repeats the HelloWorldWideWeb listing and shows its output. Line numbers here and in other examples in this chapter are added for reference only, and do not appear in the actual module.

Example 3-1: HelloWorldWideWeb

```
1. ' Chapter 3 Module definition HelloWorldWideWeb

2. Module HelloWorldWideWeb

3.    Sub Main()

4.       Console.WriteLine("Hello World Wide Web")

5.    End Sub

6. End Module
```

Sample Run:

```
Hello World Wide Web
```

This VB .NET code is structured as a **module definition**, which begins on line 2 with `Module` and ends at line 6 with `End Module`.

 In addition to module definitions, you can also write VB .NET statements in a form definition or a class definition. A **form definition** is used to create a visible graphical user interface (GUI) and is described in Chapter 8. **Class definitions** are written to represent objects and are explained and illustrated in Chapter 10.

The VB .NET statements in Example 3-1 consist of **keywords** (`Module`, `Sub`, `End Sub`) and **identifiers** (`Main`, `Console`, `WriteLine`, `HelloWorldWideWeb`). Keywords have special meaning to the VB .NET compiler. Appendix A lists the VB .NET keywords.

A VB .NET identifier is the name you assign to things such as modules, procedures, and variables. Following are the VB .NET rules for identifiers:

- Identifiers can be up to 1023 characters long.

- They can include any letter, number, or the underscore character, but no spaces.

- They cannot begin with a number.

- They cannot be a keyword.

Although the VB .NET compiler does not require it, good programming practice suggests that your identifiers be meaningful. Table 3-2 illustrates identifier names.

Table 3-2 Identifier examples

Identifier	Comment
amount	Valid, descriptive
a	Valid, might not be descriptive
firstName	Valid, descriptive
1stName	Invalid, must begin with letter
taxableAmount	Valid, descriptive
total Amount	Invalid, contains a space

The code you write in VB .NET is not case sensitive. You can type `Module` or `module`. Although the VB .NET compiler does not require you to indent code, good programming practice encourages indentation as shown in the examples in this text. Recall from Chapter 2 that the VB .NET code editor indents your code by default.

Notice that HelloWorldWideWeb in Example 3-1 consists of only six lines. Line 1 is a **comment**. You use comment lines to add explanations to your code, which the compiler ignores. A VB .NET comment begins with a single quote (`'`), and can be on a line by itself or at the end of a line of code.

Modules begin with a module header, which names the module. Line 2 is a module header line, which contains the keyword `Module` followed by the module name, `HelloWorldWideWeb`.

Lines 3 through 5 represent a **procedure**. Procedures begin with a procedure header. A **procedure header** is written to identify the beginning of the procedure and to describe some of its characteristics, such as its name. This procedure header consists of another keyword, `Sub`, and then the procedure name `Main`.

You will learn more about VB .NET procedures in subsequent chapters, but in general, a procedure contains statements that you write to do some processing. VB .NET has two types of procedures: **Sub procedures** and **Function procedures**. These are described in more detail later; however, the main difference between the two is that a Function procedure can return a value but a Sub procedure cannot.

Whenever a module has a procedure named `Main`, this procedure is automatically invoked when the module is loaded into memory; the `Main` procedure is what executes. This means that when HelloWorldWideWeb.vb file is loaded into memory, the `Main` procedure begins running.

The `Main` procedure here contains a single statement at line 4 that is executed to display your message. This statement invokes a method to do the real work of displaying the message. `Console` is a class in the `System` namespace that provides methods to accomplish various tasks. One of these methods, `WriteLine`, displays a line of text that is passed to the method. Another method in the `Console` class is `ReadLine`, which accepts input data from the keyboard. `ReadLine` is illustrated in a later example.

The information that is contained in parentheses in line 4 is called an **argument**. It is sent to the `WriteLine` method, which then displays it.

Because the argument is included between quotation marks, as in (`"Hello World Wide Web"`), VB .NET recognizes it as a character string **literal**. A literal is a value defined within a statement. `String` values are enclosed in double quotation marks.

DEFINING VISUAL BASIC .NET VARIABLES AND DATA TYPES

You create a variable to contain data. A **variable** is a memory location that contains data. All variables have a name, data type, and value. Each of these characteristics is defined in the following list:

- *Name.* A variable name is the identifier you create to refer to the variable. VB .NET programmers have adopted the convention of beginning variable names with a lowercase letter, and then capitalizing subsequent embedded words (`firstName`, and `totalAmount`, for example).

- *Data type.* The data type specifies the kind of data the variable can contain. For example, you can store numeric values without decimal positions (123), numeric values with decimal positions (456.789), a single character (Q), a string of characters (Eleanor), and so forth. The specific .NET data types are described in the next section.

- *Value.* Every variable refers to a memory location that contains data. You can specify this data value. If you do not assign a value to the variable, then VB .NET assigns a default value. Numeric variables are initialized to zero, the character variable is initialized to `Nothing`, and the `Boolean` variable to `False`. **Nothing** is a keyword representing the value of nothing—binary zeros.

Understanding VB .NET Data Types

When declaring a variable, you must specify the data type the variable will use. VB .NET has nine **primitive data types** shown in Table 3-3. These are called primitive data types to distinguish them from more complex data types, such as class names, which are discussed later in this chapter and in subsequent chapters.

Table 3-3 VB .NET primitive data types

	Type	Range of Values	Size
Numeric with no decimals	1. Byte	0 to 255	8 bits
	2. Short	-32,768 to 32,767	16 bits
	3. Integer	-2,147,483,648 to 2,147,483,647	32 bits
	4. Long	±9,223,372,036,854,775,807	64 bits
Numeric with decimals	5. Single	±1.5E-45 to ±3.4E+38; up to 6 decimal positions	32 bits
	6. Double	±5.0E-324 to ±1.7E+308; up to 14 decimal positions	64 bits
	7. Decimal	1.0E-28 to 7.9E+28; up to 28 decimal positions	128 bits
Other	8. Boolean	True or False	16 bits
	9. Char	Any Unicode character	16 bits

You use the first four data types (`Byte`, `Short`, `Integer`, and `Long`) to contain numeric data without decimals. You use the next three data types (`Single`, `Double`, and `Decimal`) to contain numeric data with decimals. Although `Single` and `Double` have greater capacities than `Decimal`, `Decimal` gives you much greater precision, up to 28 decimal positions. This is because `Single` and `Double` values are stored as floating point and `Decimal` as fixed point. In general, you use `Decimal` when doing calculations where small rounding errors are not acceptable.

The primitive data type `Boolean` contains one of two possible values: `True` or `False`. You use the primitive data type `Char` for variables that contain a single character of text. Characters in VB .NET use the **Unicode** character set, which allocates two bytes for each character. Unicode accommodates all the characters of major international languages. To store more than one character, you use the `String` class, introduced in a later section and explored more thoroughly in Chapter 4.

 Some programmers add a prefix to variable names to indicate the data type. For example, an `Integer` variable is named `intTotal` instead of `total`.

Declaring and Populating Variables

Statements that define variables are called **declaration statements**. To declare a VB .NET variable, you write the keyword `Dim` followed by the name (identifier) you want to use, the keyword `As`, and then the data type.

Example 3-2: Declaring variables

The following statements declare three variables, each as a different data type: `myInteger` is an `Integer`, `myDouble` is a `Double`, and `myBoolean` is a `Boolean`.

```
Dim myInteger As Integer
Dim myDouble As Double
Dim myBoolean As Boolean
```

You can also declare several variables in one statement.

Example 3-3: Declaring multiple variables

The following statement declares two variables: `myInteger` as an `Integer` and `myDouble` as a `Double`.

```
Dim myInteger As Integer, myDouble As Double
```

Now that you know how to declare variables, you are ready to **populate** them, or place data into the variables. You can add code to populate the variables by assigning each a value.

Example 3-4: Populating variables

The following statements assign the values of 1 and 2.5 to the variables `myInteger` and `myDouble`, respectively.

```
myInteger = 1
myDouble = 2.5
```

The equal sign (=) in these statements is called the **assignment operator**. Statements that assign values to variables are called **assignment statements**. The assignment operator assigns the value on the right side of the equal sign to the variable named on the left side. Figure 3-4 shows these variables in memory.

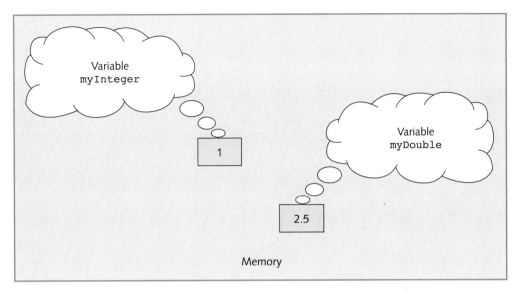

Figure 3-4   Variables containing data

You also can write code to both declare and initialize a variable in the same statement.

Example 3-5: Declaring and populating variables

The following statements declare variables, and then assign them to the values indicated.

```
Dim myInteger As Integer = 1
Dim myDouble As Double = 2.5
Dim myDecimal As Decimal = 123.456D
Dim myBoolean As Boolean = True
```

Note that in Example 3-5, the values being assigned to the variables **myInteger**, **myDouble**, and **myDecimal** are numeric literals. When you write a numeric literal, VB .NET assumes that a value *without* a decimal point is data type **Integer** and a value *with* a decimal point is data type **Double**. The literal value being assigned to **myDecimal** is written with a **D** at the end. This tells VB .NET that the value is data type **Decimal** instead of **Double**. The value **True** being assigned to **myBoolean** is a VB .NET keyword.

 You should not use commas, %, $, and so forth when writing numeric literals.

Defining Constants

It is often useful to declare a **constant**—a variable with a value that does not change. You use constants to contain values such as a company name, tax identification number, or phone number that never or seldom changes.

The code to declare a constant is identical to what you write to declare a variable, except that you write the keyword `Const` instead of `Dim`. Also, constants must be initialized in the same statement that declares them; you cannot define a constant in one statement and then populate it in another. By convention, you capitalize constant names and, if the name consists of more than one word, you separate the words with the underscore character (_).

Example 3-6: Declaring a constant

The following statement shows how you declare a constant for a sales tax rate of 7.5%.

```
Const Double SALES_TAX_RATE = 7.5
```

This code declares a constant named **SALES_TAX_RATE** of data type `Double`, and initializes it to 7.5; the value cannot be changed. If you attempt to write another statement that assigns a value to a constant, the compiler produces an error message.

Converting Data Types

Note that the seven numeric data types in Table 3–3 have different capacities. For example, a `Byte` variable can hold a maximum value of only 255, yet an `Integer` variable has a maximum value of 2.1 billion. Similarly, data type `Single` has a capacity of 3.4E+38, but `Double` has a capacity of 1.7E+308, which is significantly more.

Implicit type conversion occurs when you use the assignment operator to assign the contents of one variable to a variable with a different data type.

Example 3-7: Implicit type conversion

To illustrate implicit type conversion, assume you have defined and populated the variables **myInteger** and **myDouble** as in the following example.

```
Dim myInteger As Integer = 1
Dim myDouble As Double = 2.5
myDouble = myInteger
```

The first statement defines variable **myInteger** as data type `Integer` and populates it with 1. The second statement defines variable **myDouble** as data type `Double` and populates it with 2.5. The last statement assigns the contents of **my Integer** (containing 1) to **myDouble**. Following the execution of this statement, both variables will contain the value 1. You can assign an `Integer` value to a `Double` variable because data type `Double` has a *greater capacity* than `Integer` and there is no potential loss of data.

However, consider the result if you write the statements shown in Example 3-8. When you assign the value of one variable to another, and the first variable has a smaller capacity than the second, the results can suffer from a loss of precision. A **loss of precision** is a computing error that can occur when decimal positions are dropped, for example.

Example 3-8: Loss of precision

In the following code, the third statement causes a loss of precision error.

```
Dim myInteger As Integer = 1
Dim myDouble As Double = 2.5
myInteger = myDouble
```

Variables `myInteger` and `myDouble` are defined and populated as before; however, the third statement now assigns the contents of `myDouble` to `myInteger`, which is data type `Integer` and cannot hold decimal positions. When you attempt to assign the value 2.5 to `myInteger`, the decimal positions are truncated, resulting in a loss of precision. In this case, `myInteger` will contain 2 instead of 2.5. Note that VB .NET will *automatically round* decimal values before truncating. If the original value in `myDouble` were 2.55, the result in `myInteger` would be 3.

 You should generally avoid using implicit type conversion because of the potential for loss of precision.

The VB .NET compiler provides an option called **Option Strict** that you can enable to prevent the unintentional loss of precision when mixing data types in assignment statements. There are two ways to set this option. First, you can write `Option Strict On` or `Option Strict Off` at the beginning of your module. Alternately, you can right-click the project name in the Solution Explorer window, open the project's property window, select Build under Common Properties, and then check "Option Strict On." You should generally enable this option to prevent loss of precision when working with numeric data.

If you have set `Option Strict On`, then whenever you write an assignment statement that may result in a loss of precision, the VB .NET compiler detects the potential loss and displays an error message. You can override the compiler's objection by invoking one of the methods in the `Convert` class listed in Table 3-4. When you invoke a `Convert` method to convert data types, it is called **explicit type conversion**.

Table 3-4 Methods in the Convert class

Method	Description
ToInt16(x)	Converts the argument to Short
ToInt32(x)	Converts the argument to Integer
ToInt64(x)	Converts the argument to Long
ToSingle(x)	Converts the argument to Single
ToDouble(x)	Converts the argument to Double
ToString(x)	Converts the argument to String

Example 3-9: Explicit type conversion

To use an explicit type conversion instead of an implicit type conversion, you can modify the code in Example 3-8 as follows:

```
Dim myInteger As Integer = 1
Dim myDouble As Double = 2.5
myInteger = Convert.ToInt32(myDouble)
```

The last line of code invokes the method `ToInt32` in the `Convert` class. This method receives `myDouble` containing 2.5 as an argument, rounds it to the nearest integer value, and assigns the result, 2, to `myInteger`. Note that you assume responsibility for any loss of precision in this operation. The compiler warned you of the potential error, and by using the `Convert` methods you accepted this potential error.

 You should avoid mixing data types in statements whenever possible to avoid the loss of precision issue.

The VB .NET compiler has another option called **Option Explicit**, which is generally set On. When you use `Option Explicit On`, you must define a variable before you can use it in a statement. If you attempt to use a variable that has not been previously defined, the compiler generates an error message. However, when you set `Option Explicit Off`, the VB .NET compiler *automatically* defines a variable if you use it in a statement without first defining it. On the surface this may appear to be an attractive choice; however, if you misspell a variable name in a statement after you defined it, VB .NET defines a new variable using the misspelled name without notifying you. For example, assume you defined an `Integer` variable named `examScore`. Later in your code, however, you misspell it as `exmScore`. VB .NET creates a new variable for you named `exmScore`.

To summarize, you define variables using specific data types that determine the kind of data the variable can contain. Numeric data types have different capacities. When you assign the value of one variable to another, and the first variable has a smaller capacity than the second, loss of precision can occur. `Option Strict` prevents the unintentional loss of precision when assigning values to variables. `Option Explicit` requires that you define a variable before you can use it in a statement.

Using Reference Variables

You have seen that variables hold data. Actually, there are two kinds of variables: **primitive variables** and **reference variables**. Until now you have studied primitive variables. A primitive variable is declared with one of the nine primitive data types and it actually contains the data you put there.

In contrast, a reference variable uses a class name, such as `String`, as a data type. The variable refers to or points to an instance of that class. A reference variable does not actually contain the data; instead, it contains the memory address of an instance of a class that contains the data. For example, you may have noticed that `String` data, a collection of characters, is not one of the primitive data types. Instead, `String` data is contained in an instance of the `String` class, one of the many supplied FCL classes.

You declare a `String` reference variable just as you declared a primitive variable. You write the keyword `Dim` followed by the name you want to use, the keyword `As`, and then the data type.

Example 3-10: Declaring a String variable

```
Dim myString As String = "Hello Again"
Dim myInteger As Integer = 1
```

The first statement declares a variable named **myString**, creates an instance of the `String` class containing the characters "Hello Again," and assigns the memory address of this instance to the variable **myString**. However, **myString** does not contain "Hello Again." Instead it contains the memory location of the instance. The instance contains "Hello Again."

The second statement defines an `Integer` variable named **myInteger** and populates it with 1. **myInteger** is a primitive variable *containing* the value 1, while **myString** is a reference variable *pointing to* or *referencing* an instance of the `String` class that contains "Hello Again."

Figure 3-5 illustrates the distinction between primitive and reference variables.

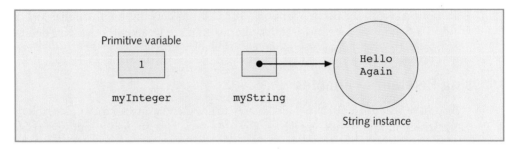

Figure 3-5 Contrasting primitive and reference variables

The distinction between primitive and reference variables becomes especially important when you work with instances, invoking their methods and accessing their attributes. Chapter 4 explores these ideas in greater detail and illustrates how to invoke methods in the `String` class.

Example 3-11: VariableDemo.vb

This example lists the code in a program module called VariableDemo, which illustrates how to declare and populate variables and shows examples of both implicit and explicit data type conversion.

```
1. ' Chapter 3 Example 3-11 - VariableDemo.vb

2. Option Strict On
3. Option Explicit On

4. Module VariableDemo

5. Sub Main()

6.    ' declare & populate variables
7.    Dim myInteger As Integer = 1
8.    Dim myDouble As Double = 2.5
9.    Dim myDecimal As Decimal = 123.456D
10.   Dim myBoolean As Boolean = True
11.   Dim myString As String = "Hello Again"

12.   ' a constant must be populated when it is declared
13.   Const SALES_TAX_RATE As Double = 7.5
```

```
14.   ' display variable contents
15.   Console.WriteLine("myInteger = " & myInteger)
16.   Console.WriteLine("myDouble = " & myDouble)
17.   Console.WriteLine("myDecimal = " & myDecimal)
18.   Console.WriteLine("myBoolean = " & myBoolean)
19.   Console.WriteLine("myString = " & myString)

20.   Console.WriteLine("SALES_TAX_RATE = " & SALES_TAX_RATE)
21.   ' illustrate implicit type conversion
22.   myDouble = myInteger
23.   Console.WriteLine("myDouble after implicit conversion = "
      & myDouble)

24.   ' illustrate explicit type conversion
25.   myDouble = 2.5
26.   myInteger = Convert.ToInt32(myDouble)
27.   Console.WriteLine("myInteger after explicit conversion =
      " & myInteger)
28.   myDouble = Convert.ToDouble(myDecimal)
29.   Console.WriteLine("myDouble after explicit conversion = "
      & myDouble)
30.   ' illustrate rounding as result of explicit conversion
31.   myDouble = 2.55
32.   myInteger = Convert.ToInt32(myDouble)
33.   Console.WriteLine("rounded results " & myInteger)
34. End Sub

35. End Module
```

Sample Run:

```
myInteger = 1
myDouble = 2.5
myDecimal = 123.456
myBoolean = True
myString = Hello Again
SALES_TAX_RATE = 7.5
myDouble after implicit conversion = 1
myInteger after explicit conversion = 2
myDouble after explicit conversion = 123.456
rounded results 3
```

Discussion:

Lines 2 and 3 enable strict type checking and explicit variable declaration, respectively.

Line 4 defines the beginning of the module and names it `VariableDemo`. Line 5 specifies the beginning of the `Main` method. Remember that whenever a module has a method named `Main`, it is the method where execution begins.

Lines 7 through 11 declare and populate several variables, and line 13 creates a constant.

Lines 15 through 20 display the contents of the variables previously defined and populated. These statements invoke the `WriteLine` method in the `Console` class to display the argument contained in parentheses. The arguments contain a `String` literal **concatenated** with a variable. For example, line 15 sends the argument (`"myInteger = " & myInteger`) to `WriteLine`. The argument consists of the `String` literal `"myInteger = "` contained within double quotation marks (`"`) followed by the VB .NET concatenate operator (`&`). This operator joins two values together, producing a `String` value suitable for display. The operator converts the numeric contents of the variable `myInteger` to `String`.

Line 22 illustrates implicit type conversion. `myInteger` is an `Integer` variable containing 1 and `myDouble` is a `Double` variable containing 2.5. Line 22 assigns the contents of `myInteger` to `myDouble`. Because `Double` has a greater capacity than `Integer`, this conversion is successful with no loss of precision.

Lines 25 through 29 illustrate explicit type conversion. Line 25 repopulates `myDouble` with 2.5. Line 26 accomplishes two things:

1. It invokes the `ToInt32` method in the `Convert` class, passing `myDouble` containing 2.5 as an argument. This method converts the `Double` value 2.5 to an `Integer` value of 2.

2. The `Integer` value 2 is returned by the `ToInt32` method and assigned to `myInteger`.

Line 28 invokes the `Convert` method `ToDouble`, passing `myDecimal` containing 123.456 as an argument. This method converts the decimal value to data type `Double` and assigns the value returned to `myDouble`.

Lines 31 and 32 illustrate rounding as a result of explicit conversion. Line 31 populates `myDouble` with 2.55. Line 32 again invokes `ToInt32` passing the argument `myDouble`. This time, however, `ToInt32` rounds 2.55 to the `Integer` value 3, which is returned and assigned to `myInteger`. The integer conversion methods in `Convert` round to the nearest `Integer` value.

WRITING BASIC COMPUTATIONAL STATEMENTS

VB .NET uses the familiar **arithmetic operators** for multiplication, division, addition, and subtraction (`*`, `/`, `+`, `-`) to specify arithmetic operations. When you write more than one arithmetic operator in an expression, they are evaluated in a predetermined order called **precedence**. The standard algebraic rules of precedence—the sequence in which operations are completed—apply to these operators. Multiplication and division are done first, followed by addition and subtraction. Operators with the same precedence are evaluated from left to right. In VB .NET and other programming languages, you can also use parentheses to group parts of an expression and establish precedence. Expressions inside parentheses are evaluated first.

To illustrate precedence, consider the following two expressions.

Expression 1:

4 / 2 + 3 * 4

Expression 2:

4 / (2 + 3) * 4

Expression 1 is evaluated in three steps:

1. Multiplication and division are evaluated first, left to right: 4 / 2 = 2

2. Multiplication and division are evaluated next, left to right: 3 * 4 = 12

3. Addition and subtraction are evaluated next: 2 + 12 = 14

Expression 2 is also evaluated in three steps:

1. Expressions in parentheses are evaluated first: (2 + 3) = 5

2. Multiplication and division are evaluated next, left to right: 4 / 5 = $\frac{4}{5}$

3. Multiplication and division are evaluated next, left to right:
   $\frac{4}{5}$ * 4 = $\frac{16}{5}$ = 3$\frac{1}{5}$

Using the Arithmetic Operators

Multiplication, addition, and subtraction of **Integer** values will produce **Integer** results, as shown in Example 3-12.

Example 3-12: Integer multiplication, addition, and subtraction

In this example, an `Integer` variable named `firstInt` is first multiplied by an `Integer` variable named `secondInt`, then `firstInt` is added to `secondInt`, and, finally, `secondInt` is subtracted from `firstInt`. In each calculation, the result is an `Integer`.

```
Dim firstInt As Integer = 11
Dim secondInt As Integer = 2
Dim integerResult As Integer = 0
integerResult = firstInt * secondInt
Console.WriteLine("firstInt * secondInt = " & integerResult)
integerResult = firstInt + secondInt
Console.WriteLine("firstInt + secondInt = " & integerResult)
integerResult = firstInt - secondInt
Console.WriteLine("firstInt - secondInt = " & integerResult)
```

Sample Run:

```
firstInt * secondInt = 22
firstInt + secondInt = 13
firstInt - secondInt = 9
```

However, when you divide two `Integer` values, the result may be a non–integer value, as shown in Example 3-13.

Example 3-13: Dividing integer values

The following code declares and populates three `Integer` variables and one `Double` variable, and then attempts to divide them.

1. `Dim firstInt As Integer = 11`
2. `Dim secondInt As Integer = 2`
3. `Dim integerResult As Integer = 0`
4. `Dim doubleResult As Double = 0`
5. `integerResult = firstInt / secondInt`
6. `doubleResult = firstInt / secondInt`

Discussion:

Line 5 attempts to divide two `Integer` variables containing 11 and 2, respectively, which produces the non-integer result of 5.5. This result cannot be assigned to the `Integer` variable `integerResult`. If you have set `Option Strict On`, then the VB .NET compiler generates an error message and will not compile your code.

Line 6, however, accommodates a non-integer value because `doubleResult` is declared in line 4 as data type `Double`, which can hold decimal positions.

You could also invoke the `Convert.ToInt32` method in line 5 to force the conversion of 11 / 2 to an integer value (5):

```
integerResult = Convert.ToInt32(firstInt / secondInt)
```

In addition to the operators for addition, subtraction, multiplication, and division, VB .NET provides operators for exponentiation, integer division, and remainder computation. The caret (^) is used for exponentiation.

3

Example 3-14: Exponentiation using the caret (^)

The following code raises `firstInt` (containing 11) to the `secondInt` (containing 2) power.

```
Dim firstInt As Integer = 11
Dim secondInt As Integer = 2
Dim doubleResult As Double = 0
doubleResult = firstInt ^ secondInt
Console.WriteLine("doubleResult = firstInt ^ secondInt: " &
doubleResult)
```

Sample Run:

```
doubleResult = firstInt ^ secondInt: 121
```

VB .NET uses the **integer division operator (\)** to produce an `Integer` result.

Example 3-15: Integer division (\)

The following code divides `firstInt` containing 11 by `secondInt` containing 2. Example 3-13 shows that the normal divide operator (/) produces a non-integer result of 5.5; however, the integer divide operator (\) is used here and the result is an integer value.

```
Dim firstInt As Integer = 11
Dim secondInt As Integer = 2
Dim integerResult As Integer = 0
integerResult = firstInt \ secondInt
Console.WriteLine("integerResult = firstInt \ secondInt: " &
integerResult)
```

Sample Run:

```
integerResult = firstInt \ secondInt: 5
```

Integer division truncates a result and does not round.

The **remainder operator (Mod)**, also called the **modulus operator**, produces a remainder resulting from the division of two integers.

Example 3-16: Determining a remainder

The following code uses the remainder operator, Mod, to divide 11 by 5, producing a remainder of 1.

```
Dim firstInt As Integer = 11
Dim secondInt As Integer = 5
Dim integerResult As Integer = 0
integerResult = firstInt Mod secondInt
Console.WriteLine("integerResult = firstInt Mod secondInt: " &
integerResult)
```

Sample Run:

```
integerResult = firstInt Mod secondInt: 1
```

The VB .NET arithmetic operators are summarized in Table 3-5 in order of precedence.

Table 3-5: VB .NET arithmetic operators

Operator	Description	Example	Result
^	Exponentiation	11 ^ 2	121
*	Multiplication	11 * 2	22
/	Division	11 / 2	5.5
\	Integer division	11 \ 2	5
Mod	Remainder	11 Mod 2	1
+	Addition	11 + 2	13
–	Subtraction	11 – 2	9

VB .NET also supports **assignment operators**, sometimes called **shortcut operators**, which are formed by combining one of the arithmetic operators with the assignment operator. For example, to add 1 to a variable named i, you can write either of the following statements:

```
i = i + 1
```

or

```
i += 1
```

Table 3-6 lists the frequently used assignment operators in order of precedence.

Table 3-6: Selected VB .NET assignment operators

Operator	Description	Example	Interpreted As
=	Assignment	a = 1	a = 1
^=	Exponentiation assignment	a ^= 2	a = a ^ 2
*=	Multiply assignment	a *= 2	a = a * 2
/=	Division assignment	a /= 2	a = a / 2
\=	Integer division assignment	a \= 2	a = a \ 2
+=	Addition assignment	a += 2	a = a + 2
-=	Subtraction assignment	a -= 2	a = a - 2

Invoking Methods in the Math Class

In addition to the arithmetic operators described in the previous section, the `System` name-space includes the `Math` class, which contains methods to accomplish exponentiation, rounding, trigonometric calculations, and numerous other tasks. Table 3-7 lists some of the `Math` class methods. You can access the .NET Help facility to explore these methods in more detail.

Table 3-7 Selected methods in the Math class

Method	Description	Data Type Returned
Abs(x)	Returns absolute value of x	Same as argument
Cos(x)	Returns cosine of angle x	Double
Exp(x)	Returns e raised to the x power	Double
Pow(x,y)	Returns x raised to the power of y	Double
Round(x, n)	Returns x rounded to n decimals	Same as argument
Sin(x)	Returns sin of angle x	Double
Sqrt(x)	Returns square root of x	Double
Tan(x)	Returns tangent of angle x	Double

To invoke one of these methods, you write the name of the class (`Math`), a period, the name of the method, and then the required arguments, as in `Math.Pow(firstInt, secondInt)`. The method returns the resulting value after doing the computation. Note that these methods return specific data types that you generally assign to variables. When assigning values being returned by these methods, you must assign the values to variables with a data type of equal or greater capacity, or use explicit type conversion.

Example 3-17: Exponentiation using the Math.Pow method

In the previous section, you saw how to use the caret (^) to accomplish exponentiation. The following example illustrates exponentiation using the `Pow` method in the `Math` class.

```
Dim firstInt As Integer = 11
Dim secondInt As Integer = 2
Dim doubleResult As Double = 0
doubleResult = Math.Pow(firstInt, secondInt)
Console.WriteLine("doubleResult = Math.Pow(firstInt,
secondInt): " & doubleResult)
```

Sample Run:

```
doubleResult = Math.Pow(firstInt, secondInt) = 121
```

The `Pow` method accepts two arguments and raises the first argument to the power of the second. In this example, `firstInt` contains 11 and `secondInt` contains 2. `Pow` raises 11 to the second power, and returns the result 121, which is assigned to `doubleResult`. Note that `Pow` returns a `Double` data type.

Example 3-18: Using the Math.Sqrt method

This example computes the square root of 121 by invoking `Math.Sqrt`, which also returns a `Double` value.

```
Dim firstInt As Integer = 121
Dim doubleResult As Double = 0
doubleResult = Math.Sqrt(firstInt)
Console.WriteLine("doubleResult = Math.Sqrt(firstInt): "
& doubleResult)
```

Sample Run:

```
doubleResult = Math.Sqrt(firstInt) = 11
```

The `Math` class also has two useful constants: PI and E. You access these by writing the class name, a period, and the constant name: `Math.PI` or `Math.E`.

Example 3-19: Using Math.PI constant

This example uses `Math.PI` to compute the area of a circle.

```
Dim radius As Integer = 1
Dim area As Double = Math.Pow(radius, 2) * Math.PI
Console.WriteLine("area = " & area)
```

Sample Run:

```
area = 3.14159265358979
```

Discussion:

Line 1 declares an `Integer` variable named `radius` and populates it with 1.

Line 2 does four things:

    1. Declares a `Double` variable named `area`

    2. Invokes the `Math.Pow` method, which raises the contents of `radius` (1) to the second power

    3. Multiplies the value returned by `Math.Pow` by the constant Math.PI

    4. Assigns the result of the multiplication in Step 3 to the variable `area`

Line 3 displays the result.

The `Math.Round` method rounds a value to the number of decimal positions specified.

Example 3-20: Using Math.Round

This example rounds the `Double` value 123.456 to one decimal place. Note that line 2 uses the variable `doubleResult` as an argument sent to `Math.Round`, and then assigns the value returned from the method to the same variable, `doubleResult`. This means that the original contents of `doubleResult` have been replaced with the rounded value 123.5.

```
Dim doubleResult As Double = 123.456
doubleResult = Math.Round(doubleResult, 1)
Console.WriteLine("Math.Round(doubleResult, 1): " & doubleResult)
```

Sample Run:

```
Math.Round(doubleResult, 1): 123.5
```

READING INPUT FROM THE KEYBOARD

Earlier you learned how to use the `Console.WriteLine` method to display information. `Console` has several additional useful methods such as `ReadLine`, which you invoke to read one or more characters from the keyboard. Because this method reads characters, you must convert any numeric data to the desired data type when assigning it to a variable.

When you want to read data from the keyboard, you should display a message called a **prompt** that explains to the user what they should type. You can use the `Console.WriteLine` method to display prompts.

Example 3-21: Using Console.ReadLine

This example shows several ways to use `ReadLine`. The shaded data in the Sample Run shows the user input.

```
Dim name As String
Dim age As Integer
Console.WriteLine("Please enter your name")
name = Console.ReadLine()
Console.WriteLine("You entered: " & name)
Console.WriteLine("Please enter your age")
age = Convert.ToInt32(Console.ReadLine())
Console.WriteLine("You entered: " & age)
```

Sample Run:

```
Please enter your name
Emily
You entered: Emily
Please enter your age
20
You entered: 20
```

Discussion:

Line 1 declares a `String` variable named `name` and Line 2 declares an `Integer` variable named `age`.

Line 3 invokes `Console.WriteLine` to display the prompt message "Please enter your name."

Line 4 invokes `Console.ReadLine` to read the characters being entered from the keyboard. The characters returned from the `ReadLine` method are then assigned to the `String` variable `name`. In this example, the value Emily was entered.

Line 5 again invokes `Console.WriteLine` to display the value that was entered.

Line 6 invokes `Console.WriteLine` to display another prompt: "Please enter your age."

Line 7 invokes `Console.ReadLine` again to read the value being entered. This time, however, the user enters a number that is to be assigned to the `Integer` variable named `age`. Because the data type returned by `ReadLine` is `String`, regardless of the actual value, you must invoke the `Convert.ToInt32` method to convert the `String` data to `Integer`. Finally, the converted value returned by `Convert.ToInt32` is then assigned to the variable `age`.

Line 8 displays the contents of `age`, which in this example is 20.

3

PROGRAMMING EXAMPLE: TEMPERATURE CONVERTER

This example demonstrates a program that converts a Fahrenheit temperature to Celsius. The program prompts the user for a Fahrenheit temperature, computes the appropriate Celsius value, and then displays the result.

Input   A Fahrenheit temperature including any decimal positions

Output   The Celsius temperature that corresponds to the Fahrenheit temperature that was input, with the results rounded to one decimal position

Problem Analysis and Algorithm Design

The purpose of this program is to convert a Fahrenheit temperature to Celsius. To perform the conversion, you subtract 32 from the Fahrenheit temperature, and then multiply the result by 5/9. Because you are prompting a user for input, you must also convert the `String` data the user provides to the `Double` data type.

Variables   Two data type `Double` variables named fahrenheit and celsius:

```
Dim fahrenheit, celsius As Double
```

Formula $C = 5/9(F - 32)$

Main Algorithm

1. Declare the variables.
2. Prompt the user for input.
3. Invoke `Console.ReadLine` to input the value from keyboard, and invoke `Convert.ToDouble` to convert the data type `String` to `Double`.
4. Compute the Celsius temperature.
5. Invoke `Math.Round` to round the computed value to one decimal position.
6. Invoke `Console.WriteLine` to display the rounded Celsius temperature.

Complete Program Listing

```
' TemperatureConverter Chapter 3 End of chapter example
Option Strict On
Option Explicit On
Module TemperatureConverter
  Sub Main()

    ' declare variables
    Dim fahrenheit, celsius As Double
    ' display prompt
    Console.WriteLine("Please enter a Fahrenheit temperature:")
    ' read fahrenheit temperature & convert to data type Double
    fahrenheit = Convert.ToDouble(Console.ReadLine())
    ' compute celsius
    celsius = 5 / 9 * (fahrenheit - 32)
    ' round to one decimal
    celsius = Math.Round(celsius, 1)
    ' display result
    Console.WriteLine(fahrenheit & " F = " & celsius & " C")
End Sub
End Module
```

Sample Runs

In the following sample runs, the user input is shaded.

```
Please enter a Fahrenheit temperature:
212
212 F = 100 C
Please enter a Fahrenheit temperature:
32
32 F = 0 C
Please enter a Fahrenheit temperature:
-22
-22 F = -30 C
Please enter a Fahrenheit temperature:
55
55 F = 12.8 C
```

QUICK REVIEW

1. The central component of Visual Basic .NET (VB .NET) is the .NET Framework. This Framework consists of compilers for VB .NET and other supported .NET languages, the Common Language Runtime (CLR), and the Framework Class Library (FCL).

2. All of the Framework compilers check syntax and translate your source code into a language called Microsoft Intermediate Language (MSIL), or simply Intermediate Language (IL). The Just-In-Time (JIT) Compiler translates IL into executable, processor-specific machine language.

3. An assembly is a file containing IL. The FCL consists of approximately 100 assemblies, each of which contains one or more classes with methods you invoke to accomplish tasks.

3

4. The classes in the FCL are organized logically into namespaces. Namespaces are arranged into a hierarchy. A namespace can contain classes and other namespaces.

5. You give the compiler access to the classes in a namespace by writing the keyword **Imports** followed by the namespace at the beginning of your module.

6. VB .NET statements consist of keywords and identifiers. Keywords have special meaning to the VB .NET compiler. A VB .NET identifier is the name you assign to things such as modules, procedures, and variables.

7. The code you write in VB .NET is *not* case sensitive.

8. You use comment lines to add explanations to your code, which the compiler ignores. A VB .NET comment begins with a single quotation mark (') and can be on a line by itself or at the end of a line of code.

9. Modules begin with a module header, which names the module. Procedures begin with a procedure header to identify the procedure and to describe some of its characteristics, such as its name.

10. VB .NET has two types of procedures: Sub procedures and Function procedures. A Function procedure can return a value to the statement that invoked it, but a Sub procedure cannot.

11. Whenever a module has a procedure named **Main**, this procedure is automatically invoked when the module is loaded into memory; the **Main** procedure is what executes.

12. A literal is what you call a value defined within a statement. **String** literals are enclosed in double quotation marks. **Decimal** literals are followed by the character D.

13. A variable is a memory location that contains data. All variables have a name, data type, and value. If you do not assign the variable a value, then VB .NET assigns a default value. Numeric variables are initialized to zero, the character variable is initialized to **Nothing** (binary zeros), and the Boolean variable to **False**.

14. VB .NET has nine primitive data types: four contain numeric data without decimals, three contain numeric data with decimals, **Boolean** contains **True** or **False**, and **Char** contains a single character of text.

15. Characters in VB .NET use the Unicode character set, which uses two bytes for each character. To store more than one character, you use the **String** class.

16. Statements that define variables are called declaration statements. To declare a VB .NET variable, you write the keyword `Dim` followed by the name (identifier) you want to use, the keyword `As`, and then the data type. You can declare several variables in one statement. You also can write code both to declare and to initialize a variable in the same statement.

17. The assignment operator is the equal sign (=). It assigns the value on the right side of the equal sign to the variable named on the left side. Statements that assign values to variables are called assignment statements.

18. A constant is a variable with a value that does not change. You declare a constant by writing the keyword `Const` instead of `Dim`. Constants must be initialized in the same statement that declares them. By convention, you capitalize constant names; if the name consists of more than one word, you separate the words with the underscore character (_).

19. Numeric data types have different capacities. When you assign the value of one variable to another, and the first variable has a smaller capacity than the second, loss of precision can occur. `Option Strict` is a compiler option that prevents the unintentional loss of precision when assigning values to variables.

20. `Option Explicit` requires that you define a variable before you can use it in a statement.

21. A primitive variable is declared with one of the nine primitive data types and contains the data.

22. A reference variable uses a class name, such as `String`, as a data type and refers to or points to an instance of that class. A reference variable does not actually contain the data; instead, it contains a memory address that refers to an instance of a class that contains the data.

23. The VB .NET concatenate operator (`&`) joins two values together, producing a `String` value suitable for display.

24. VB .NET uses the familiar arithmetic operators for addition, subtraction, multiplication, and division (+, -, *, /) that are used in other programming languages. VB .NET also uses a remainder operator (`Mod`) to produce a remainder resulting from the division of two integers, and the integer division operator (\) to produce an `Integer` result. The caret (^) is used for exponentiation.

25. VB .NET supports assignment operators, sometimes called shortcut operators, which are formed by combining one of the arithmetic operators (^, *, /, +, -, `Mod`, \) with the assignment operator (=).

26. The `Math` class in the `System` namespace contains methods to accomplish exponentiation, rounding, and numerous other tasks. To invoke one of these methods, you write the name of the class (`Math`), a period, the name of the method, and then any arguments required.

EXERCISES

1. Which of the following is *not* a valid VB .NET identifier? Why not?

   a. `name`

   b. `2ndName`

   c. `lastName`

   d. `keyword`

2. Given the following code, identify the contents of variables `c`, `d`, and `e` after the statements are executed.

   ```
   Dim a, b, c As Integer
   Dim d, e As Double
   a = 2
   b = 3
   c = (b \ a)
   d = a / b
   e = b Mod a
   ```

3. Rewrite the following algebraic expressions using VB .NET syntax.

   a. $(1+i)^y$

   b. $(b^2 - 4ac)/2a$

   c. $\sin(45)$

   d. $1/(1+i)^y$

4. Rewrite the following code as one statement using only one variable named `amount`.

   ```
   Dim amount, roundedAmount As Double
   Dim input As String
   input = Console.ReadLine
   amount = Convert.ToDouble(input)
   roundedAmount = Math.Round(amount, 2)
   ```

5. List the seven numeric primitive data types in ascending capacity sequence.

6. What is a VB .NET identifier? What are the rules for creating one?

7. What is a keyword?

8. What is a primitive variable?

9. How can you tell if an identifier is a constant?

10. What does the keyword `Nothing` mean?

11. What is an argument?

12. What is a literal?

13. What is the `Main` procedure?

14. Explain the difference between the divide (/) and the remainder operator (`Mod`).

15. Explain the difference between the divide (/) and the integer divide (\) operator.

16. Describe the differences between the `WriteLine` and `ReadLine` methods in the `Console` class.

PROGRAMMING EXERCISES

1. Design and write a program that does the following:

   a. Prompts the user to input a number containing decimals: `aNumber`

   b. Prompts the user to input the number of desired decimal positions after rounding: `numberOfDecimals`

   c. Rounds `aNumber` to `numberOfDecimals` decimal positions

   d. Displays the rounded value in `aNumber`

2. Design and write a program that does the following:

   a. Prompts the user to input a Celsius temperature: `celsius`

   b. Computes the equivalent Fahrenheit temperature: `fahrenheit`

   c. Rounds `fahrenheit` to two decimal positions

   d. Displays the rounded value in `fahrenheit`

   To review the formula for converting Celsius to Fahrenheit, refer to the Programming Example in this chapter.

3. Design and write a program that does the following:

   a. Prompts the user to input three exam scores: `exam1Score`, `exam2Score`, and `exam3Score`

   b. Computes the average of the three scores: `averageExamScore`

   c. Rounds `averageExamScore` to one decimal position

   d. Displays the rounded value in `averageExamScore`

4. Design and write a program that does the following:

   a. Prompts the user to input the number of inches: `inches`

   b. Converts `inches` to centimeters: `centimeters`

   c. Rounds `centimeters` to three decimal positions

   d. Displays the rounded value in `centimeters`

   To review the formula for converting inches to centimeters, refer to an online conversion tool.

5. Design and write a program that does the following:

   a. Prompts the user to input the base and height of a triangle: `base` and `height`

   b. Computes the triangle's area: `area`

   c. Rounds `area` to one decimal position

   d. Displays the rounded value in `area`

   To review the formula for computing the area of a triangle, refer to an online math tool.

6. Design and write a program that illustrates `Decimal` precision better than `Single` or `Double`.

3

4

Control Structures: Selection

Chapter 3 introduced you to the .NET Framework and explored some of the fundamentals of the Visual Basic .NET (VB .NET) programming language, including how to write a module definition, declare variables, and write basic computational statements.

You saw in Chapter 1 that the statements in a program are usually executed in sequence, one after the other. Sometimes, however, you will want to alter this sequential execution by selecting specific statements to run while excluding others. Also, you will often want to repeat the execution of a set of statements a certain number of times. This repeated execution is called iteration. These three types of statement execution—**sequence**, **selection**, and **iteration**—are called **control structures**. You write programs using a combination of these control structures. This chapter describes the selection structure, which uses the `If` and `Select Case` statements. The next chapter explores iteration. You continue to use the sequence structure throughout the book.

WRITING AND INTERPRETING LOGICAL EXPRESSIONS

In addition to writing a program that follows a sequence of statements, from the first to the last, you can write a program that makes a decision and executes certain statements based on that decision. You make decisions in a selection statement by writing logical expressions. A **logical expression** specifies a condition that evaluates to either `true` or `false`. You use logical expressions to compare two values. For example, you might want to compare the contents of the variable `gpa` (for grade point average) to the value 3.0. If the value of `gpa` is greater than 3.0, the logical expression evaluates to `true`. If the value is less than 3.0, the expression evaluates to `false`.

Using the VB .NET Relational Operators

You use a **relational operator** to make a comparison in a logical expression, such as determining whether one value is equal to or less than another value. VB .NET provides several relational operators for writing logical expressions. These operators are listed in Table 4-1.

Table 4-1   VB .NET relational operators

Operator	Description
=	Equal to
>	Greater than
>=	Greater than or equal to
<	Less than
<=	Less than or equal to
<>	Not equal to

Example 4-1: Using the >= relational operator

Assume `examScore` is an `Integer` variable containing the value 86. Consider the following logical expression:

```
examScore >= 90
```

As shown in Table 4-1, the `>=` symbol is a relational operator meaning "greater than or equal to." In effect, this expression asks the question: "Is the value contained in `exam-Score` *greater than or equal to* 90?" Here the answer is no or `false`, because `examScore` contains the value 86. However, if `examScore` were to contain 90, then the expression would evaluate to `true`.

4

Example 4-2: Using the < relational operator

Next, consider an expression with a different relational operator:

```
examScore < 90
```

The `<` symbol used in this expression is a relational operator meaning "less than." This expression asks the question: "Is the value contained in `examScore` *less than* 90?" If `examScore` contains 86, the answer is yes or `true`; however, if `examScore` contains 91, then the expression evaluates to `false`.

Using the VB .NET Logical Operators

In addition to the relational operators, VB .NET uses **logical operators**, which you use to combine logical expressions. Frequently used logical operators are `Not`, which negates an expression, and `And`, which joins two expressions. Table 4-2 lists the logical operators VB .NET provides to construct logical expressions.

Table 4-2 VB .NET logical operators

Operator	Description
Not	Negates an expression
And	Logically joins two expressions; if both expressions evaluate to `true`, then `And` returns `true`; otherwise it returns `false`
Or	Logically joins two expressions; if both expressions evaluate to `false`, then `Or` returns `false`; otherwise it returns `true`
Xor	Logically joins two expressions; if both expressions evaluate to `true` or both expressions evaluate to `false`, `Xor` returns `false`; otherwise it returns `true`
AndAlso	Same as `And` except it employs short-circuit logic
OrElse	Same as `Or` except it employs short-circuit logic

Later in this chapter you learn that short-circuit logic is used with statements that include more than one logical expression. The computer evaluates the first expression, and if it can determine the result of the statement from that expression, it does not evaluate the second logical expression.

The **Not** operator *negates* a logical expression by returning the opposite value of the expression. A logical expression evaluates to either **true** or **false**; therefore, when you add the **Not** operator, the expression still evaluates to **true** or **false**.

Example 4-3: Using the Not logical operator

Example 4-1 defines **examScore** as an **Integer** variable containing the value 86. In this case, the expression:

```
examScore >= 90
```

is **false**. However, if you insert the logical operator **Not** at the beginning of the expression, the expression evaluates to **true**. That is, the expression:

```
Not examScore >= 90
```

evaluates to **true**. This expression asks the question: "Is **examScore** *not greater than or equal to 90*?" The answer is yes, or **true**: **examScore** is not greater than or equal to 90.

The logical operator **And** joins two expressions, forming a **compound expression**. If both expressions evaluate to **true**, then the compound expression is **true**; otherwise, it is **false**.

Example 4-4: Using the And logical operator

Assume you are given an **Integer** variable named **examScore** containing 86, and a **Boolean** variable named **engineeringStudent** containing the value **True**. Consider the following expression:

```
examScore >= 90 And engineeringStudent
```

This is a compound expression consisting of two expressions joined with the logical operator **And**. In this example, the first expression (**examScore >= 90**) evaluates to **false** and the second (**engineeringStudent**) evaluates to **true**. Because the **And** operator returns **true** if and only if *both* expressions are **true**, the result here is **false**.

Table 4-3 lists the four types of expressions you can use with the **And** operator and shows their results.

Table 4-3 Expressions using the And operator

Expression	Result	Explanation
1 < 2 And 2 < 3	true	Both of the expressions are true
1 < 2 And 2 > 3	false	The second expression is false
1 > 2 And 2 < 3	false	The first expression is false
1 > 2 And 2 > 3	false	Both expressions are false

4

The Or operator also joins two expressions; however, it returns true if *either or both* of the expressions are true.

Example 4-5: Using the Or logical operator

Once again, using the integer variable examScore containing 86 and the Boolean variable engineeringStudent containing the value True, consider the following expression:

examScore >= 90 Or engineeringStudent

Although the first expression (examScore >= 90) is false, the second expression (engineeringStudent) is true; therefore, the compound expression is true.

Table 4-4 lists the four types of expressions you can use with the Or operator and shows their results.

Table 4-4 Expressions using the Or operator

Expression	Result	Explanation
1 < 2 Or 2 < 3	true	Both of the expressions are true
1 < 2 Or 2 > 3	true	The first expression is true
1 > 2 Or 2 < 3	true	The second expression is true
1 > 2 Or 2 > 3	false	Both expressions are false

The Xor operator also joins two expressions; however, unlike Or, Xor returns true if *one and only one* of the expressions is true; otherwise, it returns false.

Example 4-6: Using the Xor logical operator

Again, using the `Integer` variable `examScore` containing 86 and the `Boolean` variable `engineeringStudent` containing the value `True`, consider the following expression:

```
examScore >= 90 Xor engineeringStudent
```

The first expression (`examScore >= 90`) is `false`, and the second expression (`engineeringStudent`) is `true`. Because *only one* of the two expressions in the compound expression is `true`, `Xor` returns `true`. However, if both expressions were `true`, then `Xor` would return `false`.

Table 4-5 illustrates the difference between `Or` and `Xor`.

Table 4-5 Comparing logical operators Or and Xor

Expression	Result	Explanation
`1 < 2 Or 2 < 3`	true	At least one of the expressions is `true`
`1 < 2 Xor 2 < 3`	false	Both expressions are `true`
`1 < 2 Or 2 < 1`	true	At least one of the expressions is `true`
`1 < 2 Xor 2 < 1`	true	One and only one of the expressions is `true`

The logical operators `AndAlso` and `OrElse` correspond to the `And` and `Or` operators, respectively, except that they employ a **short-circuit evaluation** technique, which is described in the following examples.

Example 4-7: Using the AndAlso logical operator

To illustrate short-circuit evaluation, assume you have two expressions joined with the `AndAlso` operator:

```
2 < 1 AndAlso 2 < 3
```

The first expression (`2 < 1`) is `false` and the second (`2 < 3`) is `true`, which means the compound expression is `false`. Short-circuit evaluation recognizes that because the first expression (`2 < 1`) is `false`, the compound expression is `false`. The computer does not evaluate the second expression because it cannot alter the resulting evaluation.

Example 4-8: Using the OrElse logical operator

The `OrElse` logical operator also uses short-circuit evaluation. Consider the following statement:

```
1 < 2 OrElse 2 < 3
```

The first expression in this compound expression is **true**, making the compound expression **true**, which eliminates the need to evaluate the second expression. The compound expression will be **true** regardless of the result of its second expression.

4

In the remaining sections of this chapter, you see how to combine logical expressions, logical operators, and relational operators to write various kinds of selection statements.

WRITING ONE-WAY SELECTION STATEMENTS

A one-way selection statement evaluates a logical expression, and then executes one or more statements only if the expression is **true**. A two-way selection statement also evaluates a logical expression and executes one or more statements if it is **true**, but executes one or more different statements if it is **false**. The two-way selection statement is discussed in the next section. For now, you can concentrate on understanding the logic and syntax of a one-way selection statement. Recall that selection is one of three common control structures used in programming languages; the others are sequence and iteration.

It is often helpful to depict control structure logic using a flowchart. A **flowchart** is a graphical representation of logic. Flowcharts use symbols to represent the logical components of an algorithm. You can use a simple flowchart consisting of only four symbols to represent control structure logic. Figure 4-1 shows the flowchart for a one-way selection structure.

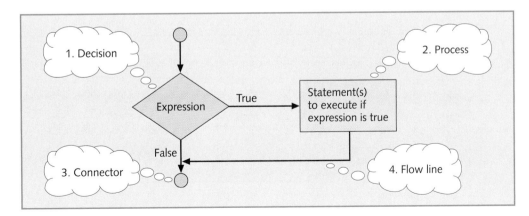

Figure 4-1   One-way selection flowchart

This flowchart consists of four symbols:

1. The diamond represents a decision. The decision is made by evaluating a logical expression to **true** or **false**.

2. A rectangle represents a process. A process contains one or more statements. As shown in Figure 4-1, if the expression is **true**, then the process is executed; otherwise it is not.

3. The small circle is a connector, which in this example is shown at both the beginning and the end of the structure. You use a connector to begin and end a flowchart and to connect various pieces of a flowchart together.

4. The flow lines indicate logic flow, or the possible paths through the diagram. If the expression is **true**, one path is followed. If it is **false**, a different path is taken.

One-way selection is implemented in VB .NET by writing either a **single-line If** or a **multi-line If** statement. A single-line **If** statement has the following form:

```
If (logical expression) Then statement
```

Example 4-9: Writing a single-line If statement

The following code illustrates a single-line **If**. In this statement, **examScore** is an **Integer** variable containing 86 and **grade** is a **String** variable that contains a space before the statement is executed.

```
If examScore >= 90 Then grade = "A"
```

This statement says: "If **examScore** contains a value greater than or equal to 90, then assign the value A to **grade**."

Figure 4-2 shows a flowchart for the statement illustrated in Example 4-9.

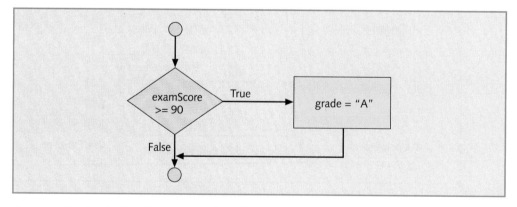

Figure 4-2   Single-line If statement flowchart

The multi-line `If` executes more than one statement when the logical expression is `true`. A multi-line `If` has the following form:

```
If (logical expression) Then
    statement
    statement
    .
    .
    statement
End If
```

Example 4-10: Executing multiple statements with a multi-line If

The following multi-line `If` executes two statements if the expression is `true`.

```
1. If examScore >= 90 Then
2.     grade = "A"
3.     Console.WriteLine("Good job!")
4. End If
```

In other words, if the value of **examScore** is greater than or equal to 90, then assign "A" to **grade** and display "Good job!" on the screen.

The multi-line `If` is different from the single-line `If` in two important ways. First, the statements to be executed when the logical expression is `true` are written on separate lines. Second, the keyword `End If` must be used to terminate the `If` statement.

Both the single-line and multi-line `If` statements can also include compound expressions.

Example 4-11: Using a multi-line If with a compound expression

The following example is a multi-line `If` statement that uses the `And` logical operator to create a compound expression.

```
1. If examScore >= 90 And numberOfAbsences < 3 Then
2.     grade = "A"
3.     Console.WriteLine("Good job!")
4. End If
```

Recall that for a compound expression of this type to be `true`, both logical expressions must be `true`. In this case, if the value of **examScore** is greater than or equal to 90 and the value of **numberOfAbsences** is less than 3, then assign "A" to **grade** and display "Good job!" on the screen.

Multi-line If statements are necessary when you want to execute more than one statement if an expression is **true**. However, you can rewrite any single-line If using the multi-line If format.

Example 4-12: Rewriting a single-line If using the multi-line If format

The following statements accomplish the same task—each assigns "A" to **grade** if the value of **examScore** is greater than or equal to 90.

```
If examScore >= 90 Then grade = "A"

If examScore >= 90 Then
      grade = "A"
End If
```

Generally, a single-line If is easier to write when you want to execute a single statement if an expression is **true** (you write one line of code instead of three). However, logic errors can be easier to identify and correct when you use the multi-line format.

Most programmers use multi-line If statements because they are generally easier to read and understand.

To summarize, you write a one-way selection statement to evaluate a logical expression and execute one or more statements when the expression is **true**. The expression can be a single logical expression or a compound expression. You can implement a one-way selection statement using a single-line or a multi-line If statement. Use the multi-line If form when you want to execute more than one statement when the logical expression is **true**.

WRITING TWO-WAY SELECTION STATEMENTS

You write a one-way selection statement to execute one or more statements when a logical expression is **true**, but you want to do *nothing* if it is **false**. In contrast, you write a two-way selection statement when you want to execute one or more statements if a logical expression is **true**, but you *also* want to execute one or more different statements if it is **false**. The flowchart in Figure 4-3 maps the logic of the two-way selection structure.

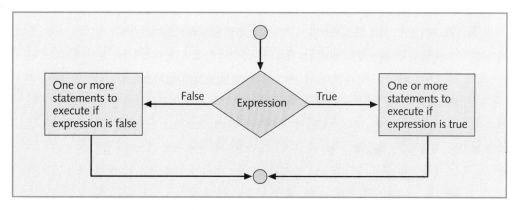

Figure 4-3 Two-way selection flowchart

You implement the two-way selection structure by writing an **If** statement together with the keyword **Else**. A two-way selection structure has the following form:

```
If (logical expression) Then
    statement(s)
Else
    statement(s)
End If
```

Example 4-13 contains statements that determine an employee's overtime pay. An employee is entitled to overtime pay if he or she works more than 40 hours in a given week and is not exempt from being paid overtime. Table 4-6 lists the variables that Example 4-13 uses to compute overtime pay.

Table 4-6 Variables to compute overtime pay

Variable Name	Data Type	Contents
hoursWorked	Double	The number of hours an employee worked in the week
rate	Double	The employee's hourly pay rate
otPay	Double	The computed overtime pay amount
exemptEmployee	Boolean	True if the employee is exempt from being paid overtime, otherwise False

Example 4-13: Computing employee pay

Using the variables defined in Table 4-6, a two-way `If` statement to calculate overtime pay is:

1. `If hoursWorked > 40 And Not exemptEmployee Then`

2. `otPay = (hoursWorked - 40) * rate * 1.5`

3. `Else`

4. `otPay = 0`

5. `End If`

Discussion:

The compound expression in line 1 is evaluated first. If the number of hours the employee worked is greater than 40 and if the employee is not exempt from the overtime pay rule, then the employee is entitled to overtime pay and line 2 is executed to compute overtime pay for the employee. In this example, overtime pay is computed at one and one-half times the rate for regular pay for hours worked above 40.

The keyword `Else` in line 3 indicates the beginning of statements to be executed when the compound expression in line 1 is `false`, which means that either the employee worked 40 hours or less, the employee is exempt from the overtime pay rule, or both. If the expression is `false`, then line 4 is executed to assign zero to the employee's overtime pay.

The flowchart in Figure 4-4 shows the logic of the two-way `If` statement in Example 4-13.

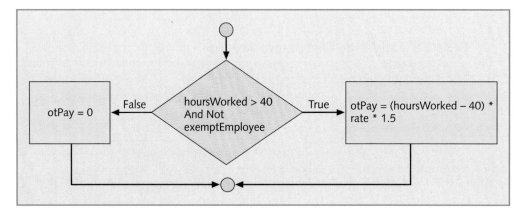

Figure 4-4   Computing employee pay flowchart

You can write more than one statement following the keyword `Else`. These statements will be executed only if the logical expression evaluates `false`.

A **nested If** is an `If` statement written inside another `If` statement. Sometimes you can replace a compound expression with a nested `If`. Example 4-11 used the following compound expression, which you can replace with the nested `If` statement shown in Example 4-14:

```
If examScore >= 90 And numberOfAbsences < 3 Then

      grade = "A"

      Console.WriteLine("Good job!")

End If
```

Example 4-14: Replacing a compound expression with a nested If

The following nested `If` statement accomplishes the same thing as the statements in Example 4-11. The shaded lines show a nested `If` statement:

```
1. If examScore >= 90 Then
2.    If numberOfAbsences < 3 Then
3.        grade = "A"
4.        Console.WriteLine("Good job!")
5.    End If
6. End If
```

Each `If` has a corresponding `End If`

Discussion:

Line 1 determines if **examScore** contains a value that is greater than or equal to 90. If it is, then line 2, which begins a nested `If` statement, is executed. Note that if the logical expression in line 1 evaluates `false`, then none of the other statements in the example are executed.

Line 2 is executed if the logical expression in line 1 is `true`. If the expression in line 2 (**numberOfAbsences < 3**) is also `true`, then lines 3 and 4 are executed. However, if this expression is `false`, then none of the remaining statements are executed.

Example 4-15: Determining a grade using single-line If statements

Consider a more complete grade-determination example using the standard 90, 80, 70, 60 logic for assigning grades. There are several ways to implement a solution for this problem. First you can use single-line **If** statements to determine if the grade is within a specific range, and assign the letter grade accordingly. The following code uses single-line **If** statements to determine the grade.

```
1. If examScore >= 90 Then grade = "A"

2. If examScore >= 80 And examScore < 90 Then grade = "B"

3. If examScore >= 70 And examScore < 80 Then grade = "C"

4. If examScore >= 60 And examScore < 70 Then grade = "D"

5. If examScore < 60 Then grade = "F"
```

Discussion:

The logic here is straightforward. Line 1 assigns a grade of A if the score is 90 or above, line 2 assigns a B if the score is between 80 and 90, and so on. Note that this solution requires only five lines of code.

Example 4-16: Determining a grade using nested If statements

Another solution to the problem presented in Example 4-15 is to use nested **If** statements. Note that this example contains 17 lines of code, considerably longer than the initial solution.

```
 1. If examScore >= 90 Then

 2.          grade = "A"

 3. Else

 4.    If examScore >= 80 Then

 5.          grade = "B"

 6.    Else

 7.       If examScore >= 70 Then

 8.             grade = "C"

 9.       Else

10.          If examScore >= 60 Then

11.                grade = "D"

12.          Else

13.                grade = "F"
```

14.   End If

15.   End If

16. End If

17. End If

You can code another shorter solution using the keyword **ElseIf**, which as the name suggests, combines **Else** and **If**.

Example 4-17: Determining a grade using ElseIf statements

1. If examScore >= 90 Then

2. grade = "A"

3. ElseIf examScore >= 80 Then

4. grade = "B"

5. ElseIf examScore >= 70 Then

6. grade = "C"

7. ElseIf examScore >= 60 Then

8. grade = "D"

9. Else grade = "F"

10. End If

 When coding solutions that can be implemented using single-line If statements, nested If statements, or **ElseIf** statements, you should choose the alternative that is the easiest for you and others to understand.

To summarize, you write a one-way selection statement when you want to execute one or more statements if a logical expression is **true**, but you want to do nothing if it is **false**. In contrast, you write a two-way selection statement when you want to execute one or more statements if a logical expression is **true**, but you *also* want to execute one or more different statements if it is **false**.

WRITING MULTI-WAY SELECTION STATEMENTS

VB .NET implements the multi-way selection structure, sometimes called the **case structure**, with the keywords **Select Case**. This type of statement acts like a multi-way **If** statement by transferring control to one or more statements, depending on the value of a variable. Use a

Select Case statement when you want to make a decision, but there are more than two values of a variable you want evaluate.

Example 4-18: Determine a grade using Select Case statements

Consider the grade assignment problem from the previous examples. You have a variable named **examScore** and you want to assign a letter grade based on its contents. You saw how to use **If** statements to assign the grade; however, you can also use the **Select Case** statement:

```
 1. Select Case examScore
 2.    Case Is >= 90
 3.        grade = "A"
 4.    Case 80 To 89
 5.        grade = "B"
 6.    Case 70 To 79
 7.        grade = "C"
 8.    Case 60 To 69
 9.        grade = "D"
10.    Case Else
11.        grade = "F"
12. End Select
```

Discussion:

The **Select Case** statement begins at line 1 with the keywords **Select Case**, followed by the variable being evaluated (**examScore**), and ends at line 12 with the keywords **End Select**. Each of the **Case** statements (lines 2, 4, 6, 8, and 10) contains an expression that is used to evaluate the contents of **examScore**. Each **Case** statement is followed by a statement to be executed if the expression is **true**.

To illustrate, line 2 contains the expression **Case Is >= 90**, which tests the contents of **examScore** for a value of 90 or greater. Line 3 assigns an "A" to **grade** if the expression in line 2 is **true**. Similarly, line 4 tests for a value 80 to 89 inclusive, and line 5 assigns a grade of "B" if **true**. Note that line 10 contains **Case Else**, which means that if none of the previous **Case** expressions were **true**, then execute the statement at line 11.

Each **Case** can specify a relational operator (**Case Is >= 90**), a range of values (**Case 80 To 99**), or a list of values (**Case 10, 15, 20**). Note the use of the keywords **Is** and **To**.

The `Select Case` is a powerful tool that can sometimes help you simplify code by replacing lengthy nested `If` statements with statements that are logically equivalent but more compact.

Another problem that lends itself to `Select Case` is determining the number of days in a month in a given year. Table 4-7 shows the number of days in each month.

Table 4-7 Number of days in each month

Month Number	Month Name	Length (Days)
01	January	31
02	February	28 or 29*
03	March	31
04	April	30
05	May	31
06	June	30
07	July	31
08	August	31
09	September	30
10	October	31
11	November	30
12	December	31

*February has 28 days except in leap years, when it has 29. Recent and upcoming leap years are 2004, 2008, 2012, and 2016.

To determine the number of days in a month, given the month number and the year, you could use nested `Select Case` statements, as shown in Example 4-19.

Example 4-19: Determine month length using Select Case statements

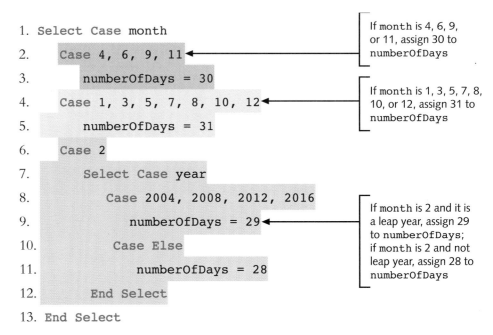

```
1. Select Case month
2.     Case 4, 6, 9, 11
3.         numberOfDays = 30
4.     Case 1, 3, 5, 7, 8, 10, 12
5.         numberOfDays = 31
6.     Case 2
7.         Select Case year
8.             Case 2004, 2008, 2012, 2016
9.                 numberOfDays = 29
10.            Case Else
11.                numberOfDays = 28
12.        End Select
13. End Select
```

If month is 4, 6, 9, or 11, assign 30 to numberOfDays

If month is 1, 3, 5, 7, 8, 10, or 12, assign 31 to numberOfDays

If month is 2 and it is a leap year, assign 29 to numberOfDays; if month is 2 and not leap year, assign 28 to numberOfDays

This solution uses a nested **Select Case** statement. Like the previous example, line 1 begins the **Select Case**, and line 13 ends it with **End Select**. However, lines 7 through 12 include a second, nested **Select Case** structure.

The logic begins at line 2 where, if **month** contains 4, 6, 9, or 11, then line 3 assigns 30 to **numberOfDays**. If the **Case** at line 2 was not met (that is, **month** contained something other than 4, 6, 9, or 11), line 4 executes. Line 4 determines if **month** contains 1, 3, 5, 7, 8, 10, or 12. If so, then line 5 assigns 31 to **numberOfDays**. If **month** is none of these values, then line 6 checks for the value 2. If **month** is 2, then the nested **Select Case** structure beginning at line 7 executes. Notice that the **Select Case** structure beginning at line 7 tests the contents of **year**. Line 8 determines if it is a leap year by checking for the values shown. If **year** matches one of the specified values, then line 9 assigns **numberOfDays** the value 29, otherwise line 11 assigns the value 28.

PROGRAMMING EXAMPLE: PAYROLL CALCULATION

This programming example demonstrates a program that calculates an employee's pay based on an hourly pay rate, number of hours worked, and eligibility for overtime pay. The program prompts the user to input overtime eligibility, hours worked, and pay rate, and then computes regular pay, overtime pay, and total pay. Finally, it displays the computation results rounded to two decimal positions.

Input   Overtime exempt "Y" or "N", hours worked, and hourly pay rate

Output   The employee's regular pay, overtime pay, and total pay, with the results rounded to two decimal positions

Problem Analysis and Algorithm Design

The purpose of this program is to calculate and print an employee's pay amount. To calculate the pay, you need to know how many hours the employee worked and the normal pay rate. You also need to know whether the employee is eligible for overtime pay; if so, the program calculates the overtime amount and adds it to the regular pay amount. The program should print the pay amount to two decimal places because this is a currency amount.

Variables   Because the program will ask users whether an employee is exempt from overtime pay, and then to enter the pay rate and number of hours worked, you need variables to store this information and the user's input. You also need a variable to store the calculated pay amount. You therefore need the following five data type `Double` variables, one `Boolean`, and one `String`.

```
Dim hoursWorked, rate, regularPay, overtimePay, totalPay As Double
Dim exemptEmployee As Boolean
Dim stringInput As String
```

Formulas   The program uses three formulas to compute the pay amount—one to calculate regular pay, another to calculate overtime pay, and a third to calculate total pay:

```
regularPay = hoursWorked * rate
overtimePay = (hoursWorked - 40) * rate * 1.5
totalPay = regularPay + overtimePay
```

Main Algorithm

1. Declare the variables.
2. Display informative messages to the user.
3. Prompt the user to input "Y" if exempt from overtime; otherwise, input "N".
4. Input the value from the keyboard. Assign `True` to `Boolean` variable `exemptEmployee` if value entered is "Y" or "y"; otherwise, assign `False`.
5. Prompt the user to input the number of hours worked.
6. Input the value from the keyboard and convert it to data type `Double`.
7. Prompt the user to enter the employee's hourly pay rate.
8. Input the value from the keyboard and convert it to data type `Double`.
9. Compute the regular pay.
10. If hours worked is greater than 40 and the employee is not exempt from overtime pay, compute overtime pay.

11. If hours worked is 40 or less or the employee is exempt from overtime pay, set overtime pay equal to 0.

12. Compute total pay.

13. Round the computed values to two decimal positions.

14. Display the rounded results for regular pay, overtime pay, and total pay.

Complete Program Listing

```
Option Strict On
Option Explicit On
Module Payroll
 Sub Main()
  ' declare variables
  Dim hoursWorked, rate, regularPay, overtimePay, totalPay As Double
  Dim exemptEmployee As Boolean
  Dim stringInput As String
  ' display descriptive message to user
  Console.WriteLine("This program inputs the type of employee
(exempt or non-exempt), ")
  Console.WriteLine("the employee's hourly pay rate, and number of
hours worked.")
  Console.WriteLine(" It then computes and displays regular pay,
overtime pay, and total pay.")
  Console.WriteLine("Enter Y if this employee is exempt from
overtime pay, otherwise enter N:")
  ' read user input
  stringInput = Console.ReadLine()
  If stringInput = "Y" Or stringInput = "y" Then
     exemptEmployee = True
  Else
     exemptEmployee = False
  End If
  ' prompt user for hoursWorked
  Console.WriteLine("Enter total hours worked for this employee:")
  ' read input, convert to data type Double & assign to hoursWorked
  hoursWorked = Convert.ToDouble(Console.ReadLine())
  ' prompt user for hourly pay rate
  Console.WriteLine("Enter hourly pay rate for this employee:")
  ' read input, convert to data type Double & assign to rate
  rate = Convert.ToDouble(Console.ReadLine())
  ' compute regular pay
  regularPay = hoursWorked * rate
  ' compute overtime pay if worked over 40 hours and not exempt
  If hoursWorked > 40 And Not exemptEmployee Then
     overtimePay = (hoursWorked - 40) * rate * 1.5
  Else
     overtimePay = 0
  End If
```

```
' compute total pay
totalPay = regularPay + overtimePay
' round computed values, then display them
Console.WriteLine("Regular Pay: " & Math.Round(regularPay, 2))
Console.WriteLine("Overtime Pay: " & Math.Round(overtimePay, 2))
Console.WriteLine("Total Pay: " & Math.Round(totalPay, 2))
End Sub
End Module
```

Sample Run   In this sample run, the user input is shaded.

```
This program inputs the type of employee (exempt or non-exempt),
the employee's hourly pay rate, and number of hours worked.
It then computes and displays regular pay, overtime pay, and total
pay.
Enter Y if this employee is exempt from overtime pay, otherwise
enter N:
N
Enter total hours worked for this employee:
45
Enter hourly pay rate for this employee:
10.37
Regular Pay: 466.65
Overtime Pay: 77.77
Total Pay: 544.42
```

QUICK REVIEW

1. You make decisions in a selection statement by writing a logical expression, which evaluates to either **true** or **false**.

2. Visual Basic .NET (VB .NET) uses relational operators (=, >, >=, <, <=, <>) and logical operators (**Not, And, Or, Xor, AndAlso, OrElse**) in writing logical expressions.

3. The logical operators join two logical expressions to form a compound expression.

4. The logical operators **AndAlso** and **OrElse** correspond to the **And** and **Or** operators, respectively, except that they employ a short-circuit evaluation technique, which does not evaluate the second logical expression of a compound expression if its evaluation will not alter the result of the compound expression.

5. A one-way selection statement evaluates a logical expression and then executes one or more statements only if the expression is true. The two-way selection statement also evaluates a logical expression and executes one or more statements if it is true, but executes one or more different statements if it is false.

6. A flowchart is a graphical representation of logic. Flowcharts use symbols to represent the logical components of an algorithm.

7. One-way selection is implemented in VB .NET by writing either a single-line or a multi-line **If** statement.

8. You generally use a multi-line **If** when more than one statement is to be executed when the logical expression is true. However, you can substitute a multi-line **If** for a single-line **If**.

9. Generally, a single-line **If** is easier to write when you want to execute a single statement if an expression is true. However, when you want to execute more than one statement, you use the multi-line **If**.

10. You implement the two-way selection structure by writing an **If** statement together with the keyword **Else**.

11. VB .NET implements the multi-way selection structure, sometimes called the case structure, with the keywords **Select Case**. This statement acts like a multi-way **If** statement by transferring control to one of several statements or group of statements, depending on the value of a variable. Use a **Select Case** statement to make a decision where there are more than two values of a variable you want to evaluate.

EXERCISES

1. Correct the following code so that it compiles and executes correctly. Assume the variables have been correctly declared and populated.

   ```
   If hoursWorked Not > 40 Then otPay = 0
   ```

2. Correct the following code so that it compiles and executes correctly. Assume the variables have been correctly declared and populated.

   ```
   If hoursWkd Not > 40 Then
   otPay = 0
   ```

3. What is the output of the following code?

   ```
   If 1 > 2 Or 5 < 6 Then
       Console.WriteLine("True")
   Else
       Console.WriteLine("False")

   End If
   ```

4. What is the output of the following code?

   ```
   If 1 > 2 Xor 5 < 6 Then
       Console.WriteLine("True")
   Else
       Console.WriteLine("False")

   End If
   ```

5. What is the output of the following code?

```
If 1 > 2 OrElse 5 < 6 Then
    Console.WriteLine("True")
Else
    Console.WriteLine("False")
End If
```

6. Correct the following code so that it compiles and executes correctly.

```
Dim gpa As Double = 2.95
Dim cscMajor As Boolean = True
Select Case gpa
    Case > 3
        Console.WriteLine("Fantastic")
    Case < 1
        If cscMajor Then Console.WriteLine("Change Majors")
    Case Else
        Console.WriteLine("Meet With Advisor")
End Select
```

4

7. What is the output of the following code?

```
If 1 < 2 AndAlso 5 < 6 Then
    Console.WriteLine("True")
Else
    Console.WriteLine("False")
End If
```

PROGRAMMING EXERCISES

1. Modify the payroll calculation program in the Programming Example to use Select Case statements wherever possible.

2. Design and write a program that will input three integer values, and then find and display the smallest of them. Draw a flowchart of your logic, and then write and test your solution code using nested If statements.

3. Redesign and rewrite Example 4-19 to determine the month length using If statements instead of Select Case statements.

4. Design and write a program to compute a consumer's electric bill. Your program will input the previous meter reading (a five-digit number), the current meter reading

(also five digits), and compute the consumption. The bill calculation is based on the following consumption chart:

KWH Consumed	Rate Per KWH
< 500	.05
500 – 1000	$25 + .055 for amount over 500
> 1000	$52.50 + .06 for amount over 1000

In addition, a sales tax rate of .085 is added to the total bill.

Input Previous meter reading and current meter reading

Output KWH consumed, electricity charge, tax, and total bill

5. Example 4–19 determines whether the year is a leap year by listing specific years. Modify the example to use the following logic to determine whether the year is a leap year:

   A year is a leap year if it is divisible by 4 except for years that are both divisible by 100 and not divisible by 400.

   Examples 2000 is divisible by 4, 100, and 400, and therefore is a leap year

   1900 is divisible by 4, 100 but *not* 400, and therefore is not a leap year

   2004 is divisible by 4, 100, and 400, and therefore is a leap year

6. In Chapter 3 you converted Fahrenheit temperature to Celsius. Select another conversion such as gallon to liter, inch to centimeter, pound to kilogram, or mile to kilometer. Find the appropriate conversion factors, and then design and write a program that will input a conversion code and the value to be converted. Compute and display the appropriate result. The conversion codes will be character values such as "GL" for gallon to liter, "IC" for inch to centimeter, and so forth.

   Several Web sites such as *www.wsdot.wa.gov/Metrics/factors.htm* provide the conversion factors.

Control Structures: Iteration

You previously learned that programs are written using a combination of the three basic control structures: sequence, selection, and iteration. The sequence structure executes statements one after another in sequence. You employed sequence structures in previous chapters and will continue to use this structure throughout the remainder of the book. You use the selection structure when you want to execute one or more statements if a logical expression is `true`. You select statements to be executed based on the truth of an expression. In Chapter 4 you implemented the selection structure using the `If` and `Select Case` statements.

Iteration is another control structure, a powerful programming tool you use to repeat the execution of one or more statements until a terminating condition occurs. You create an iteration structure, also called a loop, when you want to repeatedly execute a set of statements. These statements are executed until a terminating condition occurs that you have specified. In this chapter, you learn how to implement the iteration structure using the Visual Basic .NET (VB .NET) `Do` and `For` statements.

EXPLORING THE ITERATION STRUCTURE

You use the iteration structure, often called a **loop**, to execute one or more statements repeatedly. To illustrate, the following program inputs two exam scores, computes the average of the scores, and displays the result.

 Example 5-1: Computing the average of two exam scores

In the following example and in others throughout the chapter, line numbers are added for reference only, and do not appear in the actual program.

```
1. Dim score, sum, average As Double
2. Dim numberOfExams As Integer = 2
3. ' input the two scores
4. Console.WriteLine("Enter an Exam Score: ")
5. score = Convert.ToDouble(Console.ReadLine())
6. sum += score
7. Console.WriteLine("Enter an Exam Score: ")
8. score = Convert.ToDouble(Console.ReadLine())
9. sum += score
```

```
10. ' compute average and display

11. average = sum / numberOfExams

12. Console.WriteLine("The average is: " &
    Math.Round(average, 1))
```

Sample Run:

In the following output and in the Sample Runs throughout the chapter, user input is shaded.

```
Enter an Exam Score:
85
Enter an Exam Score:
90
The average is: 87.5
```

Discussion:

Line 1 defines `Double` variables `score`, `sum`, and `average` that will be used to input, sum, and compute the average of the exam scores being entered. Line 2 defines an `Integer` variable `numberOfExams` and populates it with 2. Line 4 displays a prompt message asking the user to enter an exam score, and line 5 invokes the `Console.ReadLine` method to read the user input. Recall that because this method returns data type `String`, you also have to invoke `Convert.ToDouble` in order to assign the value to the `Double` variable `score`. Line 6 adds `score` to the `Double` variable `sum`.

Line 7 prompts for the second exam score, line 8 inputs the second value, and line 9 adds it to `sum`. Line 11 computes `average` by dividing the sum of the scores by `numberOfExams`, which contains 2. Line 12 displays the result rounded to one decimal position by invoking `Math.Round`.

Note that lines 7, 8, and 9 are *identical to* lines 4, 5, and 6. We have, in effect, *repeated* the execution of lines 4 through 6. This example is straightforward: enter the scores, compute their average, and display the result.

Example 5-2: Computing the average of five exam scores

To solve the same problem involving five exam scores, you can simply repeat the input operation five times and change **numberOfExams** to 5.

Five exams

Lines 4, 5, and 6 are repeated to input all five scores

```
1.  Dim sum, average As Double
2.  Dim numberOfExams As Integer = 5
3.  ' input the scores
4.  Console.WriteLine("Enter an Exam Score: ")
5.  score = Convert.ToDouble(Console.ReadLine())
6.  sum += score
7.  Console.WriteLine("Enter an Exam Score: ")
8.  score = Convert.ToDouble(Console.ReadLine())
9.  sum += score
10. Console.WriteLine("Enter an Exam Score: ")
11. score = Convert.ToDouble(Console.ReadLine())
12. sum += score
13. Console.WriteLine("Enter an Exam Score: ")
14. score = Convert.ToDouble(Console.ReadLine())
15. sum += score
16. Console.WriteLine("Enter an Exam Score: ")
17. score = Convert.ToDouble(Console.ReadLine())
18. sum += score
19. ' compute average and display
20. average = sum / numberOfExams
21. Console.WriteLine("The average is: " & Math.Round(average, 1))
```

Sample Run:

```
Enter an Exam Score:
85
Enter an Exam Score:
90
Enter an Exam Score:
94
Enter an Exam Score:
89
Enter an Exam Score:
91
The average is: 89.8
```

Discussion:

Example 5-2 was created by populating **numberOfExams** with 5 and repeating lines 4, 5, and 6 four times to input all five scores.

Consider the same problem with 50 or 100 exams. Of course, you could again duplicate lines 4 through 6 in Example 5-2 the necessary number of times and populate `numberOfEx-ams` with the appropriate value to solve the problem, but this approach becomes cumbersome for larger numbers of exams. Iteration deals effectively with this kind of problem by enabling you to write a set of statements, and then repeatedly execute them until a terminating condition is reached.

Iteration Logic

Figure 5-1 maps the logic of a basic iteration structure or loop.

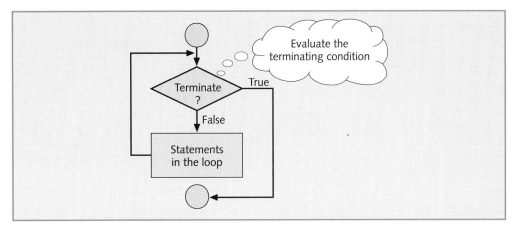

Figure 5-1 Basic iteration logic

This logic first tests to see whether the loop should terminate. The specific form of the terminating expression depends on how you write the loop. The expression can be as simple as testing a variable for a specific value (`counter = 5`) or it can be more complex.

If the loop does not terminate, then the statement or statements in the loop body are executed. After the statements in the loop body are executed, control returns to the beginning where once again the test determines whether the loop should terminate. The loop continues in this manner until the terminating condition occurs.

 If the terminating condition never occurs, then you have an **infinite loop**. An infinite loop never ends because the terminating condition never occurs. Although you want to avoid them, infinite loops are quite easy to write; you should therefore take great care to ensure that the terminating condition you specify will occur.

There are two kinds of loop logic: the **pre-test loop** and the **post-test loop**. The logic shown in Figure 5-1 uses pre-test logic: the terminating condition is checked *before* the body of the loop is executed. If the terminating condition initially exists when you use a pre-test loop, then the statements in the loop are not executed.

In contrast, a post-test loop checks for the terminating condition *after* the body of the loop is executed. When you use a post-test loop, the statements in the loop are executed at least once regardless of the terminating condition. Figure 5-2 illustrates the difference between pre-test and post-test loops.

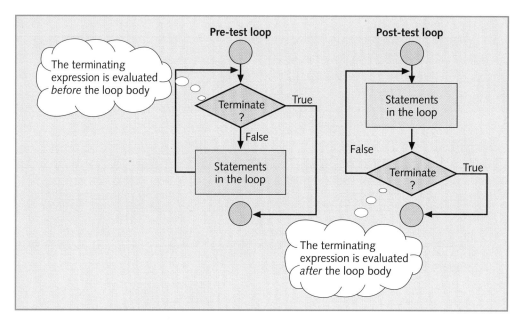

Figure 5-2   Pre-test and post-test loops

You will normally write pre-test loops because you generally do not want to execute the statements within the loop body if the terminating expression is **true**. You use post-test loops whenever you want the loop body to execute *at least once* regardless of the terminating condition and you want the terminating condition evaluated at the end of the loop.

Controlling Iteration

There are two general approaches to controlling the number of times a loop executes: **counter control** and **sentinel control**. Counter control, as the name suggests, employs an `Integer` variable called a **counter** to count the number of times the loop has executed. You update the counter each time the loop executes, and when the counter reaches a predetermined value, the loop terminates. Although you generally update the counter by adding 1, you can increment or decrement by any value that suits your logic. Figure 5-3 illustrates the logic of a counter-controlled loop applied to the exam score average example.

5

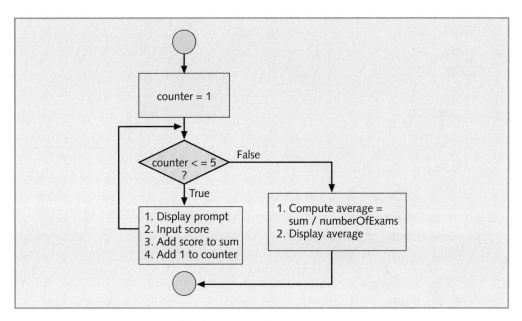

Figure 5-3   A counter-controlled loop example

Sentinel-control logic checks the user input for a specific value and terminates when this value, called a sentinel, is detected. When selecting a sentinel value, you should choose a unique value. In the exam score average example, exam scores are always in the range of 0 to 100 inclusive; therefore, you could choose a sentinel value of -999 to indicate that there is no more input and the loop should terminate. Figure 5-4 illustrates the logic of a sentinel-controlled loop applied to the exam score average example.

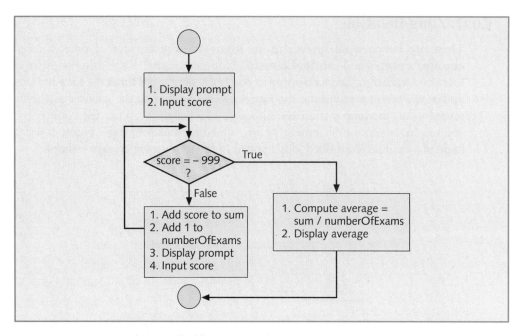

Figure 5-4   A sentinel-controlled loop example

Compare the flowcharts in Figures 5-3 and 5-4 closely. In addition to not using a counter in a sentinel-controlled loop, there are two other important differences. First, the sentinel-controlled loop logic inputs an initial value for **score** *before* the loop begins. This enables you to test for the sentinel value the first time the loop executes. Second, the sequence of steps within the loop is different. After the result of the test for the sentinel value is **false**, you add the input value to **sum**, and then input the *next* value for **score**. The loop continues until an exam score of -999 is entered; the loop then terminates and the average is computed and displayed.

To summarize, you use a counter-controlled loop when you want to iterate a specific predetermined number of times (such as five exam scores); you know how many values are to be input. In contrast, you employ a sentinel-controlled loop when: you do not know how many values are to be input; you want to use a sentinel value to indicate there is no more input; and thus, you want to terminate the iteration.

IMPLEMENTING ITERATION USING THE DO WHILE AND DO UNTIL STATEMENTS

You implement the iteration structure in VB .NET using either the `Do` statement or the `For` statement. The `Do` statement and its various forms are explored in this section and the `For` statement in the next. The `Do` statement uses two forms: `Do While` and `Do Until`. With the `Do` statement, you can use either pre-test or post-test logic, and you can create either counter-controlled or sentinel-controlled loops.

Writing Loops Using Do While

5

The basic form of the `Do While` loop is shown in Figure 5-5. Note that this is a pre-test loop; the terminating condition is tested at the beginning of the loop.

```
Do While expression◄─────────────────────────        Loop while the
    statements                                        expression is True
Loop
```

Figure 5-5   Format of the Do While loop

You begin this loop by writing `Do While` followed by a logical expression. The loop continues to execute as long as this expression is `true`. You indicate the end of the loop by writing the keyword `Loop`. Between these two statements, `Do While` and `Loop`, you write the code that you want to comprise the loop body—the statements to be executed for each iteration.

Example 5-3: Computing an exam average using a counter-controlled Do While loop

This example uses `Do While` to create a counter-controlled loop that computes the average of five exam scores.

```
1. ' define variables
2. Dim sum, average AsDouble
3. Dim numberOfExams As Integer = 5
4. Dim counter As Integer = 1
5. ' begin loop
```

```
 6. Do While (counter <= numberOfExams)
 7.    Console.WriteLine("Enter an Exam Score: ")
 8.    sum = sum + Convert.ToDouble(Console.ReadLine())
 9.    counter += 1    ' count the number of iterations
10. Loop
11. ' compute & display the average
12. average = sum / numberOfExams
13. Console.WriteLine("The average is: " &
    Math.Round(average, 1))
```

Sample Run:

```
Enter an Exam Score:
85
Enter an Exam Score:
90
Enter an Exam Score:
94
Enter an Exam Score:
89
Enter an Exam Score:
91
The average is: 89.8
```

Discussion:

From the user's perspective, Example 5-3 behaves exactly like Example 5-2. It prompts for a score, inputs a value, repeats this process a total of five times, and then computes and displays the average. The output from the Example 5-3 program is the same as for Example 5-2.

Lines 2 and 3 define the same variables `sum`, `average`, and `numberOfExams` as Example 5-2. Line 4, however, defines an `Integer` variable named `counter` and initializes it to 1. You use this variable to count the number of iterations, which in this example is five.

Lines 6 through 10 define the loop that will execute the three statements contained in lines 7, 8, and 9. Note that these statements are indented to improve readability. The `Do While` statement in line 6 tells VB .NET to "continue to loop as long as `counter` is less than or equal to 5." Line 7 displays a prompt, and line 8 inputs an exam score and adds it to `sum`. Examine line 8 closely; it actually does four things:

1. Invokes `Console.ReadLine` to read the user's input

2. Invokes `Convert.ToDouble` to convert the `String` value returned by `Console.ReadLine` to data type `Double`

3. Adds the value returned by `Convert.ToDouble` to `sum`

4. Assigns the result of the addition to `sum`

Note that line 8 could also be written as:

```
sum += Convert.ToDouble (Console.ReadLine())
```

Line 9 counts the iterations by incrementing `counter` each time it is executed. Because the terminating condition is checked at the beginning of the loop, this is a pre-test loop.

Table 5-1 shows the contents of `counter` and `sum` at the end of each iteration during the execution of Example 5-3.

Table 5-1:   Contents of variables for Example 5-3

Iteration	counter	sum
1	2	85
2	3	175
3	4	269
4	5	358
5	6	449

You can make the code in Example 5-3 more powerful by displaying prompts that ask the user to input the number of exams. This modification enables the loop to work for any number of exams. To make this change, replace line 3 with the following statements:

```
Dim numberOfExams As Integer
Console.WriteLine ("Enter the number of exams: ")
numberOfExams = Convert.ToInt32 (Console.ReadLine())
```

Example 5-3 employed a `Do While` counter-controlled pre-test loop. You can also solve the exam score average problem with a counter-controlled *post-test* loop. To write a `Do While` post-test loop, you move the `While` clause from the `Do` statement to the `Loop` statement, as shown in Example 5-4.

Example 5-4: Using a post-test Do While loop

In this example, note that you get the same result using both pre- and post-test code, unless the user enters zero (0) for the number of exams.

```
Do
    Console.WriteLine("Enter an Exam Score: ")
    sum = sum + Convert.ToDouble(Console.ReadLine())
    counter += 1    ' count the number of iterations
Loop While (counter <= numberOfExams)
```

Move the While clause to create a post-test loop

 You can also write a Do While loop using the keywords While and End While. This form is continued from earlier versions of Visual BASIC and behaves identically to the Do While form previously described.

The previous two examples contain counter-controlled loops. You can also solve the exam average problem using a sentinel-controlled loop.

Example 5-5: Computing an exam average using a sentinel-controlled Do While loop

1. ` define variables

2. Dim sum, score, average As Double

3 Dim numberOfExams As Integer = 0

4. ` enter the first value

5. Console.WriteLine ("Enter an Exam Score (-999 if no more): ")

6. score = Convert.ToDouble(Console.ReadLine())

7. ` begin loop

8. Do While (score <> -999)

9.   numberOfExams += 1

10.   sum += score

11.   Console.WriteLine("Enter an Exam Score(-999 if no more): ")

```
12.    score = Convert.ToDouble(Console.ReadLine())
13. Loop
14. ' compute & display the average
15. average = sum / numberOfExams
16. Console.WriteLine("The average is: " &
        Math.Round(average, 1))
```

Sample Run:

```
Enter an Exam Score (-999 if no more):
85
Enter an Exam Score (-999 if no more):
90
Enter an Exam Score (-999 if no more):
94
Enter an Exam Score (-999 if no more):
89
Enter an Exam Score (-999 if no more):
91
Enter an Exam Score (-999 if no more):
-999
The average is: 89.8
```

Discussion:

Lines 2 and 3 define the variables **sum**, **score**, **average**, and **numberOfExams** similarly to the previous examples.

Line 5 prompts users to input an exam score and instructs them to enter -999 if there are no more scores. Line 6 reads the input, converts it to data type **Double**, and assigns the value to **score**.

This loop begins at line 8 and ends at line 13. The statements within the loop body are contained in lines 9 through 12. This is a pre-test loop because the terminating expression is included in the **Do While** statement.

Line 9 increments **numberOfExams** and line 10 adds **score** to **sum**. Lines 11 and 12 repeat lines 5 and 6: display the prompt and read the user's input. This loop continues as long as the input value is *not equal* to -999. When the user enters an exam score of -999, line 8 terminates the loop, and execution continues after the end of the loop at line 15, which computes the exam average, and line 16 displays it.

You can convert Example 5-5 to a post-test loop by moving the **While** clause to the **Loop** statement.

Example 5-6: Using a post-test sentinel-controlled Do While loop

Move the `While` clause to the
end to create a post-test loop

```
Do
    numberOfExams += 1
    sum += score
    Console.WriteLine("Enter an Exam Score (-999 if no more): ")
    score = Convert.ToDouble(Console.ReadLine())
Loop While (score <> -999)
```

If you use a post-test loop in Example 5-6, then you must have at least one exam score because the statements inside the loop are always executed once. Even if you enter –999 for the first exam score, these statements will execute because the terminating condition is not checked until the end of the loop. You use post-test logic only when you want the loop statements to execute at least once.

To summarize, you can write a loop using the keywords `Do While` and `Loop`. Using `Do While` you can write a counter-controlled loop or a sentinel-controlled loop. You can also use either pre-test or post-test logic.

Writing Loops Using Do Until

The `Do Until` loop is similar to the `Do While` loop. The difference, as shown in Figure 5-6, is that the `Do While` executes *while* the expression is `true`, and the `Do Until` executes *until* the expression is `true`.

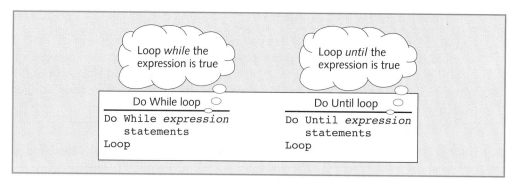

Figure 5-6   Contrasting the Do While and Do Until loops

Example 5-7: Computing an exam average using a counter-controlled Do Until loop

Example 5-3 uses: `Do While (counter <= numberOfExams)`

```
1.  ' define variables
2.  Dim sum, average As Double
3.  Dim numberOfExams As Integer = 5
4.  Dim counter As Integer = 1
5.  ' begin loop
6.  Do Until (counter > numberOfExams)
7.      Console.WriteLine("Enter an Exam Score: ")
8.      sum = sum + Convert.ToDouble(Console.ReadLine())
9.      counter += 1
10. Loop
11. ' compute & display the average
12. average = sum / numberOfExams
13. Console.WriteLine("The average is: " & Math.Round(average, 1))
```

5

Sample Run:

```
Enter an Exam Score:
85
Enter an Exam Score:
90
Enter an Exam Score:
94
Enter an Exam Score:
89
Enter an Exam Score:
91
The average is: 89.8
```

Discussion:

With the exception of line 6, Example 5-7 is identical to Example 5-3. It prompts for a score, inputs a value, repeats this process a total of five times, and then computes and displays the average. The output from Example 5-7 is the same as Example 5-3.

The `Do Until` statement in line 6 tells VB .NET to "continue to loop until the contents of variable **counter** is greater than the contents of **numberOfExams**, which contains 5."

Example 5-7 is a pre-test counter-controlled loop. Similar to the previous `Do While` examples, you can also write sentinel-controlled and post-test loops. To create a post-test `Do Until` loop, you move the `Until` clause to the `Loop` statement.

Example 5-8: Using a post-test Do Until loop

In this example, the `Loop` statement includes an `Until` clause, making this a post-test `Do Until` loop.

```
Do
    Console.WriteLine("Enter an Exam Score: ")
    sum = sum + Convert.ToDouble(Console.ReadLine())
    counter += 1
Loop Until (counter > numberOfExams)
```

Move the `Until` clause to the end to create a post-test loop

To summarize, you write a `Do` loop using the keywords `Do While` or `Do Until`. The `Do While` executes as long as an expression is `true`. In contrast, `Do Until` executes *until* an expression is `true`. You can write a counter-controlled loop or a sentinel-controlled loop using either form. You can also create pre-test or a post-test logic using either form.

IMPLEMENTING ITERATION USING THE FOR NEXT STATEMENT

Another way to write loops in VB .NET is to use the `For Next` statement. You use this statement to create counter-controlled pre-test loops only. Although theoretically possible, you do not use `For Next` to write sentinel-controlled loops. You cannot employ post-test logic using `For Next`.

The `For Next` loop initializes a counter variable and *automatically* increments the counter, which simplifies and shortens your code. You will generally want to use a `For Next` loop for counter-controlled loops. The format of the `For Next` loop is shown in Figure 5-7.

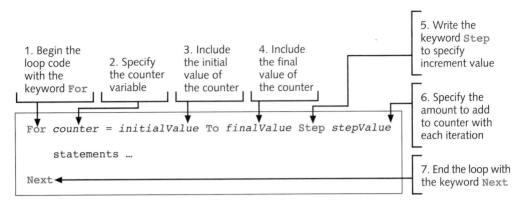

1. Begin the loop code with the keyword `For`

2. Specify the counter variable

3. Include the initial value of the counter

4. Include the final value of the counter

5. Write the keyword `Step` to specify increment value

6. Specify the amount to add to counter with each iteration

7. End the loop with the keyword `Next`

```
For counter = initialValue To finalValue Step stepValue

    statements ...

Next
```

Figure 5-7   Format of a For Next loop

You begin by writing the keyword **For** followed by the name of your loop counter variable. Then you include an equal operator and the initial value you want to use to populate your counter. Note this can be either a literal value or a variable. Next you write the keyword **To** followed by the final value of your counter. This is the last value in the counter before your loop terminates. Optionally, you write the keyword **Step** and the amount you want to increment the counter each iteration. Note that the default value is 1, which means you can omit the **Step** clause if you want your counter variable incremented by 1 each iteration.

Following the **For** statement, you write the statements within the loop body. Note that you do not increment your loop counter; this is done automatically for you. You indicate the end of the loop by writing the keyword **Next**. Figure 5-8 maps the logic of the **For Next** loop.

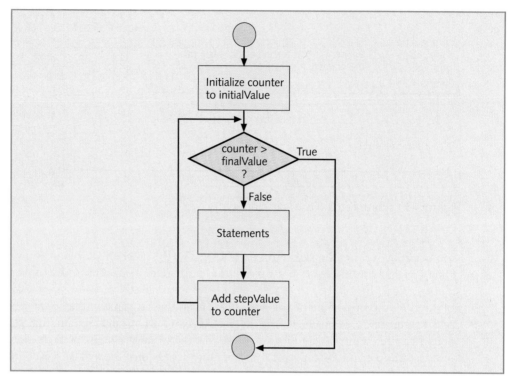

Figure 5-8   Flowchart of For Next loop

To illustrate the **For Next** statements, Example 5-9 once again computes the average of five exams, but here employs a **For Next** loop.

Example 5-9: Computing an exam average using a For Next loop

```
1.  ' define variables
2.  Dim sum, average As Double
3.  Dim numberOfExams As Integer = 5
4.  Dim counter As Integer
5.  ' begin loop
6.  For counter = 1 To 5 Step 1
7.      Console.WriteLine("Enter an Exam Score: ")
8.      sum = sum + Convert.ToDouble(Console.ReadLine())
9.  Next
10. ' compute & display the average
11. average = sum / numberOfExams
12. Console.WriteLine("The average is: " & Math.Round(average, 1))
```

Start of loop

End of loop

Sample Run:

```
Enter an Exam Score:
85
Enter an Exam Score:
90
Enter an Exam Score:
94
Enter an Exam Score:
89
Enter an Exam Score:
91
The average is: 89.8
```

Discussion:

Lines 2 and 3 define the variables `sum`, `average`, and `numberOfExams` as in the previous examples.

Line 4 defines `counter` but *does not initialize* it because the `For` statement at line 6 sets the initial value of `counter` to 1. Note that although line 6 includes `Step 1`, this clause is not necessary because if you omit it, the default increment value is 1.

Line 7 displays the user prompt and line 8 reads the user's input, converts it to data type `Double`, adds it to `sum`, and then assigns the result to `sum`.

The remainder of the example is identical to previous examples. Line 11 computes `average` and line 12 displays it.

Example 5-10: Summing the odd integers between 1 and 25 using For Next

To illustrate the use of different `Step` values, this example assumes you want to compute and display the sum of the odd integers between 1 and 25 inclusive.

```
1. ' define variables
2. Dim sum, counter As Integer
3. ' begin loop
4. For counter = 1 To 25 Step 2
5.    sum += counter
6. Next
7. '  display the sum
8. Console.WriteLine ("The sum is: " & sum)
```

Sample Run:

```
The sum is: 169
```

Discussion:

Line 2 defines two variables `sum` and `counter`, which are both data type `Integer`.

Line 4 begins the loop indicating an initial counter value of 1 and a final value of 25. Line 4 also specifies that 2 is added to the counter with each iteration. Within the loop there is a single statement—line 5 adds the contents of `counter` to `sum` and assigns the result to `sum`. Line 8 executes when the loop terminates to display the contents of `sum`.

Of course, you can also sum odd integers using a **Do** loop. Consider the following example, which also computes the sum of the odd integers between 1 and 25.

Example 5-11: Summing the odd integers between 1 and 25 using Do While

This example shows how to use a **Do While** loop to perform the same task as in Example 5-10: sum the odd integers between 1 and 25.

```
         You must initialize counter          You must also increment counter

  1.   ' define variables
  2.   Dim sum, counter As Integer
  3.   counter = 1
  4.   ' begin loop
  5.   Do While counter <= 25
  6.       sum += counter
  7.       counter += 2
  8.   Loop
  9.   ' display the sum
 10.   Console.WriteLine("The sum is: " & sum)
```

Sample Run:

```
The sum is: 169
```

Discussion:

Notice that Example 5-11 using **Do While** has two more statements than Example 5-10 using **For Next**. This is because in a **Do While** loop, you must initialize the counter (line 4) and you must also increment it (line 7).

To summarize, you can implement iteration using either Do or For Next code. Using Do, you can construct both counter and sentinel-controlled loops with either pre-test or post-test logic. With For Next code, however, you write only counter-controlled pre-test loops.

CREATING NESTED STRUCTURES

In Chapter 4 you learned how to write selection structures within other selection structures, creating nested selection structures. You can also write iteration structures within other iteration structures, creating **nested loops**. Of course you can also write selection within iteration and iteration within selection, depending on the logic you need to employ.

Example 5-9 used a For Next loop to compute the average of five exam scores. Assume you want to compute the exam average for more than one student. One way you can solve this problem is to write nested For Next loops: a loop inside another loop. The first, or outer, loop will iterate once per student. The inner loop will iterate once for each exam. The inner loop uses code similar to Example 5-9.

Example 5-12: Computing an exam average using a nested For Next loop

This example shows how to use a nested For Next loop to compute the exam average for more than one student.

```
1. ' define variables
2. Dim sum, score, average As Double
3. Dim numberOfExams As Integer = 5
4. Dim numberOfStudents As Integer = 2
5. Dim studentCounter, examCounter As Integer
6. ' begin outer loop for students
7. For studentCounter = 1 To numberOfStudents
8.     sum = 0 ' reinitialize sum
9.     ' begin inner loop for exams
10.     For examCounter = 1 To numberOfExams
11.         Console.WriteLine ("Enter an Exam Score: ")
12.         score = Convert.ToDouble (Console.ReadLine())
13.         sum += score
14.     Next ' end of inner loop
```

15.   average = sum / numberOfExams

16.   Console.WriteLine ("The average is: " &
Math.Round(average, 1))

17. **Next** ' end of outer loop

Sample Run:

```
Enter an Exam Score:
85
Enter an Exam Score:
90
Enter an Exam Score:
94
Enter an Exam Score:
89
Enter an Exam Score:
91
The average is: 89.8◀──  First student's average
Enter an Exam Score:
78
Enter an Exam Score:
83
Enter an Exam Score:
87
Enter an Exam Score:
85
Enter an Exam Score:
90
The average is: 84.6◀──  Second student's average
```

Discussion:

Line 2 defines **sum**, **score**, and **average** as in previous examples. Line 3 defines **numberOfExams** and populates it with 5. Line 4 defines **numberOfStudents** and populates it with 2.

Because this example contains two **For Next** loops, you use two counters: **studentCounter** and **examCounter** defined in line 5.

The outer loop begins at line 7 and ends at line 17. Notice that all of the statements in this loop are indented for improved readability.

Line 8 initializes **sum** to zero. You must do this because you compute the sum of exam scores for *each* student. If you failed to reinitialize **sum** to zero, then when you begin accumulating the exam score total for the second student, **sum** would still contain the total of exam scores for the first student. The outer loop executes once for each student. In this example there are two students (defined in line 4); therefore, the outer loop will execute twice.

The inner loop for exams begins at line 10 and ends at line 14. Because the purpose of this loop is to compute the sum of the five exams for each student, it will execute five times for each student. Within the inner loop, line 11 displays the prompt and line 12 reads the exam score, converts its data type to **Double**, and assigns the result to **score**. Line 13 adds **score** to **sum**.

Lines 15 and 16 are executed after the inner loop has executed five times to compute the total of a student's exam scores. Line 15 computes **average** and line 16 displays it.

Figure 5-9 contains a flowchart showing the logic of Example 5-12.

5

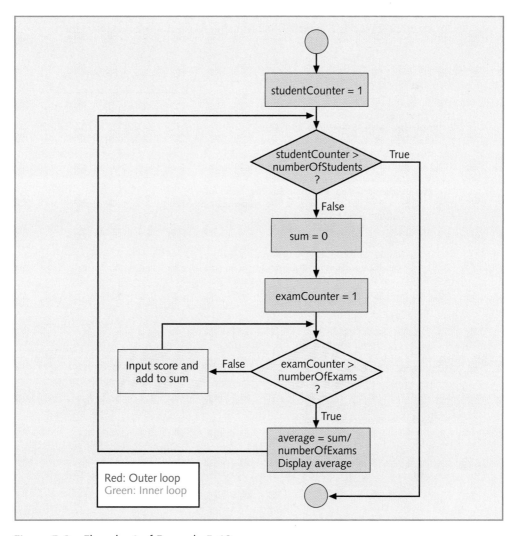

Figure 5-9 Flowchart of Example 5-12

In addition to constructing an iteration structure within another iteration structure, you can write a selection structure within an iteration, or an iteration within a selection. Example 5-13 employs a selection structure within an iteration structure to ensure that the user has entered valid data.

Consider the problem of the user entering an invalid exam score in the previous example. If exam scores are supposed to be in the range of 0 through 100, then a value that is negative or greater than 100 is invalid, and you should not use it in computing a student's average score. To make sure exam scores fall within the appropriate range, you use data validation, code that checks the data the user enters and makes sure it meets the program's requirements.

Example 5-13: Computing an exam average using data validation

This example expands Example 5-12 to include exam score data validation.

Reject score if not 0 –100

```
1    ' define variables
2.   Dim sum, score, average As Double
3.   Dim numberOfExams As Integer = 5
4.   Dim numberOfStudents As Integer = 2
5.   Dim studentCounter, examCounter As Integer
6.   ' begin outer loop for students
7.   For studentCounter = 1 To numberOfStudents
8.       sum = 0 ' reinitialize sum & examCounter
9.       examCounter = 0

10.      ' begin inner loop for exams
11.      Do Until examCounter = numberOfExams
12.         Console.WriteLine("Enter an Exam Score: ")
13.         score = Convert.ToDouble(Console.ReadLine())
14.         If score < 0 Or score > 100 Then
15.            Console.WriteLine("Invalid Exam Score. Must be 0 - 100, please re-enter: ")
16.         Else
17.            sum += score
18.            examCounter += 1
19.         End If
20.      Loop ' end of inner loop

21.      average = sum / numberOfExams
22.      Console.WriteLine("The average is: " & Math.Round(average, 1))
23.  Next ' end of outer loop
```

Sample Run:

```
Enter an Exam Score:
185
Invalid Exam Score. Must be 0 - 100, please re-enter:
Enter an Exam Score:
-85
Invalid Exam Score. Must be 0 - 100, please re-enter:
Enter an Exam Score:
```

Discussion:

This example is similar to Example 5-12, but replaces the inner For Next loop with a Do Until loop. It also adds an If statement at line 14 to ensure that the exam score entered is within the desired range (0 - 100). As you can see from the Sample Run, this statement checks the exam score entered and if it is not valid, displays a prompt to re-enter a valid score. If the score is valid, then it is added to sum.

PROGRAMMING EXAMPLE: LOAN AMORTIZATION COMPUTATION

This example demonstrates a program that computes and displays the amortization of a loan with monthly payments. (A loan amortization shows the periodic payments made to service the loan.) The user inputs the loan amount, the annual percentage rate (APR), and the duration of the loan expressed in number of months. The program then computes and displays the payment amount. For each month, it computes and displays the interest paid, the principal paid, and the remaining balance. At the end, the total amount of interest paid is displayed.

Input Loan amount, APR, and loan duration expressed in number of months

Output Payment amount, the monthly interest and principal paid, and the remaining loan balance; at the end, the total interest paid is displayed

Problem Analysis and Algorithm Design

The purpose of this program is to compute and display the amortization of a loan with monthly payments.

Variables

Double data type variables:

apr—annual percentage interest rate, input by the user

mpr—monthly interest rate, computed

loanAmount—amount of loan, input by the user

paymentAmount—monthly payment amount, computed

monthlyInterest—monthly interest amount, computed

`principalPaid`—amount of principal already paid, computed

`remainingBalance`—amount of the remaining balance, computed

`totalInterestPaid`—total interest paid to date, which is the sum of `monthlyInterest`

`Integer` data type variables:

`numberOfMonths`—loan duration, input by the user

`monthNumber`—counter used in `For` loop

Formulas

1. `mpr = apr / 12`
2. `paymentAmount = loanAmount * mpr / (1 -((1 / (1 + mpr) ^ numberOfMonths)))`
3. `monthlyInterest = remainingBalance * mpr`
4. `principalPaid = paymentAmount - monthlyInterest`
5. `remainingBalance = remainingBalance - principalPaid`

Main Algorithm

1. Declare the variables.
2. Prompt the user to input the loan amount.
3. Read the value from keyboard.
4. Prompt the user to input the loan duration in months.
5. Read the value from keyboard.
6. Prompt the user to input the annual percentage interest rate.
7. Read the value from keyboard.
8. Compute the monthly payment amount and the monthly interest rate. Round the payment amount to two decimal positions.
9. Display column headings.
10. Use a loop to calculate the payments:
    a. Use a `For Next` loop to iterate the number of months.
    b. For each month, compute the monthly interest, principal paid, and remaining balance. Round these values to two decimal positions. Add the monthly interest to the total interest paid.
    c. If it is the last month, then recompute the payment amount by adding the remaining balance to the monthly interest. Display the month number, monthly interest, principal paid, and remaining balance. At the end, display the total interest paid.

 The constant vbTab, which appears in lines 35 and 36 of the following code, inserts a tab in the line of text being displayed.

Complete Program Listing

```
Option Strict On
Option Explicit On
Module Module1
 Sub Main()
  ' declare variables
  Dim apr, mpr, loanAmount, paymentAmount As Double
  Dim monthlyInterest, totalInterestPaid, principalPaid,
      remainingBalance As Double
  Dim numberOfMonths, monthNumber As Integer
  ' prompt user for input
  Console.WriteLine ("This is a loan amortization program. ")
  Console.Write ("Enter the amount of the loan: ")
  loanAmount = Convert.ToDouble (Console.ReadLine())
  Console.Write ("Enter the duration of the loan in months: ")
  numberOfMonths = Convert.ToInt32 (Console.ReadLine())
  Console.Write ("Enter the annual percentage interest rate: ")
  apr = Convert.ToDouble(Console.ReadLine())
  ' compute monthly interest rate and the monthly payment amount
  mpr = apr / 12
  paymentAmount = loanAmount * mpr / (1 -((1 / (1 + mpr) ^
      numberOfMonths)))
  paymentAmount = Math.Round(paymentAmount, 2)
  Console.WriteLine ("Payment amount is: " & paymentAmount)
  ' display column headings
  Console.WriteLine ("Mo" & "    " & "Interest" & " " &
      "Principal" & " " &"Balance")
  remainingBalance = loanAmount
  ' iterate for the number of months
  For monthNumber = 1 To numberOfMonths
    ' compute & round interest this month
    monthlyInterest = Math.Round ((remainingBalance * mpr), 2)
    totalInterestPaid += monthlyInterest
    ' if last month, recompute payment amount
    If monthNumber = numberOfMonths Then paymentAmount =
    remainingBalance + monthlyInterest
    principalPaid = paymentAmount - monthlyInterest
    remainingBalance -= principalPaid
    remainingBalance -= Math.Round(remainingBalance 2)
    ' display payment schedule
    Console.WriteLine (monthNumber & vbTab & monthlyInterest
    & vbTab)
    Console.WriteLine (principalPaid & vbTab & remaining Balance)
  Next
  Console.WriteLine ("Total Interest Paid: " & totalInterestPaid)
 End Sub
End Module
```

Sample Run

In the following Sample Run, the user input is shaded.

```
This is a loan amortization program.
Enter the amount of the loan:
1000
Enter the duration of the loan in months:
12
Enter the annual percentage interest rate:
.07
Payment amount is: 86.53
Mo    Interest Principal Balance
1      5.83      80.7     919.3
2      5.36      81.17    838.13
3      4.89      81.64    756.49
4      4.41      82.12    674.37
5      3.93      82.6     591.77
6      3.45      83.08    508.69
7      2.97      83.56    425.13
8      2.48      84.05    341.08
9      1.99      84.54    256.54
10     1.5       85.03    171.51
11     1         85.53    85.98
12     0.5       85.98    0
Total Interest Paid: 38.31
```

QUICK REVIEW

1. You use the iteration structure, also called a loop, to execute one or more statements repeatedly.

2. Basic iteration logic first tests to see if a loop should terminate. If the loop does not terminate, the statements in the loop body are executed. Control then returns to the beginning where once again the test determines whether the loop should terminate. The loop continues in this manner until the terminating condition occurs.

3. There are two kinds of loop logic: the pre-test loop and the post-test loop. Using pre-test logic, the terminating condition is checked *before* the body of the loop is executed. A post-test loop checks for the terminating condition *after* the body of the loop is executed. When you use a post-test loop, the statements in the loop are executed at least once regardless of the terminating condition.

4. There are two general approaches to controlling the number of times a loop executes: counter control and sentinel control. Counter-control logic employs a variable called a counter to count the number of times the loop has executed. Sentinel-control logic checks the user input for a specific value and terminates when this value, called a sentinel, is detected.

5. You use a counter-controlled loop when you want to iterate a specific predetermined number of times. You employ a sentinel-controlled loop when you do not know how many values are to be input and you use a sentinel value to indicate there is no more input.

6. You implement the iteration structure in Visual Basic .NET (VB .NET) using either the `Do` statement or the `For` statement.

7. The `Do` statement uses two forms: `Do While` and `Do Until`. You indicate the end of the loop by writing the keyword `Loop`.

8. The `Do While` loop continues to execute as long as an expression is `true`.

9. The `Do Until` loop continues to execute until an expression is `true`.

10. You can write either a counter-controlled loop or a sentinel-controlled loop using the `Do` statement. You can also create either a pre-test or a post-test loop.

11. You use the `For Next` structure to create counter-controlled pre-test loops only. Although theoretically possible, you generally do not use `For Next` to write sentinel-controlled loops.

12. The `For Next` loop includes counter initialization and it *automatically* increments your counter, which simplifies and shortens your code. You write the keyword `Step` and the amount you want to counter-increment each iteration. The default value is 1; therefore, you can omit `Step 1` if you want to increment your counter variable by 1 each iteration. You indicate the end of the loop by writing the keyword `Next`.

13. You can write iteration structures within other iteration structures, creating nested loops. In addition, you can write a selection structure within an iteration, or an iteration within a selection.

14. One example of a selection structure within an iteration is data validation code, which checks the data the user enters and makes sure it is appropriate for the program.

EXERCISES

1. What is the output of the following code?

```
Dim counter As Integer
Do While counter <= 5
    Console.WriteLine(counter)
Loop
```

2. What is the output of the following code?

```
Dim counter As Integer
For counter = 1 To 5
    Console.WriteLine(counter)
Next
```

3. What is the output of the following code?

```
Dim counter As Integer
For counter = 1 To 5 Step 2
    Console.WriteLine(counter)
Next
```

4. What is the output of the following code?

```
Dim counter As Integer
For counter = 5 To 1 Step -1
    Console.WriteLine(counter)
Next
```

5. What is the output of the following code?

```
Dim counter As Integer = 6
Do
    Console.WriteLine(counter)
    counter += 1
Loop While counter <= 5
```

6. What is the output of the following code?

```
Dim counter As Integer
Do
    Console.WriteLine(counter)
    counter += 1
Loop Until counter = 5
```

7. What is the output of the following code?

```
Dim i, j As Integer
Do While i <= 2
    For j = 1 To 3
        Console.WriteLine(I & ", ")
        Console.WriteLine(j)
    Next
Loop
```

8. Rewrite the following loop using Do While.

```
Dim counter As Integer
For counter = 5 To 1 Step -1
    Console.WriteLine(counter)
Next
```

9. Rewrite the following loop using For Next.

```
Dim counter As Integer = 1
Do While counter <= 9
    Console.WriteLine(counter)
    counter += 3
Loop
```

10. Rewrite the following loop using Do Until.

```
Dim counter As Integer = 1
Do While counter <= 9
    Console.WriteLine(counter)
    counter += 3
Loop
```

PROGRAMMING EXERCISES

1. Assume a bank savings account begins with a specified balance and earns interest at a specified annual interest rate. The interest is computed at the end of each year using the following formula: `newBalance = previousBalance * (1 + apr)`

   Design and write a program that does the following:

   a. Prompts the user to input a beginning balance: `balance`

   b. Prompts the user to input the annual interest rate: `apr`

   c. Prompts the user to input the number of years: `years`

   d. Iterates to compute and display the interest earned and the new balance for each year, and rounds results to two decimal positions

2. Change the code in Example 5-12 to use nested `Do Until` loops.

3. The factorial of a positive integer, denoted n!, is the product of the integers from 1 to *n* inclusive. Design and write a program that does the following:

   a. Prompts the user to input a positive integer between 2 and 10 inclusive. Verify the integer is within the required range; display a message and reprompt if it is not.

   b. Compute and display the factorial using a `For Next` loop.

4. Redesign and rewrite Exercise 3 using a `Do While` loop.

5. Programming Exercise 4 in Chapter 3 asked you to design and write a program that does the following:

a. Prompts the user to input the number of inches: `inches`

b. Converts `inches` to centimeters: `centimeters`

c. Rounds `centimeters` to three decimal positions

d. Displays the rounded value in `centimeters`

Redesign and rewrite the program to loop until a sentinel value of –999 is entered for inches.

6. Programming Exercise 4 in Chapter 4 asked you to design and write a program to compute a consumer's electric bill. Redesign and rewrite the program to calculate the bill for one or more customers by looping until a sentinel value of –99999 is entered for the previous meter reading.

Your program will input the previous meter reading (a five-digit number), the current meter reading (also five digits), and compute the consumption. The bill calculation is based on the following consumption chart:

KWH Consumed	Rate per KWH
> 500	.05
500 – 1000	$25 + .055 for amount over 500
> 1000	$52.50 + .06 for amount over 1000

In addition, a sales tax rate of .085 is added to the total bill.

Input Previous meter reading and current meter reading

Output KWH consumed, electricity charge, tax, and total bill

7. Redesign the loan amortization program in the Programming Example at the end of this chapter to include data validation logic for the APR, number of months, and loan amount. The APR must be in the range 0.01 to 0.20 inclusive, the number of months must be 6 to 360, and the loan amount must be 1000 to 500,000 inclusive. Display a descriptive message if an invalid value is entered.

Using VB .NET Supplied Classes

In this chapter, you will:

O Learn more about the Framework Class Library
O Invoke methods in the String class
O Display message boxes
O Format numeric output
O Work with dates
O Read and write sequential files

Chapter 3 introduced you to the .NET Framework and the Framework Class Library (FCL). You learned that the FCL contains hundreds of prewritten classes providing methods you invoke to accomplish tasks ranging from computation and number formatting to establishing network connections and accessing relational databases. You saw that the FCL is shared by the various .NET languages.

This chapter shows you how to invoke methods in the **String** class to manipulate string data, introduces you to the **MessageBox** class, and shows you how to work with dates. You also learn how to format numeric data and work with sequential files. The next chapter explores arrays and continues working with the supplied classes **String**, **Array**, and **ArrayList**.

INTRODUCING THE FRAMEWORK CLASS LIBRARY

You learned in Chapter 3 that an **assembly** is a file with a .dll suffix containing Intermediate Language (IL). The Framework Class Library consists of approximately 100 assemblies, each containing one or more classes. As you have seen, each class has methods that you invoke to accomplish tasks, and several have attributes containing data you can retrieve. Methods and attributes in the .NET classes are also called **members**.

The classes in the FCL are organized logically into **namespaces**. A namespace can contain both classes and other namespaces. For example, the **System** namespace contains several classes you have already used such as **Math**, **Console**, and **String**. In addition to containing these and other classes, **System** is also the *root* of all other namespaces, which means it contains all of the other namespaces. For example, the **IO** namespace contains classes you use to accomplish file input and output. However, because the **System** namespace also contains the **IO** namespace, the complete reference is written as **System.IO**.

You have already invoked methods such as **Pow** and **Round** in the **Math** class and accessed the constant value for **PI**. Also, you invoked methods **WriteLine** and **ReadLine** in the **Console** class to input and display data.

Table 6-1 lists selected namespaces and indicates the classes with which you have previously worked or explored in this and the next chapter.

Table 6-1   Selected FCL namespaces and classes

Namespace	Selected Classes
System	Array
	Console
	Convert
	DateTime
	TimeSpan
	String
	Math
System.Collections	ArrayList
System.IO	StreamReader
	StreamWriter
System.Windows.Forms	Button
	Form
	Label
	MessageBox
	TextBox

The Framework compilers do not automatically search all namespaces for classes used by your code. Instead, you use the keyword `Imports` to tell the compiler which namespaces to access. If you omit the `Imports` statement, the compiler cannot locate the class you reference and error messages result. You specify a namespace by writing the hierarchy names separated with periods. To illustrate, you specify the `Forms` namespace by writing `System.Windows.Forms`. This means the `Forms` namespace is contained within the `Windows` namespace, which in turn is in the `System` namespace. You give the compiler access to the classes in a namespace at the beginning of your module by writing the keyword `Imports` followed by the namespace.

The `System` namespace (but not its subordinate namespaces) is accessed automatically by the compiler. This means that if you use only classes in the `System` namespace, then you do not need to include the `Imports` statement.

INVOKING METHODS IN THE STRING CLASS

As in many other languages, string data in Visual Basic .NET (VB .NET) is a collection of characters (`"Hello Again"`). However, VB .NET stores string data in instances of the `String` class, a member of the `System` namespace. Remember that because this namespace is automatically imported by the VB .NET compiler, you do not need to write an `Imports` statement at the beginning of your module.

Example 6-1: Declaring a String variable

You saw in Chapter 3 that you can declare a **String** variable using code similar to that used to declare a primitive value:

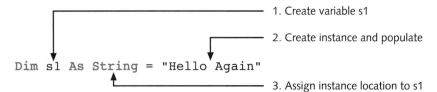

```
Dim s1 As String = "Hello Again"
```

1. Create variable s1
2. Create instance and populate
3. Assign instance location to s1

This code creates an instance of the **String** class. This is called **instantiating** a class and means you are creating an instance of the class. This statement actually does three things:

1. It first tells VB .NET to create a variable named **s1** whose data type is **String**.

2. It then creates an instance of the **String** class, and populates it with **"Hello Again"**.

3. Finally, it assigns the memory location of the new instance to the variable **s1**.

Using the data type **String** means that **s1** points to or refers to a **String** instance; it is a **reference** variable. Object-oriented programming (OOP) involves instantiating numerous classes, as you will see throughout this book. Figure 6-1 shows the **String** instance you just created.

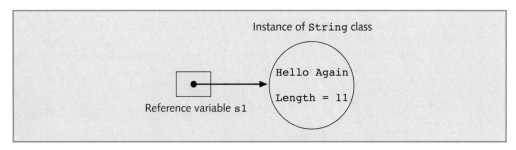

Figure 6-1 A String instance

As a class, `String` has several useful methods and properties. A **property** is a special kind of VB .NET method that you can access like a public variable. Table 6-2 lists selected methods and properties in the `String` class. Notice that most of the methods are invoked using a reference variable (`s` in these examples), but that the `Copy` method is invoked by specifying the class name, `String`.

Table 6-2 Selected String methods and properties

Name	Method	Property	Description
s.Chars(i)	x		Returns the character in the `String` instance s at index i (relative to zero)
String.Copy(s)	x		Returns a new `String` instance, which is a copy of the instance referenced by s
s.EndsWith("a")	x		Returns `Boolean` `True` if the `String` s ends with the `String` value "a"; otherwise, returns `False`
s.Equals(s1)	x		Compares values character by character in `String` instances s and s1 and returns either `True` or `False`
s.IndexOf("a")	x		Returns the index (relative to zero) of the first occurrence of the character "a" in the `String` instance referenced by s; a return of -1 means not found.
s.Insert(i,"a")	x		Inserts the `String` "a" into s beginning at index i (relative to zero) and returns the new `String` instance
s.Length		x	Returns the number of characters in the instance referenced by s
s.Replace("a","b")	x		Searches the instance referenced by s for the `String` "a", replaces it with the `String` "b", and returns the new `String` instance
s.Split("a")	x		Returns a `String` array containing substrings separated by "a" (arrays are explored in the next chapter)
s.StartsWith("a")	x		Returns `Boolean` `True` if the `String` s begins with the `String` value "a"; otherwise, returns `False`
s.Substring(i,j)	x		Returns a new `String` instance containing the characters in instance s beginning at index i for a length of j
s.ToUpper()	x		Returns a new `String` instance containing the contents of instance s converted to uppercase
s.ToLower()	x		Returns a new `String` instance containing the contents of instance s converted to lowercase

6

The following discussion and examples illustrate the use of several methods listed in Table 6-2. `String` instances have two important characteristics. First, `String` instances in VB .NET are **immutable**: they cannot be changed. Methods that appear to change a `String` value, such as `Insert`, `Replace`, `ToUpper`, and `ToLower`, actually create and return a *new* `String` instance.

Second, each character in a `String` instance has an index that indicates its position. However, index values in VB .NET begin with zero. This means that the index for the first character index is 0, the second is 1, and so on. Earlier you defined a new `String` variable named `s1`, created a `String` instance containing `"Hello Again"`, and populated `s1` by writing the single statement:

```
Dim s1 As String = "Hello Again"
```

Figure 6-2 illustrates the index values for each character in this `String`.

H	e	l	l	o		A	g	a	i	n
0	1	2	3	4	5	6	7	8	9	10

Figure 6-2   String index values

Using the Length Property

Note that in Figure 6-1 the `String` property named `Length` contains the number of characters in the `String`, which is 11 in this example. You can access the `Length` property by writing the reference variable name `s1`, a period, and the property name `Length`.

Example 6-2: Accessing the String Length property

```
Dim s1 As String = "Hello Again"

Console.WriteLine("The length of s1 is: " & s1.Length)
```

Sample Run:

```
The length of s1 is: 11
```

Discussion:

This example declares a `String` reference variable named `s1`, creates a `String` instance, populates it with `"Hello Again"`, and assigns the memory location of the instance to `s1`. The second line of code retrieves the `Length` property of the instance and displays it, showing the number of characters in `s1`.

Using the Copy Method

To explore how the **String** Copy method works, consider an example that assigns the contents of one reference variable to another.

Example 6-3: Assigning the contents of a reference variable

In the following example and in others throughout the chapter, line numbers are added for reference only, and do not appear in the actual program.

```
1. Dim s1, s2 As String
2. s1 = "Hello Again"
3. s2 = s1
```

Discussion:

The first line of code in this example creates two reference variables of the data type **String** (**s1** and **s2**). Line 2 creates a **String** instance, populates it with **"Hello Again"**, and assigns the memory address of the instance to **s1**. Line 3 then assigns the *contents* of variable **s1** to **s2**. This means that both variables contain the memory address of the instance: they both point to or reference the *same instance*. This example illustrates that you can assign the contents of a reference variable just like you can a primitive variable and that two reference variables can refer to the same instance.

Example 6-4: Invoking the String Copy method

```
1. Dim s1, s2 As String
2. s1 = "Hello Again"
3. s2 = String.Copy(s1)
```

Discussion:

Similar to the previous example, the first line of code creates two reference variables of the data type **String**, and then line 2 creates a **String** instance, populates it with **"Hello Again"**, and assigns the memory address of the instance to **s1**.

In this example, however, line 3 invokes the **String.Copy** method, sending **s1** as an argument. This method creates a copy of the **String** instance referenced by **s1**, returns a reference to this *new* instance, and assigns it to **s2**. This means that there are now two instances and the variables contain different memory addresses. **s1** points to the original instance and **s2** points to the copy.

Using the Chars Method

You saw earlier that the characters in a **String** instance have indexes. The **Chars** method returns the character located at a specified index in the instance.

Example 6-5: Invoking the String Chars method

1. `Dim s1 As String = "Hello Again"`

2. `Console.WriteLine(s1.Chars(6))`

Sample Run:

A

Discussion:

As before, line 1 creates the **String** instance and assigns its reference to **s1**. Line 2 invokes **Chars** for the **String** instance referenced by **s1**, and passes an argument of 6. The method returns the character at index 6, which is "A."

Example 6-4 invoked the **Copy** method and Example 6-5 the **Chars** method. Notice, however, that you wrote **String Copy(s1)** to invoke **Copy**, but you wrote **s1.Chars(6)** to invoke **Chars**. In other words, you invoked the first method using the class name (**String**) but you invoked the second method using the reference variable name (**s1**). Some methods such as **Copy** are called **class methods** and others such as **Chars** are called **instance methods**. Later on you explore the differences between these two, but for now remember that you invoke class methods using the class name, and instance methods using the reference variable name.

 A common error for VB .NET programmers is to attempt to invoke an instance method using a reference variable that has not yet been initialized. In other words, the variable contains nothing and *does not point to an instance*, so VB .NET cannot possibly invoke the method you request. When you make this error, VB .NET terminates the execution of your code and displays a message stating that you have a NullReferenceException. When you get this message, look for the statement containing the reference variable that caused the error and then add the code needed to initialize the reference variable.

Using the Equals Method

You saw in Chapter 4 that you use the equal sign (=) in an expression to see if two values are equal to each other. You can use this same approach to compare two **String** values. However, you can also invoke the **Equals** method to see if two **String** instances contain the same data.

Example 6-6: Invoking the String Equals method

```
1. Dim s1, s2 As String
2. s1 = "Hello Again"
3. s2 = String.Copy(s1)
4. If s1 = s2 Then
5.     Console.WriteLine("s1 = s2")
6. End If
7. If s1.Equals(s2) Then
8.     Console.WriteLine("s1.Equals(s2)")
9. End If
```

Sample Run:

```
s1 = s2

s1.Equals(s2)
```

Discussion:

Lines 1 through 3 are a copy of Example 6-4. They create two identical `String` instances containing `"Hello Again"`, referenced by the variables `s1` and `s2`. Lines 4 through 6 contain an `If` statement with the expression `s1 = s2`. Lines 7 through 9 contain another `If` statement with the expression `s1.Equals(s2)`. Both of these expressions evaluate `True`. The second `If` contains the expression `s1.Equals(s2)`, which invokes the `Equals` method for the instance referenced by `s1`, passing the argument `s2`. This method returns `True` if the two instances contain identical data, which in this example, they do.

Using the Substring Method

The purpose of the `Substring` method is to extract one or more characters from a `String` instance, and then return a new `String` instance containing the extracted characters. The first argument is the index of the first character to extract, and the second argument is the number of characters to extract. You can use the `Substring` method to retrieve parts of a string value, such as a person's last name from their complete name.

Example 6-7: Invoking the String Substring method

```
1. Dim s1, s2 As String
2. s1 = "Hello Again"
3. s2 = s1.Substring(0, 5)
4. Console.WriteLine(s2)
```

Sample Run:

```
Hello
```

Discussion:

As in the previous examples, line 1 declares two **String** reference variables **s1** and **s2**, and then line 2 creates a **String** instance containing **"Hello Again"** and references it with **s1**.

Line 3 invokes the **Substring** method for the instance referenced by **s1**, passing an argument of **(0, 5)**. This method extracts one or more characters beginning at the index specified by the first value in the argument, which here is 0. The second value in the argument tells the method how many characters to extract. In this example, five characters beginning at index 0 will be retrieved (**Hello**).

This method creates and returns a reference to a new **String** instance containing the characters retrieved. Line 3 assigns the reference of this new instance to the variable **s2** and line 4 invokes **Console.WriteLine** to display the contents of this new instance.

Using the Replace Method

As its name suggests, you invoke the **Replace** method when you want to replace one or more characters in a **String** with one or more other characters. You send two arguments to **Replace**. The first is a **String** containing the character(s) to be replaced, and the second is a **String** containing the replacement character(s). This example replaces **"Hello"** with **"Hi"** in the instance referenced by **s1**. Remember that **String** instances are immutable; they cannot be changed. Methods such as **Replace** actually create and return a new instance.

Example 6-8: Invoking the String Replace method

```
1. Dim s1, s2 As String
2. s1 = "Hello Again"
3. s2 = s1.Replace("Hello", "Hi")
4. Console.WriteLine(s2)
```

Sample Run:

```
Hi Again
```

Discussion:

Lines 1 and 2 again declare two **String** reference variables and create an instance containing **"Hello Again"**.

Line 3 invokes the **Replace** method for the instance referenced by **s1**, passing two values as an argument (**"Hello"**, **"Hi"**). This method searches the instance for the first value and replaces *all occurrences* of it with the second value. This method creates a new **String** instance containing the replaced values. Line 3 assigns the reference of this new instance to the variable **s2** and line 4 displays it.

The two arguments passed in this example are literals. You can also pass variables that reference **String** instances. In this example, the two values **"Hello"** and **"Hi"** could reside in **String** instances referenced by variables **s3** and **s4**, respectively. You would then pass the argument (**s3**, **s4**) instead of (**"Hello"**, **"Hi"**).

 The Replace method employs case-sensitive logic in its search. It *replaces all occurrences* of the first value with the second. Also, if the replacement value is **Null(" ")**, then the method *removes all occurrences* of the first value.

Using the Insert Method

You use the **Insert** method to add one or more characters into an existing **String** instance beginning at a specified index. The following example inserts the word "**There**" beginning at index 6, which follows the space after **"Hello"**.

Example 6-9: Invoking the String Insert method

```
1. Dim s1, s2 As String
2. s1 = "Hello Again"
3. s2 = s1.Insert(6, "There ")
4. Console.WriteLine(s2)
```

Sample Run:

Hello There Again

Discussion:

Lines 1 and 2 are identical to the previous examples.

Line 3 invokes the **Insert** method for the instance referenced by **s1**, passing two values as an argument (**6**, **"There "**). The first value is the index where you want to begin the insertion. Here the index value is 6, which is the character **A** of the word **Again**. The second value of the argument, **There**, contains the characters you want inserted. You can write either a literal or a reference variable pointing to a **String** instance that contains the characters you want to insert.

This method creates a new **String** instance containing the old data with the insert completed. Line 3 assigns the reference of this new instance to the variable **s2** and line 4 displays it.

Using the StartsWith and EndsWith Methods

When processing string data, you might want to identify all values that either begin with or end with a certain value. For example, you might want to identify all customers whose phone area code begins with 5. The `StartsWith` method compares a `String` argument with the beginning character(s) of a `String` instance, and then returns `True` or `False` depending on whether there is a match. `EndsWith` is similar, except it compares the *ending* characters with the argument. You can use both methods to search for text containing specified characters.

Example 6-10: Invoking the String StartsWith and EndsWith methods

```
 1. Dim s1 As String
 2. Dim s3 As String = "Again"
 3. s1 = "Hello Again"
 4. If s1.StartsWith("Hi") Then
 5.    Console.WriteLine("s1 starts with Hi")
 6. Else
 7.    Console.WriteLine("s1 does not start with Hi")
 8. End If
 9. If s1.EndsWith(s3) Then
10.    Console.WriteLine("s1 ends with Again")
11. Else
12.    Console.WriteLine("s1 does not end with Again")
13. End If
```

Sample Run:

```
s1 does not start with Hi
s1 ends with Again
```

Discussion:

Line 1 declares two `String` reference variables `s1` and `s2`.

Line 2 declares `s3` as a `String` reference variable, creates a `String` instance containing `"Again"`, and assigns its reference to `s3`.

Line 3 creates the `String` instance referenced by `s1` containing `"Hello Again"`.

Lines 4 through 8 consist of an `If` statement that contains the expression `s1.StartsWith("Hi")`. This expression invokes `StartsWith` for the instance referenced by `s1`, passing the argument `("Hi")`. This method determines if the `String` instance begins with the characters `"Hi"`, and returns `True` if it does; otherwise, the method returns `False`.

Line 5 is executed if the method returns `True`. If it returns `False`, then line 7 is executed.

Lines 9 through 13 consist of a second `If` statement containing the expression `s1.EndsWith(s3)`. This expression invokes `EndsWith` for the instance referenced by `s1`, passing the variable `s3`, which references a `String` instance containing `"Again"`. This method determines if the `String` instance ends with the characters `"Again"`, and returns `True` if it does; otherwise, the method returns `False`.

Line 10 is executed if the method returns `True`. If it returns `False`, then line 12 is executed.

6

Using the ToUpper, ToLower, IndexOf, and ToString Methods

If you want to change the case of a `String` value to uppercase or lowercase, you can invoke methods named `ToUpper` or `ToLower`. `ToUpper` returns a `String` instance containing the original value converted to uppercase. Similarly, `ToLower` returns an instance with the value converted to lowercase.

You invoke the `IndexOf` method to search a `String` instance for a specific value. This method returns the index of the first character of the value, or –1 if no matching value is found.

In Chapter 3, you saw how to invoke methods in the `Convert` class to change from one data type to another. You saw how to convert `Double` to `Integer`, `String` to `Double`, and so forth. In addition to converting `String` data to numeric, sometimes you also want to convert numeric values to a `String`. You can convert a numeric value to a `String` value by invoking the `ToString` method in the `Convert` class or by invoking the `ToString` method in one of the primitive structures (`Integer`, `Double`, etc).

 Each of the VB .NET primitive data types is represented by a **structure**. A structure is similar to a class in that it has methods, but the data is primitive and is stored in the variable instead of an instance. This means that when you declare a primitive variable, you can invoke certain methods associated with that variable, even though it is a primitive. You invoke one of these methods, `ToString`, to convert primitive data to `String`. In a later section you see how to invoke `ToString` to format numeric data with dollar signs, commas, etc.

Example 6-11: Invoking the ToString method

```
1. Dim i, j As Integer, s1, s2 As String
2. i = 5
3. j = 6
4. ' invoke Integer ToString
5. s1 = i.ToString()
6. Console.WriteLine(s1)
7. ' invoke Convert ToString
8. s2 = Convert.ToString(j)
9. Console.WriteLine(s2)
```

Sample Run:

5

6

Discussion:

Line 1 declares two **Integer** variables i and j plus two **String** variables **s1** and **s2**. Lines 2 and 3 then populate i and j with 5 and 6, respectively.

Line 5 invokes **ToString** for the **Integer** structure. This method creates a **String** instance and populates it with the contents of the primitive variable i. Line 6 displays the contents of the new instance.

Line 8 invokes the **ToString** method in the **Convert** class, passing the variable j as an argument. Similar to line 5, this method also creates a **String** instance and populates it with the contents of j. Line 9 displays the contents of the second instance.

DISPLAYING MESSAGE BOXES

You use a message box to display a message and, if you want, to get a response. The **MessageBox** class is a member of the **System.Windows.Forms** namespace, which contains numerous other GUI classes such as **Form**, **Button**, **Label**, and **TextBox**. You must import **System.Windows.Forms** to make **MessageBox** available to the compiler. You work with several of the GUI classes in Chapter 8.

MessageBox has a single method named **Show** that creates an instance of **MessageBox** and makes it visible. The **Show** method can receive up to four arguments. The first is required and the rest are optional.

1. The first argument is the message you want to display, which can be in the form of a string literal or variable.

2. The second argument is the caption you want to display in the message box.

3. The third argument specifies the buttons you want to display.

4. The last argument indicates the type of icon you want to show.

In its simplest form, you send a single argument containing the message you want to display.

Example 6-12: Displaying message boxes

The following code displays four message boxes: one with only a message, one with a message and a caption, one with a message, caption, and buttons, and another with a message, caption, buttons, and icons.

6

```
1. ' display a message
2. MessageBox.Show("Hello Again")
3. 'display a message and a caption
4. MessageBox.Show("Hello Again", "MessageBox Demo")
5. 'display message, caption, Yes/No/Cancel buttons
6. MessageBox.Show("Hello Again", "MessageBox Demo",
   MessageBoxButtons.YesNoCancel)
7. 'display message, caption, Yes/No/Cancel buttons, and Icon
8. MessageBox.Show("Hello Again", "MessageBox Demo",
   MessageBoxButtons.YesNoCancel, MessageBoxIcon.Information)
```

Discussion:

Line 2 displays the first message box shown in Figure 6-3. It contains the message "Hello Again", which was the argument passed to the Show method.

Figure 6-3   Message box with a message

Line 4 displays a message box with both the "Hello Again" message and a "MessageBox Demo" caption, as shown in Figure 6-4.

Figure 6-4   Message box with a message and caption

Line 6 passes three arguments to the **Show** method. The first two are the message and caption you previously used. The third argument is a constant, **MessageBoxButtons. YesNoCancel**, that tells the **Show** method to display three buttons: Yes, No, and Cancel, as shown in Figure 6-5. The message box is dismissed when the user clicks one of the displayed buttons.

 YesNoCancel is the constant name and **MessageBoxButtons** is the class containing the constant. VB .NET frequently uses constants written in this style.

Figure 6-5   Message box with buttons

VB .NET provides six button combinations, as shown in Figure 6-6. This list is automatically displayed by IntelliSense after you type the class name **MessageBoxButtons**. You can then select the specific buttons to be displayed from the list.

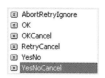

Figure 6-6   Message box button combinations

Line 8 displays the message box shown in Figure 6-7. This is similar to the previous example, but includes the information icon. This icon is displayed because you pass the constant `MessageBoxIcon.Information` as the fourth argument to the `Show` method. When you type `MessageBoxIcon`, IntelliSense displays the list shown in Figure 6-8. You select the specific icon you want to display.

Figure 6-7   Message box with information icon

Figure 6-8   Message box icon choices

When you display a message box, you can determine which button the user clicked by obtaining a return value from the `Show` method. The returned value is data type `DialogResult`, and you can compare it to specific values using an `If` statement. When you type `DialogResult`, IntelliSense lists your choices, as shown in Figure 6-9.

Figure 6-9   DialogResult values

The following example displays the Yes, No, and Cancel buttons in a message box, and then determines which button was clicked and displays a descriptive message.

Example 6-13: Identifying buttons clicked in a message box

```
1.'display message, caption, Yes/No/Cancel buttons, and Icon,
   and get result

2. Dim result As DialogResult

3. result = MessageBox.Show("Hello Again", "MessageBox
   Demo", MessageBoxButtons.YesNoCancel,
   MessageBoxIcon.Information)

4. If result = DialogResult.Yes Then

5.    Console.WriteLine("The Yes button was clicked")

6. ElseIf result = DialogResult.No Then

7.    Console.WriteLine("The No button was clicked")

8. ElseIf result = DialogResult.Cancel Then

9.    Console.WriteLine("The Cancel button was clicked")

10. End If
```

Discussion:

Line 2 declares a variable named `result` whose data type is `DialogResult`.

In line 3, the code on the right side of the equal sign displays the message box shown in Figure 6-7 with the three buttons: Yes, No, and Cancel. The message box remains visible until the user clicks one of the buttons. When a button is clicked, the name of the button is assigned to the variable `result`.

Lines 4 through 10 are a series of `If` statements that interrogate the contents of `result` to determine which button was clicked. In line 4, the expression is `result = DialogResult.Yes`. This expression compares the contents of `result` to the constant `DialogResult.Yes`. This expression evaluates to `True` if the Yes button is clicked. Similar expressions are contained in lines 6 and 8.

During processing, you might want to give the user the option of indicating yes, no, or cancel. You can then identify their button selection using this technique.

To recap, you can display a message box with a message, a message and caption, a message, a caption, and a combination of buttons, or a message, a caption, a combination of buttons, and an icon. In addition, you can determine which button was clicked to dismiss the message box.

FORMATTING NUMERIC OUTPUT

You can format your numeric output to make it more attractive and easier to read. Formatting means inserting commas, decimal places, dollar signs, percent symbols, parentheses, hyphens, and so forth.

Earlier you invoked the **ToString** method to convert primitive numbers to **String** data. You can also invoke this method to format numeric data.

You can pass two types of arguments to the **ToString** method to format numeric data. You can either pass one of the characters listed in Table 6-3 or you can pass a format mask that defines the format you want to have. A **format mask** is a series of characters that describe the format you want to use.

6

Table 6-3   ToString format characters

Character	Format Result
C	Currency
F	Fixed point
P	Percentage
N	Number
E	Exponential

The following example illustrates the use of these format characters as arguments passed to the **ToString** method.

Example 6-14: Using format characters

```
1. Dim d As Double, s As String
2. ' currency
3. d = 12345.67
4. s = d.ToString("C")
5. Console.WriteLine("Double 12345.67 with C format is " & s)
6. d = 12345.678
7. s = d.ToString("C")
8. Console.WriteLine("Double 12345.678 with C format is " & s)
9. ' fixed point
```

```
10. d = 12345.67
11. s = d.ToString("F")
12. Console.WriteLine("Double 12345.67 with F format is " & s)
13. ' percentage
14. s = d.ToString("P")
15. Console.WriteLine("Double 12345.67 with P format is " & s)
16. ' number
17. s = d.ToString("N")
18. Console.WriteLine("Double 12345.67 with N format is " & s)
19. ' exponential
20. s = d.ToString("E")
21. Console.WriteLine("Double 12345.67 with E format is " & s)
```

Sample Run:

```
Double 12345.67 with C format is $12,345.67
Double 12345.678 with C format is $12,345.68
Double 12345.67 with F format is 12345.67
Double 12345.67 with P format is 1,234,567.00 %
Double 12345.67 with N format is 12,345.67
Double 12345.67 with E format is 1.234567E+004
```

Discussion:

Line 1 declares a **Double** variable **d** and a **String** variable **s**, and line 3 populates **d**.

Line 4 invokes **ToString** for the structure, passing "C" as an argument. This method converts the contents of **d** to data type **String**, and then formats it as currency by inserting a dollar sign, comma, and decimal point. Following the conversion, **s** is assigned the reference to the new **String** instance.

Lines 6, 7, and 8 repeat the currency formatting, but illustrate rounding. When you invoke **ToString** to format, it will *round off* your number to two decimal positions.

Lines 10, 11, and 12 illustrate the use of fixed point ("F") format. Note that line 10 repopulates **d** with 12345.67. This format inserts a decimal position, but no commas or dollar sign. It will also round to two decimal positions.

Lines 14 and 15 demonstrate the percentage ("P") format argument. The contents of **d** are multiplied by 100, then formatted with commas, two decimal positions, and the percent symbol (%).

Lines 17 and 18 show the number format ("N") argument. This format is the same as currency except that no dollar sign is inserted.

Finally, lines 20 and 21 illustrate the use of the exponential ("E") format. This format expresses the number in exponential format.

You can also pass a format mask to the **ToString** method. In this example, you specify where you want the dollar sign, comma, and decimal placed. In addition, you use the pound sign (#) character to indicate whether you want to suppress leading zeros. You can substitute a zero (0) for the pound sign character if you do not want to suppress leading zeros.

6

Sometimes you need to format values such as a telephone number or Social Security number. You can invoke the **ToString** method with a format mask, as in the following example.

Example 6-15: Using a format mask

```
1. Dim d As Double, s As String
2. d = 12345.67
3. ' format mask: currency
4. s = d.ToString("$#,##0.00")
5. Console.WriteLine("Double 12345.67 with $#,##0.00 format
   is " & s)
6. ' phone no
7. Dim phoneNo As Double = 1234567890
8. s = phoneNo.ToString("(###) ###-####")
9. Console.WriteLine("Phone number format example: " & s)
10. ' social security number
11. Dim ssNo As Double = 123456789
12. s = ssNo.ToString("###-##-####")
13. Console.WriteLine("Social security number format
    example: " & s)
```

Sample Run:

Double 12345.67 with $#,##0.00 format is $12,345.67

Phone number format example: (123) 456-7890

Social security number format example: 123-45-6789

Discussion:

Lines 1 and 2 define the variables d and s and populate d as in the previous example.

Line 4 invokes **ToString**, passing (**"$#,##0.00"**) as an argument. This mask specifies where the dollar sign, comma, and decimal are to be inserted. The zeros tell the method to not suppress any leading zeros in the positions occupied by the zeros.

Lines 7, 8, and 9 illustrate how to format a phone number with area code. The argument (**"(###) ###-####"**) contains parentheses, a space, and a hyphen where they are to be inserted. The pound signs indicate where each digit is placed.

Similarly, lines 12 and 13 demonstrate how to format a Social Security number with hyphens.

To summarize, you can format a number by invoking the **ToString** method. You can pass either a format character or a format mask as an argument. This method converts the data type to **String** and then formats the number according to the argument you pass.

WORKING WITH DATES

While developing systems, you often need to work with dates. For example, many systems deal with today's date, due dates, order dates, employment dates, dates of birth, expiration dates, and so forth. VB .NET provides structures with methods that let you retrieve the current system date, retrieve the system time of day, format date values, perform arithmetic on date fields, and compare date values.

In the following examples, you use two FCL structures: **DateTime** and **TimeSpan**. A **DateTime** instance contains an actual date value. A **TimeSpan** instance contains the computed difference between two dates. These structures are in the **System** namespace, which is automatically imported by the compiler; therefore, you do not need to add an **Imports** statement.

Today is a property of **DateTime** that gets the system date and returns a **DateTime** instance. If you also want to capture the current time, then you should access the **Now** property.

Example 6-16: Retrieving and displaying today's date

```
1. ' create a DateTime instance populated with the system date
2. Dim todaysDate As DateTime, s As String
3. todaysDate = DateTime.Today
4. ' display the date in various formats
5. Console.WriteLine("Today is: " & todaysDate)
6. s = todaysDate.ToString("MMMM dd, yyyy")
7. Console.WriteLine("MMMM dd, yyyy: " & s)
8. s = todaysDate.ToString("dddd, MMMM dd, yyyy")
9. Console.WriteLine("dddd, MMMM dd, yyyy: " & s)
10. s = todaysDate.ToString("MMMM yy")
11. Console.WriteLine("MMMM yy: " & s)
```

Sample Run:

```
Today is: 2/26/2005

MMMM dd, yyyy: February 26, 2005

dddd, MMMM dd, yyyy: Thursday, February 26, 2005

MMMM yy: February 05
```

Discussion:

Line 2 defines two variables: todaysDate, which references a DateTime instance, and s, which references a String instance.

Line 3 retrieves the Today property, which references a DateTime instance containing the system date. The reference is assigned to the variable todaysDate.

Line 5 displays the date in the default format mm/dd/yyyy.

Line 6 invokes ToString for the todaysDate instance, passing the argument ("MMMM dd, yyyy"), which formats the date as month name, day of month, comma, and four-digit year. This method returns the formatted date in a String instance whose reference is assigned to s. Line 7 displays the contents of the instance.

Similarly, lines 8 through 10 format today's date as shown.

You can format the way a date is displayed by invoking its **ToString** method and passing arguments that describe the desired format.

Table 6-4 lists selected **ToString** format characters for dates that you combine to produce the display you want. Notice the difference between uppercase and lowercase "M." Lowercase indicates minute and uppercase represents month. You can insert commas, spaces, colons, and other characters into the format string.

Table 6-4 Selected date format characters

Format Characters	Description
D	Day as a number (1–7)
dd	Day as a number with leading zero (01–07)
ddd	Three-character day name (Sun)
dddd	Full day name (Sunday)
M	Month as a number (1–12)
MM	Month as a number with leading zero for single digit (01–12)
MMM	Three-character month name (Feb)
MMMM	Full month name (February)
m	Minute without leading zeros
mm	Minute with leading zeros
s	Second without leading zeros
ss	Second with leading zeros
T	Displays "A" for AM and "P" for PM
Tt	Displays "AM" or "PM"
Y	Single-digit year number without leading zeros (3)
yy	Two-digit year number (03)
yyyy	Four-digit year number (2003)

You can create a **DateTime** instance containing a specific date. The following example creates two date instances. The first, **eleanorsBirthday**, contains December 15, 1998, and the second, **emilysBirthday**, contains April 6, 2002.

■ Example 6-17: Creating specific dates

```
1. ' create specific instances of dates
2. Dim el, em As String
3. Dim eleanorsBirthday, emilysBirthday As DateTime
4. eleanorsBirthday = New DateTime(1998, 12, 15)
5. emilysBirthday = New DateTime(2002, 4, 6)
6. el = eleanorsBirthday.ToString("MMMM dd, yyyy")
7. Console.WriteLine("Eleanor's Birthday is " & el)
8. em = emilysBirthday.ToString("MMMM dd, yyyy")
9. Console.WriteLine("Emily's Birthday is " & em)
```

6

Sample Run:

Eleanor's Birthday is December 15, 1998

Emily's Birthday is April 06, 2002

Discussion:

Line 2 declares two **String** reference variables and line 3 declares two **DateTime** reference variables.

Line 4 does three things: it creates a **DateTime** instance, populates it with the date value December 15, 1998, and then assigns a reference to this new instance to the variable **eleanorsBirthday**. Note the use of the keyword **New**. You will often use this keyword to create an instance.

Line 5 is similar to line 4, but this instance is populated with April 6, 2002.

Line 6 invokes **ToString** for **eleanorsBirthday** to format the date, and line 7 displays it.

Similarly, line 8 formats **emilysBirthday**, and line 9 displays it.

Comparing Dates

The **DateTime** class has a method named **Subtract**, which you invoke to compute the number of days between two **DateTime** instances. This method returns an instance of the **TimeSpan** class that you use to hold a span of time, whether measured in hours, minutes, seconds, or days.

The **Subtract** method computes the difference between the two **DateTime** instances and returns a **TimeSpan** instance. You can then invoke the **TotalDays** method to obtain the number of days that was computed.

Example 6-18: Computing the difference between dates

```
1. ' compute the difference between two dates
2. Dim daysDifference As Double, ageDifference As TimeSpan
3. ageDifference = emilysBirthday.Subtract(eleanorsBirthday)
4. daysDifference = ageDifference.TotalDays()
5. Console.WriteLine("The age difference is " & _
   daysDifference)
```

Sample Run:

```
The age difference is 1208
```

Discussion:

Given `eleanorsBirthday` and `emilysBirthday` as `DateTime` instances from the previous example, this code computes and displays the number of days between the two birthdays (December 15, 1998, and April 6, 2002).

Line 2 defines a `Double` variable named `daysDifference` and a `TimeSpan` reference variable named `ageDifference`.

Line 3 invokes the `Subtract` method for the `emilysBirthday` instance, passing the `eleanorsBirthday` instance as an argument. This method returns an instance of `TimeSpan` and its reference is assigned to `ageDifference`.

Line 4 invokes the `TotalDays()` method for the `TimeSpan` instance referenced by `ageDifference`. This method returns a `Double` value that is assigned to `daysDifference`.

Line 5 displays the contents of `daysDifference`.

The `DateTime` class also has a method named `Compare` that compares two `DateTime` instances and returns either -1, 0, or +1, depending on whether the first `DateTime` instance is less than, equal to, or greater than the second. In the following example, `emilysBirthday` contains April 6, 2002, and `eleanorsBirthday` contains December 15, 1998. When you compare these two, `emilysBirthday` is greater than `eleanorsBirthday`, so the method returns +1.

Example 6-19: Comparing two dates

1. ' compare two dates - Compare returns -1, 0, or +1 for
   <, =, >

2. If DateTime.Compare(emilysBirthday, eleanorsBirthday)
   < 0 Then

3.   Console.WriteLine("Emily is older than Eleanor")

4. Else

5.   Console.WriteLine("Emily is younger than Eleanor")

6. End If

6

Sample Run:

Emily is younger than Eleanor

Discussion:

Given the two `DateTime` instances, `eleanorsBirthday` containing December 15, 1998, and `emilysBirthday` containing April 6, 2002, from the previous example, the `If` statement in this example compares the two dates to determine which is earlier; in other words, which person is older.

The expression in line 2 first invokes `DateTime.Compare` passing two arguments: `emilysBirthday` and `eleanorsBirthday`. This method returns -1 if the first instance contains a date before the second, 0 if they are the same, or +1 if the first instance contains a date after than the second. April 6, 2002 is *after* December 15, 1998; therefore, the method returns +1. The expression tests the value returned for < 0 which is false; therefore, the statement in line 5 is executed.

Performing Arithmetic with Dates

Sometimes you might need to perform arithmetic on a date value. For example, you might need to determine the date for a month from today or a year from today. The `DateTime` class has methods that will add a value to the month, day, or year. These are appropriately named `AddMonths`, `AddDays`, `AddYears`, and so forth. You pass these methods an argument that is the value you want added. To add one month, you invoke `AddMonths(1)`.

Example 6-20: Computing with dates

1. ' add 1 to today's month

2. Dim todaysDate, aMonthFromToday, aYearFromToday As DateTime

3. todaysDate = DateTime.Today

4. `aMonthFromToday = todaysDate.AddMonths(1)`

5. `Console.WriteLine("One month from today is " &`
   `aMonthFromToday)`

6. `' add 1 to today's year`

7. `aYearFromToday = todaysDate.AddYears(1)`

8. `Console.WriteLine("One year from today is " &`
   `aYearFromToday`

Sample Run:

`One month from today is 3/26/2005`

`One year from today is 2/26/2006`

Discussion:

Line 2 declares three `DateTime` reference variables: `todaysDate`, `aMonthFromToday`, and `aYearFromToday`.

Line 3 retrieves the current system date instance and assigns its reference to `todaysDate`.

Line 4 invokes `AddMonths` for the `DateTime` instance referenced by `todaysDate`, passing an argument of 1. This method adds one month to the date, creating a new `DateTime` instance containing the new date. The method returns a reference to this new instance and line 4 assigns the reference to `aMonthFromToday`. Line 5 displays the new date. Note that you could have displayed this date with a different format.

Similarly, line 7 adds 1 to the year and assigns the new instance's reference to `aYearFromToday`. Line 8 displays the new date.

READING AND WRITING SEQUENTIAL FILES

This section introduces you to two classes typically employed in sequential file processing: `StreamWriter` and `StreamReader`. You invoke methods in these classes to store and retrieve data in sequential files.

You can store data in relational databases and files. In a **database**, your data is organized into one or more tables, which can be related. You work with relational databases in Chapter 14. Files also contain data, but the data is organized into fields and records. A **field** is an individual data item that can be contained in a primitive variable or `String` instance. Examples include customerName, customerAddress, and customerPhoneNumber.

A **record** consists of one or more related fields. For example, if you are storing customer information that consists of name, address, and phone number, then an individual customer record will have customerName, customerAddress, and customerPhoneNumber as its fields. A **file** contains one or more related records. Therefore, if you have 1000 customers, your customer file contains 1000 customer records and each record consists of the name, address, and phone number fields.

A **sequential file** contains data that is organized with one data item following another. The name sequential means that you read and write data items in sequence. For example, to retrieve the fourth data item in a sequential file, you must first read data items 1 through 3. Figure 6-10 shows two customer records in a sequential file.

6

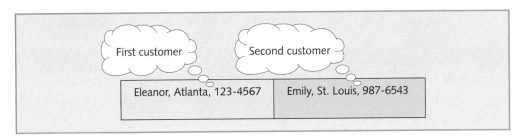

First customer   Second customer

Eleanor, Atlanta, 123-4567 | Emily, St. Louis, 987-6543

Figure 6-10   Two customer records

VB .NET uses two classes in the `System.IO` namespace to work with sequential files: `StreamWriter` and `StreamReader`. Because the VB .NET compiler does not automatically import this namespace, you must write an `Imports System.IO` statement at the beginning of your module to give the compiler access to the classes in this namespace.

You invoke the `WriteLine` method in `StreamWriter` to write items to a sequential file, and you invoke the `ReadLine` method in `StreamReader` to read items. This method returns `String` data; therefore, this example writes all `String` data to the file. You use the `StreamWriter` class to either create a new sequential file or to append data to an existing sequential file.

Example 6-21: Creating a new sequential file

```
1. Dim customerFile As New StreamWriter("C:\Customers.txt")

2. customerFile.WriteLine("Eleanor")

3. customerFile.WriteLine("Atlanta")

4. customerFile.WriteLine("123-4567")

5. customerFile.WriteLine("Emily")
```

6. `customerFile.WriteLine("St. Louis")`

7. `customerFile.WriteLine("987-6543")`

8. `customerFile.Close()`

Discussion:

Line 1 does several things. First, it declares a reference variable named `customerFile` whose data type is `StreamWriter`. Second, the **New** keyword instantiates `StreamWriter` and the statement passes the argument `("C:\Customers.txt")`. This argument contains the file specification for the new customer file you will create. Its name is `Customers.txt` and it will be written in the root directory of drive C. The instantiation of `StreamWriter` opens this file for output, which means that drive C is checked for availability and space to contain the new file. A reference for the new `StreamWriter` instance is assigned to `customerFile`.

Lines 2 through 7 write the data items to the new sequential file by invoking `WriteLine` for the `StreamWriter` instance referenced by `customerFile`. The argument passed to this method is written to the file. You can use either literals as in this example, or variable names as an argument.

Line 8 invokes the `customerFile.Close` method, which completes the file creation process. Figure 6-11 shows the data in the new sequential file that was created.

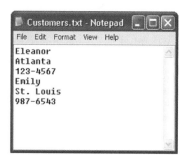

Figure 6-11   Data in the new sequential file

When you have an existing sequential file, you may want to add records to it. You can append data to an existing sequential file by making a slight addition to the argument when you instantiate StreamWriter. In addition to passing the file specification, pass the Boolean constant True. This tells StreamWriter to append to the existing file instead of creating a new file.

Example 6-22: Appending to a sequential file

Append

1. `Dim customerFile As New StreamWriter("C:\Customers.txt", True)`

2. `customerFile.WriteLine("Graham")`

3. `customerFile.WriteLine("Marietta")`

4. `customerFile.WriteLine("467-1234")`

5. `customerFile.Close()`

Discussion:

Line 1 instantiates `StreamWriter` as before, but here the argument includes the `Boolean` constant `True`.

Lines 2 through 4 write data items for the third customer, and line 5 closes the file just like the previous example.

Figure 6-12 shows the data in the sequential file after adding the third customer.

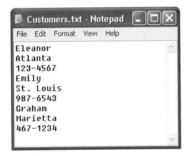

Figure 6-12   Data in the sequential file after append

You invoke the ReadLine method in the StreamReader class to read from a sequential file. When you read data from a sequential file, however, you need to know when you reach the end of the data. You receive an error if you attempt to read data after you have reached the end of file.

To avoid this error, you write a loop when reading from a sequential file. You use a pre-test loop that checks for the existence of data *before* reading data. This means that the loop terminates when there is no more data. You invoke the `Peek` method in `StreamReader` to determine if there is more data to be read. This method returns a -1 when there is no more data to be read.

Example 6-23: Reading from a sequential file

```
1. Dim inputFile As New StreamReader("C:\Customers.txt")
2. Dim name, address, phoneNo As String
3. Do Until inputFile.Peek = -1
4.     name = inputFile.ReadLine()
5.     address = inputFile.ReadLine()
6.     phoneNo = inputFile.ReadLine()
7.     Console.WriteLine(name & ", " & address & ",
       " & phoneNo)
8. Loop
9. inputFile.Close()
```

Sample Run:

```
Eleanor, Atlanta, 123-4567

Emily, St. Louis, 987-6543

Graham, Marietta, 467-1234
```

Discussion:

Line 1 accomplishes several things. First, it declares a reference variable named `inputFile` of data type `StreamReader`. Then the `New` operator creates an instance of `StreamReader`. The argument contains the file specification of the sequential file to be read and the file is verified to exist. Finally, line 1 assigns the reference of the new `StreamReader` instance to `inputFile`.

Line 2 declares three `String` reference variables. The `String` instances hold the data read from the file.

Lines 3 through 8 define a `Do Until` loop. This is a pretest loop whose expression (`inputFile.Peek = -1`) invokes the `Peek` method for the `StreamReader` instance referenced by `inputFile`. This method returns -1 when there is no more data to be read. The -1 return value causes the loop to terminate.

Within the loop body, lines 4, 5, and 6 invoke the `ReadLine` method to read data from the file, which is then assigned to the variables shown. Line 7 displays the data that was read.

Line 9, which is executed when the loop terminates, closes the input file.

PROGRAMMING EXAMPLE: EMPLOYEE REPORT

This programming example demonstrates a program that reads a sequential file containing employee information and displays a report with the data appropriately formatted.

Input Sequential file named C:\Employee.txt containing Social Security number, date employed (mm/dd/yyyy), hourly pay rate, employee first name, and employee last name; all of these fields are data type `String`

Output Employee report containing:

1. Social Security number formatted nnn-nn-nnnn
2. Date employed formatted as monthname dd, yyyy
3. Hourly pay rate formatted as currency
4. Employee name formatted as last name, (comma) first initial

At the end of the report, display the number of employees and the average hourly pay rate.

Problem Analysis and Algorithm Design

The purpose of this program is to read a sequential file containing employee data, format the data, and then produce an employee report.

Variables You need a reference variable for the `StreamReader` instance, variables to store the information read from the sequential file, and variables to count the number of employees and compute the average hourly pay rate.

```
Dim inputFile As New StreamReader("C:\Employees.txt")
Dim dateEmployed, firstName, lastName, firstInitial As String
Dim ssNo, numberOfEmployees, monthEmployed, dayEmployed,
yearEmployed As Integer
Dim hourlyPayRate, totalPayRate, averagePayRate As Double
Dim dateEmployedInstance As DateTime
```

Formulas The program counts the number of employees and sums the hourly pay rate. Upon reaching the end of file, it computes the average pay rate by dividing the total pay rate by the number of employees.

6

Main Algorithm
1. Declare the variables.
2. Instantiate `StreamReader`.
3. Display report headings.
4. Use a Do Until pretest loop to read and display each employee's data. Note that all of the data is stored in the sequential file named Employee.txt as data type `String`.
5. Within the loop body:
   a. Read the Social Security number and convert it to `Integer`.
   b. Read the date employed as `String`.
   c. Read the hourly pay rate and convert it to `Double`.
   d. Read the first name and last name data.
   e. Invoke `String Substring` to extract the month, day, and year employed into separate `Integer` variables, and then instantiate `DateTime` passing these values.
   f. Invoke `String Substring` to extract the employee's first initial.
   g. Display the formatted Social Security number.
   h. Display the formatted date employed.
   i. Display the formatted hourly pay rate.
   j. Display the employee's last name, comma, and first initial.
   k. Count the number of employees.
   l. Sum the hourly pay rate.
6. When the loop terminates, display the number of employees, compute and display the average pay rate, and close the input file.

Complete Program Listing

```
Option Strict On
Option Explicit On


Imports System.IO


Module Chapter6ProgrammingExample


Sub Main()
' declare variables
Dim inputFile As New StreamReader("C:\Employees.txt")
Dim dateEmployed, firstName, lastName, firstInitial
As String
Dim ssNo, numberOfEmployees, monthEmployed, dayEmployed,
          yearEmployed As Integer
```

```vb
Dim hourlyPayRate, totalPayRate, averagePayRate As Double
Dim dateEmployedInstance As DateTime

' display report headings
Console.WriteLine(ControlChars.Tab & "Employee Report")
Console.WriteLine()
Console.Write("Social Sec    Date Employed")
Console.WriteLine(ControlChars.Tab & "Pay Rate Employees
Name")

' loop to read the customer file and display report
Do Until inputFile.Peek = -1
ssNo = Convert.ToInt32(inputFile.ReadLine())
dateEmployed = inputFile.ReadLine()
hourlyPayRate = Convert.ToDouble
(inputFile.ReadLine())
firstName = inputFile.ReadLine()
lastName = inputFile.ReadLine()
' extract month, day, year employed (mm/dd/yyyy)
monthEmployed = Convert.ToInt32 (dateEmployed.Substring(0, 2))
dayEmployed = Convert.ToInt32 (dateEmployed.Substring(3, 2))
yearEmployed = Convert.ToInt32 (dateEmployed.Substring(6, 4))
dateEmployedInstance = New DateTime(yearEmployed,
        monthEmployed, dayEmployed)
' extract first initial
firstInitial = firstName.Substring(0, 1)
' display the employee info
Console.Write(ssNo.ToString("###-##-####") & " ")
Console.Write(dateEmployedInstance.ToString("MMMM dd, yyyy")
& "   ")
Console.Write(ControlChars.Tab & hourlyPayRate.ToString("C")
& "     ")
Console.WriteLine(lastName & ", " & firstInitial)
' sum pay rate and count
```

6

```
totalPayRate += hourlyPayRate
numberOfEmployees += 1
Loop
Console.WriteLine()
' display number of employees
Console.WriteLine("Number of employees: " &
numberOfEmployees)
' compute & display average pay rate
averagePayRate = totalPayRate / numberOfEmployees
Console.WriteLine("Average pay rate: " & average
PayRate.ToString("C"))
inputFile.Close()
End Sub


End Module
```

> **NOTE**
> Line 34 employs a constant named `ControlChars.Tab`. The ControlChars module contains constants you use as control characters. Review the Visual Studio Help facility to learn about the ControlChars module.

Sample Run:

```
      Employee Report

Social Sec    Date Employed       Pay Rate Employees Name
444-55-6666 December 15, 1998     $12.34    Bartlett, E
333-44-4455 April 06, 2002       $11.22    Kraus, E
454-54-6677 April 06, 2004       $15.67    Reed, G

Number of employees: 3
Average pay rate: $13.08
```

QUICK REVIEW

1. The classes in the Framework Class Library (FCL) are organized logically into namespaces. A namespace can contain both classes and other namespaces. The Framework compilers do not automatically search all namespaces for classes used by your code. Instead, you use the keyword **Imports** to tell the compiler which namespaces to access. The **System** namespace (but not its subordinate namespaces) is accessed automatically by the compiler.

2. Visual Basic .NET (VB .NET) stores string data in instances of the **String** class, a member of the **System** namespace. Each character in a **String** instance is identified with an index beginning with zero that indicates its position.

3. **String** has several useful methods and properties. A property is a special kind of VB method that you can access like a public variable.

4. **String** instances in VB .NET are immutable; they cannot be changed. Methods that appear to change a **String** value, such as **Insert, Replace, ToUpper**, and **ToLower**, actually create and return a *new* **String** instance.

5. The **String** property named **Length** contains the number of characters in the **String**.

6. You can convert a numeric value to a **String** value by invoking the **ToString** method in the **Convert** class or by invoking the **ToString** method in one of the primitive structures (**Integer, Double**, etc.).

7. You use the class **MessageBox** to display a message and, if you want, to get a response. **MessageBox** has a single method named **Show** that creates an instance of **MessageBox** and makes it appear. The **Show** method will receive up to four arguments. The first is required and the remainder are optional.

8. You can display a message box with a message, a message and caption, a message, a caption, and a combination of buttons, or a message, a caption, a combination of buttons, and an icon. In addition, you can determine which button was clicked to dismiss the message box.

9. You invoke the **ToString** method in one of the primitive structures to format numeric data. You can insert punctuation such as commas, decimal places, dollar signs, percent symbols, parentheses, hyphens, and spaces.

10. You use two structures, **DateTime** and **TimeSpan**, to work with dates. A **DateTime** instance contains an actual date value, and a **TimeSpan** instance contains the computed difference between two dates. You can create a **DateTime** instance containing the system date or a specific date.

11. You can format the way a date is displayed by invoking its **ToString** method and passing arguments that describe the desired format.

12. The **DateTime** method **Subtract** computes the difference between the two **DateTime** instances and returns a **TimeSpan** instance. You can then invoke the **TimeSpan TotalDays** method to obtain the number of days that was computed.

13. The **DateTime** class also has a method named **Compare** that compares two **DateTime** instances and returns -1, 0, or +1, depending on whether the first **DateTime** instance is less than, equal to, or greater than the second.

14. The **DateTime** class has methods that add a value to the month, day, or year.

15. Files contain data organized into fields and records. A field is an individual data item that can be contained in a primitive variable. A record consists of one or more related fields.

16. A sequential file contains data that is organized one data item following another. The name sequential means that you read and write data items in sequence.

17. VB .NET uses two classes in the `System.IO` namespace to work with sequential files: `StreamWriter` and `StreamReader`. You invoke the `WriteLine` method in `StreamWriter` to write items to a sequential file, and you invoke the `ReadLine` method in `StreamReader` to read items. You use the `StreamWriter` class to either create a new sequential file or to append data to an existing sequential file.

18. You invoke the `ReadLine` method in the `StreamReader` class to read from a sequential file. When reading from a sequential file, you write a pretest loop that checks for the existence of data *before* reading data. You invoke the `Peek` method in `StreamReader` to determine if there is more data to be read. This method returns a –1 when there is no more data to be read.

EXERCISES

1. Write an `Imports` statement that gives the compiler access to the following classes:

   a. `DateTime`

   b. `Math`

   c. `MessageBox`

   d. `StreamWriter`

2. What does it mean to "instantiate a class"?

3. What is the output of the following code?

   ```
   Dim s1 As String = "Hi Ellie"
   Console.WriteLine("The length of s1 is: " & s1.Length)
   ```

4. What is the output of the following code?

   ```
   Dim s1 As String = "Hi Emily"
   Console.WriteLine(s1.Chars(6))
   ```

5. What is the output of the following code?

   ```
   Dim s1, s2 As String
   s1 = "Hi Gray"
   s2 = s1.Substring(3, 4)
   Console.WriteLine(s2)
   ```

6. Describe the message box displayed by the following code.

   ```
   MessageBox.Show("We have a problem", "MessageBox Demo", _
       MessageBoxButtons.AbortRetryIgnore,_
       MessageBoxIcon.Warning)
   ```

7. What is the output of the following code?

```
Dim d As Double, s As String
d = 1234567.89
s = d.ToString("C")
Console.WriteLine(s)
```

8. What is the output of the following code?

```
Dim d As Double, s As String
d = 1234567.89
s = d.ToString("F")
Console.WriteLine(s)
```

9. What is the output of the following code?

```
Dim d As Double, s As String
d = 1234567.89
s = d.ToString("N")
Console.WriteLine(s)
```

6

10. What is the output of the following code?

```
Dim d As Double, s As String
d = 1234567.89
s = d.ToString("##,###,##0.00")
Console.WriteLine(s)
```

11. Assume today's date is May 1, 2005. What is the output of the following code?

```
Dim todaysDate As DateTime, s As String
todaysDate = DateTime.Today
s = todaysDate.ToString("MMMM dd, yyyy")
Console.WriteLine(s)
```

12. Assume today's date is May 1, 2005. What is the output of the following code?

```
Dim todaysDate As DateTime, s As String
todaysDate = DateTime.Today
s = todaysDate.ToString("dddd, MMMM dd, yyyy")
Console.WriteLine(todaysDate.ToString(s))
```

PROGRAMMING EXERCISES

1. Programming Exercise 1 in Chapter 5 asked you to design and write a savings account program that prompted the user to input the beginning balance, the annual interest rate, and number of years. The program iterated to compute and display the interest earned and the new balance for each year rounded to two decimal positions. The formula used was:

```
newBalance = previousBalance * (1 + interestRate)
```

Use the following data for three savings accounts to complete Steps a and b.

Beginning Balance	APR	Years
100.00	7.5%	5
250.00	8.25%	4
75.00	5.5%	3

a. Create a sequential file named Savings.txt containing this data. Invoke the WriteLine method to output the data items individually.

b. Modify your solution for Programming Exercise 1 in Chapter 5 to input data from this sequential file. Display the interest earned and the new balance using currency format.

2. Design and write a program that inputs a sentence. Convert the first letter of the sentence to uppercase, place a period at the end of the sentence, and then display the new sentence. None of the remaining letters in the sentence are to be uppercase.

3. Programming Exercise 7 in Chapter 5 asked you to include data validation logic for the annual percentage rate (APR), number of months, and loan amount. The APR must be in the range 0.01 to 0.20 inclusive, number of years must be 1 to 30, and the loan amount must be 1000 to 500,000 inclusive. Modify your solution to display the appropriate error message using a message box with Cancel/Retry buttons and a Warning icon. Interrogate the user response and terminate if the Cancel button is clicked. Test your solution with the following data.

Beginning Balance	APR	Years
1000.00	27.5%	5
2500.00	8.25%	400
75.00	5.5%	3

4. Design and write a program that inputs an employee's date of employment and their birthday, and then computes and displays their age at employment, expressed in years and days.

6

7

Working with Arrays

In this chapter, you will:

- ○ Define one-dimensional arrays
- ○ Create String arrays
- ○ Declare multi-dimensional arrays
- ○ Search an array
- ○ Use the ArrayList class

Arrays consist of a collection of elements with each element behaving as a variable does. Array elements, like variables, can contain either primitive data or they can be reference variables, but they must have the same data type. You access the individual elements in an array using an index.

`Array` is a class in the `System` namespace that provides you with properties and methods. Arrays can be either one-dimensional or multi-dimensional. A **one-dimensional array** consists of elements arranged in a single row. Conceptually, a **two-dimensional array** has *both* rows and columns, and a **three-dimensional array** is like a cube, with rows, columns, and pages. However, Visual Basic .NET (VB .NET) implements multi-dimensional arrays as arrays of arrays; therefore, you are not restricted by rectangles and cubes. For example, the rows in an array can be unequal lengths. Single- and two-dimensional arrays are illustrated in this chapter.

In this chapter, you learn how to declare and populate arrays. You also learn how to iterate an array and to search for specific values in an array. One disadvantage of arrays is they are static; after you create one, you cannot change the number of elements, though you can use the `ReDim` statement to create a copy of an existing array with additional elements. In addition to the `Array` class, the Framework Class Library (FCL) includes a class named `ArrayList` that you can use whenever you need a dynamically resizable array. `ArrayList` permits you to change the number of elements as your code is executing. You create dynamically resizable arrays using the `ArrayList` class.

After completing this chapter, you will understand several benefits of using arrays and be able to create and access one- and two-dimensional arrays using either the `Array` class or the `ArrayList` class.

DEFINING ONE-DIMENSIONAL ARRAYS

In Chapter 5, you worked with examples that input five exam scores and computed their average. The following example repeats this processing; however, it uses five `Integer` variables. The output is identical to the previous examples.

Example 7-1: Computing an exam average using individual variables

In the following example and in others throughout the chapter, line numbers are added for reference only, and do not appear in the actual program.

```
1. ' define variables
2. Dim exam1, exam2, exam3, exam4, exam5 As Integer
```

```
3. Dim sum, average As Double

4. Dim numberOfExams As Integer= 5

5. ' enter the exam scores

6. Console.WriteLine("Enter an Exam Score: ")    ' Exam 1

7. exam1 = Convert.ToInt32(Console.ReadLine())

8. Console.WriteLine("Enter an Exam Score: ")    ' Exam 2

9. exam2 = Convert.ToInt32(Console.ReadLine())

10. Console.WriteLine("Enter an Exam Score: ")    ' Exam 3

11. exam3 = Convert.ToInt32(Console.ReadLine())

12. Console.WriteLine("Enter an Exam Score: ")    ' Exam 4

13. exam4 = Convert.ToInt32(Console.ReadLine())

14. Console.WriteLine("Enter an Exam Score: ")    ' Exam 5

15. exam5 = Convert.ToInt32(Console.ReadLine())

16. ' compute sum and average

17. sum += exam1

18. sum += exam2

19. sum += exam3

20. sum += exam4

21. sum += exam5

22. average = sum / numberOfExams


23. Console.WriteLine("The average is: " &
    Math.Round(average, 1))
```

7

Sample Run:

In the following output and in the Sample Runs throughout the chapter, user input is shaded.

```
Enter an Exam Score:
85
Enter an Exam Score:
90
Enter an Exam Score:
94
Enter an Exam Score:
89
Enter an Exam Score:
91
The average is: 89.8
```

Discussion:

Line 2 defines five **Integer** variables to contain the five exam scores.

Line 3 defines variables to compute the sum and average, and line 4 defines and populates **numberOfExams**.

Lines 6 through 15 input the five scores, lines 17 through 21 compute the sum of the scores, line 22 computes the average, and line 23 displays the result.

The examples in Chapter 5 did not use individual variables for the individual exams. Instead, they combined the input and summing operations in single statements. One benefit of using individual variables in Example 7-1 is that you have access to all exam scores. For example, if you want to identify the highest or lowest score, you need access to all of the individual scores.

If you are working with relatively few values such as five exam scores, using individual variables is a viable approach. However, as the number of values increases, this technique quickly becomes cumbersome. To illustrate, if Example 7-1 had 10 exams, you would need to define 10 variables and input 10 values, and if there were 20 exams, you would be required to define 20 variables. Arrays are often an attractive alternative to individual variables, especially when larger numbers of values are involved.

To declare an array, you write the keyword **Dim** followed by the name of the reference variable you want to use. Next, you write the index of the last element of the array in parentheses. VB .NET numbers the array elements beginning with 0. This means the index of the first element is 0, the second element is 1, and so forth. In Example 7-2, the index of the last (fifth) element is 4.

Example 7-2: Computing an exam average using an array

The following code shows how to use an array to compute the average of five exam scores.

| Only the index changes | Create a five-element array whose elements are data type Integer | Identical statements except for index value |

```
1.   ' define variables
2.   Dim examScores(4) As Integer
3.   Dim sum, average As Double
4.   Dim numberOfExams As Integer = 5
5.   ' enter the exam scores
6.   Console.WriteLine("Enter an Exam Score: ")    ' exam 1
7.   examScores(0) = Convert.ToInt32(Console.ReadLine())
8.   Console.WriteLine("Enter an Exam Score: ")    ' exam 2
9.   examScores(1) = Convert.ToInt32(Console.ReadLine())
10.  Console.WriteLine("Enter an Exam Score: ")    ' exam 3
11.  examScores(2) = Convert.ToInt32(Console.ReadLine())
12.  Console.WriteLine("Enter an Exam Score: ")    ' exam 4
13.  examScores(3) = Convert.ToInt32(Console.ReadLine())
14.  Console.WriteLine("Enter an Exam Score: ")    ' exam 5
15.  examScores(4) = Convert.ToInt32(Console.ReadLine())
16.  ' compute sum and average
17.  sum += examScores(0)
18.  sum += examScores(1)
19.  sum += examScores(2)
20.  sum += examScores(3)
21.  sum += examScores(4)
22.  average = sum / numberOfExams
23.  Console.WriteLine("The average is: " & Math.Round(average, 1))
```

7

Sample Run:

```
Enter an Exam Score:
85
Enter an Exam Score:
90
Enter an Exam Score:
94
```

```
Enter an Exam Score:
89
Enter an Exam Score:
91
The average is: 89.8
```

Discussion:

Line 2 does three things. First, it defines a reference variable named **examScores**. Next, it creates an **Array** instance containing five elements whose data type is **Integer**. Finally, the statement assigns the reference of the new **Array** instance to **examScores**.

Identical to the previous example, line 3 defines variables to compute the sum and average, and line 4 defines and populates **numberOfExams**.

You access the individual elements of the array by writing the array reference variable **examScores** followed by the index value of the element enclosed in parentheses. For example, to access the second element, you write **examScores(1)**.

Lines 6 through 15 again input the five scores, but this time the scores entered are assigned to the five elements of the array. Line 7, for example, invokes **Console.ReadLine** to input the exam score from the keyboard, invokes **Convert.ToInt32** to convert the value returned to data type **Integer**, and then assigns the value returned to the array element located at index 0 (**examScores(0)**). Notice that lines 7, 9, 11, 13, and 15 are identical except for the index value. In line 7 the index is 0, in line 9 it is 1, and so forth.

Identical to the previous example, lines 17 through 21 compute the sum of the scores. These statements are also identical except for the index value.

Line 22 computes the average and line 23 displays the result. The output is identical to the previous example.

Figure 7-1 shows the array you created and populated in this example.

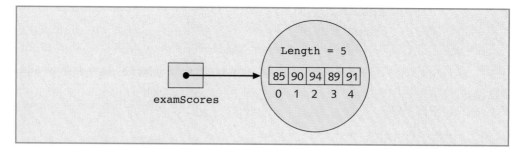

Figure 7-1   A five-element Integer array

Using a Loop to Iterate an Array

In Example 7-2, lines 7, 9, 11, 13, and 15 are identical and lines 17 through 21 are identical except for the index values. This suggests that you can write a loop instead of repeating the input and addition statements. A loop is especially appropriate when working with larger arrays. You can certainly write five statements to input and compute the sum of five exams; however, it is impractical to write 100 statements to compute the sum of an array having 100 elements.

Example 7-3 uses a **For Next** loop to input and compute the sum of the array contents.

Example 7-3: Computing exam average using an array and a loop

Index value begins at 0 and
increases by 1 each iteration

Length property contains 5

7

```
1.    ' define variables
2.    Dim examScores(4) As Integer
3.    Dim sum, average As Double
4.    Dim index As Integer

5.    ' loop to enter and sum the exam scores
6.    For index = 0 To examScores.Length - 1
7.        Console.WriteLine("Enter an Exam Score: ")
8.        examScores(index) = Convert.ToInt32(Console.ReadLine())
9.        sum += examScores(index)
10.   Next

11.   average = sum / examScores.Length
12.   Console.WriteLine("The average is: " & Math.Round(average, 1))
```

Sample Run:

```
Enter an Exam Score:
85
Enter an Exam Score:
90
Enter an Exam Score:
94
```

```
Enter an Exam Score:
89
Enter an Exam Score:
91
The average is: 89.8
```

Discussion:

Identical to Example 7-2, line 2 creates the five-element array and line 3 defines the variables to compute the sum and average.

Line 4 declares an `Integer` variable named `index` that is used both as a loop counter and as an index to access the array elements.

Lines 6 through 10 define a `For Next` loop that will input the five exam scores and populate the array. This loop uses the variable named `index` as a counter.

Line 6 initializes `index` to 0. Note that the terminating value for this loop is `examScores.Length - 1`. The `Length` property of an array contains the number of elements, which is 5 in this example.

 You can also invoke the `Ubound` function to obtain the number of elements in an array. Refer to the VB .NET Help facility to learn more about `Ubound`.

Line 7 displays a user prompt as before.

Line 8 inputs a score, converts it to `Integer`, and assigns it to the array element indexed by `index`. Note the use of a variable instead of a literal as an index. This loop executes five times. The first time, `index` contains 0, the second 1, and so forth.

Line 9 adds the array element just populated to `sum`, and line 10 indicates the end of the loop body.

Line 11 computes the exam average by dividing the `sum` by the `Length` property of the array. Line 12 displays this average.

Because the number of iterations in this example is determined by the number of array elements, you can easily change the number of exam scores to be averaged. For example, if you have 10 exams, simply change the number of elements to 10 by replacing the 4 with 9 in line 2.

Invoking Array Methods

The `Array` class has several methods that you can explore by accessing the VB .NET Help facility. Two of these methods, `Sort` and `Reverse`, are demonstrated in Example 7-4.

Example 7-4: Invoking array methods Sort and Reverse

The following code displays an unsorted array of exam scores, sorts the array, and then reverses the sorted exam scores.

```
1. ' populate the array
2. Dim examScores() As Integer = {85, 90, 94, 89, 91}
3. Dim index As Integer
4. ' display the unsorted array
5. Console.WriteLine("Unsorted array:")
6. For index = 0 To examScores.Length - 1
7.    Console.Write(examScores(index) & ", ")
8. Next

9. ' display sorted
10. Array.Sort(examScores)
11. Console.WriteLine()
12. Console.WriteLine("Sorted array:")
13. For index = 0 To examScores.Length - 1
14.    Console.Write(examScores(index) & ", ")
15. Next

16. ' display reversed
17. Array.Reverse(examScores)
18. Console.WriteLine()
19. Console.WriteLine("Reversed array:")
20. For index = 0 To examScores.Length - 1
21.    Console.Write(examScores(index) & ", ")
22. Next
23. Console.WriteLine()
```

Sample Run:

```
Unsorted array:
85, 90, 94, 89, 91,
Sorted array:
85, 89, 90, 91, 94,
Reversed array:
94, 91, 90, 89, 85,
```

Discussion:

Line 2 illustrates a convenient way to both create and populate an array when working with a small number of elements. This statement first declares the array reference variable **examScores**, creates the array with five **Integer** elements, populates the elements with the values written within the braces, and finally assigns the reference to **examScores**. Notice that when you create an array using this technique, you do not specify the number of elements; VB .NET uses the number of values you provide to determine the number of elements.

Line 3 defines the index variable as in previous examples.

Line 5 displays a heading description, and then lines 6 through 8 define a **For Next** loop to display the array contents. This loop contains one statement (line 7) that displays the contents of the array element specified by the index value.

Line 10 invokes the **Sort** method for the **examScores** array. This method rearranges the array contents into ascending order. Line 11 displays a blank line to improve readability.

Lines 12 through 15 again display the rearranged array contents.

Line 17 invokes the **Reverse** method for the **examScores** array. As the name implies, this method reverses the sequence of the array contents.

The remaining code displays the rearranged array's contents.

CREATING STRING ARRAYS

Earlier you created an array of **Integer** elements with the statement:

```
Dim testScores(4) As Integer
```

This code declares the array reference variable **testScores**, creates an **Array** instance consisting of five elements each of data type **Integer**, and then points **testScores** to the newly created array. Remember that when you define an array, you specify the index of the last element, not the number of elements. You access a specific element of the array using an index. Recall that 0 is the index of the first element, 1 the second, and so forth.

The code to create a `String` array is similar:

```
Dim stringArray(3) As String
```

This statement declares an array reference variable `stringArray`, creates an array instance containing four elements, each of which is a reference variable whose data type is `String`, and then points `stringArray` to the array instance. Note that the elements of the `testScores` array are *primitive* variables of data type `Integer`. However, the elements of `stringArray` are *reference* variables of data type `String`. This means that each element of `stringArray` will point to a `String` instance.

The following example creates and populates a four-element `String` array.

Example 7-5: Creating and accessing a String array

```
1.  ' declare a String
2.  Dim stringValue As String = "Hello World Wide Web"

3.  ' extract words delimited by space to populate a
    String array
4.  Dim stringArray() As String = stringValue.Split(" "c)

5.  ' display the array contents
6.  Dim i As Integer
7.  For i = 0 To stringArray.Length - 1
8.      Console.WriteLine(stringArray(i))
9.  Next

10. ' display the number of elements
11. Console.WriteLine(stringArray.Length & " elements")

12. ' display the number of characters in the last element
13. Console.WriteLine("length of Web is " &
       stringArray(3).Length)

14. ' invoke ToUpper method for the first element
15. Console.WriteLine(stringArray(0).ToUpper())
```

Sample Run:

```
Hello
World
Wide
Web
4 elements
length of Web is 3
HELLO
```

Discussion:

Line 2 creates a `String` instance containing "Hello World Wide Web" and referenced by `stringValue`.

Line 4 does several things:

1. It creates a new array whose data type is `String`.

2. It assigns a reference to the new array to `stringArray`.

3. It invokes the `Split` method for the `String` instance referenced by `stringValue`, passing the argument (`" "c`). The space is called a delimiter, and it can be a comma, period, or any other character.

This method extracts the substrings separated by the character value specified and uses these substrings to populate a `String` array. This example uses the character space. Note the use of the character "c" in the argument. This tells VB .NET that the data type of the literal `" "` is `Char`. Normally when you write a value in quotation marks, VB .NET assumes the data type is `String`.

Note that you could also populate `stringArray` by writing individual assignment statements:

```
stringArray(0) = "Hello"
stringArray(1) = "World"
stringArray(2) = "Wide"
stringArray(3) = "Web"
```

In addition, you could have declared and populated the array using a single statement:

```
Dim stringArray() As String = {"Hello", "World", "Wide", "Web"}
```

The `String` array created in this example is shown in Figure 7-2. This figure shows that the variable `stringArray` is a reference variable that points to the array instance. The array instance contains four elements, each of which is also a reference variable pointing to four `String` instances containing the values shown.

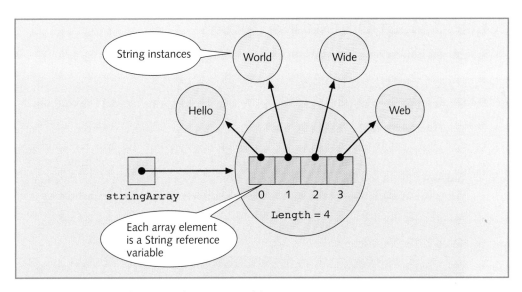

Figure 7-2   Array of String reference variables

Line 6 declares an **Integer** variable named **i** that will serve as an index.

Lines 7 through 9 use a **For Next** loop to iterate the array to display its contents.

Line 11 retrieves and displays the **Length** property for the array instance referenced by **stringArray**. There are four elements in this array.

Line 13 retrieves the **Length** property for the **String** instance referenced by the fourth element of the array. Because this **String** instance contains "Web", its **Length** property contains 3.

Line 15 invokes the **ToUpper** method for the **String** instance referenced by the first element of the array. The value "Hello" is converted to uppercase by the method.

To summarize, you can create arrays whose elements contain either primitive values such as **Integer**, or references to instances such as **String**. The **Array** class has several useful methods such as **Sort** and **Reverse**, which you invoke to manipulate the array's contents. **Array** instances have a **Length** property containing the number of array elements.

DECLARING MULTI-DIMENSIONAL ARRAYS

In addition to one-dimensional arrays, VB .NET supports multi-dimensional arrays. Recall that, conceptually, a two-dimensional array is like a table with rows and columns, and a three-dimensional array is like a cube, with rows, columns, and pages. Each dimension is has its own index. Generally you work with arrays having one or two dimensions.

You can expand the previous test scores examples to use a two-dimensional array with five rows and two columns. The two columns represent the two tests and the five rows represent the five students, as shown in Table 7-1. (Note that the column listing "Student 1, Student 2," and so on is for your reference only, and is not part of the array.) The first column contains the same values as the previous one-dimensional array, examScores.

Table 7-1 Exam scores

	Exam 1	Exam 2
Student 1	85	88
Student 2	90	85
Student 3	94	60
Student 4	89	95
Student 5	91	100

You declare a two-dimensional array similar to the way you declare a one-dimensional array, but you specify the number of rows and columns. The following example declares an **Integer** array named **testScoreTable** with five rows and two columns. Note that you specify the index of the last row (4) and the last column (1).

Example 7-6: Creating a two-dimensional array

```
1. ' testScoreTable
2. Dim testScoreTable(4, 1) As Integer
3. ' populate the elements in column 1
4. testScoreTable(0, 0) = 85
5. testScoreTable(1, 0) = 90
6. testScoreTable(2, 0) = 94
7. testScoreTable(3, 0) = 89
8. testScoreTable(4, 0) = 91
```

```
 9. ' populate the elements in column 2
10. testScoreTable(0, 1) = 88
11. testScoreTable(1, 1) = 85
12. testScoreTable(2, 1) = 60
13. testScoreTable(3, 1) = 95
14. testScoreTable(4, 1) = 100
```

Discussion:

Line 2 creates the two-dimensional array containing 10 **Integer** elements arranged in five rows and two columns and assigns its reference to the variable **testScoreTable**.

Lines 4 through 8 populate the first column and lines 10 through 14 populate the second. When working with two-dimensional arrays, you always specify the row index first, then the column index. In this example, each column represents a separate exam. Column 1 contains the scores for Exam 1 and column 2 contains the scores for Exam 2.

VB .NET implements multi-dimensional arrays by creating an array of arrays.

The two-dimensional array structure for **testScoreTable** is shown graphically in Figure 7-3.

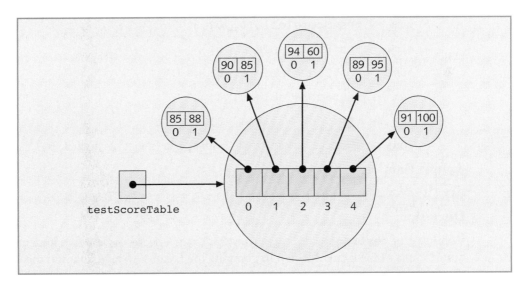

Figure 7-3   An array of arrays

You can create and populate small two-dimensional arrays using a single statement:

```
Dim testScoreTable(,) As Integer = _
    {{85, 88}, {90, 85}, {94, 60}, {89, 95}, {91, 100}}
```

Note that you do not specify the number of rows or columns using this technique. VB .NET determines these based on the number of values you code.

The reference variable `testScoreTable` points to the array instance containing five elements, one for each row. Each of these elements, in turn, is a reference to a second array instance containing two elements, one for each column. You should note that there are actually six array instances shown.

Because each row of a two-dimensional array is actually a separate array object, each row does not have to be the same length. In other words, you can create a two-dimensional array where the first row has two elements, the second row five elements, and so forth. Although you usually work with two-dimensional arrays having rows of the same length, you have the option of having rows with different lengths.

The following example shows an excerpt of code that uses a two-dimensional array to compute the average score on the first of five exams.

Example 7-7: Computing the first exam average

```
1. ' compute average of Exam 1

2. Dim sum As Double

3. sum += testScoreTable(0, 0)

4. sum += testScoreTable(1, 0)

5. sum += testScoreTable(2, 0)

6. sum += testScoreTable(3, 0)

7. sum += testScoreTable(4, 0)

8. Console.WriteLine("Exam 1 average is " & sum / 5)
```

Sample Run:

```
Exam 1 average is 89.8
```

Discussion:

Column 1 of `testScoreTable` contains the Exam 1 scores for the five students, and column 2 contains the Exam 2 scores. To compute the Exam 1 average, you sum the contents of the elements in column 1.

Line 2 defines a variable named **sum**, which will be used to compute the sum of the column 1 elements.

Lines 3 through 7 compute the sum of the first exam. Notice that these statements are identical except for the row index.

Line 8 computes and displays the average.

To compute the average of the second exam, you copy lines 3 through 7, changing the column index from 0 to 1.

Example 7-8 shows an excerpt of code that uses a loop instead of a two-dimensional array to compute the average score on the first of five exams. Note that the example assumes **testScoreTable** has been declared and populated.

Example 7-8: Computing the first exam average using a loop

```
1. ' compute Exam 1 average using a loop

2. Dim sum As Double, row As Integer

3. For row = 0 To 4

4.    sum += testScoreTable(row, 0)

5. Next

6. Console.WriteLine("Exam 1 average is " & sum / 5)
```

Sample Run:

```
Exam 1 average is 89.8
```

Discussion:

Line 2 defines the variable **sum** as before, plus a counter named **row**.

Lines 3 through 5 create a **For Next** loop to sum Exam 1. The counter in this example begins at 0 and terminates at 4. Note that you could use a variable containing 4 instead of the literal 4 in this example. These counter values are used in line 4 to specify the row index. Line 4 executes five times. The first time line 4 executes, **row** contains 0, the second time 1, and so forth.

When the loop terminates, line 6 computes and displays the average as in the previous example.

To compute the average of the second exam, you could copy statements 3, 4, and 5 and change the column index to 1.

The following example shows an excerpt of code that demonstrates how to use a nested loop instead of two separate loops to compute the average score on two exams.

Example 7-9: Computing both exam averages using a nested loop

```
1. ' compute the average test score using nested for loop
2. Dim row, col As Integer, average, sum As Double
3. For col = 0 To 1
4.    sum = 0
5.    For row = 0 To 4
6.       sum += testScoreTable(row, col)
7.    Next ' end of inner loop
8.    ' compute the column average
9.    average = sum / 5
10.   Console.WriteLine("Exam " & (col + 1) & " average is " & average)
11. Next ' end of outer loop
```

Sample Run:

```
Exam 1 average is 89.8
Exam 2 average is 85.6
```

Discussion:

Line 2 defines `Double` variables `sum` and `average`, plus two `Integer` counters named `row` and `col`.

This example uses a nested loop contained in lines 3 through 11. The outer loop iterates twice, once for each column. The inner loop, lines 5 through 7, iterates five times, once for each row.

Line 3 begins the outer loop.

Line 4 initializes `sum` to 0. This is necessary because the variable is used to compute the sum of column 1 and column 2. If you fail to reinitialize, then it will contain the total of column 1 when you begin summing column 2.

Line 5 begins the inner (`row`) loop.

Line 6 adds the contents of the element indexed by `row` and `col` to `sum`.

Line 7 defines the end of the inner loop.

Line 9 computes the average and line 10 displays it.

Line 11 ends the outer loop.

SEARCHING AN ARRAY

Sometimes you want to search an array to see if it contains a specific value. To illustrate, the following example searches the **stringArray** you created in an earlier section for the value "Web."

Example 7-10: Searching an array

```
1. Dim stringValue As String = "Hello World Wide Web"
2. Dim stringArray() As String = stringValue.Split(" "c)
3. Dim searchValue As String = "Web"
4. Dim found As Boolean = False
5. Dim i As Integer = 0
6. Do While i < stringArray.Length And Not found
7.    If stringArray(i).Equals(searchValue) Then
8.       found = True
9.    Else
10.      i += 1
11.   End If
12. Loop
13. If found Then Console.WriteLine("found " & searchValue)
```

Sample Run:

```
found Web
```

Discussion:

Lines 1 and 2 define and populate the four-element **String** array named **stringArray** with which you worked earlier.

Line 3 creates a **String** instance containing "Web" referenced by the variable **searchValue**. This is the value for which you will search in the array.

7

Line 4 declares a **Boolean** variable named **found** and initializes it to **False**. This variable will be set to **True** if the search value is found.

Line 5 declares an **Integer** variable named **i** that will serve as an index.

Lines 6 through 12 define a **Do While** loop that will iterate the array to see if the specified value exists. This loop will continue until either the end of the array is reached or the specified value is found.

Lines 7 through 11 contain an **If** statement. The expression in line 7 invokes the **Equals** method for the element indexed by **i**, passing **searchValue** as an argument. If the instance referenced by the element matches the contents of **searchValue**, the method returns **True**; otherwise, it returns **False**. If the expression is **True**, then **found** is assigned the value **True**. Note that this will terminate the loop.

 You could use the "=" operator here instead of the Equals method, but the Equals method reinforces the notion that you are dealing with instances instead of primitive values.

If the expression in line 7 is **False**, then the index is incremented and the loop continues.

Line 13 is executed when the loop terminates. It evaluates the contents of **found**, and displays the message if **True**.

USING THE ARRAYLIST CLASS

As you have seen, array elements are actually variables. As such, they may be either primitive or reference variables, depending on how you declare the array. Earlier you created an array of primitive elements and then you saw how to create an array of **String** reference elements. As powerful as they are, however, arrays have a significant limitation: they are fixed in size. It is extremely difficult to change the number of array elements as your code is executing.

You use the **ArrayList** class, a member of the **System.Collections** namespace, to create an array that is dynamically resizable. This means that you can change the number of elements of an **ArrayList** *while your code is executing*. The **ArrayList** class also provides several useful methods and properties, some of which are illustrated in this section. Table 7-2 lists several commonly used **ArrayList** methods and properties, and the remainder of this section illustrates their use.

Table 7-2 Selected ArrayList methods and properties

Method Name	Description
Add(o)	Method places a reference to the object instance o into the next available element
Contains(o)	Method determines if object o is in the **ArrayList**, and then returns **True** or **False**
Capacity	Property sets or gets the number of elements
Count	Property gets the number of populated elements
Item(i)	Property sets or gets the object referenced by the element at index i
IndexOf(o)	Returns the index of the element referencing object instance o if it exists, returns –1 if object is not found
Remove(o)	Method removes the first occurrence of object o
Reverse()	Method reverses the element sequence

7

The following example shows how to create and populate an **ArrayList** with three elements.

Example 7-11: Creating and populating an ArrayList instance

```
1. ' create an ArrayList instance with 3 elements
2. Dim anArrayList As ArrayList = New ArrayList(3)

3. ' create String instances
4. Dim s1 As String = "Hello"
5. Dim s2 As String = "World"
6. Dim s3 As String = "Wide"
7. Dim s4 As String = "Web"

8. ' populate the first two elements
9. anArrayList.Add(s1)
10. anArrayList.Add(s2)
11. Console.WriteLine("number of elements = " &
    anArrayList.Capacity)
```

```
12. Console.WriteLine("populated elements = " &
    anArrayList.Count)


13. ' iterate and display

14. Dim i As Integer

15. For i = 0 To anArrayList.Count - 1

16.     Console.WriteLine(anArrayList.Item(i))

17. Next
```

Sample Run:

```
number of elements = 3
populated elements = 2
Hello
World
```

Discussion:

Line 2 does several things. First, it declares a variable named **anArrayList** whose data type is **ArrayList**. This means that this variable will reference an instance of the **ArrayList** class. Second, the statement creates an **ArrayList** instance containing three elements. Finally, a reference to the new instance is assigned to the newly defined variable, **anArrayList**.

Note that the code in line 2 uses the keyword **New**, which creates an instance and automatically invokes a special method called the **constructor** in **ArrayList**. You will work more with constructor methods in a later chapter. For now, you should know that the constructor is invoked when you instantiate a class. The value in parentheses, 3, is an argument that is sent to the constructor method, indicating the number of elements you want to create. Note that unlike an array, where you specify the index of the last element, when instantiating an **ArrayList** you specify the actual number of elements.

Lines 4 through 7 create four **String** instances that are populated with the values shown and are referenced by the variables **s1, s2, s3,** and **s4**.

Lines 9 and 10 invoke the **Add** method for the **ArrayList** instance, passing the reference variables **s1** and **s2**, respectively. This method populated the first available element with the argument passed it. Following the execution of lines 9 and 10, the first two elements of **anArrayList** reference **String** instances containing "Hello" and "World."

Note that you can create the **String** instance and populate an **ArrayList** element using a single statement. The following statement creates the **String** instance and passes its reference to the **Add** method, which stores the reference in the next available element of the **ArrayList**. This approach eliminates the need for the additional **String** reference variable.

```
anArrayList.Add("Hello")
```

The `Capacity` property contains the number of elements in an `ArrayList`, and the `Count` property contains the number of *populated* elements. Line 11 displays the `Capacity` property which, in this example, contains 3. Line 12 displays the `Count` property containing 2 in this example.

The `Item` method returns the contents of the element at a specified index. Lines 15 through 17 create a `For Next` loop that iterates the `ArrayList` to retrieve and display the contents.

Line 15 begins the loop which will terminate when the counter (`i`) contains a value equal to the `Count` property minus 1.

Line 16 invokes the `Item` method passing the loop counter which serves as an index.

The following example shows how to add elements to an `ArrayList` instance that has three elements.

7

Example 7-12: Adding elements to an ArrayList instance

```
1. ' create an ArrayList instance with 3 elements
2. Dim anArrayList As ArrayList = New ArrayList(3)


3. ' populate the first two elements
4. anArrayList.Add("Hello")
5. anArrayList.Add("World")
6. Console.WriteLine("number of elements = " &
   anArrayList.Capacity)
7. Console.WriteLine("populated elements = " &
   anArrayList.Count)


8. ' populate two more elements
9. anArrayList.Add("Wide")
10. anArrayList.Add("Web")
11. Console.WriteLine("number of elements = " &
    anArrayList.Capacity)
12. Console.WriteLine(anArrayList.Count & " are populated")
```

```
13. ' iterate and display

14. Dim i As Integer

15. For i = 0 To anArrayList.Count - 1

16.     Console.WriteLine(anArrayList.Item(i))

17. Next
```

Sample Run:

```
number of elements = 3
populated elements = 2
number of elements = 6
4 are populated
Hello
World
Wide
Web
```

Discussion:

This example is similar to Example 7-11. It first creates an **ArrayList** with three elements and populates the first two. In this example, however, separate **String** instances are not created.

After populating the first two elements, lines 9 and 10 invoke the **Add** method to populate two more elements. However, note that the **ArrayList** instance has only three elements. Line 9 populates the third element with a reference to the **String** containing "Wide."

When line 10 invokes the **Add** method again, the **Capacity** and **Count** properties both equal 3. When this happens, the **ArrayList** automatically doubles the number of elements. In this example, when the **Add** method at line 10 is invoked, three more elements are added to the **ArrayList** instance, and the fourth element is populated with a reference to a **String** instance containing "Web."

Line 11 displays the new **Capacity** property (6) and line 12 displays the **Count** (4).

Lines 15 through 17 again iterate and display the contents of all four **String** instances referenced by the **ArrayList** elements.

The next example illustrates three of the **ArrayList** methods: **Contains**, **IndexOf**, and **Reverse**.

Example 7-13: Invoking ArrayList methods

```
1. Dim anArrayList As ArrayList = New ArrayList(4)
2. Dim s1 As String = "Hello"
3. Dim s2 As String = "World"
4. Dim s3 As String = "Wide"
5. Dim s4 As String = "Web"

6. anArrayList.Add(s1)
7. anArrayList.Add(s2)
8. anArrayList.Add(s3)
9. anArrayList.Add(s4)

10. ' search for "Hello"
11. If anArrayList.Contains(s1) Then
12.    Console.WriteLine("anArrayList Contains Hello")
13. End If

14. ' get the index of "Wide"
15. Console.WriteLine("the index of Wide = " &
    anArrayList.IndexOf(s3))

16. ' reverse the elements, then display the contents
17. anArrayList.Reverse()
18. Dim i As Integer
19. For i = 0 To anArrayList.Count - 1
20.    Console.WriteLine(anArrayList.Item(i))
21. Next
```

7

Sample Run:

```
anArrayList Contains Hello
the index of Wide = 2
Web
Wide
World
Hello
```

Discussion:

Line 1 creates a four-element `ArrayList` referenced by `anArrayList`.

Lines 2 through 5 create four `String` instances, and lines 6 through 9 populate the `ArrayList` instance with references to these `String` instances.

`ArrayList` has a built-in search method, `Contains`. This method iterates the `ArrayList` instance, searching for an element that references the object instance specified. Line 11 invokes the `Contains` method, passing `s1` as an argument. This method returns `True` if the `ArrayList` contains a reference to the argument; otherwise, it returns `False`. In this example, the `ArrayList` does contain the reference and `True` is returned.

Line 15 invokes the `IndexOf` method, passing `s3`. Because the third element contains a reference to `s3`, the method returns its index, 2.

Line 17 invokes the `Reverse` method for the `ArrayList` instance. This method is similar to the `Array Reverse` method. It rearranges the contents of the elements in reverse sequence.

Lines 19 through 21 iterate the `ArrayList` and display the contents, which are now in reverse sequence.

PROGRAMMING EXAMPLE: EMPLOYEE PAYROLL

This programming example demonstrates a program that computes the federal tax withholding amount for employees.

Input   Taxable wages and marital status

Output   Amount of federal tax to be withheld

Problem Analysis and Algorithm Design

The purpose of this program is to input an employee's taxable wages and marital status, then compute and display the amount of federal tax to be withheld formatted as currency.

Variables   The computation of federal tax withholding involves the use of two tax tables, one for single employees (see Table 7-3) and one for married employees (see Table 7-4). These tables can be stored in two-dimensional arrays.

Table 7-3 Single employee federal tax withholding table

Wages Over	But Not Over	Base Tax Amount	Plus %	Of Excess Over
0	51	0	0	
51	187	0	10	51
187	592	13.60	15	187
592	1317	74.35	25	592
1317	2860	255.60	28	1317
2860	6177	687.64	33	2860
6177		1782.25	35	6177

Table 7-4 Married employee federal tax withholding table

Wages Over	But Not Over	Base Tax Amount	Plus %	Of Excess Over
0	154	0	0	
154	429	0	10	154
429	1245	27.50	15	429
1245	2270	149.90	25	1245
2270	3568	406.15	28	2270
3568	6271	769.59	33	3568
6271		1661.58	35	6271

In addition to the arrays, you will need the following variables:

`singleTaxTable(,) As Double` references the single employee tax table

`marriedTaxTable(,) As Double` references the married employee tax table

`taxTable(,) As Double` contains a reference to either the single or married employee tax table

`marriedOrSingle As Char` contains M or S to indicate if employee is married or single

`rowIndex As Integer` row index for tax table

`wages As Double` contains the employee's wages

`fedWithholding As Double` contains the computed tax to be withheld

`found As Boolean` contains `True` if the wages amount has been found in the table; otherwise, `False`

Declaring a variable in the form `singleTaxTable(,)` creates a reference variable for a two-dimensional array.

Formulas   When the appropriate row in the tax table is located, the program computes the federal tax withholding = column 4 * (wages - column 5) + column 3.

 The index of the columns is one less than the column number.

Main Algorithm

1. Declare and populate the tax tables.
2. Declare the variables.
3. Start a `Do Until` pre-test loop to input each employee's wages and marital status:
   a. Use a sentinel value of 99999 for wages to terminate the loop.
   b. Display a prompt to input wages.
   c. Input wages and convert to `Double`.
4. Within the `Do Until` loop body:
   a. Display a prompt to input marital status.
   b. Input M for married or S for single and convert to `Char`.
   c. Assign `taxTable` reference to either married or single tax table.
   d. Initialize `rowIndex` to 0 and `found` to `False`.
5. Use a `Do While` loop to find the appropriate row in `taxTable` for wages. Within the loop body:
   a. If wages are less than or equal to the amount in column 1, then compute tax withholding amount and terminate the loop.
   b. If wages are greater than column 1, increment `index`, and loop again.
6. When the loop terminates, display the withholding amount formatted as currency.

Complete Program Listing

```
Option Explicit On

Option Strict On

Imports System.Collections.ArrayList


Module EmployeePayroll

    Sub Main()
```

```vbnet
' single employee table

Dim singleTaxTable(,) As Double = {{51, 0, 0, 0}, _

                                   {187, 0, 0.1, 51}, _

                                   {592, 13.6, 0.15, 187}, _

                                   {1317, 74.35, 0.25, 592}, _

                                   {2860, 255.6, 0.28, 1317}, _

                                   {6177, 687.64, 0.33, 2860}, _

                                   {99999, 1782.25, 0.35, 6177}}

' married employee table

Dim marriedTaxTable(,) As Double = {{154, 0, 0, 0}, _

                                    {429, 0, 0.1, 154}, _

                                    {1245, 27.5, 0.15, 429}, _

                                    {2270, 149.9, 0.25, 1245}, _

                                    {3568, 406.15, 0.28, 2270}, _

                                    {6271, 769.59, 0.33, 3568}, _

                                    {99999, 1661.58, 0.35, 6271}}


Dim taxTable(,) As Double

Dim marriedOrSingle As Char

Dim rowIndex As Integer

Dim wages, fedWithholding As Double

Dim found As Boolean


' use 99999 as sentinel value to terminate

Console.Write("Enter wage amount (99999 to stop): ")

wages = Convert.ToDouble(Console.ReadLine())

' begin the loop for each employee

Do Until wages = 99999

    Console.Write("Enter M for married, S for single: ")
```

7

```
            marriedOrSingle = Convert.ToChar(Console.ReadLine())

            ' assign taxTable reference to appropriate table
            If marriedOrSingle = "M" Then

                taxTable = marriedTaxTable
            Else

                taxTable = singleTaxTable
            End If


            rowIndex = 0

            found = False
            ' loop to find the appropriate row for the wages
            Do While rowIndex < 6 And found = False

                If wages <= taxTable(rowIndex, 0) Then

                    ' compute the withholding amount
                    fedWithholding = taxTable(rowIndex, 1) +
                    taxTable(rowIndex, 2) * _

                        (wages - taxTable(rowIndex, 3))

                    found = True ' stop the loop
                Else

                    rowIndex += 1
                End If
            Loop
        Console.WriteLine("Federal Withholding = " &
    fedWithholding.ToString("C"))

                ' input wage amount for next employee
                Console.Write("Enter wage amount (99999 to stop):")

                wages = Convert.ToDouble(Console.ReadLine())

            Loop

        End Sub


    End Module
```

Sample Run

In the following sample run, the user input is shaded.

```
Enter wage amount (99999 to stop):
500
Enter M for married, S for single:
M
Federal Withholding = $38.15
Enter wage amount (99999 to stop):
600
Enter M for married, S for single:
S
Federal Withholding = $76.35
Enter wage amount (99999 to stop):
99999
```

7

QUICK REVIEW

1. In Visual Basic .NET (VB .NET), arrays are instances of the **Array** class.

2. To declare an array, you write the keyword **Dim** followed by the name of the reference variable you want to use. Next you write the index of the last element of the array in parentheses. VB .NET numbers the array elements beginning with 0. This means the index of the first element is 0, the second element is 1, and so forth.

3. Arrays consist of elements with each element behaving as a variable does. All of an array's elements must have the same data type. Array elements, like variables, can contain either primitive data or can be reference variables. You access the individual elements in an array using an index.

4. Arrays can be either one-dimensional or multi-dimensional. A one-dimensional array consists of elements arranged in a single row. Conceptually, a two-dimensional array has both rows and columns, and a three-dimensional array is like a cube, with rows, columns, and pages.

5. You access the individual elements of a one-dimensional array by writing the array reference variable followed by the index value of the element enclosed in parentheses.

6. You access the elements of a two-dimensional array by writing the array reference variable name followed by the row index, a comma, and the column index enclosed in parentheses.

7. VB .NET supports multi-dimensional arrays. Each dimension is has its own index.

8. You declare a two-dimensional array similar to the way you declare a one-dimensional array, but you specify both the number of rows and columns.

9. VB .NET implements multi-dimensional arrays by creating an array of arrays. Because each row of a two-dimensional array is actually a separate array object, each row does not have to be the same length.

10. One disadvantage of arrays is they are static; after you create one, you cannot change the number of elements. You must use the **ReDim** statement to make a copy of the array with additional elements.

11. You use the **ArrayList** class, a member of the **System.Collections** namespace, to create an array that is dynamically resizable. This means that you can change the number of elements of an **ArrayList** while your code is executing.

12. A constructor is a special method automatically invoked when you instantiate a class.

13. The **Capacity** property contains the number of elements in an **ArrayList** and the **Count** property contains the number of *populated* elements.

EXERCISES

1. Each element in a **String** array is _____.

   a. a primitive variable

   b. null

   c. a reference variable

   d. It depends on the data type you specify.

2. To obtain the number of elements in a **String** array named **sArray**, you would write _____.

   a. sArray.Length

   b. sArray.LengthOf

   c. String.Length

   d. StringArray.Length

3. The elements of an **ArrayList** _____.

   a. begin with an index value of 0

   b. can contain only primitive values

   c. begin with an index value of 1

   d. must be data type array

4. The **ArrayList** method that returns the number of elements is _____.

   a. Size

   b. numberOfElements

   c. Capacity

   d. There is no such method.

5. It appears that you could always use an **ArrayList** instead of an array. Why should you ever use an array?

6. The **String Split** method _____.

    a. requires a delimiter

    b. returns an array of **String** instances

    c. both a and b

    d. None of the above.

7. Arrays are static, which means that _____.

    a. Once populated, you cannot change their contents.

    b. Once created, you cannot change the number of elements.

    c. You can change the number of elements only by invoking a method.

    d. All of the above.

    e. None of the above.

8. **ArrayLists** are like **Arrays** except that _____.

    a. **ArrayLists** have methods but no properties.

    b. You can add elements to **ArrayLists**.

    c. You can change the number of elements only by invoking a method.

    d. All of the above.

    e. None of the above.

9. Which of the following is true about arrays?

    a. Arrays must have a data type which is the same for all elements.

    b. Once created, you can change the data type of individual elements.

    c. You can change the data type of elements only by invoking a method.

    d. All of the above.

    e. None of the above.

10. Multi-dimensional arrays in VB .NET _____.

    a. are not limited to three dimensions

    b. can have unequal row lengths

    c. are implemented as arrays of arrays

    d. All of the above.

    e. None of the above.

7

PROGRAMMING EXERCISES

1. The following table contains quarterly sales figures for five departments.

	Quarter 1	Quarter 2	Quarter 3	Quarter 4	Total
Department 1	750	660	910	800	
Department 2	800	700	950	900	
Department 3	700	600	750	600	
Department 4	850	800	1000	950	
Department 5	900	800	960	980	
Total					

Design and write a module named SalesAnalysis that will:

a. Declare a two-dimensional integer array named `sales`.

b. Populate the first four columns using the data in the preceding table.

c. Contain a loop to compute and populate the total column. Within the loop, display each department total as it is computed.

d. Contain a loop to compute and populate the total row. Within the loop, display each quarter's total as it is computed.

2. Continue working with Programming Exercise 1 by writing a nested loop that will compute and display:

a. The percentage of total sales made by each department for each quarter.

b. The percentage of total sales made each quarter.

3. Create a four-row, three-column **String** array containing the data in the following table. Then write code to display the contents of each row with appropriate labels.

Airline Departure Information

Flight	Gate	Destination
AA 7401	C33	St. Louis
AA 431	D8	Dallas
Delta 94	A12	Atlanta
United 155	B4	Chicago

4. Continuing with Programming Exercise 3, design and code a module that will input a flight, and then search the table to display the Gate and Destination for that flight.

Writing Graphical User Interfaces

In this chapter, you will:

○ Learn about the GUI classes in VB .NET

○ Understand the code generated by the Windows Form Designer

○ Explore GUI design principles

○ Review forms, buttons, and labels

○ Handle events

○ Work with additional GUI controls

In Chapters 3 through 7, you learned fundamental Visual Basic .NET (VB .NET) programming concepts. You developed console applications that rely on the methods `WriteLine` and `ReadLine` in the `Console` class to input and display data. In Chapter 6, you saw how to use a `MessageBox` to display a message and how to read data from and write data to sequential files. In this chapter, you learn how to create graphical user interfaces (GUIs) to input and display data. You provide a GUI so that users can enter program inputs and view program outputs in a visually appealing and intuitive manner.

This chapter introduces the fundamental components and techniques you use to build a GUI. Although you can create a GUI programmatically by writing code from scratch, it is much easier to create a GUI by using the drag-and-drop features of the Windows Form Designer.

Chapter 2 introduced the visual programming techniques you use to develop GUI applications in VB .NET. In Chapter 2 you learned how to create a Windows application using the Toolbox to select GUI components and position them on a form. You also learned how to control the appearance of a form and its components by setting the values of various properties in the Properties window. Recall that as you visually arrange components on the form and set their properties in the Properties window, Visual Studio .NET generates the underlying code associated with your design. You complete the user interface by specifying the way your program is to behave when the user takes certain actions—such as clicking a button or pressing a key on the keyboard. Such actions are referred to as **user-generated events**.

After completing this chapter, you will be able to create GUI applications using a variety of controls, including buttons, labels, text boxes, radio buttons, list boxes, and several others. You will understand much of the code generated by VB .NET during the visual programming process and know how to write methods that respond to user-generated events.

INTRODUCING THE GUI CLASSES IN VB .NET

Figure 8-1 shows a window containing many different GUI components (sometimes referred to as controls). As you learned in Chapter 2, the window is called a form, and is an instance of the `Form` class. The `Form` class, like all other GUI classes, is a member of the `System.Windows.Forms` namespace. The form shown in Figure 8-1 contains several GUI components, including buttons, labels, text boxes, check boxes, radio buttons, and list boxes. Table 8-1 describes these and other GUI components introduced in this chapter. There are many other GUI components, some of which you learn about in Chapter 13. Figure 8-2 shows some GUI components that are available in the Toolbox window.

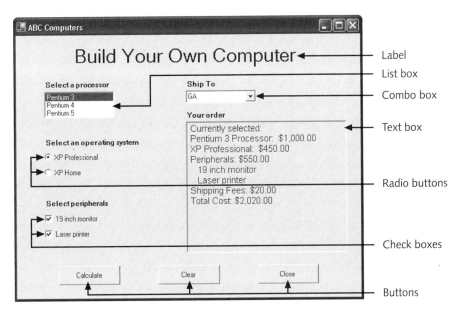

Figure 8-1   A form with GUI components

Table 8-1 Commonly used GUI components

GUI Component	Description
Button	A control that the user clicks to perform an action.
CheckBox	A two-state control that enables yes/no (true/false) options.
CheckedListBox	Enables selection of one or more predefined items from a list that includes check boxes. When an item is selected, it appears checked.
ComboBox	Enables selection of one or more predefined items from a list, or entry of a new value.
Control	The superclass of all visible GUI controls.
Form	A GUI window with a title bar. Forms usually contain other GUI components.
Label	Used to display text (but not to input text).
ListBox	Enables selection of one or more predefined items from a list.
RadioButton	A two-state control that enables yes/no (true/false) options while enforcing mutually exclusive behavior (that is, only one radio button in a radio button group may be selected at a time).
TextBox	Used to display and input text.

8

Figure 8-2 Components available in the Toolbox window

All of the GUI classes in the `System.Windows.Forms` namespace take advantage of inheritance. Recall from Chapter 1 that inheritance means a class of objects takes on, or inherits, characteristics of another class and extends them. You learn much more about inheritance in Chapter 11. For now, recognize that most of the GUI classes you use on a form are subclasses of the `Control` class and, therefore, inherit important properties and methods from `Control`. These inherited properties and methods provide basic functionality for the visible controls you use on a form. As you explore the code generated by VB .NET in this chapter and in Chapter 13, you learn about many of these properties and methods. After you become familiar with the basic concepts and techniques, you can explore the documentation within the VB .NET Help facility to learn more about other GUI classes and their associated properties and methods.

UNDERSTANDING THE CODE GENERATED BY THE WINDOWS FORM DESIGNER

When you create GUI applications in VB .NET, you use the drag-and-drop features of the Windows Form Designer as part of a visual programming process. **Visual programming** generally consists of creating a form, setting its properties, adding components to the form, setting their properties, and then adding the code necessary to handle the events users generate when they interact with your form.

As you add components and modify properties, VB .NET generates the code that handles the details of your form design. The code VB .NET generates for a GUI is called a **class definition**. The class definition specifies the attributes and methods that make the form work.

Exploring the FormDemo Program

The first example of a GUI class definition is the FormDemo program you created in Chapter 2. Recall that the form contains a label (`lblWelcome`) and a button (`btnPushMe`). When you press the button, a message box appears, as shown in Figure 8-3. The code generated by VB .NET for this application and the code you added to make the button work are shown in Figure 8-4.

8

Figure 8-3   Output of FormDemo program

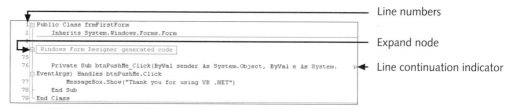

Figure 8-4   Code for FormDemo program

As shown in Figure 8-4, the class definition begins with a **class header** and ends with an **End Class** statement. The keyword **Class** identifies the first line of code as the class header, and **frmFirstForm** specifies the name of the class. The keyword **Public** means that the class can be used by anyone. The second line uses the **Inherits** keyword to indicate that this class inherits from (or is a subclass of) the **Form** class. This is important because it means that through inheritance the **frmFirstForm** class can use the properties and methods supplied in the **Form** class. Notice in Figure 8-4 that the code generated by VB .NET uses fully qualified class names—such as **System.Windows.Forms.Form**—rather than including a statement to import the **System.Windows.Forms** namespace and then using the simple version of the class name in the **Inherits** clause (for example, **Inherits Form**).

When you are working in the Integrated Development Environment (IDE), most of the remaining code generated by VB .NET is collapsed under the heading "Windows Form Designer generated code." You can view this code by clicking the expand node. The code that is revealed is shown in Figure 8-5.

```
1. Public Class frmFirstForm
2.     Inherits System.Windows.Forms.Form
3.
4. #Region " Windows Form Designer generated code "
5.
6.     Public Sub New()
7.         MyBase.New()
8.
9.         'This call is required by the Windows Form Designer.
10.        InitializeComponent()
11.
12.        'Add any initialization after the InitializeComponent() call
13.
14.    End Sub
15.
16.    'Form overrides dispose to clean up the component list.
17.    Protected Overloads Overrides Sub Dispose(ByVal disposing As
       Boolean)
18.        If disposing Then
19.            If Not (components Is Nothing) Then
20.                components.Dispose()
```

Figure 8-5   Code revealed by clicking the expand node

```
21.              End If
22.          End If
23.          MyBase.Dispose(disposing)
24.      End Sub
25.
26.      'Required by the Windows Form Designer
27.      Private components As System.ComponentModel.IContainer
28.
29.      'NOTE: The following procedure is required by the Windows Form
         Designer
30.      'It can be modified using the Windows Form Designer.
31.      'Do not modify it using the code editor.
32.      Friend WithEvents lblWelcome As System.Windows.Forms.Label
33.      Friend WithEvents btnPushMe As System.Windows.Forms.Button
34.      <System.Diagnostics.DebuggerStepThrough()> Private Sub
         InitializeComponent()
35.          Me.lblWelcome = New System.Windows.Forms.Label
36.          Me.btnPushMe = New System.Windows.Forms.Button
37.          Me.SuspendLayout()
38.          '
39.          'lblWelcome
40.          '
41.          Me.lblWelcome.Font = New System.Drawing.Font("Times New
             Roman",18.0!, System.Drawing.FontStyle.Regular,
             System.Drawing.GraphicsUnit.Point, CType(0, Byte))
42.          Me.lblWelcome.ForeColor = System.Drawing.Color.Red
43.          Me.lblWelcome.Location = New System.Drawing.Point(68, 16)
44.          Me.lblWelcome.Name = "lblWelcome"
45.          Me.lblWelcome.Size = New System.Drawing.Size(256, 48)
46.          Me.lblWelcome.TabIndex = 0
47.          Me.lblWelcome.Text = "Welcome to VB .NET"
48.          Me.lblWelcome.TextAlign =
             System.Drawing.ContentAlignment.MiddleCenter
49.          '
50.          'btnPushMe
51.          '
52.          Me.btnPushMe.BackColor = System.Drawing.Color.Yellow
53.          Me.btnPushMe.Font = New System.Drawing.Font("Arial", 9.75!,
             System.Drawing.FontStyle.Regular,
             System.Drawing.GraphicsUnit.Point, CType(0, Byte))
54.          Me.btnPushMe.Location = New System.Drawing.Point(152, 80)
55.          Me.btnPushMe.Name = "btnPushMe"
56.          Me.btnPushMe.Size = New System.Drawing.Size(88, 32)
57.          Me.btnPushMe.TabIndex = 1
58.          Me.btnPushMe.Text = "Push Me"
59.          '
60.          'frmFirstForm
61.          '
62.          Me.AutoScaleBaseSize = New System.Drawing.Size(5, 13)
63.          Me.BackColor = System.Drawing.Color.White
64.          Me.ClientSize = New System.Drawing.Size(392, 358)
65.          Me.Controls.Add(Me.btnPushMe)
66.          Me.Controls.Add(Me.lblWelcome)
```

8

Figure 8-5   Code revealed by clicking the expand node (continued)

```
67.          Me.Name = "frmFirstForm"
68.          Me.StartPosition =
             System.Windows.Forms.FormStartPosition.CenterScreen
69.          Me.Text = "My First Form"
70.          Me.ResumeLayout(False)
71.
72.      End Sub
73.
74.#End Region
75.
76.      Private Sub btnPushMe_Click(ByVal sender As System.Object, ByVal
         e As System.EventArgs) Handles btnPushMe.Click
77.          MessageBox.Show("Thank you for using VB .NET")
78.      End Sub
79.End Class
```

Figure 8-5   Code revealed by clicking the expand node (continued)

Recall that to see line numbers in the IDE, you select Options on the Tools menu to open the Options dialog box. Open the Text Editor folder, and then open the Basic subfolder. Under Display, check the Line numbers check box. Check Word wrap under Settings to enable the word wrap feature, which allows you to see long lines of code in their entirety by wrapping them to subsequent lines.

As you see in Figure 8-5, the generated code is complex. Normally, you are not concerned with the code generated by VB .NET and can leave the code in its collapsed format. However, you should be able to read and understand key aspects of this code. In the following discussion and in others throughout the chapter, line numbers are added for reference only, and do not appear in the actual program.

The expanded code begins on line 4 with the **#Region** directive and ends on line 74 with the **#End Region** directive. These directives specify that the code contained within them, by default, collapses into a single line in the Code Editor window. Collapsing this code hides the details associated with the GUI and allows you to concentrate on other portions of the program.

The first block of code (lines 6–14) defines the **constructor** of the **frmFirstForm** class. The Windows Form Designer provides a default constructor for each form you create. A constructor is a special method that is automatically invoked when an instance of a class is created. Like a class definition, a method definition begins with a method header. The keyword **Sub** on line 6 identifies this statement as the method header, and **End Sub** (line 14) identifies the end of the method. The method name **New** identifies the method as a constructor. You learn more about methods and constructors in Chapters 9 and 10. For now, recognize that the constructor performs two initialization functions. First, it calls the base class (or superclass) constructor. **MyBase** is a keyword that refers to the superclass of the current object. In this example, the current object is **frmFirstForm** and its superclass is **Form**. The statement **MyBase.New( )** calls the superclass constructor to create a new **Form** instance. The constructor then invokes the **InitializeComponent** method (defined in lines 34–72) to initialize property settings for all of the components within the form. As indicated by the comment on line 12, there are times when you may need to add code to the constructor method to specify further initialization steps. You will learn why this is sometimes necessary in Chapter 13.

The second block of code (lines 16–24) defines the `Dispose` method. The `Dispose` method is a **destructor**—which means it releases system resources when the program ends. Every form you create inherits a default version of the `Dispose` method. For now, you need not be concerned with the details of this method, but you should be aware of its purpose.

Line 27 uses the `IContainer` class to create a **container.** A container is an object that holds other components. A form is one kind of container. You learn about other containers in Chapter 13.

Lines 32 and 33 declare the controls you created visually in the Design window—`lblWelcome` and `btnPushMe`. Note once more the use of fully qualified class names (for example, `System.Windows.Forms.Label` rather than simply `Label`). The code generator declares `lblWelcome` and `btnPushMe` using the `Friend` and `WithEvents` keywords. The `Friend` keyword specifies that an object is accessible only within the files that compose the application. The `WithEvents` keyword signifies that a control instance may be the source of events and that such events will be handled by methods that include a `Handles controlName.eventName` clause in the method header. For example, in this program the control that may trigger an event is `btnPushMe`, and the event of interest is `Click`. Declaring `btnPushMe` with the `WithEvents` keyword means that clicking `btnPushMe` invokes the event-handling method that includes the clause `Handles btnPushMe.Click` in the method header. Methods that handle events are called **event handlers.** You learn more about methods and method headers in Chapter 9.

The remainder of the generated code (lines 34–72) defines the `InitializeComponent` method. The code contained within angle brackets on line 34 instructs the debugger not to stop at this method when the program executes in debug mode. The `Private` keyword indicates that this method is accessible only within this class. Lines 35 and 36 use the keyword `New` to create the label and button instances. The keyword `Me` refers to the current object, which in this case is `frmFirstForm`. Line 37 invokes the `SuspendLayout` method to suspend layout events while you manipulate the properties (such as size and location) of various controls.

Lines 41 through 48 set the properties of the `lblWelcome` instance in accordance with the values you specified through the Properties window. These statements establish the label's font, foreground color, location, name, size, tab index, text, and alignment. The tab index specifies the order in which the user moves from one control to the next by pressing the Tab key. The tab index starts with 0; thus a tab index of 0 indicates that this is first control in the tab order.

 By default, the tab order is identical to the order in which you create controls in the Windows Form Designer. You can change the tab order of a control by setting its TabIndex property in the Properties window. Alternately, you can select Tab Order from the View menu, and then click the controls in the desired order.

Similar statements on lines 52 through 69 establish the properties of the button and form instances. Each statement corresponds to an action you completed visually using the Toolbox and the Properties window. Line 70 invokes the `ResumeLayout` method to apply the pending layout events that were suspended earlier by the `SuspendLayout` method. In line 74, the `#End Region` directive identifies the end of the code block generated by the Windows Form Designer.

The last few lines of the program (lines 76-78) define the actions to take when the user clicks `btnPushMe` (the "Push Me" button). Stated another way, this block of code defines the event handler for a click event triggered by `btnPushMe`. The code generator uses the convention *controlName_eventName* (that is, `btnPushMe_Click`) to name the method. The code within parentheses specifies the method's **parameter list**. A parameter list identifies variables that receive values when a method is invoked. You learn about invoking methods in Chapter 10. Finally, notice that (as predicted) the method header (line 76) includes the clause `Handles btnPushMe.Click`.

In Chapter 2, you added the code at line 77 to specify the action to take in response to the button click. In this case, the event handler responds to a click event by displaying a message box that includes the statement "Thank you for using VB .NET."

Each time you visually create a form, the Windows Form Designer generates code of this type. The complexity of the code and the ease with which you can create sophisticated GUIs illustrates the power of the Designer. Although you usually do not modify the generated code that is collapsed under the expand node, as you will soon see, it is common to modify the code before and after the expand node. Examples in this and subsequent chapters do not include the code collapsed under the expand node but denote the existence of this code by the comment "Windows Form Designer generated code".

EXPLORING GUI DESIGN PRINCIPLES

As you work with GUI forms and components, you make many decisions about the GUI's appearance and functionality. There are many standards that guide the creative process of user interface design. Some of the basic principles include creating a consistent look and feel, ensuring ease of use, minimizing data entry errors, providing feedback to users, and adhering to standard naming conventions.

Creating a Consistent Look and Feel

The style and appearance of a form is called its **look and feel**. Many applications consist of multiple forms. For example, a payroll application might include a form for entering information about an employee, another for information about the employee's dependents, another for information about payroll deductions for insurance and retirement benefits, and yet another for entering hours worked in a given pay period. A key design goal is to provide a consistent look and feel as a user moves among various forms. For example, the size and location of buttons that perform common functions (such as navigating among forms and saving your work) should be consistent from one form to the next.

Part of the look and feel of an application is the choice of colors and fonts for various controls. Whether an application consists of a single or multiple forms, limiting the use of colors and fonts improves visual impact. When used sparingly, colors and fonts impart emphasis, but an overabundance of either distracts the user. When an application consists of multiple forms, colors and fonts should be consistent across forms. In addition, you should choose colors carefully, as certain colors or combinations of colors are not only distracting but can create difficulties for users who are color blind.

Ensuring Ease of Use and Minimizing Data-Entry Errors

Another design goal is ease of use. To the extent possible, the purpose of each control and the layout of the form should be intuitive to the user. Prompts should clearly identify the data to be entered by the user and the actions that will be taken when the user interacts with a control (such as pressing a button). The placement and grouping of controls should be logical, and the form should appear uncluttered. When placing controls on a form, strive to achieve a balanced layout, group related items, and make good use of white space.

In addition, it is good practice to design input forms in a way that minimizes the keystrokes required of the user. This can be accomplished by providing default values and using controls such as radio buttons and list boxes that allow users to make a selection rather than requiring them to type a value. Minimizing keystrokes reduces the chance of data entry errors and improves the user-friendliness of your form.

Providing Feedback to the User

Provide feedback to the user when certain actions (such as adding a record to a file) have been completed, and to inform the user when data entry errors have occurred. Such feedback should be presented to the user in a consistent manner, and with consistent verbiage, tone, and visual elements.

Naming Conventions

Another standard followed by professional programmers concerns the naming conventions for program variables. Although end users are not aware of the variable names within a program, adhering to a set of naming conventions improves program readability and facilitates program maintenance.

VB .NET includes many GUI controls and components. Recall from Chapter 2 that by default the code generator assigns variable names such as Button1, Button2, Label1, and Label2 to the controls you create in the Form Designer window. It is good programming practice to assign more meaningful variable names to these instances.

To assign a new variable to a control, you change the (Name) property for that control in the Properties window. The variable name should reflect both the type of control (button, label, etc.) and its purpose. For example, the FormDemo program names the "Push Me" button as btnPushMe and the "Welcome to VB .NET" label as lblWelcome. The "btn" and "lbl" prefixes are naming conventions that help you identify objects as buttons and labels, respectively. Naming conventions are used throughout this book to identify types of GUI controls. Table 8-2 shows the prefix naming conventions for the controls used in this chapter.

Table 8-2 Naming conventions for GUI controls

Component	Prefix
Button	btn
CheckBox	chk
CheckedListBox	chklst
ComboBox	cmb
Form	frm
Label	lbl
ListBox	lst
RadioButton	rad
TextBox	txt

Achieving these design goals requires forethought and planning. Programming teams often develop a set of standards for form design at the outset of a project. Those standards are then enforced rigorously throughout the software development process.

REVIEWING FORMS, BUTTONS, AND LABELS

The FormDemo program of Chapter 2 introduced you to some common methods and properties of the **Button**, **Form**, and **Label** classes. Recall that all GUI components with a visual representation are subclasses of the **Control** class and, therefore, inherit properties, methods, and events from **Control**. Because the **Control** class is a subclass of the **Component** class, controls such as forms, buttons, and labels also inherit properties and methods from the **Component** class. Selected properties and methods of the **Control** class (some of which are inherited from the **Component** class) are summarized in Table 8-3. Typically, you set many of these properties in the Properties window as you design the form. However, you can also manipulate them through the code you write in the event handlers. The **Control** and **Component** classes contain many other properties, methods, and events. You can learn about other members of the **Control** and **Component** classes by using the Help facility.

Table 8-3 Selected properties and methods of the Control class

Properties of the Control Class	Description
BackColor	Indicates the background color of the control.
ClientSize	Indicates the size of the client area of the control.
Controls	Identifies the collection of controls contained within the control. (The Add and Remove methods of the Control.ControlCollection class add individual controls to the collection. The AddRange and Clear methods of the Control.ControlCollection class add or remove all controls in the collection.)
Enabled	Indicates whether the user can interact with the control.
Focused	Indicates whether the control has the input focus.
Font	Indicates the font associated with the control.
ForeColor	Indicates the foreground color of the control.
Location	Indicates the coordinates of the upper-left corner of the control, relative to the upper-left corner of its container.
Name	Identifies the name assigned to the control.
Size	Indicates the size (height and width) of the control.
TabIndex	Identifies the tab order of the control within its container.
Text	Identifies the text associated with the control.
Visible	Indicates whether the control will be visible or hidden from the user.
Methods of the Control Class	
Dispose	Releases the resources used by the control.
Focus	Sets the input focus to the control.
Hide	Hides the control from the user.
ResumeLayout	Applies pending layout events previously suspended by the SuspendLayout method.
Show	Displays the control to the user.
SuspendLayout	Temporarily suspends layout events while properties of various controls are manipulated.
Common Events	
Click	Occurs when the control is clicked.
MouseEnter	Occurs when the mouse pointer enters the control.
MouseHover	Occurs when the mouse pointer hovers over the control.

8

Tables 8-4, 8-5, and 8-6 summarize selected properties, methods, and common events of the Form, Button, and Label classes.

Table 8-4 Selected properties and methods of the Form class

Properties of the Form Class	Description
	Inherits properties, methods, and events of the Control class
AcceptButton	Identifies the button that is clicked when the user presses the Enter key.
AutoScale	Identifies a value indicating whether the form adjusts its size to fit the height of the font used on the form and scales its controls.
AutoScaleBaseSize	Indicates the base size used for autoscaling the form.
CancelButton	Identifies the button that is clicked when the user presses the Esc key.
Menu	Associates a MainMenu instance with the form.
StartPosition	Indicates the starting position of the form when it executes.
Text	Identifies the text that appears in the form's title bar.
Methods of the Form Class	
Close	Closes the form and disposes all associated resources.
Common Events	
Load	Occurs before a form is displayed. You can use this event to perform various initialization activities.

Table 8-5 Selected properties, methods, and events of the Button class

Properties of the Button Class	Description
	Inherits properties, methods, and events from the Control class
Text	Text that appears on the button's label
TextAlign	Sets the alignment of the button's text
Common Events	
Click	Occurs when the user clicks the button
PerformClick	Generates a click event for the button

Table 8-6 Selected properties, methods, and events of the Label class

Properties of the Label Class	Description
	Inherits properties, methods, and events from the Control class
Text	Sets the text that appears on the label
TextAlign	Sets the alignment of the label
Common Events	
Click	Occurs when the user clicks the label

HANDLING EVENTS

When you develop forms with GUI controls, you supply the details of the event handling procedures associated with those controls. To create an event handling procedure for a control, you double-click that control in the Forms Designer window. VB .NET then places the method header for the *most commonly used* event procedure for that control in the Code window, and you add statements that handle the event.

GUI components can be the source of many different events, and at times your programs will need to respond to events other than the most commonly used event for a particular control. For example, you might want the FormDemo program to respond to a MouseEnter event for `lblWelcome` by displaying the message "Mouse entered label control". (Recall from Table 8-3 that a MouseEnter event occurs when the mouse pointer moves into the space occupied by the control.) As shown in Figure 8-6, you can add this event handling method to the FormDemo program by pressing F7 to open the Code window, selecting lblWelcome from the Class Name list box, selecting MouseEnter from the Method Name list box, and then adding a `MessageBox.Show` statement.

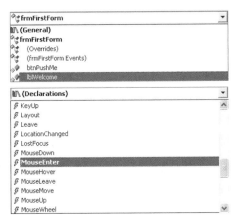

Figure 8-6   Creating an event handling method

Example 8-1: Handling MouseEnter and MouseHover events

The following example illustrates the event handling procedures for MouseEnter and MouseHover events in the Form Demo program. Figure 8-7 shows the result of the MouseEnter event, and Figure 8-8 shows the result of the MouseHover event.

Line numbers in this example and the remaining examples in this chapter are used for reference only. Because the code generated by the Windows Form Designer is omitted in these examples, line numbers used for reference may not correspond to line numbers in the IDE.

Represents code collapsed
under the expand node

```
1.   Public Class frmFirstForm
2.        Inherits System.Windows.Forms.Form
3.   'Windows Form Designer generated code

4.   'Event handler for Click event on Push Me button
5.   Private Sub btnPushMe_Click(ByVal sender As System.Object, ByVal e As
     System.EventArgs) Handles btnPushMe.Click
6.        MessageBox.Show("Thank you for using VB .NET")
7.   End Sub

8.   'Event handler for MouseEnter event on Welcome label
9.   Private Sub lblWelcome_MouseEnter(ByVal sender As Object, ByVal e As
     System.EventArgs) Handles lblWelcome.MouseEnter
10.  MessageBox.Show("Mouse entered the label control")
11.  End Sub

12.  'Event handler for MouseHover event on Push Me button
13.  Private Sub btnPushMe_MouseHover(ByVal sender As Object, ByVal e As
     System.EventArgs) Handles btnPushMe.MouseHover
14.       MessageBox.Show("Mouse hovering over the button control")
15.  End Sub
16.  End Class
```

If you create the event handler by double-clicking a component in the Designer window, the code generator defines the sender parameter as type System.Object (as shown on Line 5). If you create the event handler by selecting the Class Name and Method name from the list boxes in the Code window, the code generator defines sender as type Object (as shown in lines 9 and 13). Because all Windows applications automatically include the System namespace, either System.Object or Object is acceptable.

Sample Run:

Figure 8-7   Result of the MouseEnter event

Figure 8-8   Result of the MouseHover event

8

Discussion:

Line 1 defines the class header and line 2 specifies that the class inherits properties, methods, and events from the Form class. Line 3 denotes the existence of the code generated by the Windows Form Designer and collapsed under the expand node. (Explanations of lines 1 through 3 are not repeated in the remaining examples in this chapter.)

Lines 4 through 7 define the event handler that responds to a click event for the "Push Me" button. As before, the event handler displays a thank-you message.

Lines 8 through 11 define the actions to take when the mouse pointer enters the space occupied by the welcome label. In this case the event handler displays a message indicating that the mouse pointer entered the label control.

Lines 12 through 15 define the event handler that responds when the mouse pointer hovers over the "Push Me" button. This event handler displays a message indicating that the mouse pointer is hovering over the button control.

Line 16 signifies the end of the class.

Note that it is possible (in fact, common) to define multiple events for the same control. In this example, two event handlers respond to different events generated by the user's interaction with the "Push Me" button.

WORKING WITH ADDITIONAL GUI CONTROLS

VB .NET includes a wide variety of GUI controls. In addition to forms, buttons, and labels, some of the most typical controls are text boxes, combo boxes, check boxes, radio buttons, and list boxes. In this section, you learn these and other commonly used VB .NET GUI controls. You explore the primary properties and methods of each control and how it might be used. All of the VB .NET GUI controls have additional methods and properties that you may want to explore. You can use the Help facility to learn about any GUI class.

Using Text Boxes and Combo Boxes

Text boxes are used to display textual information to the user and to enable the inputting of text from the keyboard. When you use a text box to obtain input, the user must type text into the box. A **combo box** extends the functionality of a text box by providing the ability to select an item from a predetermined list of values, in addition to typing a value. Visually, a combo box looks like a text box, but includes a list arrow on its right. When you click the list arrow, a list of values appears and you select an item from that list. In VB .NET, the TextBox and ComboBox classes provide the functionality for these controls.

If you know that the value a user enters into a text box is frequently limited to a set of pre-defined choices, you should consider using a combo box. The user usually selects from the list, but can enter alternate text when needed. Overall, a combo box reduces the number of keystrokes, which improves the user friendliness of your program and makes it less susceptible to data-entry errors.

As with buttons and labels, you include a text box or combo box within a form by selecting the appropriate control from the Toolbox, placing it on a form, and then setting its properties through the Properties window. Tables 8-7 and 8-8 summarize frequently used properties, methods, and events for these controls.

Table 8-7 Selected properties, methods, and events of the TextBox class

Properties of the TextBox Class	Description
	Inherits properties, methods, and events from the Control class
AcceptsReturn	Indicates whether pressing the Enter key creates a new line of text (in a multiline text box) or activates the default button for the form
AcceptsTab	Indicates whether pressing the Tab key types a tab character (in a multiline text box) or moves the input focus to the next control in the tab order
BorderStyle	Indicates the border style for the text box
MaxLength	Indicates the maximum number of characters the text box can hold
Multiline	Indicates whether the text box can contain a single line of text (the default) or multiple lines of text
PasswordChar	Indicates the character that is echoed in the text box when a user types a password
ReadOnly	Indicates whether the text box is read-only or can be edited
Text	Identifies the text contained within the text box
TextAlign	Indicates how text is aligned within the text box
Methods of the TextBox Class	
AppendText	Appends text to the text currently in the text box
Clear	Clears the text currently in the text box
Common Events	
TextChanged	Occurs when the text in the text box changes
Leave	Occurs when the focus leaves the text box

8

Table 8-8 Selected properties, methods, and events of the ComboBox class

Properties of the ComboBox Class	Description
	Inherits properties, methods, and events from the Control class
Items	Identifies the items contained within the combo box
MaxDropDownItems	Indicates the maximum number of items that will be shown in the drop-down portion of the combo box
SelectedIndex	Indicates the index of the currently selected item in the combo box
SelectedItem	Identifies the currently selected item in the combo box
Sorted	Indicates whether the items in the combo box are sorted
Text	Identifies the text that is displayed by default in the combo box
Common Event	
SelectedIndexChanged	Occurs when the item selected in the combo box changes

The following example illustrates how you can use text box events to create a currency conversion application. The GUI form includes three text boxes and a button, as shown in Figure 8-9.

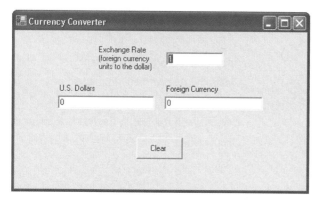

Figure 8-9 Currency conversion form

The text boxes are named txtExchangeRate, txtDollars, and txtForeignCurrency. The button is named btnClear. You type the exchange rate and then press the Tab key to move to the txtDollars or txtForeignCurrency text box. You type a value into one of these text boxes depending on whether you want to convert from dollars to foreign currency or vice versa. The application converts from one currency to the other and displays the result in the appropriate text box. The Clear button clears the form and places default values in the text boxes.

Example 8-2: The currency conversion program

The following example code uses event handlers to create a currency conversion form. Figure 8-10 shows the form that this code produces.

```
1. Public Class Form1
2.       Inherits System.Windows.Forms.Form


3.       'Define variables needed by event handlers
4.       Dim exchangeRate, dollars, foreignCurrency As Single


5.       'Windows Form Designer generated code


6.       'Event handler for Leave event on Exchange Rate text
         box
7.       Private Sub txtExchangeRate_Leave(ByVal sender
         As Object, ByVal e As System.EventArgs) Handles
         txtExchangeRate.Leave
8.           'Get exchange rate and convert to numeric value
9.           exchangeRate =
             Convert.ToSingle(txtExchangeRate.Text)
10.          'If exchange rate < 0 display error message and
             reset focus
11.          If exchangeRate <= 0 Then
12.              MessageBox.Show("You must enter an exchange
                 rate > 0")
13.              txtExchangeRate.Focus()
14.          End If
15.      End Sub
```

8

```vb
16.    'Event handler for Leave event on U.S. Dollars text box

17.    Private Sub txtDollars_Leave(ByVal sender
       As System.Object, ByVal e As System.EventArgs) Handles
       txtDollars.Leave

18.        'Get U.S. dollars convert to numeric value

19.        dollars = Convert.ToSingle(txtDollars.Text)

20.        'Calculate foreign currency equivalent

21.        foreignCurrency = dollars * exchangeRate

22.        'Format and display dollars and foreign currency
           in text boxes

23.        txtDollars.Text() =
           dollars.ToString("##,###,##0.00")

24.        txtForeignCurrency.Text =
               foreignCurrency.ToString("##,###,##0.00")

25.    End Sub


26.    'Event handler for Leave event on Foreign Currency
       text box

27.    Private Sub txtForeignCurrency_Leave(ByVal sender
       As System.Object, ByVal e As System.EventArgs) Handles
       txtForeignCurrency.Leave

28.        'Get foreign currency and convert to numeric value

29.        foreignCurrency =
           Convert.ToSingle(txtForeignCurrency.Text)

30.        'Calculate U.S. dollars equivalent

31.        dollars = foreignCurrency / exchangeRate

32.        'Format and display dollars and foreign currency in
           text boxes

33.        txtForeignCurrency.Text =
               foreignCurrency.ToString("##,###,##0.00")

34.        txtDollars.Text = dollars.ToString("##,###,##0.00")

35.    End Sub
```

```
36.     'Event handler for Click event on Clear button
37.     Private Sub btnClear_Click(ByVal sender As
        System.Object, ByVal e As System.EventArgs) Handles
        btnClear.Click
38.         'Set exchange rate to 1, dollars and foreign
            currency to 0
39.         txtExchangeRate.Text = 1
40.         txtDollars.Text = 0
41.         txtForeignCurrency.Text = 0
42.     End Sub


43.     'Event handler for Load event on the form
44.     Private Sub Form1_Load(ByVal sender As Object, ByVal e
        As System.EventArgs) Handles MyBase.Load
45.         'Generate a click event on the Clear button
46.         btnClear.PerformClick()
47.     End Sub


48. End Class
```

Sample Run:

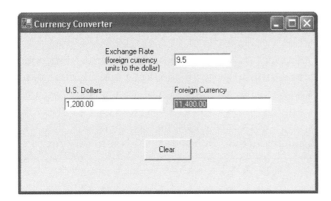

Figure 8-10   Output of the currency conversion program

Discussion:

Line 4 defines three `Single` variables to contain the exchange rate, U.S. dollars, and the foreign currency equivalent. These variables are defined at the class level so that all event handlers can access them.

Lines 6 through 15 define the event handler that responds when the cursor leaves the exchange rate text box. When the cursor is positioned within a control, that control is said to have the **focus**. A Leave event occurs when a control such as a text box loses focus—that is, when the user positions the cursor within a different control. Line 9 converts the string entered into the text box to a number and assigns the result to the variable **exchangeRate**. Line 11 checks to see if the exchange rate is less than or equal to zero. (This is necessary to ensure against division by zero at line 31). If the exchange rate is less than or equal to zero, line 12 displays an error message and line 13 resets the focus back to the Exchange Rate text box.

 If you enter non-numeric information into the Exchange Rate text box, VB .NET generates an error. You learn how to handle errors (or exceptions) of this type later in this book.

Lines 16 through 25 define the event handler that responds when the cursor leaves the txtDollars control. Line 19 converts the string entered into the U.S. Dollars text box to a number and assigns this value to the variable **dollars**. Line 21 converts dollars to the foreign currency equivalent by multiplying dollars times the exchange rate. Line 23 formats the value in the U.S. Dollars text box. Line 24 formats and displays the foreign currency equivalent.

Lines 26 through 35 define the event handler that responds when the cursor leaves the txtForeignCurrency control. Line 29 converts the string entered into the Foreign Currency text box to a number and assigns this value to the variable **foreignCurrency**. Line 31 converts the foreign currency amount into the dollar equivalent by dividing the foreign currency amount by the exchange rate. Line 33 formats the value in the Foreign Currency text box. Line 34 formats and displays the U.S. dollars equivalent.

Lines 36 through 42 define the event handler that responds when the Clear button is clicked. Line 39 sets the exchange rate to a default value of 1. Lines 40 and 41 set the default values of dollars and foreign currency to 0.

Lines 43 through 47 define the event handler that responds when the form initially loads. You can use the Load event for a form to perform additional initialization tasks. When this form loads, the default values for exchange rate, dollars, and foreign currency should be set as they are by the Clear button. Line 46 invokes the **PerformClick** method of the btnClear control to achieve this task. The **PerformClick** method generates a Click event for btnClear, causing the event handling method **btnClear_Click** to execute.

The next example illustrates the use of a combo box. This example uses text boxes to capture a student's name and address. A combo box allows you to select a zip code from a list box. Notice that in this example the ReadOnly property for the Student Name text box is set to true. This dims the text box and prohibits you from making changes to its contents.

Example 8-3: Responding to a SelectedIndexChanged event in a combo box

The following code uses an event handler to display a message after a Zip Code is selected in a combo box on a form. Figure 8-11 shows the contents of the combo box, and Figure 8-12 shows the confirmation message that appears after a Zip Code is selected.

```
1. Public Class Form1
2.      Inherits System.Windows.Forms.Form


3.      'Windows Form Designer generated code
4.      'Event handler for SelectedIndexChanged event on
        Zip Code combo box
5.      Private Sub cmbZipCode_SelectedIndexChanged(ByVal
        sender As System.Object, ByVale As System.EventArgs)
        Handles cmbZipCode.SelectedIndexChanged
6.          'Display message identifying selected zip code
7.          MessageBox.Show("You selected zip code " &
                cmbZipCode.SelectedItem)
8.      End Sub
9. End Class
```

8

Sample Run:

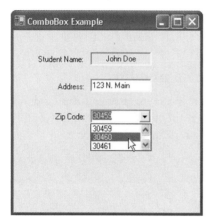

Figure 8-11   Selecting an item from a combo box

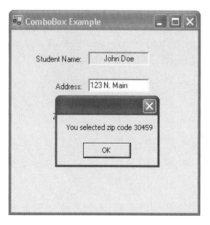

Figure 8-12   Output of the combo box program

Discussion:

Selecting an item from a combo box generates a SelectedIndexChanged event. Lines 4 through 8 define the event handler that responds to this event. Line 7 uses the SelectedItem property of the ComboBox class to display a message identifying the Zip Code selected from the list.

Using Check Boxes and Radio Buttons

Check boxes and radio buttons provide the ability to select from options presented within a GUI form. At any time, a check box or radio button is in one of two states: checked (selected) or not checked (not selected). The `CheckBox` and `RadioButton` classes include methods that enable you to determine and set the state of a check box or radio button instance. Checking or unchecking one of these controls creates an event.

A **check box** appears as a small white box and usually includes a label that identifies its purpose. You use the Text property to set the value of the caption (or label) that describes the purpose of the check box. When selected, a check mark appears in the box. It is common to use multiple check boxes on a GUI form to capture combinations of related options that each have a true or false (checked or not checked) state. For example, in a hotel reservation application, you could use two check boxes to indicate whether a guest would like a rollaway bed and a nonsmoking room. Depending on the preferences of the guest, one, both, or neither check box might be checked. When working with a multiple check boxes, there is no requirement that any check box be checked, and conversely, any or all of the check boxes may be checked simultaneously.

8

Radio buttons are similar to check boxes in many ways, but have important differences. Visually, radio buttons appear as small white circles and have captions (or labels) that identify their purpose. When a radio button is selected, a black dot appears within the circle. Like check boxes, a group of radio buttons represents a set of related options. However, you use radio buttons when the options are mutually exclusive—in other words, when one and only one of the options may be selected at any given time. For example, a hotel reservation can be made using a MasterCard or Visa, but not both. It is common to include more than one set of radio buttons on a form. In Chapter 13, you will learn how to use group boxes to manage more than one set of radio buttons.

When there are a small number of options, check boxes and radio buttons can reduce keystrokes and data entry errors. Tables 8-9 and 8-10 summarize frequently used properties, methods, and events for these controls.

Table 8-9 Selected properties, methods, and events of the CheckBox class

Properties of the CheckBox Class	Description
	Inherits properties, methods, and events from the Control class
Checked	Indicates whether the check box is checked (true) or unchecked (false)
CheckState	Indicates the state of a check box: checked (contains a checkmark), unchecked (empty), or indeterminate (checked and shaded)
Text	Identifies the text (label) associated with the check box
Common Events	
CheckedChanged	Occurs when the check property (true or false) changes (that is, each time the check box is checked or unchecked)

Table 8-10 Selected properties, methods, and events of RadioButton class

Properties of the RadioButton Class	Description
	Inherits properties, methods, and events from the Control class
Checked	Indicates whether the radio button is checked (true) or unchecked (false)
Text	Identifies the text (label) associated with the radio button
Common Events	
CheckedChanged	Occurs when the check property (true or false) changes (that is, each time the radio button is checked or unchecked)

Example 8-4: Formatting a text box

The following example illustrates the use of radio buttons and check boxes. This program allows you to select a font color and several other formatting options for a text box. Figure 8-13 shows the results of using this form to format a text box.

```
1. Public Class Form1

2.     Inherits System.Windows.Forms.Form


3.     'Windows Form Designer generated code
```

```vb
4.      'Event handler for CheckedChanged event on Black radio
        button

5.      Private Sub radBlack_CheckedChanged(ByVal sender As
        System.Object,ByVal e As System.EventArgs) Handles
        radBlack.CheckedChanged

6.          'Set color of text to black

7.          txtData.ForeColor = Color.Black

8.      End Sub


9.      'Event handler for CheckedChanged event on Blue
        radio button

10.     Private Sub radBlue_CheckedChanged(ByVal sender As
        System.Object, ByVal e As System.EventArgs) Handles
        radBlue.CheckedChanged

11.         'Set color of text to blue

12.         txtData.ForeColor = Color.Blue()

13.     End Sub


14.     'Event handler for CheckedChanged event on Red radio
        button

15.     Private Sub radRed_CheckedChanged(ByVal sender As
        System.Object, ByVal e As System.EventArgs) Handles
        radRed.CheckedChanged

16.         'Set color of text to red

17.         txtData.ForeColor = Color.Red

18.     End Sub


19.     'Event handler for CheckedChanged event on Border
        check box

20.     Private Sub chkBorder_CheckedChanged(ByVal sender As
        System.Object, ByVal e As System.EventArgs) Handles
        chkBorder.CheckedChanged

21.         'If Border check box is checked, set border to 3D
            style, otherwise to none
```

8

```
22.            If chkBorder.Checked = True Then

23.                txtData.BorderStyle = BorderStyle.Fixed3D

24.            Else

25.                txtData.BorderStyle = BorderStyle.None

26.            End If

27.        End Sub


28.        'Event handler for CheckedChanged event on Read Only
           check box

29.        Private Sub chkReadOnly_CheckedChanged(ByVal sender
           As System.Object, ByVal e As System.EventArgs) Handles
           chkReadOnly.CheckedChanged

30.            'If Read Only check box is checked, set text box as
               read only, otherwise do not

31.            If chkReadOnly.Checked = True Then

32.                txtData.ReadOnly = True

33.            Else

34.                txtData.ReadOnly = False

35.            End If

36.        End Sub


37.        'Event handler for CheckedChanged event on Password
           check box

38.        Private Sub chkPassword_CheckedChanged(ByVal sender
           As System.Object, ByVal e As System.EventArgs) Handles
           chkPassword.CheckedChanged

39.            'If Password check box is checked, set password
               character to *, otherwise set it to Nothing

40.            If chkPassword.Checked = True Then
```

```
41.                    txtData.PasswordChar = "*"
42.            Else
43.                    txtData.PasswordChar = Nothing
44.            End If
45.      End Sub
46. End Class
```

Sample Run:

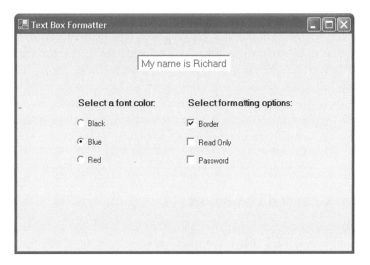

Figure 8-13   Output of the text box formatting program

Discussion:

Recall that at any time, a radio button may be checked or unchecked. Each time a radio button is selected, its check state changes and a CheckedChanged event occurs. The functionality of radio buttons is such that when one radio button is selected, the others are automatically deselected. Lines 4 through 8 define the event handler that responds when the Black radio button is selected. Line 7 sets the foreground color of the text box to black.

Lines 9 through 18 define similar event handlers for the Blue and Red radio buttons. These event handlers set the foreground color of the text box to blue and red, respectively.

Like radio buttons, check boxes may be checked or unchecked. When the check state of a check box changes, a CheckedChanged event occurs. However, unlike radio buttons, any number of check boxes may be checked (selected) or unchecked (deselected) at the same time. Lines 19 through 27 define the event handler that responds when the Border check box is checked or unchecked. If the Border check box is checked (the Checked property contains the value `True`), then the border style of the text box is set to Fixed3D, giving it a three-dimensional appearance. Otherwise, the border style is set to None.

Lines 28 through 36 define a similar event handler that responds when the check state of the Read Only check box changes. If the Read Only check box is checked, the ReadOnly property of the text box is set to `True`. The text box appears dimmed and its contents cannot be modified. Otherwise, the ReadOnly property is set to `False` and the text box appears and functions normally.

Lines 37 through 45 define the event handler that responds when the Password check box is checked or unchecked. If the Password check box is checked, line 41 sets the PasswordChar property of the text box to an asterisk (*). When the PasswordChar property contains a value, that value is used to mask the information entered into the text box. If the Password check box is not checked, line 43 sets the PasswordChar property to `Nothing`. Recall that the `Nothing` keyword represents the default value of nothing. Assigning `Nothing` to the PasswordChar property means this property will not contain a value and masking will no longer occur.

Using List Boxes and Checked List Boxes

List boxes and checked list boxes provide the ability to select one or more items from a predetermined list of values. **List boxes**, which are instances of the `ListBox` class, enable you (by default) to select one item from the list, but you can enable the selection of multiple list items by setting the SelectionMode property. **Checked list boxes** extend the functionality of a list box by including a check box to the left of each item in the list. By default, instances of the `CheckedListBox` class allow the selection of multiple items in the list. When you select an item in the list, a check mark appears in the corresponding check box.

Use a list box or checked list box when you want to force the user to select one or more items from a predetermined list of values without an option to enter alternate values. For example, in a hotel reservation program you could use a list box to enable the user to select from a list of available rooms. Tables 8-11 and 8-12 summarize frequently used properties, methods, and events for these controls.

Table 8-11   Selected properties, methods, and events of the ListBox class

Properties of the ListBox Class	Description
	Inherits properties, methods, and events from the Control class
Items	Gets the items of the list box
Multicolumn	Indicates whether the list box supports multiple columns
SelectedIndex	Indicates the index of the currently selected item in the list box
SelectedIndices	Indicates the indices of all the currently selected items in the list box
SelectedItem	Identifies the currently selected item in the list box
SelectedItems	Identifies all the currently selected items in the list box
SelectionMode	Indicates whether the user can select a single item or multiple items from the list box
Sorted	Indicates whether the items in the list box are sorted
Methods of the ListBox Class	
ClearSelected	Deselects all items in the list box
GetSelected	Indicates whether the specified item is selected in the list box
SetSelected	Selects (or deselects) the specified item in the list box
Common Event	
SelectedIndexChanged	Occurs when the item selected in the list box changes

8

Table 8-12   Selected properties, methods, and events of the CheckedListBox class

Properties of the CheckedListBox Class	Description
	Inherits properties, methods, and events from the Control and ListBox classes
CheckedIndices	Identifies the checked indexes in the checked list box
CheckedItems	Identifies the checked items in the checked list box
Methods of the CheckedListBox Class	
GetItemChecked	Indicates whether the specified item is checked
GetItemCheckState	Indicates the check state of the specified item
SetItemChecked	Sets (checks) the item at the specified index
SetItemCheckState	Sets the check state of the item at the specified index
Common Events	
ItemCheck	Occurs when the checked state of an item changes
SelectedIndexChanged	Occurs when the item selected in the checked list box changes

Example 8-5: The Fast Food Menu program

The following example illustrates the use of a list box to select items from a fast food menu and submit an order. When an order is submitted, the list of ordered items appears in the text box and the total cost of the order is calculated and displayed. Note that the list box in this example allows multiple items to be selected from the list (that is, the SelectionMode property is set to MultiSimple). Also, the text box is a multiline text box (that is, the Multiline property is set to true).

Figure 8-14 shows the results of using the form to submit an order.

```
1. Public Class Form1

2.     Inherits System.Windows.Forms.Form

3.     'Windows Form Designer generated code


4.     'Event handler for Click event on Submit button

5.     Private Sub btnSubmit_Click(ByVal sender As
       System.Object, ByVal e As System.EventArgs) Handles
       btnSubmit.Click
```

```vbnet
6.         'define variables
7.         Dim totalCost As Single
8.         Dim costArray As Single() = New Single() {1.09,
           0.89, 0.99}
9.         Dim item As String
10.        Dim index As Integer
11.        Dim output As String
12.        'clear the text box, the output string and
           total cost
13.        txtOrder.Clear()
14.        output = ""
15.        totalCost = 0
16.        'loop to add selected menu items to the output
           string
17.        For Each item In lstMenu.SelectedItems
18.            output = output & item & vbCrLf
19.            index = lstMenu.Items.IndexOf(item)
20.            totalCost = totalCost + costArray(index)
21.        Next
22.        'display the output string in the text box
23.        txtOrder.AppendText(output)
24.        'display the total cost
25.        txtOrder.AppendText(vbCrLf & "Order Total " &
               totalCost.ToString("C"))
26.    End Sub


27.    'Event handler for Click event on Clear button
28.    Private Sub btnClear_Click(ByVal sender As
       System.Object, ByVal e As System.EventArgs) Handles
       btnClear.Click
29.        Dim index As Integer
30.        'clear the text box
```

8

```
31.          txtOrder.Clear()
32.          'loop to deselect all items in the list box
33.          For index = 0 To lstMenu.Items.Count - 1
34.              lstMenu.SetSelected(index, False)
35.          Next
36.      End Sub
37. End Class
```

Sample Run:

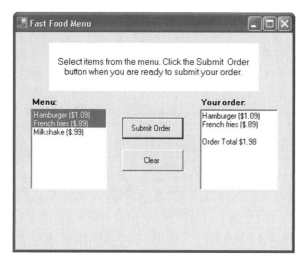

Figure 8-14 Output of the Fast Food Menu program

Discussion:

Lines 4 through 26 define the event handler that responds when the Submit Order button is clicked. Line 7 declares a variable to contain the total cost of the order.

Line 8 defines an array that contains the costs of items on the menu. Line 9 defines a `String` variable that is used as a loop control variable and to identify an item selected in the list box. Line 10 declares an `Integer` variable to represent the index of an item selected in the list box. Line 11 declares a `String` variable that is used to display information in the text box.

Lines 13, 14, and 15 clear the text box, the output string, and the total cost.

Lines 16 through 21 use a `For Each` statement to determine which items in the list box are selected. A `For Each` statement is similar to a `For Next` statement but differs in several important ways. A `For Each` statement loops through a collection of items. In this case the collection is the set of items selected in the list box. The `For Each` statement that begins on line 17 specifies a variable, `item`, and a collection, `lstMenu.SelectedItems`. The SelectedItems property identifies all of the items selected in the list box. The `For Each` statement repeats for all of these items, each time assigning the value of the item to the `String` variable `item`. Line 18 concatenates this string with the `String` variable `output` and the constant `vbCrLf` (which represents a carriage return and line feed). Line 19 uses the `IndexOf` method to determine the position (or index) of the item within the list box. Line 20 uses this index to look up the cost of the item in `costArray` and adds this cost to `totalCost`.

Line 23 displays the output string, which consists of the items ordered, in the text box, and line 25 displays the total cost of the order.

Lines 27 through 36 define the event handler that responds to a Click event for the Clear button. Line 31 clears the text box. The `For Next` loop on lines 33 through 35 uses the `SetSelected` method to deselect all items in the list box.

8

PROGRAMMING EXAMPLE: ABC COMPUTERS

This programming example combines many of the GUI components and event handlers about which you learned in this chapter. It allows you to select options for building your own computer and calculates the price based on the options you choose.

Input   Type of processor, operating system, and peripherals desired, and state of residence

Output   Order summary and total cost

Problem Analysis, GUI Design, and Algorithm Design

The purpose of this program is to create a GUI form for pricing a computer. The purchase price of a computer is determined by four factors: (1) the processor, (2) the operating system, (3) peripheral devices, and (4) the cost of shipping the computer to the buyer. Let variables `processorCost`, `osCost`, `peripheralCost`, and `shippingCost` represent these values, and `totalCost` represent the total cost. The order summary information is obtained by concatenating strings that represent the user's selections. The GUI form in Figure 8-15 contains six labels, a list box, two radio buttons, two check boxes, a multi-line text box, a combo box, and three buttons.

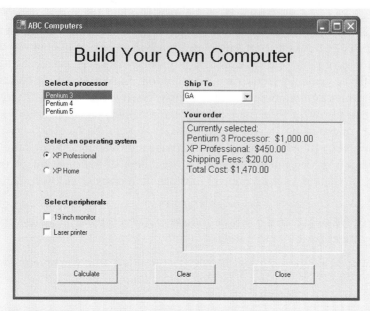

Figure 8-15   GUI form for pricing a computer

Each time the user selects an option from the GUI, the order summary information and total cost change. These changes are automatically reflected in the multiline text box. This means that all of the cost variables must be accessible to all of the individual event handlers. It also means that the list box, both radio buttons, both check boxes, and the combo box must all respond to user-generated events. Accordingly, an event handler is needed for each of these controls. The buttons must also respond to click events, and therefore also need event handlers.

Variables

`processorCost As Single` contains the processor cost

`osCost As Single` contains the operating system cost

`peripheralCost As Single` contains the sum of the peripheral costs

`shippingCost As Single` contains the shipping cost

`totalCost As Single` contains the total cost

`osString As String` references a string describing the operating system selected

`peripheralString As String` references a string describing the peripherals selected

`index As Integer` index for determining item selected in list box

`cmbString As String` references a string describing combo box items

`validState As Boolean` indicates whether a valid state has been selected in the combo box

`output As String` references a string that describes the order summary and cost

`lstProcessor As ListBox` references the processor list box

`radXPPro As RadioButton` references the XP Professional radio button

`radXPHome As RadioButton` references the XP Home radio button

`chkMonitor As CheckBox` references the 19-inch monitor check box

`chkPrinter As CheckBox` references the laser printer check box

`cmbShipTo As ComboBox` references the ship to combo box

`txtOrder As TextBox` references the text box that displays the order details

`btnCalculate As Button` references the calculate button

`btnClear As Button` references the clear button

`btnClose As Button` references the close button

`lblProcessor As Label` references the processor label

`lblOperatingSystem As Label` references the operating system label

`lblPeripherals As Label` references the peripherals label

`lblShipTo As Label` references the ship to label

`lblOutput As Label` references the output label

`lblTitle As Label` references the title label

8

Formula The formula for calculating the total cost is:

```
totalCost = processorCost + osCost + peripheralCost + shippingCost
```

Main Algorithm

Based on the GUI shown in Figure 8-15 and the recognized need for event handlers, an event-driven algorithm for this program is as follows:

1. Define cost variables at the class level.
2. Create an event handler for each control that captures data from the user.
3. When the user selects an option from one of the GUI controls, let the event handler for that control:
   a. Determine the price of that option.
   b. Calculate total cost and display the order summary.

Complete Program Listing

```vb
Public Class Form1
    Inherits System.Windows.Forms.Form

    'Define variables needed by event handlers
    Dim processorCost, osCost, peripheralCost, shippingCost,
        totalCost As Single
    Dim osString, peripheralString As String

    'Windows Form Designer generated code
    'Event handler for SelectedIndexChanged event on Processor
    list box
    Private Sub lstProcessor_SelectedIndexChanged(ByVal sender As
    System.Object, ByVal e As System.EventArgs) Handles
    lstProcessor.SelectedIndexChanged
        Dim index As Integer   'define index variable
        'Set index equal to the index of item selected on the
        list box
        index = lstProcessor.SelectedIndex
        'Assign processor cost based on the selected index
        If index = 0 Then processorCost = 1000
        If index = 1 Then processorCost = 1200
        If index = 2 Then processorCost = 1400
        'Generate click event to calculate total cost
        btnCalculate.PerformClick()
    End Sub

    'Event handler for CheckedChanged event on XP Pro radio button
    Private Sub radXPPro_CheckedChanged(ByVal sender As
    System.Object, ByVal e As System.EventArgs) Handles
    radXPPro.CheckedChanged
```

```vb
        'If XP Pro is checked set OS cost to $450, otherwise $275
        'Set OS output string accordingly
        If radXPPro.Checked = True Then
            osCost = 450
            osString = radXPPro.Text()
        Else
            osCost = 275
            osString = radXPHome.Text()
        End If
        'Generate click event to calculate total cost
        btnCalculate.PerformClick()
    End Sub

    'Event handler for CheckedChanged event on XP Home radio button
     Private Sub radXPHome_CheckedChanged(ByVal sender As
     System.Object, ByVal e As System.EventArgs) Handles
            radXPHome.CheckedChanged
        'If XP Home is checked set OS cost to $275, otherwise $450
        'Set OS output string accordingly
        If radXPHome.Checked = True Then
            osCost = 275
            osString = radXPHome.Text()
        Else
            osCost = 450
            osString = radXPPro.Text()
        End If
        'Generate click event to calculate total cost
        btnCalculate.PerformClick()
    End Sub

    'Event handler for CheckedChanged event Monitor check box
    Private Sub chkMonitor_CheckedChanged(ByVal sender As
     System.Object, ByVal e As System.EventArgs) Handles
            chkMonitor.CheckedChanged
        'If Monitor check box is checked add $300 to peripheral
        cost
        'Otherwise subtract $300 from peripheral cost
        If chkMonitor.Checked = True Then
            peripheralCost = peripheralCost + 300
        Else
            peripheralCost = peripheralCost - 300
        End If
        'Generate click event to calculate total cost
        btnCalculate.PerformClick()
    End Sub

    'Event handler for CheckedChanged event on Printer check box
```

8

```
Private Sub chkPrinter_CheckedChanged(ByVal sender As
System.Object, ByVal e As System.EventArgs) Handles
chkPrinter.CheckedChanged
    'If Printer check box is checked add $250 to peripheral
    cost
    'Otherwise subtract $250 from peripheral cost
    If chkPrinter.Checked = True Then
        peripheralCost = peripheralCost + 250
    Else
        peripheralCost = peripheralCost - 250
    End If
    'Generate click event to calculate total cost
    btnCalculate.PerformClick()
End Sub

'Event handler for TextChanged event on Ship To combo box
Private Sub cmbShipTo_TextChanged(ByVal sender As
  System.Object, ByVal e As System.EventArgs) Handles
        cmbShipTo.TextChanged
    'Define a variable to reference items in combo box
    Dim cmbString As String
    'Define a variable to indicate whether a valid state is
        selected
    '   in the combo box and set its initial value to False
    Dim validState As Boolean
    validState = False
    'Compare text entered into the combo box to each item in
    the list
    'If a match is found, set validState to True
    For Each cmbString In cmbShipTo.Items
        If cmbShipTo.Text().Equals(cmbString) Then
            validState = True
        End If
    Next
    'If an invalid state was entered into the combo box
    '  display an error message, reset selected index, and
    recalculate
    If validState = False Then
        MessageBox.Show("You must select a state from
        the list")
        cmbShipTo.SelectIndex=0
        btnCalculate.PerformClick()
    End If
End Sub

'Event handler for SelectedIndexChanged event on Ship To
combo box
```

```
Private Sub cmbShipTo_SelectedIndexChanged(ByVal sender As
System.Object, ByVal e As System.EventArgs) Handles
cmbShipTo.SelectedIndexChanged
    'Assign shipping cost based on state selected
    If cmbShipTo.SelectedIndex() = 0 Then
        shippingCost = 20
    ElseIf cmbShipTo.SelectedIndex() = 1 Then
        shippingCost = 30
    ElseIf cmbShipTo.SelectedIndex() > 1 Then
        shippingCost = 40
    End If
    'Generate click event to calculate total cost
    btnCalculate.PerformClick()
End Sub

'Event handler for Click event on Calculate button
Private Sub btnCalculate_Click(ByVal sender As System.Object,
ByVal e As System.EventArgs) Handles btnCalculate.Click
    'Define and initialize output string
    Dim output As String
    output = ""
    'Clear text box
    txtOrder.Clear()
    'Build output string based selected processor & OS
    (& their costs)
    output = "Currently selected: " & vbCrLf
    output = output & lstProcessor.SelectedItem &
    " Processor: "
    output = output & processorCost.ToString("C") & vbCrLf
    output = output & osString & ": " & osCost.ToString("C")
    & vbCrLf
    'Concatenate selected peripherals and their costs with
    output string
    If peripheralCost <> 0 Then
        output = output & "Peripherals: " &
        peripheralCost.ToString("C") & vbCrLf
        If chkMonitor.Checked = True Then
            output = output & "    " & chkMonitor.Text & vbCrLf
        End If
        If chkPrinter.Checked = True Then
            output = output & "    " & chkPrinter.Text & vbCrLf
        End If
    End If
    'Concatenate shipping fees with output string
    output = output & "Shipping Fees: " &
    shippingCost.ToString("C") & vbCrLf
    'Calculate total cost
```

8

```vbnet
        totalCost = processorCost + osCost + peripheralCost +
        shippingCost
        'Concatenate total cost with output string
        output = output & "Total Cost: " &
    (totalCost).ToString("C")
        txtOrder.AppendText(output)
    End Sub

    'Event handler for Click event on Clear button
    Private Sub btnClear_Click(ByVal sender As System.Object,
    ByVal e As System.EventArgs) Handles btnClear.Click
        'Set total cost to 0
        totalCost = 0
        'Select first item on the Processor list box
        lstProcessor.SetSelected(0, True)
        'Select first item in Ship To combo box
        cmbShipTo.SelectedIndex = 0
        'Initialize radio buttons
        radXPPro.Checked = True
        radXPHome.Checked = False
        'Initialize check boxes
        chkMonitor.Checked = False
        chkPrinter.Checked = False
        'Clear text box
        txtOrder.Clear()
    End Sub

    'Event handler for Click event on Close button
    Private Sub btnClose_Click(ByVal sender As System.Object,
    ByVal e As System.EventArgs) Handles btnClose.Click
        Close()   'Close the form
    End Sub

    'Event handler for Load event on the form
    Private Sub Form1_Load(ByVal sender As System.Object, ByVal e
    As System.EventArgs) Handles MyBase.Load
        'Set the default value of the OS string
        osString = radXPPro.Text()
        'Select first item on the Processor list box
        lstProcessor.SetSelected(0, True)
        'Select first item in the Ship To combo box
        cmbShipTo.SelectedIndex = 0
    End Sub
End Class
```

QUICK REVIEW

1. All of the graphical components you see on Visual Basic .NET (VB .NET) graphical user interface (GUI) windows are instances of classes in the `System.Windows.Forms` namespace.

2. GUI classes take advantage of inheritance. Most of the GUI classes you use on a form are subclasses of the `Control` class and, therefore, inherit important properties and methods from `Control`.

4. The code VB .NET generates for a GUI is called a class definition and specifies the attributes and methods that make the form work.

5. A class definition begins with a class header and ends with an `End Class` statement. Class definitions generated by the Windows Form Designer have the form `Public Class` classname `Inherits System.Windows.Forms.Form`. The `Inherits` clause specifies that the class inherits from the Form class in the `System.Windows.Forms` namespace.

6. Most of the remaining code generated by VB .NET is collapsed under the heading "Windows Form Designer generated code." You can view this code by clicking the expand node.

7. The code generated by the Windows Forms Designer is complex. Changes to a form and its components should be made by manipulating the items in the Properties window rather than by modifying this code.

8. The keywords `Sub` and `End Sub` identify the beginning and end of a method definition.

9. A constructor is a special method that is automatically invoked when an instance of a class is created. The Windows Form Designer provides a default constructor for each form you create. The purpose of the constructor method is to initialize the form and its components.

10. The Windows Form Designer provides a default destructor method for every form you create. A destructor releases system resources when your program ends.

11. A container is an object that holds other components. A form is one kind of container.

12. Users interact with GUIs by entering data and clicking controls such as buttons and menus. An event is a signal that the user has taken some action, such as clicking a button. An event handler is a method or procedure that responds to an event.

13. When you define a control using the `With Events` modifier, event handlers for that control are named *controlName_eventName* and include a `Handles` *controlName.eventName* clause in the method header. An event handler is invoked whenever the event specified by *eventName* occurs for the control specified by *controlName*.

14. The style and appearance of a form is called its look and feel.

8

15. When designing GUI applications, it is important to adhere to standards that lead to a consistent look and feel, improve ease of use, and reduce the likelihood of data entry errors. The application should also provide feedback to inform the user when errors have occurred.

16. Be sure to follow naming conventions for controls.

17. A form instance becomes a visible window. Forms are containers for other components.

18. Labels display data but cannot be used for input.

19. Text boxes can be used to display and input data, and can contain either a single line of text (by default) or multiple lines of text.

20. Combo boxes can be used to display and input a single line of text, but additionally enable the user to select from a predefined list of values.

21. Check boxes and radio buttons enable users to select (or deselect) from a list of options.

22. Any number of check boxes in a group of check boxes can be selected or not selected at a given time.

23. Radio buttons enforce mutually exclusive behavior, meaning that only one radio button in a group of radio buttons may be selected at a given time.

24. List boxes and checked list boxes enable users to select one or more items from a predefined list of values.

25. When you double-click a control in Design mode, the Windows Form Designer automatically inserts the method header for the *most commonly used* event procedure for that control. You then supply the details that determine how the procedure responds to the event.

26. GUI components can be the source of many different events. You can add other event handling methods to your program by pressing F7 to open the Code window, selecting the control of interest from the Class Name list box, and then selecting the event of interest from the Method Name list box.

EXERCISES

1. An instance of the **Form** class is also a _____.

   a. component

   b. container

   c. control

   d. All of the above.

2. `Label` is a subclass of _____.

   a. `Component`

   b. `Container`

   c. `Control`

   d. All of the above.

3. The style and appearance of a GUI form and its components is called its _____.

   a. charisma

   b. public persona

   c. look and feel

   d. style and look

4. When you create an instance of the `Button` class in the Forms Designer window, VB .NET automatically inserts code that _____.

   a. declares the button instance

   b. invokes the constructor method of the `Button` class

   c. sets default properties for the button instance

   d. All of the above.

5. The keyword `Me` refers to _____.

   a. a new button instance

   b. a new form instance

   c. a new component instance

   d. the current object

6. A VB .NET event for a particular control is usually _____.

   a. the result of the user interacting with that control

   b. identified by the name *eventName.controlName*

   c. difficult to detect

   d. All of the above.

7. The event handler that responds to a click event for a button named Button1 is named _____.

   a. ButtonClickEvent

   b. Button1_Click

   c. Click_Button1

   d. Button.Click

8

8. A _____ control allows you to select multiple options in a list at once.

a. radio button

b. group box

c. list box

d. text box

9. What property would be used to change the color of text in a label?

a. ForeColor

b. BackColor

c. Font

d. Color

10. Which method is used to release system resources when a program ends?

a. `Event Handler`

b. `Control`

c. `Dispose`

d. `Exit`

11. PasswordChar is a specific property of what control?

a. Label

b. TreeNode

c. Panel

d. TextBox

12. SelectedIndexChanged is a common event of the _____ and _____ controls.

a. combo box, checked list box

b. combo box, check box

c. check box, radio button

d. checked list box, radio button

13. When designing GUI applications, it is important to adhere to standards that _____.

a. lead to a consistent look and feel

b. improve ease of use

c. reduce the likelihood of data entry errors

d. All of the above.

14. A _____ control enforces mutually exclusive behavior.

    a. combo box

    b. list box

    c. label

    d. radio button

15. Labels cannot be used for inputting data. Why do you need them in a GUI program?

16. How many events may be associated with a single control on a GUI form?

17. Why is it important to adhere to variable naming conventions?

18. Summarize the actions performed within the code generated by the Windows Form Designer.

19. What do the following VB .NET statements do?

    a. `btnCalculate.PerformClick()`

    b.
```
If radOption1.Checked = True Then
      txtOutput.Text = "You selected Option 1"
End If
```

    c.
```
For Each item In lstCourse.SelectedItems
          outputString = outputString & item & vbCrLf
          index = lstCourse.SelectedItems.IndexOf(item)
          totalCreditHours = totalCreditHours +
          creditHoursArray(index)
Next
```

 Assume `lstCourse` contains a list of courses offered at your school. Assume `item` and `outputString` are both `String` variables that have been initialized to Nothing; `totalCreditHours` is an `Integer` variable initialized to 0; and `creditHoursArray` is an `Integer` array containing the credit hours associated with each course.

20. Identify the circumstances under which the following controls would be preferred and give an example of each.

    a. combo box

    b. radio button

    c. check box

    d. list box

    e. label

8

PROGRAMMING EXERCISES

1. The formula for computing the monthly payment for a loan is:
   paymentAmount = (amountOfLoan * (rate / 12)) / (1-1/(1 + rate/12) ^ months)
   where rate is the annual interest rate (represented as a number between 0 and 1), ^
   means raise to the power, and months is the number of months of the loan. Design
   a GUI application similar to the one shown in Figure 8-16 to accept amountOfLoan,
   rate, and months, and then compute and display the monthly payment amount.
   Assume that the user enters valid information for the loan amount, interest rate,
   and number of months.

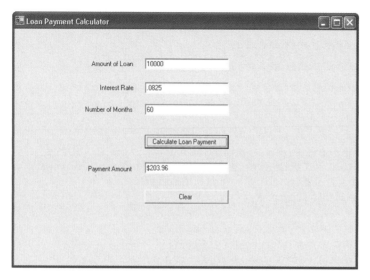

Figure 8-16   GUI for calculating a loan payment

2. Modify Programming Exercise 1 so that it generates an amortization schedule. The
   amortization should be displayed in a scrollable, multiline text box. See Figure 8-17.
   At the end of the amortization schedule, output the total interest paid.

 You can use the constant **vbTab** to align the output in the text box. The constant
   vbTab causes the output to tab to the next tab position.

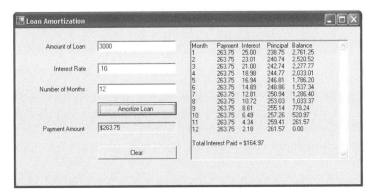

Figure 8-17   GUI to calculate a loan payment and generate an amortization schedule

8

3. Design a GUI similar to Figure 8-18 that computes your semester and cumulative grade point average (GPA). The GUI should accept the previous values of your cumulative GPA (a number between 0 and 4.0) and credit hours completed, as well as the course name, credit hours, and grade earned for each course completed this semester. Use the Add to List button to store information for a completed course in a list box. Use the Remove from List button to remove a course from the list box. When the Calculate New GPA button is pressed, calculate the semester GPA for the courses contained in the list box and calculate the new cumulative GPA. You may assume the following: (1) the user enters valid information for prior GPA and prior credit hours; (2) the user selects course credit hours and course grade from the items in the combo boxes; and (3) the user selects an item on the list before attempting to remove it from the list. (*Hint*: Use the RemoveAt method of the Items collection to remove items from the list.)

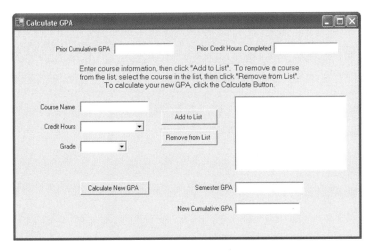

Figure 8-18   GUI to calculate cumulative GPA

4. Develop a GUI that simulates a simple calculator. The calculator should perform simple arithmetic operations between two integers. In other words, it should calculate a result for expressions such as 231 + 46, 99 / 3, or 22 * 17. Use buttons for each digit and operation key. As digit buttons are pressed, display the corresponding digits in the text box. For example, to enter the number 231, the user presses 2, then 3, then 1. Pressing an operation key signifies that the user is ready to enter the second number. When the user presses the = key, calculate the result and display it the text box. If the user attempts to perform an operation involving division by zero, display an error message in the text box. Because this calculator handles operations involving two numbers only, disable all digit and operation buttons after displaying the result until the Clear key is pressed. Your GUI should resemble Figure 8-19. (*Hint:* Use a Boolean variable to determine whether the user is entering the first or the second number.)

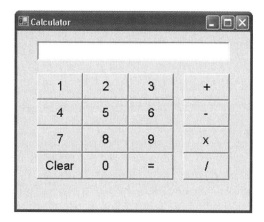

Figure 8-19   GUI form that simulates a calculator

5. Design a GUI that accepts a string and converts each word in the string to Pig Latin. To convert a word to Pig Latin, remove the first character of the word, then append it to the end of the word followed by the letters "ay". For example, the string "have a nice day" in pig Latin is "avehay aay icenay ayday". Your GUI should resemble Figure 8-20.

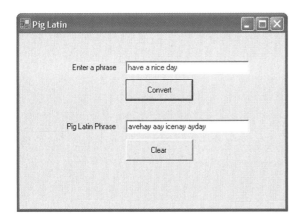

Figure 8-20   GUI that generates Pig Latin

6. Rewrite Example 8-5 (the Fast Food Menu program) so that is uses a checked list box rather than a list box to display and select menu items. Your GUI should resemble Figure 8-21.

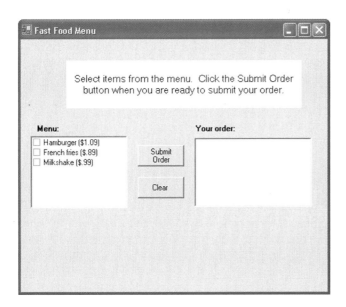

Figure 8-21   Fast food menu using checked list boxes

9 Writing Procedures

Visual Basic (VB) programmers make a distinction between a module and a class and between a procedure and a method. A module contains code to do some processing—to accomplish tasks. You have been writing modules in previous chapters and continue to do so in this chapter. Similar to a module, a class also contains code, but a class can be instantiated. For example, in previous chapters you created instances of the `String` class and invoked their methods. Sometimes classes represent real-world entities such as graphical user interface (GUI) Buttons or Customers. Chapter 10 deals with writing class definitions, instantiating classes, and writing methods.

Procedures contain code and can be invoked. Methods are simply procedures within a class. This chapter describes how to write and invoke procedures. Chapter 1 introduced you to basic object-oriented concepts such as a class, procedure, and encapsulation, and described how objects interact by sending messages. In Chapter 3, you learned that the Framework Class Library (FCL) contains hundreds of prewritten classes providing procedures you invoke to accomplish tasks ranging from computation and number formatting to establishing network connections and accessing relational databases. In Chapter 3, you also invoked procedures in the `String` and `Math` classes, and then in Chapter 6 you invoked procedures in additional classes to display message boxes, create and read sequential files, and work with dates.

In this chapter, you learn how to create user-defined procedures you invoke to accomplish tasks not provided by FCL classes. You will see the benefits of designing your code to employ procedures instead of creating monolithic processes.

Exploring the Client-Server Model

Methods are procedures within a class definition. In the previous chapters, you wrote code that invoked methods in the supplied classes. In fact, the first example in Chapter 2 invoked the `WriteLine` method in the `Console` class to display a message in the output window. Objects generally do not function alone. Instead, they interact and collaborate: their procedures provide services to other objects in a system. Object interaction is simulated when one object sends a message to another object to invoke a procedure. One way of viewing this interaction between objects is to apply the basic client-server model. The object sending the message becomes the **client object**, while the object receiving the message is the **server object**. See Figure 9-1.

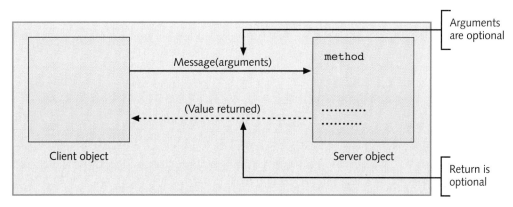

Figure 9-1   Client-server interaction

The client sends a message invoking a server procedure, optionally sending values in the form of arguments. The server procedure performs the requested task, and optionally returns a value to the client. In the Chapter 2 Hello World Wide Web example, the code to invoke the `WriteLine` method was:

```
Console.WriteLine("Hello World Wide Web")
```

`Console` is the name of the class having the method you want to invoke, `WriteLine` is the method name, and `"Hello World Wide Web"` is the argument you pass. When the method is invoked, it displays the argument in the output window. In this example, your program is the client and the `WriteLine` method in the `Console` class is the server. Here, the server does not return a value.

In another example in Chapter 3 (Example 3-18), you invoked the `Sqrt` method in the `Math` class by writing:

9

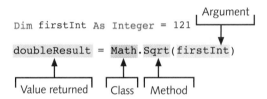

Here your code invokes the **Sqrt** method in the **Math** class, passing the contents of the variable **firstInt** as an argument. **Sqrt** computes the square root of this value and returns the answer, which is then assigned to the variable **doubleResult**.

Applying the client–server model to these examples, your statements were client code invoking server methods in the supplied classes.

A Unified Modeling Language (UML) sequence diagram maps interactions between objects. Figure 9-2 shows a sequence diagram for invoking the **Math.Sqrt** method.

 The UML provides various diagrams for modeling object-oriented systems. UML is an accepted standard by the Object Management Group (OMG), an industry association dedicated to improving object-oriented development practices. You can find complete information about UML, the diagrams, and constructs at *www.Rational.com*.

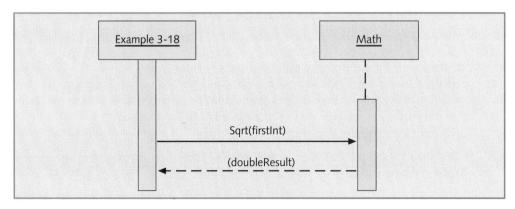

Figure 9-2   Sequence diagram to invoke Math.Sqrt

The sequence diagram shows objects as rectangles. Here there are two objects: the client object named **Example 3-18** and the server object **Math**. The vertical lines below the objects are called **lifelines** and represent a sequence of time. The lifeline is shown as either a dashed line or a narrow box. The narrow box represents a period of time when it is an **active**

object; that is, when it is executing or controlling part of the interaction. The horizontal arrows represent messages sent or received in sequence. The first horizontal line indicates the invoking of `Sqrt`. The argument is shown in parentheses. The dashed line indicates the return of execution to the client object. Data returned is shown in parentheses above the dashed line.

The following example shows a complete module that invokes `Math.Pow`.

Example 9-1: Invoking Math.Pow

In the following example and in others throughout the book, line numbers are added for reference only, and do not appear in the actual program.

```
1. Option Explicit On
2. Option Strict On

3. Module Chapter9Example1

4. Sub Main()
5.    Dim answer As Double
6.    answer = Math.Pow(4, 2)
7.    Console.WriteLine(answer)
8. End Sub

9. End Module
```

Sample Run:

16

Discussion:

This example contains a complete module. Lines 1 and 2 set `Options Explicit` and `Strict` to `On`.

Line 3 marks the beginning of the module and line 9 the end. This module name is `Chapter9Example1`.

Lines 4 through 8 define the `Main` procedure. Recall that this procedure, if it exists, automatically begins executing when the module is loaded into memory.

Line 5 declares a `Double` variable named **answer**.

9

Line 6 invokes the **Pow** method in the **Math** class. This method raises a value to a power. The **Pow** method accepts two arguments, raising the first argument to the power of the second. In this example, the first value is 4 and the second is 2. **Pow** raises 4 to the second power, and returns the result 16, which is assigned to **answer**. Note that **Pow** returns a **Double** data type.

Line 7 invokes **Console.WriteLine**, passing **answer** as an argument. This method then displays the contents of **answer** in the output window.

Figure 9–3 contains a sequence diagram for Example 9–1.

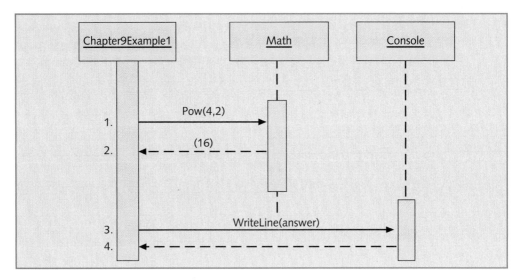

Figure 9-3 Sequence diagram for Example 9-1

This diagram shows the three objects involved in this example: **Chapter9Example1**, the **Math** class, and the **Console** class. Although normally not shown, this diagram contains line numbers for the four horizontal lines. Horizontal line 1 shows that **Chapter9Example1** is invoking the **Pow** method in the **Math** class, passing the argument (4, 2). Line 2 indicates the result (16) is being returned by **Pow**. Line 3 shows that **Chapter9Example1** is invoking **WriteLine** in the **Console** class, passing the argument (**answer**), which contains 16. **WriteLine** displays the contents of **answer** in the output window. Line 4 shows that control is returned to **Chapter9Example1**, but note that no value is being returned.

To summarize, objects frequently collaborate by interacting. This interaction is implemented by client objects invoking procedures in server objects. Some procedures accept arguments. Also, some procedures return values to the invoking client. Sequence diagrams are used to map the interaction between objects.

REVIEWING THE SYNTAX OF PROCEDURES

Designing modular processes using procedures instead of writing monolithic programs improves the clarity of your code, enhances error detection, and simplifies maintenance. It is much easier to deal with smaller cohesive units of code grouped into procedures instead of large code sections containing multiple processes.

Visual Basic .NET (VB .NET) provides two types of procedures: **Sub procedures** and **Function procedures**. The difference between the two is that a Function procedure returns a value but a Sub procedure does not.

Using Sub Procedures

A Sub procedure definition begins with a procedure header followed by one or more statements and ends with the keywords `End Sub`. This syntax is shown in Figure 9-4.

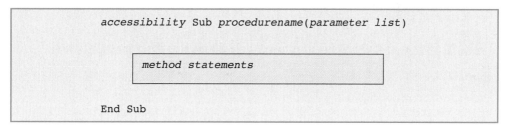

Figure 9-4   VB .NET Sub procedure syntax

The procedure header shown in Figure 9-4 consists of four parts:

1. *accessibility*—The accessibility is specified using the keywords `Public`, `Private`, `Protected`, or `Friend` to indicate which objects may invoke this procedure. In general, `Public` means that any object may invoke this procedure, and `Private` means only the module or class containing this procedure may invoke it. The keywords `Protected` and `Friend` are described in subsequent chapters. In this chapter, you use `Public` and `Private` accessibility.

2. `Sub`—This keyword indicates this is a Sub procedure as opposed to a Function procedure.

3. *procedurename*—This is an identifier that names the procedure. Procedure names generally contain a verb describing what the procedure does, and follow the identifier-naming rules described earlier. VB .NET programmers capitalize procedure names by convention.

4. *(parameter list)*—Arguments are passed into **parameters**. The parameter list consists of variable declarations that receive arguments being sent from client objects. When values are sent, VB .NET insists that the data types of the argument variables are compatible with the parameter variables. If the argument data type is not the same as the parameter data type, then the parameter data type must have equal or greater capacity. For example, you cannot pass an argument with data type `Double` into a parameter variable with data type `Integer` or `String`. If no argument is being passed to the procedure, then the parameter list is an empty set of parentheses.

To illustrate a Sub procedure, Example 9-2 includes two modules named `Client` and `Server`. `Client` invokes a procedure named `AddEmUp` in `Server`, passing two `Integer` arguments. `AddEmUp` receives the two values, then computes and displays their sum.

 To add a module using the VB .NET IDE, select the current project in the Solution Explorer window. On the Project menu, select Add New Item. Select a category, select the module template, then select Open.

Example 9-2: Writing and invoking a Sub procedure

Client Module

```
1. Option Explicit On
2. Option Strict On
3. Module Client
4. Sub Main()
5.     Server.AddEmUp(2, 3)
6. End Sub

7. End Module
```

Server Module

```
1. Option Explicit On
2. Option Strict On
3. Module Server
4. Public Sub AddEmUp(ByVal a As Integer, ByVal b As Integer)
5.     Dim sum As Integer
6.     sum = a + b
7.     Console.WriteLine("The sum is: " & sum)
8. End Sub

9. End Module
```

Argument 2 is passed into parameter a, and 3 is passed into b

Sample Run:

The sum is: 5

Client Module Discussion:

The client module in this example is named `Client` and contains a `Main` procedure consisting of the single statement at line 5:

```
Server.AddEmUp(2, 3)
```

This statement invokes the procedure named `AddEmUp` in the module named `Server`, passing the two literal arguments `(2, 3)`.

These two arguments are passed into the parameter variables `a` and `b` in the `AddEmUp` procedure.

Server Module Discussion:

The procedure named `AddEmUp` is shown in lines 4 through 8 of the module named `Server`. Line 4 is the procedure header. The accessibility is `Public`, which means any object can invoke the procedure. `Sub` indicates this is a Sub procedure, which means it will not return a value to the invoking client. The procedure name, `AddEmUp`, comes next, followed by the parameter variable definitions.

The parameter list defines two `Integer` variables named `a` and `b`, which receive the two `Integer` arguments passed by an invoking client. Note that these variable definitions use the keyword `ByVal` instead of `Dim`. When you define a parameter variable, you write either `ByVal` or `ByRef` instead of `Dim`. You can pass an argument to a procedure either by value (`ByVal`) or by reference (`ByRef`). By value means the procedure does not have direct access to the argument variable and cannot change its contents; instead, the procedure is given a copy of the variable. By reference means the procedure code is given direct access to the argument variable and therefore may change its value. Generally, you use `ByVal` when writing parameter definitions, unless you want the procedure to change the argument value. You can also make an argument optional. This technique is described in a later section.

Line 5 declares an `Integer` variable named `sum`. Line 6 adds the contents of variables `a` and `b` and assigns the result to `sum`. Line 7 then displays it.

Figure 9-5 contains the sequence diagram for Example 9-2. This example employs three objects: `Client`, `Server`, and `Console`. At line 1, code in `Client` invokes `AddEmUp` in `Server`, passing the arguments `(2, 3)`. `AddEmUp` then computes `sum`, and at line 2 invokes `WriteLine` in the `Console` class to display the sum. At line 3, control returns to `Server`, and at line 4 control returns to `Client`.

9

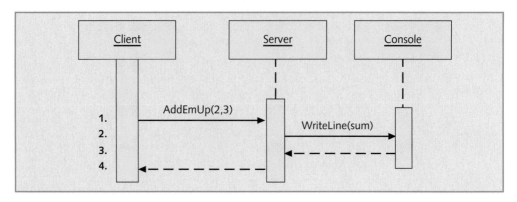

Figure 9-5 Sequence diagram for Example 9-2

Using Function Procedures

Similar to a Sub procedure, a Function procedure definition begins with a procedure header followed by one or more statements and ends with the keywords `End Function`. This syntax is shown in Figure 9-6.

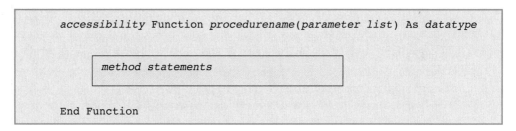

Figure 9-6 VB .NET Function procedure syntax

The procedure header shown in Figure 9-6 contains five parts:

1. *accessibility*—The accessibility (`Public`, `Private`, `Protected`, or `Friend`) as described in the previous section.

2. `Function`—This keyword indicates this is a Function procedure instead of a Sub procedure.

3. *procedurename*—The name of the procedure.

4. **(parameter list)**—The parameter list consists of variable declarations you write so the procedure can receive arguments sent from client objects.

5. **As *datatype***—Function procedures return a single variable. You write its datatype here (Integer, Double, String, etc.).

In Example 9-2, AddEmUp in Server was written as a Sub procedure and therefore did not return a value. Instead, it invoked Console.WriteLine to display the answer. Example 9-3 rewrites AddEmUp as a Function procedure that returns the result to Client, which then displays it.

Example 9-3: Writing and invoking a Function procedure

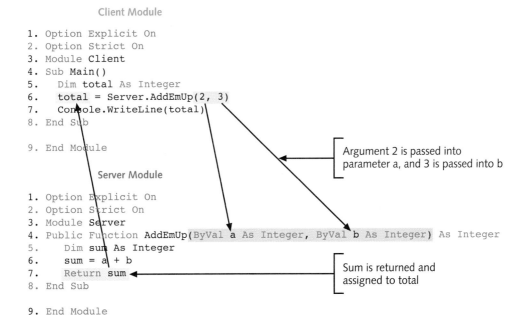

```
                    Client Module
1. Option Explicit On
2. Option Strict On
3. Module Client
4. Sub Main()
5.    Dim total As Integer
6.    total = Server.AddEmUp(2, 3)
7.    Console.WriteLine(total)
8. End Sub

9. End Module
                    Server Module
1. Option Explicit On
2. Option Strict On
3. Module Server
4. Public Function AddEmUp(ByVal a As Integer, ByVal b As Integer) As Integer
5.    Dim sum As Integer
6.    sum = a + b
7.    Return sum
8. End Sub

9. End Module
```

Argument 2 is passed into parameter a, and 3 is passed into b

Sum is returned and assigned to total

Sample Run:

5

Client Module Discussion:

Lines 1 through 4 of the client module are identical to the previous example.

Line 5 declares a new Integer variable named total.

Line 6 invokes `Server.AddEmUp`, passing the same arguments as before. In this example, however, `AddEmUp` returns a value; therefore, line 6 is written to receive the returned `Integer` value and assign it to `total`.

Line 7 then invokes `Console.WriteLine` to display the contents of `total`.

Server Module Discussion:

The procedure named `AddEmUp` is shown in lines 4 through 8 of the module named `Server`. Line 4 is the procedure header and contains two important differences from Example 9-2. First, following the keyword `Public` is the keyword `Function` instead of `Sub`, making this a Function procedure. This means it will return a value to the invoking client. Second, following the parameter list is the data type of the value being returned by the function. In this example, the data type being returned is `Integer`.

Line 5 declaring the `Integer` variable named `sum` and line 6 adding the contents of variables `a` and `b` are identical to the previous example. Line 7, however, instead of invoking `Console.WriteLine` to display `sum`, returns it to the invoking object, `Client`. You return a variable by writing the keyword `Return` followed by the variable name being returned.

 Note that the keyword `Return` returns control of execution to the invoking client. In functions, a variable is required. You can write `Return` without a variable, and you can write more than one `Return` statement in a procedure, although a single exit point is better programming. In addition, you can write `Return` in both Sub and Function procedures.

Figure 9-7 contains the sequence diagram for Example 9-3.

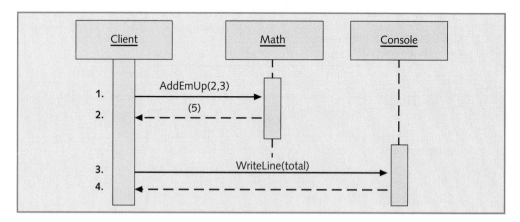

Figure 9-7   Sequence diagram for Example 9-3

WRITING USER-DEFINED PROCEDURES

User-defined procedures are procedures that you design and write. These are in contrast to the methods contained in the FCL classes, which are supplied for you. You create user-defined procedures to give your code structure and organization. In addition, you can create reusable code by designing procedures that others can invoke. There are two categories of user-defined procedures: public and private. **Private procedures** are those you write within a module to provide services only to that module; private procedures cannot be invoked by code in other objects. In contrast, **public procedures** are procedures you design specifically to be invoked by other objects. Each of these categories is described in detail in the following sections.

Writing Private Procedures

Recall that the Programming Example at the end of Chapter 3 converted a Fahrenheit temperature to Celsius. The input consisted of a Fahrenheit temperature. The example then converted the input temperature to Celsius and displayed the result. The example consisted of four separate steps:

1. Input a Fahrenheit temperature.

2. Compute the corresponding Celsius temperature.

3. Round the result to one decimal position.

4. Display the result.

Some of these steps could be written as private procedures, as shown in Example 9-4.

9

Example 9-4: Temperature converter using private procedures

```
1. Option Strict On
2. Option Explicit On

3. Module Chapter9Example4
4. ' declare variables with module scope
5.    Dim fahrenheit, celsius As Double
```

```
6.
7.   Sub Main()
8.       InputFahrenheit()
9.       ComputeCelsius()
10.      DisplayCelsius()
11.   End Sub
12.
13.   Private Sub InputFahrenheit()
14.       Console.WriteLine("Please enter a Fahrenheit temperature:")
15.       fahrenheit = Convert.ToDouble(Console.ReadLine())
16.   End Sub
17.
18.   Private Sub ComputeCelsius()
19.       celsius = 5 / 9 * (fahrenheit - 32)
20.   End Sub
21.
22.   Private Sub DisplayCelsius()
23.       celsius = Math.Round(celsius, 1)
24.       Console.WriteLine(fahrenheit & " F = " & celsius & " C")
25.   End Sub
```

26. End Module

Sample Run: In the following output and in the Sample Runs throughout the chapter, user input is shaded.

Please enter a Fahrenheit temperature:

212
212 F = 100 C

Discussion:

This module consists of four Sub procedures: `Main`, `InputFahrenheit`, `ComputeCelsius`, and `DisplayCelsius`.

Lines 1 and 2 set `Options Strict` and `Explicit` to `On`. Line 3 is the beginning of the module and line 26 ends it.

Line 5 declares two `Double` variables named **fahrenheit** and **celsius**. These variables have module **scope**, which means they can be accessed by any of the code in the module. The scope of a variable represents its visibility or accessibility and is determined by where you declare it. If you declare a variable within a procedure, then its scope is limited to that procedure: it has **procedure scope**. This means that only code within the procedure can access the variable; it is not accessible to code outside the procedure.

Variables with procedure scope are created when the procedure begins executing and are destroyed when the procedure exits. This means the variables exist only while the procedure is executing. Parameter variables have procedure scope.

On the other hand, when you declare a variable outside the procedures in a module, as done in this example in line 5, then the variable is accessible to code within all of the procedures in the module—it has **module scope**. The next example uses variables with procedure scope.

 Variables can also have what is called **block scope**. When you write code that is grouped using an `If`, `Do`, or `For`, and terminated with `End`, `Next`, or `Loop`, the code is called a block. If you declare a variable within such a code block, its scope is limited to that block.

In general, you want to use variables with the smallest or narrowest scope possible. This technique minimizes the impact that changes in one procedure may have in others. You want the code outside a procedure to be ignorant of the variables defined within the procedure. In fact, you want to hide as much as you can of the internal workings of a procedure from outside code; you want to make it as independent as possible. In order for clients to invoke procedures, they need know only the procedure name, the arguments expected, and the data type being returned, if any.

In this example, `Main` is automatically invoked when the module is loaded into memory and is listed in lines 7 through 11. It consists of only three statements that invoke procedures to input a Fahrenheit temperature, compute the Celsius temperature, and then round and display the Celsius temperature.

`InputFahrenheit` is shown in lines 13 through 16. Line 14 displays a prompt and line 15 reads the value, converts it to data type `Double`, and assigns the result to `fahrenheit`.

Lines 18 through 20 show `ComputeCelsius`, which converts the Fahrenheit temperature to Celsius.

Finally, lines 22 through 25 contain `DisplayCelsius`, which rounds the Celsius value to one decimal and then displays it.

None of the procedures in this example contains variable declarations. Instead, they share the module scope variables declared in line 5.

Also note that the three user-defined procedures have `Private` accessibility, which means that other objects cannot invoke them; they can be invoked only by code within this module. If you omit accessibility, the default is `Private`. In addition, these are all Sub procedures, which means they do not return values.

The next example uses a design alternative with Function procedures.

9

Example 9-5: Temperature converter using private functions

```
1. Option Strict On
2. Option Explicit On

3. Module Chapter9Example5

4.    Sub Main()
5.       Dim fahrenheit As Double = InputFahrenheit()
6.       Dim celsius As Double = ComputeCelsius(fahrenheit)
7.       DisplayCelsius(fahrenheit, celsius)
8.    End Sub

9.    Private Function InputFahrenheit() As Double
10.       Dim f As Double
11.       Console.WriteLine("Please enter a Fahrenheit temperature:")
12.       f = Convert.ToDouble(Console.ReadLine())
13.       Return f
14.    End Function

15.    Private Function ComputeCelsius(ByVal f As Double) As Double
16.       Dim c As Double
17.       c = 5 / 9 * (f - 32)
18.       Return c
19.    End Function

20.    Private Sub DisplayCelsius(ByVal f As Double, ByVal c As Double)
21.       c = Math.Round(c, 1)
22.       Console.WriteLine(f & " F = " & c & " C")
23.    End Sub

24. End Module
```

Sample Run:

Please enter a Fahrenheit temperature:

```
212
212 F = 100 C
```

Discussion:

This module also consists of four procedures. Note that `Main` and `DisplayCelsius` are Sub procedures, but `InputFahrenheit` and `ComputeCelsius` are written as Function procedures; they are designed to return a value.

Lines 1 and 2 again set `Options Strict` and `Explicit` to `On`. Line 3 is the beginning of the module and line 24 ends it.

The `Main` procedure is listed in lines 4 through 8 and again contains three statements. Line 5 declares a `Double` variable named `fahrenheit`, invokes the function procedure named `InputFahrenheit`, and assigns the value returned to `fahrenheit`. Note that the scope of `fahrenheit` is the `Main` procedure; it is not visible to any of the other code in the module. This example does not use variables with module scope. Generally, you want to use variables with the smallest possible scope to hide as much implementation detail as possible from other procedures.

Lines 9 through 14 define the Function procedure `InputFahrenheit`. The function header at line 9 does not include parameter variables, indicating this function does not accept arguments, but it does return a variable whose data type is `Double`. Line 10 declares a `Double` variable named `f` with procedure scope. Line 11 displays a prompt and line 12 then reads the value, converts it to data type `Double`, and assigns the result to `f`. Line 13 returns the contents of variable `f` to line 5, which then assigns it to `fahrenheit`.

Back in the `Main` procedure, line 6 declares a procedure scope variable named `celsius` of data type `Double`, invokes the function `ComputeCelsius`, passing the contents of `fahrenheit` as an argument. `ComputeCelsius` is defined at lines 15 through 19. The value returned by `ComputeCelsius` is then assigned to `celsius`.

The procedure header at line 15 declares a parameter variable named `f` whose data type is `Double` and whose scope is the procedure. This procedure returns a value whose data type is `Double`.

Line 16 declares a `Double` variable named `c` with procedure scope. Line 17 converts the Fahrenheit temperature contained in parameter variable `f` to Celsius, assigning the result to `c`. Line 18 returns the contents of `c` to line 6 where it is assigned to `celsius`.

Finally, line 7 in `Main` invokes the Sub procedure named `DisplayCelsius`, passing the two arguments `(fahrenheit, celsius)`.

`DisplayCelsius` is defined at lines 20 through 23. The header at line 20 declares two parameter variables named `f` and `c` whose data type is `Double`. Note that when line 7 invokes `DisplayCelsius`, the contents of `fahrenheit` are assigned to `f` and the contents of `celsius` to `c`. Line 21 then invokes `Math.Round` to round the contents of `c` to one decimal position. Line 22 then invokes `Console.WriteLine` to display the result.

Writing Public Procedures

You have seen that private procedures can only be invoked by the module containing the procedures. On the other hand, public procedures can be invoked by any object. You generally design public procedures to provide services that are required by multiple objects or applications. For example, sales tax computation is a process that can be shared by others.

Example 9-6 illustrates a solution using both private and public procedures.

Example 9-6: Using both public and private procedures

Chapter9Example6 Module

```
1. Option Strict On

2. Option Explicit On

3. Module Chapter9Example6


4.    Sub Main()

5.      Dim amountOfSale, salesTax As Double

6.      amountOfSale = InputAmountOfSale()

7.      Do Until amountOfSale = 99999

8.        salesTax = Server.ComputeSalesTax(amountOfSale)

9.        DisplayTotal(amountOfSale, salesTax)

10.       amountOfSale = InputAmountOfSale()

11.     Loop

12.   End Sub


13.   Private Function InputAmountOfSale() As Double

14.     Console.Write("Enter amount of sale (99999 to
          stop):  ")

15.     Dim amount As Double = Convert.ToDouble(Console.
          ReadLine())

16.     Return amount

17.   End Function


18.   Private Sub DisplayTotal(ByVal saleAmount As
          Double, ByVal tax As Double)

19.     Dim total As Double = saleAmount + tax

20.     Console.WriteLine("Amount of sale: " &
          saleAmount.ToString("C"))

21.     Console.WriteLine("Sales tax: " & tax.ToString("C"))
```

22.    ```
       Console.WriteLine("Total amount due: " &
           total.ToString("C"))
       ```

23.   `End Sub`

24. `End Module`

Server Module

1. `Option Explicit On`

2. `Option Strict On`

3. `Module Server`

4.    ```
      Public Function ComputeSalesTax(ByVal amount As
          Double) As Double
      ```

5.   `Const SALES_TAX_RATE As Double = 0.085`

6.   `Dim salesTax As Double`

7.   `salesTax = SALES_TAX_RATE * amount`

8.   `salesTax = Math.Round(salesTax, 2)`

9.   `Return salesTax`

10.   `End Function`

11. `End Module`

Sample Run:

```
Enter amount of sale (99999 to stop): 123.45
Amount of sale: $123.45
Sales tax: $10.49
Total amount due: $133.94
Enter amount of sale (99999 to stop): 99999
```

Discussion:

This example illustrates both private and public procedures and consists of two modules: `Chapter9Example6` and `Server`. `Server` contains a single public procedure named `ComputeSalesTax` listed in lines 4 through 10. This Function procedure accepts a sales amount, then computes and returns the sales tax amount. `ComputeSalesTax` is public and designed to be used by any object wanting to determine the sales tax amount.

The procedure header at line 4 indicates it is to receive a `Double` argument and that it returns a `Double` value. Line 5 declares and populates a constant for the percentage sales tax, and line 6 declares a `Double` variable that will hold the computed tax amount.

Line 7 computes the tax, line 8 rounds it to two decimal positions, and line 9 returns it to the invoking client, which in this example is the module named `Chapter9Example6`.

The client module has two private Sub procedures: `Main` at lines 4 through 12 and `DisplayTotal` at lines 18 through 23. In addition, there is one private function procedure named `InputAmountOfSale` at lines 13 through 17.

The `Main` method first declares two `Double` variables with procedure scope named `amountOfSale`, which will contain the sale amount, and `salesTax`, which will hold the computed sales tax.

Line 6 invokes `InputAmountOfSale` and assigns the value returned to `amountOfSale`. `InputAmountOfSale` continues at lines 13 through 17 and displays a prompt at line 14. Line 15 declares a `Double` variable named `amount`, invokes `Console.ReadLine` to input the value entered, invokes `Convert.ToDouble` to convert it to `Double`, and finally assigns the result to `amount`.

Lines 7 through 11 define a sentinel-controlled `Do Until` loop, which terminates when a sale amount of 99999 is entered.

Line 8 invokes `ComputeSalesTax` in the `Server` module, passing `amountOfSale` as an argument. The value returned is then assigned to `salesTax`.

Next, line 9 invokes `DisplayTotal`, passing arguments (`amountOfSale, salesTax`).

`DisplayTotal` is defined at lines 18 through 23. The procedure header at line 18 declares two parameter variables named `saleAmount` and `tax`. Line 19 declares a `Double` variable named `total` and then assigns the sum of `saleAmount` and `tax`. Lines 20 through 22 display the sale amount, the tax amount, and the total.

To summarize, you write Function procedures to return a value and Sub procedures when you do not need to return a value. You write private procedures to be invoked by code within the same module, and you write public procedures to be invoked by code outside the module. Often you will design and write public procedures to be invoked by more than one object.

Using Optional Parameters

When designing procedures, you may sometimes want to make some arguments optional. You create an optional argument by adding the keyword `Optional` to a parameter variable declaration in the procedure header and then indicating a default value. When you write an optional parameter definition, you must provide a default value. Also, you cannot follow an optional parameter definition with a non-optional one; if you have optional parameters, their definitions must come at the end of the parameter list.

The following example uses a public procedure to compute the shipping charge for an order based on the distance the order is being shipped. The procedure, named ComputeShippingCharge, has an optional parameter named distance. If the invoking object does not provide an argument, then the default distance value of 100 is used.

Example 9-7: Using an optional parameter

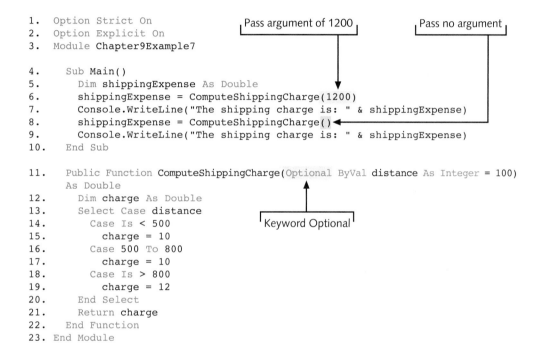

```
1.   Option Strict On
2.   Option Explicit On
3.   Module Chapter9Example7

4.     Sub Main()
5.        Dim shippingExpense As Double
6.        shippingExpense = ComputeShippingCharge(1200)
7.        Console.WriteLine("The shipping charge is: " & shippingExpense)
8.        shippingExpense = ComputeShippingCharge()
9.        Console.WriteLine("The shipping charge is: " & shippingExpense)
10.    End Sub

11.    Public Function ComputeShippingCharge(Optional ByVal distance As Integer = 100)
          As Double
12.       Dim charge As Double
13.       Select Case distance
14.         Case Is < 500
15.            charge = 10
16.         Case 500 To 800
17.            charge = 10
18.         Case Is > 800
19.            charge = 12
20.       End Select
21.       Return charge
22.    End Function
23. End Module
```

Pass argument of 1200

Pass no argument

Keyword Optional

9

Sample Run:

```
The shipping charge is: 12
The shipping charge is: 10
```

Discussion:

This example consists of a single module named Chapter9Example7 having two procedures: Main at lines 4 through 10 and ComputeShippingCharge at lines 11 through 22.

The procedure header for `ComputeShippingCharge` at line 11 has the keyword `Optional` preceding the declaration of the parameter named `distance`. Following the declaration, the default value of 100 is specified. You must always indicate a default value when you use an optional parameter. If the invoking code passes an argument, then that value is assigned to `distance`; otherwise, the default value of 100 is assigned. Lines 11 through 20 assign a value to `charge` based on the contents of `distance`, and line 21 returns the charge.

`Main` first declares a `Double` variable named `shippingExpense` at line 5.

Line 6 invokes `ComputeShippingCharge`, passing 1200 as an argument, and line 7 displays it.

Line 8 invokes `ComputeShippingCharge` but passes no argument. This causes the procedure to assign the default value of 100. Line 9 then displays the value returned.

DESIGNING AND WRITING OVERLOADED PROCEDURES

`ComputeSalesTax` in Example 9-6 accepts a `Double` argument. Because this procedure was designed to be invoked by any code wanting to compute sales tax, you want to make the procedure as flexible as possible. One way to increase its usefulness is to permit arguments with other data types. For example, if a client wants to pass `ComputeSalesTax` an argument whose data type is `Single` instead of `Double`, the procedure in its present form will not accept it because `Option Strict` is set to On. To accommodate a `Single` argument, you create an **overloaded procedure**.

A procedure's **signature** consists of both its name *and* its parameter list. When you invoke a procedure, VB .NET identifies the procedure by its signature, *not* by its name. Therefore, you can have two or more procedures with the same name, but as long as their parameter lists are different, VB .NET sees them as unique procedures. VB .NET uses the name *and* the argument list to match the procedure you invoke.

Overloading a procedure means you write multiple procedures with the *same name* but with *different signatures*. Overloading is a convenient technique to avoid using unique names for procedures.

 Note that you can overload a Function procedure with a Sub procedure and vice versa. The return data type is not a part of a procedure's signature.

Overloading is one solution to the `ComputeSalesTax` argument data type difficulty. You can write one version using a `Double` argument and a second version using a `Single` argument. You use the keyword `Overloads` to define each version of an overloaded procedure. Example 9-8 illustrates this solution.

Example 9-8: Overloading a procedure

Module Server

Use keyword Overloads

The data type of the argument is Single

```
1. Option Explicit On
2. Option Strict On
3. Module Server

4. Const SALES_TAX_RATE As Double = 0.085 ' note module scope

5.    Public Overloads Function ComputeSalesTax(ByVal amount As Single) As Double
6.       Dim salesTax As Double
7.       salesTax = SALES_TAX_RATE * amount
8.       salesTax = Math.Round(salesTax, 2)
9.       Return salesTax
10.   End Function

11.   Public Overloads Function ComputeSalesTax(ByVal amount As Double) As Double
12.       Dim salesTax As Double
13.       salesTax = SALES_TAX_RATE * amount
14.       salesTax = Math.Round(salesTax, 2)
15.       Return salesTax
16.   End Function

17.End Module
```

The data type of the argument is Double

9

Chapter9Example8

```
1. Option Strict On

2. Option Explicit On


3. Module Chapter9Example8

4.    Sub Main()

5.       Dim amount1 As Double = 100

6.       Dim amount2 As Single = 200

7.       Dim salesTax As Double

8.       salesTax = Server.ComputeSalesTax(amount1)

9.       Console.WriteLine("Sales tax for amount1 is: " &
          salesTax.ToString("C"))

10.      salesTax = Server.ComputeSalesTax(amount2)

11.      Console.WriteLine("Sales tax for amount2 is: " &
          salesTax.ToString("C"))

12.    End Sub


13. End Module
```

Sample Run:

```
Sales tax for amount1 is: $8.50
Sales tax for amount2 is: $17.00
```

Discussion:

The **Server** module in this example now has two procedures named **ComputeSalesTax**. The first, in lines 5 through 10, accepts an argument whose data type is **Single**. The second procedure in lines 11 through 16 accepts an argument whose data type is **Double**. Note that these two procedures are identical except for their parameter variables data types: they have different signatures.

Recall that when you write an overloaded procedure you add the keyword **Overloads** to the procedure header. This tells the VB .NET compiler that you are creating a different version of the procedure.

Note that the constant **SALES_TAX_RATE** has module scope in this example instead of repeating it in each procedure. This change avoids duplication and facilitates changing its value at some future time.

The client in this example is named **Chapter9Example8** and consists of the single procedure **Main** at lines 4 through 12.

Line 5 declares a **Double** variable named **amount1** and populates it with 100.

Line 6 declares a **Single** variable named **amount2** and populates it with 200.

Line 7 declares a **Double** variable named **salesTax** that will hold the computed tax.

Line 8 invokes **Server.ComputeSalesTax** passing **amount1** as an argument. The value returned is assigned to **salesTax**. Line 9 displays this value.

Line 10 invokes **Server.ComputeSalesTax** passing **amount2** as an argument. The value returned is assigned to **salesTax**. Line 11 displays this value.

In the **Chapter9Example8** module, when line 8 is executed, the procedure at line 11 in the **Server** module is invoked because the argument being passed is data type **Double**. When line 10 is executed, the procedure at line 5 in the **Server** module is invoked because the argument being passed is data type **Single**. VB .NET matches both the name and argument data type when invoking a procedure.

To summarize, you write overloaded procedures when you want to use the same procedure name but different arguments. VB .NET identifies a procedure using its signature, which consists of the name and parameter list.

PROGRAMMING EXAMPLE: ELECTRICITY BILLING

This Programming Example demonstrates a program that inputs previous and current electric meter readings, computes the electricity charge and sales tax, and then displays the electricity consumed, electricity charge, sales tax, and total bill. It uses a sentinel-controlled loop to process several bills.

Input   Previous and current meter reading

Output   Electric bill containing:
1. Kilowatt hours (kwh) consumed
2. Electric charge formatted as currency
3. Sales tax formatted as currency
4. Bill total formatted as currency

Problem Analysis and Algorithm Design

The purpose of this program is to input previous and current electric meter readings, and then compute and display the total bill using a sentinel-controlled loop.

Variables   You need `Integer` variables to store the previous and current meter readings, and the amount of kilowatt hours (kwh) consumed; you need `Double` variables to contain the electricity charge, sales tax, and total bill.

Formulas   Subtract the previous meter reading from the current meter reading to obtain the kwh consumed. The charge for electricity uses the following table:

KWH Consumed	Rate per KWH
< 500	.05
500—1000	$25 + .055 for amount over 500
> 1000	$52.50 + .06 for amount over 1000

Use the `ComputeSalesTax` procedure from Example 9-6 to compute the sales tax. The total bill is computed by adding the electricity charge to the sales tax.

Main Algorithm and Design

Use a modular design consisting of two modules: a main module named `Chapter9EOCExample` and a server module named `Server` containing the `ComputeSalesTax` procedure, which is copied without change from Example 9-6.

The main module will have five procedures:

1. `Main`: this Sub procedure is automatically invoked when the application begins.
   a. Declare variables with procedure scope.
   b. Invoke `GetPreviousReading` to get previous meter reading.
   c. Begin a sentinel-controlled `Do Until` loop that terminates when the previous meter reading is 99999.
      - Invoke `GetCurrentReading` to get current meter reading.
      - Compute kwh consumed.
      - Invoke `ComputeElectricityCharge` passing KWH consumed.
      - Invoke `ComputeSalesTax` passing electricity charge.
      - Invoke `DisplayBill` passing kwh consumed, electricity charge, and sales tax.

2. `GetPreviousReading`: This Function procedure inputs and returns the previous meter reading.

3. `GetCurrentReading`: This Function procedure inputs and returns the current meter reading.

4. `ComputeElectricityCharge`: This Function procedure computes the electricity charge based on the preceding table using the `Select Case` structure.

5. `DisplayBill`: This Sub procedure displays kwh consumed, electricity charge, sales tax, and total bill. Dollar amounts are formatted as currency.

Complete Program Listing

Chapter9EOCExample Module

```
Option Explicit On
Option Strict On
Module Chapter9EOCExample

    Sub Main()
        Dim electricityCharge, salesTax As Double
        Dim previousMeterReading, currentMeterReading, _
        kwhConsumed As Integer
        previousMeterReading = GetPreviousReading()

        Do Until previousMeterReading = 99999
            currentMeterReading = GetCurrentReading()
            kwhConsumed = currentMeterReading - _
            previousMeterReading
            electricityCharge = ComputeElectricityCharge _
            (kwhConsumed)
```

```vbnet
            salesTax = Server.ComputeSalesTax(electricityCharge)
            DisplayBill(salesTax, kwhConsumed, electricityCharge)
            previousMeterReading = GetPreviousReading()
        Loop
    End Sub
    Private Function GetPreviousReading() As Integer
        Console.WriteLine("This program computes an electric
        bill for customers")
        Console.Write("Enter previous meter reading (99999 to
        stop):  ")
        Dim reading As Integer = Convert.ToInt32(Console. _
        ReadLine())
        Return reading
    End Function
    Private Function GetCurrentReading() As Integer
        Console.Write("Enter current meter reading:  ")
        Dim reading As Integer = _
        Convert.ToInt32(Console.ReadLine())
        Return reading
    End Function
    Private Function ComputeElectricityCharge(ByVal kwh As
    Integer) As Double
        Dim amount As Double
        Select Case kwh
            Case Is < 500
                amount = kwh * 0.05
            Case 500 To 1000
                amount = 25 + (kwh - 500) * 0.055
            Case Is > 1000
                amount = 52.5 + (kwh - 1000) * 0.06
        End Select
        amount = Math.Round(amount, 2)
        Return amount
    End Function
    Private Sub DisplayBill(ByVal tax As Double, ByVal kwh
    As Integer, ByVal charge As Double)
        Dim totalBill As Double
        totalBill = tax + charge
        Console.WriteLine("KWH Consumed: " & kwh)
        Console.WriteLine("Electricity charge: " & _
        charge.ToString("C"))
        Console.WriteLine("Sales Tax: " & tax.ToString("C"))
        Console.WriteLine("Total Bill: " & totalBill. _
    ToString("C"))
    End Sub
End Module
```

9

Server Module

```
Option Explicit On
Option Strict On
Module Server
    Public Function ComputeSalesTax(ByVal amount As Double) _
    As Double
        Const SALES_TAX_RATE As Double = 0.085
        Dim salesTax As Double
        salesTax = SALES_TAX_RATE * amount
        salesTax = Math.Round(salesTax, 2)
        Return salesTax
    End Function
End Module
```

Sample Run

In the following Sample Run, the user input is shaded.

```
This program computes an electric bill for customers
Enter previous meter reading (99999 to stop): 00000
Enter current meter reading: 400
KWH Consumed: 400
Electricity charge: $20.00
Sales Tax: $1.70
Total Bill: $21.70
This program computes an electric bill for customers
Enter previous meter reading (99999 to stop): 1000
Enter current meter reading: 1500
KWH Consumed: 500
Electricity charge: $25.00
Sales Tax: $2.12
Total Bill: $27.12
This program computes an electric bill for customers
Enter previous meter reading (99999 to stop): 99999
```

QUICK REVIEW

1. Objects frequently collaborate by interacting. Applying the basic client–server model, the object sending a message is the client object, and the object receiving the message is the server object. Some procedures accept arguments and some procedures return procedures to the invoking client.

2. The Unified Modeling Language (UML) provides various diagrams for modeling object-oriented systems, including the sequence diagram, which maps interactions between objects.

3. Visual Basic .NET (VB .NET) provides two types of procedures: Sub procedures and Function procedures. The difference between the two is that a Function procedure returns a value but a Sub procedure does not.

4. A Sub procedure definition begins with a procedure header containing the keyword `Sub` followed by one or more statements and ends with the keywords `End Sub`.

5. Arguments are passed into parameters. The parameter list consists of variable declarations that receive arguments being sent from client objects.

6. A Function procedure definition begins with a procedure header containing the keyword `Function` followed by one or more statements, and ends with the keywords `End Function`. Function procedures return a single variable. You write its data type at the end of the procedure header.

7. User-defined procedures are procedures that you design and write. These are in contrast to the methods contained in the Framework Class Library (FCL) classes.

8. There are two categories of user-defined procedures: public and private. Private procedures are those you write within a module to provide services to that object; private procedures cannot be invoked by code in other objects. In contrast, public procedures are procedures you write specifically designed to be invoked by other objects.

9. The scope of a variable represents its visibility or accessibility and is determined by where you declare it. A variable declared within a procedure has procedure scope. However, a variable declared outside the procedures within a module is accessible to code within all of the procedures in the module—it has module scope.

10. Variables can also have what is called block scope. When you write code that is grouped using an `If`, `Do`, or `For`, and terminated with `End`, `Next`, or `Loop`, the code is called a block. If you declare a variable within such a code block, its scope is limited to that block.

11. You create an optional argument by adding the keyword `Optional` to a parameter variable declaration in the procedure header and then indicating a default value.

12. A procedure's signature consists of both its name and its parameter list. When you invoke a procedure, VB .NET identifies the procedure by its signature, *not* by its name.

13. Overloading a procedure means you write multiple procedures with the *same name* but with *different signatures*. Overloading is a convenient technique to avoid using unique names for procedures.

14. You can overload a Function procedure with a Sub procedure and vice versa. The return data type is not a part of a procedure's signature.

Exercises

1. How can you tell whether a procedure returns a value?
2. Distinguish between `Private` and `Public` accessibility.
3. Explain the difference between an argument and a parameter.
4. Draw a sequence diagram for Example 9-6.

5. What is an `Optional` parameter? What are the rules for writing one?

6. What is a user-defined procedure?

7. What is scope? Distinguish between module and procedure scope.

8. What is block scope?

9. What is a procedure's signature?

10. What is an overloaded procedure?

PROGRAMMING EXERCISES

1. The `ComputeCelsius` procedure in Example 9-5 accepts a `Double` argument and returns a `Double` value. Write an overloaded version of `ComputeCelsius` that accepts `Integer` and returns `Single`. Modify the `Main` procedure in this example to invoke both versions of `ComputeCelsius`.

2. Example 4-18 in Chapter 4 contains code using the `Select Case` structure to determine a student's grade based upon an exam score. Design and write a public Function procedure that accepts an exam score as an argument and then determines and returns the grade, using the code from Example 4-18. Write a client module to test your code.

3. The Programming Example at the end of Chapter 7 contains code that computes the federal withholding tax for employees based on their wages and marital status. Using this example as a guide, design and write a public Function procedure that accepts wages and marital status as arguments and returns the federal withholding tax. Write a client module to test your code, using the values from the Chapter 7 Programming Example as test data.

4. The Programming Example at the end of Chapter 5 produces a loan amortization report. The input is the amount of the loan, the annual percentage rate, and the duration expressed in number of months. Redesign the example to use procedures. Design public procedures to compute the monthly payment and the monthly interest, and place these into a module named Server.

10

Writing Class Definitions

In this chapter, you will:

- Examine the three-tier design model
- Write a class definition
- Design and write overloaded constructors
- Create polymorphic methods
- Write properties
- Create shared attributes and methods

In the previous chapter, you wrote modules and procedures. In earlier chapters, you invoked methods within some of the supplied classes. In this chapter, you write class definitions containing attribute definitions, methods, and properties.

A class is similar to a module in that it contains code, but classes have some important differences. First, classes often represent real-world entities such as GUI Buttons, Message Boxes, or Customers and Students. Second, you can create instances of classes and then invoke methods for the instances. In previous chapters, for example, you instantiated GUI classes such as Button and MessageBox and then made them visible. You have also created instances of non-visible classes such as String and ArrayList and invoked their methods. In this chapter you write class definitions.

EXAMINING THE THREE-TIER DESIGN MODEL

Object-oriented (OO) developers have adopted an approach to OO systems development called **three-tier design**. This approach places the objects in an OO system into three categories of classes—**problem domain**, **GUI**, and **data access**. Problem domain (PD) classes represent objects specific to a business application, such as Customers, Orders, and Products. GUI classes define the objects that make up the user interface to the application, including forms, buttons, labels, list boxes, and text boxes. You worked with several of these GUI classes in Chapter 8 and will develop more complex GUI classes in Chapter 13.

The third category of classes in three-tier design is called data access classes. These interact with database management systems to store and retrieve information needed for processing. Figure 10-1 illustrates three-tier design.

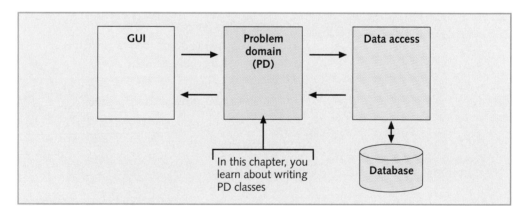

Figure 10-1   Three-tier design

Three-tier design requires that OO system developers define these three categories of classes when designing and building a system. First, the developers identify and specify the problem domain classes. Once these are specified, the developers then define how GUI classes will be used to allow the user to interact with the problem domain classes. Finally, they specify data access classes to allow problem domain classes to interact with the database. Once all three tiers are completed, they are ready to work together as a complete system.

WRITING A CLASS DEFINITION

You begin developing an OO system by writing a **class definition** for each of the problem domain classes. The Visual Basic .NET (VB .NET) code you write representing a class is called a class definition. These class definitions are based on some of the features of their real-world counterparts. Features you want to capture in your model include the object's characteristics and behavior.

For example, to model a Customer you could choose to include the customer's name, address, and telephone number as characteristics. You model an object's characteristics by defining **attributes**. Attributes are variables that are populated with data describing the object.

You model an object's behavior by writing methods that mimic the desired behavior. To illustrate, a Customer could tell you their address and telephone number. You would then write methods to report the address and telephone number for the particular customer. Each class definition will contain the attributes and methods that make the objects behave as required by the system.

10

Drawing a Class Diagram

In Chapter 9 you drew Unified Modeling Language (UML) sequence diagrams to model object interaction. Another useful UML model is the **class diagram**. You draw a class diagram to model classes. Given a system involving customers, you could create a `Customer` class that represents all of the customers in the system. First, you identify the relevant attributes you want to model and then write a class definition representing a software model of the `Customer` class.

 The UML provides various diagrams for modeling OO systems. UML is an accepted standard by the Object Management Group (OMG), an industry association dedicated to improving OO development practices. You can find complete information about UML, the diagrams, and the constructs at *www.Rational.com*.

Figure 10-2 shows a class diagram for the **Customer** class, which represents the customers in a system. In this example, you capture three customer attributes: name, address, and phone number. In the next section, you write a class definition for **Customer**.

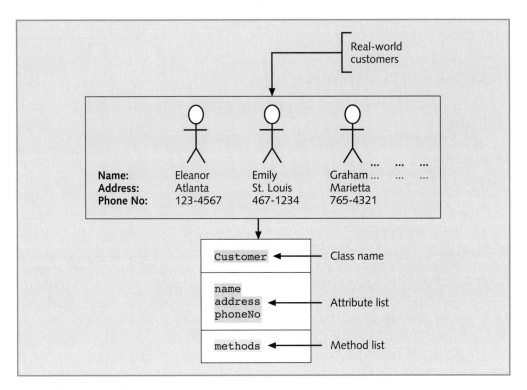

Figure 10-2   The Customer class represents customers

The class diagram uses a rectangle to model a class. The body of the rectangle has three parts. The class name goes in the top part, the attribute list in the middle, and the method list in the bottom part. Chapter 11 deals with inheritance and association, and illustrates more complex class diagrams showing relationships between classes.

Class Definition Syntax

The syntax of a class definition begins with a **class header** followed by attribute definitions, then method code, and ends with the keywords **End Class**. The class header is a line of code that identifies the class and some of its characteristics. Figure 10-3 shows the structure of a VB .NET class definition.

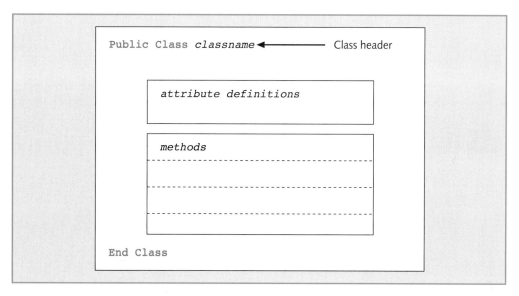

Figure 10-3   VB .NET class definition structure

The keyword `Public` indicates this class has public accessibility, meaning anyone can use it. The keyword `Class` indicates this line of code is a class header, which is followed by the class name, such as `Customer`.

Following the class header, you write attribute definitions and methods. The keywords `End Class` terminate the class definition code.

Defining Attributes

The `Customer` class diagram in Figure 10-2 shows three attributes for name, address, and phone number. You define attributes by declaring variables for each one. You declare a variable by writing the keyword `Dim`, the variable name, the keyword `As`, and then its data type followed by its name. You write an attribute definition the same way, except you replace the keyword `Dim` with the accessibility. Similar to procedures, you specify the accessibility of a variable by writing `Public` or `Private`. `Public` allows any class to access the variable directly, while `Private` prohibits direct access, and the variable is accessible only within the class where it is defined.

 When defining the accessibility of a variable or procedure, you can write `Public`, `Private`, `Protected`, or `Friend`. The keyword `Protected` allows subclasses to have direct access, while `Friend` permits classes within the same **assembly** access. An assembly is a collection of one or more projects that are deployed as an application. You can assign your project and all of its classes to a specific assembly. You will use `Protected` in the next chapter.

Example 10-1 shows a class definition, which is part of an existing project. To add a class definition to a project in VB.NET, click Project on the menu bar, and then click Add Class to open the Add New Item window. Select the Class icon in the Templates section, and enter the class name in the Name box. Then click the Open button.

Example 10-1 shows the definition for the `Customer` class shown in Figure 10-2.

Example 10-1: Class definition for Customer

```
1. Public Class Customer
2.     Public name As String
3.     Public address As String
4.     Public phoneNo As String
5. End Class
```

Discussion:

This class definition begins with the class header in line 1 and ends at line 5 with the keywords **End Class**. Lines 2, 3, and 4 declare attributes for the customer's name, address, and phone number. Later you add methods to this class.

The next example includes a `Client` module to create instances of `Customer`.

VB .NET programmers have adopted a style for naming classes, attributes, and methods:
Class names begin with a capital letter (`Customer`, `Student`);
Attribute names begin with a lowercase character, and subsequent words in the name start with a capital letter (`address`, `phoneNo`);
Method names begin with a capital letter, with subsequent words also starting with a capital letter. In addition, method names usually contain an imperative verb describing what the method does, followed by a noun. Examples of method names are `GetPhoneNo`, `SetAddress`, and `ComputeLease`.

Instantiating a Class

You create instances of a class with each instance representing specific occurrences of the class. In this example, you instantiate `Customer` to represent real-world customers. The following example creates an instance representing the customer named Eleanor.

Example 10-2: Client module to instantiate Customer

```
1. Option Strict On
2. Option Explicit On
3. Module Client
4. Sub Main()
5.    Dim aCustomer As Customer
6.    ' create a Customer instance
7.    aCustomer = New Customer
8.    ' populate the attributes
9.    aCustomer.name = "Eleanor"
10.   aCustomer.address = "Atlanta"
11.   aCustomer.phoneNo = "123-4567"
12.   ' retrieve & display the attribute contents
13.   Console.WriteLine(aCustomer.name)
14.   Console.WriteLine(aCustomer.address)
15.   Console.WriteLine(aCustomer.phoneNo)
16. End Sub
17. End Module
```

Sample Run:

```
Eleanor
Atlanta
123-4567
```

Discussion:

This module named `Client` contains the single procedure `Main`, which executes when it is loaded.

Line 5 declares a reference variable named `aCustomer` whose data type is `Customer`.

Line 7 instantiates `Customer` using the keyword `New` and assigns its reference to the instance to the reference variable `aCustomer`. Figure 10-4 shows the new `Customer` instance.

10

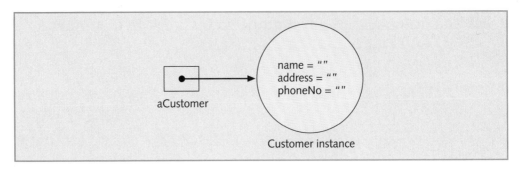

Figure 10-4   A Customer instance

Note that the attributes in the new instance are not yet populated. Lines 9, 10, and 11 populate the instance attributes by assigning them values. You are able to access these attributes from code in the **Client** module because their accessibility is coded **Public**. This means any object has permission to access these attributes.

Figure 10-5 shows the instance with its attributes populated.

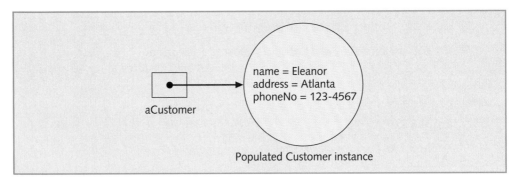

Figure 10-5   Customer instance with attributes populated

Lines 13, 14, and 15 retrieve the contents of the three attributes and display them.

Writing Accessor Methods

The **Customer** class definition in the previous example had attributes with **Public** accessibility. This means that all objects have direct access to the attribute variables. Although this approach is simple and works, it violates the OO principle of **encapsulation**. Encapsulation requires that the internal data and structure of a class be hidden from outside objects. This requires that the class have methods providing access to attributes. These methods are called **accessor methods**.

`Customer` has three attributes, each with private accessibility, which prevents client objects from accessing them directly. Instead, clients invoke accessor methods to store and retrieve attribute values.

Accessor methods are often called **standard methods** and are typically not shown on class diagrams because developers assume they are included. In contrast, methods that you write to perform other functions are called **custom methods**, and *are* shown on class diagrams.

There are two types of accessor methods: those that *get* attribute values and those that *set* attribute values. Accessors that retrieve values are called **get accessor methods**, or simply **getters**, and are named with the prefix "get" followed by the attribute name. Because `Customer` has three attributes, you write three getter methods named `getName`, `getAddress`, and `getPhoneNo` for the `Customer` class definition. Similarly, accessor methods that change attribute values are called **set accessor methods**, or **setters**, and are named with the prefix "`set`" followed by the attribute name. You also write a setter for each attribute: `setName`, `setAddress`, and `setPhoneNo`. You write Sub procedures for setters and Function procedures for getters because they return a value. The general format for accessor methods is shown in Figure 10-6.

```
// getter format
Public Function getAttributeName() As attributeDataType
   Return attributeName
End Function

// setter format
Public Sub setAttributeName(ByVal parameterName As attributeDataType)
    attributeName = parameterName
End Sub
```

Figure 10-6   Accessor method syntax

The getter method header specifies the data type of the attribute it will return and has an empty parameter list because it does not receive arguments. In this example, the getter method has a single statement using the keyword `Return` to send the contents of the attribute variable to the invoking client object. Sometimes getter methods format data before returning it to a client. Methods can return only a single variable value, although it can be a reference variable pointing to an instance that can contain numerous values.

Client objects send arguments to the setter method that they use to populate attributes. Therefore, you must declare a parameter variable to receive this argument. Setter methods sometimes have data validation code to verify that the values they receive are valid.

Example 10-3 lists the Customer class with the accessor methods included.

Example 10-3: Customer class definition with accessor methods

```
1. Public Class Customer
2.    'attribute definitions with Private accessibility
3.    Private name As String
4.    Private address As String
5.    Private phoneNo As String
6.
7.    'get accessor methods
8.    Public Function GetName() As String
9.      Return name
10.   End Function
11.
12.   Public Function GetAddress() As String
13.     Return address
14.   End Function
15.
16.   Public Function GetPhoneNo() As String
17.     Return phoneNo
18.   End Function
19.
20.   'set accessor methods
21.   Public Sub SetName(ByVal aName As String)
22.     name = aName
23.   End Sub
24.
25.   Public Sub SetAddress(ByVal anAddress As String)
26.     address = anAddress
27.   End Sub
```

```
28.
29.    Public Sub SetPhoneNo(ByVal aPhoneNo As String)
30.       phoneNo = aPhoneNo
31.    End Sub
32.  End Class
```

Now, when a client instantiates **Customer**, it invokes the set methods to populate attributes and it invokes get methods to retrieve attribute values. Example 10-4 shows this code.

Example 10-4: Client invoking accessor methods in Customer

```
1.   Option Strict On
2.   Option Explicit On
3.   Module Client
4.   Sub Main()
5.     Dim aCustomer As Customer
6.     ' instantiate Customer
7.     aCustomer = New Customer

8.     ' invoke set methods to populate attributes
9.     aCustomer.SetName("Eleanor")
10.    aCustomer.SetAddress("Atlanta")
11.    aCustomer.SetPhoneNo("123-4567")

12.    ' invoke get methods to retrieve attributes
13.    Console.WriteLine(aCustomer.GetName)
14.    Console.WriteLine(aCustomer.GetAddress)
15.    Console.WriteLine(aCustomer.GetPhoneNo)
16.  End Sub
17.  End Module
```

10

Sample Run:

```
Eleanor
Atlanta
123-4567
```

Discussion:

This module named `Client` contains the single procedure `Main`, which executes when it is loaded.

Line 5 declares a reference variable named `aCustomer` whose data type is `Customer`.

Line 7 instantiates `Customer` using the keyword `New` and assigns the instance reference to `aCustomer`. This means that `aCustomer` now points to, or refers to, the new `Customer` instance.

Line 9 invokes `SetName` for the instance referenced by `aCustomer`, passing the argument (`"Eleanor"`). This method, shown in line 21 in Example 10-3, receives the argument `"Eleanor"` into the parameter variable named `aName`. Line 22 in the method then assigns this value to the attribute variable `name`.

Similarly, line 10 in `Client` invokes `SetAddress` in the `Customer` instance, passing the argument (`"Atlanta"`), and line 11 in `Client` invokes `SetPhoneNo` passing (`"123-4567"`). All three attribute variables are now populated.

Line 13 in `Client` invokes `GetName` for the instance referenced by `aCustomer`, passing the value returned to `Console.WriteLine`, which displays it. Similarly, lines 14 and 15 retrieve and display the customer's address and phone numbers.

Writing a Parameterized Constructor

In the previous section, you saw how to create a customer instance and invoke its setter methods to populate the attributes. Although this approach works, you can simplify it by adding a constructor to your `Customer` class definition. A **constructor** is a special method that is *automatically* invoked whenever you create an instance of a class using the keyword `New`. The constructor is always named `New` and is written as a Sub procedure because it cannot return a value.

Even if you do not write a constructor, VB .NET creates a default constructor that is invoked when you instantiate a class, although it doesn't do anything. The default constructor consists of only a header and an `End Sub` statement. The default constructor for `Customer` is shown in Figure 10-7.

```
Public Sub New()
End Sub
```

Figure 10-7   Default constructor for Customer

You can write your own constructor, called a **parameterized constructor**, because it can contain a parameter list to receive arguments that are used to populate the instance attributes. You want the constructor method for `Customer` to receive arguments for the three attributes: name, address, and phone number. The constructor will then invoke the setter methods to populate the attributes. This saves the `Client` code by eliminating the need for it to invoke each setter method to populate the three attributes.

The `Customer` class definition with a parameterized constructor is shown in Example 10-5.

Example 10-5: Customer class definition with parameterized constructor

```
1. Public Class Customer
2.    private name As String
3.    Private address As String
4.    Private phoneNo As String

5. ' parameterized constructor
6.    Public Sub New(ByVal aName As String, ByVal anAddress
         As String, ByVal aPhoneNo As String)
7.       SetName(aName)
8.       SetAddress(anAddress)
9.       SetPhoneNo(aPhoneNo)
10. End Sub

11.    'get accessor methods
12.    Public Function GetName() As String
13.       Return name
14.    End Function
```

10

```
15.   Public Function GetAddress() As String
16.      Return address
17.   End Function

18.   Public Function GetPhoneNo() As String
19.      Return phoneNo
20.   End Function
21.   'set accessor methods
22.   Public Sub SetName(ByVal aName As String)
23.      name = aName
24.   End Sub

25.   Public Sub SetAddress(ByVal anAddress As String)
26.      address = anAddress
27.   End Sub

28.   Public Sub SetPhoneNo(ByVal aPhoneNo As String)
29.      phoneNo = aPhoneNo
30.   End Sub
31. End Class
```

Discussion:

This **Customer** class definition is a copy of Example 10-3 with the addition of a constructor listed in lines 6 through 10.

You give this constructor method **Public** access because you want clients to invoke it, and name it **New** as required by VB .NET. The parameter list consists of variable declarations named **aName, anAddress**, and **aPhoneNo**, each of data type **String**, which will receive attribute values for the three **Customer** attributes. The body of the constructor method invokes the three set accessor methods, passing the parameter variables containing the attribute values that were received.

Line 7 invokes the setter for name passing **aName. SetName** receives **aName** and uses it to populate the name attribute. Similarly, line 8 invokes **SetAddress** and line 9, **SetPhoneNo**.

An alternate design is to have the constructor assign the values directly to the attribute variables instead of invoking the setter methods. Generally you avoid doing this because often you will include data validation code in set methods and you want this code invoked when you instantiate the class. Chapter 12 includes examples of set methods with data validation code.

The next example shows a **Client** that instantiates **Customer** passing arguments to populate the attributes for the newly created instance.

Example 10-6: Client invoking parameterized constructor in Customer

```
1. Option Strict On
2. Option Explicit On
3. Module Client
4. Sub Main()
5.    Dim aCustomer As Customer
6.    ' instantiate Customer
7.    aCustomer = New Customer("Eleanor", "Atlanta",
      "123-4567")

8. ' invoke get methods to retrieve attributes
9.    Console.WriteLine(aCustomer.GetName)
10.   Console.WriteLine(aCustomer.GetAddress)
11.   Console.WriteLine(aCustomer.GetPhoneNo)
12.   End Sub
13. End Module
```

Sample Run:

```
Eleanor
Atlanta
123-4567
```

Discussion:

Line 5 declares a reference variable named **aCustomer** whose data type is **Customer**.

Line 7 instantiates **Customer** by using the keyword **New**. This statement invokes the constructor at line 6 in Example 10-5, passing the values to populate the attributes for the new instance.

Lines 9, 10, and 11 then invoke the getters to retrieve and display the customer's name, address, and telephone number.

Creating Multiple Instances

Figure 10-2 illustrated three customers: Eleanor in Atlanta, Emily in St. Louis, and Graham in Marietta. Given the `Customer` class definition in Example 10-5, you can create several customers as illustrated in Example 10-7.

Example 10-7: Creating multiple Customer instances

```
1. Option Strict On
2. Option Explicit On
3. Module Client
4. Sub Main()
5.    Dim customer1, customer2, customer3 As Customer

6.    ' create 3 instances of Customer
7.    customer1 = New Customer("Eleanor", "Atlanta",
      "123-4567")
8.    customer2 = New Customer("Emily", "St. Louis",
      "467-1234")
9.    customer3 = New Customer("Graham", "Marietta",
      "765-4321")

10.   ' invoke get methods to retrieve attributes
11.   Console.WriteLine(customer1.GetName)
12.   Console.WriteLine(customer2.GetName)
13.   Console.WriteLine(customer3.GetName)
14. End Sub
15. End Module
```

Sample Run:

```
Eleanor
Emily
Graham
```

Discussion:

This example shows a module named `Client` that creates three customer instances, then retrieves and displays their names.

Line 5 declares three `Customer` reference variables named `customer1`, `customer2`, and `customer3`.

Line 7 once again creates a `Customer` instance for Eleanor and assigns its reference to `customer1`.

Line 8 also creates a `Customer` instance, though this time it is for Emily in St. Louis, and assigns its reference to `customer2`.

Line 9 then creates a `Customer` instance for Graham in Marietta and assigns its reference to `customer3`.

Figure 10-8 illustrates the three `Customer` instances created in Example 10-7.

10

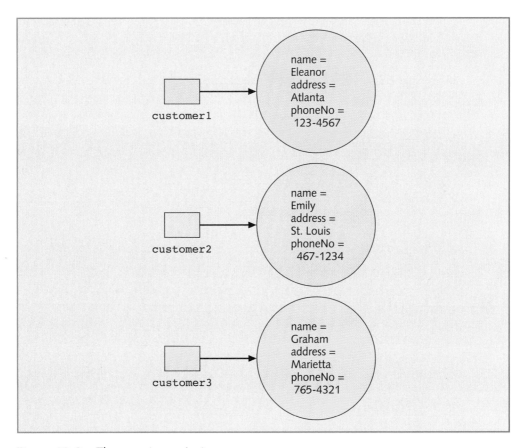

Figure 10-8   Three customer instances

Line 11 invokes `GetName` for the instance referenced by `customer1`. This method returns the contents of the name attribute for the `Customer` instance referenced by `customer1` and then passes this value to the `WriteLine` method in the `Console` class, which displays it.

Line 12 repeats this process, except the `Customer` reference is `customer2`, which points to the instance for Emily. Finally, line 13 invokes `GetName` for the third instance and passes the value returned to the `WriteLine` method in the `Console` class, which displays it.

DESIGNING AND WRITING OVERLOADED CONSTRUCTORS

In Chapter 9 you learned how to write overloaded procedures. You saw that VB .NET identifies a procedure by its signature, which consists of *both* its name and its parameter list. Because a constructor is also a procedure, you can overload a constructor.

Numerous applications use telephone information. For example, Customers, Students, and Employees all have telephones, often more than one. You can create a `Phone` class to contain this information. Figure 10-9 shows a class diagram for the `Phone` class. This class has attributes for area code (data type `Integer`), number (data type `Integer`), and type of phone (data type `String`: for example, home, mobile, or office).

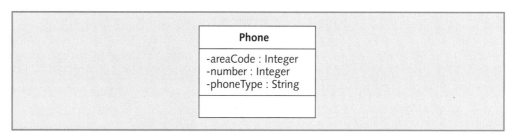

Figure 10-9   Phone class diagram

Example 10-8 lists the class definition for `Phone`.

Example 10-8: Phone class definition

```
1. Public Class Phone
2.     Private areaCode As Integer
3.     Private number As Integer
4.     Private phoneType As String
5.     ' constructor
```

```
6.   Public Sub New(ByVal anAreaCode As Integer, ByVal aNumber
       As Integer, ByVal aPhoneType As String)

7.     SetAreaCode(anAreaCode)

8.     SetNumber(aNumber)

9.     SetPhoneType(aPhoneType)

10.  End Sub


11.  'get accessor methods

12.  Public Function GetAreaCode() As Integer

13.     Return areaCode

14.  End Function


15.  Public Function GetNumber() As Integer

16.     Return number

17.  End Function


18.  Public Function GetPhoneType() As String

19.     Return phoneType

20.  End Function


21.  'set accessor methods

22.  Public Sub SetAreaCode(ByVal anAreaCode As Integer)

23.     areaCode = anAreaCode

24.  End Sub


25.  Public Sub SetNumber(ByVal aNumber As Integer)

26.     number = aNumber

27.  End Sub
```

10

28.   `Public Sub SetPhoneType(ByVal aPhoneType As String)`

29.   `phoneType = aPhoneType`

30.   `End Sub`

31. `End Class`

Discussion:

This example lists the definition for the **Phone** class, which, like the **Customer** class definition, has attribute definitions, a constructor, and accessor methods.

Lines 2 through 4 declare the three attribute variables.

Lines 6 through 10 define the **Phone** constructor. It receives three arguments containing the values for area code, number, and phone type. It then invokes the set methods to populate the three phone attributes.

Lines 11 through 20 list the get three accessor methods and lines 22 through 30 the set accessors.

Example 10-9 lists a **Client** module that creates three phone instances.

Example 10-9: Creating three phone instances

```
1.  Option Strict On
2.  Option Explicit On
3.  Module Client
4.    Sub Main()
5.      Dim phone1, phone2, phone3 As Phone

6.      ' create 3 instances of Phone
7.      phone1 = New Phone(314, 1234567, "Home")
8.      phone2 = New Phone(314, 5556789, "Mobile")
9.      phone3 = New Phone(314, 4321234, "Home")

10.     ' invoke get methods to retrieve, format
        & display phone 1 info
11.     Console.Write(phone1.GetPhoneType())
12.     Console.Write(" " &
          phone1.GetAreaCode().ToString("(###)"))
13.     Console.WriteLine(" " &
          phone1.GetNumber().ToString("###-####"))
14.   End Sub
15. End Module
```

Step 3: Invoke WriteLine to display the formatted result

Step 2: Invoke ToString for the Integer area code to format it

Step 1: Invoke GetAreaCode for the phone1 instance

Sample Run:

```
Home (314) 123-4567
```

Discussion:

This example lists a module named `Client` that instantiates the `Phone` class.

Lines 4 through 14 contain the `Main` procedure where execution begins.

Line 5 declares three reference variables whose data type is `Phone`. This means they will refer to or point to instances of the `Phone` class.

Lines 7, 8, and 9 create three instances of `Phone`, assigning their references to the variables `phone1`, `phone2`, and `phone3`, respectively. When the `Phone` class is instantiated, the constructor is invoked and the arguments passed to it are used to populate the instance attributes.

Lines 11 through 13 retrieve the attributes for the first `Phone` instance, and then format and display the data retrieved. Line 11 invokes `phone1.GetPhoneType` and passes the value returned to `Console.Write`. This method displays the argument passed, but does not go to a new line.

Line 12 does three things. First, it invokes `GetAreaCode` for the `phone1` instance, which returns the `Integer` area code value. Second, it invokes `ToString` for the `Integer` area code, passing the format mask `"(###)"` to format the area code. Finally, the `String` value returned by `ToString` is passed to `Console.Write` for display.

10

Similarly, line 13 retrieves, formats, and displays the phone number attribute.

Notice that the area code for all three of the phones in Example 10-9 have the same value, 314. If many of the phone instances you are creating have the same area code, you can create a default area code value of 314, and then pass only the number and phone type to the constructor.

However, you need to write a 2-parameter constructor to overload the original 3-parameter constructor.

Example 10-10: Creating a 2-parameter constructor

```
1.  Public Class Phone
2.     Private areaCode As Integer
3.     Private number As Integer
4.     Private phoneType As String
5.     Const defaultAreaCode As Integer = 314

6.     ' 3 parameter constructor
7.     Public Sub New(ByVal anAreaCode As Integer, ByVal
       aNumber As Integer, ByVal aPhoneType As String)
8.        SetAreaCode(anAreaCode)
9.        SetNumber(aNumber)
10.       SetPhoneType(aPhoneType)
11.    End Sub

12.    ' 2 parameter constructor using default area code
13.    Public Sub New(ByVal aNumber As Integer, ByVal
       aPhoneType As String)
14.       Me.New(defaultAreaCode, aNumber, aPhoneType)
15.    End Sub
```

Me is this instance
New is the constructor name

```
16.    'get accessor methods
17.    . .

18.    'set accessor methods
19.    . .

20. End Class
```

Discussion:

This listing of the Phone class shows two constructors. The original 3-parameter constructor is contained in lines 7 through 11.

Lines 13 through 15 show the 2-parameter constructor. The header in line 13 has two parameter variable definitions; one for number and one for phone type.

Line 14 invokes the 3-parameter constructor passing the default area code plus the number and phone type values it receives as arguments. The keyword Me tells VB .NET to invoke the specified method for the instance executing the code. The specified method name in this example is New, which is the name of the constructor.

The default area code value is declared at line 5.

Example 10-11 illustrates a `Client` module that invokes both the 3-parameter constructor and the 2-parameter constructor.

Example 10-11: Invoking overloaded constructors

```
1. Option Strict On

2. Option Explicit On

3. Module Client

4.    Sub Main()

5.       Dim phone1, phone2 As Phone


6.       ' create 2 instances of Phone

7.       phone1 = New Phone(1234567, "Home")      ' 2 arguments

8.       phone2 = New Phone(417, 7654321, "Home") ' 3 arguments


9.       ' invoke get methods to retrieve, format, & display
         phone info

10.      Console.Write(phone1.GetPhoneType())

11.      Console.Write(" " &
         phone1.GetAreaCode().ToString("(###)"))

12.      Console.WriteLine(" " &
         phone1.GetNumber().ToString("###-####"))

13.      Console.Write(phone2.GetPhoneType())

14.      Console.Write(" " &
         phone2.GetAreaCode().ToString("(###)"))

15.      Console.WriteLine(" " &
         phone2.GetNumber().ToString("###-####"))

16.   End Sub

17. End Module
```

10

Sample Run:

```
Home (314) 123-4567

Home (417) 765-4321
```

Discussion:

The **Client** in this example creates two instances of the **Phone** class. The first instance is created passing two arguments and the second by passing three.

Lines 4 through 16 contain the **Main** procedure.

Line 5 declares two reference variables whose data type is **Phone**.

Line 7 creates an instance of **Phone** by passing only two arguments to the **Phone** constructor. Because VB .NET identifies a procedure using its signature, the 2-parameter constructor at line 13 in Example 10-10 is invoked. As described earlier, this constructor invokes the 3-parameter constructor passing the default area code plus the number and phone type values it received as arguments.

Line 8 in **Client** creates a second **Phone** instance. This time, however, three arguments are passed to the **Phone** constructor and the 3-parameter constructor is invoked.

Lines 10 through 12 display the attributes for the first **Phone** instance, and lines 13 through 15 the second.

CREATING POLYMORPHIC METHODS

Polymorphism means "many forms." In object-oriented systems, polymorphism means that you can have different methods in different classes with the same signature that do different things. For example, a dialog box, a network connection, and a document all may have a method named **Close**. However, the implementation for each **Close** method is different.

Similarly, given a Banking application with different types of accounts such as checking, money market, and loan, you would have class definitions for **CheckingAccount**, **MoneyMarketAccount**, and **LoanAccount**. Each of these may have a method **CalculateInterest**. However, the implementation of each of these methods will be different; they will each calculate interest using a different algorithm. Figure 10-10 illustrates polymorphism for two different types of bank accounts.

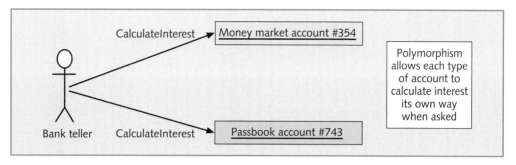

Figure 10-10   Polymorphism illustrated

In the previous section, you developed a class definition for **Phone**, then created a **Client** module that instantiated **Phone**. **Client** contained code to retrieve the attribute values from an instance, format these values, and then display them. You can relieve the **Client** of some work by adding a method to **Phone** that will return all three attribute values formatted. Example 10-12 adds a method named **TellAboutSelf** that accomplishes this.

Example 10-12: Phone with TellAboutSelf method

```
 1. Public Class Phone
 2.     Private areaCode As Integer
 3.     Private number As Integer
 4.     Private phoneType As String
 5.     Const defaultAreaCode As Integer = 314
 6.     ' 3 parameter constructor
 7.     ..
 8.     ' 2 parameter constructor using default area code
 9.     ..
10.     'get accessor methods
11.     ..
12.     'set accessor methods
13.     ..
14.     Public Function TellAboutSelf() As String
15.        Dim info, areaCodeInfo, numberInfo, typeInfo As String
16.        typeInfo = Me.GetPhoneType()
```

```
17.     areaCodeInfo = Me.GetAreaCode().ToString("(###)")
18.     numberInfo = Me.GetNumber().ToString("###-####")
19.     info = typeInfo & " " & areaCodeInfo & " " & numberInfo
20.   Return info
21. End Function
22. End Class
```

Discussion:

For brevity, this listing omits the two constructors and the accessor methods. These are identical to those in the previous **Phone** class definition.

TellAboutSelf is shown in lines 14 through 20. It is written as a function procedure because it will return a **String** value containing the formatted attribute values.

Line 15 declares three **String** variables used to contain the formatted attribute values.

Line 16 invokes **GetPhoneType()** and assigns the value returned to **typeInfo**. For clarity, the specified instance is **Me**, although you could have omitted it because it is the default.

Line 17 first invokes **GetAreaCode**, and then invokes **ToString** passing the argument **("(###)")** to format the area code. The value returned from **ToString** is then assigned to **areaCodeInfo**.

Similarly, line 18 invokes **GetNumber**, invokes **ToString** to format the number, and then assigns the value returned to **numberInfo**.

Line 19 concatenates the type, area code, and number values along with appropriate spacing and assigns the result to **info**. Line 20 then returns **info** to the invoking client.

Example 10-13 lists a **Client** to invoke the **Phone TellAboutSelf** method.

Example 10-13: Invoking the Phone TellAboutSelf method

```
1. Option Strict On
2. Option Explicit On
3. Module Client
4.    Sub Main()
5.      Dim phone1, phone2 As Phone

6.      ' create 2 instances of Phone
7.      phone1 = New Phone(1234567, "Home")
```

8.   phone2 = New Phone(417, 7654321, "Home")

9.   ' display phone info

10.   Console.WriteLine(phone1.TellAboutSelf())

11.   Console.WriteLine(phone2.TellAboutSelf())

12.   End Sub

13. End Module

Sample Run:

Home (314) 123-4567

Home (417) 765-4321

Discussion:

This example is identical to Example 10-11, except here the Client invokes TellAboutSelf in Phone to retrieve and format the attribute values.

Lines 7 and 8 create two Phone instances referenced by the variables phone1 and phone2.

Line 10 invokes TellAboutSelf for the instance referenced by phone1, passing the returned value to Console.WriteLine for display. Similarly, line 11 does the same thing for the instance referenced by phone2.

10

At the beginning of this section, you learned polymorphism means that you have different methods in different classes with the same signature that do different things. TellAboutSelf in the Phone class retrieves the instance attributes, formats them, and returns a formatted string to the invoking Client.

You can create a TellAboutSelf method for the Customer class that was developed earlier.

Example 10-14: Customer with TellAboutSelf method

1. Public Class Customer

2.   Private name As String

3.   Private address As String

4.   Private phoneNo As String

5.   ' parameterized constructor

6.   ..

7.   'get accessor methods

```
8.   ..
9.   'set accessor methods
10.  ..
11.  Public Function TellAboutSelf() As String
12.     Dim info As String
13.     info = GetName() & ", " & GetAddress() & ", " &
        GetPhoneNo()
14.     Return info
15.  End Function
16. End Class
```

Discussion:

This **Customer** class definition is a copy of the one shown in Example 10-5 with the addition of the **TellAboutSelf** method in lines 11 through 15. Once again, the constructor and accessor methods are not shown in order to reduce the listing size.

Line 11 is the method header, which is the same as that in the **Phone** class definition shown in Example 10-12.

Line 12 declares a **String** variable named **info** that is used to contain the **Customer** instance attribute values formatted.

Line 13 populates **info** by invoking the getter methods and concatenating the values returned with commas and spaces to improve readability. Note that in this example, the keyword **Me** has been omitted.

Example 10-15 is similar to Example 10-7, but here the **Client** module invokes **TellAboutSelf** to retrieve the **Customer** attribute values.

Example 10-15: Invoking the Customer TellAboutSelf method

```
1. Option Strict On
2. Option Explicit On
3. Module Client
4.    Sub Main()
5.       Dim customer1, customer2, customer3 As Customer
6.       ' create 3 instances of Customer
7.       customer1 = New Customer("Eleanor", "Atlanta",
          "123-4567")
```

```
8.    customer2 = New Customer("Emily", "St. Louis",
      "467-1234")

9.    customer3 = New Customer("Graham", "Marietta",
      "765-4321")

10.   ' invoke get methods to retrieve attributes

11.   Console.WriteLine(customer1.TellAboutSelf())

12.   Console.WriteLine(customer2.TellAboutSelf())

13.   Console.WriteLine(customer3.TellAboutSelf())

14. End Sub

15. End Module
```

Sample Run:

```
Eleanor, Atlanta, 123-4567
Emily, St. Louis, 467-1234
Graham, Marietta, 765-4321
```

Discussion:

Line 5 declares three reference variables whose data type is `Customer`, and then lines 7, 8, and 9 create three `Customer` instances, populating their attributes.

Line 11 invokes `TellAboutSelf` for the instance referenced by `customer1`, and then passes the value returned to `Console.WriteLine` for display.

Lines 12 and 13 repeat this for the `Customer` instances referenced by `customer2` and `customer3`, respectively.

To summarize, polymorphic methods are methods with the same signature residing in different classes. You have seen that `TellABoutSelf` in `Phone` returns the `Phone` instance attributes, while `TellABoutSelf` in `Customer` returns the `Customer` instance attributes.

WRITING PROPERTIES

In previous chapters, you accessed properties in the supplied classes. Specifically, a **property** is similar to an accessor method, but to client objects it appears as a public attribute. In other words, you do not write code to *invoke* a property. Instead, you retrieve the contents of a property as if it were a variable.

10

You can also create properties to set and get attribute values in user-defined classes. A property begins with a header indicating that you are writing a property definition and ends with **End Property**. Because the property contains code to both set and get an attribute value, as shown in Example 10-16, the header also specifies the data type of the attribute being returned. The get section returns the attribute and the set section populates the attribute with the value received.

Example 10-16 lists the **Customer** class definition using properties instead of accessor methods.

Example 10-16: Customer class definition with properties

```
1.   Public Class Customer
2.      Private name As String
3.      Private address As String
4.      Private phoneNo As String

5.      ' parameterized constructor
6.      Public Sub New(ByVal aName As String, ByVal anAddress
        As String, ByVal aPhoneNo As String)
7.         CustomerName = aName
8.         CustomerAddress = anAddress
9.         CustomerPhoneNo = aPhoneNo
10.     End Sub

11.     ' property named CustomerName
12.     Public Property CustomerName() As String
13.        Get
14.           Return name
15.        End Get
16.        Set(ByVal aName As String)
17.           name = aName
18.        End Set
19.     End Property

20.     ' property named CustomerAddress
21.     Public Property CustomerAddress() As String
22.        Get
23.           Return address
24.        End Get
25.        Set(ByVal anAddress As String)
26.           address = anAddress
27.        End Set
```

> CustomerAddress appears as a public variable to Client objects

> This code retrieves the attribute value

> This code populates the attribute value

```
28.    End Property

29.    ' property named CustomerPhoneNo
30.    Public Property CustomerPhoneNo() As String
31.      Get
32.        Return phoneNo
33.      End Get
34.      Set(ByVal aPhoneNo As String)
35.        phoneNo = aPhoneNo
36.      End Set
37.    End Property

38.    Public Function TellAboutSelf() As String
39.      Dim info As String
40.      info = CustomerName & ", " & CustomerAddress & "," &
          CustomerPhoneNo
41.      Return info
42.    End Function
43. End Class
```

10

Discussion:

Lines 2, 3, and 4 declare the attribute variables the same as the previous **Customer** class definition.

Lines 6 through 10 contain the parameterized constructor. However, in this code the constructor assigns the received arguments to the properties.

Lines 12 through 19 create a property for the name attribute. Line 12 is the property header, which names the property **CustomerName**, and specifies the data type of the attribute, **String**.

A property contains code to both get and set the attribute value. The get section of the property **CustomerName** is coded in lines 13 through 15. Line 14 returns the contents of the **name** attribute to the **Client**. The set part of the property is shown in lines 16 through 18. Line 16 includes a parameter variable definition to receive the value sent by the client. Line 17 assigns the contents of the parameter variable to the **name** attribute.

Lines 21 through 28 contain the property named **CustomerAddress** and lines 30 through 37 contain the property named **CustomerPhoneNo**.

Both the constructor and the **TellAboutSelf** method use the properties instead of accessor methods because the accessor methods have been replaced with properties.

You can include *both* properties and accessor methods in a class definition. `Customer` could include the three properties, three get accessor methods, and three set accessor methods.

Example 10-17 shows a `Client` module using the `Customer` class definition in Example 10-16.

Example 10-17: Client accessing Customer properties

```
1.  Option Strict On
2.  Option Explicit On
3.  Module Client
4.    Sub Main()
5.      Dim customer1, customer2, customer3 As Customer
6.      ' create 3 instances of Customer
7.      customer1 = New Customer("Eleanor", "Atlanta",
            "123-4567")
8.      customer2 = New Customer("Emily", "St. Louis",
            "467-1234")
9.      customer3 = New Customer("Graham", "Marietta",
            "765-4321")
10.     ' invoke get methods to retrieve attributes
11.     Console.WriteLine(customer1.TellAboutSelf())
12.     Console.WriteLine(customer2.TellAboutSelf())
13.     Console.WriteLine(customer3.TellAboutSelf())

14.     ' change Eleanor's address
15.     customer1.CustomerAddress = "Marietta"
16.     Console.WriteLine(customer1.TellAboutSelf())
17.   End Sub
18. End Module
```

Use the CustomerAddress property to change Eleanor's address

Sample Run:

```
Eleanor, Atlanta, 123-4567
Emily, St. Louis, 467-1234
Graham, Marietta, 765-4321
Eleanor, Marietta, 123-4567
```

Discussion:

Note that lines 1 through 13 in this example are *identical* to the `Client` in Example 10-15; the first three lines of output are also identical.

Line 15, however, changes the address of the `Customer` instance referenced by `customer1` by assigning a new value to the property. Note that the `Client` cannot distinguish between a property named `CustomerAddress` and a public variable named `CustomerAddress`.

To summarize, accessor methods are invoked to set and get attribute values in a class definition. You can also write properties that accomplish the same thing; however, to a client, properties appear to be public variables.

CREATING SHARED ATTRIBUTES AND METHODS

In the previous examples, you created instances of Customers and Phones. Each instance of `Customer` contained three attributes: `name`, `address`, and `phoneNo`. Similarly, each instance of `Phone` had three attribute variables: `areaCode`, `number`, and `phoneType`. Whenever you create an instance of `Customer`, the new instance has three variables, and whenever you instantiate `Phone`, the new instance has three variables.

In addition, each instance of `Customer` and `Phone` had their own accessor methods.

Sometimes, however, you may need to declare an attribute or a method that is not copied for each instance you create. Instead, you create an attribute or method that is *shared* by all instances of the class, instead of each instance getting its own copy.

Consider a class named `Circle` with attributes center coordinates x and y, radius, and PI. Each instance of `Circle` will have unique values for x, y, and radius; however, each instance does not need an attribute for PI; PI can be a shared attribute, as shown in Example 10-18.

10

Example 10-18: Class definition for Circle with shared attribute and method

```
1.  Public Class Circle
2.     Private x, y As Integer
3.     Private radius As Double
4.     ' shared attribute
5.     Private Shared PI As Double = 3.14159
```

This attribute is shared by all instances of Circle

```
6.     Public Sub New(ByVal centerX As Integer, ByVal centerY
          As Integer, ByVal aRadius As Double)
7.        SetX(centerX)
8.        SetY(centerY)
9.        SetRadius(aRadius)
10.    End Sub

11.    'get accessor methods
12.    Public Function GetX() As Integer
13.       Return x
14.    End Function
15.    Public Function GetY() As Integer
16.       Return y
17.    End Function
18.    Public Function GetRadius() As Double
19.       Return radius
20.    End Function

21.    ' shared method
22.    Public Shared Function GetPI() As Double
23.       Return PI
24.    End Function
```

This method is shared by all instances of Circle

```
25.    'set accessor methods
26.    Public Sub SetX(ByVal centerX As Integer)
27.       x = centerX
28.    End Sub
29.    Public Sub SetY(ByVal centerY As Integer)
30.       y = centerY
31.    End Sub
32.    Public Sub SetRadius(ByVal aRadius As Double)
33.       radius = aRadius
34.    End Sub
```

```
35.  'custom method to compute circumference
36.   Public Function ComputeCircumference() As Double
37.      Dim circumference As Double
38.      circumference = PI * radius * radius
39.   Return circumference
40. End Function

41. End Class
```

Discussion:

Lines 2 and 3 declare attribute variables for x, y, and the radius. Note that these attributes are not shared; each instance receives its own copy.

Line 5 declares a shared attribute named `PI` and populates it. To declare a shared attribute, you write the keyword `Shared`.

Lines 6 through 10 define the constructor. When `Circle` is instantiated, it receives the three arguments and invokes the set methods to populate the three attributes.

Lines 12 through 20 contain the get accessor methods.

Lines 22 through 24 define a get accessor for the shared attribute, `PI`. Note that this method is also shared; one copy can be invoked by all of the `Circle` instances. It also can be invoked by any client object because it has `Public` accessibility.

Lines 26 through 34 define the set accessor methods for `Circle`.

Lines 36 through 39 contain a method named `ComputeCircumference`, which computes and returns to the invoking client the circle's circumference.

Example 10-19 illustrates how a client can access shared attributes and invoke shared methods.

Example 10-19: Accessing shared attribute and methods

```
1. Option Strict On

2. Option Explicit On

3. Module Client

4.   Sub Main()

5.      Dim circle1, circle2, circle3 As Circle

6.      ' create 3 instances of circle

7.      circle1 = New Circle(5, 5, 2)
```

8.   `circle2 = New Circle(15, 25, 9)`

9.   `circle3 = New Circle(40, 30, 15)`

10.   `' invoke get methods to retrieve attributes`

11.   `Console.WriteLine(circle1.ComputeCircumference())`

12.   `Console.WriteLine(circle2.ComputeCircumference())`

13.   `Console.WriteLine(circle3.ComputeCircumference())`

14.   `Console.WriteLine(Circle.GetPI())`

15.   `End Sub`

16. `End Module`

Sample Run:

```
12.56636
254.46879
706.85775
3.14159
```

Discussion:

Line 5 declares three reference variables whose data type is `Circle`.

Lines 7, 8, and 9 create three instances of `Circle`, each with different attribute values. References to these instances are assigned to the three reference variables.

Lines 11, 12, and 13 invoke `ComputeCircumference` for the three `Circle` instances, and then invoke `WriteLine` to display the result.

Line 14 invokes the get accessor for `PI` and displays the result. This method is shared by all of the `Circle` instances; therefore, you invoke it by specifying the class name, `Circle`. Note that lines 11–13 invoke `ComputeCircumference` by specifying the instance reference variables `circle1`, `circle2`, and `circle3`, respectively. This is because you are calculating the circumference for a specific instance of `Circle`. However, when you invoke `GetPI`, you are not doing it for a specific instance. Rather, you are invoking a method that is shared by all of the instances. You specify the class name when invoking shared methods, and you specify reference variable names when invoking non-shared methods. Because of this difference, shared methods and attributes are also called **class methods** and **class attributes**. Non-shared methods and attributes are also called **instance methods** and **instance attributes**.

 You can also invoke a shared method by specifying an instance reference variable because VB .NET will know which class is associated with the instance. Your code will be easier to understand, however, if you use the class name when invoking shared methods.

To summarize, you declare shared attributes and write shared methods when you want them to be shared with all instances of the class. You invoke shared or class methods by specifying the class name instead of the instance name.

PROGRAMMING EXAMPLE: ELECTRICITY BILLING

This programming example demonstrates a redesign of the Electricity Billing Programming Example at the end of Chapter 9. This new design includes a class named `ElectricBill` to represent electricity bills, the Chapter 9 Server module to compute sales tax, and a Client to instantiate `ElectricBill`. The design invokes the Client methods to compute the electricity charge, sales tax, and then display the electricity consumed, electricity charge, sales tax, and total bill.

Problem Analysis and Algorithm Design

As shown in Figure 10-11, the class definition for ElectricBill includes the three attributes, a parameterized constructor, standard accessor methods, plus the custom methods `ComputeElectricityCharge` and `DisplayBill`. `ComputeElectricityCharge` uses the same logic as the procedure with the same name in the Chapter 9 Programming Example. Similarly, `DisplayBill` produces the same output as the procedure named `DisplayBill` in Chapter 9.

10

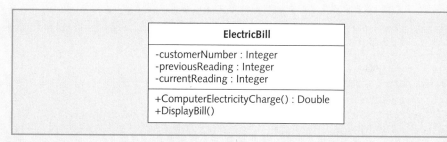

ElectricBill
-customerNumber : Integer -previousReading : Integer -currentReading : Integer
+ComputerElectricityCharge() : Double +DisplayBill()

Figure 10-11   ElectricBill class diagram

The Server used in this example is an exact copy of the one in the Chapter 9 Programming Example.

Formulas Subtract the previous meter reading from the current meter reading to obtain the KWH consumed. The charge for electricity uses the following table:

KWH Consumed	Rate per KWH
< 500	.05
500 – 1000	$25 + .055 for amount over 500
> 1000	$52.50 + .06 for amount over 1000

Complete Program Listing

ElectricBill Class

```
Public Class ElectricBill
    Private customerNumber As Integer
    Private previousReading As Integer
    Private currentReading As Integer
    Dim electricityCharge As Double

    Public Sub New(ByVal custNo As Integer, ByVal prevReading As _
        Integer, ByVal currReading As Integer)
        SetCustomerNumber(custNo)
        SetPreviousReading(prevReading)
        SetCurrentReading(currReading)
    End Sub
    'get accessor methods
    Public Function GetCustomerNumber() As Integer
        Return customerNumber
    End Function
    Public Function GetPreviousReading() As Integer
        Return previousReading
    End Function
    Public Function GetCurrentReading() As Integer
        Return currentReading
    End Function
    'set accessor methods
    Public Sub SetCustomerNumber(ByVal custNo As Integer)
        customerNumber = custNo
    End Sub
    Public Sub SetPreviousReading(ByVal prevReading As Integer)
        previousReading = prevReading
    End Sub
    Public Sub SetCurrentReading(ByVal currReading As Integer)
        currentReading = currReading
```

```
End Sub

    Public Function ComputeElectricityCharge() As Double
        Dim amount As Double
        Dim kwh As Integer = GetCurrentReading() - _
        GetPreviousReading()
        Select Case kwh
            Case Is < 500
                amount = kwh * 0.05
            Case 500 To 1000
                amount = 25 + (kwh - 500) * 0.055
            Case Is > 1000
                amount = 52.5 + (kwh - 1000) * 0.06
        End Select
        amount = Math.Round(amount, 2)
        Return amount
    End Function
    Public Sub DisplayBill(ByVal tax As Double, ByVal charge As _
    Double)
        Dim totalBill As Double
        Dim kwh As Integer = GetCurrentReading() - _
        GetPreviousReading()
        totalBill = tax + charge
        Console.WriteLine("Customer number:" & GetCustomerNumber())
        Console.WriteLine("KWH Consumed: " & kwh)
        Console.WriteLine("Electricity charge: " &
        charge.ToString("C"))
        Console.WriteLine("Sales Tax: " & tax.ToString("C"))
        Console.WriteLine("Total Bill: " & totalBill.ToString("C"))
        Console.WriteLine()
    End Sub

End Class
```

10

Server Module

```
Option Strict On
Option Explicit On
Module Server
    Public Function ComputeSalesTax(ByVal amount As Double) _
    As Double
        Const SALES_TAX_RATE As Double = 0.085
        Dim salesTax As Double
        salesTax = SALES_TAX_RATE * amount
        salesTax = Math.Round(salesTax, 2)
        Return salesTax
    End Function

End Module
```

Client Module

```
Option Strict On
Option Explicit On
Module Client
    Sub Main()
        Dim electricBill1, electricBill2 As ElectricBill
        Dim electricityCharge, salesTax As Double
        ' create 2 instances of ElectricBill
        electricBill1 = New ElectricBill(1, 0, 400)
        electricBill2 = New ElectricBill(2, 1000, 1500)

        ' compute & display first bill
        electricityCharge =
        electricBill1.ComputeElectricityCharge()
        salesTax = Server.ComputeSalesTax(electricityCharge)
        electricBill1.DisplayBill(salesTax, electricityCharge)
        ' compute & display second bill
        electricityCharge =
        electricBill2.ComputeElectricityCharge()
        salesTax = Server.ComputeSalesTax(electricityCharge)
        electricBill2.DisplayBill(salesTax, electricityCharge)
    End Sub

End Module
```

Sample Run

```
Customer number: 1
KWH Consumed: 400
Electricity charge: $20.00
Sales Tax: $1.70
Total Bill: $21.70

Customer number: 2
KWH Consumed: 500
Electricity charge: $25.00
Sales Tax: $2.12
Total Bill: $27.12
```

QUICK REVIEW

1. A class is similar to a module, but often represents real-world entities. You can create instances of classes and then invoke methods for the instances.

2. Three-tier design places objects into three categories of classes—problem domain, graphical user interface (GUI), and data access.

3. The Visual Basic .NET (VB .NET) code you write representing a class is called a class definition. The syntax of a class definition begins with a class header followed by attribute definitions, then method code, and then ends with the keywords `End Class`.

4. Class definitions are based on some of the object's characteristics (attributes) and behavior (methods).

5. You draw a class diagram to model classes. The class diagram uses a rectangle to model a class. The body of the rectangle has three parts. The class name goes in the top part, the attribute list in the middle, and the method list in the bottom part.

6. When defining the accessibility of a variable or procedure, you can write `Public`, `Private`, `Protected`, or `Friend`. The keyword `Protected` allows subclasses to have direct access, while `Friend` permits classes within the same assembly to have access. An assembly is a collection of one or more projects that are deployed as an application. You can assign your project and all of its classes to a specific assembly.

7. VB .NET programmers have adopted a style for naming classes, attributes, and methods. Class names begin with a capital letter. Attribute names begin with a lowercase character, and subsequent words in the name start with a capital letter. Method names begin with a capital letter, with subsequent words also starting with a capital letter. In addition, method names usually contain an imperative verb describing what the method does, followed by a noun.

8. You create instances of a class using the keyword `New` with each instance representing specific occurrences of the class.

9. Class definitions have methods providing access to attributes. These are accessor methods, often called standard methods, and are typically not shown on class diagrams.

10. There are two types of accessor methods: those that *get* attribute values and those that *set* attribute values.

11. Accessors that retrieve values are called get accessor methods, or simply getters, and are named with the prefix "`get`" followed by the attribute name.

12. Accessor methods that change attribute values are called set accessor methods, or setters, and are named with the prefix "`set`" followed by the attribute name.

13. A constructor is a special method that is *automatically* invoked whenever you create an instance of a class using the keyword `New`. The constructor is always named `New` and is written as a Sub procedure because it cannot return a value.

14. If you do not write a constructor, VB .NET creates a default constructor that is invoked when you instantiate a class, although it doesn't do anything.

15. You can write your own constructor, called a parameterized constructor, because it can contain a parameter list to receive arguments that are used to populate the instance attributes.

16. VB .NET identifies a procedure by its signature which consists of *both* its name and its parameter list. Because a constructor is also a procedure, you can overload a constructor.

17. The keyword `Me` tells VB .NET to invoke the specified method for the instance executing the code.

10

18. In object-oriented systems, polymorphism means that you can have different methods in different classes with the same signature that do different things.

19. A property is similar to an accessor method, but to client objects, it appears as a public attribute. You can include *both* properties and accessor methods in a class definition.

20. A property begins with a header indicating that you are writing a property definition and ends with **End Property**. The property contains code to both set and get an attribute value.

21. You declare shared attributes and write shared methods when you want them to be shared with all instances of the class. You invoke shared or class methods by specifying the class name instead of the instance name.

EXERCISES

1. Explain the difference between a class and a module.

2. Describe three-tier design.

3. What is a class diagram?

4. Explain the difference between public and private accessibility for an attribute and for a method.

5. Explain and give examples of the style adopted by VB .NET programmers for naming classes, attributes, and methods.

6. What is an accessor method?

7. Distinguish between a default constructor and a parameterized constructor.

8. What does the keyword **Me** do?

9. What is polymorphism?

10. What is a property? How is a property different from a method? From an attribute?

11. What is a shared attribute? A shared method?

PROGRAMMING EXERCISES

1. Write a 1-parameter constructor for **Phone** in Example 10-10.

2. Using the **Phone** class definition from Example 10-12 and the **Customer** class definition from Example 10-14, write a client that creates a **Customer** instance and a **Phone** instance, and then invokes **TellAboutSelf** for each.

3. Rewrite **Circle** in Example 10-18 using properties.

4. Modify **ComputeCircumference** in Example 10-18 to use **PI** in the **Math** class instead of **PI** in the **Circle** class.

5. Redesign the **Client** in Example 10-15 to use an array instead of individual reference variables.

11

Implementing Inheritance and Association

In this chapter, you will:
- O Explore inheritance
- O Create subclasses
- O Write abstract classes and methods
- O Define interfaces
- O Create association links

In the previous chapter, you wrote class definitions and learned how to create constructors and accessor methods. You also saw how to overload constructors and to write polymorphic methods. In this chapter, you explore and implement relationships between classes. Classes can be related either by **inheritance** or **association**.

In Chapter 1, you were introduced to several object-oriented concepts including inheritance. You learned that in an inheritance hierarchy, the superclass specifies the general characteristics of an object, and then the subclass inherits characteristics (attributes and methods) from the superclass and adds more specialized attributes and methods. Inheritance is sometimes called a generalization/specialization hierarchy, and is a powerful tool in systems development, promoting code reuse, and improving maintainability.

Association means that two or more classes are linked. Given classes for `Customer`, `Order`, `Student`, `Course`, `Person`, and `Phone`, `Customer` *places* an `Order`, `Student` *enrolls* in a `Course`, and `Person` *has* a `Phone`. These are association relationships. In this chapter, you see how to create these links between classes.

EXPLORING INHERITANCE

In Chapter 10, you worked with the `Customer` class. In this chapter, `Customer` becomes a subclass of the more general class named Person, as shown in Figure 11-1. `Person` is also called a **base** class because it serves as a base for its subclasses. Subclasses are also called **derived** classes because they derive some of their attributes and behavior from their superclass.

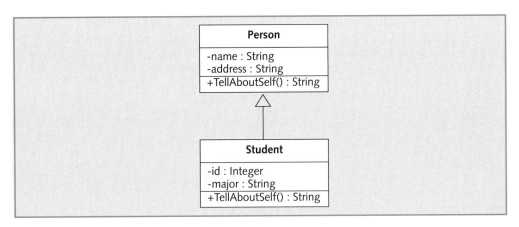

Figure 11-1 Person and Student class diagram

In this scenario, **Student** is a specialized type of **Person**; it is derived from **Person**. **Person** contains two general attributes: **name** and **address**. **Student** has two attributes: **id** and **major**. Both classes contain a **TellAboutSelf** method that returns the attribute values formatted in a string that is suitable for display.

Here you can instantiate either **Person** or **Student**. A person instance will contain attributes for **name** and **address**. However, when you instantiate **Student**, the resulting instance will have four attribute values: **name** and **address** from **Person** plus **id** and **major** from **Student**. In other words, when you instantiate a subclass you actually instantiate the inheritance hierarchy. In this example, instantiating **Student** creates a composite instance consisting of both **Person** and **Student**.

Writing a Superclass Definition

To illustrate this inheritance hierarchy, you first write a class definition for **Person**.

Example 11-1: Person class definition

```
1. Public Class Person
2.    Private name As String
3.    Private address As String

4. ' parameterized constructor
5.    Public Sub New(ByVal aName As String, ByVal anAddress
       As String)
6.       SetName(aName)
7.       SetAddress(anAddress)
8.    End Sub

9.    'get accessor methods
10.   Public Function GetName() As String
11.      Return name
12.   End Function
13.   Public Function GetAddress() As String
14.      Return address
15.   End Function

16.   'set accessor methods
17.   Public Sub SetName(ByVal aName As String)
18.      name = aName
19.   End Sub
20.   Public Sub SetAddress(ByVal anAddress As String)
```

11

```
21.      address = anAddress
22.   End Sub
23.   Public Overridable Function TellAboutSelf() As String
24.      Dim info As String
25.      info = GetName() & ", " & GetAddress()
26.      Return info
27.   End Function
28. End Class
```

This method may be overridden

Discussion:

This class definition is similar to the **Customer** class definition you developed in Chapter 10. It consists of attribute definitions for **name** and **address**, a parameterized constructor, two get accessors, two set accessors, and **TellAboutSelf**.

Note that the **TellAboutSelf** header in line 23 contains the keyword **Overridable**. This keyword tells Visual Basic .NET (VB .NET) that overriding this method is permitted. You **override** a superclass method when you write a method with the same signature in a subclass. Figure 11-1 shows the method **TellAboutSelf** in both **Person** and **Student**. Note that these are *different* methods. **TellAboutSelf** in **Person** returns **name** and **address**, yet **TellAboutSelf** in **Student** returns **id** and **major**.

Instantiating Superclasses

Next, you create a **Client** to create **Person** instances.

Example 11-2: Instantiating Person

```
1. Option Strict On
2. Option Explicit On
3. Module Client
4.    Sub Main()
5.       Dim person1, person2, person3 As Person
6.       ' create 3 instances of Person
7.       person1 = New Person("Eleanor", "Atlanta")
8.       person2 = New Person("Emily", "St. Louis")
9.       person3 = New Person("Graham", "Marietta")
10.      ' invoke get methods to retrieve attributes
11.      Console.WriteLine(person1.TellAboutSelf())
12.      Console.WriteLine(person2.TellAboutSelf())
```

13.   `Console.WriteLine(person3.TellAboutSelf())`

14.   `End Sub`

15. `End Module`

Sample Run:

```
Eleanor, Atlanta
Emily, St. Louis
Graham, Marietta
```

Discussion:

In line 5, this Client module declares three reference variables whose data type is `Person`.

Lines 7, 8, and 9 create and populate three `Person` instances.

Lines 11, 12, and 13 invoke `TellAboutSelf` for each instance, displaying the result.

CREATING SUBCLASSES

Writing a definition for a subclass is similar to writing any class definition, except that the subclass must perform three tasks:

    1. Specify its superclass using the keyword `Inherits`

    2. Invoke the superclass constructor as the *first* statement in its constructor

    3. Add the keyword `Overrides` to methods overriding superclass methods

Example 11-3 illustrates these points in the `Student` class definition.

11

Example 11-3: Student class definition

```
1. Public Class Student
2.     Inherits Person                    ┐ 1. Specify the
3.     Private id As Integer              ┘    superclass
4.     Private major As String

5.     ' parameterized constructor
6.     Public Sub New(ByVal aName As String, ByVal
       anAddress As String, ByVal anId As Integer, ByVal
       aMajor As String)
7.         ' invoke superclass constructor to populate name
           & address attributes
8.         MyBase.New(aName, anAddress)    ┐ 2. Invoke superclass
9.         ' populate id and major attributes ┘    constructor
```

```
10.        SetId(anId)
11.        SetMajor(aMajor)
12.     End Sub

13.     'get accessor methods
14.     Public Function GetId() As Integer
15.        Return id
16.     End Function
17.     Public Function GetMajor() As String
18.        Return major
19.     End Function
20.     'set accessor methods
21.     Public Sub SetId(ByVal anId As Integer)
22.        id = anId
23.     End Sub
24.     Public Sub SetMajor(ByVal aMajor As String)
25.        major = aMajor
26.     End Sub
27.     Public Overrides Function TellAboutSelf() As String
28.        Dim info As String
29.        info = MyBase.TellAboutSelf() & ", " & GetId()
           & ", " & GetMajor()
30.        Return info
31.     End Function
32. End Class
```

3. Specify Overrides for overriding methods

Invoke TellAboutSelf in superclass

Discussion:

Line 2 uses the keyword `Inherits` to tell VB .NET that `Student` is a subclass of `Person`; this creates the inheritance hierarchy.

Lines 3 and 4 declare the attribute variables for `id` and `major`.

Lines 6 through 12 define the parameterized constructor for `Student`. Note that this constructor has *four* parameter variable definitions because it receives four arguments. When you instantiate `Student`, you are creating a composite instance consisting of both `Student` and `Person`. `Person` has two attributes (`name` and `address`) and `Student` has two attributes (`id` and `major`). Therefore, when you instantiate `Student` you must supply values for all four attributes.

Line 8 invokes the constructor in the superclass `Person` passing the arguments `aName` and `anAddress`, which are used to populate the attributes in `Person`. The keyword `MyBase` indicates the base class (`Person`), and `New` is the constructor name.

The first statement in a subclass constructor *must* invoke the superclass constructor. If you fail to do this, then VB .NET automatically attempts to invoke the default constructor in the superclass. If you replace the default constructor as was done here, then you receive an error and your code terminates.

Lines 10 and 11 of the constructor invoke the setter methods to populate `id` and `major` in `Student`.

The accessor methods are contained in lines 14 through 26.

Lines 27 through 31 show the `TellAboutSelf` method. The header contains the keyword `Overrides`, which indicates this method is overriding the superclass method with the same signature. This means when you invoke `TellAboutSelf` for a `Student` instance, this is the method that executes. Notice that line 29 invokes `TellAboutSelf` in the superclass to retrieve the attribute values from `Person`. The `String` value returned is then concatenated with the values returned by `GetId` and `GetMajor`.

Instantiating an Inheritance Hierarchy

When you instantiate `Student`, you create a composite instance containing the attributes and methods of both `Person` and `Student`. Actually, Client does not need to know that the `Person` class exists; you can instantiate `Student` without reference to `Person`. From the Client's perspective, there is no superclass. The inheritance hierarchy is hidden from outside classes.

11

Example 11-4: Instantiating Student

```
1. Option Strict On

2. Option Explicit On

3. Module Client

4.    Sub Main()

5.       Dim student1, student2, student3 As Student

6.       ' create 3 instances of student

7.       student1 = New Student("Eleanor", "Atlanta", 1234567,
          "Zoology")

8.       student2 = New Student("Emily", "St. Louis", 7654321,
          "Art")
```

9.   `student3 = New Student("Graham", "Marietta", 4569876, "Computer Science")`

10. `' invoke get methods to retrieve attributes`

11. `Console.WriteLine(student1.TellAboutSelf())`

12. `Console.WriteLine(student2.TellAboutSelf())`

13. `Console.WriteLine(student3.TellAboutSelf())`

14. `End Sub`

15. `End Module`

Sample Run:

```
Eleanor, Atlanta, 1234567, Zoology
Emily, St. Louis, 7654321, Art
Graham, Marietta, 4569876, Computer Science
```

Discussion:

This client creates and populates three **Student** instances, and then their attribute values.

Line 5 declares three **Student** reference variables.

Lines 7, 8, and 9 create and populate the three **Student** instances. Note that four attribute values are passed to the **Student** constructor.

Lines 11, 12, and 13 invoke **TellAboutSelf** for each instance, passing the value returned to **Console.WriteLine** for display.

Notice that no code in Client recognizes the existence of **Person**. For example, you could rewrite **Student** to contain all four attributes (name, address, id, and major) without requiring changes to Client.

Understanding Private versus Protected Access

The **Person** class definition listed in Example 11-1 specifies **Private** accessibility for the two attributes **name** and **address**. This means that no other object, including its subclass **Student**, may access these attributes directly. You provide access to subclasses by specifying **Protected** accessibility. Attributes and methods with **Protected** accessibility are accessible only within the class and its subclasses.

To illustrate, Example 11-5 shows the **Person** class with **Private** attributes, but with **Protected** methods.

Example 11-5: Person with Protected methods

```
1. Public Class Person
2.    Private name As String
3.    Private address As String
4.    ' parameterized constructor
5.    Protected Sub New(ByVal aName As String, ByVal
        anAddress As String)
6.       SetName(aName)
7.       SetAddress(anAddress)
8.    End Sub

9.    'get accessor methods
10.   Protected Function GetName() As String
11.      Return name
12.   End Function
13.   Protected Function GetAddress() As String
14.      Return address
15.   End Function
16.   'set accessor methods
17.   Protected Sub SetName(ByVal aName As String)
18.      name = aName
19.   End Sub
20.   Protected Sub SetAddress(ByVal anAddress As String)
21.      address = anAddress
22.   End Sub
23. End Class
```

11

Discussion:

In this example, the `Person` class definition has been modified by removing its `TellAboutSelf` method and giving the remaining methods, including the constructor, `Protected` accessibility. This means that only `Person` and its subclasses may invoke them.

Example 11-6 lists the `Student` class definition with its `TellAboutSelf` method modified to invoke get accessor in `Person`.

Example 11-6: Student invoking Protected methods in Person

```
1. Public Class Student
2.    Inherits Person
3.    Private id As Integer
4.    Private major As String

5.    ' parameterized constructor
6.    Public Sub New(ByVal aName As String, ByVal anAddress
         As String, ByVal anId As Integer, ByVal aMajor As
         String)
7.      ' invoke superclass constructor to populate name &
        address attributes
8.      MyBase.New(aName, anAddress)
9.      ' populate id and major attributes
10.     SetId(anId)
11.     SetMajor(aMajor)
12.   End Sub

13.   'get accessor methods
14.   Public Function GetId() As Integer
15.      Return id
16.   End Function
17.   Public Function GetMajor() As String
18.      Return major
19.   End Function
20.   'set accessor methods
21.   Public Sub SetId(ByVal anId As Integer)
22.      id = anId
23.   End Sub
24.   Public Sub SetMajor(ByVal aMajor As String)
25.      major = aMajor
26.   End Sub
27.   Public Function TellAboutSelf() As String
28.      Dim info As String
29.      info = GetName() & ", " & GetAddress()
            & ", " & GetId() & ", " & GetMajor()
30.      Return info
31.   End Function
32. End Class
```

Invoke protected
superclass methods

Discussion:

This version of `Student` has two changes, both in the `TellAboutSelf` method. First, because `TellAboutSelf` was removed from the superclass `Person`, the keyword `Overrides` is removed from the method header. Second, instead of invoking `MyBase.TellAboutSelf` to retrieve `name` and `address`, this code invokes `GetName` and `GetAddress`, which have `Protected` access.

You could have written `MyBase.GetName()` and `MyBase.GetAddress()` to invoke the accessor methods. However, because these methods are inherited from `Person`, specifying `MyBase` is not necessary.

Adding a Second Subclass

One of the many benefits of inheritance is that it gives you the ability to add more subclasses without changing the superclass. In fact, the superclass does not know the subclasses exist. Figure 11-2 contains a class diagram showing a second subclass named `Professor`. This new subclass has two attributes, `rank` and `department`. Because it is a subclass of `Person`, when you instantiate `Professor`, the resulting composite instance contains four attributes: `name` and `address` from `Person` plus `rank` and `department` from `Professor`.

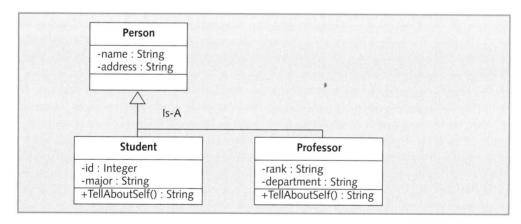

11

Figure 11-2 Subclasses Student and Professor

Example 11-7 lists a class definition for `Professor`.

Example 11-7: Professor class definition

```
1. Public Class Professor
2.    Inherits Person
3.    Private rank As String
4.    Private department As String

5.    ' parameterized constructor
6.    Public Sub New(ByVal aName As String, ByVal anAddress
      As String, ByVal aRank As String, ByVal aDepartment
      As String)
7.      ' invoke superclass constructor to populate name &
        address attributes
8.      MyBase.New(aName, anAddress)
9.      ' populate rank and department attributes
10.     SetRank(aRank)
11.     SetDepartment(aDepartment)
12.   End Sub

13.   'get accessor methods
14.   Public Function GetRank() As String
15.     Return rank
16.   End Function
17.   Public Function GetDepartment() As String
18.     Return department
19.   End Function
20.   'set accessor methods
21.   Public Sub SetRank(ByVal aRank As String)
22.     rank = aRank
23.   End Sub
24.   Public Sub SetDepartment(ByVal aDepartment As String)
25.     department = aDepartment
26.   End Sub
27.   Public Function TellAboutSelf() As String
28.     Dim info As String
29.     info = GetName() & ", " & GetAddress()
          & ", " & GetRank() & ", " & GetDepartment()
30.     Return info
31.   End Function
32. End Class
```

Discussion:

The class definition for **Professor** is similar to that for **Student**.

Line 2 specifies that **Professor** is also a subclass of **Person**.

Lines 6 through 12 define the **Professor** parameterized constructor. Note that the method header defines four parameter variables: **aName**, **anAddress**, **aRank**, and **aDepartment**. Line 8 invokes the **Person** constructor to populate **name** and **address**, and lines 10 and 11 invoke setter methods to populate **rank** and **department**.

Lines 14 through 19 define the get accessor methods for **rank** and **department**, and lines 21 through 26 the set accessor.

Lines 27 through 31 list the **TellAboutSelf** method, which invokes the (still **Protected**) **Person** methods **GetName** and **GetAddress**, and then invokes **GetRank** and **GetDepartment**. These values are concatenated to populate **info**, which is then returned to the invoking client.

The next example shows a Client module that creates two instances of **Professor**.

Example 11-8: Instantiating Professor

```
1. Option Strict On

2. Option Explicit On

3. Module Client

4.    Sub Main()

5.       Dim student1, student2, student3 As Student

6.       ' create 3 instances of student

7.       student1 = New Student("Eleanor", "Atlanta", 1234567,
          "Zoology")

8.       student2 = New Student("Emily", "St. Louis", 7654321,
          "Art")

9.       student3 = New Student("Graham", "Marietta", 4569876,
          "Computer Science")

10.      ' invoke get methods to retrieve attributes

11.      Console.WriteLine(student1.TellAboutSelf())

12.      Console.WriteLine(student2.TellAboutSelf())

13.      Console.WriteLine(student3.TellAboutSelf())
```

11

```
14.    Dim professor1, professor2 As Professor

15.    ' create 2 instances of professor

16.    professor1 = New Professor("Susan", "Atlanta", "Dept
       Head", "CSC")

17.    professor2 = New Professor("Reed", "St. Louis",
       "Emeritus", "CIS")

18.    ' invoke get methods to retrieve attributes

19.    Console.WriteLine(professor1.TellAboutSelf())

20.    Console.WriteLine(professor2.TellAboutSelf())

21.  End Sub

22. End Module
```

Sample Run:

```
Eleanor, Atlanta, 1234567, Zoology
Emily, St. Louis, 7654321, Art
Graham, Marietta, 4569876, Computer Science
Susan, Atlanta, Dept Head, CSC
Reed, St. Louis, Emeritus, CIS
```

Discussion:

The first 13 lines of Client are the same as Example 11-4. These statements create three `Student` instances, populate them, and then invoke `TellAboutSelf` and display the values returned.

Line 14 declares two variables whose data type is `Professor`.

Lines 16 and 17 then create two instances of `Professor`, populating them with the values passed as arguments.

Lines 19 and 20 invoke the `Professor TellAboutSelf` to retrieve the attribute values, and then invoke `Console.WriteLine` to display these values.

WRITING ABSTRACT CLASSES AND METHODS

In an object-oriented system, you can have both abstract and concrete classes. An **abstract class** is a class that you do not instantiate, and a **concrete class** is a class that you do instantiate. In Example 11-8, `Person` is a superclass with subclasses `Student` and `Professor`. Although the Client did not instantiate `Person`, code could have been added to do so. In your system, if all of the objects are either `Students` or `Professors`, you will never want to create an instance of `Person`; therefore, you make `Person` an abstract class. `Student` and `Professor` are concrete classes because you will instantiate them.

You create an abstract class by including the keyword `MustInherit` in its header. To make `Person` an abstract class, you write its header as:

```
Public MustInherit Class Person
```

An **abstract method** is a method that consists only of a signature; it has no code. When you include an abstract method in a superclass, you require all of its subclasses to implement the method. You create an abstract method by writing a method signature containing the keyword `MustOverride`.

If you add the abstract method `TellAboutSelf` to `Person`, then both `Student` and `Professor` must contain `TellAboutSelf` and `Person` must be made abstract because you cannot instantiate a class containing an abstract method.

Example 11-9: Abstract Person class with abstract method

```
1. Public MustInherit Class Person          The keyword
2.    Private name As String                MustInherit makes a class
3.    Private address As String             abstract

4. ' parameterized constructor
5.    Public Sub New(ByVal aName As String, ByVal
        anAddress As String)
6.       SetName(aName)
7.       SetAddress(anAddress)
8.    End Sub

9.    'get accessor methods
10.   Public Function GetName() As String
11.      Return name
12.   End Function
13.   Public Function GetAddress() As String
14.      Return address
```

11

```
15.  End Function

16.  'set accessor methods
17.  Public Sub SetName(ByVal aName As String)
18.     name = aName
19.  End Sub
20.  Public Sub SetAddress(ByVal anAddress As String)
21.     address = anAddress
22.  End Sub
23.  Public MustOverride Function TellAboutSelf() As String
24.  End Class
```

The keyword MustOverride makes a method abstract

Discussion:

This version of **Person** is the same as Example 11-1 except that in line 1, the keyword **MustInherit** has been inserted, and in line 23, the **TellAboutSelf** method has been made abstract by adding the keyword **MustOverride** and deleting the statements in **TellAboutSelf**.

DEFINING INTERFACES

Adding an abstract method to the **Person** superclass is one way to require that its subclasses override the method. Requiring a method in a set of classes assures and enforces standardization.

Another way to require that methods be included in classes is to define an interface. An **interface** is a VB .NET component that defines abstract methods that must be implemented by classes using the interface. If you want to ensure that a class has a defined set of methods, you define an interface containing abstract methods and then require that classes implement the methods in the interface.

Example 11-10 lists an interface named **IPersonInterface** containing the abstract method **TellAboutSelf**.

Example 11-10: IPersonInterface

```
Public Interface IPersonInterface
    Function TellAboutSelf() As String
End Interface
```

Discussion:

Similar to a class definition, an interface begins with a header `Public Interface` and ends with the key words `End Interface`. An interface name begins with a capital letter "I" by convention, and using the word "interface" in the name helps to identify it is an interface instead of a class.

This interface contains a single abstract method named `TellAboutSelf`. All classes implementing this interface *must* contain a method with this signature. No code is included for the method. All functionality must be defined by the class that implements the interface. Note that when you write an abstract method in an interface, you do not write the keyword `MustOverride`.

Classes inherit from superclasses and implement interfaces.

 A VB .NET class can inherit from only one superclass, but can also implement one or more interfaces.

In the examples here, you want both `Student` and `Professor` to include the `TellAboutSelf` method; therefore, you include the statement in each of these classes, as shown in Example 11-11.

Example 11-11: Student and Professor implementing IPersonInterface

11

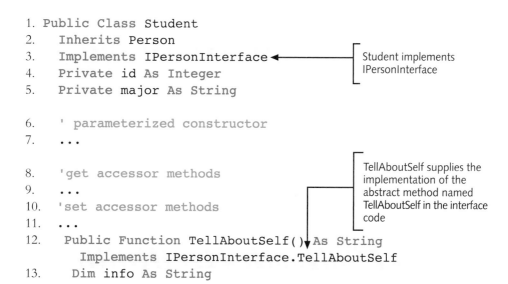

```
1.  Public Class Student
2.     Inherits Person
3.     Implements IPersonInterface          Student implements
4.     Private id As Integer                IPersonInterface
5.     Private major As String

6.     ' parameterized constructor
7.     ...
                                             TellAboutSelf supplies the
8.     'get accessor methods                 implementation of the
9.     ...                                    abstract method named
10.    'set accessor methods                  TellAboutSelf in the interface
11.    ...                                     code
12.    Public Function TellAboutSelf() As String
           Implements IPersonInterface.TellAboutSelf
13.        Dim info As String
```

```
14.     info = GetName() & ",  " & GetAddress()
            & ",  " & GetId() & ",  " & GetMajor()
15.     Return info
16.   End Function
17. End Class
```

```
1. Public Class Professor
2.    Inherits Person
3.    Implements IPersonInterface
4.    Private rank As String
5.    Private department As String

6.    ' parameterized constructor
7.    ...

8.    'get accessor methods
9.    ...
10.   'set accessor methods
11.   ...
12.    Public Function TellAboutSelf() As String
            Implements IPersonInterface.TellAboutSelf
13.     Dim info As String
14.     info = GetName() & ",  " & GetAddress()
            & ",  " & GetRank() & ",  " & GetDepartment()
15.     Return info
16.   End Function
17. End Class
```

Discussion:

For brevity, the constructor and accessor method code has been omitted from these listings.

This example lists both the Student and Professor class definitions modified to implement the IPersonInterface. Line 3 of both definitions contains the Implements statement and line 12 in each definition shows the Implements code added to the TellAboutSelf method.

To summarize, you can require a subclass to implement a method either by adding the abstract method to the superclass or by writing an Interface containing the abstract method, and then implementing the Interface in the subclasses.

CREATING ASSOCIATION LINKS

Two or more classes often have association relationships. Customers *place* Orders, Students *enroll* in Courses, and Persons *have* Phones. You implement association relationships by creating links between instances of classes.

Figure 11-3 shows a class diagram indicating an association between **Person** and **Phone**: **Person** *Has-A* **Phone**. The **Phone** class is copied from Example 10–12 in Chapter 10 and is used in the following examples without change. The **Phone** class definition is not listed again here.

 Because **Student** and **Professor** are subclasses of **Person**, they inherit the association relationship: **Student** Has-A Phone and **Professor** Has-A Phone.

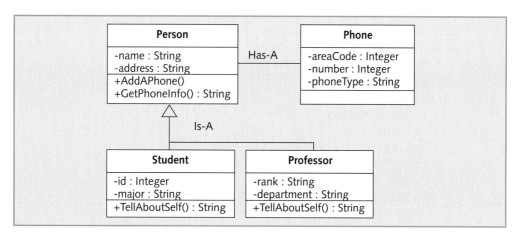

Figure 11-3   Class diagram showing inheritance and association

Implementing One-to-One Association

In a one-to-one association, each person has one phone and each phone is owned by one person. In the real world, people generally have more than one phone; home, mobile, fax, and so forth. The next section illustrates the implementation of one-to-many association relationships. This example shows how to connect one person with one phone.

Example 11-12: Person class definition with phone association

```
1. Public MustInherit Class Person
2.    Private name As String
3.    Private address As String
4.    Private phone As Phone          ◄——————————— phone attribute added
5.    ' parameterized constructor
6.    Protected Sub New(ByVal aName As String, ByVal
      anAddress As String)
7.       SetName(aName)
8.       SetAddress(anAddress)
9.    End Sub

10.   'get accessor methods
11.   Protected Function GetName() As String
12.      Return name
13.   End Function
14.   Protected Function GetAddress() As String
15.      Return address
16.   End Function
17.   'set accessor methods
18.   Protected Sub SetName(ByVal aName As String)
19.      name = aName
20.   End Sub
```

```
21.    Protected Sub SetAddress(ByVal anAddress As String)
22.       address = anAddress
23.    End Sub
```
┌ Method to add a
└ phone

```
24.    Public Sub AddAPhone(ByVal anAreaCode As Integer,
   ByVal aNumber As Integer, ByVal aPhoneType As String)
25.       phone = New Phone(anAreaCode, aNumber, aPhoneType)
26.    End Sub

27.    Public Function GetPhoneInfo() As String
28.       Dim info, formattedAreaCode, formattedNumber
          As String
29.       formattedAreaCode =
          phone.GetAreaCode().ToString("(###)")
30.       formattedNumber =
          phone.GetNumber().ToString("###-####")
31.       info = phone.GetPhoneType() & " "
             & formattedAreaCode & " " & formattedNumber
32.       Return info
33.    End Function

34. End Class
```
┌ Method to return
└ formatted phone info

11

Discussion:

This **Person** class definition is similar to those in previous examples, but has code added to accommodate the association with **Phone**.

In line 4, the attribute **phone**, a reference variable whose data type is **Phone**, is added. This variable will reference an instance of the **Phone** class.

Lines 24 through 26 contain a method named **AddAPhone** that will receive **phone** attribute values, instantiate **Phone**, and assign the instance reference to **phone**. The header at line 24 declares parameter variables for the area code, phone number, and type of phone. Line 25 instantiates **Phone** and assigns the reference to **phone**.

Lines 27 through 33 define a method that will retrieve, format, and return the phone information.

Line 28 declares **String** variables to contain the formatted information.

Line 29 invokes **GetAreaCode** for the **Phone** instance, passes the value returned to the **ToString** method to format it, and then assigns the resulting formatted value to **formattedAreaCode**. Similarly, line 30 invokes **GetNumber**, passes the value returned to the **ToString** method to format it, and then assigns the resulting formatted value to **formattedNumber**.

Line 31 invokes `GetPhoneType` for the `Phone` instance, and then concatenates the value returned with `formattedAreaCode` and `formattedNumber`. Line 32 returned the concatenated result to the invoking client.

Example 11-13: Creating Student and Professor with phones

```
1. Option Strict On

2. Option Explicit On

3. Module Client

4.    Sub Main()

5.       Dim student1 As Student, professor1 As Professor


6.       ' create an instance of student & add their phone

7.       student1 = New Student("Eleanor", "Atlanta", 1234567,
          "Zoology")

8.       student1.AddAPhone(314, 4667899, "Home")


9.       ' create an  instance of professor & add their phone

10.      professor1 = New Professor("Susan", "Atlanta", "Dept
         Head", "CSC")

11.      professor1.AddAPhone(912, 7654321, "Office")


12.      ' retrieve and display student & their phone details

13.      Console.WriteLine(student1.TellAboutSelf())

14.      Console.WriteLine(student1.GetPhoneInfo())


15.      ' retrieve and display professor & their phone details

16.      Console.WriteLine(professor1.TellAboutSelf())

17.      Console.WriteLine(professor1.GetPhoneInfo())

18.   End Sub

19. End Module
```

Sample Run:

```
Eleanor, Atlanta, 1234567, Zoology
Home (314) 466-7899
Susan, Atlanta, Dept Head, CSC
Office (912) 765-4321
```

Discussion:

This Client creates an instance of **Student** and **Professor** and links each of them to a **Phone**.

Line 5 declares a **Student** reference variable named **student1** and a **Professor** reference variable named **professor1**.

Line 7 creates the **Student** instance.

Line 8 invokes **AddAPhone** for the new **Student** instance, passing the **phone** attribute values. Recall from the previous example that this method instantiates **Phone** and populates the **phone** attribute in **Person** (**Student** superclass) with the reference.

Line 10 creates a **Professor** instance, and line 11 invokes **AddAPhone** for the new **Professor** instance.

Line 13 invokes **TellAboutSelf**, and line 14 invokes **GetPhoneInfo** for the **Student** instance, passing the results to **Console.WriteLine** for display.

Similarly, lines 16 and 17 invoke **TellAboutSelf** and **GetPhoneInfo** for the **Professor** instance and pass the results to **Console.WriteLine** for display.

11

Figure 11-4 shows the **Student** and **Professor** instances linked to their **Phone** instances.

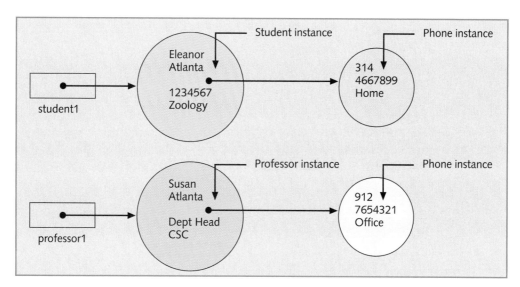

Figure 11-4   Student and Professor instances linked to Phone instances

Implementing One-to-Many Associations

Association relationships include one-to-one, one-to-many, and many-to-many. Often these relationships are implemented using arrays or ArrayLists.

To illustrate, many people have more than one phone. Example 11-14 lists the `Person` class with the `phones` attribute changed from data type `Phone` to data type `ArrayList`, which can contain references to several `Phone` instances. In addition, the methods `AddAPhone` and `GetPhoneInfo` have been modified to accommodate the addition of the `ArrayList`. Note that the class definitions for `Phone`, `Student`, and `Professor` remain unchanged.

Example 11-14: Person class definition with multiple phones

```
1. Public MustInherit Class Person
2.    Private name As String
3.    Private address As String
4.    Private phones As ArrayList           phones attribute references
                                            an ArrayList instance
5.    ' parameterized constructor
6.    Protected Sub New(ByVal aName As String, ByVal
        anAddress As String)
7.      SetName(aName)
8.      SetAddress(anAddress)
9.      ' create a 4 element ArrayList to reference
        up to 4 phones
10.     phones = New ArrayList(4)            Constructor instantiates
                                            ArrayList
11. End Sub

12.   'get accessor methods
13.   Protected Function GetName() As String
14.     Return name
15.   End Function
16.   Protected Function GetAddress() As String
17.     Return address
18.   End Function
19.   'set accessor methods
20.   Protected Sub SetName(ByVal aName As String)
21.     name = aName
22.   End Sub
23.   Protected Sub SetAddress(ByVal anAddress As String)
24.     address = anAddress
```

```
25.    End Sub                                    ──────── Method to add a phone

26.    Public Sub AddAPhone(ByVal anAreaCode As Integer,
       ByVal aNumber As Integer, ByVal aPhoneType As String)
27.       Dim aPhone As Phone = New Phone(anAreaCode,
          aNumber, aPhoneType)
28.       phones.Add(aPhone)              ─┐    Method to return String
29.    End Sub                            │    array of formatted phone
                                          │    info
30.    Public Function GetPhoneInfo() As String()
31.       Dim info, formattedAreaCode, formattedNumber
          As String
32.       Dim phoneInfo(phones.Count) As String
33.       Dim thisPhone As Phone, i As Integer

34.       ' iterate the phones ArrayList
35.       For i = 0 To phones.Count - 1
36.         thisPhone = phones.Item(i)
37.         formattedAreaCode =
            thisPhone.GetAreaCode().ToString("(###)")
38.         formattedNumber =
            thisPhone.GetNumber().ToString("###-####")
39.         info = formattedAreaCode & " "
              & formattedNumber & " " &
              thisPhone.GetPhoneType()
40.         phoneInfo(i) = info
41.       Next

42.       Return phoneInfo
43.    End Function

44. End Class
```

11

Discussion:

Four modifications were made to the **Person** class definition to accommodate multiple phones.

First, line 4 declares an attribute variable named **phones** as data type **ArrayList**. This attribute will reference an **ArrayList** instance that will contain references to **Phone** instances.

Line 10 is added to the constructor to create an `ArrayList` instance when `Person` is instantiated. Note that line 4 *does not* instantiate `ArrayList`; it only declares a reference variable. In this example, the `ArrayList` instance has four elements.

The `AddAPhone` method was modified to invoke the `Add` method for the `ArrayList` instance referenced by phones to populate the next available element of the `ArrayList` with a reference to the `Phone` instance. Line 27 instantiates `Phone`, and line 28 invokes the `Add` method.

Finally, `GetPhoneInfo` in lines 30 through 43 is rewritten to retrieve `Phone` information from the `ArrayList`.

The method header in line 30 now returns the reference to a `String` array.

Line 31 declares the same `String` variables as before to hold the formatted phone information.

Line 32 creates a `String` array with the same number of elements as the `ArrayList` referenced by phones. The reference to this new array is assigned to `phoneInfo`.

Line 33 declares two variables: `thisPhone` whose data type is `Phone`, and `i` whose data type is `Integer`.

The `For Next` loop in lines 35 through 41 iterates the `ArrayList` to retrieve the `Phone` information and populate the `String` array `phoneInfo`. Line 36 retrieves the next `Phone` instance reference and assigns it to `thisPhone`. Lines 37, 38, and 39 retrieve and format the phone information. Line 40 stores a reference to the information in the array `phoneInfo`. When the `For Next` loop terminates, line 42 returns a reference to `phoneInfo` to the invoking client.

Example 11-15: Creating Student and Professor with multiple phones

```
1. Option Strict On
2. Option Explicit On
3. Module Client
4.    Sub Main()
5.       Dim student1 As Student, professor1 As Professor
6.       Dim phoneInfo() As String, i As Integer

7.       ' create an instance of student & add their phones
8.       student1 = New Student("Eleanor", "Atlanta",
           1234567, "Zoology")
9.       student1.AddAPhone(314, 1234567, "Home")
10.      student1.AddAPhone(314, 4445555, "Mobile")
```

phoneInfo is a reference to a String array

```
11.        ' create an  instance of professor & add their
           phones
12.        professor1 = New Professor("Susan", "Atlanta",
           "Dept Head", "CSC")
13.        professor1.AddAPhone(912, 7654321, "Office")
14.        professor1.AddAPhone(417, 2233445, "Home")
15.        professor1.AddAPhone(912, 6584747, "Mobile")
16.        professor1.AddAPhone(912, 7651111, "Fax")

17.        ' retrieve and display student & their phone details
18.        Console.WriteLine(student1.TellAboutSelf())
19.        phoneInfo = student1.GetPhoneInfo()
20.        For i = 0 To phoneInfo.Length - 1
21.          Console.WriteLine(phoneInfo(i))
22.        Next

23.        ' retrieve and display professor & their phone
           details
24.        Console.WriteLine(professor1.TellAboutSelf())
25.        phoneInfo = professor1.GetPhoneInfo()
26.        For i = 0 To phoneInfo.Length - 1
27.          Console.WriteLine(phoneInfo(i))
28.        Next

29.    End Sub
30. End Module
```

Sample Run:

```
Eleanor, Atlanta, 1234567, Zoology
(314) 123-4567 Home
(314) 444-5555 Mobile
Susan, Atlanta, Dept Head, CSC
(912) 765-4321 Office
(417) 223-3445 Home
(912) 658-4747 Mobile
(912) 765-1111 Fax
```

Discussion:

This Client has been modified to add and retrieve multiple phones for **Person**.

Line 5 declares **Student** and **Professor** reference variables.

Line 6 declares a **String** array reference variable and an **Integer** variable.

Line 8 instantiates a `Student`.

Lines 9 and 10 add two phones for the student by invoking `AddAPhone`.

Line 12 instantiates `Professor`, and lines 13 through 16 add four phones for the professor.

Line 18 invokes `TellAboutSelf` for the `Student` instance and displays the result.

Line 19 invokes `GetPhoneInfo` for the `Student` instance, and assigns the value returned to `phoneInfo`. Recall that this method now returns a reference to a `String` array that has been populated with the information for all of the phones associated with the `Person` (`Student` or `Professor`).

Lines 20 through 22 define a `For Next` loop that iterates the `String` array referenced by `phoneInfo` and displays the contents of each `String` element.

Similarly, line 24 invokes `TellAboutSelf` for the `Professor` instance, and lines 25 through 27 retrieve and display the information for all of the phones associated with the `Professor` instance.

To summarize, classes can have association relationships. These associations can be one-to-one, one-to-many, or many-to-many. You implement association relationships by connecting instances of the classes having the association relationships. Connections are accomplished by creating and populating attribute reference variables.

PROGRAMMING EXAMPLE: STUDENT ENROLLS IN COURSE

This programming example demonstrates the implementation of inheritance and a many-to-many association involving a subclass. It illustrates many-to-many association implementation using the ArrayList class.

Problem Analysis and Algorithm Design

Figure 11-5 shows a class diagram with a many-to-many association between **Student** and **Course**. A student can enroll in multiple courses and a course can enroll multiple students. **Student** remains a subclass of **Person**, but the association is between **Student** and **Course**, not **Person** and **Course**.

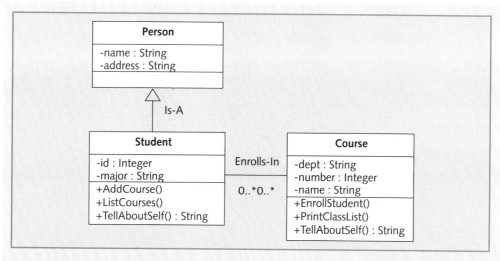

Figure 11-5 Student enrolls in Course

The **Person** class definition is copied from Example 11-5 without modification.

The class definition for **Student** is modified to include a new **ArrayList** attribute reference variable named **courses**, which will contain references to all of the courses the student takes. Two new methods are added. **AddCourse** will receive an argument containing a reference to the added **Course** instance, add its reference to the **ArrayList courses**, and then invoke **EnrollStudent** in the **Course** instance, passing a reference to the **Student** instance. **ListCourses** will iterate **courses**, retrieving and displaying the information for each course in which the student is enrolled.

The class definition for **Course** will contain attribute variable definitions for **department**, **course number** and **course name**, plus an **ArrayList** attribute reference variable named **students**, which will contain references to all of the students enrolled. In addition to accessor methods, **Course** will have three custom methods. **EnrollStudent** will receive a reference to a **Student** instance and add it to the **students ArrayList**, **PrintClassList** will display information for all of the students enrolled, and **TellAboutSelf** will return a formatted **String** containing **Course** attribute values.

Complete Program Listing

Student Class Definition

```
Public Class Student
    Inherits Person
    Private id As Integer
```

```
Private major As String
Private courses As New ArrayList(5)
' parameterized constructor
Public Sub New(ByVal aName As String, ByVal anAddress As _
String, ByVal anId As Integer, ByVal aMajor As String)
    ' invoke superclass constructor to populate name & address
    attributes
    MyBase.New(aName, anAddress)
    ' populate id and major attributes
    SetId(anId)
    SetMajor(aMajor)
End Sub

'get accessor methods
Public Function GetId() As Integer
    Return id
End Function
Public Function GetMajor() As String
    Return major
End Function
'set accessor methods
Public Sub SetId(ByVal anId As Integer)
    id = anId
End Sub
Public Sub SetMajor(ByVal aMajor As String)
    major = aMajor
End Sub
Public Function TellAboutSelf() As String
    Dim info As String
    info = GetName() & ", " & GetAddress() & ", " & GetId() & _
    ", " & GetMajor()
    Return info
End Function
' enroll this student in the course
Public Sub AddCourse(ByVal newCourse As Course)
    courses.Add(newCourse)
    newCourse.EnrollStudent(Me) ' Note: keyword Me references
    this Student instance
End Sub
' list the courses for this student
Public Sub ListCourses()
    Console.WriteLine("Enrolled in: ")
    Dim i As Integer, course As Course
    For i = 0 To courses.Count - 1
        course = courses.Item(i)
        Console.WriteLine(course.TellAboutSelf)
```

```
        Next
    End Sub
End Class
```

Course Class Definition

```
Public Class Course
    Private dept As String
    Private number As Integer
    Private name As String
    Private students As New ArrayList(15)

    ' constructor
    Public Sub New(ByVal aDept As String, ByVal aNumber As Integer, _
ByVal aName As String)
        SetDept(aDept)
        SetNumber(aNumber)
        SetName(aName)
    End Sub
    'get accessor methods
    Public Function GetDept() As String
        Return dept
    End Function
    Public Function GetNumber() As Integer
        Return number
    End Function
    Public Function GetName() As String
        Return name
    End Function

    'set accessor methods
    Public Sub SetDept(ByVal aDept As String)
        dept = aDept
    End Sub
    Public Sub SetNumber(ByVal aNumber As Integer)
        number = aNumber
    End Sub
    Public Sub SetName(ByVal aName As String)
        name = aName
    End Sub
    Public Function TellAboutSelf() As String
        Dim info As String
        info = GetDept() & ", " & GetNumber() & ", " & GetName()
        Return info
    End Function
    ' enroll the student
    Public Sub EnrollStudent(ByVal newStudent As Student)
        students.Add(newStudent)
    End Sub
```

11

```vbnet
    ' display a list of all students enrolled in this course
    Public Sub PrintClassList()
        Console.Write("Class List for: ")
        Console.WriteLine(Me.TellAboutSelf())    ' Me is implied and
        could be omitted
        Dim i As Integer, student As Student
        For i = 0 To students.Count - 1
            student = students.Item(i)
            Console.WriteLine(student.TellAboutSelf())
        Next
    End Sub
End Class
```

Client Module

```vbnet
Option Strict On
Option Explicit On
Module Client
    Sub Main()
        Dim student1, student2 As Student
        Dim course1, course2, course3 As Course

        ' create an instance of students & courses
        student1 = New Student("Eleanor", "Atlanta", 1234567, _
        "Zoology")
        student2 = New Student("Emily", "St. Louis", 7654321, _
        "Art")
        course1 = New Course("Computer Science", 101, "Intro to _
        Comp Sci")
        course2 = New Course("Information Systems", 483, "OO _
        Programming")
        course3 = New Course("Spanish", 202, "Advanced Grammar")

        ' enroll Eleanor in two courses
        student1.AddCourse(course1)
        student1.AddCourse(course3)
        ' enroll Emily in three course
        student2.AddCourse(course1)
        student2.AddCourse(course2)
        student2.AddCourse(course3)

        ' retrieve and display student  info
        Console.WriteLine(student1.TellAboutSelf())
        student1.ListCourses()
        Console.WriteLine()
        Console.WriteLine(student2.TellAboutSelf())
        student2.ListCourses()
```

```
       ' retrieve and display course & their student info
       Console.WriteLine()
       course1.PrintClassList()
       ' retrieve and display course & their student info
       Console.WriteLine()
       course2.PrintClassList()
       ' retrieve and display course & their student info
       Console.WriteLine()
       course3.PrintClassList()
   End Sub
End Module
```

Sample Run

```
Eleanor, Atlanta, 1234567, Zoology
Enrolled in:
Computer Science, 101, Intro to Comp Sci
Spanish, 202, Advanced Grammar

Emily, St. Louis, 7654321, Art
Enrolled in:
Computer Science, 101, Intro to Comp Sci
Information Systems, 483, OO Programming
Spanish, 202, Advanced Grammar

Class List for: Computer Science, 101, Intro to Comp Sci
Eleanor, Atlanta, 1234567, Zoology
Emily, St. Louis, 7654321, Art

Class List for: Information Systems, 483, OO Programming
Emily, St. Louis, 7654321, Art

Class List for: Spanish, 202, Advanced Grammar
Eleanor, Atlanta, 1234567, Zoology
Emily, St. Louis, 7654321, Art
```

11

QUICK REVIEW

1. Inheritance is sometimes called a generalization/specialization hierarchy, where the superclass specifies the general characteristics of an object, and then the subclass inherits characteristics (attributes and methods) from the superclass and adds more specialized attributes and methods. It is a powerful tool in systems development, promoting code reuse and improving maintainability.

2. A superclass is also called a base class because it serves as a base for its subclasses. Subclasses are also called derived classes because they derive some of their attributes and behavior from their superclass. The superclass does not know the subclasses exist.

4. Writing a definition for a subclass is similar to writing any class definition, except that the subclass must do three things: specify its superclass using the keyword `Inherits`; Invoke the superclass constructor as the *first* statement in its constructor; and add the keyword `Overrides` to methods overriding superclass methods.

5. You use the keyword `Overridable` to tell Visual Basic .NET (VB .NET) that overriding a method is permitted. You override a superclass method when you write a method with the same signature in a subclass.

6. When you instantiate a subclass, you create a composite instance containing the attributes and methods of both the superclass and the subclass.

7. When you assign `Private` accessibility to attributes and methods it means that no other object, including a subclass, may access them directly. You provide access to subclasses by specifying `Protected` accessibility. Attributes and methods with `Protected` accessibility are accessible only within the class and its subclasses.

8. You invoke methods in a superclass using the keyword `MyBase` plus the method name. You do not need to write `MyBase` to invoke inherited methods (methods with `Protected` accessibility).

9. The first statement in a subclass constructor *must* invoke the superclass constructor. If you fail to do this, then VB .NET will automatically attempt to invoke the default constructor in the superclass.

10. An abstract class is a class that you do not instantiate and a concrete class is a class that you do instantiate. You create an abstract class by including the keyword `MustInherit` in its header.

11. An abstract method is a method that consists only of a signature; it has no code. When you include an abstract method in a superclass, you require all of its subclasses to implement the method. You create an abstract method by writing a method signature containing the keyword `MustOverride`.

12. Another way to require that methods be included in classes is to define an interface. An interface is a VB .NET component that defines abstract methods that must be implemented by classes using the interface.

13. An interface name begins with a capital letter "I" by convention, and using the word "interface" in the name helps to identify it is an interface instead of a class.

14. Classes *inherit* from superclasses and *implement* interfaces. A VB .NET class can inherit from only one superclass but can also implement one or more interfaces.

15. Association means that two or more classes are linked. Given classes for `Customer`, `Order`, `Student`, `Course`, `Person`, and `Phone`, `Customer` *places* an `Order`, `Student` *enrolls* in a `Course`, and `Person` *has* a `Phone`.

16. Association relationships include one-to-one, one-to-many, and many-to-many.

17. You implement association relationships by connecting instances of the classes having the association relationships. Connections are accomplished by creating and populating attribute reference variables.

18. One-to-many and many-to-many relationships are implemented using arrays or ArrayLists.

EXERCISES

1. Explain the difference between a Class and an Interface.

2. Distinguish between an abstract class and a concrete class.

3. Explain why you cannot instantiate a class with an abstract method.

4. Why is an inheritance hierarchy also called a generalization/specialization hierarchy?

5. What is a derived class? What is a base class?

6. How does a subclass identify its superclass?

7. How does a superclass identify its subclasses?

8. What does it mean to "override" a method?

9. What is Protected accessibility?

10. What must the first statement in a subclass constructor do? Why?

11

PROGRAMMING EXERCISES

1. The `Person` class definition in Example 11-12 implements a one-to-one association between `Person` and `Phone`. `Person` includes a method named `AddAPhone` that instantiates `Phone`, passing three arguments: `area code`, `number`, and `phone type`. `Phone` has both a 3-parameter constructor and a 2-parameter constructor using the default `area code` value 314. Add an overloaded 2-parameter `AddAPhone` method to `Person` and modify the Client module in Example 11-13 to invoke this new method.

2. Example 11-14 implements a one-to-many relationship between `Person` and `Phone` using an ArrayList. Modify `Person` to implement this association with a four-element array.

3. The Programming Example at the end of this chapter implements a many-to-many relationship between `Student` and `Course`: a `Student` enrolls in several courses and each `Course` has several students. Modify `Course` to include an attribute containing the maximum enrollment for the course. Modify `Client` as needed to implement this new attribute.

4. Add a current enrollment attribute to `Course` in the end-of-chapter Programming Example. Increment this attribute in the `Course` constructor. Modify the `TellAboutSelf` method in the `Course` class to include this new attribute.

5. Students sometimes drop courses. Modify the end-of-chapter Programming Example to include a method to drop a course.

12

Advanced Topics: Exception Handling

In this chapter, you will:

○ Examine the VB .NET exception-handling model

○ Explore the supplied Exception classes

○ Write user-defined Exception classes

○ Add data validation code to methods

○ Explore the debugging tool

In previous chapters, you worked with supplied classes and wrote user-defined class definitions and methods. In this chapter, you explore the Visual Basic .NET (VB .NET) exception-handling model and write exception class definitions. An exception, like many other things in VB .NET, is an object instance. Specifically it is an instance of the Framework Class Library (FCL)-supplied Exception class or one of its subclasses. VB .NET uses exceptions to notify you of errors, problems, and other unusual conditions that may occur while your system is running. Applying the now-familiar client-server model, a client invokes a server method, perhaps passing along arguments. The server performs its assigned task and may return a value to the invoking client. The server uses exceptions to inform the client of a problem or unusual situation. Perhaps the client sent an inappropriate or invalid argument, or perhaps the server cannot complete its normal processing because of some other condition. In this chapter, you learn how to work with exceptions in both client and server code.

Exception handling is an important tool in developing fault-tolerant applications. In this chapter, you see how to employ exception handling to improve the applications you develop.

EXAMINING THE VB .NET EXCEPTION-HANDLING MODEL

In Chapter 6, you explored the `String` class and invoked some of its methods to manipulate string data. One of these methods, `Insert`, inserts a `String` argument at a specified index into an existing `String` instance, returning a new instance with the inserted value. Example 12-1 illustrates the use of this method.

Example 12-1: Invoking the String Insert method

```
1. Option Strict On
2. Option Explicit On
3. Module Chapter12Example1
4.    Sub Main()
5.       Dim s1 As String = "Hello Again"
6.       Dim s2 As String = s1.Insert(6, "There ")
7.       Console.WriteLine(s2)
8.    End Sub
9. End Module
```

Sample Run:

Hello There Again

Discussion:

Line 5 first declares a `String` reference variable `s1`, then creates a `String` instance, populates it with `"Hello Again"`, and assigns its reference to `s1`.

Line 6 declares a second `String` reference variable `s2`, invokes the `Insert` method for the instance referenced by `s1`, passing two values as an argument `(6, "There ")`. The first value is the index where you want to begin the insertion. Here the index value is 6, which is the character "A" of the word "Again." The second value of the argument, `"There "`, contains the characters you want inserted. You can write either a literal or a reference variable pointing to a `String` instance that contains the characters you want to insert.

The reference for the newly created `String` instance returned by `Insert` is assigned to `s2`.

Line 7 invokes `Console.WriteLine` to display the contents of the new `String` instance.

Causing an Exception

In Example 12-1, the original `String` value "Hello Again" contains 11 characters including the space. The index values are 0 through 10. Example 12-1 inserted a value beginning at index 6.

The next example contains a deliberate error. The index of the value is changed from 6 to 16. In other words, you are asking the `Insert` method to insert a value at index 16, which does not exist. What can the method do?

Example 12-2: Invoking the String Insert method with an invalid argument

12

```
1. Option Strict On

2. Option Explicit On

3. Module Chapter12Example2

4.    Sub Main()

5.       Dim s1 As String = "Hello Again"

6.       Dim s2 As String = s1.Insert(16, "There ")

7.       Console.WriteLine(s2)

8.    End Sub

9. End Module
```

Sample Run:

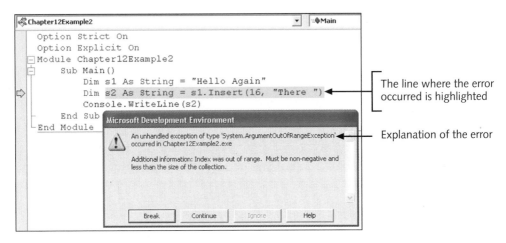

Figure 12-1 Output from Example 12-2

Discussion:

In this example, you passed an invalid argument to the `Insert` method. The method *cannot* insert the additional characters beginning at index 16 because there is no index 16. The `Insert` method has attempted to notify you by sending, or **throwing**, you an exception. The message in the dialog box in Figure 12-1 states:

```
"An unhandled exception of type 'System.ArgumentOutOfRangeException'
occurred in Chapter12Example2.exe."
```

This message means that the method *threw an exception* to you, but your code *did not deal with it* appropriately and execution was interrupted. The documentation for the `Insert` method states that it will throw an `ArgumentOutOfRangeException` if the index argument is negative or greater than the length of the `String` instance.

Exception-Handling Syntax

When errors arise, such as in Example 12-2, the server method can create an exception instance containing information about the situation. The server then sends, or throws, the exception instance to the invoking client. Of course, the client must be prepared to receive the exception and take appropriate action. In Example 12-2, the client was unprepared to deal with the exception and execution stopped.

VB .NET uses five keywords to deal with exceptions: `Try`, `Catch`, `Finally`, `End Try`, and `Throw`. The first four are used by the client, while the last, `Throw`, is used by the server.

Figure 12-2 illustrates the interaction between client and server methods dealing with exceptions.

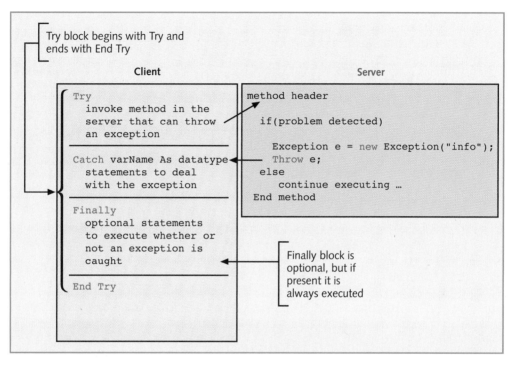

Figure 12-2   Client-server exception handling

Whenever a client invokes a method that may create and throw an exception, the invoking code is placed within a **Try block**. A `Try` block begins with the keyword `Try` and ends with the keyword `End Try`. The client invokes the server method within the `Try` block. Then, if the server detects an exception, the server method creates an exception instance and sends it to the invoking client using the keyword `Throw`. The client *catches* the exception instance in a **Catch block** and executes statements to deal with the exception. The **Finally block** is optional, but will execute regardless of whether an exception is caught.

Example 12-3 repeats Example 12-2, but this time illustrates the use of a `Try` block to deal with the exception.

Example 12-3: Invoking the Insert method using Try-Catch

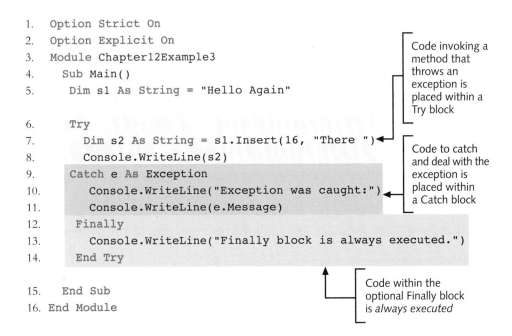

```
1.   Option Strict On
2.   Option Explicit On
3.   Module Chapter12Example3
4.     Sub Main()
5.       Dim s1 As String = "Hello Again"

6.       Try
7.         Dim s2 As String = s1.Insert(16, "There ")
8.         Console.WriteLine(s2)
9.       Catch e As Exception
10.        Console.WriteLine("Exception was caught:")
11.        Console.WriteLine(e.Message)
12.      Finally
13.        Console.WriteLine("Finally block is always executed.")
14.      End Try

15.    End Sub
16. End Module
```

Code invoking a method that throws an exception is placed within a Try block

Code to catch and deal with the exception is placed within a Catch block

Code within the optional Finally block is *always executed*

Sample Run:

```
Exception was caught:
Index was out of range. Must be non-negative
and less than the size of the collection.
Parameter name: startIndex
Finally block is always executed.
```

Discussion:

In this example, the code invoking **Insert** is contained within a **Try** block at lines 6 through 14.

Line 7 invokes **Insert**, passing an invalid argument. As promised, **Insert** creates and throws an Exception instance. Because line 7 invoked a method that threw an exception, execution is transferred to the **Catch** block and line 8 is not executed.

The **Catch** statement at line 9 receives a reference to the Exception instance, which is stored in the variable **e**. Lines 10 and 11 within the **Catch** block are then executed. Line 11 retrieves the **Message** property for the instance referenced by **e**, and passes it to **Console.WriteLine** for display. As you can see in the output, the **Message** property contains an explanation of the error.

The **Finally** block beginning at line 12 is executed whether or not an exception is caught.

To summarize, VB .NET uses exceptions to notify you of errors, problems, and other unusual conditions that may occur while your system is running. You add exception-handling code to write fault-tolerant programs. VB .NET uses the keywords `Try`, `Catch`, `Finally`, `End Try`, and `Throw` to deal with exceptions. All are used by the client, except `Throw`, which is used by the server.

EXPLORING THE SUPPLIED EXCEPTION CLASSES

Figure 12-3 contains a partial class diagram of the VB .NET `Exception` class hierarchy.

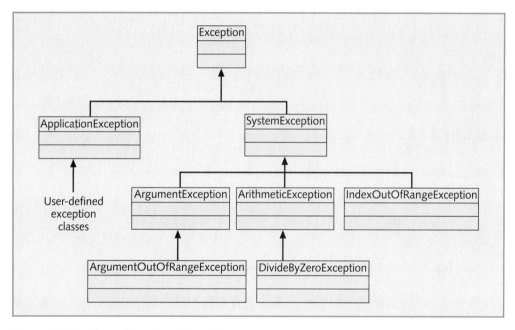

Figure 12-3 Exception class hierarchy

The base class of all exceptions is the `Exception` class. This class contains a constructor and, as you have seen, the `Message` property.

The `Exception` class has two immediate subclasses: `ApplicationException` and `SystemException`. When you write user-defined exception class definitions, you extend `ApplicationException`. `SystemException` is the base class for the exceptions used by VB .NET. Subclasses of `SystemException` are instantiated and thrown by methods in the FCL classes and also by the Common Language Runtime (CLR). Recall from Chapter 3 that the CLR manages the execution of your code. Part of that management process is to detect runtime error conditions and to instantiate and throw exceptions. `ArgumentOutOfRangeException` was thrown by `String.Insert` in Examples 12-2 and 12-3.

Properties also throw exceptions. Recall that properties are really accessor methods disguised as public variables. For example, the String Chars property returns a character at a specified index. Because an index could be invalid, it will throw `IndexOutOfBoundsException`.

The following example illustrates the CLR throwing an exception.

Example 12-4: Triggering an exception from the CLR

```
1. Option Strict On

2. Option Explicit On

3. Module Chapter12Example4

4.    Sub Main()

5.       Dim s1, s2 As String

6.          s1 = "Hello Again"

7.          s2 = s2.Insert(6, "There ")

8.          Console.WriteLine(s2)

9.    End Sub

10. End Module
```

Sample Run:

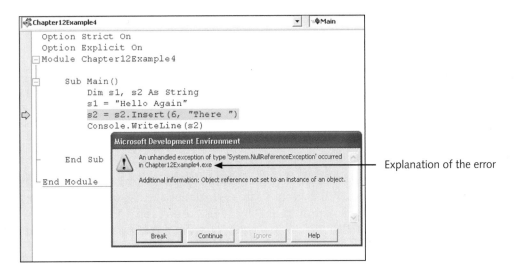

Figure 12-4   Output from Example 12-4

Discussion:

Line 5 declares two `String` reference variables named `s1` and `s2`.

Line 6 creates a `String` instance and populates `s1` with its reference.

Line 7 attempts to invoke `Insert` for the instance referenced by `s2`. However, because `s2` has not been populated, it references nothing; it contains no value. Reference variables containing no value are said to contain **null**. Obviously you cannot invoke a method for an instance that does not exist. The CLR detects this error and creates and throws the `NullReferenceException`.

You can also write code to create and throw instances of `Exception`, `SystemException`, and its subclasses. You can also write your own exception class definitions which will extend `ApplicationException`. Writing user-defined exceptions is described in the next section.

Example 12-5 uses the client-server model to illustrate a method that instantiates one of the supplied exception classes.

Example 12-5: Instantiating the supplied exception classes

Server Module

```
1. Option Strict On
2. Option Explicit On
3. Module Server
4.    Public Function Divide(ByVal a As Integer, ByVal b As
         Integer) As Double
5.       Dim e As DivideByZeroException
6.       If b = 0 Then
7.          e = New DivideByZeroException("You cannot divide by
            zero")
8.          Throw e
9.       Else
10.         Return a / b
11.      End If
12.   End Function
13. End Module
```

12

Client Module

```
1. Option Strict On
2. Option Explicit On
3. Module Client
4.    Sub Main()
5.       Dim result As Double
6.       Try
7.          result = Server.Divide(10, 3)
8.          Console.WriteLine("Result = " & result)
9.          result = Server.Divide(10, 0)
10.         Console.WriteLine("Result = " & result)
11.      Catch x As DivideByZeroException
12.         Console.WriteLine(x.Message)
13.      End Try
14.   End Sub
15. End Module
```

Sample Run:

```
Result = 3.33333333333333
You cannot divide by zero
```

Server Module Discussion:

The Server module in this example contains a single method named `Divide`. This method accepts two `Integer` arguments, divides the first value by the second, and returns a `Double` result. The method will create and throw an instance of `DivideByZeroException` if an attempt to divide by zero is detected.

Line 5 declares a reference variable named e whose data type is `DivideByZeroException`.

Line 6 tests to see if the second parameter contains zero. If it does, line 7 instantiates `DivideByZeroException`, passing a message to the constructor. Line 8 then throws the instance to the Client.

If the second parameter does not contain zero, then the divide operation is completed and the result is returned to the Client.

Client Module Discussion:

In the Client module, line 5 declares a `Double` variable named `result`.

Lines 6 through 13 define a `Try` block. Line 7 invokes `Server.Divide`, passing the arguments `(10, 3)`. Because these are valid arguments, the method computes the quotient and returns it to the Client, where it is assigned to `result`.

Line 8 invokes `Console.WriteLine` to display the result.

Line 9 again invokes `Server.Divide`; however, this time it passes the arguments `(10, 0)`. Because the second argument is zero, the `Divide` method instantiates and throws `DivideByZeroException`. When an exception is thrown, execution of the statements in the `Try` block is interrupted and control is passed to the `Catch` block.

Line 11 is written to specifically catch `DivideByZeroException`. Note that if a different exception class had been instantiated, it would not have been caught here.

 Line 11 could have been written to catch a superclass of `DivideByZeroException`. If `Exception` was specified, then the `Catch` would catch any exception because `Exception` is the superclass of all `Exception` classes.

Line 12 retrieves the message property and displays it.

To summarize, numerous exception classes are supplied as part of the FCL. The base class of them is named `Exception`. Immediate subclasses of `Exception` are `ApplicationException` and `SystemException`. The supplied classes and the FCL use subclasses of `SystemException`. When you write user-defined exception class definitions, you extend `ApplicationException`.

12

WRITING USER-DEFINED EXCEPTION CLASSES

Writing a user-defined exception class is essentially the same as writing any class definition. You can include attribute definitions, accessor methods, and one or more constructors. Recall, however, that a subclass constructor must invoke its superclass constructor as its first statement. This requirement remains the same for an exception class definition. Also, VB .NET programmers include the word "Exception" as a part of the class name.

ADDING DATA VALIDATION CODE TO METHODS

Example 10-12 in Chapter 10 listed a class definition for the `Phone` class. The class diagram for `Phone` is repeated in Figure 12-5 and listed in Example 12-6.

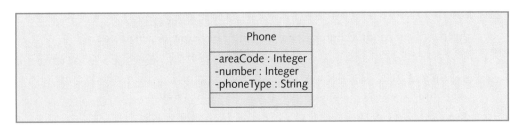

Figure 12-5   Phone class diagram

Example 12-6: Phone class definition

```
1. Public Class Phone
2.    Private areaCode As Integer
3.    Private number As Integer
4.    Private phoneType As String
5.    Const defaultAreaCode As Integer = 314
6.    ' 3 parameter constructor
7.    ..
8.    ' 2 parameter constructor using default area code
9.    ..
10.   'get accessor methods
11.   ..
12.   'set accessor methods
13.   ..
14.   Public Function TellAboutSelf() As String
15.      Dim info, areaCodeInfo, numberInfo, typeInfo As String
16.      typeInfo = Me.GetPhoneType()
17.      areaCodeInfo = Me.GetAreaCode().ToString("(###)")
18.      numberInfo = Me.GetNumber().ToString("###-####")
19.      info = typeInfo & " " & areaCodeInfo & " " & numberInfo
20.   Return info
21. End Function
22. End Class
```

Discussion:

This example lists the definition for the **Phone** class, which has attribute definitions, a 3-parameter constructor, a 2-parameter constructor using the default area code 314, and accessor methods plus a **TellAboutSelf** method.

Although the class definition in Example 12-6 appears complete, it does not include **data validation** code. Data validation code is added to methods to ensure valid arguments are passed. In Example 12-6, the **Phone** constructor accepts arguments to populate the attributes without checking the values for validity. For example, if the only valid values for **phoneType** are "Home," "Mobile," "Office," and "Fax," then code should be added to verify that the argument submitted for **phoneType** is one of these values.

When a client instantiates **Phone**, passing an invalid argument for **phoneType**, you want the **SetPhoneType** accessor method to detect this error, and then create and throw an exception. In this example, you could either use one of the supplied **Exception** classes, such as **Exception**, or you can write a user-defined exception. You choose to write a user-defined exception whenever you want to add attributes and methods that are not included in the supplied classes.

Example 12-7 lists the user-defined class for **InvalidPhoneTypeException**.

Example 12-7: InvalidPhoneTypeException class definition

```
1.   Public Class InvalidPhoneTypeException        ApplicationException is the
2.      Inherits ApplicationException   ◄─────     base class for user-defined
3.      Private phoneTypeSubmitted As String       exception classes
4.      Public Sub New(ByVal aType As String, ByVal message
         As String)
5.        MyBase.New(message)
6.        phoneTypeSubmitted = aType
7.      End Sub

8.      Public Function GetPhoneType() As String
9.        Return phoneTypeSubmitted
10.     End Function
11. End Class
```

12

Discussion:

This class definition includes one attribute, a single constructor, and a get accessor method.

Line 2 specifies that **InvalidPhoneTypeException** extends **ApplicationException** as required.

Line 3 declares the attribute variable named `phoneTypeSubmitted`. This attribute will contain the submitted argument value for the phone type.

The constructor is shown in lines 4 through 7. The header at line 4 declares two parameter variables. The first is the phone type submitted and the second will contain a message value that will populate the message property of the superclass `Exception`. Line 5 invokes the superclass constructor, passing the message value as an argument. Line 6 then populates `phoneTypeSubmitted`.

Lines 8 through 10 define the get accessor method for `phoneTypeSubmitted`.

Next, the `Phone` class definition is modified to provide data validation.

Example 12-8: Phone class definition with data validation

```
1. Public Class Phone
2.    Private areaCode As Integer
3.    Private number As Integer
4.    Private phoneType As String
5.    Const defaultAreaCode As Integer = 314
6.    ' 3 parameter constructor
7.    ..
8.    ' 2 parameter constructor using default area code
9.    ..
10.   'get accessor methods
11.   ..

12.   Public Sub SetPhoneType(ByVal aPhoneType As String)
13.      Dim e As InvalidPhoneTypeException
14.      Dim typeOK As Boolean = False

15.      Select Case aPhoneType
16.        Case "Home", "home", "HOME"
17.          typeOK = True
18.          aPhoneType = "Home"
19.        Case "Mobile", "mobile", "MOBILE"
20.          typeOK = True
21.          aPhoneType = "Mobile"
22.        Case "Office", "office", "OFFICE"
23.          typeOK = True
24.          aPhoneType = "Office"
25.        Case "Fax", "fax", "FAX"
26.          typeOK = True
27.          aPhoneType = "Fax"
```

See if the phone type is one of the acceptable values

```
28.        End Select
29.        If typeOK Then
30.           phoneType = aPhoneType  ◄───────────────┐
31.        Else                                        │
32.           e = New InvalidPhoneTypeException(aPhoneType,
                 "Phone type must be Home, Mobile, Office, or Fax")
33.           Throw e
34.        End If
35.     End Sub
```

> If the phone type is valid, then populate the attribute, otherwise instantiate and throw InvalidPhoneTypeException

```
36.     'set accessor methods for areaCode and number
37.     ..
38.     Public Function TellAboutSelf() As String
39.        Dim info, areaCodeInfo, numberInfo,
              typeInfo As String
40.        typeInfo = Me.GetPhoneType()
41.        areaCodeInfo = Me.GetAreaCode().ToString("(###)")
42.        numberInfo = Me.GetNumber().ToString("###-####")
43.        info = typeInfo & " " & areaCodeInfo & " " &
              numberInfo
44.        Return info
45.     End Function

46. End Class
```

12

Discussion:

This class definition for **Phone** has data validation code added to the set accessor method **SetPhoneType** defined in lines 12 through 35.

Line 13 declares a reference variable named **e** whose data type is **InvalidPhoneTypeException**.

Line 14 then declares a **Boolean** variable named **typeOK** and initializes it to **False**. This variable will be set to **True** if a valid phone type is detected in the **Select Case** statement beginning at line 15.

The **Select Case** statement contained in lines 15 through 28 tests the contents of the argument passed to the set method for one of the acceptable values. Note that variations of each value are checked. For example, Home, home, and HOME are all acceptable values, however, Home is not. If an acceptable value is detected, **typeOK** is set to **True** and the appropriate capitalization is stored for the attribute.

Lines 29 through 34 contain an **If** statement that interrogates **typeOK**. If it evaluates True, then the phone type attribute is populated with the submitted argument. However, if it is False, this means an invalid phone type was detected and **InvalidPhoneTypeException** is instantiated and thrown at lines 32 and 33.

An alternative design here is to use the Case Else to instantiate and throw
`InvalidPhoneTypeException`.

Example 12-9 lists a Client that instantiates **Phone**, sending an invalid phone type as an
argument.

Example 12-9: Phone class throwing InvalidPhoneTypeException

```
1. Option Strict On
2. Option Explicit On
3. Module Client
4.    Sub Main()
5.       Dim phone1, phone2 As Phone

6.       Try
7.          ' create a valid Phone
8.          phone1 = New Phone(1234567, "Home")
9.          Console.WriteLine(phone1.TellAboutSelf())

10.         ' now pass an invalid type
11.         phone2 = New Phone(1234567, "Cell")
12.         Console.WriteLine(phone2.TellAboutSelf())


13.      Catch e As InvalidPhoneTypeException
14.         Console.WriteLine(e.Message)
15.         Console.WriteLine("Argument submitted = " &
            e.GetPhoneType)
16.
17.      End Try
18.   End Sub
19. End Module
```

Instantiate Phone within Try block
because SetPhoneType can throw
an exception

If SetPhoneType throws an exception,
it will be caught in this block

Sample Run:

```
Home (314) 123-4567
Phone type must be Home, Mobile, Office, or Fax
Argument submitted = Cell
```

Discussion:

This Client module first instantiates **Phone**, passing valid attribute values, and then attempts
to instantiate **Phone**, passing an invalid phone type argument.

Line 5 declares two reference variables for `Phone` named `phone1` and `phone2`.

A `Try` block begins at line 6. The code to instantiate `Phone` is placed in a `Try` block because `SetPhoneType` can create and throw an `InvalidPhoneTypeException`.

Line 8 instantiates `Phone`, passing two valid attribute values, which invokes the 2-parameter constructor.

Line 9 invokes `TellAboutSelf` for this new `Phone` instance and passes the value returned to `Console.WriteLine` for display.

Line 11 then attempts to instantiate `Phone`, but this time passes an invalid phone type value. The constructor in `Phone` invokes the individual set accessor methods to populate the `Phone` attributes. When the constructor invokes `SetPhoneType`, it passes the invalid phone type value that was sent by the Client module. `SetPhoneType` detects the invalid type, and as a result it instantiates and throws `InvalidPhoneTypeException`.

The instance of `InvalidPhoneTypeException` is caught at Client line 13 and its reference is stored in the reference variable `e`.

Line 14 retrieves the `Message` property from the instance referenced by `e` and passes the value returned to `Console.WriteLine` for display.

Line 15 then invokes `GetPhoneType` for the instance referenced by `e` and again passes the value returned to `Console.WriteLine` for display.

EXPLORING THE DEBUGGING TOOL

12

In Chapter 2, you were introduced to the Visual Studio .NET debugger. You recall that a **debugger** is a software tool provided to assist you in finding errors that keep your program from running as intended. In Chapter 2, you used the debugger to set a breakpoint, a flag to tell the debugger to temporarily suspend execution of your program at a particular point. In this chapter, you continue working with breakpoints, plus you learn how to create a **watch window** and see how to step through the execution of code a line at a time. A watch window is a window where you can view the contents of variables and expressions.

Setting a Breakpoint

Recall that a breakpoint is a flag in your program that tells the debugger to pause execution of the program at a specific line of code. Breakpoints are an important debugging tool provided by Visual Studio. While your program is suspended at a breakpoint, you can view and alter the contents of variables and you can alter the sequence of a statement execution by specifying the next statement to be executed.

Example 12-10 expands on Example 9-5 in Chapter 9 that converts Fahrenheit temperatures to Celsius.

Example 12-10: Setting a breakpoint

```
Chapter12Example10                        ▼  Main
 1   Option Strict On
 2   Option Explicit On
 3   Imports System.windows.forms
 4 ⊟ Module Chapter12Example10
 5 ⊟     Sub Main()
 6           Dim fahrenheit, celsius As Double
 7           fahrenheit = InputFahrenheit()
 8           Do Until fahrenheit = 999
 9               celsius = ComputeCelsius(fahrenheit)
10               DisplayCelsius(fahrenheit, celsius)
11               fahrenheit = InputFahrenheit()
12           Loop
13       End Sub
14 ⊟     Private Function InputFahrenheit() As Double
15           Dim f As Double
16           Console.WriteLine("Please enter a Fahrenheit temperature (999 to stop
17           f = Convert.ToDouble(Console.ReadLine())
18           Return f
19       End Function
20 ⊟     Private Function ComputeCelsius(ByVal f As Double) As Double
21           Dim c As Double
22           c = 5 / 9 * (f - 32)
23           Return c
24       End Function
25 ⊟     Private Sub DisplayCelsius(ByVal f As Double, ByVal c As Double)
26           c = Math.Round(c, 1)
27           MessageBox.Show(f & " F = " & c & " C")
28       End Sub
29   End Module
```

Sample Run:

```
Please enter a Fahrenheit temperature (999 to stop):
212
```

Discussion:

This module consists of a **Main** procedure and three **Private** procedures.

The **Main** procedure at lines 5 through 13 contains a **Do Until** loop that continues until a sentinel value of 999 is entered. **Main** invokes the **InputFahrenheit** method, then **ComputeCelsius**, and finally **DisplayCelsius**.

InputFahrenheit is listed in lines 14 through 19. Line 15 declares a **Double** variable named **f** that will contain the Fahrenheit temperature entered. Line 16 displays a prompt message, and line 17 inputs the temperature. Line 18 returns the value entered.

ComputeCelsius is shown in lines 20 through 24. Line 21 declares a **Double** variable named **c** that contains the computed Celsius temperature. Line 22 computes Celsius and line 23 returns it. Note that line 22 has a breakpoint set. You set a breakpoint by right-clicking the statement where the breakpoint is to be set, and then selecting Insert Breakpoint from the menu, as shown in Figure 12-6.

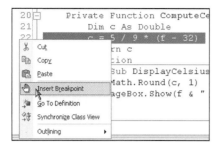

```
20 □    Private Function ComputeCe
21         Dim c As Double
22         c = 5 / 9 * (f - 32)
   Cut              rn c
   Copy             tion
   Paste            Sub DisplayCelsius
   Insert Breakpoint  Math.Round(c, 1)
                     ageBox.Show(f & "
   Go To Definition
   Synchronize Class View
   Outlining        ►
```

Figure 12-6   Setting a breakpoint

`DisplayCelsius` is listed at lines 25 through 28. Line 26 invokes `Math.Round` to round the Celsius value to one decimal position, and line 27 displays the result in a MessageBox.

When you execute the program, the breakpoint at line 22 suspends execution, as shown in Figure 12-7. Clicking Continue resumes execution, and the output is displayed in the MessageBox shown in Figure 12-8. Entering the sentinel value 999 terminates the program's execution.

```
20 □    Private Function ComputeCelsius(ByVal f As Double) As Double
21         Dim c As Double
22         c = 5 / 9 * (f - 32)
23         Return c
24 └    End Function
```

Figure 12-7   Execution stopped at breakpoint

12

212 F = 100 C

OK

Figure 12-8   MessageBox with output

Breakpoints have two additional features that increase their usefulness. First, you can specify the number of times a breakpoint is encountered before stopping. This value is called the **hit count**. The default hit counter value is 1. Second, you can attach a logical expression to a breakpoint and execution will then stop if the expression evaluates true.

Figure 12-9 displays the Breakpoint Properties dialog box. To view this window, right-click the breakpoint line, and then select Breakpoint Properties from the shortcut menu.

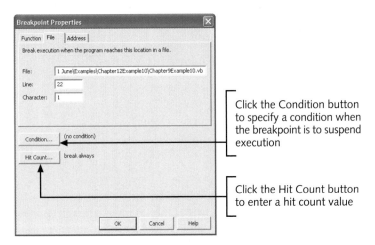

Click the Condition button to specify a condition when the breakpoint is to suspend execution

Click the Hit Count button to enter a hit count value

Figure 12-9   Breakpoint Properties dialog box

You click the Condition button to specify a condition when the breakpoint is to become active, and click the Hit Count button to enter a Hit Count value.

Creating a Watch Window

You use a **watch window** to display the contents of variables while your program is suspended at a breakpoint. It is available only when the execution of your program is suspended at a breakpoint. To display a watch window, click Debug on the menu bar, point to Windows, point to Watch, and then click Watch 1. Figure 12-10 illustrates this sequence.

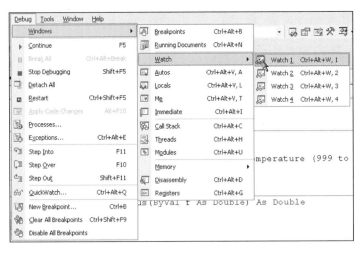

Figure 12-10   Displaying a watch window

When the watch window appears, you enter the variable names whose contents you want to display, as shown in Figure 12-11.

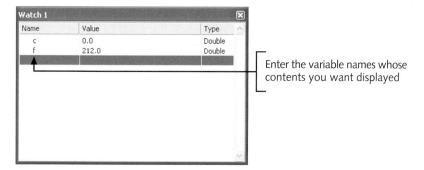

Enter the variable names whose contents you want displayed

Figure 12-11   Watch window contents

Using the Step Feature

Another powerful feature of the Debugger tool is the Step feature. You use Step when you want to execute one line of code at a time. VB .NET provides two different Step options: Step Into and Step Over. Both cause the debugger to execute the next line of code; however, they differ in how they behave if the code invokes a procedure. Step Into executes the line of code and stops. Step Over also executes the next line of code, but if that code invokes a procedure, all of the statements in the procedure are executed and then the debugger stops. In other words, if you want to execute the statements in an invoked procedure one at a time, use Step Into. However if you prefer to execute all of the statements in an invoked procedure and then stop, use Step Over.

You activate Step Into by pressing F11 or by selecting Step Into from the Debug menu, as shown in Figure 12-12.

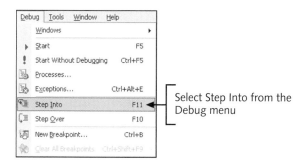

Select Step Into from the Debug menu

Figure 12-12   Activating Step Into

12

Figure 12-13 shows that Step Into has been activated for Example 12-10. The statement being executed is shown with a yellow highlight.

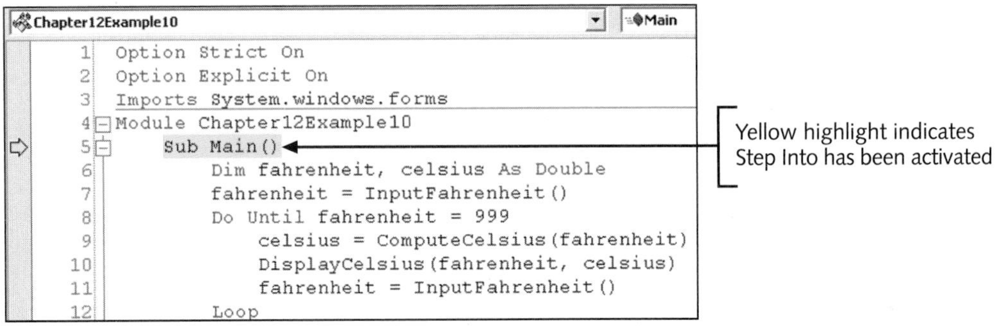

```
Chapter12Example10                                    ▼  Main
     1   Option Strict On
     2   Option Explicit On
     3   Imports System.windows.forms
     4 □ Module Chapter12Example10
⇨    5 □    Sub Main()◄──────────────       Yellow highlight indicates
     6           Dim fahrenheit, celsius As Double       Step Into has been activated
     7           fahrenheit = InputFahrenheit()
     8           Do Until fahrenheit = 999
     9               celsius = ComputeCelsius(fahrenheit)
    10               DisplayCelsius(fahrenheit, celsius)
    11               fahrenheit = InputFahrenheit()
    12           Loop
```

Figure 12-13   Example 12-10 with Step Into activated

Because execution has just begun, the **Main** procedure header is highlighted. When you press F11 again or select Step Into from the Debug menu, line 7 will be highlighted, as shown in Figure 12-14. This means that line 7 is the next statement to be executed.

```
Chapter12Example10                                    ▼  Main
     1   Option Strict On
     2   Option Explicit On
     3   Imports System.windows.forms
     4 □ Module Chapter12Example10
     5 □    Sub Main()
     6           Dim fahrenheit, celsius As Double
⇨    7           fahrenheit = InputFahrenheit()
     8           Do Until fahrenheit = 999
     9               celsius = ComputeCelsius(fahrenheit)
    10               DisplayCelsius(fahrenheit, celsius)
    11               fahrenheit = InputFahrenheit()
    12           Loop
    13 └    End Sub
```

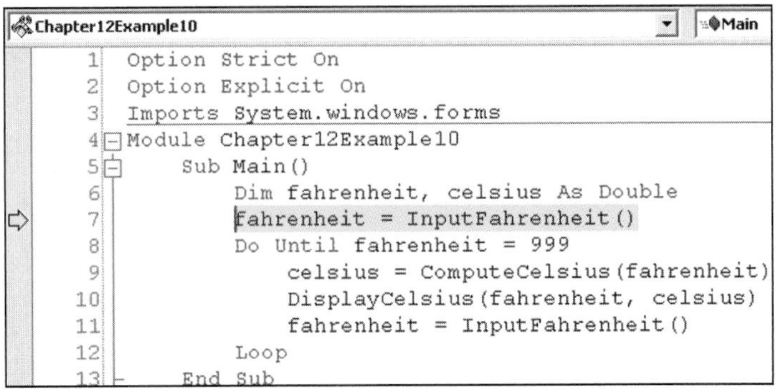

Figure 12-14   Line 7 will be executed next

Because line 7 invokes **InputFahrenheit**, the next statement to be executed after line 7 is line 14, as shown in Figure 12-15.

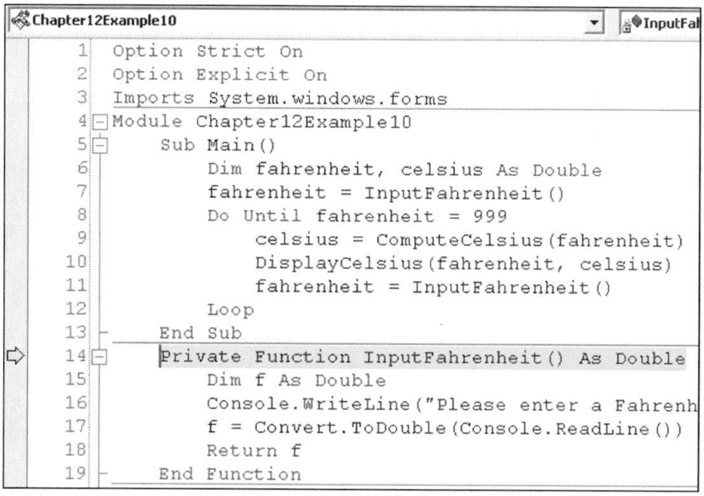

```
Chapter12Example10                                    ▼  ₐ♦InputFal
    1  Option Strict On
    2  Option Explicit On
    3  Imports System.windows.forms
    4 ⊟Module Chapter12Example10
    5 ⊟    Sub Main()
    6          Dim fahrenheit, celsius As Double
    7          fahrenheit = InputFahrenheit()
    8          Do Until fahrenheit = 999
    9              celsius = ComputeCelsius(fahrenheit)
   10              DisplayCelsius(fahrenheit, celsius)
   11              fahrenheit = InputFahrenheit()
   12          Loop
   13  ┤    End Sub
⇨  14 ⊟    Private Function InputFahrenheit() As Double
   15          Dim f As Double
   16          Console.WriteLine("Please enter a Fahrenh
   17          f = Convert.ToDouble(Console.ReadLine())
   18          Return f
   19  ┤    End Function
```

Figure 12-15   Line 14 will be executed next

Note that if you were using Step Over instead of Step Into after line 7 was executed, the debugger would stop at line 8 *after* executing all of the statements in `InputFahrenheit`.

To summarize, you can instruct the debugger to execute statements one at a time. You use Step Into to execute each statement one at a time and use Step Over to execute all of the statements in an invoked procedure.

12

Programming Example: Data Validation with User-Defined Exception Classes

This Programming Example extends the Chapter 7 end-of-chapter programming example. It demonstrates the implementation of user-defined `Exception` classes used in data validation. This example employs a Server module, a Client module, and two user-defined exception class definitions.

This example computes the federal withholding tax for employees based on their wages and marital status. It accepts wages and marital status as arguments and returns the federal withholding tax. Marital status must be "M", "m", "S", or "s", or an instance of `InvalidMaritalStatusException` is created and thrown. Wages must be greater than zero and less than or equal to $4,000.00 or an instance of `InvalidWagesException` is created and thrown. (For this employer, $4,000 is the maximum wage.)

Problem Analysis and Algorithm Design

The Server module in this example consists of a single method named `ComputeWithHolding` that receives wages and marital status as arguments, then computes and returns the federal withholding tax. `ComputeWithHolding` validates marital status, which must be "M", "m", "S", or "s", or an instance of `InvalidMaritalStatusException` is created and thrown. Similarly, wages must be greater than zero and less than or equal to $4,000.00 or an instance of `InvalidWagesException` is created and thrown.

Variables   The computation of federal tax withholding is copied from the Programming Example in Chapter 7. It involves the use of two tax tables, one for single employees (see Table 12-1) and one for married employees (see Table 12-2). These tables are stored in two-dimensional arrays.

Table 12-1 Single employee federal tax withholding table

Wages Over	But Not Over	Base Tax Amount	Plus %	Of Excess Over
0	51	0	0	
51	187	0	10	51
187	592	13.60	15	187
592	1317	74.35	25	592
1317	2860	255.60	28	1317
2860	6177	687.64	33	2860
6177		1782.25	35	6177

Table 12-2 Married employee federal tax withholding table

Wages Over	But Not Over	Base Tax Amount	Plus %	Of Excess Over
0	154	0	0	
154	429	0	10	154
429	1245	27.50	15	429
1245	2270	149.90	25	1245
2270	3568	406.15	28	2270
3568	6271	769.59	33	3568
6271		1661.58	35	6271

Formulas   When the appropriate row in the tax table is located, the program computes the federal tax withholding = column 4 * (wages - column 5) + column 3

> **NOTE** Note that the index of the columns is 1 less than the column number.

Main Client Algorithm

1. Start a `Do Until` pre-test loop to input each employee's wages and marital status.
2. Use a sentinel value of 99999 for wages to terminate the loop.
3. Display a prompt to input wages.
4. Input wages and convert to `Double`.
5. Within the `Do Until` loop body:
   a. Display a prompt to input marital status.
   b. Input M for married or S for single and convert to `Char`.
   c. Within a `Try` block:
      - Invoke `ComputeWithHolding`.
      - Invoke `Console.WriteLine` to display the federal withholding formatted as currency.
      - If a subclass of ApplicationException is thrown, display the message property.
   d. Initialize rowIndex to 0 and found to `False`.

12

Complete Program Listing

InvalidMaritalStatusException Class Definition

```
Option Explicit On
Option Strict On
Public Class InvalidMaritalStatusException
    Inherits ApplicationException
    Private maritalStatusSubmitted As String
    Public Sub New(ByVal maritalStatus As String, ByVal message _
    As String)
        MyBase.New(message)
        maritalStatusSubmitted = maritalStatus
    End Sub
    Public Function GetMaritalStatus() As String
        Return maritalStatusSubmitted
    End Function

End Class
```

InvalidWagesException Class Definition

```
Option Explicit On
Option Strict On
Public Class InvalidWagesException
    Inherits ApplicationException
    Private wagesSubmitted As Double
    Public Sub New(ByVal wages As Double, ByVal message As String)
        MyBase.New(message)
        wagesSubmitted = wages
    End Sub
    Public Function GetWagesSubmitted() As Double
        Return wagesSubmitted
    End Function
End Class
```

Client Module

```
Option Explicit On
Option Strict On
Imports System.Windows.Forms
Module Client
    Public Sub main()
        Dim wages, fedWithholding As Double, marriedOrSingle As Char
        ' use 99999 as sentinel value to terminate
        Console.Write("Enter wage amount (99999 to stop):")
        wages = Convert.ToDouble(Console.ReadLine())
        ' begin the loop for each employee
        Do Until wages = 99999
            Console.Write("Enter M for married, S for single:")
            marriedOrSingle = Convert.ToChar(Console.ReadLine())
            Try
                fedWithholding = ComputeWithHolding(wages, marriedOrSingle)
                Console.WriteLine("Federal Withholding = :" & _
                  fedWithholding.ToString("C"))
            Catch ex As ApplicationException
                MessageBox.Show(ex.Message)
            End Try
            ' input wage amount for next employee
            Console.Write("Enter wage amount (99999 to stop):")
            wages = Convert.ToDouble(Console.ReadLine())
        Loop
    End Sub
End Module
```

Server Module

```vb
Option Explicit On
Option Strict On
Module Server

    Public Function Compute WithHolding(ByVal wages As Double, ByVal _
    marriedOrSingle As Char) As Double
        ' single employee table
        ' table format
        ' wages not over, withholding amount is, plus %, of excess over
        Dim singleTaxTable(,) As Double = {{51, 0, 0, 0}, _
                                           {187, 0, 0.1, 51}, _
                                           {592, 13.6, 0.15, 187}, _
                                           {1317, 74.35, 0.25, 592}, _
                                           {2860, 255.6, 0.28, 1317}, _
                                           {6177, 687.64, 0.33, 2860}, _
                                           {99999, 1782.25, 0.35, 6177}}
        ' married employee table
        Dim marriedTaxTable(,) As Double =  {{154, 0, 0, 0}, _
                                            {429, 0, 0.1, 154}, _
                                            {1245, 27.5, 0.15, 429}, _
                                            {2270, 149.9, 0.25, 1245}, _
                                            {3568, 406.15, 0.28, 2270}, _
                                            {6271, 769.59, 0.33, 3568}, _
                                            {99999, 1661.58, 0.35, 6271}}

        Dim taxTable(,) As Double
        Dim msIndex, rowIndex As Integer
        Dim fedWithholding As Double
        Dim found, maritalStatusOK, wagesOK As Boolean
        Dim maritalStatusException As InvalidMaritalStatusException
        Dim wagesException As InvalidWagesException
        Dim message As String
        Const MAXIMUM_WAGE_ALLOWED As Double= 4000

        ' validate marital status
        maritalStatusOK = False
        If marriedOrSingle = "M" Or marriedOrSingle = "m" Then
            maritalStatusOK = True
            taxTable = marriedTaxTable
        ElseIf marriedOrSingle = "S" Or marriedOrSingle = "s" Then
            maritalStatusOK = True
            taxTable = singleTaxTable
        End If
```

12

```
        If Not maritalStatusOK Then
            message = "Marital Status must be M or S"
            maritalStatusException = New _
                InvalidMaritalStatusException(marriedOrSingle, message)
            Throw maritalStatusException
        End If
        ' validate wages
        wagesOK = False
        If wages <= 0 Or wages > MAXIMUM_WAGE_ALLOWED Then
            message = "Wages must be 1 - " & MAXIMUM_WAGE_ALLOWED
            wagesException = New InvalidWagesException(wages, message)
            Throw wagesException
        End If
        ' marital status and wages are valid
        rowIndex = 0
        found = False
        ' loop to find the appropriate row for the wages
        Do While rowIndex < 6 And found = False
            If wages <= taxTable(rowIndex, 0) Then
                ' compute the withholding amount
                fedWithholding = taxTable(rowIndex, 1) + _
                taxTable(rowIndex, 2) * (wages - taxTable(rowIndex, 3))
                found = True ' stop the loop
            Else
                rowIndex += 1
            End If
        Loop

        Return fedWithholding
    End Function

End Module
```

Sample Run

In the Sample Runs, user input is shaded. Figure 12-16 shows the message that appears for invalid wages. Figure 12-17 shows the message that appears for invalid marital status.

```
Enter wage amount (99999 to stop):
500
Enter M for married, S for single:
M
Federal Withholding = $38.15
Enter wage amount (99999 to stop):
600
Enter M for married, S for single:
S
```

```
Federal Withholding = $76.35
Enter wage amount (99999 to stop):
0
Enter M for married, S for single:
S
```

Figure 12-16   MessageBox displayed for invalid wages

```
Enter wage amount (99999 to stop):
500
Enter M for married, S for single:
A
```

Figure 12-17   MessageBox displayed for invalid marital status

```
Enter wage amount (99999 to stop):
99999
```

12

QUICK REVIEW

1. Visual Basic .NET (VB .NET) uses exceptions to notify you of errors, problems, and other unusual conditions that may occur while your system is running.

2. An exception is an instance of the Framework Class Library (FCL)-supplied `Exception` class or one of its subclasses.

3. When errors arise, server methods can create an exception instance containing information about the situation. The server then sends or throws the exception instance to the invoking client. The client must be prepared to receive the exception and take appropriate action.

4. Properties also throw exceptions.

5. VB .NET uses five keywords to deal with exceptions: `Try`, `Catch`, `Finally`, `End Try`, and `Throw`. The first four are used by the client, while the last, `Throw`, is used by the server.

6. Whenever a client invokes a method that may create and throw an exception, the invoking code is placed in a `Try` block.

7. A `Try` block begins with the keyword `Try` and ends with the keyword `End Try`.

8. The client invokes the server method within the `Try` block. Then, if a situation warranting an exception is detected, the server method creates an exception instance and sends it to the invoking client using the keyword `Throw`.

9. The client *catches* the exception instance in a `Catch` block and executes statements to deal with the exception.

10. The `Finally` block is optional, but if included will execute regardless of whether an exception is caught.

11. The base class of all exceptions is the `Exception` class.

12. The `Exception` class has two immediate subclasses: `ApplicationException` and `SystemException`.

13. When you write user-defined exception class definitions, you extend `ApplicationException`.

14. `SystemException` is the base class for the exceptions used by VB .NET. Subclasses of `SystemException` are instantiated and thrown by methods in the FCL classes and also by the Common Language Runtime (CLR).

15. You can also write code to create and throw instances of `Exception`, `SystemException`, and its subclasses. You can also write your own exception class definitions, which extend `ApplicationException`.

16. Writing a user-defined exception class is essentially the same as writing any class definition. You can include attribute definitions, accessor methods, and one or more constructors.

17. The Visual Studio debugger is a software tool provided to assist you in finding errors that keep your program from running as intended.

18. A breakpoint is a flag in your program that tells the debugger to pause execution of the program at a specific line of code.

19. While your program is suspended at a breakpoint, you can view and alter the contents of variables and you can alter the sequence of statement execution by specifying the next statement to be executed.

20. You can specify the number of times a breakpoint is encountered before stopping. This value is called the hit count. The default hit counter value is 1.

21. You can attach a logical expression to a breakpoint and execution will then stop if the expression evaluates true.

22. You use a watch window to display the contents of variables while your program is suspended at a breakpoint.

23. You use a Step option when you want to execute one line of code at a time. VB .NET provides two different Step options: Step Into and Step Over.

24. Step Into executes the line of code and stops.

25. Step Over also executes the next line of code, but if that code invokes a procedure, all of the statements in the procedure are executed and then the debugger stops.

EXERCISES

1. What are the two immediate subclasses of `Exception`?

2. Explain the purpose of the five keywords VB .NET uses to deal with exceptions.

3. What is the purpose of `SystemException`?

4. What is the purpose of `ApplicationException`?

5. Why would you need to write a user-defined `Exception` class definition?

6. What is the debugger?

7. What is a breakpoint?

8. What is a breakpoint hit count?

9. What does a watch window accomplish?

10. Distinguish between Step Into and Step Over.

12

PROGRAMMING EXERCISES

1. In Chapter 10, Example 10-18 illustrated a `Circle` class and a Client module. Modify `Circle` to provide data validation for its three attributes: x, y, and radius.
   x and y must be > 0 and <= 100. Radius must be > 0 and <= 75.
   Instantiate and throw an Exception containing an appropriate error message when an invalid value is detected. Modify Client to test your modifications.

2. Extend Exercise 1 by writing an exception class named `InvalidArgumentException`. Modify `Circle` to instantiate and throw `InvalidArgumentException` containing an appropriate error message when an invalid value is detected.

3. Example 12-9 contained the `Phone` class with data validation for phone type. Extend this example to include data validation for area code and number. Area code must be > 0 and <= 999. Phone number must be > 0 and <= 9999999. Whenever an invalid value is detected, instantiate and throw `InvalidArgumentException` (from Exercise 2) containing an appropriate error message when an invalid value is detected.

4. Programming Exercise 3 in Chapter 11 asked you to modify the end-of-chapter Programming Example by changing **Course** to include an attribute containing the maximum enrollment for the course, and then changing **Student** and **Client** as needed to implement this new attribute. Extend this exercise by adding data validation code to ensure that the maximum enrollment is not exceeded.

   Write an **Exception** class definition named **CourseFullException** and modify **Client** to catch this exception whenever an attempt is made to enroll a student in a course that is full.

13

Advanced GUI and Graphics

In this chapter, you will:

O Work with additional GUI controls

O Draw lines, rectangles, and ovals

O Develop GUI classes that interact with a PD class

O Create applications with multiple forms

O Simulate a DA class

O Create an integrated system that simulates interaction with a database

In Chapter 8, you learned how to write a graphical user interface (GUI) class to display a form containing various GUI components such as labels, text boxes, and buttons, as well as how to write methods to handle events. This chapter introduces new GUI components and some graphics capabilities of Visual Basic .NET (VB .NET).

This chapter also shows you how to create an integrated system using multiple forms and a simulated database. First, you learn how to develop GUI classes that interact with the **Customer** problem domain (PD) class you worked with in Chapter 10. You then create a main menu form that integrates these classes into a single system. Finally, you see how to develop a data access (DA) class and create an integrated system that uses an **ArrayList** to simulate interaction with a database.

WORKING WITH ADDITIONAL GUI CONTROLS

Figure 13-1 shows a form containing many GUI controls. The form contains several GUI components you are familiar with, such as buttons, labels, text boxes, and radio buttons. It also includes several new controls, namely menus, group boxes, and tab pages. Table 13-1 describes these and other GUI components introduced in this chapter, together with those you learned about in Chapter 8. Naming conventions are also shown in Table 13-1. Components introduced in Chapter 13 are shown in bold.

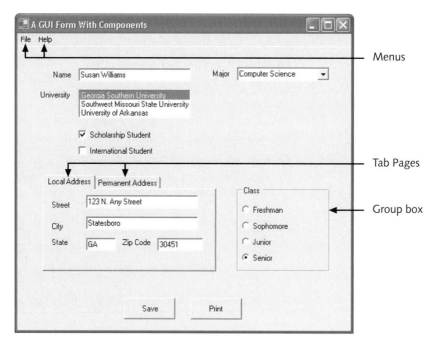

Figure 13-1   A form with GUI components

Table 13-1   Commonly used GUI components and naming conventions

GUI Component	Prefix	Description
Button	btn	Control that the user clicks to perform an action
CheckBox	chk	Two-state control that enables yes/no (true/false) options
CheckedListBox	chklst	Component that enables selection of one or more predefined items from a list of check boxes; when an item is selected, it appears checked
ComboBox	cmb	Control that enables selection of one or more predefined items from a list, or entry of a new value
Form	frm	GUI window with a title bar; forms usually contain other GUI components
GroupBox	**grp**	**Container for other GUI components, and usually includes a border and a title, but not scroll bars**
Label	lbl	Control used to display text (but not to input text)
ListBox	lst	Control that enables selection of one or more predefined items from a list
MainMenu	**mnu**	**Control that provides drop-down menus on a form**
MenuItem	**mnuitm**	**Component that provides individual menu options for drop-down menus**
Panel	**pnl**	**Container for other GUI components, and usually includes scroll bars, but not a title or border**
RadioButton	rad	Two-state control that enables yes/no (true/false) options while enforcing mutually exclusive behavior (i.e., only one radio button in a radio button group may be selected at a given time)
TabControl	**tab**	**Control that enables the inclusion of tab pages on a form**
TabPage	**tabpg**	**Component that provides individual tab pages for a tab control**
TextBox	txt	Control used to display and input text
TreeNode	**trn**	**Component that provides individual nodes within a tree view**
TreeView	**trv**	**Component that displays expandable outlines**

13

Recall that all of the GUI classes in the `System.Windows.Forms` namespace take advantage of inheritance and that most of the GUI classes you use on a form are subclasses of the `Control` class. Properties and methods inherited from `Control` provide basic functionality for the visible controls you use on a form.

Using Group Boxes and Panels

Group boxes and **panels** are containers that enable you to visually and logically organize groups of related controls. After you create an instance of the `GroupBox` or `Panel` class, you add components (such as buttons, labels, and text boxes) by drawing them inside the group box or panel. If you place a group box (or panel) on the form after creating other controls, the controls may appear to be inside the group box, but they are not. You can add controls to a group box (or panel) by cutting and pasting them inside the group box (or panel), or by dragging them into it.

When you move the panel or group box, all the controls within it move together. A group box appears with a border (or frame) around the controls contained within it. A panel does not include a border by default, but you can change the BorderStyle property if necessary. Panels may include vertical and horizontal scroll bars, but do not have captions. Group boxes, on the other hand, do not include scroll bars, but usually have a caption. You set the caption using the Text property. Panels and group boxes may be nested—in other words, a group box or panel may contain other group boxes or panels.

Although they may contain any of the GUI controls, a common use of group boxes and panels is to group a set of radio buttons. Several group boxes and panels may be used within a single form to group multiple sets of radio buttons. Mutually exclusive behavior is enforced separately for each group. This means that only one radio button in a radio button group can be selected at a given time. When you select any radio button in the group, the others are automatically deselected. If you have more than one radio button group, this behavior is enforced within each group. Group boxes and panels can be the source of several different events, but your programs do not typically need to respond to these events. Tables 13-2 and 13-3 summarize frequently used methods and properties for these controls.

Table 13-2 Selected properties, methods, and events of the GroupBox class

Properties of the GroupBox Class	Description
	Inherits properties, methods, and events from the Control class
Controls	Identifies the collection of controls contained within the group box. (The Add and Remove methods of the `Control.ControlCollection` class add individual controls to the collection. The AddRange and Clear methods of the `Control.ControlCollection` class add or remove all controls in the collection.)
Text	Identifies the text (caption) associated with the group box

Table 13-3 Selected properties, methods, and events of the Panel class

Properties of the Panel Class	Description
	Inherits properties, methods, and events from the Control class
AutoScroll	Indicates whether the panel allows the user to use scroll bars to view portions of the panel that would otherwise be out of view
BorderStyle	Indicates the border style for the panel (default is none)
Controls	Identifies the collection of controls contained within the panel. (The `Add` and `Remove` methods of the `Control.ControlCollection` class add individual controls to the collection. The `AddRange` and `Clear` methods of the `Control.ControlCollection` class add or remove all controls in the collection.)

The following example illustrates the use of group boxes and panels. It creates the GUI shown in Figure 13-2.

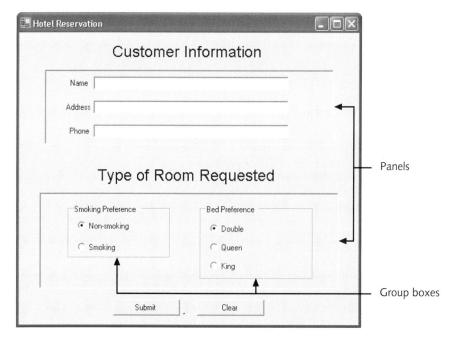

Figure 13-2 Hotel Reservation GUI

13

Example 13-1: Using group boxes and panels

As shown in Figure 13-2, the GUI contains two panels, two group boxes, three labels, three text boxes, five radio buttons, and two buttons. Mutually exclusive behavior is enforced within each group box. Users enter their name, address, and phone number, and then select preferences for the type of hotel room they want.

The program includes two event handlers—one for the Submit button and one for the Clear button. When the user clicks the Submit button, the program checks to see that all customer information was entered. This is accomplished by verifying that the length of the string in each text box is greater than zero. If so, the program displays a confirmation message. Otherwise, the program displays an error message. When the user clicks the Clear button, the program clears the text boxes and resets room preferences to their default values.

 Many method headers in this chapter are long and do not fit on a single printed line. However, when you type the code in your IDE, you should type the method headers as a single line. (Code other than method headers use an underscore as the continuation character to indicate that a statement continues on the next line.)

The complete program listing follows:

```
Public Class frmHotelReservation
    Inherits System.Windows.Forms.Form

    'Windows Form Designer generated code

    'Event handler for click event on Submit button
    Private Sub btnSubmit_Click(ByVal sender As System.Object, ByVal
    e As System.EventArgs) Handles btnSubmit.Click
        'Declare variables
        Dim output, smoking, bedType As String
        Dim name, address, phone As String
        'Get values from text boxes
        name = txtName.Text
        address = txtAddress.Text
        phone = txtPhone.Text
        'Validate that the user has entered all customer information
        If name.Length = 0 Or address.Length = 0 _
        Or phone.Length = 0 Then
            MessageBox.Show _
            ("Please enter all requested customer information")
    Else
        'All required data entered - check preferences
        output = "Thank you, " & name & "." & vbCrLf
        'Determine smoking preference
        If radSmoking.Checked = True Then
            smoking = radSmoking.Text
        Else
            smoking = radNonSmoking.Text
        End If
```

```
                    'Append smoking preference to output string
                    output = output & "Your request for a " & smoking & ", "
                    'Determine bed preference
                    If radKing.Checked = True Then
                        bedType = radKing.Text
                    ElseIf radQueen.Checked = True Then
                        bedType = radQueen.Text
                    Else
                        bedType = radDouble.Text
                    End If
                    'Append bed preference to output string
                    output = output & bedType & " room is confirmed."
                    'Display confirmation message
                    MessageBox.Show(output)
                End If
            End Sub

            Private Sub btnClear_Click(ByVal sender As System.Object, ByVal e
        As System.EventArgs) Handles btnClear.Click
                'Clear text boxes and reset default radio buttons
                txtName.Clear()
                txtAddress.Clear()
                txtPhone.Clear()
                radNonSmoking.Checked = True
                radDouble.Checked = True
            End Sub
        End Class
```

Sample Run:

Figure 13-3 shows the output of this program.

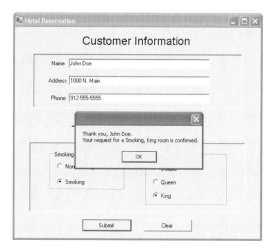

Figure 13-3   Output of Hotel Reservation program

Using Tree Nodes and Tree Views

A **tree view**, which is supported by the `TreeView` class, displays a group of hierarchically related items, where each item (or **tree node**) is represented as an instance of the `TreeNode` class. As shown in Figure 13-4, a tree view and its associated tree nodes appear as an expandable outline. To expand or collapse a node, you click the plus or minus box to the left of the node.

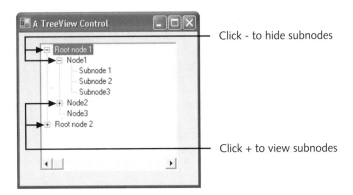

Figure 13-4   Tree view control

Each node in the tree contains a value. A node that contains one or more subnodes is called a **parent node**. Subnodes are referred to as **child nodes**. A child node may be a parent to other subnodes. Child nodes that have the same parent are called **sibling nodes**. The top-level parent node is referred to as the **root node**. A tree view can have more than one root node.

Tree views are useful for displaying hierarchical information. For example, when you select Contents from the Help menu in VB .NET, you see a tree view. Each node in the tree contains the name of a help topic, many of which are expandable into subtopics. Each subtopic may also have subtopics of its own. Another common example is the directory structure of a computer. The top-level directory (such as C:) contains folders that may each contain subfolders of their own. In this case, the root node is C: and each folder of C: is a child node. Each child node (representing a folder of C:) would have child nodes of its own to represent its subfolders.

Tables 13-4 and 13-5 summarize frequently used properties, methods, and events of the `TreeView` and `TreeNode` classes.

Table 13-4 Selected properties, methods, and events of the TreeView class

Properties of the TreeView Class	Description
CheckBoxes	Indicates whether check boxes are displayed next to the nodes in the tree
Indent	Indicates the distance to indent each level in the tree
Nodes	Identifies the collection of tree nodes assigned to the tree
Scrollable	Indicates whether the tree view control displays scroll bars when needed
SelectedNode	Identifies the currently selected node in the tree
ShowLines	Indicates whether lines are drawn between nodes in the tree
ShowPlusMinus	Indicates whether plus (+) and minus (-) signs are displayed next to nodes that contain subnodes. Plus and minus signs indicate that a node can be expanded or collapsed, respectively.
ShowRootLines	Indicates whether lines are drawn between nodes that are at the root of the tree
Sorted	Indicates whether the nodes in the tree are sorted
Methods of the TreeView Class	
CollapseAll	Collapses all the nodes in the tree
ExpandAll	Expands all the nodes in the tree
GetNodeAt	Retrieves the node at the specified location in the tree
GetNodeCount	Retrieves the number of nodes in the tree, optionally including the nodes in all subtrees
Common Event	
AfterSelect	Occurs after a tree node is selected

13

Table 13-5 Selected properties, methods, and events of the TreeNode class

Properties of the TreeNode Class	Description
Checked	Indicates whether a tree node is checked or unchecked
FirstNode	Gets the first child node in the tree
FullPath	Gets the path from the root to the current node
Index	Identifies the position of the specified node in the tree
LastNode	Gets the last child node in the tree
NextNode	Gets the next sibling node in the tree
Nodes	Identifies the collection of tree nodes assigned to the current node
Parent	Gets the parent node of the current node in the tree
SelectedNode	Identifies the currently selected node
Text	Identifies the text that appears in the label of the tree node
Methods of the TreeNode Class	
Collapse	Collapses the tree node
ExpandAll	Expands all nodes in the tree
GetNodeCount	Identifies the number of child nodes
Remove	Removes the current node from the tree

The following example illustrates the use of tree node and tree view controls. This program displays the GUI shown in Figure 13-5.

Figure 13-5   Computer Science Courses GUI

Example 13-2: Using tree views and tree nodes

13

As shown in Figure 13-5, this program contains a tree view, a multiline text box, and two buttons. The names of these controls are `trvCSC`, `txtOutput`, `btnFill`, and `btnCollapse`, respectively. The program includes three event handlers—one for each button and one to respond to the selection of a node in the tree.

When the user clicks the Fill Tree button, the event handler declares necessary loop index and tree node variables. It then removes any existing nodes in the tree. This is necessary to prevent the tree from being populated with duplicate entries each time the Fill Tree button is pressed.

```
'Declare loop index and tree node variables
Dim profIndex, courseIndex As Integer
Dim rootNode, profNode As TreeNode
'Clear the tree view each time the method is called
trvCSC.Nodes.Clear()
```

Next, a one-dimensional array, `profArray`, is populated with the names of three professors, and a two-dimensional array, `courseArray`, is populated with the names of nine courses. For this example, assume that the first three courses are taught by the first professor, the next three by the second professor, and the last three by the third professor.

```
'Fill arrays with values to be contained in the tree
profArray = New String() _
{"Professor Doke", "Professor Rebstock", "Professor Williams"}

courseArray = New String(,) _
{{"CSC 1236", "CSC 3301", "CSC 5502"}, _
{"CSC 1301", "CSC 1302", "CSC 4134"}, _
{"CSC 2230", "CSC 3130", "CSC 4238"}}
```

One way to add a node to a tree is to write a statement of the form as follows:

control.Nodes.Add(*myString*)

where `control` is a tree view or tree node control and `myString` is the value to be added. Root nodes are added to the tree view control. All other nodes are added to their parent node.

To populate the tree, first add a root node for the Computer Science Department. Note that the root node is added to the tree view control.

```
'Add root node for the Computer Science Department
rootNode = trvCSC.Nodes.Add("Computer Science Department")
```

Nested `For` `Next` loops are used to add a child node for each professor, and subsequent child nodes for each course.

```
1. 'Add a child node to the root node for each professor
2. For profIndex = 0 To 2
3.     profNode = rootNode.Nodes.Add(profArray(profIndex))
4.     'Add child nodes for each course taught by this
       professor
5.     For courseIndex = 0 To 2
6.         profNode.Nodes.Add(courseArray(profIndex,
           courseIndex))
7.     Next
8. Next
```

Lines 2-8 define the outer `For` loop. Line 3 adds a child node to the root node. The value of the child node is the string located at the `profIndex` position of `profArray`. Lines 5-7 define the inner `For` loop. Line 6 adds a child node to the professor node. The value of the child node is the string located at the `courseIndex` column in the `profIndex` row of the two-dimensional course array.

When the user selects a node within the tree, an `AfterSelect` event is generated. The `AfterSelect` event handler displays a message in the text box identifying the selected node, its parent node, its previous sibling node, and its next sibling node. This is accomplished by first creating a variable of the type `TreeNode`.

```
Dim myNode As TreeNode = New TreeNode
```

Later, `myNode` is set equal to the selected node by using the `SelectedNode` property of the `TreeView` class.

```
myNode = trvCSC.SelectedNode
```

A series of `If` statements is used to test for the existence of the parent and previous and next sibling nodes using the `Parent`, `PrevNode`, and `NextNode` properties of the `TreeNode` class. For example, the following statement tests for the existence of a parent node:

```
If myNode.Parent Is Nothing Then
    'display appropriate message
Else
    'display message identifying parent node
End If
```

When the user clicks the Collapse Tree button, the `CollapseAll` method of the `TreeView` class is called to collapse the tree. The complete program listing is as follows:

```
Public Class frmTreeView
    Inherits System.Windows.Forms.Form
    'Declare ArrayLists to hold professor and course information
    Dim profArray As String()
    Dim courseArray As String(,) 'two dimensional array

    'Windows Forms Designer generated code

    'Event handler for Click event on Fill button
    Private Sub btnFill_Click(ByVal sender As System.Object, ByVal e
    As System.EventArgs) Handles btnFill.Click
        'Declare loop index and tree node variables
        Dim profIndex, courseIndex As Integer
        Dim rootNode, profNode As TreeNode
        'Clear the tree view each time the method is called
        trvCSC.Nodes.Clear()
        'Fill arrays with values to be contained in the tree
        profArray = New String() _
            {"Professor Doke", "Professor Rebstock", _
            "Professor Williams"}
        'In the course array:
        '   first row contains courses taught by Professor Doke
        '   second row contains courses taught by Professor Rebstock
        '   third row contains courses taught by Professor Williams
        courseArray = New String(,) _
            {{"CSC 1236", "CSC 3301", "CSC 5502"}, _
            {"CSC 1301", "CSC 1302", "CSC 4134"}, _
            {"CSC 2230", "CSC 3130", "CSC 4238"}}

        'Add root node for the Computer Science Department
        rootNode = trvCSC.Nodes.Add("Computer Science Department")
```

13

```vb
        'Add a child node to the root node for each professor
        For profIndex = 0 To 2
            profNode = rootNode.Nodes.Add(profArray(profIndex))
            'Add child nodes for each course taught by this professor
            For courseIndex = 0 To 2
                profNode.Nodes.Add(courseArray(profIndex, _
                courseIndex))
            Next
        Next
    End Sub

    'Event handler for AfterSelect event
    Private Sub trvProfessor_AfterSelect(ByVal sender As
    System.Object, ByVal e
    As System.Windows.Forms.TreeViewEventArgs) Handles
    trvCSC.AfterSelect
        'Create a variable of type TreeNode
        Dim myNode As TreeNode = New TreeNode
        'Create a variable of type String to hold the output text
        Dim output As String
        'Clear the text box
        txtOutput.Clear()
        'Set myNode equal to the node selected
        myNode = trvCSC.SelectedNode
        'Initialize output string
        output = "Selected node is " & myNode.Text
        'Check for existence of parent node & append result to
        'output string
        If myNode.Parent Is Nothing Then
            output += vbCrLf & "Node has no parent"
        Else
            output += vbCrLf & "Parent node is " & myNode.Parent.Text
        End If
        'Check for previous sibling node & append result to output
        'string
        If myNode.PrevNode Is Nothing Then
            output += vbCrLf & "Node has no previous sibling node"
        Else
            output += vbCrLf & "Previous sibling node is " & _
            myNode.PrevNode.Text
        End If
        'Check for next sibling node & append result to output string
        If myNode.NextNode Is Nothing Then
            output += vbCrLf & "Node has no next sibling node"
        Else
            output += vbCrLf & "Next sibling node is " & _
            myNode.NextNode.Text
        End If
        'Display the output string in the text box
```

```
        txtOutput.AppendText(output)
    End Sub

    'Event handler for Click event on Collapse button
    Private Sub btnCollapse_Click(ByVal sender As System.Object,
    ByVal e As System.EventArgs) Handles btnCollapse.Click
        'Collapse the tree
        trvCSC.CollapseAll()
        'Clear the output text
        txtOutput.Clear()
    End Sub
End Class
```

Sample Run:

The output of this program is shown in Figure 13-6.

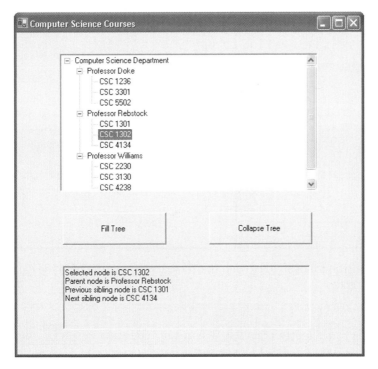

13

Figure 13-6   Output of the Computer Science Courses program

Using Tab Controls and Tab Pages

A **tab control** (which is an **instance** of the `TabControl` class) provides the functionality for a set of tab pages. Each tab page is an instance of the `TabPage` class (a subclass of `Panel`). **Tab pages** are useful when a form requires a large number of controls (too many to fit on a single screen), and those controls can easily be grouped into logical subsets. Each tab page contains one of those subsets and a tab identifying its purpose. The user switches between subsets by clicking the appropriate tab. An example of a form using tab pages that you are already familiar with is the dialog box that appears when you select the Customize option from the Tools menu in VB .NET. This dialog box, shown in Figure 13-7, contains a tab control with three tab pages. When you click one of the tabs, you see a set of controls that pertain to a particular aspect of the VB .NET environment. For example, when you click the Toolbars tab, you see the controls shown in Figure 13-7a; when you click the Commands tab, you see the controls shown in Figure 13-7b.

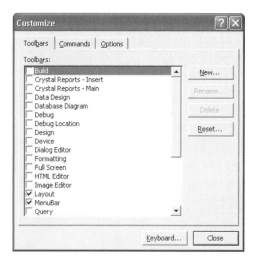

Figure 13-7   The Customize dialog box with the Toolbars tab selected and the Commands tab selected

When you design a form, tab pages can help you organize information and simplify the user interface. For example, most university students have both a permanent and a local address. In a student information form, you could use a tab control consisting of two tab pages to capture this information. As shown in Figure 13-8, one tab page could include controls pertaining to a student's permanent address and the other could include controls pertaining to a student's local address. (You develop this form in a Programming Exercise at the end of this chapter.)

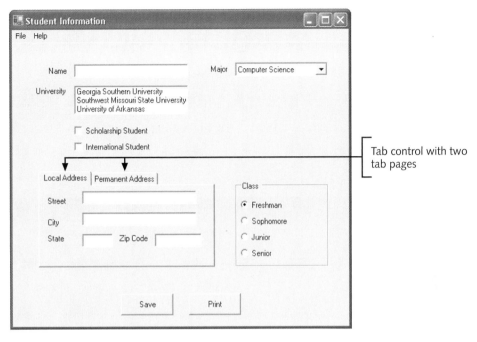

Figure 13-8   Student information form

Tables 13-6 and 13-7 summarize frequently used properties and events for the `TabControl` and `TabPage` classes.

Table 13-6 Selected properties, methods, and events of the TabControl class

13

Properties of the TabControl Class	Description
	Inherits properties, methods, and events from the Control class
Alignment	Identifies the area of the control in which tabs are aligned (default is top)
Multiline	Indicates whether more than one row of tabs can be displayed
SelectedIndex	Identifies the index of the currently selected tab page
SelectedTab	Identifies the currently selected tab page
ShowToolTips	Indicates whether a tool tip will be displayed when the mouse moves across a tab
TabCount	Identifies the number of tab pages in the tab control
TabIndex	Identifies the tab order of the control within its container

Table 13-6 Selected properties, methods, and events of the TabControl class (continued)

Properties of the TabControl Class	Description
TabPages	Identifies the collection of tab pages within the tab control
Common event	
SelectedIndexChanged	Occurs each time one of the tabs in the tab control is selected

Table 13-7 Selected properties, methods, and events of the TabPages class

Properties of the TabPage Class	Description
	Inherits properties, methods, and events from the Control class
Text	Identifies the text that appears on the tab
ToolTipText	Identifies the text that appears in the tab's tool tip
Common Event	
Click	Occurs when the tab page is clicked

Although you commonly use tab pages to include a large number of controls on a single form, you can also use them effectively in forms that require only a few controls. The following example illustrates the use of a tab control and tab pages to alter the appearance of a label. The example is deliberately simple, demonstrating the functionality of tab pages with just a few lines of code. The GUI for this program contains a label and a tab control with three tab pages, as shown in Figure 13-9. Each tab page contains controls of its own.

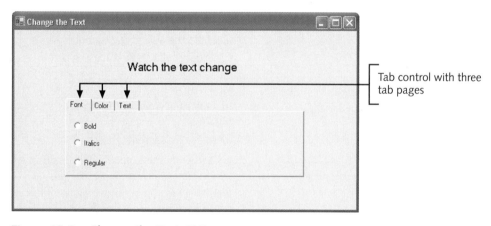

Figure 13-9 Change the Text GUI

Example 13-3: Using tab controls and tab pages

The Font tab page contains three radio buttons: Bold, Italics, and Regular. When the user selects one of these radio buttons, the font style of the label text changes accordingly. To select the Color tab page, the user clicks the Color tab. The Color tab page also contains three radio buttons: Red, Blue, and Black, as shown in Figure 13-10.

Figure 13-10   The Color tab page

When the user selects one of these radio buttons, the color of the label text changes to that color. Similarly, to select the Text tab page, the user clicks the Text tab. As shown in Figure 13-11, the Text tab page contains a text box and a button. The user enters new text in the text box, then clicks the Change Text button to change the label text.

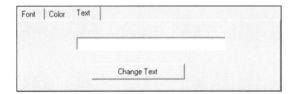

Figure 13-11   The Text tab page

13

The program includes seven event handlers: one for each of the six radio buttons on the Font and Color tab pages, and one for the button on the Text tab page. The event handlers for the radio buttons on the Font tab page use the Font property of the label and the Font class constructor to change the appearance of the label text. The version of the Font constructor used here requires a Font object and a font style. The Font object in this case is the current font of the label. Font styles are referred to in VB .NET as FontStyle.Bold, FontStyle.Italic, and so on.

The complete program listing follows:

```
Public Class frmTabControl
    Inherits System.Windows.Forms.Form

    'Windows Forms Designer generated code

    Private Sub radBold_CheckedChanged(ByVal sender As System.Object,
    ByVal e As System.EventArgs) Handles radBold.CheckedChanged
        lblDisplay.Font = New Font(lblDisplay.Font, FontStyle.Bold)
    End Sub

    Private Sub radItalics_CheckedChanged(ByVal sender As
    System.Object, ByVal e As System.EventArgs) Handles
    radItalics.CheckedChanged
        lblDisplay.Font = New Font(lblDisplay.Font, FontStyle.Italic)
    End Sub

    Private Sub radRegular_CheckedChanged(ByVal sender As
    System.Object, ByVal e As System.EventArgs) Handles
    radRegular.CheckedChanged
        lblDisplay.Font = New Font(lblDisplay.Font, _
        FontStyle.Regular)
    End Sub

    Private Sub radBlue_CheckedChanged(ByVal sender As System.Object,
    ByVal e As System.EventArgs) Handles radBlue.CheckedChanged
        lblDisplay.ForeColor = Color.Blue
    End Sub

    Private Sub radRed_CheckedChanged(ByVal sender As System.Object,
    ByVal e As System.EventArgs) Handles radRed.CheckedChanged
        lblDisplay.ForeColor = Color.Red
    End Sub

    Private Sub radBlack_CheckedChanged(ByVal sender As
    System.Object, ByVal e As System.EventArgs) Handles
    radBlack.CheckedChanged
        lblDisplay.ForeColor = Color.Black
    End Sub

    Private Sub btnChange_Click(ByVal sender As System.Object, ByVal
    System.EventArgs) Handles btnChange.Click
        lblDisplay.Text = txtText.Text
    End Sub
End Class
```

Sample Run:

An example of the output generated by this program is shown in Figure 13-12.

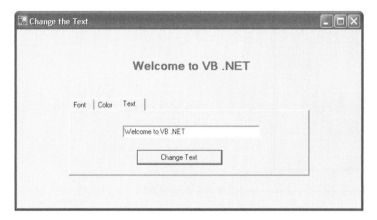

Figure 13-12   Output of the Change the Text program

Using Main Menus and Menu Items

The `MainMenu` and `MenuItem` classes allow you to create a set of menus and submenus for a form. The **main menu** control serves as a container for the menu structure. **Menu items** represent individual menu choices within that structure.

To add a menu to a form, double-click the MainMenu control in the Toolbox. When the Toolbox slides out of view, you see the MainMenu control in the tray just below the form in the Designer window and a placeholder for the first menu item (indicated by the words "Type Here"). See Figure 13-13.

 If the placeholder is not visible, select the MainMenu control in the tray.

13

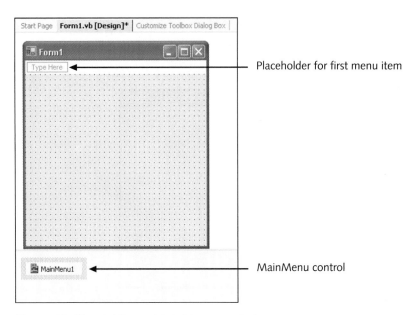

Figure 13-13   Adding a MainMenu control

To add a menu item, click the placeholder. New placeholders appear for the menu item beneath it and the menu item to its left, as shown in Figure 13-14.

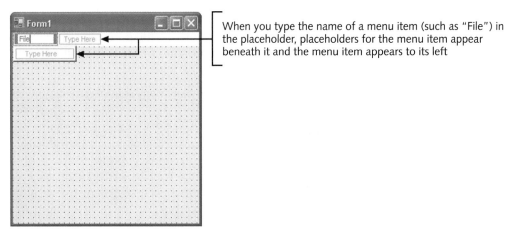

Figure 13-14   Adding menu items

You continue to add menu items into the placeholders until you achieve the desired menu structure. To associate the menu structure with the form, assign the **MainMenu** instance to the form's Menu property in the Property window. See Figure 13-15.

Set the Menu property to the name of the MainMenu control

Figure 13-15 Assigning a menu structure to a form

Menus are used for many purposes. In complex systems such as VB .NET, menus provide functionality for common tasks, such as opening and closing files, editing text, and accessing help features. In simple programs, you can use menus instead of buttons to perform many tasks. For example, in the program presented in the previous section, you could use menus rather than radio buttons to change the font and style of the text. Tables 13-8 and 13-9 summarize frequently used properties and events for these controls.

13

Table 13-8 Selected properties of the MainMenu class

Properties of the MainMenu Class	Description
	Inherits properties, methods, and events from the Control class
MenuItems	Identifies the collection of menu items associated with the menu

Table 13-9 Selected properties and events of the MenuItem class

Properties of the MenuItem Class	Description
	Inherits properties, methods, and events from the Control class
Index	Indicates the position of a menu item within the menu
MenuItems	Identifies the collection of menu items associated with the current menu selection
Shortcut	Identifies the shortcut key or key combination for the menu item
ShowShortcut	Indicates whether the shortcut key associated with the menu item will be displayed
Text	Indicates the text that appears on the menu for this menu item
Common Event	
Click	Occurs when a menu item is clicked

The following example illustrates the use of menus to achieve much of the same functionality as the previous programming example. As shown in Figure 13-16, the GUI consists of a label and a menu. The menu structure includes 14 menu items, only two of which (Edit and Close) are visible in Figure 13-16.

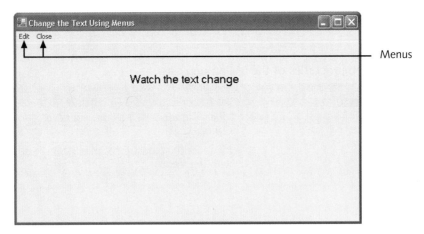

Figure 13-16 Change the Text Using Menus GUI

As shown in Figure 13-17, the Edit menu includes submenus for Font, Color, and Text. The Font submenu (not shown) includes choices for Bold, Italics, and Regular; the Color submenu (also not shown) contains choices for Blue, Red, and Black; and the Text menu (as shown in Figure 13-17) includes choices for "Hello World", "Thank You", and "Enjoy VB .NET".

Figure 13-17 The Edit menu and one of its submenus

Example 13-4: Using menus

This program includes ten event handlers: one for each of the three choices on the Font submenu, one for each of the three choices on the Color submenu, one for each of the three choices on the Text submenu, and one for the Close option. All event handlers respond to Click events. The code within each event handler is very similar to the code in the event handlers in the previous example.

The complete program listing follows:

```
Public Class frmMenu
    Inherits System.Windows.Forms.Form

    'Windows Forms Designer generated code

    Private Sub mnuitmBold_Click(ByVal sender As System.Object, ByVal
    e As System.EventArgs) Handles mnuitmBold.Click
        lblDisplay.Font = New Font(lblDisplay.Font, FontStyle.Bold)
    End Sub

    Private Sub mnuitmItalic_Click(ByVal sender As System.Object,
    ByVal e As System.EventArgs) Handles mnuitmItalic.Click
        lblDisplay.Font = New Font(lblDisplay.Font, FontStyle.Italic)
    End Sub

    Private Sub mnuitmRegular_Click(ByVal sender As System.Object,
    ByVal e As System.EventArgs) Handles mnuitmRegular.Click
        lblDisplay.Font = New Font(lblDisplay.Font, _
        FontStyle.Regular)
    End Sub
```

13

```
    Private Sub mnuitmBlue_Click(ByVal sender As System.Object, ByVal
    e As System.EventArgs) Handles mnuitmBlue.Click
        lblDisplay.ForeColor = Color.Blue
    End Sub

    Private Sub mnuitmRed_Click(ByVal sender As System.Object, ByVal
    e As System.EventArgs) Handles mnuitmRed.Click
        lblDisplay.ForeColor = Color.Red
    End Sub

    Private Sub mnuitmBlack_Click(ByVal sender As System.Object,
    ByVal e As System.EventArgs) Handles mnuitmBlack.Click
        lblDisplay.ForeColor = Color.Black
    End Sub

    Private Sub mnuitmClose_Click(ByVal sender As System.Object,
    ByVal e As System.EventArgs) Handles mnuitmClose.Click
        Me.Close()
    End Sub

    Private Sub mnuitmHello_Click(ByVal sender As System.Object,
    ByVal e As System.EventArgs) Handles mnuitmHello.Click
        lblDisplay.Text = mnuitmHello.Text
    End Sub

    Private Sub mnuitmThanks_Click(ByVal sender As System.Object,
    ByVal e As System.EventArgs) Handles mnuitmThanks.Click
        lblDisplay.Text = mnuitmThanks.Text
    End Sub

    Private Sub mnuitmEnjoy_Click(ByVal sender As System.Object,
    ByVal e As System.EventArgs) Handles mnuitmEnjoy.Click
        lblDisplay.Text = mnuitmEnjoy.Text
    End Sub
End Class
```

Sample Run:

An example of the output produced by this program is shown in Figure 13-18.

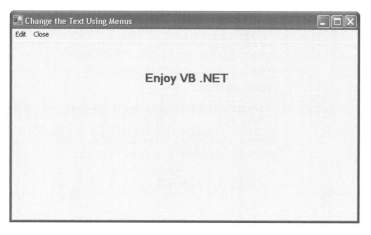

Figure 13-18   Output of the Change the Text Using Menus program

DRAWING LINES, RECTANGLES, AND OVALS

In addition to GUI controls, VB .NET includes a rich set of classes for drawing lines, rectangles, circles, polygons, and other graphical elements. This section introduces a few of the classes that provide this functionality.

The `System.Drawing` namespace contains the classes and **structures** you need for drawing graphical objects. A structure is similar to a class in that both have members that can include constructors, methods, properties, and events. However, structures are **value types** whereas classes are **reference types**. This means that when you declare a variable to store a structure (a value type), that variable contains the actual data for the structure, rather than a memory address as is the case when you declare a variable to reference a class (a reference type). Classes and structures in the `System.Drawing` namespace that you use in this chapter are shown in Table 13-10.

13

Table 13-10 Selected classes of the System.Drawing namespace

Classes and Structures of the System.Drawing namespace	Description
Color	Contains properties for a predefined set of colors and methods for creating new colors
Font	Contains properties and methods for formatting text, including point size, font face, and style attributes
Graphics	Contains methods for drawing shapes such as rectangles, circles, and lines
Pen	Defines an object used to draw lines and curves in an outline style
SolidBrush	Defines a solid color brush used to fill shapes such as rectangles and circles

The **System.Drawing** namespace is automatically available in Windows applications, so you do not need to import it to make use of the methods in these classes and structures. In this chapter, the methods you use for drawing are found in the **Graphics** class and are listed in Table 13-11.

Table 13-11 Selected methods of the Graphics class

Classes of the System.Drawing namespace	Description
DrawEllipse	Draws an ellipse within a rectangle defined by a pair of (x, y) coordinates, a height, and a width
DrawLine	Draws a line connecting two points defined by a pair of (x, y) coordinates
DrawRectangle	Draws a rectangle defined by a pair of (x, y) coordinates, a height, and a width
DrawString	Draws text at a location specified by a pair of (x, y) coordinates, using specified Brush and Font objects
FillEllipse	Fills the interior of an ellipse
FillRectangle	Fills the interior of a rectangle

The following example illustrates the use of classes and methods in the **System.Drawing** namespace to draw lines, rectangles, circles, and text. (Note that a circle is an ellipse whose height and width are equal.) The GUI contains four group boxes and a button. The first three group boxes contain radio buttons for selecting a shape (rectangle, circle, or line), a size (small or large), and a fill style (fill or outline). The fourth group box contains a list box for selecting a color (blue, red, green, yellow, pink, brown, or black). See Figure 13-19.

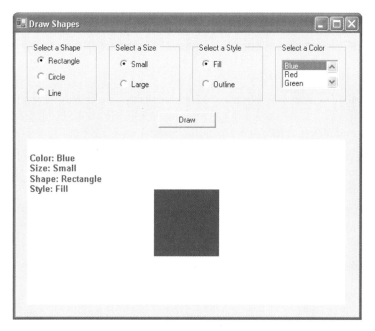

Figure 13-19   Draw Shapes GUI

Example 13-5: Using graphics

This program responds to three events: a Click event on the Draw button, a Paint event for the form, and a Load event for the form. In this case, the event handler for the Draw button simply invokes the `Invalidate` method of the `Form` class. The `Invalidate` method generates a Paint event for the form, causing it to be redrawn.

13

```
'Event handler for Click event on Draw button
Private Sub btnDraw_Click(ByVal sender As System.Object, ByVal e As
System.EventArgs) Handles btnDraw.Click
'call the Invalidate method to generate a Paint event for the form
    Invalidate()
End Sub
```

As with other event handlers, the Paint event handler provides two parameters. The first parameter, `sender`, provides a reference to the object that raised the event. The second parameter, `e`, passes an object specific to the event that is being handled. Until now, the events you have worked with have passed a value for `e` that is of the `System.EventArgs` type. `EventArgs` is the base class for classes containing event data. In the Paint event handler, `e` is of the `System.Windows.Forms.PaintEventArgs` type. `PaintEventArgs` is a subclass of `EventArgs` and provides data for the Paint event. The `PaintEventArgs` instance specifies the Graphics object that is to be used to paint (or redraw) the control. The first statement within the Paint event handler declares a reference variable `g` (of type `Graphics`) to store a reference to the Graphics object passed to the event handler.

```
'Event handler for Paint event for the form
Private Sub frmDrawShapes_Paint(ByVal sender As Object, ByVal e As
System.Windows.Forms.PaintEventArgs) Handles MyBase.Paint
    'get reference to the Graphics object passed to the event handler
    Dim g As Graphics = e.Graphics
```

Next, the event handler defines variables needed for drawing. These include references to a Color object (used to determine the color of a shape), a SolidBrush object (used to fill the interior of a shape), and a Pen object (used to outline a shape).

```
'declare variables needed for drawing
Dim instrumentColor As Color
Dim myBrush As SolidBrush
Dim myPen As Pen
```

Variables that define a shape's coordinates, height, and width are then declared, along with a variable used to display output.

```
'declare variables for a shape's (x, y) coordinates, height,
'and width
Dim shapeX, shapeY, shapeHeight, shapeWidth As Integer
'declare output string
Dim output As String
```

Next, the event handler draws a white rectangle to serve as a drawing canvas.

```
'draw a white rectangle to serve as drawing canvas
g.FillRectangle(New SolidBrush(Color.White), 18, 160, 492, 248)
```

The color selected in the list box is added to the output string, and then converted to a **Color** instance named **instrumentColor** using the **FromName** method of the Color structure. The **FromName** method creates a Color structure from the name of a predefined color. SolidBrush and Pen instances of this color are then instantiated.

```
'add color to output string
output = "Color: " + lstColor.SelectedItem + vbCrLf
'convert selected color String to Color instance
instrumentColor = Color.FromName(lstColor.SelectedItem)
'Define a brush using the selected Color
myBrush = New SolidBrush(instrumentColor)
'Define a pen using the selected Color
myPen = New Pen(instrumentColor)
```

Based on radio button selections for the type of shape and its size, the event handler determines the (x, y) coordinates for the upper-left corner of the shape, its height, and its width. Size and shape information is appended to the output string.

```
'Determine XY position and size based on radio button
'selections and add size to output string
If radSmall.Checked Then
    shapeX = 215
    shapeY = 235
```

```
    shapeWidth = 100
    shapeHeight = 100
    output = output + "Size: " + radSmall.Text + vbCrLf
Else
    shapeX = 165
    shapeY = 185
    shapeWidth = 200
    shapeHeight = 200
    output = output + "Size: " + radLarge.Text + vbCrLf
End If
```

The event handler then uses a series of `If` statements to determine the type of shape being drawn (rectangle, circle, or line). If the shape is a rectangle or circle, a nested `If` is used to determine whether the shape is to be filled or drawn in outline form, and methods that fill or draw shapes are invoked accordingly. Information about the shape and its fill or outline style are also appended to the output string.

```
'Determine shape and style and add these to output string
If radRectangle.Checked Then
    'radRectangle is checked
    output = output + "Shape: " + radRectangle.Text + vbCrLf
    If radFill.Checked Then
        g.FillRectangle(myBrush, shapeX, shapeY, shapeWidth, _
        shapeHeight)
        output = output + "Style: " + radFill.Text
    Else
        g.DrawRectangle(myPen, shapeX, shapeY, shapeWidth, _
        shapeHeight)
        output = output + "Style: " + radOutline.Text
    End If
End If

If radCircle.Checked Then
    'radCircle is checked
    output = output + "Shape: " + radCircle.Text + vbCrLf
    If radFill.Checked Then
        g.FillEllipse(myBrush, shapeX, shapeY, shapeWidth, _
        shapeHeight)
        output = output + "Style: " + radFill.Text
    Else
        g.DrawEllipse(myPen, shapeX, shapeY, shapeWidth, shapeHeight)
        output = output + "Style: " + radOutline.Text
    End If
End If
```

13

If the shape is a line, the current values of the (x, y) coordinates `shapeX` and `shapeY` specify the beginning point of the line. The ending point is determined by adding the current value of `shapeWidth` to each of these coordinates.

```
If radLine.Checked Then
    'radLine is checked
    output = output + "Shape: " + radLine.Text + vbCrLf
    g.DrawLine(myPen, shapeX, shapeY, shapeX + shapeWidth, shapeY +
    shapeWidth)
End If
```

Finally, the `DrawString` method is used to display the output. The version of the `DrawString` method used here requires five arguments: the output string, a font, a brush, and a pair of (x, y) coordinates that designates where the string will be positioned. A new instance of the `Font` class is instantiated using the version of the Font constructor that requires three parameters: a font face, point size, and font style.

```
'draw output string
Dim fntOutput As New Font("Arial", 10, FontStyle.Bold)
g.DrawString(output, fntOutput, myBrush, 20, 180)
```

The third event handler in this example responds to a Load event. When the form loads, VB.NET generates a Paint event to draw the form. This means that the Paint event handler executes before the user has an opportunity to select a color from the list. The event handler for the Load event selects the first color in the list box as a default.

```
Private Sub frmDrawShapes_Load(ByVal sender As Object, ByVal e As
System.EventArgs) Handles MyBase.Load
'if no color is selected in the list box, set selected index to 0
    If lstColor.SelectedIndex = -1 Then
        lstColor.SelectedIndex = 0
    End If
End Sub
```

The complete program listing follows.

```
Public Class frmDrawShapes
    Inherits System.Windows.Forms.Form
    'Windows Form Designer generated code

    'Event handler for Click event on Draw button
    Private Sub btnDraw_Click(ByVal sender As System.Object, ByVal e
    As System.EventArgs) Handles btnDraw.Click
        'call the Invalidate method to generate a Paint event for
        'the form
        Invalidate()
    End Sub

    'Event handler for Paint event for the form
    Private Sub frmDrawShapes_Paint(ByVal sender As Object, ByVal e
    As System.Windows.Forms.PaintEventArgs) Handles MyBase.Paint
        'get reference to the Graphics object passed to the event
        'handler
        Dim g As Graphics = e.Graphics
```

```vbnet
'declare variables needed for drawing
Dim instrumentColor As Color
Dim myBrush As SolidBrush
Dim myPen As Pen
'declare variables for a shape's (x, y) coordinates, height,
'and width
Dim shapeX, shapeY, shapeHeight, shapeWidth As Integer
'declare output string
Dim output As String
'draw a white rectangle to serve as drawing canvas
g.FillRectangle(New SolidBrush(Color.White), 18, 160,
492, 248)
'add color to output string
output = "Color: " + lstColor.SelectedItem + vbCrLf
'convert selected color String to Color instance
instrumentColor = Color.FromName(lstColor.SelectedItem)
'Define a brush using the selected Color
myBrush = New SolidBrush(instrumentColor)
'Define a pen using the selected Color
myPen = New Pen(instrumentColor)
'Determine XY position and size based on radio button
'selections and add size to output string
If radSmall.Checked Then
    shapeX = 215
    shapeY = 235
    shapeWidth = 100
    shapeHeight = 100
    output = output + "Size: " + radSmall.Text + vbCrLf
Else
    shapeX = 165
    shapeY = 185
    shapeWidth = 200
    shapeHeight = 200
    output = output + "Size: " + radLarge.Text + vbCrLf
End If
'Determine shape and style and add these to output string
If radRectangle.Checked Then
    'radRectangle is checked
    output = output + "Shape: " + radRectangle.Text + vbCrLf
    If radFill.Checked Then
        g.FillRectangle(myBrush, shapeX, shapeY, shapeWidth, _
        shapeHeight)
        output = output + "Style: " + radFill.Text
    Else
        g.DrawRectangle(myPen, shapeX, shapeY, shapeWidth, _
        shapeHeight)
        output = output + "Style: " + radOutline.Text
```

13

```
            End If
        End If

        If radCircle.Checked Then
            'radCircle is checked
            output = output + "Shape: " + radCircle.Text + vbCrLf
            If radFill.Checked Then
                g.FillEllipse(myBrush, shapeX, shapeY, shapeWidth, _
                shapeHeight)
                output = output + "Style: " + radFill.Text
            Else
                g.DrawEllipse(myPen, shapeX, shapeY, shapeWidth, _
                shapeHeight)
                output = output + "Style: " + radOutline.Text
            End If
        End If

        If radLine.Checked Then
            'radLine is checked
            output = output + "Shape: " + radLine.Text + vbCrLf
            g.DrawLine(myPen, shapeX, shapeY, shapeX + shapeWidth, _
            shapeY + shapeWidth)
        End If

        'draw output string
        Dim fntOutput As New Font("Arial", 10, FontStyle.Bold)
        g.DrawString(output, fntOutput, myBrush, 20, 180)
    End Sub

    Private Sub frmDrawShapes_Load(ByVal sender As Object, ByVal e As
    System.EventArgs) Handles MyBase.Load
        'if no color is selected in the list box, set selected
        'index to 0
        If lstColor.SelectedIndex = -1 Then
            lstColor.SelectedIndex = 0
        End If
    End Sub
End Class
```

Sample Run:

An example of the output of this program is shown in Figure 13-20.

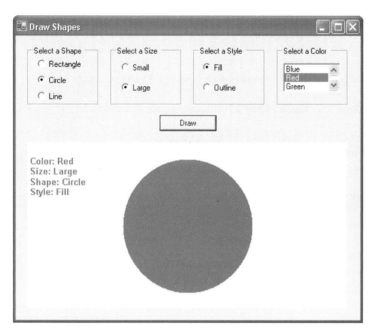

Figure 13-20   Output of the Draw Shapes program

DEVELOPING GUI CLASSES THAT INTERACT WITH A PD CLASS   **13**

In this section, you learn how to create GUIs that interact with a problem domain (PD) class. The first example in this section develops a GUI to input customer attribute values and create instances of the **Customer** PD class you learned about in Chapter 10. The GUI in the second example allows the user to select a customer from a list box, and then displays that customer's address and phone number. The **Customer** PD class used in these examples (first presented in Example 10-5 and shown again in the following code) contains three attributes: **name**, **address**, and **phoneNo**, a parameterized constructor, as well as get and set accessor methods for each of the three attributes.

```
Public Class Customer
    Private name As String
    Private address As String
    Private phoneNo As String
```

```
'Parameterized constructor
Public Sub New(ByVal aName As String, ByVal anAddress As String,
ByVal aPhoneNo As String)
    SetName(aName)
    SetAddress(anAddress)
    SetPhoneNo(aPhoneNo)
End Sub

'Get accessor methods
Public Function GetName() As String
    Return name
End Function

Public Function GetAddress() As String
    Return address
End Function

Public Function GetPhoneNo() As String
    Return phoneNo
End Function

'Set accessor methods
Public Sub SetName(ByVal aName As String)
    name = aName
End Sub

Public Sub SetAddress(ByVal anAddress As String)
    address = anAddress
End Sub

Public Sub SetPhoneNo(ByVal aPhoneNo As String)
    phoneNo = aPhoneNo
End Sub
End Class
```

Adding a Customer

The GUI form to add a new customer is shown in Figure 13-21. The form contains a label for the logo of a fictitious company called ABC Computers. It also contains three labels and three text boxes for inputting customer information, and three buttons.

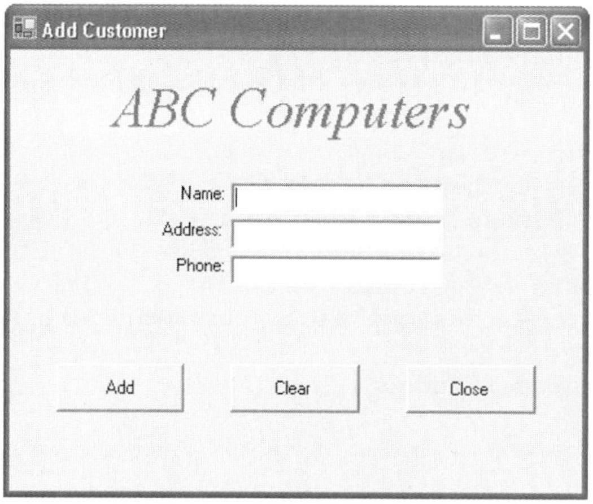

Figure 13-21   Add Customer GUI

The form in Figure 13-21 uses the text boxes (txtName, txtAddress, and txtPhone) to input the customer name, address, and phone number. The buttons (btnAdd, btnClear, and btnClose) are used to add a new customer after the data has been entered, to clear the text boxes, and to close the form and terminate processing.

As you have seen, the visual programming process generates the variables necessary to create the GUI, but does not generate all the variables needed to respond to events that result from interaction with the GUI. These variables must be added to the source code through the Code Editor window. For this example, a Customer reference variable is needed to create a new customer instance from the data entered by the user. Three `String` variables are used to contain the customer data that is retrieved from the text boxes.

```
'Declare customer reference variable
Private aCustomer As Customer
'Declare string variables for name, address, and phone
Private customerName, customerAddress, customerPhone As String
```

This example uses three push buttons that correspond to three events: add a customer, clear the form, or close it. The event handler for the Add button retrieves the values from the text boxes, and then checks that the information was entered for each attribute by verifying that the length of each string is greater than zero. If any of the information is missing, the program displays an error message. Otherwise, it creates an instance of the `Customer` class, displays a confirmation message, and then calls the `ClearForm` method to clear the form.

```
'Event handler for Add button
Private Sub btnAdd_Click(ByVal sender As System.Object, ByVal e
As System.EventArgs) Handles btnAdd.Click
    'Get values from the text boxes
    customerName = txtName.Text
    customerAddress = txtAddress.Text
```

13

```
        customerPhone = txtPhone.Text
        'Validate that the user has entered values for name,
        'address, and phone
        If customerName.Length = 0 Or _
           customerAddress.Length = 0 Or _
           customerPhone.Length = 0 Then
               MessageBox.Show("Please Enter All Data")
        Else
           'Data is valid — create a Customer instance
           aCustomer = New Customer(customerName, customerAddress, _
           customerPhone)
           MessageBox.Show("Customer Added")
           'Clear the form
           ClearForm()
        End If
    End Sub
End Sub
```

The `ClearForm` method stores an empty string in each of the text boxes, then invokes the `Focus` method for the txtName control. The `Focus` method positions the cursor within the Name text box and sets the input focus to this control.

```
Private Sub ClearForm()
    txtName.Text = ""
    txtAddress.Text = ""
    txtPhone.Text = ""
    txtName.Focus()
End Sub
```

The event handler for the Clear button calls the `ClearForm` method, and the event handler for the Close button closes the form. The complete program listing is given in Example 13-6.

Example 13-6: A GUI interacting with a PD class to add a customer

```
Public Class frmAddCustomer
    Inherits System.Windows.Forms.Form

    'Declare customer reference variable
    Private aCustomer As Customer
    'Declare string variables for name, address, and phone
    Private customerName, customerAddress, customerPhone As String

    'Windows Form Designer generated code

    'Event handler for Add button
    Private Sub btnAdd_Click(ByVal sender As System.Object, ByVal e
    As System.EventArgs) Handles btnAdd.Click
        'Get values from the text boxes
        customerName = txtName.Text
```

```vb
        customerAddress = txtAddress.Text
        customerPhone = txtPhone.Text
        'Validate that the user has entered values for name,
        'address, and phone
        If customerName.Length = 0 Or _
         customerAddress.Length = 0 Or _
         customerPhone.Length = 0 Then
            MessageBox.Show("Please Enter All Data")
        Else
            'Data is valid — create a Customer instance
            aCustomer = New Customer(customerName, customerAddress, _
            customerPhone)
            MessageBox.Show("Customer Added")
            'Clear the form
            ClearForm()
        End If
    End Sub

    'Event handler for Clear button
    Private Sub btnClear_Click(ByVal sender As System.Object, ByVal e
    As System.EventArgs) Handles btnClear.Click
        ClearForm()
    End Sub

    'Event handler for Close button
    Private Sub btnClose_Click(ByVal sender As System.Object, ByVal e
    As System.EventArgs) Handles btnClose.Click
        Me.Close()
    End Sub

    'Method to clear the textboxes on the form and reset focus
    Private Sub ClearForm()
        txtName.Text = ""
        txtAddress.Text = ""
        txtPhone.Text = ""
        txtName.Focus()
    End Sub
End Class
```

13

Sample Run:

The output of the Add Customer GUI is shown in Figure 13-22.

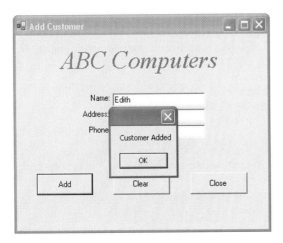

Figure 13-22   Output of the Add Customer GUI

Finding a Customer

The second example of a GUI interacting with a PD class is a form that allows you to search for a specific customer of ABC Computers, display that customer's address and phone number, and optionally update that information. Figure 13-23 shows the form for finding a customer.

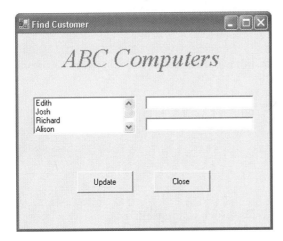

Figure 13-23   Find Customer GUI

As in the previous example, the form in Figure 13-23 contains a label for the ABC Computers logo. It also contains a list box, two text boxes, and two buttons. The form uses the list box to display customer names. When you select a customer from the list, the form displays the customer's address and phone number in the text boxes. You can modify the customer's address or phone number by changing the text in the text boxes. The Update button records these changes, and the Close button closes the form.

The technique for finding a customer uses an `ArrayList` to simulate interaction with a database. The GUI for finding a customer simulates this interaction by creating multiple customer instances, and then populating an `ArrayList` with the customer references. Recall that `ArrayList` is a member of the `System.Collections` namespace; thus, frmFindCustomer begins by importing this namespace and then declaring an `ArrayList` to hold the customer references. It also declares a `Customer` reference variable to store the customer instance that is found.

```
Imports System.Collections
Public Class frmFindCustomer
    Inherits System.Windows.Forms.Form

    'Declare customer reference variable
    Private aCustomer As Customer
    'Declare array to simulate customer database
    Private customers As New ArrayList
```

In Chapter 5 you learned that an `ArrayList` works like an array but is dynamic rather than fixed in size. The `Add` method of the `ArrayList` class appends an element to the end of an `ArrayList`. A method named `CreateCustomers` adds customer instances to the `ArrayList`.

```
'Method to create customers instances
Private Sub CreateCustomers()
  'Create customer instances - simulate database
  customers.Add(New Customer("Edith", "Batesville", "123-4567"))
  customers.Add(New Customer("Josh", "Springfield", "234-5678"))
  customers.Add(New Customer("Richard", "Statesboro", "345-6789"))
  customers.Add(New Customer("Alison", "Blackshear", "987-6543"))
  customers.Add(New Customer("Truman", "West Plains", "876-5432"))
  customers.Add(New Customer("Kyle", "Savannah", "765-4321"))
End Sub
```

13

 Because this chapter *simulates* interaction with a database, customer instances are created from hard-coded data. Normally, you do not hard-code data of this kind— you read it from a file. In Chapter 14, you learn to implement the more powerful and realistic approach of reading this information from the database.

The `CreateCustomers` method is invoked by a method named PopulateListBox. The `PopulateListBox` method uses the customer instances to add customer names to the list box on the form.

```
'Method to populate the list box
Private Sub PopulateListBox()
    'Create the customer instances
    CreateCustomers()
    'Add the name of each customer to the list
    Dim i As Integer
    For i = 0 To customers.Count - 1
        aCustomer = customers(i)
        lstCustomer.Items.Add(aCustomer.GetName())
    Next
End Sub
```

Because customer names should appear within the list box when the form opens, the PopulateListBox method is invoked by the event handler for the Load event.

```
Private Sub frmFindCustomer_Load(ByVal sender As Object, ByVal e
As System.EventArgs) Handles MyBase.Load
    'Populate the customer list box
    PopulateListBox()
End Sub
```

The GUI responds to three additional events: clicking a name in the list box, clicking the Update button, and clicking the Close button. When you click a name in the list box, the index of the customer within the list box identifies the location of the corresponding Customer instance within the ArrayList. Accessor methods of the Customer class are used to retrieve the customer's address and phone number, which are then displayed in the text boxes.

```
'Event handler for Click event on customer list box
Private Sub lstCustomer_Click(ByVal sender As System.Object, ByVal e
As System.EventArgs) Handles lstCustomer.Click
    Dim i As Integer
    'Identify the selected index in the list box
    i = lstCustomer.SelectedIndex
    'Find this customer in the ArrayList
    aCustomer = customers(i)
    'Retrieve and display this customer's address and phone
    txtCustomerAddress.Text = aCustomer.GetAddress()
    txtCustomerPhone.Text = aCustomer.GetPhoneNo()
End Sub
```

Similarly, the event handler for the Update button uses accessor methods of the Customer class to set new values for address and phone number.

```
'Event handler for Update button
Private Sub btnUpdate_Click(ByVal sender As System.Object, ByVal e As
System.EventArgs) Handles btnUpdate.Click
    Dim i As Integer
    'Identify the selected index in the list box
    i = lstCustomer.SelectedIndex
    'Find this customer in the ArrayList
    aCustomer = customers(i)
```

```
'Set this customer's address and phone to the values
'entered by the user
aCustomer.SetAddress(txtCustomerAddress.Text)
aCustomer.SetPhoneNo(txtCustomerPhone.Text)
'Store the updated customer in the ArrayList
customers(i) = aCustomer
MessageBox.Show("Customer Updated")
End Sub
```

The complete program listing is given in Example 13-7.

Example 13-7: A GUI interacting with a PD class to find a customer

```
Imports System.Collections
Public Class frmFindCustomer
    Inherits System.Windows.Forms.Form

    'Declare customer reference variable
    Private aCustomer As Customer
    'Declare array to simulate customer database
    Private customers As New ArrayList

    'Windows Form Design generated code

    'Event handler for Click event on customer list box
    Private Sub lstCustomer_Click(ByVal sender As System.Object,
    ByVal e As System.EventArgs) Handles lstCustomer.Click
        Dim i As Integer
        'Identify the selected index in the list box
        i = lstCustomer.SelectedIndex
        'Find this customer in the ArrayList
        aCustomer = customers(i)
        'Retrieve and display this customer's address and phone
        txtCustomerAddress.Text = aCustomer.GetAddress()
        txtCustomerPhone.Text = aCustomer.GetPhoneNo()
    End Sub

    'Event handler for Update button
    Private Sub btnUpdate_Click(ByVal sender As System.Object, ByVal
    e As System.EventArgs) Handles btnUpdate.Click
        Dim i As Integer
        'Identify the selected index in the list box
        i = lstCustomer.SelectedIndex
        'Find this customer in the ArrayList
        aCustomer = customers(i)
        'Set this customer's address and phone to the values
        'entered by the user
        aCustomer.SetAddress(txtCustomerAddress.Text)
```

13

```vb
        aCustomer.SetPhoneNo(txtCustomerPhone.Text)
        'Store the updated customer in the ArrayList
        customers(i) = aCustomer
        MessageBox.Show("Customer Updated")
    End Sub

    'Event handler for Close button
    Private Sub btnClose_Click(ByVal sender As System.Object, ByVal e
    As System.EventArgs) Handles btnClose.Click
        Me.Close()
    End Sub

    'Method to create customers instances
    Private Sub CreateCustomers()
        'Create customer instances - simulate database
        customers.Add(New Customer("Edith", "Batesville", _
        "123-4567"))
        customers.Add(New Customer("Josh", "Springfield", _
        "234-5678"))
        customers.Add(New Customer("Richard", "Statesboro", _
        "345-6789"))
        customers.Add(New Customer("Alison", "Blackshear", _
        "987-6543"))
        customers.Add(New Customer("Truman", "West Plains", _
        "876-5432"))
        customers.Add(New Customer("Kyle", "Savannah", "765-4321"))
    End Sub

    'Method to populate the list box
    Private Sub PopulateListBox()
        'Create the customer instances
        CreateCustomers()
        'Add the name of each customer to the list
        Dim i As Integer
        For i = 0 To customers.Count - 1
            aCustomer = customers(i)
            lstCustomer.Items.Add(aCustomer.GetName())
        Next
    End Sub

    Private Sub frmFindCustomer_Load(ByVal sender As Object, ByVal e
    As System.EventArgs) Handles MyBase.Load
        'Populate the customer list box
        PopulateListBox()
    End Sub
End Class
```

Sample Run:

The output of the Find Customer GUI is shown in Figure 13-24.

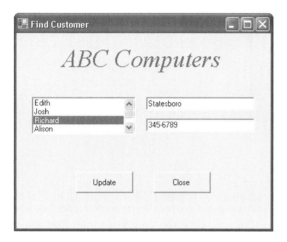

Figure 13-24   Output of the Find Customer GUI

CREATING APPLICATIONS WITH MULTIPLE FORMS

Thus far, you have created simple applications that contain a single form. Applications used by organizations today are usually more complex and require the use of multiple forms. For example, an order entry system would require forms to capture information about products, customers, orders, and salespersons, as well as forms that enable the completion of tasks such as generating invoices and creating sales reports. Although you can design a system with separate, stand-alone GUI classes for each task—such as adding or finding a customer—a better approach is to link them through a GUI that allows you to navigate between forms. A GUI that enables such navigation is referred to as a main menu GUI.

Navigating multiple forms through a main menu GUI makes it easier for you to go from one task (such as adding a new customer) to a second (such as retrieving information about an existing customer). The main menu GUI displays buttons for the available tasks, such as adding a customer and finding a customer. You click one of these buttons to instantiate and display the appropriate GUI. After completing that task, you click a button to return to the main menu.

A main menu form that links the GUIs for adding and finding a customer is shown in Figure 13-25. The form contains two labels—one for the ABC Computers logo and the other to identify the form as the main menu. The form also contains three buttons—one to navigate to the form for adding a customer, one to navigate to the form for finding a customer, and one to close the application.

13

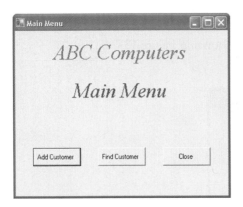

Figure 13-25   Main Menu GUI

The sequence of GUI forms to find and add a customer is shown in Figure 13-26. When you click the Add Customer button on the main menu, the main menu closes and the form to add a customer appears. Similarly, when you click the Find Customer button on the main menu, the main menu closes and the form for finding a customer appears. If you click the Return to Main Menu button on the form for adding or the form for finding a customer, the form closes and the main menu reappears.

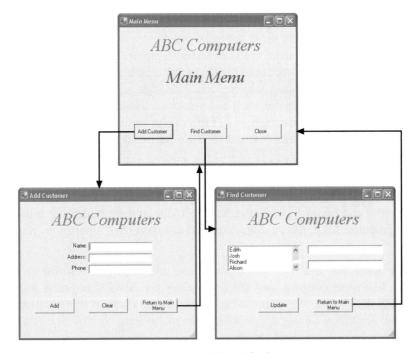

Figure 13-26   GUI sequence to add and find a customer

Event handlers are needed for each of the three buttons on the main menu. The event handler for the Add Customer button hides the main menu form using the `Hide` method of the `Form` class, and then creates an instance of the form for adding a customer (`frmAddCustomer`) and displays the form using the `ShowDialog` method.

```
'Event handler for the Add Customer button
Private Sub btnAdd_Click(ByVal sender As System.Object,
ByVal e As System.EventArgs) Handles btnAdd.Click
    'Hide the main menu form
    Me.Hide()
    'Create and display AddCustomer form
    Dim frmAddCustomerGUI = New frmAddCustomer
    frmAddCustomerGUI.ShowDialog()
    'Make the main menu form visible
    Me.Show()
End Sub
```

Displays frmAddCustomer as a modal dialog box

Because frmAddCustomer is displayed modally, this line of code does not execute until after frmAddCustomer is closed

The `ShowDialog` method shows a form as a **modal** dialog box. When shown a modal dialog box, a form must be dismissed before the next statement in the procedure will be executed. This means that once the form for adding a customer is shown, it must later be hidden or closed before the other forms in the system can be made visible.

After the form for adding a customer closes, the hidden main menu is made visible again by invoking the `Show` method of the `Form` class. The `Show` method (rather than `ShowDialog`) is used here because although hidden, by default the main menu is already displayed modally.

The event handler for the Find Customer button is nearly identical, except that it instantiates and displays the form for finding a customer rather than the form for adding a customer. The event handler for the Close button closes the main menu. The entire program listing for the main menu form is shown in Example 13-8.

13

Example 13-8: Creating a main menu for navigating multiple forms

```
Public Class frmMainMenu
    Inherits System.Windows.Forms.Form

    'Windows Form Designer generated code

    'Event handler for the Close button
    Private Sub btnClose_Click(ByVal sender As System.Object, ByVal e
    As System.EventArgs) Handles btnClose.Click
```

```
        Me.Close()
    End Sub

    'Event handler for the Add Customer button
    Private Sub btnAdd_Click(ByVal sender As System.Object, ByVal e
    As System.EventArgs) Handles btnAdd.Click
        'Hide the main menu form
        Me.Hide()
        'Create and display AddCustomer form
        Dim frmAddCustomerGUI = New frmAddCustomer
        frmAddCustomerGUI.ShowDialog()
        'Make the main menu form visible
        Me.Show()
    End Sub

    'Event handler for the Find Customer button
    Private Sub btnFind_Click(ByVal sender As System.Object, ByVal e
    As System.EventArgs) Handles btnFind.Click
        'Hide the main menu form
        Me.Hide()
        'Create and display FindCustomer form
        Dim frmFindCustomerGUI = New frmFindCustomer
        frmFindCustomerGUI.ShowDialog()
        'Make the main menu form visible
        Me.Show()
    End Sub
End Class
```

Although this example enables navigation from one form to the next, there is one major shortcoming—each form functions independently. Therefore, the data associated with one form is not shared with the other forms in the system. This means that new customer information entered into the Add Customer form will not appear on the Find Customer form. Although you could pass an **ArrayList** of **Customer** instances from one form to the next, a more general and elegant approach is to use a DA class to enable sharing of data among forms. The following section demonstrates this approach.

SIMULATING A DA CLASS

In Chapter 14, you learn how to design data access (DA) classes that use a relational database. The focus in this chapter, however, is multiple GUI forms; therefore, here you simulate the interaction with a database by using an **ArrayList** of customers.

In Chapter 10, you learned that object-oriented systems employ a three-tier design consisting of GUI classes, problem PD classes, and DA classes. As their names suggest, the GUI classes provide a graphical interface for the input and display of data, PD classes model the objects specific to the application, and DA classes provide data storage and retrieval services.

A major advantage of three-tier design is that classes in each tier can be independent of those in another. For example, the GUI or PD classes only need to be able to invoke methods to store and retrieve data; they don't need to know how the DA classes store data. Similarly, the DA classes are not aware of the GUI classes. This independence can dramatically simplify future maintenance chores because modifications to classes in one tier do not require changes to classes in another tier. For example, because the PD and GUI classes are unaware of how the DA classes store and retrieve data, a change from one type of database to another will not affect the GUI and PD classes.

Five of the DA methods—`Initialize`, `GetAll`, `AddNew`, `Find`, and `Update`—are introduced here. The GUI classes invoke these methods but are unaware of their implementation. This means that later you can convert to a real database management system and achieve data persistence (rather than storing data in an `ArrayList`) without changing the GUI classes. The following list identifies the purpose of the five DA methods.

- *Initialize*—This method performs initialization tasks in preparation for database access.

- *GetAll*—This method retrieves references to all instances of the `Customer` class that are stored in the database.

- *AddNew*—This method stores a reference to a new `Customer` instance into the database.

- *Find*—This method finds a specific `Customer` instance in the database.

- *Update*—This method replaces a reference to a particular `Customer` instance that is stored in the database with a reference to a new `Customer` instance.

The DA methods are defined in a separate class named `CustomerDA`. Because the `CustomerDA` class uses an `ArrayList` to simulate the database, it begins by importing the `System.Collections` namespace. An `ArrayList` named customers and a Customer reference variable named `aCustomer` are then declared, each with class scope and `Shared` access. As you learned in Chapter 10, `Shared` access means that these variables are shared by all instances of the class.

13

```
'CustomerDA class definition
Imports System.Collections
Public Class CustomerDA

    'Declare array to simulate customer database
    Private Shared customers As New ArrayList

    'Declare Customer reference variable
    Private Shared aCustomer As Customer
```

In the simulated database, the `Initialize` method of the DA class creates multiple customer instances and stores their references into an `ArrayList`. Declaring the `Initialize` method with `Shared` access means that it is not associated with a specific instance and can be invoked from other modules by qualifying it with the CustomerDA class name.

```
Public Shared Sub Initialize()
   'Create customer instances - simulate database
   customers.Add(New Customer("Edith", "Batesville", "123-4567"))
   customers.Add(New Customer("Josh", "Springfield", "234-5678"))
   customers.Add(New Customer("Richard", "Statesboro", "345-6789"))
   customers.Add(New Customer("Alison", "Blackshear", "987-6543"))
   customers.Add(New Customer("Truman", "West Plains", "876-5432"))
   customers.Add(New Customer("Kyle", "Savannah", "765-4321"))
End Sub
```

The `GetAll` method returns a reference to the `customers ArrayList`.

```
Public Shared Function GetAll() As ArrayList
   Return customers
End Function
```

When a new customer instance is created, it is added to the `ArrayList` of customers. The `AddNew` method receives a reference to a `Customer` instance through the parameter list, then invokes the `Add` method of the `ArrayList` class to add the customer reference to the `customers ArrayList`.

```
Public Shared Function AddNew(ByRef newCustomer As Customer)
   customers.Add(newCustomer)
End Function
```

The `Update` method receives two parameters. The first parameter identifies the location in the `ArrayList` of the customer whose information is to be changed. The second is a reference to a `Customer` instance containing the updated data. The `Update` method stores the reference to the updated `Customer` instance at the specified location in the `ArrayList`.

```
Public Shared Function Update(ByVal index As Integer, ByRef
thisCustomer As Customer)
   customers(index) = thisCustomer
End Function
```

The complete listing for the `CustomerDA` class is given in Example 13-9.

Example 13-9: CustomerDA class

```
'CustomerDA class definition
Imports System.Collections
Public Class CustomerDA

   'Declare array to simulate customer database
   Private Shared customers As New ArrayList

   'Declare Customer reference variable
   Private Shared aCustomer As Customer

   Public Shared Sub Initialize()
```

```
          'Create customer instances - simulate database
          customers.Add(New Customer("Edith", "Batesville", _
          "123-4567"))
          customers.Add(New Customer("Josh", "Springfield", _
          "234-5678"))
          customers.Add(New Customer("Richard", "Statesboro", _
          "345-6789"))
          customers.Add(New Customer("Alison", "Blackshear", _
          "987-6543"))
          customers.Add(New Customer("Truman", "West Plains", _
          "876-5432"))
          customers.Add(New Customer("Kyle", "Savannah", "765-4321"))
      End Sub

      Public Shared Function GetAll() As ArrayList
          Return customers
      End Function

      Public Shared Function AddNew(ByRef newCustomer As Customer)
          customers.Add(newCustomer)
      End Function

      Public Shared Function Find(ByVal index As Integer) As Customer
          aCustomer = customers(index)
          Return aCustomer
      End Function

      Public Shared Function Update(ByVal index As Integer, ByRef
      thisCustomer As Customer)
          customers(index) = thisCustomer
      End Function
  End Class
```

13

CREATING AN INTEGRATED SYSTEM THAT SIMULATES INTERACTION WITH A DATABASE

With the DA class in place, the forms in the ABC Computers application can easily share data. To accomplish this, each of the three forms requires minor modifications.

Modifying the Main Menu Form

The main menu form now performs one additional task: it initializes the simulated database by invoking the `Initialize` method of the `CustomerDA` class. Because database initialization should take place when the main menu loads, the `Initialize` method is invoked by the event handler for the Load event.

```
Private Sub frmMainMenu_Load(ByVal sender As Object, ByVal e As
System.EventArgs) Handles MyBase.Load
    'Initialize the simulated database
    CustomerDA.Initialize()
End Sub
```

Note that because the `Initialize` method was declared with `Shared` access in the `CustomerDA` class, it is not associated with a specific instance and can be invoked by qualifying it with the class name—in other words, by specifying `CustomerDA.Initialize()`.

Modifying the Add Customer Form

The GUI for adding a customer also requires a simple modification. As before, the program retrieves customer information from the text boxes, verifies that nothing has been left blank, and then uses this information to create a `Customer` instance. However, the event handler for the Add Customer button now invokes the `AddNew` method of the DA class to add the `Customer` instance to the simulated database.

```
Private Sub btnAdd_Click(ByVal sender As System.Object,
ByVal e As System.EventArgs) Handles btnAdd.Click
    'Get values from the text boxes
    customerName = txtName.Text
    customerAddress = txtAddress.Text
    customerPhone = txtPhone.Text
    'Validate that the user has entered values for name,
    'address, and phone
    If customerName.Length = 0 Or _
      customerAddress.Length = 0 Or _
      customerPhone.Length = 0 Then
        MessageBox.Show("Please Enter All Data")
    Else
        'Data is valid -- create Customer instance
        aCustomer = New Customer(customerName, _
                customerAddress, customerPhone)
        'Add customer to simulated database
        CustomerDA.AddNew(aCustomer)
        MessageBox.Show("Customer Added ")
        'Clear the form
        ClearForm()
    End If
End Sub
```

This line of code invokes the DA method AddNew to add the Customer instance to the simulated database

Modifying the Find Customer Form

In the earlier example, frmFindCustomer had a method named `CreateCustomers`, which was invoked by the `PopulateListBox` method. The purpose of this method was to create customer instances and store their references in an `ArrayList`. The new version of `FindCustomer` does not include the `CreateCustomers` method. Instead of invoking the `CreateCustomers` method to obtain an `ArrayList` of customers, the `PopulateListBox` method now invokes the DA class method `GetAll` to obtain the `ArrayList`.

```
Private Sub PopulateListBox()
    'Retrieve all customer data from simulated database
    customers = CustomerDA.GetAll()
    'Add the name of each customer retrieved to the list
    Dim i As Integer
    For i = 0 To customers.Count - 1
        aCustomer = customers(i)
        lstCustomer.Items.Add(aCustomer.GetName())
    Next
End Sub
```

This line of code invokes the DA method GetAll to obtain the ArrayList of Customer instances from the simulated database

The event handler for the list box now invokes the DA class method `Find` to retrieve a reference to the `Customer` instance that corresponds to the name selected on the list box. Similarly, the event handler for the Update button now invokes the DA class method `Update` to store the reference to the updated `Customer` instance in the simulated database.

13

```
Private Sub lstCustomer_Click(ByVal sender As System.Object,
ByVal e As System.EventArgs) Handles lstCustomer.Click
    Dim i As Integer
    'Identify the selected index in the list box
    i = lstCustomer.SelectedIndex
    'Find this customer in the simulated database
    aCustomer = CustomerDA.Find(i)
    'Retrieve and display this customer's address and phone
    txtCustomerAddress.Text = aCustomer.GetAddress()
    txtCustomerPhone.Text = aCustomer.GetPhoneNo()
End Sub
```

The line of code invokes the DA method Find to retrieve a reference to the selected Customer from the simulated database

```
Private Sub btnUpdate_Click(ByVal sender As System.Object,
ByVal e As System.EventArgs) Handles btnUpdate.Click
```

```
Dim i As Integer
'Identify the selected index in the list box
i = lstCustomer.SelectedIndex
'Find this customer in the simulated database
aCustomer = customers(i)
'Set this customer's address and phone to the values
'entered by the user
aCustomer.SetAddress(txtCustomerAddress.Text)
aCustomer.SetPhoneNo(txtCustomerPhone.Text)
'Update this customer in the simulated database
CustomerDA.Update(i, aCustomer)
MessageBox.Show("Customer Updated")
End Sub
```

The line of code invokes the DA method Update to store the reference
to the updated Customer instance in the simulated database

A complete listing of the three GUI programs in this application (excluding most of the code generated by the Windows Form Designer) is shown in Example 13-10. The CustomerDA class is identical to Example 13-9 and is not listed again here.

Example 13-10: An integrated system that simulates interaction with a database

Main Menu GUI

```
Public Class frmMainMenu
    Inherits System.Windows.Forms.Form

    'Windows Form Designer generated code

    Private Sub btnClose_Click(ByVal sender As System.Object, ByVal e
    As System.EventArgs) Handles btnClose.Click
        Me.Close()
    End Sub

    Private Sub btnAdd_Click(ByVal sender As System.Object, ByVal e
    As System.EventArgs) Handles btnAdd.Click
        'Hide the main menu form
        Me.Hide()
        'Create and display AddCustomer form
        Dim frmAddCustomerGUI = New frmAddCustomer
        frmAddCustomerGUI.ShowDialog()
        'Make the main menu form visible
        Me.Show()
    End Sub

    Private Sub btnFind_Click(ByVal sender As System.Object, ByVal e
    As System.EventArgs) Handles btnFind.Click
```

```vb
        'Hide the main menu form
        Me.Hide()
        'Create and display FindCustomer form
        Dim frmFindCustomerGUI = New frmFindCustomer
        frmFindCustomerGUI.ShowDialog()
        'Make the main menu form visible
        Me.Show()
    End Sub

    Private Sub frmMainMenu_Load(ByVal sender As Object, ByVal e As
    System.EventArgs) Handles MyBase.Load
        'Initialize the simulated database
        CustomerDA.Initialize()
    End Sub

End Class
```

Add Customer GUI

```vb
Public Class frmAddCustomer
    Inherits System.Windows.Forms.Form

    'Declare customer reference variable
    Private aCustomer As Customer
    'Declare string variables for name, address, and phone
    Private customerName, customerAddress, customerPhone As String

    'Windows Form Designer generated code

    Private Sub btnAdd_Click(ByVal sender As System.Object, ByVal e
    As System.EventArgs) Handles btnAdd.Click
        'Get values from the text boxes
        customerName = txtName.Text
        customerAddress = txtAddress.Text
        customerPhone = txtPhone.Text
        'Validate that the user has entered values for name,
        'address, and phone
        If customerName.Length = 0 Or _
         customerAddress.Length = 0 Or _
         customerPhone.Length = 0 Then
            MessageBox.Show("Please Enter All Data")
        Else
            'Data is valid — create Customer instance
            aCustomer = New Customer(customerName, customerAddress, _
            customerPhone)
            'Add customer to simulated database
            CustomerDA.AddNew(aCustomer)
            MessageBox.Show("Customer Added ")
            'Clear the form
            ClearForm()
        End If
    End Sub
```

13

```
      Private Sub ClearForm()
          txtName.Text = ""
          txtAddress.Text = ""
          txtPhone.Text = ""
          txtName.Focus()
      End Sub

      Private Sub btnClear_Click(ByVal sender As System.Object, ByVal e
      As System.EventArgs) Handles btnClear.Click
          ClearForm()
      End Sub

      Private Sub btnReturn_Click(ByVal sender As System.Object, ByVal
      e As System.EventArgs) Handles btnReturn.Click
          Me.Close()
      End Sub
  End Class
```

Find Customer GUI

```
Imports System.Collections
Public Class frmFindCustomer
    Inherits System.Windows.Forms.Form

    'Declare customer reference variable
    Private aCustomer As Customer

    'Declare array to simulate customer database
    Private customers As New ArrayList

    'Windows Form Designer generated code

    Private Sub lstCustomer_Click(ByVal sender As System.Object,
    ByVal e As System.EventArgs) Handles lstCustomer.Click
        Dim i As Integer
        'Identify the selected index in the list box
        i = lstCustomer.SelectedIndex
        'Find this customer in the simulated database
        aCustomer = CustomerDA.Find(i)
        'Retrieve and display this customer's address and phone
        txtCustomerAddress.Text = aCustomer.GetAddress()
        txtCustomerPhone.Text = aCustomer.GetPhoneNo()
    End Sub

    Private Sub btnUpdate_Click(ByVal sender As System.Object, ByVal
    e As System.EventArgs) Handles btnUpdate.Click
        Dim i As Integer
        'Identify the selected index in the list box
        i = lstCustomer.SelectedIndex
        'Find this customer in the simulated database
        aCustomer = customers(i)
```

```vb
        'Set this customer's address and phone to the values
        'entered by the user
        aCustomer.SetAddress(txtCustomerAddress.Text)
        aCustomer.SetPhoneNo(txtCustomerPhone.Text)
        'Update this customer in the simulated database
        CustomerDA.Update(i, aCustomer)
        MessageBox.Show("Customer Updated")
    End Sub

    Private Sub btnReturn_Click(ByVal sender As System.Object, ByVal
    e As System.EventArgs) Handles btnReturn.Click
        Me.Close()
    End Sub

    Private Sub PopulateListBox()
        'Retrieve all customer data from simulated database
        customers = CustomerDA.GetAll()
        'Add the name of each customer retrieved to the list
        Dim i As Integer
        For i = 0 To customers.Count - 1
            aCustomer = customers(i)
            lstCustomer.Items.Add(aCustomer.GetName())
        Next
    End Sub

    Private Sub frmFindCustomer_Load(ByVal sender As Object, ByVal e
    As System.EventArgs) Handles MyBase.Load
        'Populate the customer list box
        PopulateListBox()
    End Sub
End Class
```

13

PROGRAMMING EXAMPLE: INTERACTING WITH MULTIPLE PD CLASSES

This programming example demonstrates the interaction of GUI forms with multiple PD classes. It uses the **Person**, **Student**, **Professor**, and **Phone** PD classes you studied in Chapter 11, and implements the one-to-one association between **Person** and **Phone** demonstrated in Example 11-12.

Problem Analysis, GUI Design, and Algorithm Design

Figure 13-27 shows the GUI sequence for this application. Five GUI classes comprise an integrated system. The GUIs include a main menu form, a form to add a student, a form to add a professor, a form to list all students, and a form to list all professors.

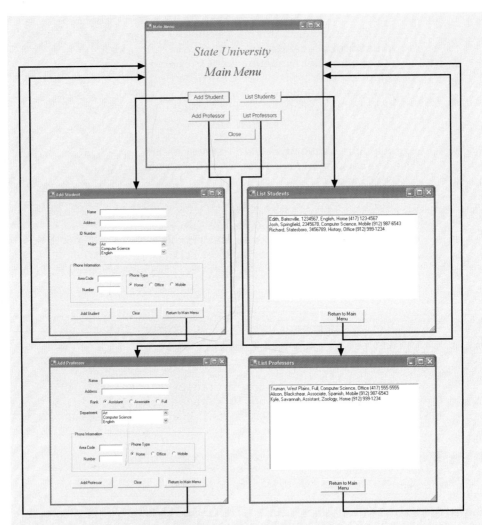

Figure 13-27 GUI sequence for Programming Example

In addition to the four PD classes previously mentioned (`Person`, `Student`, `Professor`, and `Phone`), two DA classes (one for `Student` and one for `Professor`) are needed to add and retrieve students and professors to and from the simulated database. The PD classes are copied from Chapters 10 and 11 without modification. Recall that the one-to-one association between `Person` and `Phone` is implemented through the `AddAPhone` method of the `Person` class. This method is inherited by the `Student` and `Professor` subclasses.

The DA classes are similar to the `CustomerDA` class presented in Example 13-9. Only three DA methods are required in this example: `Initialize`, `AddNew`, and `GetAll`. Although not invoked in this example, the `Find` and `Update` methods are included for completeness.

The main menu GUI invokes the `StudentDA.Initialize` and
`ProfessorDA.Initialize` methods to populate the simulated database. As in earlier
examples, the `Initialize` methods include hard-coded data. (In the next chapter, you
learn to read this data from a database.) The form to add a student retrieves student
attributes (name, address, id, and major) and the student's phone information (area code,
number, and phoneType) from the GUI controls, creates a corresponding `Student`
instance, invokes the `AddAPhone` method of the `Person` class to associate the `Student`
instance with his or her `Phone` instance, and then invokes the `StudentDA.AddNew`
method to add the `Student` instance to the simulated database. The form to add a
professor functions in a nearly identical manner.

The form to list students responds to a Load event by invoking the `StudentDA.GetAll`
method in response to a Load event, and then populating a multiline text box with
information about each student and his or her phone. This information is obtained
invoking the `TellAboutSelf` and `GetPhoneInfo` methods, respectively.

Complete program listings for each of the nine classes in this application follow.

Person

```
Public MustInherit Class Person
    Private name As String
    Private address As String
    Private phone As Phone
    ' parameterized constructor
    Protected Sub New(ByVal aName As String, ByVal anAddress As
    String)
        SetName(aName)
        SetAddress(anAddress)
    End Sub

    'get accessor methods
    Protected Function GetName() As String
        Return name
    End Function
    Protected Function GetAddress() As String
        Return address
    End Function
    'set accessor methods
    Protected Sub SetName(ByVal aName As String)
        name = aName
    End Sub
    Protected Sub SetAddress(ByVal anAddress As String)
        address = anAddress
    End Sub
    Public Sub AddAPhone(ByVal anAreaCode As Integer, ByVal aNumber
    As Integer, ByVal aPhoneType As String)
        phone = New Phone(anAreaCode, aNumber, aPhoneType)
    End Sub
```

13

```
        Public Function GetPhoneInfo() As String
            Dim info, formattedAreaCode, formattedNumber As String
            formattedAreaCode = phone.GetAreaCode().ToString("(###)")
            formattedNumber = phone.GetNumber().ToString("###-####")
            info = phone.GetPhoneType() & " " & formattedAreaCode & _
            " " & formattedNumber
            Return info
        End Function
    End Class
```

Student

```
Public Class Student
    Inherits Person
    Private id As Integer
    Private major As String

    ' parameterized constructor
    Public Sub New(ByVal aName As String, ByVal anAddress As
    String, ByVal anId As Integer, ByVal aMajor As String)
        ' invoke superclass constructor to populate name & address
        ' attributes
        MyBase.New(aName, anAddress)
        ' populate id and major attributes
        SetId(anId)
        SetMajor(aMajor)
    End Sub

    'get accessor methods
    Public Function GetId() As Integer
        Return id
    End Function
    Public Function GetMajor() As String
        Return major
    End Function
    'set accessor methods
    Public Sub SetId(ByVal anId As Integer)
        id = anId
    End Sub
    Public Sub SetMajor(ByVal aMajor As String)
        major = aMajor
    End Sub
    Public Function TellAboutSelf() As String
        Dim info As String
        info = GetName() & ", " & GetAddress() & ", " & GetId() & _
        ", " & GetMajor()
        Return info
    End Function
End Class
```

Professor

```
Public Class Professor
    Inherits Person
    Private rank As String
    Private department As String

    ' parameterized constructor
    Public Sub New(ByVal aName As String, ByVal anAddress As
    String, ByVal aRank As String, ByVal aDepartment As String)
        ' invoke superclass constructor to populate name & address
        attributes
        MyBase.New(aName, anAddress)
        ' populate rank and department attributes
        SetRank(aRank)
        SetDepartment(aDepartment)
    End Sub

    'get accessor methods
    Public Function GetRank() As String
        Return rank
    End Function
    Public Function GetDepartment() As String
        Return department
    End Function
    'set accessor methods
    Public Sub SetRank(ByVal aRank As String)
        rank = aRank
    End Sub
    Public Sub SetDepartment(ByVal aDepartment As String)
        department = aDepartment
    End Sub
    Public Function TellAboutSelf() As String
        Dim info As String
        Info = GetName() & ", " & GetAddress() & ", " & GetRank() _
        & ", " & GetDepartment()
        Return info
    End Function
End Class
```

13

Phone

```
Public Class Phone
    Private areaCode As Integer
    Private number As Integer
    Private phoneType As String
    Const defaultAreaCode As Integer = 314
    ' 3 parameter constructor
    Public Sub New(ByVal anAreaCode As Integer, ByVal aNumber As
    Integer, ByVal aPhoneType As String)
```

```
        SetAreaCode(anAreaCode)
        SetNumber(aNumber)
        SetPhoneType(aPhoneType)
    End Sub
    ' 2 parameter constructor using default area code
    Public Sub New(ByVal aNumber As Integer, ByVal aPhoneType As
    String)
        Me.New(defaultAreaCode, aNumber, aPhoneType)
    End Sub

    'get accessor methods
    Public Function GetAreaCode() As Integer
        Return areaCode
    End Function
    Public Function GetNumber() As Integer
        Return number
    End Function
    Public Function GetPhoneType() As String
        Return phoneType
    End Function

    'set accessor methods
    Public Sub SetAreaCode(ByVal anAreaCode As Integer)
        areaCode = anAreaCode
    End Sub
    Public Sub SetNumber(ByVal aNumber As Integer)
        number = aNumber
    End Sub
    Public Sub SetPhoneType(ByVal aPhoneType As String)
        phoneType = aPhoneType
    End Sub
End Class
```

StudentDA

```
'studentDA class definition
Imports System.Collections
Public Class StudentDA

    'Declare array to simulate student database
    Private Shared students As New ArrayList

    'Declare student reference variable
    Private Shared aStudent As student

    Public Shared Sub Initialize()
        Dim student1, student2, student3 As Student
        'Create student instances - simulate database
```

```
        student1 = New Student("Edith", "Batesville", 1234567, _
        "English")
        student1.AddAPhone(417, 1234567, "Home")
        students.Add(student1)
        student2 = New Student("Josh", "Springfield", 2345678, _
        "Computer Science")
        student2.AddAPhone(912, 9876543, "Mobile")
        students.Add(student2)
        student3 = New Student("Richard", "Statesboro", 3456789, _
        "History")
        student3.AddAPhone(912, 9991234, "Office")
        students.Add(student3)
    End Sub

    Public Shared Function GetAll() As ArrayList
        Return students
    End Function

    Public Shared Function AddNew(ByRef newstudent As Student)
        students.Add(newstudent)
    End Function

    Public Shared Function Find(ByVal index As Integer) As Student
        aStudent = students(index)
        Return aStudent
    End Function

    Public Shared Function Update(ByVal index As Integer, ByRef
    thisstudent As Student)
        students(index) = thisstudent
    End Function
End Class
```

ProfessorDA

```
'professorDA class definition
Imports System.Collections
Public Class ProfessorDA

    'Declare array to simulate professor database
    Private Shared professors As New ArrayList

    'Declare professor reference variable
    Private Shared aprofessor As Professor

    Public Shared Sub Initialize()
        Dim professor1, professor2, professor3 As Professor
        'Create professor instances - simulate database
```

13

```
        professor1 = New Professor("Truman", "West Plains", _
        "Full", "Computer Science")
        professor1.AddAPhone(417, 5555555, "Office")
        professors.Add(professor1)
        professor2 = New Professor("Alison", "Blackshear", _
        "Associate", "Spanish")
        professor2.AddAPhone(912, 9876543, "Mobile")
        professors.Add(professor2)
        professor3 = New Professor("Kyle", "Savannah", _
        "Assistant", "Zoology")
        professor3.AddAPhone(912, 9991234, "Home")
        professors.Add(professor3)
    End Sub

    Public Shared Function GetAll() As ArrayList
        Return professors
    End Function

    Public Shared Function AddNew(ByRef newprofessor As Professor)
        professors.Add(newprofessor)
    End Function

    Public Shared Function Find(ByVal index As Integer) As
    Professor
        aprofessor = professors(index)
        Return aprofessor
    End Function

    Public Shared Function Update(ByVal index As Integer, ByRef
    thisprofessor As Professor)
        professors(index) = thisprofessor
    End Function
End Class
```

Main Menu

```
Public Class frmMainMenu
    Inherits System.Windows.Forms.Form

    'Windows Form Designer generated code

    'Event handler for the Close button
    Private Sub btnClose_Click(ByVal sender As System.Object, ByVal
    e As System.EventArgs) Handles btnClose.Click
        Me.Close()
    End Sub

    'Event handler for the Add Student button
```

```vb
Private Sub btnAddStudent_Click(ByVal sender As System.Object,
ByVal e As System.EventArgs) Handles btnAddStudent.Click
    'Hide the main menu form
    Me.Hide()
    'Create and display AddStudent form
    Dim frmAddStudentGUI = New frmStudent
    frmAddStudentGUI.ShowDialog()
    'Make the main menu form visible
    Me.Show()
End Sub


'Event handler for the Add Professor button
Private Sub btnAddProfessor_Click(ByVal sender As
System.Object, ByVal e As System.EventArgs) Handles
btnAddProfessor.Click
    'Hide the main menu form
    Me.Hide()
    'Create and display AddProfessor form
    Dim frmAddProfessorGUI = New frmProfessor
    frmAddProfessorGUI.ShowDialog()
    'Make the main menu form visible
    Me.Show()
End Sub


Private Sub btnListStud_Click(ByVal sender As System.Object,
ByVal e As System.EventArgs) Handles btnListStud.Click
    'Hide the main menu form
    Me.Hide()
    'Create and display List Students form
    Dim frmListStudentsGUI = New frmListStudents
    frmListStudentsGUI.ShowDialog()
    'Make the main menu form visible
    Me.Show()
End Sub


Private Sub btnListProf_Click(ByVal sender As System.Object,
ByVal e As System.EventArgs) Handles btnListProf.Click
    'Hide the main menu form
    Me.Hide()
    'Create and display List Professors form
    Dim frmListProfessorsGUI = New frmListProfessors
    frmListProfessorsGUI.ShowDialog()
    'Make the main menu form visible
    Me.Show()
End Sub


Private Sub frmMainMenu_Load(ByVal sender As Object, ByVal e As
System.EventArgs) Handles MyBase.Load
```

13

```vb
        'Initialize simulated database
        StudentDA.Initialize()
        ProfessorDA.Initialize()
    End Sub
End Class
```

Add Student

```vb
Public Class frmStudent
    Inherits System.Windows.Forms.Form
    'Declare variables
    Private studName, address, major, phoneType As String
    Private id, areaCode, number As Integer
    Private aStudent As Student
    'Windows Form Designer generated code
    Private Sub btnAdd_Click(ByVal sender As System.Object, ByVal e
    As System.EventArgs) Handles btnAdd.Click
        'Get values from the GUI controls
        Try
            studName = txtName.Text
            address = txtAddress.Text
            id = System.Convert.ToInt32(txtID.Text)
            major = lstMajor.SelectedItem
            areaCode = System.Convert.ToInt16(txtAreaCode.Text)
            number = System.Convert.ToInt32(txtNumber.Text)
            If radHome.Checked Then
                phoneType = radHome.Text
            End If
            If radOffice.Checked Then
                phoneType = radOffice.Text
            End If
            If radMobile.Checked Then
                phoneType = radMobile.Text
            End If

            'Validate that the user has entered values for name and
            'address and made a selection in the list box
            If studName.Length = 0 Or address.Length = 0 Or _
                lstMajor.SelectedIndex = -1 Then
                MessageBox.Show("Please Enter All Data")
            Else
                'Data is valid -- create a Student instance
                aStudent = New Student(studName, address, id, _
                major)
                'Add the student's phone
                aStudent.AddAPhone(areaCode, number, phoneType)
                'Add the student the simulated database
                StudentDA.AddNew(aStudent)
```

```vbnet
                MessageBox.Show("Student Added")
                'Clear the form
                ClearForm()
            End If
        Catch ex As Exception
            MessageBox.Show("You must enter numbers for "& _
            "Student ID, Area Code, and Number")
        End Try
    End Sub

    Private Sub btnClear_Click(ByVal sender As System.Object, ByVal
    e As System.EventArgs) Handles btnClear.Click
        ClearForm()
    End Sub

    Private Sub btnReturn_Click(ByVal sender As System.Object,
    ByVal e As System.EventArgs) Handles btnReturn.Click
        Me.Close()
    End Sub

    Private Sub ClearForm()
        txtName.Clear()
        txtAddress.Clear()
        txtID.Clear()
        lstMajor.SelectedIndex = -1
        txtAreaCode.Clear()
        txtNumber.Clear()
        radHome.Checked = True
        txtName.Focus()
    End Sub
End Class
```

Add Professor

```vbnet
Public Class frmProfessor
    Inherits System.Windows.Forms.Form
    'Declare variables
    Private profName, address, rank, dept, phoneType As String
    Private areaCode, number As Integer
    Private aProfessor As Professor
    'Windows Form Designer generated code
    Private Sub btnAdd_Click(ByVal sender As System.Object, ByVal e
    As System.EventArgs) Handles btnAdd.Click
        'Get values from the GUI controls
        Try
            profName = txtName.Text
            address = txtAddress.Text
            If radAssistant.Checked Then
                rank = radAssistant.Text
```

13

```
            End If
            If radAssociate.Checked Then
                rank = radAssociate.Text
            End If
            If radFull.Checked Then
                rank = radFull.Text
            End If
            dept = lstDept.SelectedItem
            areaCode = System.Convert.ToInt16(txtAreaCode.Text)
            number = System.Convert.ToInt32(txtNumber.Text)
            If radHome.Checked Then
                phoneType = radHome.Text
            End If
            If radOffice.Checked Then
                phoneType = radOffice.Text
            End If
            If radMobile.Checked Then
                phoneType = radMobile.Text
            End If

            'Validate that the user has entered values for name and
            'address and made a selection in the list box
            If profName.Length = 0 Or address.Length = 0 Or _
                lstDept.SelectedIndex = -1 Then
                MessageBox.Show("Please Enter All Data")
            Else
                'Data is valid -- create a Professor instance
                aProfessor = New Professor(profName, address, _
                rank, dept)
                'Add the Professor's phone
                aProfessor.AddAPhone(areaCode, number, phoneType)
                'Add the professor to the simulated database
                ProfessorDA.AddNew(aProfessor)
                MessageBox.Show("Professor Added")
                'Clear the form
                ClearForm()
            End If
        Catch ex As Exception
            MessageBox.Show("You must enter numbers for "& _
            "Area Code and Number")
        End Try
    End Sub

    Private Sub btnClear_Click(ByVal sender As System.Object, ByVal
e As System.EventArgs) Handles btnClear.Click
        ClearForm()
    End Sub
```

```
    Private Sub btnReturn_Click(ByVal sender As System.Object,
    ByVal e As System.EventArgs) Handles btnReturn.Click
        Me.Close()
    End Sub

    Private Sub ClearForm()
        txtName.Clear()
        txtAddress.Clear()
        radAssistant.Checked = True
        lstDept.SelectedIndex = -1
        txtAreaCode.Clear()
        txtNumber.Clear()
        radHome.Checked = True
        txtName.Focus()
    End Sub
End Class
```

List Students

```
Public Class frmListStudents
    Inherits System.Windows.Forms.Form
    Private students As New ArrayList
    Private aStudent As Student
    'Windows Form Designer generated code
    Private Sub btnReturn_Click(ByVal sender As System.Object,
    ByVal e As System.EventArgs) Handles btnReturn.Click
        Me.Close()
    End Sub

    Private Sub frmListStudents_Load(ByVal sender As Object, ByVal
    e As System.EventArgs) Handles MyBase.Load
        'Retrieve all student data from simulated database
        students = StudentDA.GetAll()
        'Add the name of each student retrieved to the list
        Dim i As Integer
        For i = 0 To students.Count - 1
            aStudent = students(i)
            txtList.AppendText(aStudent.TellAboutSelf & ", ")
            txtList.AppendText(aStudent.GetPhoneInfo() & vbCrLf)
        Next
    End Sub
End Class
```

List Professors

```
Public Class frmListProfessors
    Inherits System.Windows.Forms.Form
    Private professors As New ArrayList
    Private aProfessor As Professor
    'Windows Form Designer generated code
```

13

```
    Private Sub btnReturn_Click(ByVal sender As System.Object,
    ByVal e As System.EventArgs) Handles btnReturn.Click
        Me.Close()
    End Sub

    Private Sub frmListProfessors_Load(ByVal sender As Object,
    ByVal e As System.EventArgs) Handles MyBase.Load
        'Retrieve all professor data from simulated database
        professors = ProfessorDA.GetAll()
        'Add the name of each student retrieved to the list
        Dim i As Integer
        For i = 0 To professors.Count - 1
            aProfessor = professors(i)
            txtList.AppendText(aProfessor.TellAboutSelf & ", ")
            txtList.AppendText(aProfessor.GetPhoneInfo() & vbCrLf)
        Next
    End Sub
End Class
```

QUICK REVIEW

1. Group boxes and panels are containers that enable you to visually and logically organize groups of related controls. A common use of group boxes and panels is to group sets of radio buttons.

2. A tree view displays a group of hierarchically related items as an expandable outline. Each item in the tree is called a tree node. Each node may contain subnodes.

3. A tab control provides the functionality for a set of tab pages. Tab pages are useful when a form requires a large number of controls and those controls can be grouped into logical subsets.

4. The main menu control serves as a container for the menu structure. Menu items represent individual menu choices within that structure.

5. Visual Basic .NET (VB .NET) includes a rich set of classes for drawing lines, rectangles, circles, polygons, and other graphical elements. The `System.Drawing` namespace contains the classes and structures you need for drawing graphical objects.

6. The `Graphics` class contains methods for drawing shapes such as rectangles, circles, and lines.

7. A structure is similar to a class in that both have members that can include constructors, methods, properties, and events. However, structures are value types, whereas classes are reference types.

8. When you declare a variable to store a value type, that variable contains the actual data for the structure, rather than a memory address as is the case when you declare a variable to reference a class (a reference type).

9. Event handlers provide two parameters. The first parameter, `sender`, provides a reference to the object that raised the event. The second parameter, `e`, passes an object specific to the event that is being handled. For the Paint event, e is of the `System.Windows.Forms.PaintEventArgs` type and specifies the Graphics object that is to be used to paint (or redraw) the control.

10. Graphical user interface (GUI) classes can interact with problem domain (PD) and data access (DA) classes to create integrated systems.

11. The visual programming process generates the variables necessary to create a GUI, but may not generate all the variables needed to respond to events that result from interaction with the GUI. These variables must be added to the source code through the Code Editor window.

12. An `ArrayList` can be used to simulate interaction with a database.

13. Many real-world applications consist of multiple forms. A main menu GUI can be used to navigate among these forms.

14. The `ShowDialog` method shows a form as a modal dialog box. When shown a modal dialog box, a form must be dismissed before the next statement in the procedure will be executed.

15. In applications with multiple forms, it is often necessary for the forms to share data. Data sharing can be implemented through the use of DA classes.

16. Object-oriented systems employ a three-tier design consisting of GUI classes, PD classes, and DA classes. As their names suggest, the GUI classes provide a graphical interface for the input and display of data, PD classes model the objects specific to the application, and DA classes provide data storage and retrieval services.

17. A major advantage of the three-tier design is that classes in each tier can be independent of those in another. This independence can dramatically simplify future maintenance chores because modifications to classes in one tier do not require changes to classes in another tier.

13

18. DA methods introduced in this chapter perform the following tasks: initialize the (simulated) database; insert a new record; retrieve an existing record; update an existing record; and return the set of all records.

19. PD, DA, and GUI classes can work together to create an integrated system that simulates interaction with a database.

20. An integrated system using multiple PD, DA, and GUI classes can implement associations between classes.

EXERCISES

1. Under what circumstances would you use the following controls on a GUI form?

   a. Group box

   b. Tab control with tab pages

   c. Tree view with tree nodes

   d. Main menu with menu items

2. What are the common event(s) for each of the controls listed in Exercise 1?

3. What are the similarities and differences between a panel and a group box?

4. Which namespace provides capabilities for drawing lines, rectangles, circles, and other shapes? Is it necessary to import this namespace when working with graphical elements in a GUI form? Why or why not? Which class in this namespace provides the primary methods for drawing these graphical elements?

5. Event handlers provide two parameters. What are they and what do they tell you?

6. What are the similarities and differences between a structure and a class? Between a value type and a reference type?

7. Describe the three-tier design employed by many OO applications. What is the purpose of each tier? What is the major advantage of this design?

8. Identify the five DA methods introduced in this chapter. What is the purpose of each method?

9. Describe how a main menu form can be used to navigate among multiple forms in an integrated system.

10. What is a modal dialog box? Which method do you use to show a dialog box modally? Under what circumstances would you not want a dialog box to be displayed modally?

11. Many of the examples in this book use intermediate variables to store values. This approach usually improves code readability, but reduces code efficiency. For example, in several of the examples in this chapter, the PopulateListBox method uses the intermediate variable "aCustomer" to store the Customer instance obtained from the ArrayList.

```
Private Sub PopulateListBox()
    'Declare a customer reference variable
    Dim aCustomer As Customer
    'Create the customer instances
    CreateCustomers()
    'Add the name of each customer to the list
    Dim i As Integer
    For i = 0 To customers.Count - 1
        aCustomer = customers(i)
        lstCustomer.Items.Add(aCustomer.GetName())
    Next
End Sub
```

Rewrite this method to be more efficient by eliminating the use of the intermediate variable "aCustomer".

PROGRAMMING EXERCISES

1. Most university students have both a permanent and a local address. Figure 13-28 shows a student information form that uses a tab control with two tab pages to capture this information. One tab page includes controls pertaining to a student's permanent address and the other includes an identical set of controls pertaining to a student's local address. Create the GUI shown in Figure 13-28. Include three items in the Major combo box: Computer Science, Information Systems, and Information Technology. When the form loads, display Computer Science in the combo box as the default major.

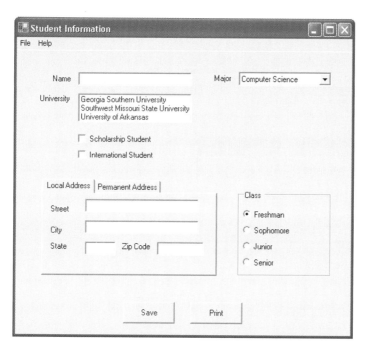

Figure 13-28   GUI to capture student information

13

2. Develop a Student PD class to interact with the GUI class you created in Programming Exercise 1.

   - Include the following attributes: name, major, university, scholarship, international, localStreet, localCity, localState, localZip, permanentStreet, permanentCity, permanentState, permanentZip, and studentClass.

   - Include a fully parameterized constructor, get and set methods for each attribute, and a TellAboutSelf method.

- When the user clicks the Save button, create a Student instance and display a message confirming that the student information was saved. Ensure that all student information has been entered before saving.

- Use the TellAboutSelf method to display student information in the message box. See Figure 13-29. When the message box closes, clear the form.

- Add a Save option and a Close option to the File menu. The Save menu option should function exactly as the Save button does. When the user clicks the Close menu option, close the form.

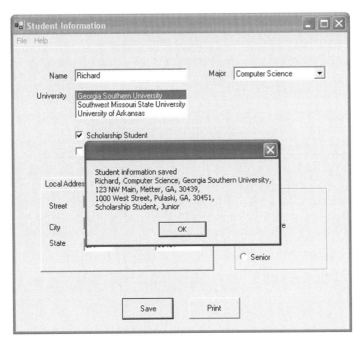

Figure 13-29 GUI to capture student information with confirmation message

3. Add a StudentDA class to the application you developed in Programming Exercise 2.

- Include the DA methods AddNew and GetAll methods. (Other DA methods can be included but are not needed for this application.)

- Use an ArrayList to simulate a student database.

- When the user clicks the Print button, display a second form (similar to the one shown in Figure 13-30) listing information for all students that have been entered on the first form.

- When the user clicks the Close button on the second form, display the original form to allow the entry of information about another student.

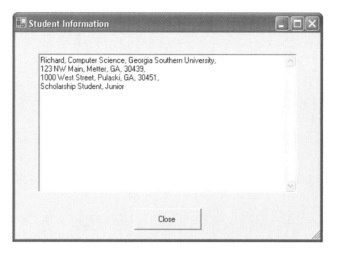

Figure 13-30   GUI to display student information

4. Example 2 of this chapter populated a tree view using two String arrays—one for professors and one for courses. Modify Example 2 so that it interacts with two PD classes—Professor and Course.

- Define a Professor PD class with two attributes: profName and courses, where profName is a String and courses is an ArrayList. Include the following methods: a constructor that requires a single parameter (professor name); a method that adds a course to the courses ArrayList; and GetName and GetCourses accessor methods.

- Define a Course PD class with the single attribute courseName. Include a parameterized constructor and a GetName accessor method.

- Create the entries for the tree utilizing instances of the Course and Professor PD classes. Use the methods of these PD classes to populate the tree. (Use professor names and course names of your choosing.)

- Change the output that appears in the text box so that it displays the full path to the selected node and all siblings of the selected node (excluding the selected node itself). See Figure 13-31. If the selected node has no siblings, display an appropriate message.

13

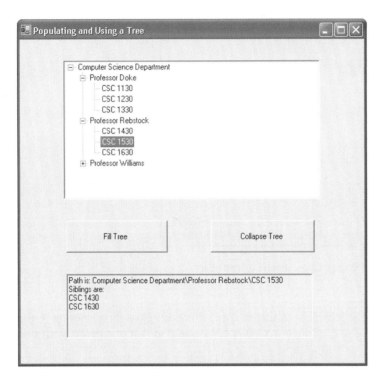

Figure 13-31   Sample output of Programming Exercise 4

5. The Circle PD class introduced in Chapter 10 (Example 10-18) defines three attributes representing a pair of (x, y) coordinates and a radius. The (x, y) coordinates define the upper-left corner (in pixels) of the circle's bounding rectangle. Modify the Circle PD class so that it uses an integer value (rather than a double) for the radius. Add a Draw method to the Circle PD class that will draw the circle defined by x, y, and radius. The Draw method requires two parameters: a reference to a Pen instance and a reference to a Graphics instance. Develop a GUI that accepts three integers representing the (x, y) coordinates and radius of a circle, each in pixels. Include a Draw button that creates the corresponding instance of the Circle class, invokes the Draw method to draw the circle on the form, and displays the circumference (in pixels). Include error-checking to ensure that the user enters valid numbers for the three integers. Sample output is shown in Figure 13-32.

(*Hint:* VB .NET invokes the Paint method when the form loads. However, when the form loads, the text boxes that capture the (x, y) coordinates and radius do not contain values that can be converted to integers. Use a Boolean variable to determine when the Paint event handler is invoked for the first time. Do not read values from the text boxes, create a Circle instance, nor draw the circle the first time the Paint event handler is invoked.)

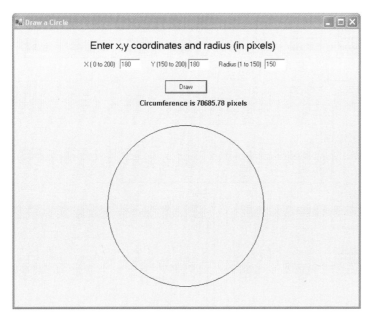

Figure 13-32   Sample output of Programming Exercise 5

6. Modify the Programming Example at the end of this chapter so that it implements a one-to-many association between Person and Phone. Replace the Phone Information group boxes on the Add Student and Add Professor GUIs with a tab control containing three tab pages: one for adding a home phone number, one for adding an office phone number, and one for adding a mobile phone number. Test your program by entering multiple phone numbers for a student or a professor. When the user clicks the List Students (or List Professors) button on the main menu, display all phones for each student (or professor) in the simulated database. The GUI sequence is shown in Figure 13-33.

13

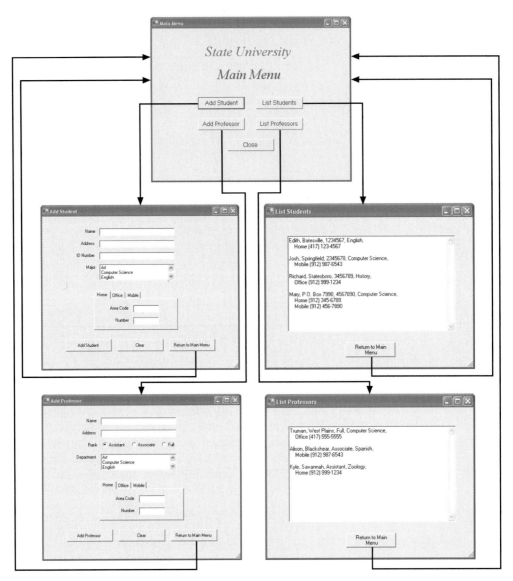

Figure 13-33 GUI sequence for Programming Exercise 6

14

Advanced Topics: DBMS, SQL, and ASP.NET

In this chapter, you will:

O Explore the relational database model

O Construct database queries using SQL

O Write VB .NET programs that interact with a relational database

O Explore ASP.NET

In Chapter 13, you learned how to develop data access (DA) classes and create integrated systems that simulate interaction with a database. In this chapter, you extend your knowledge to create integrated systems that interact with a relational database. Because relational databases provide capabilities to extract and manage the data contained within them, they are sometimes referred to as database management systems (DBMS).

This chapter introduces the fundamentals of the relational database model. You learn how to use Structured Query Language (SQL) commands to extract and change the information contained within a relational database. You then see how to develop Visual Basic .NET (VB .NET) applications that interact with a relational database.

The .NET Framework was designed to help you develop both Windows and Web applications. In previous chapters, you worked with supplied classes and wrote user-defined class definitions and methods to develop Windows applications that run on a single machine. Many applications run today in networked environments and especially the World Wide Web. In this chapter, you explore ASP.NET, which is used to develop Web-based applications.

ASP stands for Active Server Pages. These Web pages contain controls and code that let users interact with data. You may write the code using any .NET-supported language; however, in this chapter, you use VB .NET. After completing this chapter, you should understand the basic concepts of Web development and be able to create interactive Web pages using ASP.NET.

EXPLORING THE RELATIONAL DATABASE MODEL

In Chapter 13, you used data access classes to simulate interaction with a database. While this approach enabled objects to be available across different forms within an application, it did not make those objects persistent over time. Once you closed the application, the data contained within the objects was no longer available. Many real-world applications require data persistence. VB .NET provides several mechanisms for achieving data persistence. In Chapter 6, you saw how to implement data persistence in VB .NET using sequential files. In this chapter, you implement data persistence using a relational database.

Understanding Tables, Rows, Columns, and Primary and Foreign Keys

A relational database enables you to organize data into tables. Usually, a relational database consists of many different tables that are related to each other in some way. However, in simple applications, a relational database may contain only one table. Each table is comprised of rows and columns. Sometimes, a table corresponds directly to a VB .NET problem domain (PD) class. For example, the **Customer** PD class presented in Chapter 10 defines three attributes: name, address, and phoneNo.

```
Public Class Customer
  Public name As String
  Public address As String
  Public phoneNo As String
End Class
```

A relational database table for this class is shown in Figure 14-1.

Name	Address	PhoneNumber
Eleanor	Atlanta	123-4567
Josh	Springfield	987-6543
Callie	Statesboro	555-1234

Figure 14-1   The Customer table

In this example, each column in the Customer table corresponds to an attribute defined for the `Customer` class, and each row represents an individual instance of the `Customer` class. In database terminology, columns (attributes) are referred to as **fields** and rows (instances) are referred to as **records**.

 Columns in the Customer table correspond to Customer attributes in the code. It is good practice to assign similar names to corresponding columns and attributes. However, there is no requirement that they be identical. For example, it is common to begin attribute names in the code with a lowercase letter (such as "address") and to begin field names in tables with an uppercase letter (such as "Address").

Each table in a relational database has a **primary key**. A primary key is a field (or set of fields) that uniquely identifies each record. In the Customer table shown in Figure 14-1, customers are uniquely identified by their phone number, so this field could serve as a primary key. However, good database design calls for a primary key whose value is not likely to change over time and whose value is not null for any instance. Because a person's phone number is likely to change over time and some people may not have a phone number, this field is not a good choice for the primary key. A preferred solution adds a unique, identifying attribute (such as customer number) to the Customer table and the `Customer` class. See Figure 14-2.

14

CustomerNumber	Name	Address	PhoneNumber
13912	Eleanor	Atlanta	123-4567
28570	Josh	Springfield	987-6543
36409	Callie	Statesboro	555-1234

Figure 14-2   The Customer table with CustomerNumber as primary key

Unless noted otherwise, database fields in the examples in this chapter are defined as text fields.

When a relational database consists of more than one table, the tables are usually related to each other in some way. For example, suppose that in addition to the Customer table, you also have a CustOrder table that contains the following information for each order: order number, order date, order amount, and the customer number of the customer who placed the order. The CustOrder table is shown in Figure 14-3.

OrderNumber	OrderDate	OrderAmount	CustomerNumber
1001	01/19/2005	250.93	28570
1002	01/22/2006	92.18	13912
1003	03/10/2006	60.75	28570
1004	04/03/2006	132.47	36409

Figure 14-3   The CustOrder table

 OrderAmount is stored as a single precision number in the CustOrder table.

Notice that the customer number attribute, which serves as primary key in the Customer table, is also an attribute in the CustOrder table. As shown in Figure 14-4, this enables each record in the CustOrder table to be linked to the corresponding record in the Customer table.

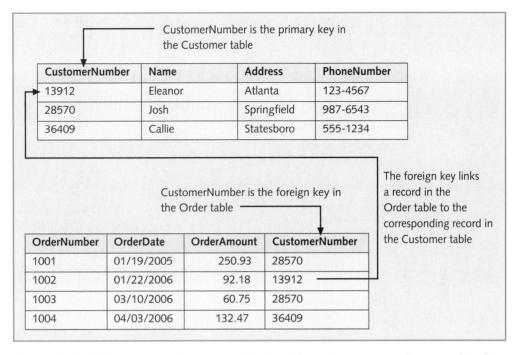

CustomerNumber is the primary key in the Customer table

CustomerNumber	Name	Address	PhoneNumber
13912	Eleanor	Atlanta	123-4567
28570	Josh	Springfield	987-6543
36409	Callie	Statesboro	555-1234

The foreign key links a record in the Order table to the corresponding record in the Customer table

CustomerNumber is the foreign key in the Order table

OrderNumber	OrderDate	OrderAmount	CustomerNumber
1001	01/19/2005	250.93	28570
1002	01/22/2006	92.18	13912
1003	03/10/2006	60.75	28570
1004	04/03/2006	132.47	36409

Figure 14-4   Linking a record in the CustOrder table to the corresponding record in the Customer table

In database terminology, a field (or set of fields) that links information in one table to information in another table is called a **foreign key**. A field that is a foreign key in one table must be a primary key (or part of a primary key) in the other table. In this example, the customer number attribute is the primary key in the Customer table and a foreign key in the CustOrder table. Foreign keys provide the links between tables and are the power behind the relational database model.

Mapping PD Attributes to Database Tables

In simple cases, mapping PD classes to database tables is straightforward. However, in more complex situations, you have many different choices for organizing attributes into relational tables. Sometimes the attributes in a PD class are mapped to more than one table. Other times, as with the Customer table described earlier, you add fields that were not originally contained within a PD class. When PD classes are related to each other through inheritance, the choices for table design are even greater.

To illustrate, consider the Programming Example at the end of Chapter 13. This application contains four PD classes: **Person**, **Student**, **Professor**, and **Phone**. Figure 14-5 shows a Unified Modeling Language (UML) class diagram for this example

14

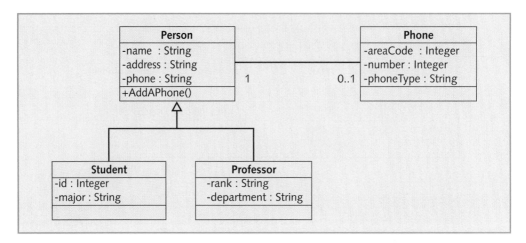

Figure 14-5   UML class diagram for the Chapter 13 Programming Example

One possible database design for this example includes four tables, one for each PD class. The **Person** class has three attributes: name, address, and phone. Recall from Chapter 13 that this example assumes a one-to-one relationship between **Person** and **Phone**, so phone could serve as a primary key. However, as discussed earlier, phone is not a good choice for the primary key because the value for a person's phone number may change over time and could be null. Thus, a better design adds an attribute to the Person table that is guaranteed to be unique, have a non-null value for each instance, and whose value will not change over time. This attribute (PersonID) serves as the primary key of the Person table.

Student and **Professor** are subclasses of the **Person** class. Tables for each of these subclasses would include the attributes unique to each subclass, plus the PersonID attribute. The PersonID field is needed in the Student and Professor tables to uniquely identify each record in these tables and to link records in these tables to corresponding records in the Person table. Note that the **id** attribute defined in the **Student** subclass maps to the PersonID field.

The fourth table includes the attributes from the **Phone** class. Once again, the PersonID field is added so that a record in the Phone table can be linked to the appropriate records in the other tables. Good database design also minimizes redundancy. Because the phone number data is stored in the Phone table, a phone number field is not needed in the Person table. Figure 14-6 illustrates the design.

Person table

PersonID	Name	Address

Student table

PersonID	Major

Professor table

PersonID	Rank	Department

Phone table

PersonID	PhoneType	AreaCode	Number

Figure 14-6 Database design using four tables

At the other extreme, the PD classes in this application could be collapsed into a single table, as shown in Figure 14-7.

PersonID	Name	Address	Major	Rank	Department	PhoneType	AreaCode	Number

Figure 14-7   Database design using a single table

Several other database designs involving two or three tables are possible for this application. Each has advantages and disadvantages. For example, a disadvantage of the design that uses four tables is that you must read records from multiple tables to obtain complete information for each person; the advantage is that there is little wasted space—each column usually contains a value for every instance. Conversely, a disadvantage of the single table design is that some columns will contain many empty values; professor-specific attributes will be empty for each student record and student-specific attributes will be empty for each professor record. As the database grows, this design becomes increasingly inefficient. The advantage of the single table solution is that you read only one table to obtain complete information for each person. Which table design is better? For this example, assuming there are a relatively small number of records, the single table solution is preferable. In general, the answer depends on a number of factors, including the nature of the application, the expected growth of the database, and the platform upon which the application runs.

A complete discussion of database design principles and performance trade-off issues is beyond the scope of the book. For now, recognize that there is seldom a single choice for mapping PD attributes to a relational database. Inefficient use of space and multiple table lookups each have performance implications. You should weigh the benefits and drawbacks of several possible designs and choose the design that best fits the needs of your application.

CONSTRUCTING QUERIES USING SQL

In this section, you learn to construct queries using Structured Query Language (SQL). A **query** is a request for information. You use queries to extract information from the database. A query usually specifies one or more conditions that the extracted information must meet. For example, in a database that contains customer order information, you might want to see a list of customer names and addresses for orders that exceed $100. In a student database, you might request a list of students whose home state is Georgia. Each of these requests can be specified as a query using SQL.

In addition to specifying queries, SQL enables you to perform other common database operations. In this section, you also write SQL statements that insert new records into a table, update records contained within a table, and delete records from a table. Later in this chapter, you use these SQL statements in VB .NET programs to interact with a Microsoft Access database.

Extracting Records from a Database

To extract records from a table (or set of tables) in a relational database you use the SQL SELECT statement. The format of the SELECT statement is:

```
SELECT attribute1, attribute2, ... , attributeN FROM table
WHERE condition
```

In a SELECT statement, each *attribute* specifies the name of a column; *table* specifies the name of a table; and *condition* specifies the criteria for selecting records (or rows) from the table. SELECT, FROM, and WHERE are SQL keywords. Although SQL is not case sensitive, this book adopts the convention of using uppercase for SQL keywords.

To illustrate the SELECT statement, consider the table shown in Figure 14-8. (This table is an expanded version of the Customer table shown in Figure 14-2.)

CustomerNumber	FirstName	LastName	City	State	PhoneNumber
13912	Eleanor	Doke	Atlanta	GA	123-4567
28570	Josh	Rebstock	Springfield	MO	987-6543
36409	Callie	Williams	Statesboro	GA	555-1234
70832	Caleb	Gilleon	Springfield	GA	876-5432

Figure 14-8   Expanded Customer table

14

A query to extract the first and last names of customers who live in the state of Georgia is:

```
SELECT FirstName, LastName FROM Customer WHERE State = 'GA'
```

The output is:

```
FirstName    LastName
Eleanor      Doke
Callie       Williams
Caleb        Gilleon
```

Note that when specifying criteria in the WHERE clause, you enclose string values in single quotes.

In SQL, you can use the keywords AND and OR to specify compound conditions. For example, a query to extract the customer number, first name, and last name of customers who live in Springfield, MO is:

```
SELECT CustomerNumber, FirstName, LastName FROM Customer
WHERE City = 'Springfield' AND State = 'MO'
```

The output is:

CustomerNumber	FirstName	LastName
28570	Josh	Rebstock

You can use a SELECT statement to extract attributes from multiple tables. Consider, for example, the Customer and CustOrder tables presented in Figure 14-4. A query to extract a list of customer names, order dates, and order amounts for orders greater than $100 is:

```
SELECT Name, OrderDate, OrderAmount
FROM Customer, CustOrder
WHERE OrderAmount > 100
AND Customer.CustomerNumber = CustOrder.CustomerNumber
```

The output is:

Name	OrderDate	OrderAmount
Josh	01/19/2005	250.93
Callie	04/03/2006	132.47

The WHERE clause in this example serves two purposes. First, it specifies the condition that the order amount must be greater than $100. It also links information in the Customer table to information in the CustOrder table. The link is established by specifying that the primary key attribute (CustomerNumber) in the Customer table must match the foreign key attribute (CustomerNumber) in the CustOrder table. Note that when you reference a field name that appears in more than one table (such as CustomerNumber), you must precede the field name with the table name using the dot notation *tableName.attributeName* (Customer.CustomerNumber, for example). Also notice that single quotes are not used when specifying criteria for fields stored in the database as numeric data types. That is, to specify the condition for extracting orders with an order amount greater than $100, you write `OrderAmount > 100` rather than `OrderAmount > '100'`.

Inserting Records into a Database

The INSERT statement allows you to insert a new record into a table. You can use one of two formats for the INSERT statement. The first requires you to specify values for all fields in the table. SQL maps these values to table attributes (or columns) in order from left to right, starting from the leftmost column in the table.

```
INSERT INTO table VALUES (value1, value2, ... , valueN)
```

The second format allows you to specify the order of the fields. When you use this format, SQL maps the first value in the value list to the first attribute in the attribute list (which may or may not be the first column in the table), the second value in the value list to the second attribute in the attribute list, and so forth.

```
INSERT INTO table (attribute1, attribute2, ... , attributeN)  VALUES
(value1, value2, ... , valueN)
```

This book uses the first format when writing INSERT statements. To use this format, you must know the order of the fields in the underlying table. For example, the order of the fields in the Customer table in Figure 14-8 is CustomerNumber, FirstName, LastName, City, State, and PhoneNumber. A statement that inserts a new customer record into this table is:

```
INSERT INTO Customer
VALUES ('51954', 'John', 'Doe', 'Miami', 'FL', '345-6789')
```

After the insert, the contents of the Customer table appear, as shown in Figure 14-9.

CustomerNumber	FirstName	LastName	City	State	PhoneNumber
13912	Eleanor	Doke	Atlanta	GA	123-4567
28570	Josh	Rebstock	Springfield	MO	987-6543
36409	Callie	Williams	Statesboro	GA	555-1234
70832	Caleb	Gilleon	Springfield	GA	876-5432
51954	John	Doe	Miami	FL	345-6789

Figure 14-9 Customer table after inserting a new record

Updating Records in a Database

To update records that already exist in a table, you use the UPDATE statement. The format of the UPDATE statement is:

```
UPDATE table
SET attribute1=value1, attribute2=value2, ..., attributeN=valueN
WHERE condition
```

In the SET clause, you assign values to each attribute that you wish to modify. The WHERE clause specifies to which record (or records) the UPDATE command applies. For example, suppose you want to change the values in the State column from the two-character postal code to the full state name. To make this change for all records that currently have the value 'GA' in the State column, you write:

```
UPDATE Customer SET State = 'Georgia' WHERE State = 'GA'
```

After the update, the contents of the Customer table appear as shown in Figure 14-10.

14

CustomerNumber	FirstName	LastName	City	State	PhoneNumber
13912	Eleanor	Doke	Atlanta	Georgia	123-4567
28570	Josh	Rebstock	Springfield	MO	987-6543
36409	Callie	Williams	Statesboro	Georgia	555-1234
70832	Caleb	Gilleon	Springfield	Georgia	876-5432
51954	John	Doe	Miami	FL	345-6789

Figure 14-10   Customer table after updating records

Deleting Records from a Database

The DELETE statement deletes records from the database. The format of the DELETE statement is:

```
DELETE FROM table WHERE condition
```

The WHERE clause specifies the condition(s) that determine the record (or records) to delete. Assuming the Customer table appears, as shown in Figure 14-10, a statement to delete records for all customers living in Georgia is:

```
DELETE FROM Customer WHERE State = 'Georgia'
```

Figure 14-11 shows the contents of the Customer table after the DELETE statement executes.

CustomerNumber	FirstName	LastName	City	State	PhoneNumber
28570	Josh	Rebstock	Springfield	MO	987-6543
51954	John	Doe	Miami	FL	345-6789

Figure 14-11   Customer table after deleting records

WRITING VB .NET PROGRAMS THAT INTERACT WITH A RELATIONAL DATABASE

The VB .NET Framework provides support for several database management systems, including Oracle, Microsoft Access, and Microsoft SQLServer. VB .NET **data providers** are used to connect to a database, execute commands, and retrieve results. The data provider for Microsoft Access databases is Microsoft.Jet.OLEDB.4.0.

Programs that interact with a Microsoft Access database use a number of classes contained within the **System.Data** and **System.Data.OleDb** namespaces. The **System.Data** namespace provides general capabilities for working with a database. The **System.Data.OleDb** namespace provides additional features designed to work with Microsoft Access. (OleDb stands for "object linking and embedding for database.") Table 14–1 describes the classes in these namespaces that are introduced in this section.

Table 14-1 Selected classes in the System.Data and System.Data.OleDb namespaces

Class	Description
DataRow	Represents a row of data in a data table
DataSet	Represents a set of database tables in memory
DataTable	Represents a single database table in memory
OleDbCommand	Executes an SQL statement against an Access database
OleDbConnection	Establishes a connection to an Access database
OleDbDataAdapter	Populates a data set and updates an Access database
OleDbException	Indicates that the data provider encountered an error

To better understand the purpose of these classes, consider the diagram shown in Figure 14–12. The actual database (or data source) resides on a physical device such as C:. A data connection links the database to a data adapter. The data adapter contains properties and methods that handle SQL SELECT, INSERT, UPDATE, and DELETE commands. The data adapter uses the results of a SELECT command to populate a data set. The data set, which resides in memory, has the same structure and is comprised of the same tables as the underlying data source. A data table is a memory-resident representation of a single table in the data source, and a data row is a memory-resident representation of a single row within a given table. When you modify the contents of a data set using the INSERT, UPDATE, or DELETE commands, the data adapter updates the data source to reflect the changes made to the data set.

14

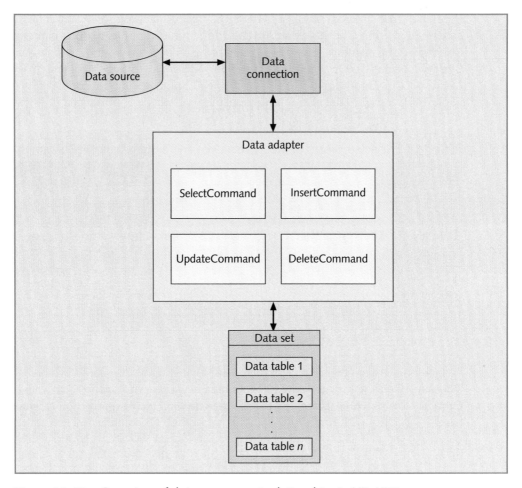

Figure 14-12 Overview of data component relationships in VB .NET

The `OleDbDataAdapter` class is designed to work with Access databases. The properties and methods of the `OleDbDataAdapter` class used in this section are shown in Table 14-2.

Table 14-2 Selected properties and methods of the OleDbDataAdapter class

Properties of the OleDbDataAdapter Class	Description
DeleteCommand	Identifies an SQL statement used to delete records from a data source
InsertCommand	Identifies an SQL statement used to insert records into a data source
SelectCommand	Identifies an SQL statement used to select records in a data source

Table 14-2 Selected properties and methods of the OleDbDataAdapter class (continued)

Properties of the OleDbDataAdapter Class	Description
UpdateCommand	Identifies an SQL statement used to update records in a data source
Methods of the OleDbDataAdapter Class	
Fill	Adds rows from the data source to a data set stored in memory

Understanding the Examples in this Section

The examples in this section build on the Programming Example presented at the end of Chapter 13. This example developed an integrated system for adding students and professors to a simulated database and producing lists of students and professors. Here, the application is limited to students only, but extends the functionality to allow for updating and deleting student records, as well as inserting and extracting them. The database design consists of only one table. As shown in Figure 14-13, the columns in the table reflect the attributes in the `Person`, `Student`, and `Phone` classes.

ID	Name	Address	Major	AreaCode	PhoneNumber	PhoneType
1234567	Edith	Batesville	English	417	1234567	Home
2345678	Josh	Springfield	Computer Science	912	9876543	Mobile
3456789	Richard	Statesboro	History	912	9991234	Office

Figure 14-13   The Student table

14

 In the Student table, ID, AreaCode, and PhoneNumber are designated as numeric fields.

In a three-tier design, the PD and GUI classes are unaware of how the DA class implements data persistence. The DA class handles all interaction with the database and carries out the tasks of inserting, updating, deleting, and extracting information. The GUI classes that capture and display information simply invoke the DA methods.

The `StudentDA` class in Chapter 13 introduced the `Initialize`, `GetAll`, `Find`, `AddNew`, and `Update` methods. You used these methods with an array list to simulate interaction with a database. In this chapter, you see how to modify these DA methods to work with a relational database. In addition, you learn how to create two new DA methods, `Delete` and `Terminate`.

Making the StudentDA Class Work with an Access Database

To make the `StudentDA` class work, you must first import the namespaces that provide the functionality to interact with a Microsoft Access database. Because ArrayLists will be used within the DA class to manipulate information extracted from the database, the `System.Collections` namespace is also imported.

```
Imports System.Data
Imports System.Data.OleDb
Imports System.Collections
```

Next, the `StudentDA` class declares a variable of the `OleDbConnection` class to represent a connection to the database. It also declares variables of type `ArrayList` and `Student` as intermediate storage areas for data that is written to or extracted from the database. Variables to capture individual Student attributes are also defined.

```
Public Class StudentDA
    'declare a connection
    Shared cnnStudent As OleDbConnection

    'declare array to hold intermediate data
    Private Shared students As New ArrayList

    'declare student reference variable
    Private Shared aStudent As Student

    'declare variables for Student attributes
    Shared id, areaCode, number As Integer
    Shared name, address, major, phoneType As String
    Shared aPhone As Phone
```

The Initialize Method

The `Initialize` method of the `StudentDA` class creates and opens the connection to the database. There are several ways to specify a connection. The approach in this book uses a connection string that identifies the data provider and the data source. The data provider for Access 2000 and later is Microsoft.Jet.OLEDB.4.0. The data source portion of the connection string specifies the name and location of the physical database file. Once the connection is created, you open it by invoking the `Open` method of the `OleDbConnection` class. Notice that the attempt to open the connection is enclosed within a Try-Catch block. If the attempt fails, the program displays an error message. Once the connection to the database is open, you can use SQL statements to perform a variety of database operations.

```
Public Shared Sub Initialize()
    'define strings for the data provider and data source file name
    Dim provider As String = "Microsoft.Jet.OLEDB.4.0; "
    Dim fileName As String = "Student.mdb"
    'create the connection instance
    cnnStudent = New OleDbConnection("Provider = " & provider & _
        "Data Source = " & fileName)
```

```
    Try   'Try to open the connection
        cnnStudent.Open()
    Catch ex As OleDbException
        MessageBox.Show("Unable to connect " & ex.ToString)
    End Try
End Sub
```

 The portion of the connection string specifying the data source will vary depending upon the name and location of the database file you are working with. By default, VB .NET looks for the database file in the bin subfolder of the folder that contains your application.

The GetAll Method

When working with a relational database, the **GetAll** method issues a SELECT command to retrieve all records from the database. Once a database connection is open, the general approach for executing a SELECT command within a VB .NET the program is as follows:

1. Create a data set instance.

2. Create a data adapter instance.

3. Define a **String** variable containing the SELECT statement.

4. Use the SelectCommand property of the data adapter to create a command instance and execute the command against the database.

5. Invoke the **Fill** method of the data adapter class to populate the data set.

The **GetAll** method uses this approach to extract all student records from the database. Accordingly, the **GetAll** method begins as follows:

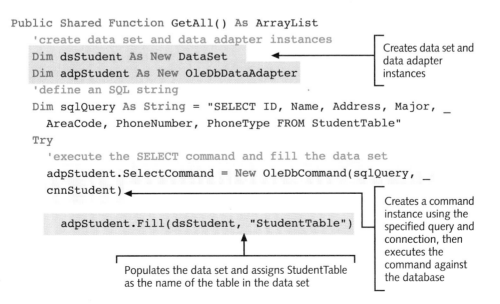

```
Public Shared Function GetAll() As ArrayList
    'create data set and data adapter instances
    Dim dsStudent As New DataSet
    Dim adpStudent As New OleDbDataAdapter
    'define an SQL string
    Dim sqlQuery As String = "SELECT ID, Name, Address, Major, _
        AreaCode, PhoneNumber, PhoneType FROM StudentTable"
    Try
        'execute the SELECT command and fill the data set
        adpStudent.SelectCommand = New OleDbCommand(sqlQuery, _
        cnnStudent)

        adpStudent.Fill(dsStudent, "StudentTable")
```

Creates data set and data adapter instances

Creates a command instance using the specified query and connection, then executes the command against the database

Populates the data set and assigns StudentTable as the name of the table in the data set

14

Next, the `GetAll` method checks to see if the SELECT command returned any records. This is determined by comparing the number of rows in StudentTable to zero. If the number of rows is greater than zero, the `GetAll` method uses a `For Each–Next` loop to process each row. For each row, the program obtains the values in each column, then uses these values to create a corresponding `Student` instance. The Student instance is then added to an array list. If the SELECT command does not return any records, the number of rows in the data set will be equal to zero. In this case, the `GetAll` method throws a `NotFoundException`. (`NotFoundException` is a custom exception class defined later in this chapter.) The `GetAll` method returns the array list to the calling program.

```vb
'if there are rows in the data table to process
If dsStudent.Tables("StudentTable").Rows.Count > 0 Then
    'declare a data row instance
    Dim studentRow As DataRow
    'clear the array list
    students.Clear()
    'process each row in the data table
    For Each studentRow In dsStudent.Tables("StudentTable").Rows
        'get the values for each column
        id = studentRow("ID")
        name = studentRow("Name")
        address = studentRow("Address")
        major = studentRow("Major")
        areaCode = studentRow("AreaCode")
        number = studentRow("PhoneNumber")
        phoneType = studentRow("PhoneType")
        'create a Student instance (complete with phone information)
        Dim aStudent As New Student(name, address, id, major)
        aStudent.AddAPhone(areaCode, number, phoneType)
        'add the Student instance to the array list
        students.Add(aStudent)
    Next
Else
    'no records in data table
    Throw New NotFoundException
End If
Catch ex As OleDbException
    MessageBox.Show("Error: " & ex.ToString)
End Try
Return students
End Function
```

Specifies the names of columns in the database

The Find Method

The **Find** method is nearly identical to the **GetAll** method, and uses the same general approach. The only difference is that the SELECT statement issued within the **Find** method returns at most one record (rather than many). Thus you do not need a **For Each–Next** to process the data set. The **Find** method is as follows:

```
Public Shared Function Find(ByVal studentID As Integer) As Student
    'create data set and data adapter instances
    Dim dsStudent As New DataSet
    Dim adpStudent As New OleDbDataAdapter
    'define an SQL string
    Dim sqlQuery As String = "SELECT ID, Name, Address, Major, _
      AreaCode, PhoneNumber, PhoneType FROM StudentTable _
      WHERE ID = " & studentID
    Try
    'execute the SELECT command and fill the data set
    adpStudent.SelectCommand = New OleDbCommand(sqlQuery, _
      cnnStudent)
    adpStudent.Fill(dsStudent, "StudentTable")
    'if there is a row in the data table to process
    If dsStudent.Tables("StudentTable").Rows.Count > 0 Then
        'declare a data row instance
        Dim studentRow As DataRow
        'get the data row from the data table
        studentRow = dsStudent.Tables("StudentTable").Rows(0)
        'get the values for each column
        id = studentRow("ID")
        name = studentRow("Name")
        address = studentRow("Address")
        major = studentRow("Major")
        areaCode = studentRow("AreaCode")
        number = studentRow("PhoneNumber")
        phoneType = studentRow("PhoneType")
        'create a Student instance (complete with phone information)
        aStudent = New Student(name, address, id, major)
        aStudent.AddAPhone(areaCode, number, phoneType)
    Else
        'no matching record found
        Throw New NotFoundException
    End If
Catch ex As OleDbException
    MessageBox.Show("Error: " & ex.ToString)
End Try
Return aStudent
End Function
```

Gets the single row of data from the data set

14

The AddNew Method

The purpose of the **AddNew** method is to insert a new record into the database. Unlike queries that extract information from a database, the INSERT command alters the database. To create and execute an INSERT command in VB. NET:

1. Create a data adapter instance.

2. Create an instance of the **OleDbCommand** class and assign this instance to the data adapter's InsertCommand property. As before, the **OleDbCommand** constructor requires two arguments: a **String** variable specifying the SQL statement, and a reference variable for the database connection.

3. Invoke the **ExecuteNonQuery** method of the **OleDbCommand** class to execute the INSERT command. The **ExecuteNonQuery** method changes the data in the database.

 In the next section, you'll see a similar approach to create and execute UPDATE or DELETE commands, substituting the UpdateCommand or DeleteCommand property for the SelectCommand property, respectively.

The **AddNew** method begins by getting the attribute values contained within the **Student** instance passed to it in the parameter list. It then defines an SQL statement to insert these values into the database. Recall that the SQL INSERT statement requires all values to be separated by commas and text values to be enclosed in single quotes. Although the INSERT statement in the **AddNew** method substitutes variable names for text values, the commas and single quotes must still be included. This accounts for the unusual appearance of the **sqlInsert** string.

Before attempting to insert the record, the **AddNew** method invokes the **Find** method to see if the database already contains a record for this student. If so, the **AddNew** method throws a **DuplicateException**. (**DuplicateException** is a custom exception defined later in this chapter.) Otherwise, the **AddNew** method catches the **NotFoundException** thrown by the **Find** method and creates and executes the INSERT command using the approach outlined earlier. The general form of the INSERT statement for this example is:

```
INSERT INTO StudentTable VALUES(id, 'name', 'address', 'major',
areaCode, number, 'phoneType')
```

where *id*, *name*, *address*, *major*, *areaCode*, *number*, and *phoneType* represent the values to insert into the table.

 Recall that in a SQL statement, you enclose string values in single quotes. In the Student table, ID, AreaCode, and PhoneNumber are defined as numeric fields. Thus, the values that correspond to these attributes are not enclosed in single quotes.

```
Public Shared Sub AddNew(ByVal aStudent As Student)
    'get student information from the Student instance
    id = aStudent.GetId
    name = aStudent.GetName
    address = aStudent.GetAddress
    major = aStudent.GetMajor
    areaCode = aStudent.GetPhone.GetAreaCode
    number = aStudent.GetPhone.GetNumber
    phoneType = aStudent.GetPhone.GetPhoneType
    'declare SQL statement
    Dim sqlInsert As String = "INSERT INTO StudentTable " & _
        "VALUES (" & id & ", '" & name & "', '" & address & "', '" _
                  & major & "', " & areaCode & ", " & number & ", _
                  '" & phoneType & " ')"
    Try
        'check to see if student with this id already exists
        'if so, throw a DuplicateException
        'otherwise, catch the NotFoundException and add the record
        Dim studentToFind As Student = Find(id)
        Throw New DuplicateException
    Catch notFound As NotFoundException
        Try
            'create a data adapter instance
            Dim adpStudent As New OleDbDataAdapter
            'create and execute the INSERT command
            adpStudent.InsertCommand = New OleDbCommand(sqlInsert,
            cnnStudent)
            adpStudent.InsertCommand.ExecuteNonQuery()
        Catch ex As OleDbException
            MessageBox.Show("Error: " & ex.ToString)
        End Try
    End Try
End Sub
```

14

The Update Method

The Update method is similar to the AddNew method. It also begins by getting the
attribute values contained within the Student instance passed to it in the parameter list.
It then defines an SQL statement to update the database with these values. The Update
method invokes the Find method to ensure that the record to be updated already exists in
the database. If so, it uses the approach outlined earlier for executing SQL statements that
alter the database. That is, after creating a data adapter instance, it creates an instance of the
OleDbCommand class, assigns this command instance to the UpdateCommand property of
the data adapter, and invokes the ExecuteNonQuery method to update the record in the
database. The Update method is as follows:

```
Public Shared Sub Update(ByVal aStudent As Student)
    'get values from the Student instance
    id = aStudent.GetId
    name = aStudent.GetName
    address = aStudent.GetAddress
    major = aStudent.GetMajor
    areaCode = aStudent.GetPhone.GetAreaCode
    number = aStudent.GetPhone.GetNumber
    phoneType = aStudent.GetPhone.GetPhoneType
    'define an SQL string
    Dim sqlUpdate As String = "UPDATE StudentTable " & _
        "SET Name = '" & name & "', Address = '" & address & "', _
        Major = '" & major & "', AreaCode = " & areaCode & ", _
        PhoneNumber = " & number & ", PhoneType = '" & phoneType & _
        "'  WHERE ID = " & id
    Try
        'locate the student record to be updated
        Dim studentToFind As Student = StudentDA.Find(id)
        'create a data adapter instance
        Dim adpStudent As New OleDbDataAdapter
        'create and execute the UPDATE command
        adpStudent.UpdateCommand = New OleDbCommand(sqlUpdate,
        cnnStudent)
        adpStudent.UpdateCommand.ExecuteNonQuery()
    Catch ex As OleDbException
        MessageBox.Show(ex.ToString)
    End Try
End Sub
```

The Delete Method

The **Delete** method is much like the **Update** method, but simpler. The **Delete** method receives a single parameter specifying the primary key of the record that is to be deleted. The **Delete** method defines an SQL DELETE statement, then invokes the **Find** method to confirm that the database contains this record. If so, it deletes the record from the database using the approach discussed earlier. The code for the **Delete** method is as follows:

```
Public Shared Sub Delete(ByVal id As Integer)
    'define an SQL string
    Dim sqlDelete As String = "DELETE FROM StudentTable WHERE ID _
    = " & id
    Try
        'locate the student record to be deleted
        Dim studentToFind As Student = StudentDA.Find(id)
        'create a data adapter instance
        Dim adpStudent As New OleDbDataAdapter
        'create and execute the DELETE command
        adpStudent.DeleteCommand = New OleDbCommand(sqlDelete, _
        cnnStudent)
        adpStudent.DeleteCommand.ExecuteNonQuery()
```

```
    Catch ex As OleDbException
        MessageBox.Show(ex.ToString)
    End Try
End Sub
```

The Terminate Method

Applications that open a connection to a database should also close the connection. The DA method `Terminate` performs this task by invoking the `Close` method of the `OleDbConnection` class. The `Terminate` method is as follows:

```
Public Shared Sub Terminate()
    Try
        'close the connection
        cnnStudent.Close()
    Catch ex As OleDbException
        MessageBox.Show("Unable to close connection")
    End Try
End Sub
```

The NotFoundException and DuplicateException Classes

The `StudentDA` method throws a `NotFoundException` when the `Find` and `GetAll` methods do not retrieve the desired record(s). StudentDA throws a `DuplicateException` when an attempt is made to insert a duplicate record. `NotFoundException` and `DuplicateException` are custom exception classes. The code for these classes is as follows:

```
Public Class NotFoundException
    Inherits Exception
    Public Sub New()
    End Sub
End Class

Public Class DuplicateException
    Inherits Exception
    Public Sub New()
        MyBase.New()
    End Sub
End Class
```

Recognizing the Benefits of the Three-Tier Design

With the `StudentDA` method in place, you are ready to create three-tier applications that interact with a relational database. The power of the three-tier design is that very little, if any, changes are required to the PD and GUI classes to make them work with the new `StudentDA` class.

14

Example 14-1: Retrieving records from a relational database

The first example demonstrates the use of the use of the DA methods to retrieve records from a database. The example integrates the **StudentDA** class with the **Person**, **Student**, and **Phone** PD classes and the **ListStudents** GUI class given in the Programming Example at the end of Chapter 13.

The **Student** and **Phone** PD classes require *no modification*. However, to facilitate manipulation of phone number information, a **GetPhone** accessor method is added to the **Person** class. Additionally, the accessibility modifier for all get accessors in the **Person** class is changed from Protected to Public. The revised **Person** PD class is as follows:

 Many method headers in this chapter are long and do not fit on a single printed line. However, when you type the code in your IDE, you should type the method headers as a single line. (Code other than method headers use an underscore as the continuation character to indicate that a statement continues on the next line.)

```
Public MustInherit Class Person
    Private name As String
    Private address As String
    Private phone As Phone
    ' parameterized constructor
    Protected Sub New(ByVal aName As String, ByVal anAddress
    As String)
        SetName(aName)
        SetAddress(anAddress)
    End Sub
    'get accessor methods
    Public Function GetName() As String        ◄─── Get accessor methods are
        Return name                                 now Public rather than
    End Function                                     Protected methods
    Public Function GetAddress() As String
        Return address
    End Function
    'get accessor method added for Chapter 14 examples
    Public Function GetPhone() As phone ◄
        Return phone
    End Function                                 A GetPhone accessor
    'set accessor methods                        method is added
    Protected Sub SetName(ByVal aName As String)
        name = aName
    End Sub
    Protected Sub SetAddress(ByVal anAddress As String)
        address = anAddress
    End Sub
    Public Sub AddAPhone(ByVal anAreaCode As Integer, ByVal
      aNumber As Integer, ByVal aPhoneType As String)
        phone = New Phone(anAreaCode, aNumber, aPhoneType)
```

```
        End Sub
    Public Function GetPhoneInfo() As String
        Dim info, formattedAreaCode, formattedNumber As String
        formattedAreaCode = phone.GetAreaCode().ToString("(###)")
        formattedNumber = phone.GetNumber().ToString("###-####")
        info = phone.GetPhoneType() & " " & formattedAreaCode & _
          " " & formattedNumber
        Return info
    End Function
End Class
```

The `ListStudents` GUI requires only two additional lines of code: one to connect to the database, and another to terminate the connection.

```
Public Class frmListStudents
    Inherits System.Windows.Forms.Form
    Private students As New ArrayList
    Private aStudent As Student

  'Windows Form Designer generated code

    Private Sub btnClose_Click(ByVal sender As System.Object,
      ByVal e As System.EventArgs) Handles btnClose.Click
        'disconnect from the database
        StudentDA.Terminate()  ◄──────  Code added to terminate the
        Me.Close()                       connection to the database
    End Sub

    Private Sub frmListStudents_Load(ByVal sender As Object,
      ByVal e As System.EventArgs) Handles MyBase.Load
        'connect to the database            Code added to connect
        StudentDA.Initialize()  ◄───────    to the database
        'Retrieve all student data from relational database
        students = StudentDA.GetAll()
        'Add information for each student to the text box
        Dim i As Integer
        For i = 0 To students.Count - 1
            aStudent = students(i)
            txtList.AppendText(aStudent.TellAboutSelf & ", ")
            txtList.AppendText(aStudent.GetPhoneInfo() & vbCrLf)
        Next
    End Sub
End Class
```

14

No other changes in the GUI are required. Although it is not necessary, for convenience a vertical scroll bar is added to the multiline text box. A sample output of the program is shown in Figure 14-14.

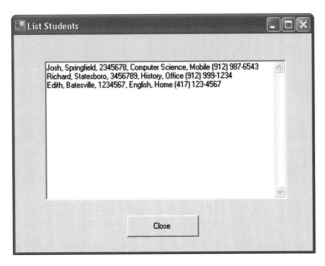

Figure 14-14 Sample output of the ListStudents program

Example 14-2: Adding records to a relational database

The second example demonstrates the use of the **StudentDA** class to add records to a relational database. The **Person**, **Student**, and **Phone** PD classes remain exactly as in the previous example.

The **AddStudent** GUI from the Programming Example at the end of Chapter 13 requires very little modification. As with the **ListStudents** GUI, statements must be added to connect and disconnect from the database. In this case, the connection to the database is established when the form initially loads; thus the statement that invokes the **Initialize** method is placed within an event handler for the Load event. Because the attempt to insert a record may generate a **DuplicateException**, the **AddStudent** GUI now includes a **Catch** block to handle this possibility.

```vb
Public Class frmStudent
    Inherits System.Windows.Forms.Form
    'Declare variables
    Private studName, address, major, phoneType As String
    Private id, areaCode, number As Integer
    Private aStudent As Student

    'Windows Form Designer generated code

    Private Sub btnAdd_Click(ByVal sender As System.Object,
      ByVal e As System.EventArgs) Handles btnAdd.Click
        'Get values from the GUI controls
        Try
            studName = txtName.Text
            address = txtAddress.Text
            id = System.Convert.ToInt32(txtID.Text)
            major = lstMajor.SelectedItem
            areaCode = System.Convert.ToInt16(txtAreaCode.Text)
            number = System.Convert.ToInt32(txtNumber.Text)
            If radHome.Checked Then
                phoneType = radHome.Text
            End If
            If radOffice.Checked Then
                phoneType = radOffice.Text
            End If
            If radMobile.Checked Then
                phoneType = radMobile.Text
            End If

            'Validate that the user has entered values for name
                and address
            'and made a selection in the list box
            If studName.Length = 0 Or address.Length = 0 Or _
                lstMajor.SelectedIndex = -1 Then
                MessageBox.Show("Please Enter All Data")
            Else
                'Data is valid -- create a Student instance
                aStudent = New Student(studName, address, id, major)
                'Add the student's phone
                aStudent.AddAPhone(areaCode, number, phoneType)
                'Add the student to the simulated database
                StudentDA.AddNew(aStudent)
                MessageBox.Show("Student Added")
                'Clear the form
                ClearForm()
            End If
```

14

```
        Catch duplicate As DuplicateException
            MessageBox.Show("Student With This ID Exists")
            'set the focus to the id text box
            txtID.Focus()                                  Code added to catch
        Catch ex As Exception                              DuplicateExceptions
            MessageBox.Show("You must enter numbers for Student ID,
            Area Code, and Number")
        End Try
    End Sub

    Private Sub btnClear_Click(ByVal sender As System.Object,
      ByVal e As System.EventArgs) Handles btnClear.Click
        ClearForm()
    End Sub

    Private Sub btnClose_Click(ByVal sender As System.Object,
      ByVal e As System.EventArgs) Handles btnClose.Click
        'disconnect from the database and close the form
        StudentDA.Terminate()                      Code added to terminate
        Me.Close()                                 the connection to the
    End Sub                                         database

    Private Sub ClearForm()
        txtName.Clear()
        txtAddress.Clear()
        txtID.Clear()
        lstMajor.SelectedIndex = -1
        txtAreaCode.Clear()
        txtNumber.Clear()                          Code added to establish
        radHome.Checked = True                     the connection to the
        txtName.Focus()                            database
    End Sub

    Private Sub frmStudent_Load(ByVal sender As Object,
      ByVal e As System.EventArgs) Handles MyBase.Load
        'connect to the database
        StudentDA.Initialize()
    End Sub
End Class
```

No other changes are needed. A sample output of the program is shown in Figure 14-15.

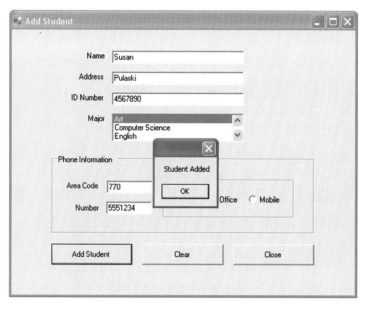

Figure 14-15   Sample output of the AddStudent program

PROGRAMMING EXAMPLE: UPDATING AND DELETING RECORDS IN A RELATIONAL DATABASE

In addition to retrieving records from and adding records to a database, applications often need to update or delete records already in the database. This Programming Example demonstrates how to update and delete records from a relational database in a three-tier design, using methods of the StudentDA class.

Problem Analysis, GUI Design, and Algorithm Design

The relational database for this example is the Student database presented earlier in chapter. This database contains the Student table shown in Figure 14-13. The PD tier consists of the **Person**, **Student**, and **Phone** classes used throughout this chapter. The **StudentDA** class comprises the DA tier. The GUI tier uses the form shown in Figure 14-16.

14

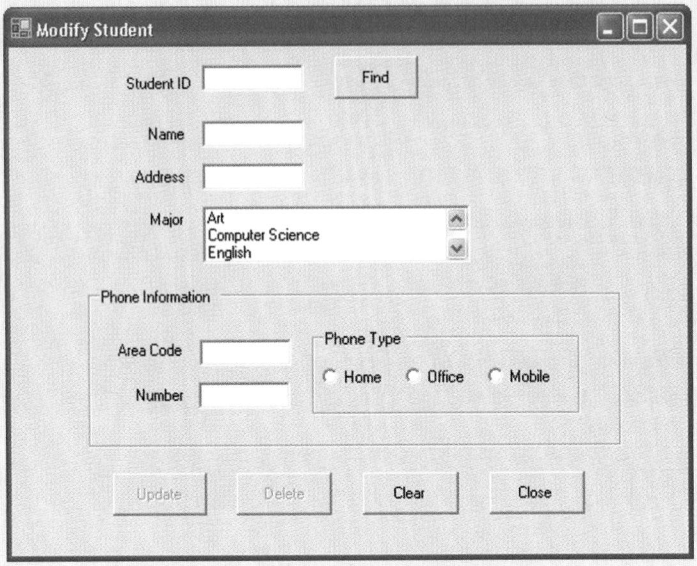

Figure 14-16 GUI for updating and deleting student records

A major benefit of three-tier design is that you can add new GUIs without having to make any changes in the PD and DA tiers. *The PD and DA classes are used without modification.* Thus, the only new code that is needed is the code behind the GUI. The GUI in Figure 14-16 accepts a student ID from the user. When the user clicks the Find button, the GUI invokes the **Find** method of the DA class to retrieve the corresponding student record from the database. The GUI then displays the student's information. Note that the user must click the Find button to retrieve a record before attempting to update or delete a record. The GUI indicates this by disabling (and, therefore, graying out) the Update and Delete buttons until after a student record is retrieved. Once the record is displayed, the read only property of the ID text box is set to true so that the user cannot change the value of the primary key. When the user clicks the Update or Delete button, the GUI invokes the corresponding DA method to perform the requested action. When a record is updated or deleted, the GUI displays an appropriate confirmation message. The GUI displays error messages when various exceptions are encountered. The complete UpdateStudent GUI program is as follows:

```
Public Class frmUpdate
    Inherits System.Windows.Forms.Form
    'declare variables
    Private studName, address, major, phoneType As String
    Private id, areaCode, number As Integer
    Private aStudent As Student

    'Windows Form Designer generated code
```

```
Private Sub btnClose_Click(ByVal sender As System.Object,
   ByVal e As System.EventArgs) Handles btnClose.Click
     'disconnect from the database and close the form
     StudentDA.Terminate()
     Me.Close()
End Sub

Private Sub ClearForm()
     txtName.Clear()
     txtAddress.Clear()
     txtId.Clear()
     lstMajor.SelectedIndex = -1
     txtAreaCode.Clear()
     txtNumber.Clear()
     radHome.Checked = True
     txtId.Focus()
     'disable update and delete buttons
     btnUpdate.Enabled = False
     btnDelete.Enabled = False
     'turn off read only property for id text box
     txtId.ReadOnly = False
End Sub

Private Sub frmUpdate_Load(ByVal sender As Object,
   ByVal e As System.EventArgs) Handles MyBase.Load
     'connect to the database
     StudentDA.Initialize()
End Sub

Private Sub btnFind_Click(ByVal sender As System.Object,
   ByVal e As System.EventArgs) Handles btnFind.Click
     'declare variables
     Dim studentID As Integer
     Dim aStudent As Student
     Try
          'get student id from the GUI
          studentID = System.Convert.ToInt32(txtId.Text)
          'locate the student in the database
          aStudent = StudentDA.Find(studentID)
          'set the name and address text boxes
          txtName.Text = aStudent.GetName
          txtAddress.Text = aStudent.GetAddress
          'select major in list box
          lstMajor.SelectedIndex =
          lstMajor.FindString(aStudent.GetMajor)
          'set the area code and phone number text boxes
          txtAreaCode.Text = aStudent.GetPhone.GetAreaCode
          txtNumber.Text = aStudent.GetPhone.GetNumber
```

14

```
                    'set the appropriate radio button for the phone type
                    Dim phoneType As String
                    'trim trailing blanks
                    phoneType = Trim(aStudent.GetPhone.GetPhoneType)
                    If phoneType = "Home" Then
                        radHome.Checked = True
                    ElseIf phoneType = "Office" Then
                        radOffice.Checked = True
                    Else
                        radMobile.Checked = True
                    End If
                    'enable the update and delete buttons
                    btnUpdate.Enabled = True
                    btnDelete.Enabled = True
                    'set the read only property of id text box to true
                    txtId.ReadOnly = True
                Catch notFound As NotFoundException
                    MessageBox.Show("Student Not Found")
                    ClearForm()
                End Try
        End Sub

        Private Sub btnUpdate_Click(ByVal sender As System.Object, _
          ByVal e As System.EventArgs) Handles btnUpdate.Click
            Try
                'get values from the GUI
                studName = txtName.Text
                address = txtAddress.Text
                id = System.Convert.ToInt32(txtId.Text)
                major = lstMajor.SelectedItem
                areaCode = System.Convert.ToInt32(txtAreaCode.Text)
                number = System.Convert.ToInt32(txtNumber.Text)
                If radHome.Checked Then
                    phoneType = radHome.Text
                End If
                If radOffice.Checked Then
                    phoneType = radOffice.Text
                End If
                If radMobile.Checked Then
                    phoneType = radMobile.Text
                End If

                'validate that the user has entered values for name and
                address
                If studName.Length = 0 Or address.Length = 0 Then
```

```vbnet
                    MessageBox.Show("Please Enter All Data")
                ElseIf areaCode < 0 Or areaCode > 999 Then
                    MessageBox.Show("Area Code must be a number > 0 and
                    < 999")
                Else
                    'data is valid -- create a Student instance
                    aStudent = New Student(studName, address, id,
                    major)
                    'add the student's phone
                    aStudent.AddAPhone(areaCode, number, phoneType)
                    'update the student record
                    StudentDA.Update(aStudent)
                    'display confirmation message and clear the form
                    MessageBox.Show("Student Updated")
                    ClearForm()
                End If
            Catch notFound As NotFoundException
                MessageBox.Show("Student Not Found")
            Catch ex As Exception
                MessageBox.Show("You must enter numbers for id, area
                code, and number")
            End Try
        End Sub

        Private Sub btnDelete_Click(ByVal sender As System.Object,
          ByVal e As System.EventArgs) Handles btnDelete.Click
            Try
                'get student id from the GUI
                id = System.Convert.ToInt32(txtId.Text)
                'delete the student record
                StudentDA.Delete(id)
                'display confirmation message and clear the form
                MessageBox.Show("Student Deleted")
                ClearForm()
            Catch notFound As NotFoundException
                MessageBox.Show("Student Not Found")
            End Try
        End Sub

        Private Sub btnClear_Click(ByVal sender As System.Object,
          ByVal e As System.EventArgs) Handles btnClear.Click
            ClearForm()
        End Sub
End Class
```

14

INTRODUCING ASP.NET

Reviewing Web Basics

Web pages employ a standard language called Hypertext Markup Language (HTML) telling browsers how to display the pages. This standard enables browsers to display the Web pages on a variety of computing platforms. The Web is based on the client-server architecture you have seen in previous chapters. When a client requests a Web page, the server locates the page and returns it to the client computer, where a browser displays it.

Understanding URLs

Every Web page has an address describing its location. This address is called a **Uniform Resource Locator** (URL).

Consider the URL shown in Figure 14-17:

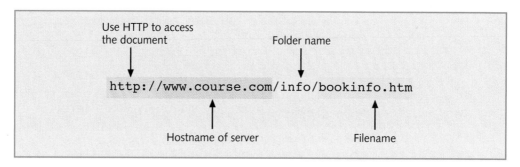

Figure 14-17 Example URL

"http:// " tells the system that Hypertext Transfer Protocol (HTTP) will be used to access the HTML document.

"*www.course.com*" is the name of the server that has the document. This server is referred to as the **host computer** or simply **host**. In this example, the name of the HTML file is "bookinfo.htm," and it is located in the info folder.

Working with HTML

HTML is a descriptive language, not a procedural language. HTML tells a browser how to display a page, but lacks procedural statements. Previous versions of ASP allowed you to include script code with HTML to produce interactivity. Now, Web pages developed using ASP.NET can contain HTML plus related files containing code to provide interactivity.

Web pages are actually files containing HTML code and have an extension of .htm or .html. HTML contains tags that define the format of a Web page. They indicate text that should appear bold or italic, or as a heading or part of a paragraph. HTML tags consist of a left angle bracket (<), the tag name, and a right angle bracket (>). Many tags come in pairs, a start tag and an end tag. The end tag uses a slash (/) to differentiate it from a start tag, and tags may have attributes. HTML is not case sensitive. ASP.NET generates lowercase HTML code.

HTML documents are text files that can be created using any text editor such as Notepad. ASP.NET generates HTML for you. Table 14-3 provides a few common HTML tags and their usage, and Example 14-3 illustrates how to use some of these tags.

Table 14-3 Common HTML tags

Tag	Description
`<html>`, `</html>`	Start, end of document
`<!--`, `-->`	comment
`<head>`, `</head>`	Head element
`<body>`, `</body>`	Body element
`<p>`, `</p>`	Paragraph element
`<h1> </h1>`... `<h6> </h6>`	Header element with six font sizes; h1 is the largest
`<a>`, `</a>`	Anchor element (used to insert links)
`<i> </i>`	Italic
`<b> </b>`	Bold
`<big> </big>`	Font size one size larger than the current font
`<small> </small>`	Font size one size smaller than the current font
` `	Line break (carriage return)

14

Example 14-3: Using HTML to create a Web page

```
1. <html>
2.    <!-- this is a comment -->
3.    <head>
4.       <title>This Appears on the Browser Title Bar</title>
5.       <h1 align=center>this is a heading with h1 font</h1>
6.       <h2 align=center>this is a heading with h2 smaller
         font</h2>
```

```
7.      <h6 align=center>this is a heading with h6 smaller
        font</h6>
8.   </head>

9.   <body>
10.     <p align=center>
11.        the body of the page begins here <br>
12.     </p>
13.     <p>
14.        <b>this is a bold paragraph</b> <br>
15.        <small><i> smaller italicized font </i>
           </small> <br>
16.        <big> larger non-italicized font </big> <br>
17.     </p>
18.   </body>
19. </html>
```

Sample Run:

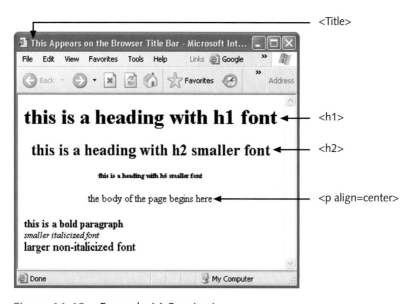

Figure 14-18   Example 14-3 output

Discussion:

The line numbers in examples are added for identification purposes and are not part of the code. The HTML code in this example was created using Notepad and saved with an extension of .htm. To display the output, you open the file with a browser.

Line 1 contains `<html>`, which indicates the beginning of the HTML document, and line 19 contains the ending tag `</html>`.

Line 2 illustrates a comment which is ignored by the browser.

Lines 3 through 8 outline the statements comprising the heading portion of the Web page. Generally you separate a page into a heading section and body section.

Line 4 contains a title, which is displayed in the browser's title bar.

Lines 5, 6, and 7 contain heading statements illustrating different font sizes.

Lines 9 through 18 outline the statements comprising the body of the page. Note the body contains one or more paragraphs. In this example, lines 10 through 12 contain the first paragraph, and lines 13 through 17 contain the second.

Line 10, in addition to indicating the beginning of a paragraph, contains an attribute specifying center alignment for this paragraph.

Line 11 contains data to be displayed followed by the line break tag.

Line 14 in the second paragraph also contains data to be displayed, however, because the second paragraph did not specify center alignment, the data is aligned left. Line 14 contains the bold tag which bolds the displayed data.

Line 15 also displays data and illustrates smaller italicized font.

Line 16 illustrates larger, non–italicized font.

Creating ASP.NET Projects

14

The .NET Framework provides tools to develop both Windows and Web applications. Web development using ASP.NET is quite similar to developing GUI applications for Windows.

 Microsoft's Internet Information Services (IIS) resides on servers running Microsoft Web applications. During development you will generally use the same machine as both a Web client and a Web server; therefore, you must have IIS installed on your machine. IIS is included with Windows 2000 and XP; however, it may not be installed. Please refer to Appendix A: Setting Up an IIS Server if you need to install IIS.

Previous versions of ASP mixed HTML tags and programming script together, which added complexity to both development and maintenance. In contrast, ASP.NET separates procedural code from the Web form (HTML) code. The Web form file has a suffix of .aspx, and the code has the familiar suffix of .vb. The .vb file is called the **code-behind file**.

Creating Your First ASP.NET Application

In Chapter 2 you created a Windows Application that displayed the form shown in Figure 14-19. In this section, you create a similar form using ASP.NET.

Figure 14-19   Output from Chapter 2 FormDemo Project

1. First, launch Visual Studio .NET.

2. If it is not already selected, click the **Start Page** tab in the document window, and then click the **Projects** tab.

3. Click the **New Project** button. The New Project dialog box appears.

4. In the New Project dialog box, click the **Visual Basic Projects** folder in the Project Types pane. Click the **ASP.NET Web Application** icon in the Templates pane.

5. If this is your first Web application, the Location text box contains the default project URL name http://localhost/WebApplication1. The default name of the server on your machine is localhost. Delete the default name and type **http://localhost/ASPDemo** in the Location text box.

6. Click **OK**. If necessary, display and pin the **Toolbox**, **Solution Explorer**, and **Properties** windows. Your screen should appear similar to Figure 14-20.

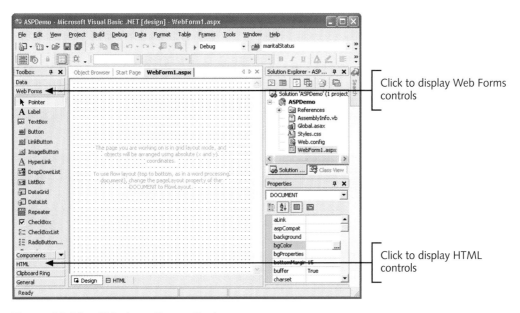

Figure 14-20   Windows Forms Designer

7. Select the form and change its Title property to **"My First Web Form"** and its bgColor property to **yellow**.

8. In the Solution Explorer window, change the name of the .aspx file to **ASPDemo.aspx**. Note the Toolbox has a button to display either Web Forms controls or HTML controls, as shown in Figure 14-20. This example uses Web Forms controls.

 You can use either Web Forms or HTML Controls or a combination. HTML controls are included to correspond to the HTML Tags.

14

9. Select the **Web Forms** controls in the Toolbox, and double-click **Label** to add a label to the form. Drag the new Label to the center of the form. Change the Label's ID property to **lblWelcome**, its Text property to **Welcome to ASP.NET**, and its ForeColor property to **red**.

10. Click the **Font** property list arrow, and then click **Large**. Resize the Label to display this larger text without wrapping, if necessary.

11. Double-click **Button** in the Toolbox to add a Button control to the form. Reposition it so that it is directly beneath the Label. Change the Button's ID property it to **btnPushMe** and its Text property to **Push Me**.

12. Double-click the **Button** to open the Code window. Add the following line of code to the Button's click event procedure named **btnPushMe_Click**:

```
lblWelcome.Text = "Thanks for Using ASP.NET"
```

13. Save your work and click the **Run** icon. Your output is displayed in a browser window, and should appear similar to Figure 14-21. After clicking the Push Me Button, your output should be similar to Figure 14-22. Figure 14-23 lists the HTML statements generated by ASP for ASPDemo.

 This chapter includes some code examples in figures so you can examine the code as it appears in the IDE with line numbers without lengthening the chapter unnecessarily.

Figure 14-21   Output from ASPDemo

Figure 14-22   Output from ASPDemo after clicking Button

Click to display your form

Click to display the HTML code

14

Figure 14-23   ASP-generated HTML code for ASPDemo

Temperature Converter Using ASP.NET

Chapter 9 included several examples of Console Applications that converted Fahrenheit temperatures to Celsius. In this section, you develop an interactive Web-based temperature converter using ASP.NET.

Example 14-4: Converting temperatures

The form used for this example is shown in Figure 14-24. This form has three Labels, two Textboxes, and three Buttons.

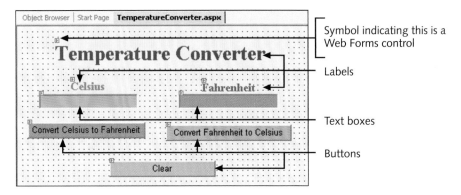

Figure 14-24   Example 14-4 form design

Discussion:

The code behind this form is shown in Figure 14-25. There are three event procedures, one for each Button.

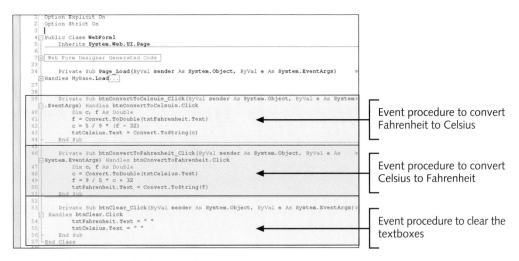

Figure 14-25   Example 14-4 code

The event procedure to convert Fahrenheit to Celsius is shown in lines 39 through 44. Line 40 declares two `Double` variables, line 41 retrieves the contents of the Fahrenheit TextBox, converts the value to `Double`, and assigns it to variable `f`. Recall that the Text property of TextBoxes contains `String` data. Line 42 computes the Celsius equivalent temperature and assigns the result to variable `c`. Line 43 then converts the contents of `c` to `String` and assigns the result to the Text property of the Fahrenheit TextBox.

The event procedure to convert Celsius to Fahrenheit is shown in lines 46 through 51. The logic of this procedure is similar to the previous one that converts Fahrenheit to Celsius.

The Clear Button click event procedure is listed in lines 53 through 57. Line 54 populates the Text property of the Fahrenheit TextBox with spaces, and line 55 does the same for the Celsius TextBox.

Sample Run:

Figure 14-26 shows the output of the code shown in Figure 14-25.

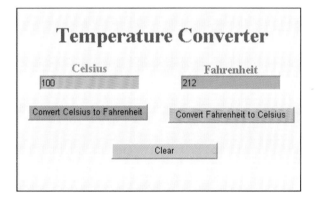

Figure 14-26 Example 14-4 output

14

Computing a Loan Payment using ASP.NET

The formula for computing the monthly payment for a loan is: paymentAmount = (amountOfLoan * (apr / 12)) / (1–1/(1 + apr/12) ^ months) where apr is the annual percentage interest rate (represented as a number between 0 and 1), ^ means raise to the power, and months is the number of months of the loan. In this section, you design a Web-based application to accept amountOfLoan, rate, and months, and then compute and display the monthly payment amount.

Example 14-5: Computing a loan payment

The form used for this example is shown in Figure 14-27. This form has six Labels, two Textboxes, two Buttons, and a RadioButtonList. This list is similar to adding RadioButtons to a GroupBox. You use a RadioButtonList to create a set of radio buttons. Each radio button is referenced using its index.

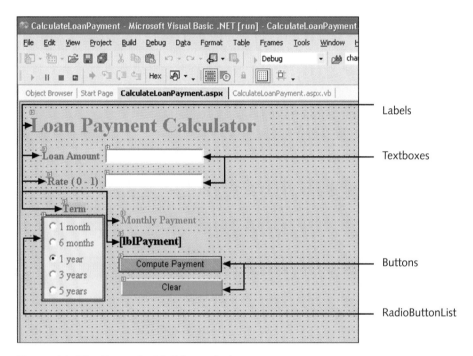

Figure 14-27   Example 14-5 form design

Discussion:

The code behind this form is shown in Figure 14-28. There are two event procedures, one for each Button, plus a private procedure written to determine the term of the loan.

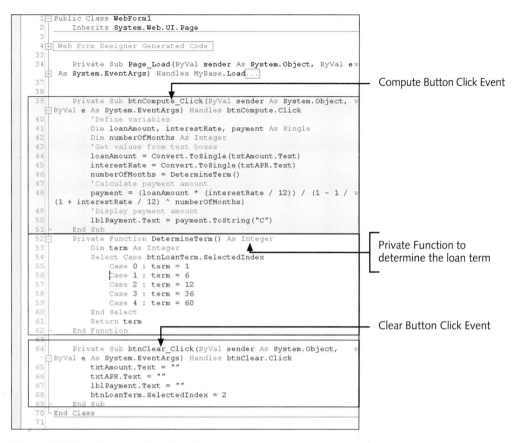

```
 1 ⊟ Public Class WebForm1
 2        Inherits System.Web.UI.Page
 3
 4 ⊞  Web Form Designer Generated Code
33
34        Private Sub Page_Load(ByVal sender As System.Object, ByVal e⤶
   ⊞  As System.EventArgs) Handles MyBase.Load...
37
38
39        Private Sub btnCompute_Click(ByVal sender As System.Object, ⤶
   ⊟ ByVal e As System.EventArgs) Handles btnCompute.Click
40            'Define variables
41            Dim loanAmount, interestRate, payment As Single
42            Dim numberOfMonths As Integer
43            'Get values from text boxes
44            loanAmount = Convert.ToSingle(txtAmount.Text)
45            interestRate = Convert.ToSingle(txtAPR.Text)
46            numberOfMonths = DetermineTerm()
47            'Calculate payment amount
48            payment = (loanAmount * (interestRate / 12)) / (1 - 1 / ⤶
   (1 + interestRate / 12) ^ numberOfMonths)
49            'Display payment amount
50            lblPayment.Text = payment.ToString("C")
51        End Sub
52 ⊟      Private Function DetermineTerm() As Integer
53            Dim term As Integer
54            Select Case btnLoanTerm.SelectedIndex
55                Case 0 : term = 1
56                Case 1 : term = 6
57                Case 2 : term = 12
58                Case 3 : term = 36
59                Case 4 : term = 60
60            End Select
61            Return term
62        End Function
63
64        Private Sub btnClear_Click(ByVal sender As System.Object, ⤶
   ⊟ ByVal e As System.EventArgs) Handles btnClear.Click
65            txtAmount.Text = ""
66            txtAPR.Text = ""
67            lblPayment.Text = ""
68            btnLoanTerm.SelectedIndex = 2
69        End Sub
70 ⊔ End Class
71
```

— Compute Button Click Event

— Private Function to determine the loan term

— Clear Button Click Event

Figure 14-28   Example 14-5 code

14

The event procedure to compute the loan payment is shown in lines 39 through 51. Lines 41 and 42 declare the variables. Lines 44 and 45 retrieve the loan amount and annual percentage interest rate. Line 46 invokes the private procedure named DetermineTerm listed at lines 52 through 62. This procedure determines which of the five radio buttons are selected by evaluating the SelectedIndex property employing a `Select Case` statement.

The Clear Button click event procedure is listed in lines 64 through 69. Line 65 populates the Text property of the Amount TextBox with spaces, line 66 does the same for the APR TextBox, and line 67 for the Payment label. Line 68 selects the third radio button (1 year term).

Sample Run:

Figure 14–29 shows the output of the code shown in Figure 14–28.

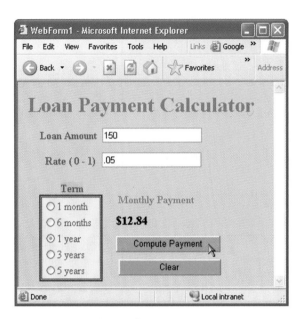

Figure 14-29   Example 14-5 output

Using ASP.NET Validation Controls

As you have seen, data validation represents an important part of any application that accepts user input. ASP.NET includes validation controls that facilitate adding data validation to an application. Table 14-4 shows the ASP.NET validation controls and describes how to use them.

Table 14-4   Validation Controls

Validation Control	Description
RequiredFieldValidator	Requires that a field have an entry
CompareValidator	Compares data to a specified value or the value of another control
RangeValidator	Checks to see whether a value is between a lower and upper boundary
RegularExpressionValidator	Checks that the entry matches a pattern defined by a regular expression
CustomValidator	Creates custom code for validation
ValidationSummary	Displays a summary of all the validation controls on the page

These controls appear in the Toolbox and can be placed on the Web page just as any other controls. Their properties can be accessed in the Properties window. To use the RequiredFieldValidator control, for example, place the control on the form, set its ControlToValidate property to the control you want to check for a value, and then set its ErrorMessage property to the text you want to display if the validation is triggered. A common use is to ensure text boxes are not left blank. However, it can also be used with controls such as radio button lists if you require the user to make a selection.

The CompareValidator control compares the input value of a control such as a text box to the value of another control or a constant value. For example, if the user must enter or select two dates, and the second date has to be larger than the first date, use the CompareValidation control. Specify the input control to validate with the ControlToValidate property and set either the ControlToCompare or ValueToCompare, depending on whether you want to compare to the value of a control or a constant value. You can use pattern-matching characters for constants to validate input patterns such as e-mail addresses and phone numbers.

The RangeValidator control provides MinimumValue and MaximumValue properties to check that a control's input is within the range. It also has a Type property to specify the data type of the data to be compared. As in the previous validation controls, you need to specify the ControlToValidate and ErrorMessage properties.

Custom validation controls let you provide your own data validation logic. To create the validation logic, provide a handler for the ServerValidate event. Set the control's ClientValidationFunction to the name of the function that contains the code logic. Depending on the particular validation, you may or may not need to set the ControlToValidate property.

You can use multiple validation controls for the same Web control. For example, you can check to see that the user enters data and that the values fall within a range. Use the RequiredFieldValidator and the CompareValidator and assign the ControlToValidate properties of both validation controls to the control you are checking.

The next example expands the Loan Payment Calculation example to include ASP.NET validation controls.

14

Example 14-6: Computing a loan payment with validation controls

This example adds two RequiredFieldValidator and two RangeValidator controls to the Loan Payment Calculator developed in the previous example. The first RequiredFieldValidator is associated with the Loan Amount TextBox. Its ControlToValidate property is set to the name of the Loan Amount TextBox (txtAmount) and its ErrorMessage property to "Amount is Required."

The second RequiredFieldValidator is associated with the Rate TextBox. Its ControlToValidate property is set to the name of the Rate TextBox (txtAPR) and its ErrorMessage property to "Rate is Required."

The two RangeValidator controls are also associated with the Loan Amount and Rate TextBoxes. The first RangeValidator has its ControlToValidate property set to txtAmount, its ErrorMessage property to "Amount must be 1 to 999999," its MinimumValue to 1, and its MaximumValue to 999999.

Similarly, the second RangeValidator has its ControlToValidate property set to txtAPR, its ErrorMessage property to "Rate must be .001 to 1," its MinimumValue to .001, and its MaximumValue to 1. Figure 14-30 shows the form design for this example.

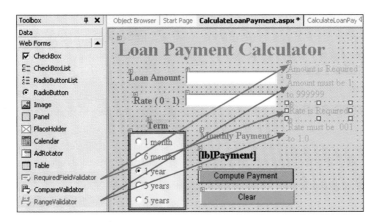

Figure 14-30 Example 14-6 form design

Sample Runs:

Figure 14-31 shows the form when the amount and rate are missing. Figure 14-32 shows the form when an invalid amount is entered. Figure 14-33 shows the form when an invalid rate is entered.

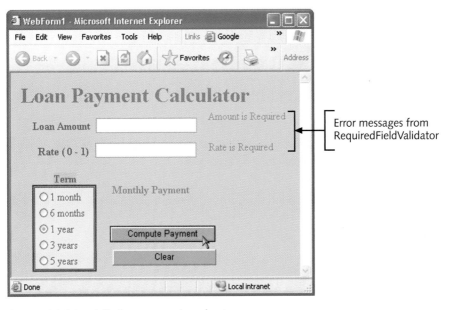

Figure 14-31   Missing amount and rate

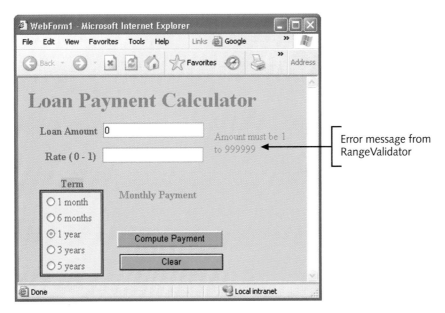

Figure 14-32   Invalid amount

14

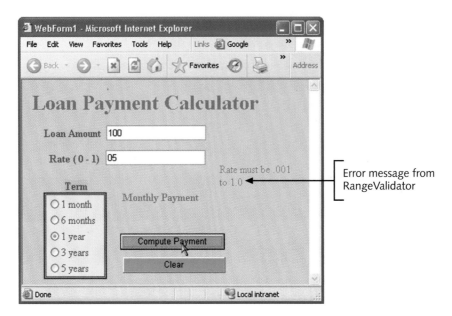

Figure 14-33   Invalid rate

PROGRAMMING EXAMPLE: ELECTRICITY BILLING

This Programming Example deploys the Electricity Billing Programming Example at the end of Chapter 10 as an ASP.NET Web-based application. The Chapter 10 design included a class named `ElectricBill` to represent electricity bills, a Server module to compute sales tax, and a Client to instantiate `ElectricBill`, invoke its methods to compute the electricity charge and sales tax, and then display the electricity consumed, electricity charge, sales tax, and total bill.

This example copies the `ElectricBill` class from Chapter 10, then copies and renames the Server module to TaxModule. In this example, the client is the ASP.NET GUI shown in Figure 14-34, which inputs and validates Customer Number, Previous, and Current Meter Readings. Validator Controls are employed to validate the data. Once valid data is entered, `ElectricBill` is instantiated, sales tax is computed, and the billing information is displayed.

Object Browser | Start Page | **WebForm1.aspx** * | WebForm1.aspx.vb | ElectricBill.vb | TaxModule.vb ◀ ▶ ✕

ASP Programming Example: Compute Electric Bill

Customer Number: [   ]   Customer Number Required

Previous Meter Reading: [   ]   Previous Reading Required
Previous Reading Must be
Between 0 and 99999

Current Meter Reading: [   ]   Current Reading Required
Current reading not > previous
Current Reading Must be
between 1 and 99999

KWH Used: [lblKWHUsed]

Electricity Charge: [lblElectricityCharge]

Sales Tax: [lblSalesTax]

Total Amount: [lblTotalAmount]

[Submit   ]   [Clear   ]

◻ Design   ⊞ HTML

Figure 14-34   Electricity billing form design

Problem Analysis and Algorithm Design

Figure 14–35 shows the class diagram for the **ElectricBill** class.

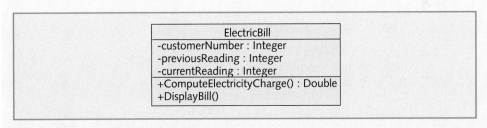

ElectricBill
-customerNumber : Integer
-previousReading : Integer
-currentReading : Integer
+ComputeElectricityCharge() : Double
+DisplayBill()

Figure 14-35   ElectricBill class diagram

The class definition for `ElectricBill` includes the three attributes, a parameterized constructor, standard accessor methods, plus the custom method `ComputeElectricityCharge`. `DisplayBill` was removed from the Chapter 10 class because the bill is displayed on the GUI in this example. The Server used in this example is an exact copy of the one in the Chapter 10 Programming Example; however, its name has been changed to `TaxModule`.

Data Validation

- Customer Number is required.
- Previous Reading is required and must be in the range 0–99999.
- Current Reading is required and must be in the range 0–99999. It also must be greater than or equal to the Previous Reading.

Formulas   Subtract the previous meter reading from the current meter reading to obtain the kwh consumed. The charge for electricity uses the following table:

KWH Consumed	Rate per KWH
< 500	.05
500—1000	$25 + .055 for amount over 500
> 1000	$52.50 + .06 for amount over 1000

Complete Program Listing

ElectricBill Class

```
Public Class ElectricBill
    Private customerNumber As Integer
    Private previousReading As Integer
    Private currentReading As Integer
    Dim electricityCharge As Double

    Public Sub New(ByVal custNo As Integer, ByVal prevReading As
    Integer, ByVal currReading As Integer)
        SetCustomerNumber(custNo)
        SetPreviousReading(prevReading)
        SetCurrentReading(currReading)
    End Sub
    'get accessor methods
    Public Function GetCustomerNumber() As Integer
        Return customerNumber
    End Function
```

```vb
    Public Function GetPreviousReading() As Integer
        Return previousReading
    End Function
    Public Function GetCurrentReading() As Integer
        Return currentReading
    End Function
    'set accessor methods
    Public Sub SetCustomerNumber(ByVal custNo As Integer)
        customerNumber = custNo
    End Sub
    Public Sub SetPreviousReading(ByVal prevReading As Integer)
        previousReading = prevReading
    End Sub
    Public Sub SetCurrentReading(ByVal currReading As Integer)
        currentReading = currReading
    End Sub

    Public Function ComputeElectricityCharge() As Double
        Dim amount As Double
        Dim kwh As Integer = GetCurrentReading() - _
        GetPreviousReading()
        Select Case kwh
            Case Is < 500
                amount = kwh * 0.05
            Case 500 To 1000
                amount = 25 + (kwh - 500) * 0.055
            Case Is > 1000
                amount = 52.5 + (kwh - 1000) * 0.06
        End Select
        amount = Math.Round(amount, 2)
        Return amount
    End Function

End Class
```

TaxModule

```vb
Option Strict On
Option Explicit On
Module TaxModule
    Public Function ComputeSalesTax(ByVal amount As Double)
    As Double
        Const SALES_TAX_RATE As Double = 0.085
        Dim salesTax As Double
        salesTax = SALES_TAX_RATE * amount
        salesTax = Math.Round(salesTax, 2)
        Return salesTax
    End Function
End Module
```

14

Code Behind ASP Programming Example

Figure 14-36 shows the code behind the ASP Programming Example.

```
1   Option Strict On
2   Option Explicit On
3 □ Public Class WebForm1
4       Inherits System.Web.UI.Page
5
6 ⊞  Web Form Designer Generated Code
47
48      Private Sub Page_Load(ByVal sender As System.Object, ByVal e
    □ As System.EventArgs) Handles MyBase.Load
49          'Put user code to initialize the page here
50  └     End Sub
51
52      Private Sub btnSubmit_Click(ByVal sender As System.Object,
    □ ByVal e As System.EventArgs) Handles btnSubmit.Click
53          Dim electricBill As ElectricBill
54          Dim electricityCharge, salesTax, totalAmount As Double
55          Dim customerNo, previousReading, currentReading, kwhUsed
    As Integer
56          customerNo = Convert.ToInt32(txtCustomerNo.Text)
57          previousReading = Convert.ToInt32(txtPreviousReading.
    Text)
58          currentReading = Convert.ToInt32(txtCurrentReading.Text)
59          electricBill = New ElectricBill(customerNo,
    previousReading, currentReading)
60          electricityCharge = electricBill.
    ComputeElectricityCharge()
61          salesTax = TaxModule.ComputeSalesTax(electricityCharge)
62          totalAmount = electricityCharge + salesTax
63          kwhUsed = currentReading - previousReading
64          lblKWHUsed.Text = kwhUsed.ToString()
65          lblElectricityCharge.Text = electricityCharge.ToString("
    C")
66          lblSalesTax.Text = salesTax.ToString("C")
67          lblTotalAmount.Text = totalAmount.ToString("C")
68          lblKWHUsedLabel.Visible = True
69          lblElectricityChargeLabel.Visible = True
70          lblSalesTaxLabel.Visible = True
71          lblTotalAmountLabel.Visible = True
72  └     End Sub
73
74      Private Sub btnClear_Click(ByVal sender As System.Object,
    □ ByVal e As System.EventArgs) Handles btnClear.Click
75          txtCustomerNo.Text = ""
76          txtPreviousReading.Text = ""
77          txtCurrentReading.Text = ""
78          lblKWHUsed.Text = ""
79          lblElectricityCharge.Text = ""
80          lblSalesTax.Text = ""
81          lblTotalAmount.Text = ""
82          lblKWHUsedLabel.Visible = False
83          lblElectricityChargeLabel.Visible = False
84          lblSalesTaxLabel.Visible = False
85          lblTotalAmountLabel.Visible = False
86
87  └     End Sub
88 └End Class
```

Figure 14-36   Code behind ASP Programming Example

Sample Run

Figure 14–37 shows the output of the code shown in Figure 14–36.

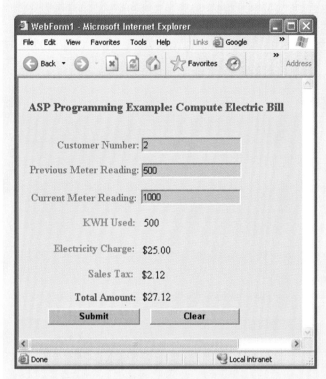

Figure 14-37   ASP Programming Example output

14

QUICK REVIEW

1. Many real-world applications require data to be persistent (or available over time). One way to achieve data persistence in Visual Basic .NET (VB .NET) is through the use of relational databases.

2. A relational database enables you to organize data into tables. A database can consist of one or many tables.

3. Each column in a relational database table represents an attribute. Each row represents an instance. In database terminology, columns are also referred to as fields and rows are referred to as records.

4. A primary key is a field (or set of fields) that uniquely identifies each record in a table.

5. Good database design calls for a primary key whose value is not likely to change over time and whose value is not null for any instance. Good database design also minimizes redundancy.

6. A field (or set of fields) that links information in one table to information in another table is called a foreign key. A field that serves as a foreign key in one table must be a primary key (or part of a primary key) in the other table.

7. A query is a request for information. You use queries to extract information from the database. A query usually specifies one or more conditions that the extracted information must meet.

8. Structured Query Language (SQL) allows you to specify queries and perform other common database operations, such as inserting new records into a table, updating records already contained within a table, and deleting records from a table.

9. VB .NET provides support for several database management systems, including Microsoft Access, Microsoft SQLServer, and Oracle.

10. Programs that interact with a Microsoft Access database use a number of classes contained within the System.Data and System.Data.OleDb namespaces.

11. Data adapters link a physical data source to a data set in memory.

12. In a three-tier design, the problem domain (PD) and GUI classes are unaware of how the data access (DA) class implements data persistence. The DA class handles all interaction with the database and carries out the tasks of inserting, updating, deleting, and extracting information. The GUI classes that capture and display information simply invoke the DA methods.

13. The .NET Framework provides you tools to develop both Windows and Web applications. Web development using ASP.NET is quite similar to developing GUI applications for Windows. ASP stands for Active Server Pages.

14. Web pages employ a standard language called Hypertext Markup Language (HTML) telling browsers how to display the pages. HTML is a descriptive language, not a procedural language. HTML tells a browser how to display a page, but it lacks procedural statements.

15. Web pages are files containing HTML code and have an extension of .htm or .html. HTML contains tags that define the format of a Web page. They indicate text that should appear bold or italic, or as a heading or as part of a paragraph.

16. Previous versions of ASP allowed you to include script code with HTML to produce interactivity; however, mixing HTML tags and programming script together added complexity to both development and maintenance.

17. ASP.NET separates procedural code from the Web form (HTML) code. The Web form file has a suffix of .aspx and the code files have the familiar suffix of .vb. The .vb files are called the code-behind files.

18. Every Web page has an address describing its location. This address is called a Uniform Resource Locator (URL).

19. ASP.NET includes validation controls that facilitate adding data validation to an application. These controls appear in the Toolbox and can be placed on the Web page just as any other controls. Their properties can be accessed in the Properties window.

EXERCISES

1. Describe the relational database model. In your description, include definitions of the following terms:

   a. table

   b. record

   c. column

   d. primary key

   e. foreign key

2. State two principles of good database design.

3. Identify performance trade-offs that should be considered when mapping PD attributes to relational tables.

4. Refer to Figure 14-6. Why is it necessary to read data from all four tables to obtain information for a given person? What would be the advantage of adding a discriminator column that specifies whether a person is a student or a professor to the Person table? Would there be an advantage in adding this column to the table shown in Figure 14-7? Why or why not?

5. Refer again to Figure 14-6.

   a. Develop a database design for this problem that consists of three tables.

   b. Develop a database design for this problem that consists of two tables.

   c. For this problem, do you prefer the design with one table, two tables, three tables, or four tables? Why?

14

6. Consider the relational tables shown in Figure 14–38. Assume that grade point average (GPA) is a numeric field.

Faculty table

FacultyID	LastName	FirstName	Department
F1000	Bradford	Douglas	IS
F1010	Cook	Bryan	CS
F1020	Thomas	Janet	CS
F1030	Brown	Randall	IT
F1040	Campbell	Deborah	CS

Student table

StudentID	LastName	FirstName	GPA	Advisor
S2000	Gillis	Michael	2.57	F1030
S2010	Thackston	Lauren	3.95	F1000
S2020	McDonald	Christopher	3.03	F1020
S2030	Kent	Richard	2.98	F1010
S2040	Warren	Paige	3.25	F1010
S2050	Smith	Mitchell	2.16	F1040
S2060	Butler	Kate	3.43	F1020

Figure 14-38 Relational tables for Exercise 6

Write an SQL statement to perform each of the following tasks:

a. Insert a record for a new faculty member into the Faculty table. (Use attribute values of your choice.)

b. Delete the record for student S2050 from the Student table.

c. Change the last name of faculty member F1040 to Wilson.

d. Produce a list of all students with a GPA of 3.0 or higher. The list should include student ID, first name, last name, and GPA.

e. Produce a list of all faculty in the Computer Science (CS) Department. The list should include faculty ID, last name, first name, and department.

    f. Produce a list of all students who are advised by Dr. Cook or Dr. Brown.

    g. Produce a list of students who have a GPA of 3.0 or higher and are advised by the Computer Science faculty. The list should include the student's first and last name, GPA, and last name of the student's advisor.

7. Refer again to the tables in Exercise 6.

    a. Identify all primary and foreign keys.

    b. What difficulty does the following INSERT statement pose?

```
INSERT INTO Student VALUES ('S3000', 'Tindell', 'Matt',
3.82, 'F1212')
```

    c. What problem would result from executing the following DELETE statement?

```
DELETE FROM Faculty WHERE LastName = 'Cook'
```

8. Describe the purpose of the following data classes and explain how they relate to each other.

    a. OleDbCommand

    b. OleDbDataAdapter

    c. DataSet

    d. DataTable

    e. DataRow

9. What does ASP stand for?

10. How is ASP.NET significantly different than previous ASP versions?

11. What does HTML mean?

12. What is HTML?

13. What is a URL?

14. What is an ASP Validation Control?

14

PROGRAMMING EXERCISES

This book assumes that you have some familiarity with Microsoft Access and know how to create and populate tables.

1. The AddStudent GUI presented in Example 14-2 includes limited error-checking capabilities. Modify this program and create custom exception classes to ensure that the user:

    a. Enters a value for name and address. If either text box is left blank, throw a custom exception named TextException.

    b. Selects a value on the list box. If not, throw a custom exception named ListException.

   c. Enters an appropriate value for area code (a number between 100 and 999), and seven digits for the number. If not, throw a custom exception named PhoneException.

   d. Enters a valid number (a value > 0 and < 1000000) for Student ID. If not, throw a custom exception named IDException.

When any of these exceptions are caught, display an appropriate error message. In addition, VB .NET throws a FormatException when an attempt to convert a value entered into a text to a number fails. Include a catch block to respond to this potential data entry error. Test your modifications to ensure that your GUI always responds gracefully to data entry errors.

2. Make similar modifications to the UpdateStudent GUI presented in the Programming Example at the end of this chapter. Test your modifications. What happens when you enter a non-numeric value for Student ID and then click the Find button? Why does this occur? What should be done to fix the problem?

3. Add the necessary exception handling to correct the problem identified with the UpdateStudent GUI in Programming Exercise 2. Use the corrected version of the UpdateStudent GUI, the revised AddStudent GUI (from Programming Exercise 1), and the Person, Student, Phone, StudentDA, and ListStudent programs (presented in the Programming Example at the end of this chapter) to create an integrated system driven by the main menu GUI shown in Figure 14-39. Change the "Close" button on the ListStudent, AddStudent, and UpdateStudent GUIs to read "Return to Main Menu". Test the application.

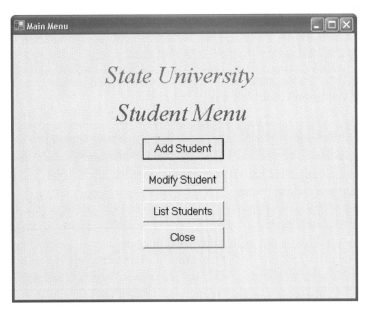

Figure 14-39 Main menu GUI for Programming Exercise 3

4. Design and write an ASP application that will input an employee's date of employment and their birthday, then compute and display their age at employment, expressed in years and days. (*Hint*: See Chapter 6.)

5. The Programming Example at the end of Chapter 5 produces a loan amortization report. The input is the amount of the loan, the annual percentage rate, and the duration expressed in number of months. Redesign the example to use ASP.NET. Employ Validation Controls as appropriate. Review Example 14-3.

6. Programming Exercise 4-6 asked you to design and write an application to make conversions such as gallon to liter, inch to centimeter, pound to kilogram, and mile to kilometer. Redesign your solution to use ASP.NET. Employ Validation Controls as appropriate. Several Web sites such as *www.wsdot.wa.gov/Metrics/factors.htm* provide the conversion factors.

7. Consider the Pet class diagram shown in Figure 14-40.

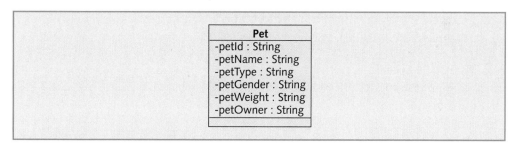

Figure 14-40   Pet class diagram

a. Create a Pet PD class based upon Figure 14-40. Include get and set accessors for each attribute.

b. Design and create a corresponding Pet table in Access.

c. Create a PetDA class containing DA methods Initialize, Find, AddNew, and Terminate.

d. Develop a GUI similar to the one shown in Figure 14-41 that allows you to add new records to the Pet table. By default, the GUI should select "Dog" as the pet type and "Male" as the gender. Weight should be a number greater than 0 and less than 200. Include exception handling for any type of data entry error, including attempts to insert duplicate records.

14

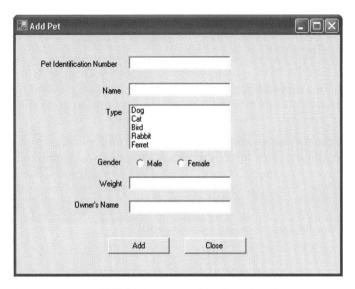

Figure 14-41 GUI for Programming Exercise 7

e. Use your GUI to add records to the Pet table.

15

Advanced Topics: Introducing Data Structures and Recursion

In this chapter, you will:

○ Create linked lists
○ Create a stack
○ Create a queue
○ Understand recursion
○ Write recursive methods

In this chapter, you learn to use data structures and recursive methods. A data structure is a collection of data. Examples of data structures you have already worked with include arrays. You worked with the **Array** and the **ArrayList** classes in Chapter 7. You learned that arrays were static data structures but that **ArrayLists** could be dynamically resized as your application executes. In this chapter, you explore additional data structures such as linked lists, stacks, and queues. In addition, you work with the Framework Class Library (FCL) classes **Stack** and **Queue**.

You also explore the principle of recursion and write programs that use recursive methods (methods that call themselves) to solve problems.

While this chapter introduces you to the advanced topics of data structures and recursion, these are important topics in computer science, and are explored in more depth in many upper-division computer science courses.

INTRODUCING DATA STRUCTURES

In this section, you learn about linked lists, stacks, and queues. A **linked list**, as the name suggests, is a list of object instances that are linked together much like a chain. Objects may be added to the beginning of the list, to the end, or somewhere in between. Objects are also removed from the beginning, the end, or the middle.

A **stack** can be implemented as a specialized case of a linked list with objects being added and removed only at the beginning of the list. A stack employs LIFO (last in, first out) logic.

A queue can also be implemented as a linked list with objects added at the end and removed from the beginning. Queues employ FIFO (first in, first out) logic. Figures 15-1, 15-2, and 15-3 show a linked list, a stack, and a queue, respectively. You work with each of these in the following sections.

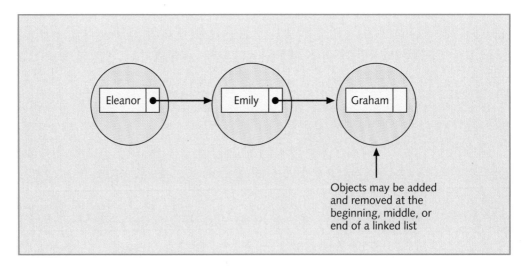

Figure 15-1 A linked list

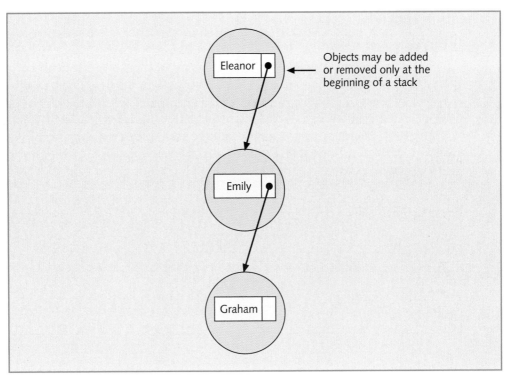

Figure 15-2   A stack

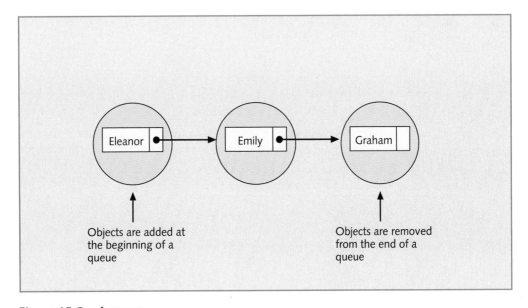

Figure 15-3   A queue

Creating Linked Lists

Each instance in a linked list is called a **node**, and contains data and a reference attribute linking it to the next node. You can maintain references to the first and last item in the list to facilitate their access.

Figure 15-4 shows a class diagram for a class named **LinkedListNode**. This class has two attributes: **data** and **nextNode**. The data type of data can be whatever you want, including a primitive or a reference data type. **nextNode** is a reference variable whose data type is **LinkedListNode**. When you have a class that references instances of that class, it is called a **self-referencing** class.

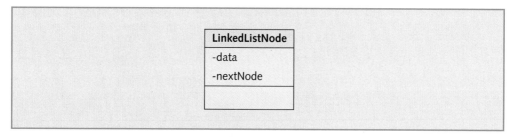

Figure 15-4 Class diagram for LinkedListNode

When you create instances of this class, populate the data attribute with **String** values, and then connect the instances as a linked list, they appear as shown in Figure 15-5. In this example, the data type of data is **String**, though it can be anything. The data type in the end-of-chapter example is **Customer**.

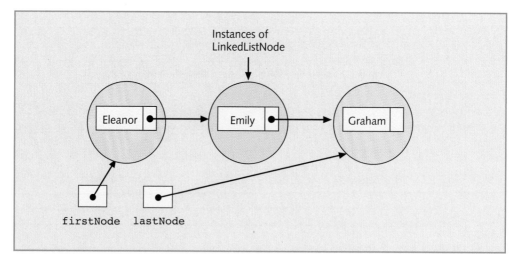

Figure 15-5 A linked list using instances of LinkedListNode

The reference variables `firstNode` and `lastNode` are data type `LinkedListNode` and are populated with references to the first and last nodes in the list.

The first node's data attribute contains "Eleanor" and its `nextNode` attribute references the second node. The second node's data attribute contains "Emily" and its `nextNode` attribute references the third node. Note that `lastNode` contains the same reference. Finally, the last node's data attribute contains "Graham" and its `nextNode` attribute is not populated: it contains `Nothing`.

Example 15-1 illustrates the creation of this linked list. You use three classes in this example: `LinkedListNode`, `LinkedList`, and a `Client` module. `LinkedListNode` is instantiated to create the individual nodes in the linked list. The `LinkedList` class manages the linked list, and `Client` invokes methods in `LinkedList` to add nodes to the list.

Figure 15-6 shows a class diagram for `LinkedList`. This class contains two attributes, `firstNode` and `lastNode`. It also has two methods. `InsertAtBeginning` adds a new instance of `LinkedListNode` to the beginning of the list. `DisplayAllNodes` traverses the list, displaying the data contained in each instance.

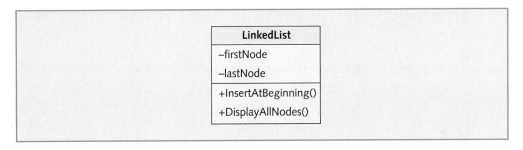

Figure 15-6   Class diagram for LinkedList

Example 15-1: A simple linked list

15

Figure 15-7 shows the code for the `LinkedListNode` class, Figure 15-8 shows the code for the `LinkedList` class, and Figure 15-9 shows the code for the `Client` module.

 This chapter includes some code examples in figures so you can examine the code as it appears in the Integrated Development Environment (IDE) with line numbers without lengthening the chapter unnecessarily.

```
 1  Option Explicit On
 2  Option Strict On
 3  Public Class LinkedListNode
 4      Private data As String
 5      Private nextNode As LinkedListNode
 6
 7      Public Sub New(ByVal newData As String, ByVal newNextNode As
    LinkedListNode)
 8          SetData(newData)
 9          SetNextNode(newNextNode)
10      End Sub
11      Public Function GetData() As String
12          Return data
13      End Function
14      Public Sub SetData(ByVal newdata As String)
15          data = newdata
16      End Sub
17      Public Function GetNextNode() As LinkedListNode
18          Return nextNode
19      End Function
20      Public Sub SetNextNode(ByVal newNextNode As LinkedListNode)
21          nextNode = newNextNode
22      End Sub
23  End Class
```

Figure 15-7   LinkedListNode listing

```
 1  Option Explicit On
 2  Option Strict On
 3  Public Class LinkedList
 4      Private firstNode, lastNode As LinkedListNode
 5      Public Sub New()
 6          firstNode = Nothing
 7          lastNode = Nothing
 8      End Sub
 9      Public Sub DisplayAllNodes()
10          Dim currentNode As LinkedListNode, data As String
11          currentNode = firstNode
12          If currentNode Is Nothing Then
13              Console.WriteLine("Empty linked list")
14          Else
15              Do Until currentNode Is Nothing
16                  data = currentNode.GetData()
17                  Console.WriteLine(data)
18                  currentNode = currentNode.GetNextNode()
19              Loop
20          End If
21      End Sub
22      Public Sub InsertAtBeginning(ByVal data As String)
23          Dim newNode As LinkedListNode
24          ' create the node
25          newNode = New LinkedListNode(data, firstNode)
26          If firstNode Is Nothing Then ' creating first node in list
27              lastNode = newNode
28          End If
29          firstNode = newNode 'the new node becomes the first
30      End Sub
31  End Class
```

Figure 15-8   LinkedList listing

```
 1  Option Explicit On
 2  Option Strict On
 3  Module Client
 4      Sub Main()
 5          Dim linkedList As LinkedList = New LinkedList
 6          linkedList.InsertAtBeginning("Graham")
 7          linkedList.InsertAtBeginning("Emily")
 8          linkedList.InsertAtBeginning("Eleanor")
 9          linkedList.DisplayAllNodes()
10      End Sub
11
12  End Module
```

Figure 15-9   Client module listing for Example 15-1

Sample Run:

```
Eleanor
Emily
Graham
```

Discussion:

The `LinkedListNode` class definition is similar to previous class definitions you have written. It has two attribute definitions in lines 4 and 5, a constructor in lines 7 through 10, and two `Get` accessors and two `Set` accessors.

The `LinkedList` class definition corresponds to its class diagram, which is shown in Figure 15-6. It has two attribute variables defined in line 4, a constructor in lines 5 through 8, `DisplayAllNodes` in lines 9 through 21, and `InsertAtBeginning` listed in lines 22 through 30. These two methods are invoked by the `Client` module.

The `Client` module is brief, containing only five lines of code.

Line 5 instantiates `LinkedList`, populating `LinkedList` with a reference to the instance. At this point there are no instances of `LinkedListNode`; therefore, the attributes in the `LinkedList` instances `firstNode` and `lastNode` contain `Nothing`.

Line 6 in `Client` invokes `InsertAtBeginning` in the `LinkedList` instance, passing the `String` argument "Graham." This method, listed in lines 22 through 30 in `LinkedList`, does two things: creates a new node and updates `firstNode` and `lastNode`. First, in line 25, it instantiates `LinkedListNode`, passing the data and `firstNode` variables. The `LinkedListNode` constructor receives these arguments and uses them to populate the two attributes in the newly created node instance. Second, in line 26, `InsertAtBeginning` checks to see if this is the first node being created for this list. If it is, then both `firstNode` and `lastNode` are assigned a reference to the new node. If this is not the first node being created, then `firstNode` is assigned a reference to the new node.

Similarly, lines 7 and 8 create and add two more nodes.

Line 9 invokes `DisplayAllNodes` in the `LinkedList` instance. This method is listed in lines 9 through 21 in the `LinkedList` class definition listing in Figure 15-8. Line 10 defines a reference variable `currentNode`, whose data type is `LinkedListNode`, used to reference the node whose data is being displayed, and a `String` variable named `data`. Line 11 assigns `firstNode` to `currentNode`. Line 12 checks to see if the list is empty and displays a message if it is. If the list is not empty, lines 15 through 19 define a loop that executes until the `currentNode` contains `Nothing`, indicating there are no more nodes to access. Line 16 invokes `GetData` for the current node and line 17 displays it. Line 18 invokes `GetNextNode` to obtain a reference to the next node in the list. The value returned is then assigned to `currentNode`.

15

In Example 15-1, `LinkedList` has a single method to add nodes to the list: `InsertAtBeginning`. In addition, it does not have a method to remove nodes from the list. Figure 15-10 shows a class diagram for `LinkedList` with the additional methods `InsertAtEnd`, `RemoveFromBeginning`, and `RemoveFromEnd`.

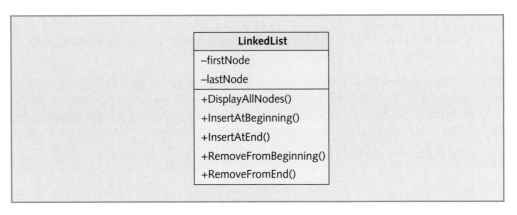

Figure 15-10   Enhanced LinkedList class diagram

Example 15-2 creates a linked list as before, but also illustrates the additional methods: `InsertAtEnd`, `RemoveFromBeginning`, and `RemoveFromEnd`. The `LinkedListNode` class is copied from Example 15-1 without modification. The `Client` module contains additional code to invoke the new methods in `LinkedList`.

Example 15-2: LinkedList with additional methods

LinkedList Class

```
1.   Option Explicit On
2.   Option Strict On
3.   Public Class LinkedList
4.     Private firstNode, lastNode As LinkedListNode
5.     Public Sub New()
6.       firstNode = Nothing
7.       lastNode = Nothing
8.     End Sub

9.     Public Sub DisplayAllNodes()
10.      Dim currentNode As LinkedNode, data As String
11.      currentNode = firstNode
12.      If currentNode Is Nothing Then
13.        Console.WriteLine("Empty linked list")
```

```
14.    Else
15.      Do Until currentNode Is Nothing
16.        data = currentNode.GetData()
17.        Console.WriteLine(data)
18.        currentNode = currentNode.GetNextNode()
19.      Loop
20.    End If
21.    End Sub
```

```
22. Public Sub InsertAtBeginning(ByVal data As String)
23.    Dim newNode As LinkedListNode
24.    newNode = New LinkedListNode(data, firstNode) ' create the node
25.    If firstNode Is Nothing Then ' create first node in list
26.      lastNode = newNode
27.    End If
28.    firstNode = newNode         'the new node becomes the first
29. End Sub
30.    Public Sub InsertAtEnd(ByVal data As String)
31.    Dim newNode As LinkedListNode
32.    newNode = New LinkedListNode(data, Nothing) ' create the node
33.    If firstNode Is Nothing Then ' creating first node in list
34.      firstNode = newNode
35.    End If
36.    'point the previous last node to the new node
37.    lastNode.SetNextNode(newNode)
38.    lastNode = newNode             'the new node becomes the last
39. End Sub
```

```
40.
41.    Public Function RemoveFromBeginning() As LinkedListNode
42.    Dim nodeToRemove, nextNode As LinkedListNode
43.    nodeToRemove = firstNode ' retrieve the node
44.    nextNode = nodeToRemove.GetNextNode() ' get next node in list
45.    If nextNode Is Nothing Then ' removing only node in list
46.      lastNode = Nothing
47.    End If
48.    firstNode = nextNode ' the next node becomes first
49.    Return nodeToRemove
50.    End Function
```

15

```
51. Public Function RemoveFromEnd() As LinkedListNode
52.  Dim nodeToRemove, nextNode, nextToLastNode As LinkedListNode
53.  nodeToRemove = lastNode ' retrieve the last node
54.  nextNode = firstNode
55.  If nextNode.GetNextNode() Is Nothing Then ' removing only node
56.    firstNode = Nothing
57.    lastNode = Nothing
58.  Else
59.    nextToLastNode = firstNode ' find the next to last node
60.    ' loop to end of list
61.    Do Until nextNode.GetNextNode() Is Nothing
62.      nextToLastNode = nextNode ' get next node
63.      nextNode = nextNode.GetNextNode()
64.    Loop
65.    ' update nextNode in the new last node of list
66.    nextToLastNode.SetNextNode(Nothing)
67.  End If
68.  Return nodeToRemove
69. End Function

70. End Class
```

Client Module

```
 1  Option Explicit On
 2  Option Strict On
 3  Module Client
 4      Sub Main()
 5          Dim node As LinkedListNode
 6          Dim linkedList As LinkedList = New LinkedList
 7          Console.WriteLine("Original list")
 8          linkedList.InsertAtBeginning("Graham")
 9          linkedList.InsertAtBeginning("Emily")
10          linkedList.InsertAtBeginning("Eleanor")
11          linkedList.DisplayAllNodes()
12          Console.WriteLine("List with Reina added at end")
13          linkedList.InsertAtEnd("Reina")
14          linkedList.DisplayAllNodes()
15          Console.WriteLine("List with Eleanor removed from beginning")
16          node = linkedList.RemoveFromBeginning()
17          linkedList.DisplayAllNodes()
18          Console.WriteLine("List with Reina removed from end")
19          node = linkedList.RemoveFromEnd()
20          linkedList.DisplayAllNodes()
21          Console.WriteLine("Remove last two nodes")
22          node = linkedList.RemoveFromEnd()
23          node = linkedList.RemoveFromBeginning()
24          linkedList.DisplayAllNodes()
25      End Sub
26
27  End Module
```

Figure 15-11   Client module listing for Example 15-2

Sample Run:

```
Original list
Eleanor
Emily
Graham
List with Reina added at end
Eleanor
Emily
Graham
Reina
List with Eleanor removed from beginning
Emily
Graham
Reina
List with Reina removed from end
Emily
Graham
Remove last two nodes
Empty linked list
```

LinkedList Discussion:

The LinkedList class definition now contains five methods. The two methods DisplayAllNodes and InsertAtBeginning are the same as in Example 15-1, but three methods have been added: InsertAtEnd listed in lines 30 through 39, RemoveFromBeginning in lines 41 through 50, and RemoveFromEnd in lines 51 through 69.

InsertAtEnd begins with line 31 declaring the reference variable newNode, which is data type LinkedListNode, and line 32 instantiates LinkedListNode, assigning its reference to newNode. Line 33 checks to see if the list is empty. If it is, then firstNode is assigned a reference to the new LinkedListNode instance; otherwise, the previous last node is linked to the new node. Line 38 updates the contents of lastNode.

RemoveFromBeginning in lines 41 through 50 begins with the declaration of two reference variables in line 42. Line 43 populates nodeToRemove with firstNode. Note that both RemoveFromBeginning and RemoveFromEnd in this example assume a non-empty linked list. The next example deals with an empty list.

Line 44 obtains a reference to the next node in the list, and line 45 checks to see if there is only one node. Line 48 populates firstNode, and line 49 returns a reference to the removed node.

RemoveFromEnd begins with line 51 declaring three reference variables of the data type LinkedListNode. Line 53 retrieves a reference to the last node in the list and assigns its reference to nodeToRemove. Line 54 assigns the contents of firstNode to nextNode.

Line 55 checks to see if there is only one node. If so, `firstNode` and `lastNode` are set to `Nothing`. Lines 61 through 64 define a loop to locate the next to the last node and assign its reference to `nextToLastNode`. This is because when the last node is removed, the nextNode attribute of the new last node must be set to `Nothing`, which is done in line 66. Finally, line 68 returns a reference to the removed node.

Client Module Discussion:

Lines 12 through 24 are code that has been added to the `Client` module from Example 15-1. This code was added to exercise the three new methods in `LinkedList`.

Line 13 invokes `InsertAtEnd`, passing the argument "Reina," and line 14 invokes `DisplayAllNodes`.

Line 16 invokes `RemoveFromBeginning`, and line 17 displays the new list.

Line 19 invokes `RemoveFromEnd`, and line 20 displays the new list.

Finally, lines 22 and 23 invoke `RemoveFromEnd` and `RemoveFromBeginning`, respectively, to remove the final two nodes.

Except for the `DisplayAllNodes` method, the `LinkedList` class in Example 15-2 does not recognize the possibility that a linked list may have no nodes. This creates an error if one of the remove methods is invoked and an empty list exists.

You learned in Chapter 12 that exceptions are an excellent technique to deal with errors such as attempting to remove a node from an empty linked list. This approach is illustrated in the next example.

First, a new exception class definition named `EmptyLinkedListException` is written. Then, the remove methods have statements added to create and throw `EmptyLinkedListException` if an empty list is detected. Finally, `Try-Catch` statements are added to the `Client` module.

Example 15-3: Adding exceptions to deal with an empty list

EmptyListException class definition

```
1. Public Class EmptyLinkedListException
2.    Inherits ApplicationException
3.    Public Sub New(ByVal message As String)
4.      MyBase.New(message)
5.    End Sub
6. End Class
```

Figure 15-12 shows the code for creating **LinkedList** remove methods with exceptions, and Figure 15-13 shows a **Client** module that includes a **Try-Catch** block.

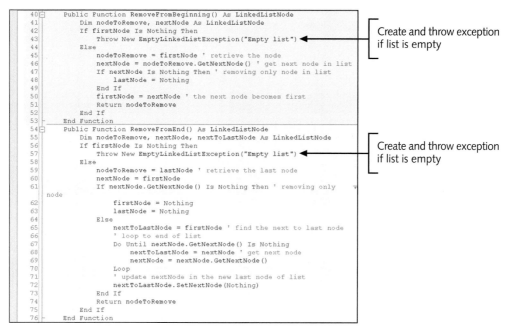

```
40   Public Function RemoveFromBeginning() As LinkedListNode
41       Dim nodeToRemove, nextNode As LinkedListNode
42       If firstNode Is Nothing Then
43           Throw New EmptyLinkedListException("Empty list")
44       Else
45           nodeToRemove = firstNode ' retrieve the node
46           nextNode = nodeToRemove.GetNextNode() ' get next node in list
47           If nextNode Is Nothing Then ' removing only node in list
48               lastNode = Nothing
49           End If
50           firstNode = nextNode ' the next node becomes first
51           Return nodeToRemove
52       End If
53   End Function
54   Public Function RemoveFromEnd() As LinkedListNode
55       Dim nodeToRemove, nextNode, nextToLastNode As LinkedListNode
56       If firstNode Is Nothing Then
57           Throw New EmptyLinkedListException("Empty list")
58       Else
59           nodeToRemove = lastNode ' retrieve the last node
60           nextNode = firstNode
61           If nextNode.GetNextNode() Is Nothing Then ' removing only
     node
62               firstNode = Nothing
63               lastNode = Nothing
64           Else
65               nextToLastNode = firstNode ' find the next to last node
66               ' loop to end of list
67               Do Until nextNode.GetNextNode() Is Nothing
68                   nextToLastNode = nextNode ' get next node
69                   nextNode = nextNode.GetNextNode()
70               Loop
71               ' update nextNode in the new last node of list
72               nextToLastNode.SetNextNode(Nothing)
73           End If
74           Return nodeToRemove
75       End If
76   End Function
```

Create and throw exception if list is empty

Create and throw exception if list is empty

Figure 15-12   LinkedList remove methods with exceptions added

```
1   Option Explicit On
2   Option Strict On
3   Module Client
4       Sub Main()
5           Dim node As LinkedListNode
6           Dim linkedList As LinkedList = New LinkedList
7           Console.WriteLine("Original list")
8           linkedList.InsertAtBeginning("Graham")
9           linkedList.InsertAtBeginning("Emily")
10          linkedList.InsertAtBeginning("Eleanor")
11          linkedList.DisplayAllNodes()
12          Console.WriteLine("List with Reina added at end")
13          linkedList.InsertAtEnd("Reina")
14          linkedList.DisplayAllNodes()
15          Console.WriteLine("List with Eleanor removed from beginning")
16          node = linkedList.RemoveFromBeginning()
17          linkedList.DisplayAllNodes()
18          Try
19              Console.WriteLine("List with Reina removed from end")
20              node = linkedList.RemoveFromEnd()
21              linkedList.DisplayAllNodes()
22              Console.WriteLine("Remove last two nodes")
23              node = linkedList.RemoveFromEnd()
24              node = linkedList.RemoveFromBeginning()
25              linkedList.DisplayAllNodes()
26              ' now try to remove from empty list
27              node = linkedList.RemoveFromBeginning()
28          Catch e As EmptyLinkedListException
29              Console.WriteLine("Exception caught: " & e.Message())
30          End Try
31      End Sub
32   End Module
```

15

Figure 15-13   Client module with Try-Catch added

Sample Run:

```
Original list
Eleanor
Emily
Graham
List with Reina added at end
Eleanor
Emily
Graham
Reina
List with Eleanor removed from beginning
Emily
Graham
Reina
List with Reina removed from end
Emily
Graham
Remove last two nodes
Empty linked list
Exception caught: Empty list
```

EmptyLinkedListException Class Definition Discussion:

This exception class is nearly identical to those you developed in Chapter 12. Line 2 specifies that this class extends `ApplicationException`. The constructor in lines 3 through 5 receives a message argument, and then invokes the superclass constructor to pass along the message.

LinkedList Discussion:

Only the two remove methods were modified here, and they are listed earlier in Figure 15-12. In `RemoveFromBeginning`, line 42 tests the contents of `firstNode` for `Nothing`, which would indicate an empty list. If the list is empty, an instance of `EmptyLinkedListException` is created and thrown.

Identical logic is used in `RemoveFromEnd` in lines 56 and 57.

Client Module Discussion:

The statements in `Client` that invoke the remove methods in `LinkedList` are placed in a `Try` block shown in lines 18 through 30. If an exception is caught in line 28, its message is displayed in line 29. In this example, line 27 attempts to remove a node from an empty list. `LinkedList` then throws the exception, which is caught and displayed by `Client`.

Creating a Stack

A `Stack` can be implemented as a `LinkedList`. You can add and remove nodes at either the beginning or the end of a linked list. However, a stack is a LIFO structure: you can add and remove nodes from only the beginning or top of a `Stack`. You can employ inheritance to create a `Stack` class, as shown in Figure 15-14.

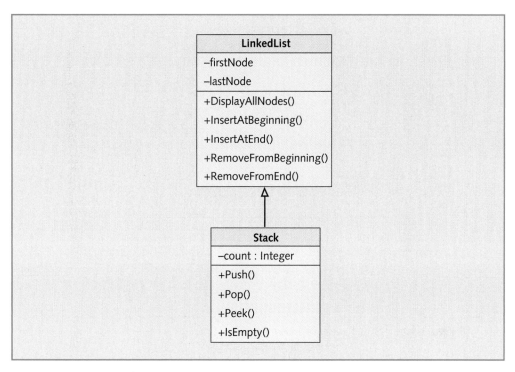

Figure 15-14   Class diagram of Stack as subclass of LinkedList

15

As shown in the class diagram, `Stack` has one attribute and four methods. `count` is the number of nodes in the stack. `Push` adds a node to the top, and `Pop` removes a node from the top and returns a reference to the removed node. `Peek` returns a reference to the top node, but does not remove it. `IsEmpty` returns a Boolean `True` if there are no nodes in the stack; otherwise, it returns `False`. Note that `Pop` and `Peek` both throw `EmptyStackException` if the stack is empty.

Because `Stack` is a `LinkedList` subclass, `Push` can invoke `InsertAtBeginning` and `Pop` can invoke `RemoveFromBeginning`. The next example illustrates the creation of the `Stack` class definition.

Example 15-4: Creating a Stack class definition

Figure 15-15 shows the code for defining a `Stack` class, and Figure 15-16 shows the code for the `Client` module.

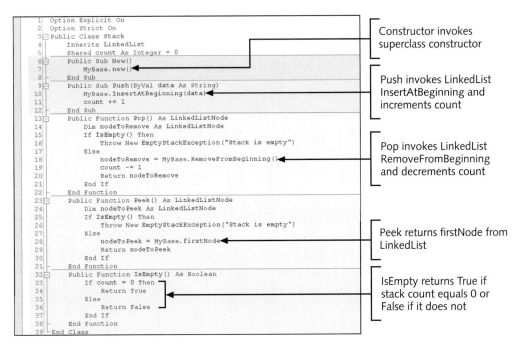

```
1   Option Explicit On
2   Option Strict On
3   Public Class Stack
4       Inherits LinkedList
5       Shared count As Integer = 0
6       Public Sub New()
7           MyBase.new()
8       End Sub
9       Public Sub Push(ByVal data As String)
10          MyBase.InsertAtBeginning(data)
11          count += 1
12      End Sub
13      Public Function Pop() As LinkedListNode
14          Dim nodeToRemove As LinkedListNode
15          If IsEmpty() Then
16              Throw New EmptyStackException("Stack is empty")
17          Else
18              nodeToRemove = MyBase.RemoveFromBeginning()
19              count -= 1
20              Return nodeToRemove
21          End If
22      End Function
23      Public Function Peek() As LinkedListNode
24          Dim nodeToPeek As LinkedListNode
25          If IsEmpty() Then
26              Throw New EmptyStackException("Stack is empty")
27          Else
28              nodeToPeek = MyBase.firstNode
29              Return nodeToPeek
30          End If
31      End Function
32      Public Function IsEmpty() As Boolean
33          If count = 0 Then
34              Return True
35          Else
36              Return False
37          End If
38      End Function
39  End Class
```

Constructor invokes superclass constructor

Push invokes LinkedList InsertAtBeginning and increments count

Pop invokes LinkedList RemoveFromBeginning and decrements count

Peek returns firstNode from LinkedList

IsEmpty returns True if stack count equals 0 or False if it does not

Figure 15-15   Stack class definition listing

```
1   Option Explicit On
2   Option Strict On
3   Module Client
4       Sub Main()
5           Dim node As LinkedListNode
6           Dim aStack As Stack = New Stack
7           Console.WriteLine("Original stack")
8           aStack.Push("Graham")
9           aStack.Push("Emily")
10          aStack.DisplayAllNodes()
11          Console.WriteLine("stack with Eleanor added")
12          aStack.Push("Eleanor")
13          aStack.DisplayAllNodes()
14          Console.WriteLine("stack with Eleanor removed")
15          node = aStack.Pop()
16          aStack.DisplayAllNodes()
17          Try
18              node = aStack.Peek()
19              Console.WriteLine("node data after Peek: " & node.GetData())
20              Console.WriteLine("stack with Emily removed")
21              node = aStack.Pop()
22              aStack.DisplayAllNodes()
23              Console.WriteLine("Remove last node")
24              node = aStack.Pop()
25              ' now try to remove from empty stack
26              Console.WriteLine("try to pop empty stack")
27              node = aStack.Pop()
28          Catch e As EmptyStackException
29              Console.WriteLine("Exception caught: " & e.Message())
30          End Try
31      End Sub
32  End Module
```

Figure 15-16   Client module listing for Example 15-4

Sample Run:

```
Original stack
Emily
Graham
stack with Eleanor added
Eleanor
Emily
Graham
stack with Eleanor removed
Emily
Graham
node data after Peek: Emily
stack with Emily removed
Graham
Remove last node
try to pop empty stack
Exception caught: Stack is empty
```

Discussion:

This example employs five class definitions plus a `Client` module.

1. `LinkedList` is copied from the previous example and the accessibility for its two attributes `firstNode` and `lastNode` are changed from Private to Protected to provide Stack access.

2. `LinkedListNode` is copied *without change* from the previous example.

3. `EmptyLinkedListException` is copied *without change* from the previous example.

4. `EmptyStackException` is a new class definition nearly identical to `EmptyLinkedListException`.

5. `Stack` is a new class definition and is discussed in the following text.

Stack Class Discussion:

As indicated by its class diagram, the `Stack` class definition has four methods plus a constructor. It also has a shared attribute named `count` that contains the number of nodes in the stack.

The constructor in lines 6 through 8 simply invokes the superclass (`LinkedList`) constructor.

The `Push` method in lines 9 through 12 receives the data argument, and then invokes the superclass method `InsertAtBeginning`, passing the argument that was received. In addition, `Push` increments the `count` variable.

The `Pop` method listed in lines 13 through 22 removes a node from the top of the stack, which is really the beginning of the linked list. However, because a node cannot be removed from an empty stack, line 15 invokes `IsEmpty` to see if the stack is empty. If so, an instance

15

of `EmptyStackException` is created and thrown in line 16. If the stack is not empty, then line 18 invokes the superclass method `RemoveFromBeginning`, line 19 decrements `count`, and line 20 returns a reference to the node removed.

The purpose of the `Peek` method in lines 23 through 31 is to return a reference to the node at the top of the stack. However, if the stack is empty, this method throws `EmptyStackException`. Line 25 invokes `IsEmpty` to see if the stack is empty. If so, an instance of `EmptyStackException` is created and thrown in line 26. If the stack is not empty, then line 28 retrieves `firstNode` from the superclass and returns a reference to it in line 29.

The `IsEmpty` method in lines 32 through 38 checks to see if `count` is zero and returns `True` if it is; otherwise, it returns `False`.

Client Module Discussion:

The `Client` module in this example is similar to that shown in the previous example.

Line 6 instantiates `Stack`.

Lines 8 and 9 invoke `Push` to add two nodes to the stack, and line 10 invokes `DisplayAllNodes`, a method inherited from `LinkedList`, to display the two nodes.

Line 12 adds a third node and line 13 again displays the nodes.

Line 15 invokes `Pop` to remove the top node, and line 16 again displays the stack.

Lines 17 through 30 contain a `Try` block.

Line 18 invokes `Peek` and line 19 displays the data contained in the top node.

Line 21 again invokes `Pop` to remove the top node, and line 22 displays the current stack.

Line 24 removes the final node and line 27 attempts to invoke `Pop` for an empty stack. An `EmptyStackException` is thrown, caught in line 28, and displayed in line 29.

Note that in this example, the `Stack` method `Pop` does not invoke the superclass method `RemoveItemFromBeginning` if the stack is empty. This means that `RemoveItemFromBeginning` never throws `EmptyLinkedListException`.

Exploring the FCL Stack Class

The FCL includes a `Stack` class with some of the same methods you included in the `Stack` class developed in Example 15-4. The FCL `Stack` class stores nodes as instances of `Object`. In addition to the now familiar `Push`, `Pop`, and `Peek` methods, this class includes the method `ToArray`, which copies the objects in the stack into an array.

The next example illustrates using the FCL `Stack` class. The `Client` module from the previous example is used with several modifications, which are discussed in Example 15-5.

Example 15-5: Exploring the FCL Stack class

Figure 15-17 shows the **Client** module listing for this example.

```
1  Option Explicit On
2  Option Strict On
3  Module Client
4      Dim data As String, aStack As Stack
5      Sub Main()
6          aStack = New Stack
7          Console.WriteLine("Original stack")
8          aStack.Push("Graham")
9          aStack.Push("Emily")
10         DisplayAll()
11         Console.WriteLine("stack with Eleanor added")
12         aStack.Push("Eleanor")
13         DisplayAll()
14         Console.WriteLine("stack with Eleanor removed")
15         data = Convert.ToString(aStack.Pop())
16         DisplayAll()
17         Try
18             data = Convert.ToString(aStack.Peek())
19             Console.WriteLine("node data after Peek: " & data)
20             Console.WriteLine("stack with Emily removed")
21             data = Convert.ToString(aStack.Pop())
22             DisplayAll()
23             Console.WriteLine("Remove last node")
24             data = Convert.ToString(aStack.Pop())
25             ' now try to remove from empty stack
26             Console.WriteLine("try to pop empty stack")
27             data = Convert.ToString(aStack.Pop())
28         Catch e As InvalidOperationException
29             Console.WriteLine("Exception caught: " & e.Message())
30         End Try
31     End Sub
32     Private Sub DisplayAll()
33         Dim i As Integer
34         Dim arrayOfData() As Object = aStack.ToArray()
35         For i = 0 To arrayOfData.Length - 1
36             data = Convert.ToString(arrayOfData(i))
37             Console.WriteLine("data # " & (i + 1) & ": " & data)
38         Next
39     End Sub
40 End Module
```

DisplayAll method retrieves and displays all items in the Stack

Figure 15-17   Client module listing for Example 15-5

Sample Run:

```
Original stack
data # 1: Emily
data # 2: Graham
stack with Eleanor added
data # 1: Eleanor
data # 2: Emily
data # 3: Graham
stack with Eleanor removed
data # 1: Emily
data # 2: Graham
node data after Peek: Emily
stack with Emily removed
data # 1: Graham
Remove last node
try to pop empty stack
Exception caught: Stack empty.
```

15

Discussion:

The `Client` module in this example contains two methods: `Main` and `DisplayAll`. `Main` executes when the module is loaded. `DisplayAll`, listed in lines 32 through 39, was added to display all of the items in the stack. In Example 15-4, `LinkedList` had a `DisplayAllNodes` method; however, the FCL `Stack` class had no similar method.

Line 4 declares two variables with module scope. The `String` variable data will hold the data from an item in the stack. `aStack` will contain a reference to the `Stack` instance created in `Main`.

Line 6 in `Main` instantiates the FCL `Stack` class, assigning its reference to `aStack`.

Lines 8 and 9 add two items to the `Stack`, similar to Example 15-4.

Line 10 invokes `DisplayAll`. Line 33 in `DisplayAll` declares an `Integer` variable named `i`, which is used in the `For Next` loop in lines 35 through 38. Line 34 declares an array reference variable named `arrayOfData`. The data type of the array elements is `Object`. Line 34 then invokes the `Stack` method `ToArray`, which copies the `Stack` elements into an array. The array reference is then assigned to `arrayOfData`. The `For Next` loop then iterates the array. Line 36 retrieves the element indexed by `i`, converts its data type from `Object` to `String`, and assigns its reference to `data`. Line 37 then displays the `String` data.

Next, line 12 in `Main` adds another item to the stack, and line 13 again invokes `DisplayAll`.

Line 15 then removes the top item, and line 16 redisplays the stack contents.

Similar to Example 15-4, lines 17 through 30 contain a `Try` block.

Within the `Try`, line 18 invokes `Peek`, line 21 removes the next item from the stack, and line 24 removes the final item. `DisplayAll` is invoked after each operation to show the stack contents.

Line 27 attempts to invoke `Pop` for a now empty stack. This method throws `InvalidOperationException`, which is caught in line 28, and the message is displayed in line 29.

Creating a Queue

You saw earlier that a queue can be implemented as a linked list, but with objects added only at the end and removed only from the beginning, employing FIFO logic. Figure 15-3 showed a queue example. The method to add an object to a queue is named `Enqueue`, and the method to remove an object is named `Dequeue`. Figure 15-14 depicted a class diagram showing `Stack` as a subclass of `LinkedList`. Because a `Queue` is also a specialized version of a linked list, you can create `Queue` as a subclass of `LinkedList`. Figure 15-18 contains a class diagram showing both `Stack` and `Queue` as subclasses of `LinkedList`.

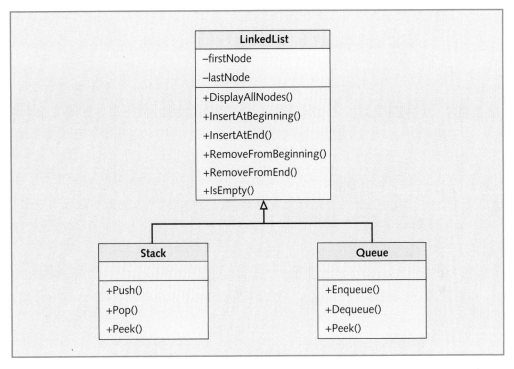

Figure 15-18   Class diagram of Queue and Stack as subclasses of LinkedList

Because the `Queue` class also needs a `count` attribute, it is removed from `Stack` and added to `LinkedList`, where it is inherited by both subclasses. Similarly, because `IsEmpty` is also required by `Queue`, it is removed from `Stack` and added to `LinkedList`. Placing common attributes and methods in the superclass eliminates redundancy in subclasses. Although the `Peek` method appears in both `Stack` and `Queue`, it has a different implementation, making it a polymorphic method. In `Stack`, `Peek` throws `EmptyStackException`, and in `Queue` it throws `EmptyQueueException`.

15

Example 15-6: Creating a Queue class

Figure 15-19 shows the code for a complete `LinkedList` class. Figure 15-20 shows the code for the `Queue` class, and Figure 15-21 shows the code for the `Client` module for this example.

```
1    Option Explicit On
2    Option Strict On
3  Public Class LinkedList
4        Protected firstNode, lastNode As LinkedListNode
5        Shared count As Integer = 0
6        Public Sub New()
7            firstNode = Nothing
8            lastNode = Nothing
9        End Sub
10       Public Sub DisplayAllNodes()
11           Dim currentNode As LinkedListNode, data As String
12           currentNode = firstNode
13           If currentNode Is Nothing Then
14               Console.WriteLine("Empty linked list")
15           Else
16               Do Until currentNode Is Nothing
17                   data = currentNode.GetData()
18                   Console.WriteLine(data)
19                   currentNode = currentNode.GetNextNode()
20               Loop
21           End If
22       End Sub
23       Public Sub InsertAtBeginning(ByVal data As String)
24           Dim newNode As LinkedListNode
25           newNode = New LinkedListNode(data, firstNode) ' create the node
26           If firstNode Is Nothing Then ' creating first node in list
27               lastNode = newNode
28           End If
29           firstNode = newNode            'the new node becomes the first
30           count += 1
31       End Sub
32       Public Sub InsertAtEnd(ByVal data As String)
33           Dim newNode As LinkedListNode
34           newNode = New LinkedListNode(data, Nothing) ' create the node
35           If firstNode Is Nothing Then ' creating first node in list
36               firstNode = newNode
37           Else
38               'point the previous last node to the new node
39               lastNode.SetNextNode(newNode)
40           End If
41           lastNode = newNode             'the new node becomes the last
42           count += 1
43       End Sub
44       Public Function RemoveFromBeginning() As LinkedListNode
45           Dim nodeToRemove, nextNode As LinkedListNode
46           If firstNode Is Nothing Then
47               Throw New EmptyLinkedListException("Empty list")
48           Else
49               nodeToRemove = firstNode ' retrieve the node
50               nextNode = nodeToRemove.GetNextNode() ' get next node in list
51               If nextNode Is Nothing Then ' removing only node in list
52                   lastNode = Nothing
53               End If
54               firstNode = nextNode ' the next node becomes first
55               count -= 1
56               Return nodeToRemove
57           End If
58       End Function
59       Public Function RemoveFromEnd() As LinkedListNode
60           Dim nodeToRemove, nextNode, nextToLastNode As LinkedListNode
61           If firstNode Is Nothing Then
62               Throw New EmptyLinkedListException("Empty list")
63           Else
64               nodeToRemove = lastNode ' retrieve the last node
65               nextNode = firstNode
66               If nextNode.GetNextNode() Is Nothing Then ' removing only node
67                   firstNode = Nothing
68                   lastNode = Nothing
69               Else
70                   nextToLastNode = firstNode ' find the next to last node
71                   ' loop to end of list
72                   Do Until nextNode.GetNextNode() Is Nothing
73                       nextToLastNode = nextNode ' get next node
74                       nextNode = nextNode.GetNextNode()
75                   Loop
76                   ' update nextNode in the new last node of list
77                   nextToLastNode.SetNextNode(Nothing)
78               End If
79               count -= 1
80               Return nodeToRemove
81           End If
82       End Function
83       Public Function IsEmpty() As Boolean
84           If count = 0 Then
85               Return True
86           Else
87               Return False
88           End If
89       End Function
90  End Class
```

Figure 15-19   Complete LinkedList class definition listing

```
 1  Option Explicit On
 2  Option Strict On
 3  Public Class Queue
 4      Inherits LinkedList
 5      Public Sub New()
 6          MyBase.new()
 7      End Sub
 8      Public Sub Enqueue(ByVal data As String)
 9          MyBase.InsertAtEnd(data)
10
11      End Sub
12      Public Function Dequeue() As LinkedListNode
13          Dim nodeToRemove As LinkedListNode
14          If IsEmpty() Then
15              Throw New EmptyQueueException("Queue is empty")
16          Else
17              nodeToRemove = MyBase.RemoveFromBeginning()
18              Return nodeToRemove
19          End If
20      End Function
21      Public Function Peek() As LinkedListNode
22          Dim nodeToPeek As LinkedListNode
23          If IsEmpty() Then
24              Throw New EmptyQueueException("Queue is empty")
25          Else
26              nodeToPeek = MyBase.firstNode
27              Return nodeToPeek
28          End If
29      End Function
30  End Class
```

Figure 15-20   Queue class definition listing

```
 1  Option Explicit On
 2  Option Strict On
 3  Module Client
 4      Sub Main()
 5          Dim node As LinkedListNode
 6          Dim aQueue As Queue = New Queue
 7          Console.WriteLine("Original Queue")
 8          aQueue.Enqueue("Graham")
 9          aQueue.Enqueue("Emily")
10          aQueue.DisplayAllNodes()
11          Console.WriteLine("Queue with Eleanor added")
12          aQueue.Enqueue("Eleanor")
13          aQueue.DisplayAllNodes()
14          Console.WriteLine("Queue with Graham removed")
15          node = aQueue.Dequeue()
16          aQueue.DisplayAllNodes()
17          Try
18              node = aQueue.Peek()
19              Console.WriteLine("node data after Peek: " & node.GetData())
20              Console.WriteLine("Queue with Emily removed")
21              node = aQueue.Dequeue()
22              aQueue.DisplayAllNodes()
23              Console.WriteLine("Remove last node")
24              node = aQueue.Dequeue()
25              ' now try to remove from empty Queue
26              Console.WriteLine("try to Dequeue empty Queue")
27              node = aQueue.Dequeue()
28          Catch e As EmptyQueueException
29              Console.WriteLine("Exception caught: " & e.Message())
30          End Try
31      End Sub
32  End Module
```

Figure 15-21   Client module listing for Example 15-6

15

Sample Run:

```
Original Queue
Graham
Emily
Queue with Eleanor added
Graham
Emily
Eleanor
Queue with Graham removed
Emily
Eleanor
node data after Peek: Emily
Queue with Emily removed
Eleanor
Remove last node
try to Dequeue empty Queue
Exception caught: Queue is empty
```

Queue Class Discussion:

The Queue class definition extends LinkedList and contains no attributes. However, it does have a constructor and three methods: Enqueue in lines 8 through 11, Dequeue in lines 12 through 20, and Peek in lines 21 through 29. Enqueue simply invokes the inherited method InsertAtEnd.

In line 14, Dequeue first checks for an empty queue by invoking the inherited method IsEmpty, throwing an EmptyQueueException if True. If the queue is not empty, then the inherited method RemoveFromBeginning is invoked.

Similarly, Peek first checks for an empty queue, and throws an exception if it is. If the queue is not empty, Peek retrieves the firstNode reference from LinkedList and returns it to Client.

Client Module Discussion:

This version of the Client module is similar to the one in the previous example.

Line 6 instantiates Queue, assigning the reference to aQueue.

Lines 8 and 9 invoke Enqueue, adding the first two items to the queue, and line 10 displays the queue.

Line 12 adds a third item to the queue, and line 13 again displays the queue.

Line 15 removes the first item from the queue and displays the revised queue.

A Try block is defined in lines 17 through 30. Line 18 invokes Peek, and line 19 displays the value returned.

Line 21 removes another item and line 22 redisplays the queue.

Line 24 removes the last item from the queue, and line 27 attempts to remove an item from the empty queue. `Dequeue` throws an `EmptyQueueException`, which is then caught and displayed in line 29.

Exploring the FCL Queue class

The FCL also includes a `Queue` class with some of the same methods you included in the class you developed in Example 15-6. Similar to the FCL `Stack` class, the supplied `Queue` class stores nodes as instances of `Object`. In addition to `Enqueue`, `Dequeue`, and `Peek` methods, this class also includes the method `ToArray`, which copies the objects in the queue into an array.

The next example illustrates using the FCL `Queue` class. The `Client` module from Example 15-6 is used with several modifications, which are discussed in the following example.

Example 15-7: Exploring the FCL Queue class

Figure 15-22 shows the code for the Client module for this example.

```
1   Option Explicit On
2   Option Strict On
3 ☐ Module Client
4       Dim data As String, aQueue As Queue
5 ☐     Sub Main()
6           aQueue = New Queue
7           Console.WriteLine("Original Queue")
8           aQueue.Enqueue("Graham")
9           aQueue.Enqueue("Emily")
10          DisplayAll()
11          Console.WriteLine("Queue with Eleanor added")
12          aQueue.Enqueue("Eleanor")
13          DisplayAll()
14          Console.WriteLine("Queue with Graham removed")
15          data = Convert.ToString(aQueue.Dequeue())
16          DisplayAll()
17          Try
18              data = Convert.ToString(aQueue.Peek())
19              Console.WriteLine("node data after Peek: " & data)
20              Console.WriteLine("Queue with Emily removed")
21              data = Convert.ToString(aQueue.Dequeue())
22              DisplayAll()
23              Console.WriteLine("Remove last node")
24              data = Convert.ToString(aQueue.Dequeue())
25              ' now try to remove from empty Queue
26              Console.WriteLine("try to Dequeue empty Queue")
27              data = Convert.ToString(aQueue.Dequeue())
28          Catch e As InvalidOperationException
29              Console.WriteLine("Exception caught: " & e.Message())
30          End Try
31      End Sub
32 ☐   Private Sub DisplayAll()
33          Dim i As Integer
34          Dim arrayOfData() As Object = aQueue.ToArray()
35          For i = 0 To arrayOfData.Length - 1
36              data = Convert.ToString(arrayOfData(i))
37              Console.WriteLine("data # " & (i + 1) & ": " & data)
38          Next
39      End Sub
40  End Module
```

Figure 15-22   Client module listing for Example 15-7

15

Sample Run:

```
Original Queue
data # 1: Graham
data # 2: Emily
Queue with Eleanor added
data # 1: Graham
data # 2: Emily
data # 3: Eleanor
Queue with Graham removed
data # 1: Emily
data # 2: Eleanor
node data after Peek: Emily
Queue with Emily removed
data # 1: Eleanor
Remove last node
try to Dequeue empty Queue
Exception caught: Queue empty.
```

Discussion:

The `Client` module in this example is nearly identical to that in Example 15-5. The references to `Stack` have been changed to `Queue`, and the statements invoking `Push` and `Pop` have been changed to `Enqueue` and `Dequeue`, respectively.

Line 4 declares two variables with module scope. The `String` variable data will be used to hold the data from an item in the stack. `aQueue` will contain a reference to the `Queue` instance created in `Main`.

Line 6 in `Main` instantiates the `Queue` class, assigning its reference to `aQueue`.

Lines 8 and 9 add two items to the new queue.

Line 10 invokes `DisplayAll` listed in lines 32 through 39. This method is copied from Example 15-5 with references to `Stack` changed to `Queue`.

Next, line 12 in `Main` adds another item to the queue, and line 13 again invokes `DisplayAll`.

Line 15 then invokes `Dequeue` to remove the last item in the queue, and line 16 redisplays the queue contents.

Similar to Example 15-6, lines 17 through 30 contain a `Try` block.

Within the `Try`, line 18 invokes `Peek`, line 21 removes the next item from the queue, and line 24 removes the final item. `DisplayAll` is invoked after each operation to show the queue contents.

Line 27 attempts to invoke `Dequeue` for a now empty queue. This method throws `InvalidOperationException`, which is caught in line 28, and the message is displayed in line 29.

PROGRAMMING EXAMPLE: RESERVATION APPLICATION

This Programming Example implements a reservation system, which uses several previously developed classes: `Customer` from Example 10-16 in Chapter 10, plus `LinkedList`, `LinkedListNode`, `Queue`, and `EmptyQueueException` from this chapter. This Programming Example also includes a new class named `ReservationList`, which extends `Queue`, and a new `Client` module patterned after the clients in this chapter.

Problem Analysis and Algorithm Design

Figure 15-23 shows the class diagram for `ReservationList`.

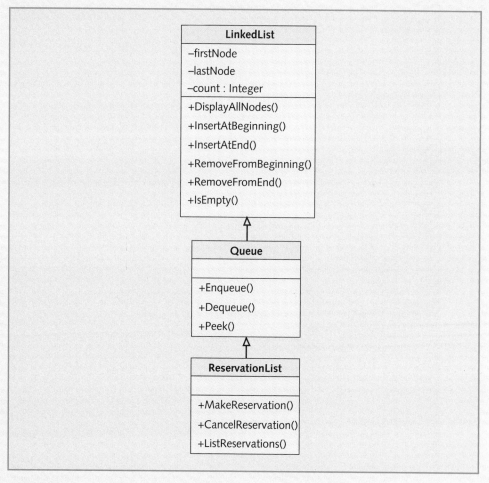

Figure 15-23   Reservation class diagram

Reservation is a subclass of Queue, which is a subclass of LinkedList. In addition to a constructor, Reservation has three other methods: MakeReservation, CancelReservation, and ListReservations.

MakeReservation:

This method receives an argument whose data type is Customer, and then invokes the inherited method Enqueue, passing the Customer reference as an argument.

CancelReservation:

This method receives an argument whose data type is Customer. It then searches the reservation list (queue) attempting to locate a Customer instance whose phone number matches that of the Customer instance received as an argument. If the queue is empty or if no matching customer is found, then an instance of EmptyQueueException is created and thrown. If a matching customer is found, then its node is removed from the queue.

ListReservations:

This method traverses the queue. For each node, the customer reference is retrieved. TellAboutSelf is invoked for each customer instance, and the String returned is displayed. If there are no reservations, a message is displayed.

Complete Program Listing

Customer, LinkedListNode, LinkedList, Queue, and EmptyQueueException were copied without change and are therefore not listed again here.

Many method headers in this chapter are long and do not fit on a single printed line. However, when you type the code in your IDE, you should type the method headers as a single line. (Code other than method headers uses an underscore as the continuation character to indicate that a statement continues on the next line.)

Reservation Class

```
Public Class ReservationList
    Inherits Queue
    Public Sub New()
        MyBase.new()
    End Sub
    Public Sub MakeReservation(ByVal customer As Customer)
        Enqueue(customer)
    End Sub
    Public Sub CancelReservation(ByVal customerToCancel As
    Customer)
        Dim currentNode, nodeToRemove, previousNode, nextNode As
        LinkedListNode
        Dim i As Integer, thisCustomer As Customer, found As
        Boolean
```

```
            If IsEmpty() Then
                Throw New EmptyQueueException("Empty list")
            Else
                ' try to find this customer in list
                found = False
                previousNode = firstNode
                currentNode = firstNode
                nodeToRemove = Nothing
                nextNode = currentNode.GetNextNode()
                Do Until found Or currentNode Is Nothing
                    thisCustomer = currentNode.GetData()
                    If thisCustomer.CustomerPhoneNo =
                    customerToCancel.CustomerPhoneNo Then
                        nodeToRemove = currentNode
                        found = True
                    Else
                        previousNode = currentNode
                        currentNode = currentNode.GetNextNode()
                        nextNode = currentNode.GetNextNode()
                    End If
                Loop
                If nodeToRemove Is Nothing Then
                    Throw New EmptyQueueException("Customer has no
                    reservation")
                Else
                    previousNode.SetNextNode(nextNode)
                End If
            End If
        End Sub
        Public Function ListReservations()
            Dim currentNode As LinkedListNode, customer As Customer
            currentNode = firstNode
            If currentNode Is Nothing Then
                Console.WriteLine("No reservations")
            Else
                Do Until currentNode Is Nothing
                    customer = currentNode.GetData()
                    Console.WriteLine(customer.TellAboutSelf())
                    currentNode = currentNode.GetNextNode()
                Loop
            End If
        End Function
    End Class
```

Client Module

```
Option Strict On
Option Explicit On
Module Client
    Sub Main()
        Dim customer1, customer2, customer3 As Customer
```

15

```
        ' create 3 instances of Customer
        customer1 = New Customer("Eleanor", "Atlanta", "123-4567")
        customer2 = New Customer("Emily", "St. Louis", "467-1234")
        customer3 = New Customer("Graham", "Marietta", "765-4321")
        ' create reservation list
        Dim node As LinkedListNode
        Dim reservations As ReservationList = New ReservationList
        Console.WriteLine("Original list")
        reservations.MakeReservation(customer1)
        reservations.MakeReservation(customer2)
        reservations.ListReservations()
        Console.WriteLine("list with Graham added")
        reservations.MakeReservation(customer3)
        reservations.ListReservations()
        Console.WriteLine("list with Emily removed")
        reservations.CancelReservation(customer2)
        reservations.ListReservations()
        Try
            Console.WriteLine("list with Graham removed")
            reservations.CancelReservation(customer3)
            reservations.ListReservations()
            Console.WriteLine("Remove last reservation")
            reservations.CancelReservation(customer1)
            ' now try to remove from empty list
            Console.WriteLine("try to remove non-existent
            customer")
            reservations.CancelReservation(customer1)
        Catch e As EmptyQueueException
            Console.WriteLine(customer1.TellAboutSelf & " has no
            reservation")
        End Try
    End Sub
End Module
```

Sample Run

```
Original list
Eleanor, Atlanta,123-4567
Emily, St. Louis,467-1234
list with Graham added
Eleanor, Atlanta,123-4567
Emily, St. Louis,467-1234
Graham, Marietta,765-4321
list with Emily removed
Eleanor, Atlanta,123-4567
Graham, Marietta,765-4321
list with Graham removed
Eleanor, Atlanta,123-4567
Remove last reservation
try to remove non-existent customer
```

UNDERSTANDING RECURSION

The methods you have written until now have been methods that call other methods in a straightforward manner. Method A calls method B, method B calls method C, and so forth. **Recursion** is a programming technique in which a method calls itself. Although the idea of a method calling itself may seem odd, for some problems a recursive approach leads to a simple and elegant solution.

Conceptually, the recursive problem-solving approach divides a complex problem into successively smaller but similar subproblems, solves each of those subproblems, and then assembles the result. To better understand the principle of recursion, think of a large box. When you open the large box (Box A), you find a smaller box (Box B). When you open Box B, you find an even smaller box (Box C). Each time you open a box, you find a smaller box within it. The steps you follow to open a box are the same for every box. Suppose that you continue to open smaller and smaller boxes until you open a box that is too small to contain another box. At this point, there are no more boxes to open and the recursive process of opening boxes stops. A recursive program that simulates this problem (assuming there are 10 different box sizes) is shown in Example 15-8.

Example 15-8: Using a recursive method to simulate opening boxes

```
Module OpenBoxesRecursively
    Sub Main()
        'open largest box (size 10)
        OpenBox(10)                                    Initial invocation of the
        System.Console.WriteLine("Done")               OpenBox method
    End Sub

                                                       When this condition (called
                                                       the base case) is recognized,
    Sub OpenBox(ByVal boxSize As Integer)              recursive calls stop
        If boxSize = 0 Then
            System.Console.WriteLine("No more boxes to open")
        Else
            System.Console.WriteLine("Box " & boxSize & _
            " opened")
                                                       Recursive call—the OpenBox
            OpenBox(boxSize - 1)                       method is called within the
        End If                                          OpenBox method
    End Sub
End Module
```

15

Discussion:

The **Main** method initially invokes the **OpenBox** method, passing to it the number 10 (which represents the size of the largest box). The **OpenBox** method first checks to see if the base case (boxSize = 0) has occurred. In this case, it has not, so the **OpenBox** method prints a message indicating that the box of size 10 has been opened, and then calls itself with the next smaller box size (boxSize = 9).

The new copy of the **OpenBox** method checks to see if the base case has occurred. Once again, it has not, so this copy of the **OpenBox** method prints a message indicating that the box of size 9 has been opened, and then calls itself with the next smaller box size (boxSize = 8).

This pattern of recursive calls continues until the **OpenBox** method calls itself with boxSize equal to 0. This copy of the **OpenBox** method recognizes the base case (boxSize = 0) and prints a message indicating that there are no more boxes to open. There are no further statements to execute in this last copy of the method, so control returns the calling method (the method where box size is equal to 1).

Again, in this copy of the method, there are no statements to execute following the line of code containing the recursive call, so control returns the next previous caller (the method where box size is equal to 2). This pattern of returns to the previous caller continues until control is returned to the method where box size is equal to 10. At this point, control returns to the **Main** method and the line of code following the initial invocation of the **OpenBox** method executes, printing the "Done" message.

Figure 15-24 depicts this procession of recursive calls and returns.

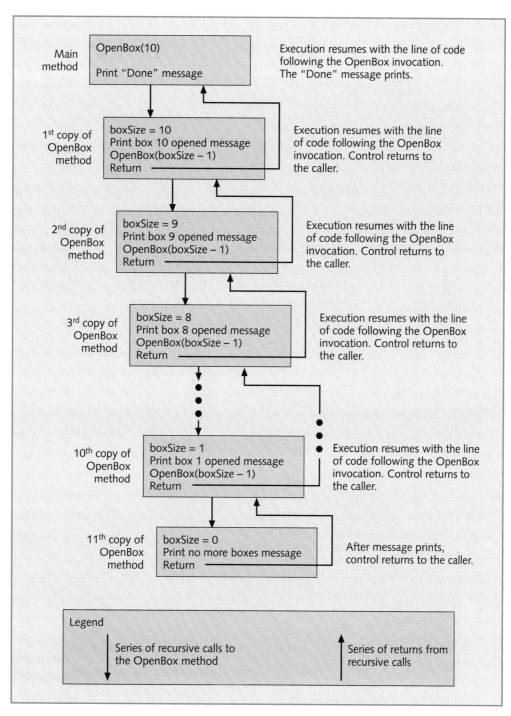

Figure 15-24 Procession of recursive calls and returns for the OpenBox method

15

Sample Run:

```
Box 10 opened
Box 9 opened
Box 8 opened
Box 7 opened
Box 6 opened
Box 5 opened
Box 4 opened
Box 3 opened
Box 2 opened
Box 1 opened
No more boxes to open
Done
```

This simple example illustrates a critical and necessary feature of a recursive solution: it must have a stopping point. If it did not, theoretically, the method would call itself indefinitely and never stop. The stopping point is also referred to as the **base case**. When the base case is recognized (usually via an `If` statement), the recursion stops. Otherwise, the method calls itself with a simpler version of the problem.

Each time a recursive method (such as `OpenBox`) calls itself, a fresh copy of the method is created. Each copy has its own set of values and parameters and remains unfinished until the base case is recognized. At that time, control returns to each immediate previous caller in succession. Upon each return, execution resumes within that copy at the line of code immediately following the recursive call.

Recursion is similar in many ways to iteration. In fact, any problem that can be solved iteratively can also be solved recursively, and vice versa. For example, the problem in Example 15-8 could be solved iteratively as follows:

```
Module OpenBoxesIteratively
    Sub Main()
        'open largest box (size 10)
        Dim boxSize As Integer
        For boxSize = 10 To 1 Step -1
            System.Console.WriteLine("Box " & boxSize & " opened")
        Next
        System.Console.WriteLine("No more boxes to open")
        System.Console.WriteLine("Done")
    End Sub
End Module
```

Usually, recursive solutions are less efficient in terms of computer resources. For example, each time a recursive method is invoked, the system allocates memory for the parameters and variables associated with that copy of the method; it then deallocates memory when that copy of the method terminates. As a result, a recursive solution for a given problem usually executes more slowly than an iterative one and requires more memory. However, for some problems, such as the Programming Example at the end of this chapter, a recursive solution is much less complex. Analyzing the efficiency of recursive solutions is an important area of study in advanced computer science courses.

WRITING RECURSIVE METHODS

To write a recursive method, you must think recursively—in other words, you must think of a problem in terms of a series of successively smaller but virtually identical subproblems. The smallest subproblem (the base case) must be one that can be solved directly—that is, without requiring another recursive call.

Computing Factorials

A classic example of recursion involves computing factorials. By definition, the factorial of a number n (designated as $n!$) is:

$n! = n * (n - 1) * (n - 2) * \ldots * 1$, where n is a positive integer

$0! = 1$

 By definition, 0! = 1. Factorials are undefined for negative integers.

For example:

$4! = 4 * 3 * 2 * 1 = 24$

In this equation, recognize that 3 * 2 * 1 is equal to 3!. Thus, thinking recursively, 4! can be defined as 4 * 3!. Likewise, 3! can be defined as 3 * 2!, and so forth. The evaluation of 4! using this recursive problem-solving approach is shown in Figure 15-25.

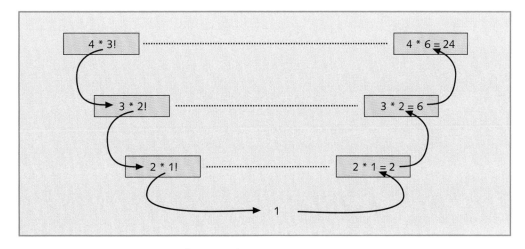

Figure 15-25   Recursive evaluation of 4!

15

In the general case, n! can be defined recursively as n * (n–1)!. With this in mind, you can develop a Windows application that uses a recursive method for finding the factorial of a number. The GUI for this application is shown in Figure 15-26.

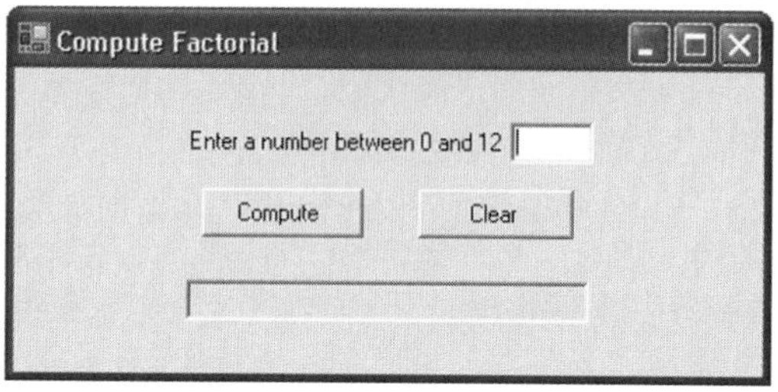

Figure 15-26 GUI for the factorial program

The code for this program is given in Example 15-9.

Example 15-9: Computing factorials

```
Public Class frmFactorial
    Inherits System.Windows.Forms.Form

    'Windows Form Designer generated code

    Private Sub btnCompute_Click(ByVal sender As System.Object,
    ByVal e As System.EventArgs) Handles btnCompute.Click
        Dim n, result As Integer
        Try
            n = System.Convert.ToInt32(txtNumber.Text)
            If n < 0 Or n > 12 Then
                MessageBox.Show _
                ("You must enter a number >= 0 and <= 12")
            Else
                result = factorial(n)
                txtResult.Text = "The factorial of " & n & _
                " is " & result.ToString("#,###")
            End If
        Catch ex As Exception
```

```
        MessageBox.Show _
          ("Invalid data entry. Please try again.")
      End Try
  End Sub


  Private Function factorial(ByVal n As Integer) As Integer
      Dim x as Integer
      If n = 0 Then
          Return 1
      Else
          x = n * factorial(n - 1)
          Return x
      End If
  End Function


  Private Sub btnClear_Click(ByVal sender As System.Object,
  ByVal e As System.EventArgs) Handles btnClear.Click
      txtNumber.Clear()
      txtResult.Clear()
      txtNumber.Focus()
  End Sub


End Class
```

Factorials become large numbers very quickly. Calculating factorials can produce a number that is too large to be represented in the memory space allocated to a particular variable. For example, the largest positive number that can be stored in a variable of type `Integer` is 2,147,483,647. The factorial of 13 is 6,227,020,800. Therefore, 12! is the largest factorial that can be computed using the `Integer` data type to hold the result.

Discussion:

15

The section of code shown in the green box handles a Click event on the Compute button. A **Try-Catch** block ensures that the user enters a value that can be converted to an integer. Within the **Try** block, an **If** statement tests to see that the value entered is an integer between 0 and 12. If so, the event handler invokes the **factorial** function, passing to it the value entered by the user. Otherwise, the event handler displays an error message.

The **factorial** function (shown in the second shaded box) is a recursive function. The **factorial** function first tests to see if the base case (n = 0) has occurred. If not, the function calls itself with the value n − 1. The pattern of recursive calls continues until the base case is recognized.

The copy of the method where the base case occurs returns the value 1 to the previous caller (recall that 0! = 1). The previous caller uses this value to calculate the value of 1! as 1 * 0! or 1 * 1, which equals 1, then returns the value 1 to its previous caller. This previous copy of the method uses this value to calculate the value of 2! as 2 * 1! or 2 * 1, which equals 2. It then returns the value 2 to its previous caller. The previous copy uses this value to calculate 3 * 2! or 3 * 2, which equals 6. This sequence of returns continues until there are no more previous copies of the method, when control returns to the event handler for the Click event. Execution resumes at the line of code following the initial invocation of the `factorial` method, which displays the result in the text box.

Figure 15-27 depicts this procession of recursive calls and returns when $n = 4$.

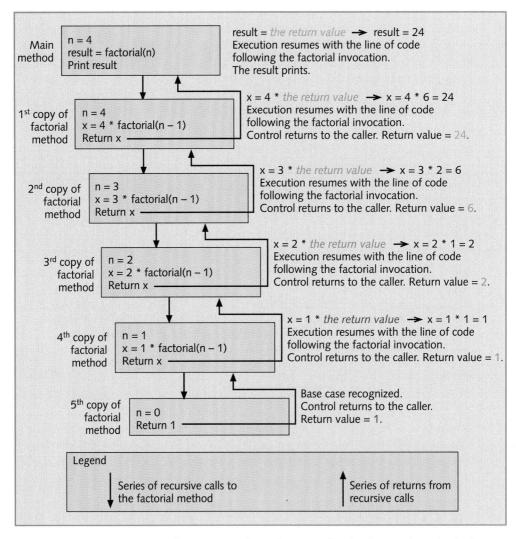

Figure 15-27   Procession of recursive calls and returns for the factorial method when $n = 4$

The code in the blue box simply clears the information in the text boxes and sets the focus to the text box that accepts the next value from the user.

A sample output of this program is shown in Figure 15-28.

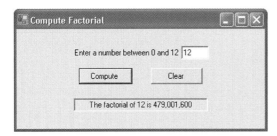

Figure 15-28   Sample output of the factorial program

Displaying a Directory Tree

In Chapter 13, you used the `TreeNode` and `TreeView` classes to display hierarchically related information. You can use these GUI classes, together with a recursive algorithm, to generate and display a tree containing the directories and subdirectories on your hard drive. A partial directory tree is shown in Figure 15-29.

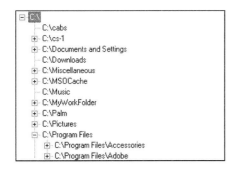

Figure 15-29   A partial directory tree

15

Figure 15-30 shows a GUI for generating and displaying the tree.

Figure 15-30 GUI for the directory tree program

Depending on the size of your hard drive and the speed of your computer, initially creating the directory tree may take a few minutes. Thus the GUI displays a wait message while it constructs the tree, as shown in Figure 15-31.

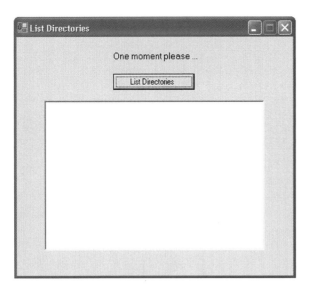

Figure 15-31 Wait message

The code for this program is shown in Example 15-10.

Example 15-10: Displaying a directory tree

```
Public Class frmListDirectory
    Inherits System.Windows.Forms.Form

    'Windows Form Designer generated code
    Friend WithEvents trvDirectory As System.Windows.Forms.TreeView

    Private Sub btnList_Click(ByVal sender As Object, ByVal e As
    System.EventArgs) Handles btnList.Click
        'display wait message
        lblWait.Text = "One moment please ..."
        lblWait.Update()
        'declare variables for root directory
        Dim rootName As String = "C:\"
        Dim rootNode As TreeNode
        'add root directory to the tree
        trvDirectory.Nodes.Add(rootName)
        rootNode = trvDirectory.Nodes(0)  'root node is node(0)
        'invoke recursive method to create the directory listing
        CreateDirectoryListing(rootName, rootNode)
        'hide wait message
        lblWait.Text = "Click + or - to expand or collapse nodes"
        lblWait.Update()
        'disable button
        btnList.Enabled = False
    End Sub

    Private Sub CreateDirectoryListing(ByVal directoryName As
    String, ByVal parentNode As TreeNode)
        'declare variables
        Dim dirArray As String()
        Dim directory As String
        Dim childNode As TreeNode
        Try
            'get all subdirectories of current directory
            dirArray = System.IO.Directory.GetDirectories(directoryName)
            'sort the array
            Array.Sort(dirArray)
            'continue recursion while there are subdirectories,
            otherwise exit
                If dirArray.Length > 0 Then
```

The Windows Form Designer generates code that includes this statement

15

```
                    'create a child node for each subdirectory
              For Each directory In dirArray
                 childNode = New TreeNode(directory)
                 'add child node to parent node
                 parentNode.Nodes.Add(childNode)
                 'begin next recursion
                 CreateDirectoryListing(directory, childNode)
              Next
           End If
     Catch ex As Exception
        MessageBox.Show("Access Denied")
        parentNode.Nodes.Add("Unable to access directory")
     End Try
   End Sub

End Class
```

Discussion:

The code in the green box is the event handler for a Click event on the List Directories button. Because the building of the directory tree can take a few minutes, the event handler uses a label to display a "One moment please" message. It then creates a node representing C: and adds this node to the tree as the root node. The event handler then makes the initial call to the recursive method `CreateDirectoryListing` passing to it the name of the root node ("C:") and the root node itself.

The `CreateDirectoryListing` method obtains the immediate subdirectories of the node passed to it, stores them in an array, and then sorts the array. If the array is empty, no subdirectories were found (the base case) and the recursion stops. Otherwise, *for each subdirectory* in the array, the `CreateDirectoryListing` method adds a child node to the directory tree, then invokes itself to find the child directories of that particular subdirectory. Because access to some directories may be prohibited, this code is enclosed within a **Try-Catch** block.

Once control returns to the event handler, the "One moment please" message is replaced by a message informing the user how to expand and collapse the tree nodes. The event handler then disables the List Directories button to avoid unnecessary replication.

A sample output for the directory tree program is shown in Figure 15-32.

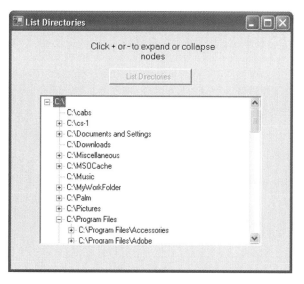

Figure 15-32   Sample output of the directory tree program

Sorting an Array

Recursive methods are frequently used for array processing. This includes tasks such as finding the minimum or maximum value in an array, printing the contents of an array in forward or reverse order, and sorting an array. One recursive technique for sorting a one-dimensional array is known as Quicksort. The Quicksort technique begins by selecting an array element to serve as the **pivot**. The objective is to move the pivot to its correct position in the array—that is, to position the pivot such that all array elements to its right are greater than or equal to the pivot, and all array elements to its left are less than or equal to the pivot. Elements to the right of the pivot comprise one subarray; elements to the left of the pivot comprise another subarray. The Quicksort technique is then applied recursively to each subarray.

To illustrate, consider the following array of 10 integers:

14   25   74   12   58   4   27   18   54   28

By default, choose the first element in the array as the pivot. It is useful to keep track of a top index and a bottom index. Initially the bottom index is 0 (the index of the first element in the array) and the top index is 9 (the index of the last element in the array). The goal is to move the pivot, in this case the number 14, to its correct position. The pivot will be in its

15

correct position when the top index and the bottom index are equal. The steps for moving the pivot to its correct position are as follows:

1. Starting with the top index (9) and working from right to left, compare each element to the pivot. When you find an element less than or equal to the pivot, or reach the bottom index (0), swap the pivot and that element. The number 4 is less than 14, so swap 14 and 4. The modified array is:

   4   25   74   12   58   **14**   27   18   54   28

   The pivot position now represents the top index (5).

2. Starting with the bottom index and working from left to right, compare each element to the pivot. When you find an element greater than or equal to the pivot, or reach the top index (5), swap the pivot and that element. The number 25 is greater than 14, so swap 14 and 25. The new array is:

   4   **14**   74   12   58   25   27   18   54   28

   The pivot position now represents the bottom index (1).

3. Starting from the right, but beginning with the top index (5), compare each element to the pivot. When you find an element less than or equal to the pivot, or reach the bottom index, swap that element and the pivot. The number 12 is less than 14, so swap 14 and 12. The array contents are:

   4   12   74   **14**   58   25   27   18   54   28

   The pivot position now represents the top index (3).

4. Starting from the left, but beginning with the bottom index (1), compare each element to the pivot. When you find an element greater than or equal to the pivot, or reach the top index, swap that element and the pivot. The number 74 is greater than 14, so swap 74 and 14. The result is:

   4   12   **14**   74   58   25   27   18   54   28

   The pivot position now represents the bottom index (2).

5. Starting from the right, but beginning with the top index (3), compare each element to the pivot. When you find an element less than or equal to the pivot, or reach the bottom index (2), swap that element and the pivot. In this case, there is only one element to consider and that element is the pivot. Swap the pivot with itself. The array contents do not change:

   4   12   **14**   74   58   25   27   18   54   28

   The pivot position now represents the top index (2). The top index (2) and the bottom index (2) are now equal, indicating that the pivot is in its correct position.

With the initial pivot in its correct position, the recursive nature of the Quicksort technique begins. The elements to the left of the pivot form a subarray, and the elements to the right of the pivot form another subarray. The subarray to the left of the pivot contains elements 4 and 12. The subarray to the right of the pivot contains elements 74, 58, 25, 27, 18, 54, and 28. The Quicksort technique is applied recursively to each subarray. When there are no more subarrays to sort (the base case), recursion stops and the array is sorted.

Figure 15-33 shows a GUI that uses the Quicksort technique to sort an array. The user clicks a button to generate an array of 10 integers between 0 and 100, and then clicks another button to sort the array, as shown in Figure 15-34.

Figure 15-33   GUI for the Quicksort program

Figure 15-34   GUI for the Quicksort program after clicking the Generate Array button

15

Example 15-11 shows the code for this example.

Example 15-11 Sorting an array using the Quicksort algorithm

```
Public Class frmQuicksort
    Inherits System.Windows.Forms.Form
    Dim numbers As Integer()

    'Windows Form Designer generated code

    Private Sub btnGenerate_Click(ByVal sender As System.Object,
    ByVal e As System.EventArgs) Handles btnGenerate.Click
        'declare variables
        Dim n, i As Integer
        Dim origOutput As String = ""
        'initialize array
        numbers = New Integer(10) {}
        'initialize the random number generator
        Randomize()
        'fill array with random numbers
        For i = 0 To 9
            n = Int(100 * Rnd()) + 1 'generate a number between 1
            'and 100
            numbers(i) = n
            'build output string
            origOutput = origOutput & n.ToString
            If i < 9 Then
                origOutput = origOutput & ", "
            End If
        Next
        'display values in original array
        txtOriginal.Text = origOutput
        'clear text box containing sorted values
        txtSorted.Clear()
    End Sub

    Private Sub btnSort_Click(ByVal sender As System.Object, ByVal
    e As System.EventArgs) Handles btnSort.Click
        'declare variables
        Dim startIndex, endIndex, n, i As Integer
        Dim sortedOutput As String
        'initialize starting and ending indices
        startIndex = 0
```

```
    endIndex = 9
    'invoke quick sort procedure
    Quicksort(startIndex, endIndex)
    'display sorted array values
    For i = 0 To 9
        n = numbers(i)
        sortedOutput = sortedOutput & n.ToString
        If i < 9 Then
            sortedOutput = sortedOutput & ", "
        End If
        txtSorted.Text = sortedOutput
    Next
End Sub
```

```
Public Sub Quicksort(ByVal startIndex As Integer, ByVal
endIndex As Integer)
    'declare variables
    Dim pivotValue, top, bottom As Integer
    'if startIndex >= endIndex, the list is sorted
    If startIndex >= endIndex Then
        Return
    Else
        'pivot is first element (by default)
        pivotValue = numbers(startIndex)
        'save startIndex and endIndex
        bottom = startIndex
        top = endIndex
        'determine correct position of the pivot
            '(all numbers to the right of the pivot are >= the
            'pivot and ' all numbers to the left of the pivot are
            '<= the pivot)
        Do
            'search from top to bottom for a value less than
            the pivot
            While (numbers(top) >= pivotValue And top > bottom)
                top = top - 1
            End While
            'swap
            numbers(bottom) = numbers(top)
            numbers(top) = pivotValue
```

15

```
          'search from bottom to the top for a value greater
          than the pivot
          While (numbers(bottom) <= pivotValue And bottom < top)
              bottom = bottom + 1
          End While
          'swap
          numbers(top) = numbers(bottom)
          numbers(bottom) = pivotValue
          If top = bottom Then
              'pivot is in its correct position
              Exit Do
          End If
      Loop

      'Sort the two subarrays
      Quicksort(startIndex, bottom - 1)
      Quicksort(bottom + 1, endIndex)
    End If
  End Sub

End Class
```

Discussion:

The code in the first shaded box is the event handler for the Generate Array button. This event handler uses the random number generator to generate 10 numbers between 0 and 100. It fills an array with these values and displays them in the first text box.

The code in the second shaded box is the event handler for the Sort Array button. This event handler invokes the Quicksort method, passing to it a starting and ending index (in this case, 0 and 9, respectively).

The recursive Quicksort method first checks to see if the base case (starting index ≥ ending index) has occurred. If so, control returns to the previous caller. Otherwise, the Quicksort method moves the pivot its correct position, and invokes itself again for each subarray.

Sample Run:

Sample output for this program is shown in Figure 15-35.

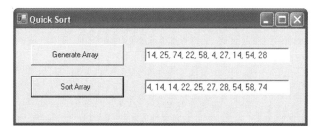

Figure 15-35   Sample output for the Quicksort program

PROGRAMMING EXAMPLE: TOWERS OF HANOI

This Programming Example presents a classic computer science problem known as the Towers of Hanoi. According to legend, priests in a Far Eastern temple were given the task of moving a stack of 64 disks from one pole to another. Each of the disks was a slightly different size, and the disks were arranged on the pole from top to bottom in order of increasing size. An intermediate pole was also available to hold disks. The priests were to move all 64 disks to the third pole using the following rules:

1. Only one disk can be moved at a time.
2. A removed disk must be placed on one of the other poles.
3. Under no circumstance may a larger disk be placed upon a smaller disk.

The priests were told that the world would end when they completed their task.

Problem Analysis, GUI Design, and Algorithm Design

Although the priests were assigned the task of moving 64 disks, consider the problem when there are a small number of disks, as depicted in Figure 15-36.

15

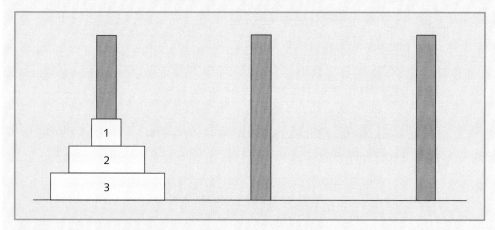

Figure 15-36   The Towers of Hanoi problem with three disks

If there is only one disk, the solution is straightforward—simply move the disk from pole 1 to pole 3. If there are two disks, move the smaller disk from pole 1 to pole 2, move the larger disk from pole 1 to pole 3, and then move the smaller disk from pole 2 to pole 3. A solution for the case when there are three disks is shown in Figure 15-37.

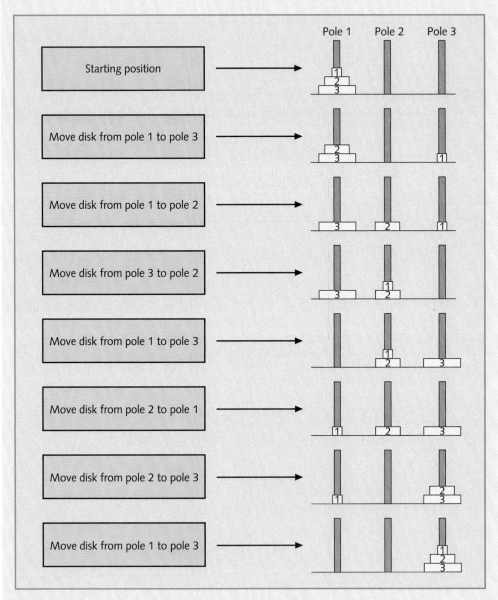

Figure 15-37 Solution for the Towers of Hanoi problem with three disks

Thinking recursively, this solution can be summarized as follows:

1. Move the top two disks from pole 1 to pole 2, using pole 3 to temporarily hold disks.
2. Move the bottom (largest) disk from pole 1 to pole 3.
3. Move the two disks on pole 2 to pole 3, using pole 1 to temporarily hold disks.

This recursive algorithm can be generalized to any number of disks, n, as follows:

1. Move the top n-1 disks from pole 1 to pole 2, using pole 3 to temporarily hold disks.
2. Move the bottom (nth) disk from pole 1 to pole 3.
3. Move the n-1 disks on pole 2 to pole 3, using pole 1 to temporarily hold disks.

Notice that the number of moves required to move the disks is $2^{64}-1$. When n = 1, the number of moves is $2^1-1 = 1$. When n = 2, the number of moves is $2^2-1 = 3$, and when n = 3, the number of moves is $2^3-1 = 7$. Similarly, when n = 64, the number of moves is $2^{64}-1$. To gain an appreciation for just how large this number is, consider that 2^n-1 is approximately equivalent to $1.85 * 10^{19}$. The number of seconds in a year is $60*60*24*365$, which is approximately $3.15 * 10^7$. Assuming that the priests could move one disk per second, the number of years it would take them to move all 64 disks is equal to $(1.85 * 10^{19}) / (3.15 * 10^7)$ or 590 billion years!

A GUI for the Towers of Hanoi problem is shown in Figure 15-38.

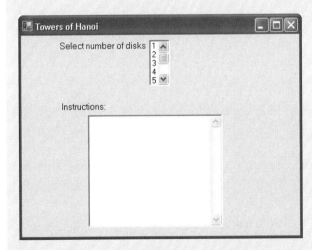

Figure 15-38   GUI for the Towers of Hanoi program

The GUI includes a list box containing the numbers 1 through 9. Once the user selects a number on the list box, the program displays the instructions for moving that number of disks from pole 1 to pole 3.

Complete Program Listing

```
Public Class frmTowersOfHanoi
    Inherits System.Windows.Forms.Form
    Dim numberOfMoves As Integer

    'Windows Form Designer generated code

    Private Sub lstNumDisks_SelectedValueChanged(ByVal sender As
    System.Object, ByVal e As System.EventArgs) Handles
    lstNumDisks.SelectedValueChanged
        Dim numberOfDisks, pole1, pole2, pole3 As Integer
        numberOfDisks = lstNumDisks.SelectedItem
        txtOutput.Clear()
        'initialize variables
        pole1 = 1    'pole1 is the pole initially holding the disks
        pole2 = 2    'pole2 is the pole used as a temporary holding
                     'area
        pole3 = 3    'pole3 is the pole to which disks are to be moved
        numberOfMoves = 0
        'invoke towers method
        '1st parameter is number of disks to be moved
        '2nd parameter specifies the pole initially holding the disks
        '3rd parameter specifies the pole to be used for intermediate
        'storage
        '4th parameter specifies the pole to which disks are to be
        moved
        towers(numberOfDisks, pole1, pole2, pole3)
        txtOutput.AppendText("Number of moves = " & numberOfMoves)
    End Sub


    Private Sub towers(ByVal numberOfDisks As Integer, ByVal pole1
    As Integer, ByVal pole2 As Integer, ByVal pole3 As Integer)
        'increment the number of moves by 1
        numberOfMoves += 1
        'if only one disk on pole 1 move it to pole 3 (base case)
        If numberOfDisks = 1 Then
            txtOutput.AppendText("Move disk from pole " & pole1 & _
            " to pole " _ & pole3 & vbCrLf)
            Return
        Else
            'move top n-1 disks from pole 1 to pole 2
```

```
            towers(numberOfDisks - 1, pole1, pole3, pole2)
            'move bottom disk from pole 1 to pole 3
            txtOutput.AppendText("Move disk from pole " & pole1 & _
            " to pole " & pole3 & vbCrLf)
            'move disks temporarily stored on pole 2 to pole 3
            towers(numberOfDisks - 1, pole2, pole1, pole3)
        End If
    End Sub
End Class
```

Sample Run

A sample output for the Towers of Hanoi program is shown in Figure 15-39.

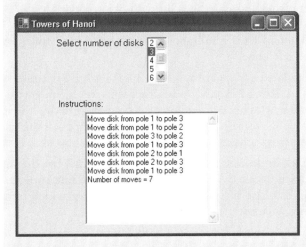

Figure 15-39   Sample output of the Towers of Hanoi program

15

QUICK REVIEW

1. A linked list, as the name suggests, is a list of object instances that are linked together much like a chain.

2. Each instance in a linked list is called a node. Each instance contains data and a reference attribute linking it to the next node.

3. The `LinkedList` class definition contains five methods: `DisplayAllNodes`, `InsertAtBeginning`, `InsertAtEnd`, `RemoveFromBeginning`, and `RemoveFromEnd`.

4. A `Stack` can be implemented as a special form of a `LinkedList`. You can add and remove nodes at either the beginning or end of a linked list. However a stack is a LIFO (last in, first out) structure: you can add and remove nodes from only the beginning or top of a Stack. Stacks generally have three methods: `Push` adds a node to the top, `Pop` removes a node from the top and returns a reference to the removed node, and `Peek` returns a reference to the top node, but does not remove it. Note that `Pop` and `Peek` will both throw `EmptyStackException` if the stack is empty.

5. You can employ inheritance to create a `Stack` class by making it a subclass of `LinkedList`. Because `Stack` is a `LinkedList` subclass, `Push` can invoke the inherited method `InsertAtBeginning` and `Pop` can invoke `RemoveFromBeginning`.

6. The Framework Class Library (FCL) includes a `Stack` class that stores nodes as instances of `Object`. In addition to `Push`, `Pop`, and `Peek` methods, this class includes the method `ToArray`, which copies the objects in the stack into an array.

7. A queue can also be implemented as a linked list with objects added at the end and removed from the beginning. Queues employ FIFO (first in, first out) logic. The `Enqueue` method adds a node at the end, and `Dequeue` removes a node from the beginning, returning its reference.

8. When `Queue` is implemented as a specialized version of a linked list, you can create `Queue` as a subclass of `LinkedList`. `Enqueue` simply invokes the inherited method `InsertAtEnd`. `Dequeue` first checks for an empty queue by invoking the inherited method `IsEmpty`, throwing an `EmptyQueueException` if `True`. If the queue is not empty, then the inherited method `RemoveFromBeginning` is invoked.

9. The FCL also includes a `Queue` class. Similar to the FCL `Stack` class, the supplied `Queue` class stores nodes as instances of `Object`. In addition to `Enqueue`, `Dequeue`, and `Peek` methods, this class also includes the method `ToArray`, which copies the objects in the queue into an array.

10. A recursive problem-solving approach divides a problem into a series of successively smaller (but similar) problems, solves each of those subproblems, and then assembles the result.

11. A recursive method is a method that calls itself.

12. A recursive method must have a stopping point (also known as a base case).

13. Each time a recursive method is invoked, a fresh copy of the method is created. Each copy has its own set of values and parameters and remains unfinished until the base case is recognized.

14. Recursion is similar in many ways to iteration. Any problem that can be solved recursively can be solved iteratively, and vice versa.

15. Recursion is usually less efficient than iteration in terms of computer resources, but for some problems yields a solution that is much less complex.

16. A recursive definition for n! is n* (n − 1)!

17. Quicksort is a recursive technique for sorting an array. The Quicksort technique partitions an array into two subarrays, based on upon the value of an arbitrarily selected array element known as the pivot.

EXERCISES

1. Describe a linked list.

2. What is a node?

3. Describe a stack.

4. Describe a queue.

5. What does it mean for a method to be recursive?

6. Describe the characteristics of a problem that can be solved recursively.

7. Suppose an array contains the numbers 5, 1, 9, 3, and 2. Illustrate a recursive problem-solving approach to find the largest number in an array. (*Hint:* The largest number in an array can be thought of as the larger of (a) the first element and (b) the largest number in the subarray containing the remaining elements.)

8. What is a base case? Why must recursive programs have a base case?

9. What does the following program do? Is this a recursive program? Why or why not? If so, what is the base case?

```
Module MysteryProgram

    Sub Main()
        mystery(1)
    End Sub

    Sub mystery(ByVal n As Integer)
        System.Console.WriteLine(n)
        If (n < 10) Then
            mystery(n + 1)
        End If
        System.Console.WriteLine(n)
    End Sub
End Module
```

10. Compare and contrast recursion and iteration.

15

PROGRAMMING EXERCISES

1. Develop an application that will accept 10 lines of data input from the keyboard. Store each line of data that is entered in a data structure. Retrieve and display the lines of data LIFO.

2. Repeat Exercise 1 using FIFO logic.

3. A doubly linked list is a linked list where each node includes a reference to the previous node in the list. Expand Example 15-2 to be a doubly linked list. Modify the Client module to verify that your previous links work properly.

4. Use your answer to Exercise 7 to write a program that uses a recursive method to find the largest number in an array.

5. A palindrome is a word or group of words that is spelled the same forward and backward. Some examples of palindromes are madam, radar, and noon. A classic palindrome (ignoring spaces) is "a man a plan a canal panama". Write a program that accepts a string, and then uses a recursive method to determine if that string is a palindrome. Your method should ignore spaces, and return a value of **True** if the string is a palindrome, **False** otherwise.

6. In mathematics, the Fibonacci sequence is defined recursively as:

   fibonacci(0) = 0
   fibonacci(1) = 1
   fibonacci(n) = fibonacci(n − 1) + fibonacci(n − 2), for n > 1

   The first eight numbers in the Fibonacci sequence are: 0, 1, 1, 2, 3, 5, 8, and 13. The Fibonacci value of 2, denoted fibonacci(2), is fibonacci(1) + fibonacci(0) = 1 + 0 = 1, and the Fibonacci value of 3 is fibonacci(2) + fibonacci(1) = 1 + 1 = 2. Similarly, the Fibonacci value of 7 is fibonacci(6) + fibonacci(5) = 8 + 5 = 13. Write a program that accepts a positive integer between 0 and 40 and uses a recursive method to find the Fibonacci value of that number.

7. The greatest common divisor of two integers is the largest integer that divides them both without a remainder. A recursive definition for finding the greatest common divisor of integers a and b, denoted gcd(a, b), is:

   gcd(a, b) = gcd(b, a Mod b)　　　where b ≠ 0 and Mod is the modulus operator
   If b = 0, gcd(a, b) = a.

    Recall that the modulus operator (a Mod b) divides integer b by integer b and returns the remainder as the result. For example, 7 Mod 3 returns the value 1.

   Write a program that accepts two integers and then uses a recursive method to find the greatest common divisor.

Setting Up
an IIS Server

When you use Microsoft's Web development technology, you must use their server software, Internet Information Services (IIS). Applications usually run on one computer, and IIS is installed on a different computer that is used only as a server. However, during development you can have IIS installed on the same computer, allowing it to work as both a Web server and a Web client. If the Web server you are using is a Web server other than your computer, see your instructor or network administrator for instructions on accessing the server.

IIS ships with Windows 2000 and Windows XP Professional, but might not have been installed on your computer. The following steps guide you through installing IIS so you can use your computer as a Web server. Because the installation steps are almost identical in Windows 2000 Professional and Windows XP, the steps for both versions of Windows are covered together. Start by checking to see whether IIS is already installed on your computer.

To install IIS in Windows 2000 and Windows XP:

1. Open the Control Panel. (In Windows 2000, click **Start**, point to **Settings**, and then click **Control Panel**. In Windows XP, click **Start**, and then click **Control Panel**.)

2. Double-click the **Add or Remove Programs** icon (**Add/Remove Programs** in Windows 2000). The Add or Remove Programs dialog box opens, as shown in Figure A-1, listing the programs currently installed on your computer.

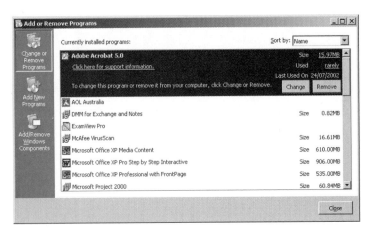

Figure A-1   Add or Remove Programs dialog box

3. In the left panel of the dialog box, click the **Add/Remove Windows Components** icon. The Windows Components Wizard dialog box opens, listing the components that are available for installation, as shown in Figure A–2. Locate the Internet Information Services (IIS) component.

    ■ If the Internet Information Services (IIS) box is checked, IIS is already installed on your computer. Select **Internet Information Services (IIS)** (the text, not the check box), and then skip to Step 4.

    ■ If the Internet Information Services (IIS) box is not checked, click to check the box. You may be asked to insert your Windows 2000 or Windows XP Professional installation disk into your computer's CD drive.

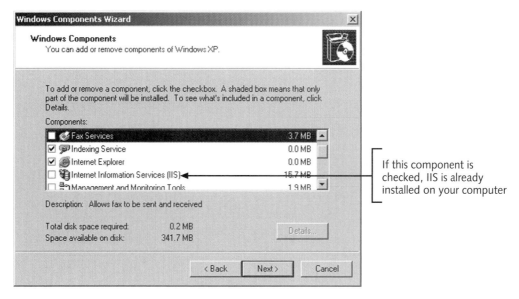

Figure A-2   Windows Components Wizard dialog box

4. With IIS selected in the Windows Components Wizard dialog box, click the **Details** button. The Internet Information Services (IIS) dialog box opens, listing subcomponents for IIS, as shown in Figure A-3.

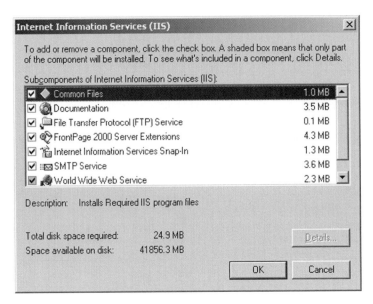

Figure A-3 Internet Information Services (IIS) dialog box

5. If necessary, select the check boxes for the following options: **World Wide Web Service**, **FrontPage 2000 Server Extensions**, and **Internet Information Services Snap-In**. If you are using IIS 5.0 distributed with Windows 2000, also scroll through the list and select the **Script Debugger** check box, if necessary. Click the **OK** button.

6. Click the **Next** button to complete the IIS installation. When the installation is complete, click **Finish** and then close the Control Panel.

When you use IIS, the default home directory for publishing Web files on your computer is c:\inetpub\wwwroot. In the following steps, you verify that these folders have been created, and then test the installation to ensure that IIS is serving Web pages as expected. IIS creates the name of your Web server based on the name of your computer; however, you can change your computer's name. Because you will use "localhost" for your examples, you do not need to change your computer's name.

To test the IIS installation:

1. Open Windows Explorer or My Computer, navigate to the c:\inetpub\wwwroot folder, and locate the **localstart.asp** file, which is the test Web page.

2. To determine your computer's name in Windows 2000, click the **Start** button, select **Settings**, and then select **Control Panel**. Double-click the **Network and Dial-up Connections** entry in the Control Panel. Click **Advanced** on the menu bar, and then click **Network Identification**. Click the **Properties** button to view the name of your computer. (You can also use

the Properties button to change the computer name.) You use this computer name in the following step. Close all open windows.

To determine your computer's name in Windows XP, click the **Start** button, and then click **Control Panel**. Double-click the **System** icon to open the System Properties dialog box, and then click the **Computer Name** tab. Click the **Change** button to view the name of your computer. (You can also use the Change button to change the computer name.) You use this computer name in the following step. Close all open windows.

3. To browse Web pages on this server, start Internet Explorer. (You might be able to double-click an **Internet Explorer** icon on the desktop to start Internet Explorer, or click the **Start** button and then click **Internet Explorer**.)

4. In the Address text box, type **http://*your_computer_name*/localstart.asp** where *your_computer_name* is the name you found in Step 2. Then press **Enter**. Two Web pages open, one a test page similar to the one shown in Figure A-4.

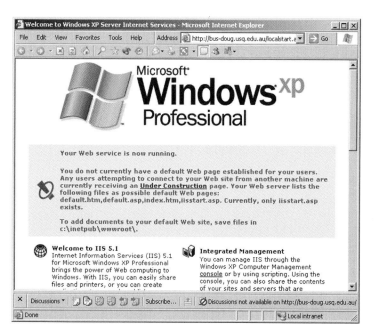

Figure A-4   IIS installation test Web page

5. Because you are using the same computer for the server and the client, you can also use "localhost" as the name of your computer. (This text uses "localhost" for its examples.) In the Address text box, type **http://localhost/localstart.asp** and press **Enter**. The same Web page shown in Figure A-4 appears again, but the URL will have *localhost* instead of your computer name in the URL.

Index